First Edition

Bali and Lombok

The complete guide, thoroughly up-to-date

Packed with details that will make your trip

The must-see sights, off and on the beaten path

What to see, what to skip

Mix-and-match vacation itineraries

City strolls, countryside adventures

Smart lodging and dining options

Essential local do's and taboos

Transportation tips, distances, and directions

Key contacts, savvy travel tips

When to go, what to pack

Clear, accurate, easy-to-use maps

Background essays

Fodor's Travel Publications •
www.fodors.com

Fodor's Bali and Lombok

EDITOR: Bonnie Bills

Editorial Contributors: Denise Dowling, Margaret Feldstein, Laura M. Kidder, Holly S. Smith, Gisela Williams

Editorial Production: Kristin Milavec

Maps: David Lindroth, Inc.; Mapping Specialists; *cartographers;* Rebecca Baer and Robert Blake, *map editors*

Design: Fabrizio La Rocca, *creative director;* Guido Caroti, *art director;* Jolie Novak, *senior picture editor;* Melanie Marin, *photo editor*

Cover Design: Pentagram

Production/Manufacturing: Bob Shields

Cover Photograph: Wendy Chan/The Image Bank

Copyright

First Edition

ISBN 0–679–00789–X

ISSN 1533–3396

Important Tip

Although all prices, opening times, and other details in this book are based on information supplied to us at press time, changes occur all the time in the travel world, and Fodor's cannot accept responsibility for facts that become outdated or for inadvertent errors or omissions. So **always confirm information when it matters,** especially if you're making a detour to visit a specific place.

Special Sales

Fodor's Travel Publications are available at special discounts for bulk purchases for sales promotions or premiums. Special editions, including personalized covers, excerpts of existing guides, and corporate imprints, can be created in large quantities for special needs. For more information contact your local bookseller or write to Special Markets, Fodor's Travel Publications, 280 Park Avenue, New York, NY 10017. Inquiries from Canada should be directed to your local Canadian bookseller or sent to Random House of Canada, Ltd., Marketing Department, 2775 Matheson Boulevard East, Mississauga, Ontario L4W 4P7. Inquiries from the United Kingdom should be sent to Fodor's Travel Publications, 20 Vauxhall Bridge Road, London SW1V 2SA, England.

PRINTED IN THE UNITED STATES OF AMERICA

10 9 8 7 6 5 4 3 2 1

CONTENTS

ON THE ROAD WITH FODOR'S

EVERY TRIP IS SIGNIFICANT. Acutely aware of that fact, we've pulled out all stops in preparing *Fodor's Bali and Lombok.* To guide you in planning your island experience, we've created multiday itineraries, driving tours, and neighborhood walks. And to direct you to the places that are truly worth your time and money in this important year, we've rallied the team of endearingly picky know-it-alls we're pleased to call our writers. Having seen all corners of Bali and Lombok, they're real experts. If you knew them, you'd poll them for tips yourself.

Denise Dowling, who covered Lombok, first studied the language and culture of Indonesia during a semester abroad in Bali and later returned as a journalist. She currently teaches journalism and is a freelance writer and editor for American, British, and Australian publications.

Northern Bali was covered by **Margaret Feldstein,** who has traveled extensively in Southeast Asia and has been to Bali three times, beginning in 1995. From her home in New York City, she dreams of sipping a lime squash under the palm trees of Bali.

You've probably seen **Holly S. Smith**—who covered the southern and eastern regions of the island—trekking around Bali with her two-year-old daughter in a backpack, her six-month-old son in a stroller, her camera over her shoulder, and her tape recorder and notebook in hand. After nearly a decade of writing travel books and articles about Southeast Asia and Indonesia, she has literally walked every street, visited every hotel and restaurant, and participated in every activity on Bali (except parachuting into the sea). She is looking forward to a long vacation at her home near Seattle, Washington, before starting on her next book, a humorous account of her adventures as a travel writer.

Gisela Williams, who wrote about western Bali, first went to the island in 1992 as a student of the School for International Training and studied Bahasa Indonesia while living with a Balinese family near Ubud. She is now a freelance writer for several travel and fashion magazines.

We'd also like to thank Cathy Pacific; Continental Micronesia; Emerald Tulamben Resort; Gray Line Bali; Holiday Inn Resort Lombok; Krakatoa Business Center; Mark and Lisa Savage of Indovillas; Anna and Niels van Dijk of Ombak Putih; guide Mia Bondue of Ombak Putih cruises; Komangs and Ketuts I, II, and III; Pak Eddy at Wisma Triguna; Pak Kadek; Pak Nyoman I; Pak Nyoman II; Sacred Mountain Sanctuary; Sea Trek cruises; driver and guide Biantara of Toyota; Reefseekers Pro Dive; Unda River Rafting; Sue from Biyu Nasak; John Flood of the Damai; Diana von Cranach of Puri Ganesha Villas; Richard from Rambutan Beach Cottages; and the staff, owners, and managers of villas Ratu Ayu, Puri Lumbung, Taman Wana, Ambara Ulangan, Ele Bianco, Puri Sienna, Umalas Stables, Sawah, Tugu, Pasti Indah, Sanctuary, Balquisse, and Ganesha.

Don't Forget to Write

Keeping a travel guide fresh and up-to-date is a big job. So we love your feedback—positive and negative—and follow up on all suggestions. Contact the Bali and Lombok editor at editors@fodors.com or c/o Fodor's, 280 Park Avenue, New York, New York 10017. And have a wonderful trip!

Karen Cure

Karen Cure
Editorial Director

Bali and Lombok

N

| 0 | 10 miles |
| 0 | 20 km |

KEY
Ferry

Bali Sea

Bali Sea

Kubutambahan

Singaraja

TO GILIMANUK, BALI BARAT
NATIONAL PARK

Seririt

Lovina

Lake Buyan

Lake Tamblingan

Lake Bratan

Bedugul

Penulisan

Kintamani

Gunung (Mount) Batur

Lake Batur

GUNUNG BATUKAU

Penelokan

Batukau

B A L I

GUNUNG AGUNG

Tulamben

Mt. Seraya

TO NEGARA,
GILIMANUK,
BALI BARAT
NATIONAL PARK,
AND JAVA

Tampaksiring

Sengeh

Bukit Sari

Tabanan

Mengwi

Ubud

Pejeng

Bedulu

Gianyar

Bangli

Semarapura

Goa Lawah

Balina
Beach and
Manggis

Amuk Bay

Padangbai

Tenganan

Candidasa

Karango

Strait

Canggu

Kerobokan

Kuta, Legian,
and Seminyak

Kuta Bay

Jimbaran Bay

Denpasar

Sanur

Turtle
Island

Benoa Port

Benoa Harbor

Benoa

Nusa Dua

Badung Strait

Nusa Lembongan

Nusa Ceningan

Toya
Pakeh

Semaya

NUSA PENIDA

Bali Strait

BUKIT BADUNG

Uluwatu

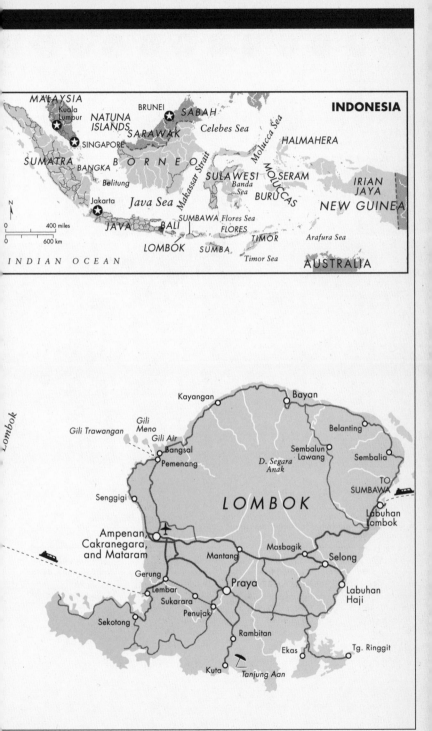

World Time Zones

Numbers below vertical bands relate each zone to Greenwich Mean Time (0 hrs).
Local times frequently differ from these general indications,
as indicated by light-face numbers on map.

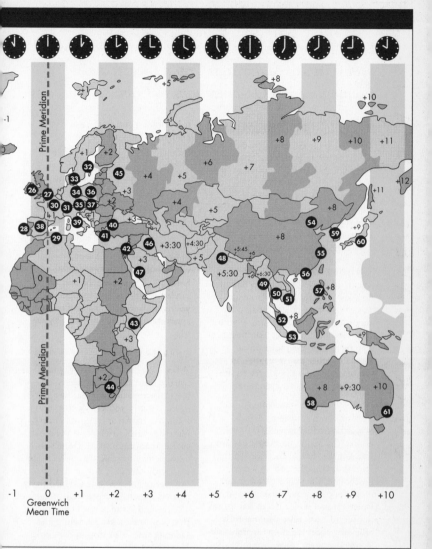

SMART TRAVEL TIPS A TO Z

Basic Information on Traveling in Bali and Lombok, Savvy Tips to Make Your Trip a Breeze, and Companies and Organizations to Contact

AIR TRAVEL

There are no nonstop flights from the United States to Bali. Your choices are a direct flight, which requires at least one stop, or a connecting flight, which necessitates at least one change of plane. Some flights are scheduled only on certain days of the week. There are many flights from London to Bali, most with at least one stopover in Asia (usually Bangkok or Singapore). You can also fly from Auckland, New Zealand, to Bali on Air New Zealand, or fly from any of Australia's large cities to Bali on major international carriers. If your destination is Lombok, your best bet is to **fly to Bali, then take an air shuttle or other transportation to Lombok,** since Lombok isn't an official point of entry to Indonesia.

From the United States and Canada there are both transpacific and transatlantic flights to Bali. Westbound, the major gateway cities are Los Angeles; San Francisco; Seattle; Portland, Oregon; and Vancouver. Eastbound, the major gateways are New York, Detroit, Chicago, and Dallas. If you're headed to Bali from the West Coast, **take Continental's relatively short Los Angeles–Honolulu–Guam–Denpasar route** (less than six hours for each flight leg). Otherwise your best bet is to **stop over in Hong Kong, Singapore, Taipei, or Tokyo;** many airlines fly nonstop to these cites, and they have the greatest number of connecting flights. If you're leaving from the midwestern or eastern United States, you can often **add a stopover in Europe or the Middle East to your transatlantic flight** for a small charge. You can also **take advantage of international routes that utilize less common entry points to Indonesia**: Davao, the Philippines, to Manado, Sulawesi; Darwin, Australia, to Kupang, Timor; Kuching, Malaysia, to Pontianak, Kalimantan (on Borneo); and Port Moresby, New Guinea, to Jayapura, Irian Jaya—although the latter requires a special visa.

If you'll be island hopping in Indonesia or even just seeing one other island besides Bali, such as Lombok, your travel is likely to be by air. Unless you'll have time to examine your options after you arrive, it's best to **buy all your air tickets for travel within Indonesia before you leave home.** Also, **compare the cost of buying one ticket that includes all your stopovers with the cost of buying separate tickets for each leg of your trip.**

CARRIERS

When flying internationally, you usually must choose between a domestic carrier, the national flag carrier of the country you are visiting, and a foreign carrier from a third country. National flag carriers have the greatest number of nonstops. Domestic carriers may have better connections to your hometown and serve a greater number of gateway cities. Third-party carriers may have a price advantage. Continental is the major U.S. airline that flies to Bali, via Honolulu and Guam; routes also stop in Bangkok, Hong Kong, Manila, Seoul, Singapore, Taipei, and Tokyo.

Garuda Indonesia, along with some smaller airlines, flies between Bali and other points in Indonesia. Note, however, that at press time much air service was suspended because of the economic crisis; **call the airlines for updates.** For information on carriers that fly between Bali and Lombok, *see* Lombok A to Z *in* Chapter 6.

➤ To Bali: **Air Canada** (☎ 800/776–3000 in the U.S.; 514/393–3333 in Montréal; 416/925–2311 in Toronto). **Cathay Pacific** (☎ 800/233–2742 in the U.S.; 604/682–9747 in Vancouver). **China Airlines** (☎ 800/227–

5118 in North America). **Continental** (☎ 800/525–0280 in the U.S.). **EVA** (☎ 800/695–1188 in the U.S.). **Garuda Indonesia** (☎ 212/370–0707 or 800/342–7832 in North America). **Japan Airlines** (☎ 800/525–3663 in North America). **Malaysia Airlines** (☎ 800/552–9264 in the U.S.; 416/928–6670 in Toronto; 604/681–7741 in Vancouver). **Northwest Airlines** (☎ 800/225–2525 in North America). **Singapore Airlines** (☎ 800/742–3333 in the U.S.; 604/682–9747 in Vancouver; 800/663–3046 toll-free in Canada). **Thai Airways International** (☎ 800/426–5204 in the U.S.; 416/971–7907 in Toronto; 604/687–1412 in Vancouver).

➤ FROM THE U.K.: **British Airways** (☎ 0845/222–1111). **Garuda Indonesia** (☎ 020/7486–3011). **Malaysia Airlines** (☎ 020/8740–2626).

➤ FROM AUSTRALIA AND NEW ZEALAND: **Air New Zealand** (☎ 09/357–3000 in Auckland; 13/2476 in Australia). **Qantas** (☎ 13/1313 in Australia).

➤ AROUND INDONESIA: **Bouraq** (☎ 021/628–8827 in Jakarta). **Merpati** (☎ 021/424–7404 in Jakarta). **Sempati** (☎ 021/835–1612 in Jakarta).

CHECK-IN & BOARDING

Because of the recent economic and political crises and subsequent uprisings in Indonesia, airport security has become more stringent in recent months, even on peaceful Bali. Make sure to **allow ample time to check in** for your flights to and from the country, and plan for delays. Security checkpoints and customs inspections can be lax or thorough. Detailed luggage checks can take place at any time, so set all questionable items at the top of your bags and be prepared to boot up laptop computers and strip off metal belt buckles; items that look remotely dangerous—even unusual ballpoint pens—may be confiscated.

Assuming that not everyone with a ticket will show up, airlines routinely overbook planes. When everyone does, airlines ask for volunteers to give up their seats. In return, these volunteers usually get a certificate for a free flight and are rebooked on the next flight out. If there are not enough volunteers, the airline must choose who will be denied boarding. The first to get bumped are passengers who checked in late and those flying on discounted tickets, so **get to the gate and check in as early as possible,** especially during peak periods.

Always **bring a government-issued photo I.D. to the airport.** You may be asked to show it before you are allowed to check in.

CUTTING COSTS

The least expensive airfares to Bali must usually be purchased in advance and are nonrefundable. It's smart to **check out air ticket Web sites** or **call a number of airlines, and when you find a good price, book it on the spot**—the same fare may not be available the next day. Always **check different routings** and look into using different airports. Travel agents, especially low-fare specialists, are helpful.

If you plan to visit other countries in Southeast Asia, **check into Circle Pacific fares or around-the-world Globetrotter fares.** These are flat-rate fares subject to advance-purchase restrictions, usually 7–14 days, and other rules. Circle Pacific fares allow four stopovers, although travel may not be allowed to Vietnam, Burma, Laos, and Cambodia. Additional stopovers can be purchased for $50–$100. Around-the-world fares also have routing restrictions and require one transatlantic and one transpacific crossing. These tickets are based on either direction or mileage, and both have their advantages: direction-based fares can be less expensive, but mileage-based fares allow backtracking and multiple visits to a single city.

If you only plan to travel to Indonesia, **consider purchasing Garuda Indonesia's Visit Indonesia Pass.** This pass is $300, good for three flights within Indonesia and additional flight coupons for $100 each. It's best to buy the pass before your arrival (allow at least a week for processing), but if you don't have time to purchase a pass before your trip, you can buy one in Indonesia if you show a

Garuda office a copy of your international tickets. One hitch to the deal is that you must fly in and out of the country on Garuda Indonesia; otherwise a surcharge of $60 is added.

Consolidators are another good source. They buy tickets for scheduled international flights at reduced rates from the airlines, then sell them at prices that beat the best fare available directly from the airlines, usually without restrictions. Sometimes you can even get your money back if you need to cancel the ticket. Carefully read the fine print detailing penalties for changes and cancellations, and **confirm your consolidator reservation with the airline.**

➤ CONSOLIDATORS: **Cheap Tickets** (☎ 800/377–1000). **Discount Airline Ticket Service** (☎ 800/576–1600). **Unitravel** (☎ 800/325–2222). **Up & Away Travel** (☎ 212/889–2345). **World Travel Network** (☎ 800/409–6753).

➤ COURIERS: **Global Courier Travel** (✉ Box 3051, Nederland, CO 80466). **International Association of Air Travel Couriers** (✉ 220 S. Dixie Hwy., Box 1349, Lake Worth, FL 33460, ☎ 561/582-8320). **Now Voyager** (✉ 74 Varick St., Suite 307, New York, NY 10013, ☎ 212/431-1616).

➤ ROUND-THE-WORLD DISCOUNTERS: **Air Brokers International** (☎ 800/883–3273, www.airbrokers.com). **AirTreks** (☎ 800/350–0612, www.airtreks.com). **Avia Travel** (☎ 800/950–2842, www.avia.com). **Ticket Planet** (☎ 800/799–8888, www.ticketplanet.com).

ENJOYING THE FLIGHT

For more legroom **request an emergency-aisle seat.** Don't sit in the row in front of the emergency aisle or in front of a bulkhead, where seats may not recline. If you have dietary concerns, **ask for special meals when booking.** These can be vegetarian, low-cholesterol, or kosher, for example. On long flights try to maintain a normal routine in order to help fight jet lag. At night, **get some sleep.** By day, **eat light meals, drink water** (not alcohol), and **move around the cabin** to stretch your legs. Flights within

Indonesia permit smoking, so **ask for a seat toward the front if you're not a smoker.**

FLYING TIMES

Transpacific flying times to Bali are approximately 19 hours from Los Angeles, 23 hours from Chicago, 25 hours from New York, and 22 hours from Vancouver. Flying the eastbound route to Bali, the flight time from New York is 25 hours; allowing for stops, it's 28 hours from Toronto or Montreal to Bali. From London it's 18 hours to Bali; from Sydney and Melbourne it's, respectively, 7 and 4 hours to Bali. From Auckland it takes 9 hours to reach Bali.

Flying from Bali to other points within Indonesia requires patience and flexibility, as schedules run on the infamous *jam karet,* or "rubber time," and long hauls may incorporate unscheduled stops. From Bali it's 1½ hours to Jakarta, 40 minutes to Mataram on Lombok, and almost 1½ hours to Ujung Pandang.

HOW TO COMPLAIN

If your baggage goes astray or your flight goes awry, complain right away. Most carriers require that you **file a claim immediately.**

➤ AIRLINE COMPLAINTS: U.S. Department of Transportation **Aviation Consumer Protection Division** (✉ C-75, Room 4107, Washington, DC 20590, ☎ 202/366–2220, airconsumer@ost.dot.gov, www.dot.gov/airconsumer). **Federal Aviation Administration Consumer Hotline** (☎ 800/322–7873).

RECONFIRMING

Although the airlines may not require you to do so, always **reconfirm both international and domestic flights** from and within Indonesia between 24 and 48 hours in advance. This also gives you a chance to **ask about flight changes**; the airlines aren't always able to reach passengers to inform them of delays or cancellations.

AIRPORTS

Bali's Ngurah Rai International Airport, in Tuban, is a major international gateway. Lombok's Selaparang Airport is in Mataram. Since the airport doesn't have immigration facilities, most travelers fly to Bali first.

➤ AIRPORT INFORMATION: **Ngurah Rai International Airport** (☎ 0361/751026). **Selaparang Airport** (☎ no phone).

TRANSFERS

Most hotels can arrange for a car or minivan to meet you at Ngurah Rai International Airport, on Bali. Otherwise, order a taxi at the counter outside customs. The fixed fare varies depending on the location of your hotel; it's around 60¢ to Kuta and $4.75 to Ubud; count on about 25¢ per mile. You can also catch a *bemo* (public minibus) outside the airport, but make sure that you're going in the right direction and that if you enter an empty vehicle, you're not hiring and paying for the entire van—unless that's your intention.

BIKE TRAVEL

Outside Denpasar, Bali is a wonderful—and challenging—place for bicycle (*sepeda*) trips. Favorite places for two-wheel adventure travel are the hills of Ubud and the eastern and western coastal roads, where the back lanes are uncrowded and spectacularly scenic. Rentals, ranging from top-grade mountain bikes to rickety antique models, are widely available at hotels, car rental agencies, and travel agencies in tourist areas; expect to pay around $3 per day, with discounted weekly rates. The colorful and detailed Periplus Travel Maps are useful for bicycle trips; they're found in travel agencies and bookstores throughout Indonesia.

➤ BIKE MAPS: **Periplus** (✉ Tuttle Publishing, 153 Milk St., Boston, MA 02109, ☎ 617/951–4080, ℻ 617/951–4045).

➤ BIKE RENTALS: **Akira Bali** (✉ Jl. Pengosekan, Ubud, Bali, ☎ 0361/973131). **Jineng Wisata** (Jl. Hanoman 22X, Ubud, Bali, ☎ 0361/976006). **Pande Wayan Ardana** (✉ Jl. Pengosekan, Ubud, Bali, ☎ 0361/974615).

BIKES IN FLIGHT

Most airlines accommodate bikes as luggage, provided they are dismantled and boxed. For bike boxes, often free at bike shops, you'll pay about $5 from airlines (at least $100 for bike bags). International travelers can sometimes substitute a bike for a piece of checked luggage at no charge; otherwise, the cost is about $100. Domestic and Canadian airlines charge $25–$50.

BOAT & FERRY TRAVEL

On Bali and Lombok and throughout this nation of thousands of islands, boats and ferries are a major mode of travel. State-owned Pelni has many passenger-boat routes that stop at Lembar, on Lombok's west side, as well as at Benoa, the port on Bali's southeast coast; make sure to **book tickets early for these routes,** particularly around Muslim holidays. Ferries make the 35-minute crossing every hour between Banyuwangi's Ketapang ferry terminal, in eastern Java, and Gilimanuk, in western Bali, for about Rp 4,000 for passengers and Rp 11,000 for vehicles. A ferry takes passengers between Padangbai, on Bali's east coast, and Lembar, on Lombok; ferries leave every two hours, and the trip takes about four hours. For more details on boat travel around Bali and Lombok, *see* the A to Z sections *in* individual chapters.

➤ BOAT & FERRY INFORMATION: **Padangbai harbor office** (☎ 0363/41840). **Pelni** (✉ Benoa Harbor, Bali, ☎ 0361/721377; ✉ Jl. Angkasa 18, Jakarta, Java, ☎ 021/421–1921; ✉ Jl. Martadinata 38, Ujung Pandang, Sulawesi, ☎ 0411/331393).

BUS TRAVEL

Outside of the scheduled bus tours between major island sites, most local travel is by public minibus, or bemo. Rather than operating on a set schedule, bemos usually circle until they are full. The main stumbling block for local bemo travel is language, so **get written directions** from a hotel staff member to show your driver—just in case. Local bemos are well worn, packed, and don't mind animal passengers. Smoking is permitted on bemos and buses, so if you need fresh air, **sit toward the front.**

FARES & SCHEDULES

Bemo routes and fares are posted at all terminals, but most don't run on a

SMART TRAVEL TIPS A TO Z

set schedule; they just fill up with people and go. Prices for bemo routes are set by the number of kilometers.

In southern Bali the Batu Bulan terminal, north of Denpasar, is for bemos traveling to towns to the north and east. Denpasar's Ubung terminal is for bemos going to places west and north of the capital, including Java. The Tegal terminal, west of Denpasar, is the place to connect with vehicles heading south to the tourist towns, the Bukit Peninsula, and the airport. The Suci terminal is for bemos to Benoa Harbor. The Kereneng terminal, home of the famous night market, is now just a stopping point to catch bemos heading to the other terminals. On Lombok bemos can be hailed just about anywhere; they also gather at the central bus terminal, Mandalika.

PAYING

Bemo drivers or their helpers collect money when the vehicle is full; you pay based on the destination you state. Fares are posted at all main terminals; if you're flagging down a vehicle on the road, **know the approximate fare** so you're not overcharged. If you plan to frequently ride bemos around Bali, carry lots of small bills (Rp 1,000 notes or less).

➤ BUS AND BEMO INFORMATION: **Batu Bulan terminal** (✉ Jl. Raya Batubulan, 6 km [4 mi] north of Denpasar, Bali). **Kereneng terminal** (✉ Jl. Kamboja, Denpasar, Bali). **Mandalika bus station** (✉ Bertais, 2 km [1 mi] east of Sweta, Lombok, ☎ 0370/667017 to restaurant). **Suci terminal** (✉ Jl. Diponegoro and Jl. Hasanuddin, Denpasar, Bali). **Tegal terminal** (✉ Jl. G. Wilis and Jl. Imam Bonjol, Denpasar, Bali). **Ubung terminal** (✉ Jl. Cokroaminoto, Denpasar, Bali).

BUSINESS HOURS

Stores and restaurants are usually open daily throughout the islands. Don't expect anything to be open on major local holidays. In addition, you may find shops, hotels, and restaurants closed—during the day, at least—during the fasting month of Ramadan. Shops and restaurants in rural areas are also subject to frequent closings for temple ceremonies

and family celebrations. For restaurant hours *see* Mealtimes *in* Dining, *below.*

BANKS & OFFICES

Banks are open Monday through Friday from around 9 to 3 or 4, but they may close during the lunch hour; bank branches in hotels may stay open later. Government offices are open Monday through Thursday from 8 to around 3 and Friday to 11:30. Some are also open on Saturday 8 until 2. Offices have varied hours, usually 9–5 weekdays and a half day on Saturday.

GAS STATIONS

Most gas stations and kiosks are open daily, from sunrise to sunset, except on major holidays.

MUSEUMS & SIGHTS

Most museums are open daily 9–5.

PHARMACIES

Pharmacies are generally open 9–8, although they will open at other times to accommodate emergencies.

SHOPS

In cities and tourist areas stores and malls are usually open daily 10–9. In smaller towns shops are generally open daily 9–6.

CAMERAS & PHOTOGRAPHY

On Bali and Lombok, the older generations can be reserved about being photographed. On the other hand, in tourist areas children will sometimes pester foreigners to take their photograph—and then demand money. However, most locals are willing to have their photo taken if you seem genuinely interested in their culture; in fact, some might even want to get into the picture with you and request that you send them a copy. Be sensitive, though, to the wishes for privacy in the more conservative rural areas, and avoid photographing military sites.

Bali and Lombok have plenty of scenic backdrops: vivid sunsets, forested mountain slopes, quiet fishing villages on stilts, brightly dressed dancers, and the ever-present smiles of children. Some classic photos to take are the smoking volcanic panorama of Bali's Gunung Batur and Gunung Agung; southern Bali's Tanah Lot at sunset; northern Bali's Pura Ulun Danu Bratan, its shrines perched on tiny islands in a shimmering lake; the lonely white-sand beaches of Lombok's Gili Islands; and sunrise from Gunung Rinjani.

➤ PHOTO HELP: **Kodak Information Center** (☎ 800/242–2424). *Kodak Guide to Shooting Great Travel Pictures,* available in bookstores or from Fodor's Travel Publications (☎ 800/533–6478; $18 plus $5.50 shipping).

EQUIPMENT PRECAUTIONS

Always **keep your film and tape out of the sun,** and **beware of flying sand** on the beach. Tropical rain and humidity can also wreak havoc on cameras, so protect your equipment accordingly. Carry an extra supply of batteries, and **be prepared to turn on your camera or camcorder** to prove to security personnel that the device is real. Always **ask for hand inspection of film,** which becomes clouded after repeated exposure to airport X-ray machines, and **keep videotapes away from metal detectors.**

FILM & DEVELOPING

You can find good-quality camera film in the tourist areas of Bali, but **check the expiration date,** and **make sure the box hasn't faded** from exposure to sunlight. Fuji film (around $3 for a roll of 36 prints and $4 for a roll of 36 slides) is less expensive than other brands, and it tends to highlight the country's scenic blues and greens better. One-hour photo development (around $1.25 per roll of 36) is available in tourist areas, as is 24-hour film developing; slide development (about $1 per roll of 36) usually takes two days.

VIDEOS

Film for video cameras can be found in tourist areas, but it isn't widely available elsewhere; it's wisest to bring your own. A Western-brand roll of VHS tape runs about $4.

CAR RENTAL

Other than traffic-choked Denpasar, Bali is perfect for self-drive tours. This small, scenic island invites visitors to linger—perhaps for a picnic beside a rice field or a sunset walk on a quiet beach. Most rentals are standard (manual) shift, and the mountains have very steep, twisted roads, so **practice at home before you venture out with a stick-shift vehicle.** If you're planning to make a longer trip on your own, or if you'll be traveling between islands, make sure to **rent the most comfortable vehicle you can afford.**

The main two-lane thread of highway from the south to Ubud is crowded with tourist buses and commuter vehicles, and other cultural sites on the island can take several hours to reach. If you're prone to road rage, or you're trying to cover a lot of territory in a short time, **hire a car with a driver** so you can just sit back and enjoy the scenery. Hiring a car and driver through your hotel or a travel agent generally costs 25%–50% more than simply renting a car, but it's still relatively inexpensive.

Daily car rental rates are, roughly: $10–$15 for a Suzuki Katana (similar to a Samaurai); $12–$17 for a Daihatsu Feroza (like a Ford Explorer); $17–$25 for a Kijang sport utility vehicle, $25–$30 with driver; and $30–$35 for an Isuzu Panther (like a Ford Expedition), with driver only. Add $12–$48 per day for insurance depending on the vehicle model and year.

The most popular and best-run car rental outfit on Bali is Toyota Rent-a-Car, which has a fleet of small to luxury vehicles, 24-hour roadside assistance, 24-hour repair service, and a team of professionally trained, English-speaking drivers. You can log onto their Web site to check out their services, ask questions, and book a vehicle before you arrive.

Bali Taksi has a fleet of luxury vehicles, under the name Golden Bird Bali, which are often hired out by visiting dignitaries and media stars. You can rent the large sedans, SUVs, or vans with or without drivers; rates are approximately $30–$75 per day. You'll find Golden Bird offices at the domestic and international airport arrival terminals, as well as at the Grand Hyatt Bali, Bali Hyatt, Shera-

SMART TRAVEL TIPS A TO Z

ton Laguna, Nikko Bali, Ramada Bintang Bali, Bali Cliff, and Ritz-Carlton hotels.

➤ MAJOR AGENCIES: **Alamo** (☎ 800/522–9696 in the U.S.; 020/8759–6200 in the U.K.). **Avis** (☎ 800/331–1084 in the U.S.; 800/331–1084 in Canada; 02/9353–9000 in Australia; 09/525–1982 in New Zealand). **Budget** (☎ 800/527–0700 in the U.S.; 0870/607–5000 in the U.K., through affiliate Europcar). **Dollar** (☎ 800/800–6000 in the U.S.; 0124/622–0111 in the U.K., through affiliate Sixt Kenning; 02/9223–1444 in Australia). **Hertz** (☎ 800/654–3001 in the U.S.; 800/263–0600 in Canada; 020/8897–2072 in the U.K.; 02/9669–2444 in Australia; 09/256–8690 in New Zealand). **National Car Rental** (☎ 800/227–7368 in the U.S.; 020/8680–4800 in the U.K., where it is known as National Europe).

➤ LOCAL AGENCIES: For smaller agencies *see* the A to Z sections *in* individual chapters. **Andika** (✉ Jl. Batur 12 A, Denpasar, Bali, ☎ 0361/240032). **Bagus Rent Car** (✉ Jl. Duyung, Sanur, Bali, ☎ 0361/287794). **Bali Taksi** (☎ 0361/701111 on Bali, www.bluebirdgroup.com). **Lina Biro Jasa** (✉ Jl. Bakungsari, Kuta, Bali, ☎ 0361/51820). **P. T. Multi Sri Bali** (✉ Jl. Raya Uluwatu 8A, Jimbaran, Bali, ☎ 0361/701770). **Toyota Rent-a-Car** (☎ 021/840–4040 in Jakarta; 0361/763333 in Jimbaran, Bali; 061/870909 in Medan, Sumatra, www.astra.co.id).

CUTTING COSTS

To get the best deal, **book through a travel agent who will shop around.** Book several weeks in advance of your trip, too—even during off-peak seasons—for lower prices and a better selection of vehicles.

INSURANCE

When driving a rented car, you are generally responsible for any damage to or loss of the vehicle as well as for any property damage or personal injury that you may cause. Before you rent, see what coverage your personal auto-insurance policy and credit cards already provide.

REQUIREMENTS & RESTRICTIONS

Most car rental companies on Bali and Lombok require (or would like you to have) your license from home *and* an International Driver's License. You can get one through the American or Canadian automobile association, or, in the United Kingdom, through the Automobile Association or Royal Automobile Club. Most Western companies also have age requirements. For example, Avis requires that you be at least 25 years old, Hertz 21 years old, and National 18 years old.

Always discuss your itinerary with the agent before signing the contract. Some rental contracts may limit the areas to which you can drive. For example, you need to **obtain a special permit to cross from Bali to Lombok—** really just a letter from the rental agency.

SURCHARGES

Before you pick up a car in one city and leave it in another, **ask about drop-off charges or one-way service fees,** which can be substantial. Note, too, that some rental agencies charge extra if you return the car before the time specified in your contract. To avoid a hefty refueling fee, **fill the tank just before you turn in the car,** but be aware that gas stations near the rental outlet may overcharge.

CAR TRAVEL

The stunning countryside, charming villages, and hospitable cultures of Bali and Lombok make for memorable road trips. However, you should **plan to stay off the roads during holidays and monsoons.** When traveling by car, delays are bound to arise, so **build some flexibility into your schedule.**

In Bali and Lombok you drive on the left side of the road. If you're not comfortable traveling at top speeds, **avoid the passing (right) lane.** And if you're a U.S. or Canadian citizen, remember to **look both ways** when you cross an intersection.

A highway runs around Bali's perimeter, and most interior roads run north to south because of the mountains. Around Denpasar, highways are four-lane, but elsewhere the roads are two-lane and curvy, though mostly paved. A very twisty two-lane highway runs west to east across central Lombok, with branches heading to the north and south coasts; most other Lombok roads are narrow dirt lanes. You can expect to drive at a speed of about 75 kph (47 mph) on the four-lane highways when there's no traffic; on smaller roads you'll be lucky to reach 40 kph (25 mph).

AUTO CLUBS

➤ IN THE U.S.: **American Automobile Association** (☎ 800/564–6222).

➤ IN CANADA: **Canadian Automobile Association** (CAA; ☎ 613/247–0117).

➤ IN THE U.K.: **Automobile Association** (AA; ☎ 0990/500–600). **Royal Automobile Club** (RAC; ☎ 0990/722–722 for membership; 0345/121–345 for insurance).

➤ IN AUSTRALIA: **Australian Automobile Association** (☎ 02/6247–7311).

➤ IN NEW ZEALAND: **New Zealand Automobile Association** (☎ 09/377–4660).

EMERGENCY SERVICES

There is no emergency roadside assistance on Bali or Lombok. **Call the police, your car rental company, or medical services,** if necessary. For local ambulance and police phone numbers, *see* the A to Z sections *in* individual chapters.

➤ CONTACTS: **Ambulance** (☎ 118 across Indonesia). **Fire** (☎ 113 across Indonesia). **Police** (☎ 110 across Indonesia).

GASOLINE

Gas (*petrol*) stations are prevalent throughout southern Bali and around the major towns in other parts of the island. Outside these areas, you have to rely on small local kiosks. Pertamina is the major gas-station chain. On Lombok the only stations are around the port of Lembar, in the towns of Ampenan and Mataram, and in the Senggigi area; otherwise, you'll need to search for local gasoline vendors, who often operate out of roadside stores. For gas-station hours *see* Business Hours, *above.*

Gas costs about 10¢–12¢ per liter, or around 50¢ per U.S. gallon. Credit cards are accepted in cities; however, it's cash only in the small towns. Most station pumps are self-serve; if full service is provided, you can tip the attendant 10¢–20¢. Remember that premium gas is standard. **Don't fill up with *solar* (diesel) unless that's what your vehicle requires.** Stations are few and far between, so **don't set out with less than a quarter tank,** and **check your fuel gauge frequently to make sure it works.**

ROAD CONDITIONS

Modern highways connect the major cities and towns, although they're often snarled with traffic. Vehicles on main roads whip by over the speed limit when the lanes are clear, but traffic slows to a typical rush-hour crawl at peak commute times. Back roads are better, often secluded and scenic, although they are also often unpaved and even undrivable. If you're planning to travel off the main roads or during the rainy season, make sure you have a sturdy vehicle and enough supplies for substantial delays.

Curving mountain roads pose many potential hazards—steep cliffs, landslides, and head-on collisions among them—so **take it slow, make sure there's no oncoming traffic** before you pass lumbering buses, and **beep your horn** before entering blind hairpin curves. When passing through villages, **beware of children and animals** suddenly running into the road, and be ready for curious onlookers to crowd around the vehicle for a chat before you can move on.

A few road signs to note: HATI-HATI (Be careful), PELAN-PELAN (Slow), and AWAS! (Watch out!). On Bali you'll regularly run into hand-lettered signs that read UPACARA (Ceremony), meaning a procession is going on in the street ahead and you'll need to be especially careful.

ROAD MAPS

You can find road maps at most bookstores, many news kiosks, and some gas stations. Large hotels often carry detailed road maps as well.

RULES OF THE ROAD

The official highway speed limit is 75 kph (47 mph). Back roads usually don't have speed limits—and don't need them; you travel as fast as you can between the potholes and farm animals. Foreigners occasionally are stopped for driver's permit and vehicle registration checks; just smile, be polite, and show your documents. Although there is no official seatbelt law—and no carseat requirement for children—cars move fast, and animals, vehicles, and carts often cut into the road unexpectedly, so buckle up. There are no drunk driving laws, either, but it is strongly recommended, due to the unpredictability of driving conditions on the islands, that you never attempt to drive while under the influence of alcohol or other inebriants.

CHILDREN ON BALI & LOMBOK

Bali and Lombok are wonderful places to travel with children, as many large hotels have playgrounds and activities for wee ones; smaller places often have more personalized services. **Check to see what types of kid-friendly amenities a hotel offers.** Some resorts on the scenic Sayan ridge in Ubud don't permit children under 12 because their grounds have steep steps and drop-offs. If you are renting a car, don't forget to **arrange for a car seat** when you reserve.

BABY-SITTING

There are no formal sitting agencies on Bali. Large hotels and resorts have their own activity programs and baby-sitting services; smaller establishments usually recruit a trusted family member or neighbor to provide any assistance you need. Rates are $3–$5 per hour, plus meals and overtime for full days and late nights. Many travelers hire one sitter per child for younger kids so that each one gets individual attention.

FLYING

If your children are two or older, **ask about children's airfares.** As a general rule, infants under two not occupying

a seat fly at greatly reduced fares or even for free. When booking, **confirm carry-on allowances** if you're traveling with infants. In general, for babies charged 10% of the adult fare you are allowed one carry-on bag and a collapsible stroller; if the flight is full, the stroller may have to be checked or you may be limited to less.

Experts agree it's a good idea to use safety seats aloft for children weighing less than 40 pounds. Airlines set their own policies: U.S. carriers usually require that the child be ticketed, even if he or she is young enough to ride free, since the seats must be strapped into regular seats. Do **check your airline's policy about using safety seats during takeoff and landing.** And since safety seats are not allowed just everywhere in the plane, get your seat assignments early.

When reserving, **request children's meals or a freestanding bassinet** if necessary. But note that bulkhead seats, where you must sit to use the bassinet, may lack an overhead bin or storage space on the floor.

FOOD

Indonesian food appeals to even the pickiest child's palate. There's a vast selection of sweet fruits and sticky rice treats, and you can find tasty, inexpensive dishes everywhere, including *nasi goreng* (fried rice), *mie goreng* (fried noodles), satay (grilled meat on sticks), and a variety of curries. Most food is fairly bland, but if it looks fiery, **ask for it without hot peppers (*tidak pedas*).** For kids who like their food bland, you can easily find steamed rice, boiled noodles, grilled meat, and soups. Average Western fare is found at the larger hotel restaurants, and there are fast-food chains on Bali in the tourist areas of Kuta, Legian, Sanur, and Ubud.

LODGING

Most hotels on Bali and Lombok allow children under 12 to stay in their parents' room at no extra charge, but some charge adult rates for children; be sure to **find out the cutoff age for children's discounts.** Baby cribs and children's cots are usually available even at the smallest hotels, so **ask for extra bedding when you book.**

▶ BEST CHOICES: **Bali Hyatt** (✉ Jl. Tamblingan, Sanur, ☎ 0361/281234). **Club Mediterraneé** (✉ Jl. Raya Nusa Dua, Nusa Dua, Bali, ☎ 0361/771246). **Grand Hyatt Bali** (✉ Jl. Nusa Dua, Nusa Dua, ☎ 0361/771234; 800/233–1234 in the U.S.). **Holiday Inn Resort Lombok** (✉ Jl. Raya Mangsit, Senggigi, ☎ 0370/693444). **Kokokan Hotel** (✉ Jl. Pengosekan, Ubud, Bali, ☎ 0361/975742). **Ritz-Carlton, Bali** (✉ Jl. Karang Mas Sejahtera, Jimbaran, ☎ 0361/702222). **Sheraton Laguna** (✉ Jl. Nusa Dua, Nusa Dua, Bali, ☎ 0361/771327; 800/325–3535 in the U.S.). **Sheraton Senggigi** (✉ Jl. Raya Senggigi Km 8, Senggigi, Lombok, ☎ 0370/693333; 800/325–3535 in the U.S.).

PRECAUTIONS

If you have young children, keep a careful watch on what goes into their mouths, and **make sure they know not to drink the water out of the tap;** this should be especially emphasized when bathing. Indonesian adults love to pick up babies and pass them around, and Indonesian children will surely roughhouse with your kids. To minimize germs, **keep moist towelettes available for wiping off hands and faces.** Also **make sure your children know not to pet the local animals,** particularly the dogs and cats that hover around looking for scraps; animals typically aren't regarded as pets in this region, and they don't behave like them. In addition, even the most placid shorelines can have a strong undertow, and no beaches have lifeguards, so **have your children stay in shallow water.**

SIGHTS & ATTRACTIONS

Places that are especially appealing to children are indicated by a rubber duckie icon 🐤 in the margin.

SUPPLIES & EQUIPMENT

Disposable diapers, wipes, bottles, and formulas are available at supermarkets in tourist areas. These can cost up to twice as much as in the United States, though, so **bring your own baby supplies if you can,** particularly if you're venturing off the main

tourist routes. Toys and children's clothes can be found in every town, and these make memorable souvenirs.

TRANSPORTATION

Children under 16 usually receive reduced fares on public transportation; those under two usually travel free. **Place babies securely in a front carrier or backpack,** especially if you need to hold the hand of an older child in crowded stations. **Bring blankets for long bus rides,** as no bassinets are available. Car seats are not the law in Indonesia, so **bring your own or request one from your rental agent** before you arrive. When traveling by boat or ferry, be aware that there are no child safety rails and there may be steep steps to climb, so **stay with young children,** especially during rough seas.

COMPUTERS ON THE ROAD

Electricity is unreliable, even in the main tourist areas, so if you must travel with a laptop, **bring a spare battery.** Also **make sure to bring an adapter and a surge protector;** you can pick these up at most general stores in Indonesia. If you need to check e-mail and download files, first **use a modem tester** (such as the pen-size IBM model) to make sure the hotel line is compatible for modem use. Always **make copies of your files,** and **keep your computer and disks protected** from the tropical heat and humidity. **Be prepared to boot up your laptop** at major security checkpoints.

CONSUMER PROTECTION

Whenever shopping or buying travel services on Bali, **pay with a major credit card** so you can cancel payment or get reimbursed if there's a problem. **Consult this guidebook and ask other travelers for recommendations** before making local purchases. If you're doing business with a particular company for the first time, **contact your local Better Business Bureau and the attorney general's offices** in your own state and the company's home state, as well. Have any complaints been filed? Finally, if you're buying a package or tour, always **consider travel insurance** that includes default coverage (☞ Insurance, *below*).

SMART TRAVEL TIPS A TO Z

SMART TRAVEL TIPS A TO Z

➤ **BBBs: Council of Better Business Bureaus** (✉ 4200 Wilson Blvd., Suite 800, Arlington, VA 22203, ☎ 703/276–0100, FAX 703/525–8277, www.bbb.org).

CRUISE TRAVEL

There are many tour operators on Bali that specialize in cruises around the island; to Nusa Penida and Nusa Lembongan, off the southeast coast; and to other Indonesian islands. Choices for these trips range from a traditional ocean liner to a clipper-type tall ship to a luxury yacht. If you're interested in visiting several Southeast Asian or Indonesian cities, also **consider an international cruise that docks on Bali for a night or two.** To get the best deal, **book with a cruise-only travel agency.**

➤ CRUISE LINES IN THE U.S.: **Crystal Cruises** (✉ 2121 Ave. of the Stars, Los Angeles, CA 90067, ☎ 800/446–6620). **Cunard Line Limited** (✉ 555 5th Ave., New York, NY 10017, ☎ 800/528–6273). **Orient Lines** (✉ 1510 S.E. 17th St., Suite 400, Fort Lauderdale, FL 33316, ☎ 305/527–6660 or 800/333–7300). **Princess Cruises** (✉ 10100 Santa Monica Blvd., Los Angeles, CA 90067, ☎ 310/553–1770). **Radisson Seven Seas Cruises** (✉ 600 Corporate Dr., Suite 410, Fort Lauderdale, FL 33334, ☎ 800/333–3333). **Renaissance Cruises** (✉ 1800 Eller Dr., Suite 300, Box 350307, Fort Lauderdale, FL 33335-0307, ☎ 800/525–2450). **Royal Caribbean Cruise Line** (✉ 1050 Caribbean Way, Miami, FL 33132, ☎ 305/539–6000). **Seabourn Cruise Line** (✉ 55 Francisco St., San Francisco, CA 94133, ☎ 415/391–7444 or 800/929–9595). **Silversea Cruises** (✉ 110 E. Broward Blvd., Fort Lauderdale, FL 33301, ☎ 305/522–4477 or 800/722–9955). **Star Clippers** (✉ 4101 Salzedo Ave., Coral Gables, FL 33146, ☎ 800/442–0551).

➤ LOCAL CRUISE LINES: **Bali Hai** (✉ Benoa Harbor, Bali, ☎ 0361/720331). **P. T. Island Explorer** (Jl. Sekar Waru 14D, Sanur, Bali, ☎ 0361/289856). **Quicksilver** (✉ Jl. Segara Kedul 3, Benoa Harbor, Bali, ☎ 0361/771997). **Waka Louka** (✉ Jl. Pratama, Tanjung Benoa, ☎ 0361/261129).

CUSTOMS & DUTIES

When shopping, **keep receipts** for all purchases. Upon reentering the country, **be ready to show customs officials what you've bought.** If you feel a duty is incorrect or object to the way your clearance was handled, note the inspector's badge number and ask to see a supervisor. If the problem isn't resolved, write to the appropriate authorities, beginning with the port director at your point of entry.

IN INDONESIA

Two liters of liquor and 200 cigarettes may be brought into Indonesia duty-free. Restrictions apply to the import of radios and television sets. No drugs, weapons, or pornography are allowed; nor are cassette players or printed matter in Indonesian or Chinese. **Carry all prescription medicines in their original containers** and keep a copy of the prescription with you.

You may not export more than 50,000 rupiah per person. Other forbidden exports include antiques—generally more than 100 years old and worth more than $100; check with customs for current specifications—artifacts, cultural treasures, and products made from endangered plants and animals, such as furs, feathers, and the tortoiseshell items sold in Bali.

IN THE U.S.

U.S. residents who have been out of the country for at least 48 hours (and who have not used the $400 allowance or any part of it in the past 30 days) may bring home $400 worth of foreign goods duty-free.

U.S. residents 21 and older may bring back 1 liter of alcohol duty-free. In addition, regardless of your age, you are allowed 200 cigarettes and 100 non-Cuban cigars. Antiques, which the U.S. Customs Service defines as objects more than 100 years old, enter duty-free, as do original works of art done entirely by hand, including paintings, drawings, and sculptures.

You may also mail or ship packages home duty-free: up to $200 worth of goods for personal use, with a limit of one parcel per addressee per day (except alcohol or tobacco products or perfume worth more than $5); label the package PERSONAL USE and attach a list of its contents and their retail value. Do not label the package UNSOLICITED GIFT, or your duty-free exemption drops to $100. Mailed items do not affect your duty-free allowance on your return.

➤ INFORMATION: **U.S. Customs Service** (✉ 1300 Pennsylvania Ave. NW, Washington, DC 20229, www. customs.gov; inquiries ☎ 202/354–1000; complaints c/o ✉ 1300 Pennsylvania Ave. NW, Room 5.4D, Washington, DC 20229; registration of equipment c/o ✉ Resource Management, ☎ 202/354–1000).

IN CANADA

Canadian residents who have been out of Canada for at least seven days may bring home C$500 worth of goods duty-free. If you've been away less than seven days but more than 48 hours, the duty-free allowance drops to C$200; if your trip lasts 24–48 hours, the allowance is C$50. You may not pool allowances with family members. Goods claimed under the C$500 exemption may follow you by mail; those claimed under the lesser exemptions must accompany you. Alcohol and tobacco products may be included in the seven-day and 48-hour exemptions but not in the 24-hour exemption. If you meet the age requirements of the province or territory through which you reenter Canada, you may bring in, duty-free, 1.14 liters (40 imperial ounces) of wine or liquor *or* 24 12-ounce cans or bottles of beer or ale. If you are 16 or older, you may bring in, duty-free, 200 cigarettes and 50 cigars. Check ahead of time with Revenue Canada or the Department of Agriculture for policies regarding meat products, seeds, plants, and fruits.

You may send an unlimited number of gifts worth up to C$60 each duty-free to Canada. Label the package UNSOLICITED GIFT—VALUE UNDER $60. Alcohol and tobacco are excluded.

➤ INFORMATION: **Revenue Canada** (✉ 2265 St. Laurent Blvd. S, Ottawa, Ontario K1G 4K3, Canada, ☎ 613/993–0534; 800/461–9999 in Canada, FAX 613/991–4126, www.ccra-adrc. gc.ca).

IN THE U.K.

From countries outside the EU, including Indonesia, you may bring home, duty-free, 200 cigarettes or 50 cigars; 1 liter of spirits or 2 liters of fortified or sparkling wine or liqueurs; 2 liters of still table wine; 60 milliliters of perfume; 250 milliliters of toilet water; plus £136 worth of other goods, including gifts and souvenirs. If returning from outside the EU, prohibited items include meat products, seeds, plants, and fruits.

➤ INFORMATION: **HM Customs and Excise** (✉ Dorset House, Stamford St., Bromley, Kent BR1 1XX, U.K., ☎ 020/7202–4227, www.hmce. gov.uk).

IN AUSTRALIA

Australian residents who are 18 or older may bring home $A400 worth of souvenirs and gifts (including jewelry), 250 cigarettes or 250 grams of tobacco, and 1,125 milliliters of alcohol (including wine, beer, and spirits). Residents under 18 may bring back $A200 worth of goods. Prohibited items include meat products. Seeds, plants, and fruits need to be declared upon arrival.

➤ INFORMATION: **Australian Customs Service** (Regional Director, ✉ Box 8, Sydney, NSW 2001, Australia, ☎ 02/9213–2000, FAX 02/9213–4000, www. customs.gov.au).

IN NEW ZEALAND

Homeward-bound residents 17 or older may bring back $700 worth of souvenirs and gifts. Your duty-free allowance also includes 4.5 liters of wine or beer; one 1,125-milliliter bottle of spirits; and either 200 cigarettes, 250 grams of tobacco, 50 cigars, or a combination of the three up to 250 grams. Prohibited items include meat products, seeds, plants, and fruits.

➤ INFORMATION: **New Zealand Customs** (Custom House, ✉ 50 Anzac Ave., Box 29, Auckland, New Zealand, ☎ 09/300–5399, FAX 09/359–6730, www.customs.govt.nz).

SMART TRAVEL TIPS A TO Z

DINING

Indonesian cuisine takes basic, earthy ingredients and mixes them with rich spices for an amazing variety of tastes. Fried rice (*nasi goreng*) and fried noodles (*mie goreng*), the staples on any menu, can still be masterpieces of color that pop with fresh bits of meat and vegetables. Simple street food—satay, *soto ayam* (chicken soup), *gado-gado* (boiled vegetable salad with peanut sauce)—can be as good as that served in the best hotels, although the more expensive restaurants add other Asian and European entrées to the typical Indonesian listings. Chinese restaurants are found throughout the islands, and there are usually at least one or two Western items on every menu in tourist areas. Bali, of course, has its own specialties, such as roast suckling pig and duck. Most top restaurants are in the tourist hubs; not all are expensive, but a meal for two (excluding drinks) in an expensive resort restaurant could cost around $50. A meal for two at a midrange hotel restaurant might run about $20; in a regular *rumah makan* restaurant, $10. In a small, open-walled *warung* a meal for two might cost less than $5; at a street stall a typical dish is less than $2. Most places are casual, although you probably want to don better clothes for your evening meal. Only the most opulent establishments require a jacket.

The restaurants listed in this book are the cream of the crop in each price category. Restaurants are denoted by the crossed knife-and-fork icon, ✕ .

Dining price categories throughout the book are based on the following ranges:

CATEGORY	COST*
$$$$	over $30
$$$	$20–$30
$$	$10–$20
$	under $10

per person for a three-course dinner, excluding tax, service, and drinks.

MEALS & SPECIALTIES

Breakfast on Bali is typically light: fruit and coffee or tea and perhaps some toast. Most Western hotel chains offer a breakfast buffet, and many *losmen* (small hotels) include fruit, toast, and tea in their room price. Lunch is also light, usually steamed rice, fish, and vegetables; nasi or mie goreng; or gado-gado. Dinner, served after sundown, is a repeat of lunch at its simplest; at its most extravagant, though, it can include flavorful curries, grilled seafood, and roasted meat. Look for rijsttafel buffets, which give you a sample of many local dishes. Indonesians generally are light eaters and thus regularly snack between meals. Popular midmorning and afternoon treats are peanuts, puffed rice, colorful rice-paste and sticky rice squares, and sliced fruits on sticks.

Bali is famous for its *babi guleg* (roasted, shredded pork), roast duck, and black-rice pudding—you usually order these a day in advance of your meal. The name Lombok actually comes from the Indonesian word for chili pepper, and you can expect spicy food on this island. Look for the word *pelecing* (served with chili sauce) on menus. You won't find much pork on Lombok; it's mostly chicken and fish. A Lombok specialty is *ayam taliwang,* grilled or fried chicken served with chili sauce.

MEALTIMES

Hotel restaurants and street warung are usually open from about 7 AM until 11 PM; other establishments open for lunch around 11 AM and close around 9 PM. On Saturday night (*Malam Minggu*), many Indonesian restaurants and clubs are open through the wee hours, particularly in Kuta.

Unless otherwise noted, the restaurants listed in this guide are open daily for lunch and dinner.

PAYING

Credit cards are widely accepted at larger restaurants in the main tourist hubs. At smaller restaurants and outside the major towns, cash is your only option.

RESERVATIONS & DRESS

Reservations are always a good idea: we mention them only when they're essential or not accepted. Book as far ahead as you can, and reconfirm as soon as you arrive. We mention dress only when men are required to wear a jacket or a jacket and tie.

WINE, BEER, & SPIRITS

Although Indonesia is a Muslim country, on Bali—the lone Hindu island—you can find alcohol almost anywhere. Most tourist restaurants and city dining establishments offer a range of alcoholic beverages to complement your meal. In the Senggigi area of Lombok you can find beer, wine, and spirits at all of the resorts and beer at Chinese restaurants. Outside of Senggigi, though, the island is dry.

Local brands of beer are cheap, about 30¢ a 12-ounce can, while imported beer can run to $3 a bottle. One-liter bottles and six-packs of domestic and imported brands are available at most stores, even in small towns. Imported wine and liquor, available at grocery stores and hotel shops in tourist areas, can cost double the prices back home. Local alcohol, known as *arak* or *tuak*, can be unpleasant, but it's effective even in very small doses. In rural areas it is often served in bamboo tubes.

DISABILITIES & ACCESSIBILITY

Travelers with disabilities who are planning a trip to Bali will find facilities adequate in the major international chain hotels built in the last decade. For example, the Four Seasons Resort in Jimbaran, the Grand Hyatt Bali in Nusa Dua, and the Amandari in Ubud all offer wheelchair access and other features for travelers with disabilities. Other hotels and restaurants, however, may present challenges, such as steep steps, rough paths, and narrow doors and hallways; call and ask (or have an Indonesian-speaking travel agent do so) before you plan a visit.

LODGING

When discussing accessibility with an operator or reservations agent, **ask hard questions.** Are there any stairs, inside *or* out? Are there grab bars next to the toilet *and* in the shower/tub? How wide is the doorway to the room? To the bathroom? For the most extensive facilities meeting the latest legal specifications, **opt for newer accommodations.**

SIGHTS & ATTRACTIONS

Most of Bali's and Lombok's tourist sites—temples, museums, performance areas, and shopping areas—have limits for travelers with disabilities. The countryside is hilly, paths are rugged, and temples such as Pura Besakih on Bali have many steps. Markets are in narrow, crowded alleys, and performance seating is usually hip to hip, without room to move. Still, ask your tour operator for advice; even if you can't visit the more famous places, he or she may have ideas about areas that are more accessible and just as enticing.

TRANSPORTATION

Although car rental agencies don't have vehicles with hand controls, you can **hire a driver and large-model vehicle** such as a Kijang or a Land Cruiser. Most ferries between islands have narrow passages and steep steps, but there are numerous boat-tour and day-cruise operators with large vessels that might suit travelers with disabilities. Expect the same facilities on Indonesia's domestic airlines as on any other carrier.

➤ COMPLAINTS: **Disability Rights Section** (✉ U.S. Department of Justice, Civil Rights Division, Box 66738, Washington, DC 20035-6738; ☎ 202/514–0301 or 800/514–0301; 202/514–0383 TTY; 800/514–0383 TTY; 𝔽𝔸𝕏 202/307–1198; www.usdoj.gov/crt/ada/adahom1.ht) for general complaints. **Aviation Consumer Protection Division** (☞ Air Travel, *above*) for airline-related problems. **Civil Rights Office** (✉ U.S. Department of Transportation, Departmental Office of Civil Rights, S-30, 400 7th St. SW, Room 10215, Washington, DC 20590, ☎ 202/366–4648, 𝔽𝔸𝕏 202/366–9371) for problems with surface transportation.

TRAVEL AGENCIES

In the United States, the Americans with Disabilities Act requires that travel firms serve the needs of all travelers. Some agencies specialize in working with people with disabilities.

➤ TRAVELERS WITH MOBILITY PROBLEMS: **Access Adventures** (✉ 206 Chestnut Ridge Rd., Scottsville, NY

14624, ☎ 716/889–9096, dltravel@prodigy.net), run by a former physical-rehabilitation counselor. **Flying Wheels Travel** (✉ 143 W. Bridge St., Box 382, Owatonna, MN 55060, ☎ 507/451–5005 or 800/535–6790, FAX 507/451–1685, thq@ll.net, www.flyingwheels.com).

DISCOUNTS & DEALS

Be a smart shopper and **compare all your options** before making decisions. A plane ticket bought with a promotional coupon from a travel club, coupon book, or direct-mail offer may not be cheaper than the least expensive fare from a discount ticket agency. And always keep in mind that what you get is just as important as what you save.

DISCOUNT RESERVATIONS

To save money, **look into discount reservations services** with toll-free numbers, which use their buying power to get a better price on hotels, airline tickets, even car rentals. When booking a room, always **call the hotel's local toll-free number** (if one is available), rather than the central reservations number, or go to the hotel's Web site; you'll often get a better price. Always ask about special packages or corporate rates.

When shopping for the best deal on hotels and car rentals, **look for guaranteed exchange rates,** which protect you against a falling dollar. With your rate locked in, you won't pay more, even if the price goes up in the local currency.

➤ HOTEL ROOMS: Steigenberger Reservation Service (☎ 800/223–5652, www.srs-worldhotels.com). **Travel Interlink** (☎ 800/888–5898, www.travelinterlink.com). **Vacation-Land** (☎ 800/245–0050, sales@vacationasia.com, www.vacation-land.com).

PACKAGE DEALS

Don't confuse packages and guided tours. When you buy a package, you travel on your own, just as though you had planned the trip yourself. Fly/drive packages, which combine airfare and car rental, are often a good deal.

ECOTOURISM

Ecotourism is quickly catching on in Indonesia, Bali and Lombok included. The islands' many parks, historic sites, and cultural hubs are treasured commodities that the government is working hard to promote and preserve with the help of international travel companies and nonprofit organizations. Educational programs encourage respect for Indonesia's natural resources, and local citizens are being trained as trip guides. You may pay more for an ecotour than for a regular group trip, but consider the advantages: more money goes to those at the local level, your leader will be more knowledgeable about the local environment, and more interest shown to this type of trip will help promote the preservation of this rich country's amazing natural and cultural wealth.

Other trends on the islands are the discouragement of littering and the encouragement of recycling. Don't drop your trash out of car windows or along the trail; find a can or carry it with you. Although you probably won't find recycling bins yet, ask if there is a special place to store used cans, bottles, and papers.

ELECTRICITY

To use your U.S.-purchased electric-powered equipment, **bring a converter and adapter.** The electrical current in Indonesia is 220 volts, 50 cycles alternating. There can be electrical surges and sags at any time, even in Bali. Carry a small flashlight with extra batteries and keep computers charged just in case.

If your appliances are dual-voltage, you need only an adapter. Don't use 110-volt outlets marked FOR SHAVERS ONLY for high-wattage appliances such as blow-dryers. Most laptops operate equally well on 110 or 220 volts and so require only an adapter.

EMBASSIES & CONSULATES

➤ CANADA: **Jakarta Embassy** (✉ Jl. Jendral Sudirman Kav. 29, 5th floor, Wisma Metropolitan 1, ☎ 021/510709).

➤ UNITED STATES: **Denpasar Consulate** (✉ Jl. Hayam Wuruk 188,

☎ 0361/233605). **Jakarta Embassy** (✉ Jl. Medan Merdeka Selatan 5, ☎ 021/3442211). **Medan Consulate** (✉ Jl. Imam Bonjol 13, ☎ 061/322200). **Sanur Consulate** (✉ Jl. Segara Ayu 5, ☎ 0361/288478). **Surabaya Consulate** (✉ Jl. Raya Dr. Sutomo 33, ☎ 031/568–2287).

➤ UNITED KINGDOM: **Jakarta Embassy** (✉ Jl. M. H. Thamrin 75, ☎ 021/330904). **Medan Consulate** (✉ Jl. Ahmad Yani 2, ☎ 061/518699).

➤ AUSTRALIA: **Denpasar Consulate** (✉ Jl. Prof. Mochtar Yamin Kav 51, Renon, ☎ 0361/235092). **Jakarta Embassy** (✉ Jl. H. R. Rasuna Said Kav. C15–16, ☎ 021/522–7111).

➤ NEW ZEALAND: **Jakarta Embassy** (✉ Jl. Diponegoro 41, ☎ 021/330680).

EMERGENCIES

Health and road emergencies are the most common problems for travelers to Bali. For medical emergencies **call an ambulance or the hospital emergency room.** You can also find 24-hour medical clinics and pharmacies in the larger towns. For after-hours dental emergencies, the larger hotels and main dental clinics will usually have someone on call. For traffic accidents and vehicle breakdowns, **call the police and your car rental agency.** Most Indonesians will go out of their way to help visitors who are in trouble.

➤ CONTACTS: **Ambulance** (☎ 118 across Indonesia). **Fire** (☎ 113 across Indonesia). **Police** (☎ 110 across Indonesia). For information on emergency contacts *see* the A to Z sections *in* individual chapters.

ENGLISH-LANGUAGE MEDIA

You can find English-language newspapers and magazines at most newsstands and hotel shops on Bali and Lombok. Except for romances and spy novels found in hotel shops, there is a limited selection of new titles; your best bet is to scour the used-book stores in the backpacker areas. Several English-language programs are aired weekly on the radio, and you find English-language news broadcasts, such as CNN and ESPN, at hotels that have cable service.

BOOKS

Book superstores aren't around yet, and small bookshops sell mostly Indonesian-language titles. Hotel shops may carry only a few current Western bestsellers, but you can find hundreds of titles at book exchange outlets in the budget tourist areas. Although in these outlets the books are cheap and well-worn, you can exchange your old titles for new ones. Bought new, books can run 30%–50% more than in the United States.

➤ BOOKSTORES: **Ary's Book Shop** (✉ Jl. Ubud, Ubud, Bali, ☎ 0361/978203). **Bagus Drugstore** (✉ Jl. Tamblingan at Jl. Duyung, Sanur, Bali, ☎ 0361/287794).

NEWSPAPERS & MAGAZINES

The *Jakarta Post* is the most prominent paper, covering all the bases: international, local, entertainment, and sports news and classifieds for the islands. The *Singapore Straits–Times* has a broader focus on news throughout Southeast Asia. You can also find the *Wall Street Journal* at most shops, along with *Time, Newsweek,* and other magazines. The weekly *AsiaWeek* newsmagazine has the most comprehensive coverage of Southeast Asian headline news, as well as a thorough exchange-rate chart in the back.

The *Bali Plus* booklet—distributed free at travel offices, hotels, and grocery stores—is full of listings for performances and temple celebrations. *Bali News,* a free newspaper, lists music, dances, and some temple activities. A new guide to Bali's entertainment scene is *The Beat,* which is distributed free in restaurants throughout the island and covers restaurants, nightlife, movies, and music around Ubud, southern Bali, and the Jakarta area. A new magazine, *Balio,* is an eye-catching publication that has the inside story on Bali's hot spots. The English-Japanese *Bali Tribune* monthly details island happenings—look for its free postcards in shops and restaurants around the island. The glossy *Bali Echo, Hello Bali,* and even *Surf Time* are good sources of information on island activities. Ask at a travel agency or tourist office to see a copy of the phonebook-size *Bali Tourist Guide,* which lists addresses and phone numbers for all major hotels and businesses on the island and describes regional cultures, performances, and festivals.

RADIO & TELEVISION

You can usually find at least one station that carries a BBC news broadcast on Bali or Lombok. Interspersed with Indonesian programming, you can find English-language radio shows and news in Bali. Shortwave Voice of America broadcasts are on 6110, 11760, and 15425 KHz. Large hotels usually have cable TV, which gives guests access to CNN, ESPN, MTV, and other Western programs.

ETIQUETTE & BEHAVIOR

The Balinese are extremely polite. Begin encounters with locals by saying "*Selamat pagi*" ("Good morning"), "*Selamat siang*" ("Good day"), "*Selamat sore*" ("Good afternoon"), or "*Selamat malam*" ("Good evening"), depending on the time of day. Two phrases you use often are "*Terima kasih*" ("Thank you") and "*Ma'af*" ("Excuse me," or "I'm sorry"). Shaking hands has become a common practice, and Indonesians are very tactile, so expect to be touched often in conversation. Smiling is the national pastime, so do it frequently, and you'll have a much easier time transcending language barriers. It's best if you **don't point with your index finger (gesture with your whole hand instead), cross your arms, or place your hands on your hips**; these are signs of anger. Most important, **avoid touching food or people with your left hand,** which is considered unclean.

The more formal or sacred an occasion, the more formally dressed you should be. When visiting mosques, **women should wear something on the head, and men should wear long trousers and have at least their upper arms covered.** Women shouldn't enter during menstruation. Don't walk in front of those who are praying. **You must wear a sash to enter Balinese temples.** Sashes are usually rented onsite for a few thousand rupiah. It's

considered improper to wear shorts and other above-the-knee clothing in temples, so avoid them or take a sarong when visiting a holy place.

If a temple fee is required to enter a temple, it will clearly be noted on a sign at the entrance. However, though most small, rural complexes have no admission fee, it's always nice to make a donation of Rp 1,000–Rp 5,000 at the entrance.

As for modesty, remember that this is Indonesia, so **keep bikini tops on and Speedos in the suitcase except where designated on tourist beaches.** Public displays of affection are frowned upon, so **keep your business inside your room.** Finally, because this is a culture deeply rooted in respect for religion, community, and family, you should be respectful in return toward the Balinese.

BUSINESS ETIQUETTE

As in the West, Indonesians greet one another by shaking right hands. **Extend your business card with both hands,** and when someone gives you a card, **take a few seconds to examine it,** as this is a sign of respect. Even formal meetings usually begin with chitchat and an offer of tea; **don't be in a hurry to get right down to business.** The manner of negotiation here is quiet, polite, and indirect; even the fiercest deals are cut with patient smiles. Remember to **thank your hosts when you leave.**

GAY & LESBIAN TRAVEL

Homosexuality is not readily accepted in this overwhelmingly Muslim country. Gay and lesbian travelers should practice discretion, even on relatively carefree Bali. On Lombok, the hotel Puri Mas, in Senggigi, is especially gay-friendly.

➤ GAY- & LESBIAN-FRIENDLY TOUR OPERATORS: **Hanns Ebensten Travel** (✉ 513 Fleming St., Key West, FL 33040, ☎ 305/294–8174). **Toto Tours** (✉ 1326 W. Albion Ave., Suite 3W, Chicago, IL 60626, ☎ 773/274–8686 or 800/565–1241, ℻ 773/274–8695).

➤ GAY- & LESBIAN-FRIENDLY TRAVEL AGENCIES: **Different Roads Travel** (✉ 8383 Wilshire Blvd., Suite 902,

Beverly Hills, CA 90211, ☎ 323/651–5557 or 800/429–8747, FAX 323/651–3678, leigh@west.tzell.com). **Kennedy Travel** (✉ 314 Jericho Turnpike, Floral Park, NY 11001, ☎ 516/352–4888 or 800/237–7433, FAX 516/354–8849, kennedytravel1@yahoo.com, www.kennedytravel.com). **Now Voyager** (✉ 4406 18th St., San Francisco, CA 94114, ☎ 415/626–1169 or 800/255–6951, FAX 415/626–8626, www.nowvoyager.com). **Skylink Travel and Tour** (✉ 1006 Mendocino Ave., Santa Rosa, CA 95401, ☎ 707/546–9888 or 800/225–5759, FAX 707/546–9891, skylinktvl@aol.com, www.skylinktravel.com), serving lesbian travelers.

HEALTH

Denpasar has several well-run hospitals with modern facilities and 24-hour service. Many tourist hubs have round-the-clock medical and dental clinics as well. Outside these areas, however, you will have to know some Indonesian—or find an English-speaking Balinese to translate—to get the assistance you need. For serious medical emergencies and long-term care, most Westerners choose to fly to Singapore.

DIVERS' ALERT

Do not fly within 24 hours of scuba diving.

FOOD & DRINK

On Bali and Lombok the major health risk is traveler's diarrhea, caused by eating contaminated fruit or vegetables or drinking contaminated water. So **watch what you eat.** Stay away from ice, uncooked food, and unpasteurized milk and milk products, and **drink only bottled water** or water that has been boiled for at least 20 minutes. Mild cases of diarrhea may respond to Imodium (known generically as loperamide) or Pepto-Bismol (not as strong), both of which can be purchased over the counter. Drink plenty of purified water or tea—chamomile is a good folk remedy. In severe cases, rehydrate yourself with a salt-sugar solution (½ teaspoon salt and 4 tablespoons sugar per quart of water), or bring along a bottle of Pedialyte. As a tastier option for rehydrating sick children, **bring Pedialyte popsicles with you** and freeze them at your hotel.

MEDICAL PLANS

No one plans to get sick while traveling, but it happens, so **consider signing up with a medical-assistance company.** Members get doctor referrals, emergency evacuation or repatriation, hot lines for medical consultation, cash for emergencies, and other assistance.

➤ MEDICAL-ASSISTANCE COMPANIES: **International SOS Assistance** (✉ 8 Neshaminy Interplex, Suite 207, Trevose, PA 19053, ☎ 215/245–4707 or 800/523–6586, FAX 215/244–9617, www.internationalsos.com; ✉ 12 Chemin Riantbosson, 1217 Meyrin 1, Geneva, Switzerland, ☎ 4122/785–6464, FAX 4122/785–6424; ✉ 331 N. Bridge Rd., 17-00, Odeon Towers, Singapore 188720, ☎ 65/338–7800, FAX 65/338–7611).

OVER-THE-COUNTER REMEDIES

You can find over-the-counter remedies such as aspirin, Tylenol, and Tums—as well as sunscreen, bug repellent, mosquito coils, Band-Aids, Bactine, iodine, and hydrogen peroxide—at most grocery stores and pharmacies. Each tourist area usually has at least one all-night pharmacy; for details *see* the A to Z sections *in* individual chapters.

PESTS & OTHER HAZARDS

According to the Centers for Disease Control and Prevention (CDC) there is no risk of malaria or dengue on Bali, though there is some risk in areas of Lombok. In most urban or easily accessible areas you need not worry. However, if you plan to visit remote regions or stay for more than six weeks, **check with the CDC.** In areas where malaria and dengue, both of which are carried by mosquitoes, are prevalent, use mosquito nets, wear clothing that covers the body, apply repellent containing DEET, and use spray for flying insects in living and sleeping areas. Also **consider taking antimalarial pills.** There is no vaccine against dengue.

SHOTS & MEDICATIONS

Although the islands of Indonesia do not require or suggest vaccinations before traveling, the CDC offers the following recommendations:

Tetanus-diphtheria and polio vaccinations should be up-to-date; if it has been more than 10 years since your last tetanus vaccination, you should get another. You should also be immunized against measles, mumps, and rubella. If you plan to visit rural areas, where there's questionable sanitation, you need to **get an immune-serum globulin vaccination as protection against hepatitis A.** If you are staying for longer than three weeks and traveling into rural areas, antimalarial pills and a typhoid vaccination are recommended. If staying for a month or more, you should be vaccinated against rabies and Japanese encephalitis; for six months or more, against hepatitis B as well. For news on current outbreaks of infectious diseases, ask your physician and check with your state or local department of health.

➤ HEALTH WARNINGS: **National Centers for Disease Control** (CDC; National Center for Infectious Diseases, Division of Quarantine, Traveler's Health Section, ✉ 1600 Clifton Rd. NE, M/S E-03, Atlanta, GA 30333, ☎ 888/232–3228 or 800/311–3435, FAX 888/232–3299, www.cdc.gov).

HOLIDAYS

Hindu, Muslim, Chinese, and Christian holidays are all celebrated on Bali. When planning your trip, check with the tourist office to see which holidays are scheduled during your proposed travel dates: perhaps you can see a fantastic temple ceremony—or avoid a time when everything is closed. In addition to the general religious observances, each temple has its own annual birthday ceremony, and there are full-moon and new-moon temple celebrations around the island. Bali's central settlements observe the island's religious holidays and celebrations more strictly than towns elsewhere, so travelers have a chance to observe a multitude of island traditions throughout the year here. Because the Balinese lunar year is just 210 days, Balinese holidays can occur twice in a single Western year. Festivities are listed in the monthly *Bali Plus* guidebook.

Throughout Lombok Muslim festivals honoring Muhammad are a tradition.

Colorful Hindu processions are more common in the west, where most of the Balinese population resides. The Islamic calendar is slightly shorter than that of the West, so festivals fall on different dates of the Western calendar each year. The Regional Office of Tourism in Ampenan has a calendar of events for West Nusa Tenggara.

INSURANCE

The most useful travel-insurance plan is a comprehensive policy that includes coverage for trip cancellation and interruption, default, trip delay, and medical expenses (with a waiver for preexisting conditions).

Without insurance you will lose all or most of your money if you cancel your trip, regardless of the reason. Default insurance covers you if your tour operator, airline, or cruise line goes out of business. Trip-delay covers expenses that arise because of bad weather or mechanical delays. Study the fine print when comparing policies.

If you're traveling internationally, a key component of travel insurance is coverage for medical bills incurred if you get sick on the road. Such expenses are not generally covered by Medicare or private policies. U.K. residents can buy a travel-insurance policy valid for most vacations taken during the year in which it's purchased (but check preexisting-condition coverage). British and Australian citizens need extra medical coverage when traveling overseas.

Always **buy travel policies directly from the insurance company;** if you buy them from a cruise line, airline, or tour operator that goes out of business, you probably will not be covered for the agency or operator's default, a major risk. Before making any purchase, **review your existing health and home-owner's policies** to find what they cover away from home.

➤ TRAVEL INSURERS: In the U.S.: **Access America** (✉ 6600 W. Broad St., Richmond, VA 23230, ☎ 804/285–3300 or 800/284–8300, FAX 804/673–1586, www.previewtravel.com). **Travel Guard International** (✉ 1145

Clark St., Stevens Point, WI 54481, ☎ 715/345–0505 or 800/826–1300, FAX 800/955–8785, www.noelgroup.com).

➤ INSURANCE INFORMATION: In Canada: **Voyager Insurance** (✉ 44 Peel Center Dr., Brampton, Ontario L6T 4M8, ☎ 905/791–8700, 800/668–4342 in Canada). In the U.K.: **Association of British Insurers** (✉ 51–55 Gresham St., London EC2V 7HQ, ☎ 020/7600–3333, FAX 020/7696–8999, info@abi.org.uk, www.abi.org.uk). In Australia: **Insurance Council of Australia** (☎ 03/9614–1077, FAX 03/9614–7924). In New Zealand: **Insurance Council of New Zealand** (✉ Box 474, Wellington, ☎ 04/472–5230, FAX 04/473–3011, www.icnz.org.nz).

LANGUAGE

Although some 300 languages are spoken in Indonesia, Bahasa Indonesia has been the national language since independence. The Balinese also have their own language, which differs slightly based on the castes of the participants. On Lombok, the Sasaks have their own dialect, and Chinese is spoken by many immigrants. English is widely spoken in tourist areas. You can begin learning the Indonesian language with a dictionary or workbook and cassette tapes, which will help you find the rhythm and pronunciation of words. You can also find language classes and services on the Internet. Once you're in the country, you will probably be approached by countless students requesting to practice their English—this is the perfect time for you to try out your Indonesian skills as well. For some language tips and basic vocabulary *see* Vocabulary at the back of this book.

In Bali and Lombok names of towns, geographical features, and attractions may have a slightly different spelling from sign to sign and map to map—usually the variation is a changed or added vowel. This book generally uses the most modern or common spelling.

LODGING

Accommodations on Bali range from shoebox-size rooms with shared or "squat" toilets to five-star luxury lodgings. Every major city and important resort has at least one international-style hotel known for its service and amenities; many are part of chains, such as Sheraton, Regent, Hyatt, Hilton, Holiday Inn, and Inter-Continental. Lombok has plenty of small losmen that appeal to back-packing types; most upscale establishments are in Senggigi, though you can find a few ocean-side resorts in other areas. If you can afford to splurge, a resort in Bali or Lombok is the place to do it. The prices of even the very top hotels are still far lower than comparable digs in Europe and North America, particularly with the recent drop in exchange rates and airfares to the region.

A good rule for medium and large hotels in popular areas is to **reserve your rooms at least two months before arrival.** This is especially true in December and January; during Nyepi and the Chinese New Year; at the end of Ramadan; and during peak tourist season in July and August. The international chains have U.S. reservations offices. If you arrive in Bali or Lombok without a hotel reservation, you will find a reservations desk at the airport that may be able to provide an immediate booking. This service is usually efficient and free, and special discounts are often available.

Most bottom-end accommodations are clustered in certain areas of cities or tourist hubs—and they're usually a little off the beaten path. Always **ask to see the room before committing to a stay in a budget hotel,** and **comparison-shop for the best deal.** On Bali the budget area is the back streets of Kuta Beach, and on Lombok the budget places are the Gili Islands and Kuta, on the southern coast.

Budget hotels are classified as *wisma* (a comfortable hotel or homestay-type establishment), *losmen* (a small hotel with simple rooms and shared baths and living areas), and *penginapan* (a bare-bones losmen, the simplest type of accommodation available). No reservations are necessary for these establishments; just show up and ask for a room. Be sure to **arrive early around holidays,** however, because rooms can fill up quickly.

The lodgings we list are the cream of the crop in each price category. We always list the facilities available—but we don't specify whether they cost extra. When pricing accommodations, always **ask what's included and what costs extra.** Lodgings are denoted by a little house icon, ⌂.

Lodging price categories throughout the book are based on the following ranges:

CATEGORY	COST*
$$$$	over $250
$$$	$150–$250
$$	$100–$150
$	$50–$100
¢	under $50

for a standard double room in high season, excluding 10% service charge and 11% tax.

Assume that hotels operate on the **European Plan** (EP, with no meals) unless we specify they use either the **Continental Plan** (CP, with a Continental breakfast), **Breakfast Plan** (BP, with a full breakfast), or the **Modified American Plan** (MAP, with breakfast and dinner) or are **all-inclusive** (including all meals and most activities).

APARTMENT & VILLA RENTALS

If you want a home base that's roomy enough for a family and comes with cooking facilities, **consider a furnished rental.** These can save you money, especially if you're traveling with a group. Home-exchange directories sometimes list rentals as well as exchanges. Larger resort hotels may also have apartment complexes next to their properties.

With rising numbers of long-term tourists, international employees, and retirees in Bali and Lombok, apartment, house, and villa rentals have become a popular way to enjoy the culture while cutting costs and maintaining an independent lifestyle. Numerous rental companies provide city and resort homes to corporate employers; hotel chains often have villas for lease; and consortiums and individuals may have small houses or apartments to rent. Real-estate agencies can also handle such deals. On

Bali one recommended rental agency is Indovillas, which has a variety of homes and villas available throughout the island; these range from comfortable budget properties to luxurious five-acre estates, and most have pools, gardens, kitchens, laundries, modern electronics, and an on-site staff.

➤ INTERNATIONAL AGENTS: **Hideaways International** (✉ 767 Islington St., Portsmouth, NH 03801, ☎ 603/430–4433 or 800/843–4433, FAX 603/430–4444, info@hideaways.com, www.hideaways.com; membership $99).

➤ LOCAL AGENTS: **Indovillas** (✉ Jl. Daksina 5, Batu Belig, Kerobokan, Bali, ☎ 0811/392985, ☎ FAX 0361/733031, balihq@idola.net.id, www.indovillas.com).

CAMPING

There are no Western-style camping areas on Bali or Lombok. In natural areas with hiking trails, such as Bali Barat National Park and Gunung Agung on Bali and Gunung Rinjani on Lombok, a guide can help plan your route and choose your sleeping spot for the night—whether it be a vacant hunting pavilion in the forest, a mountain hut, or a friend's home. If you're in a park area, make sure to **get the proper permits;** elsewhere, make sure to **get permission to camp from the leader of the nearest village.**

HOSTELS

No matter what your age, you can **save on lodging costs by staying at hostels.** In some 5,000 locations in more than 70 countries around the world, Hostelling International (HI), the umbrella group for a number of national youth-hostel associations, offers single-sex, dorm-style beds and, at many hostels, rooms for couples and family accommodations. Membership in any HI national hostel association, open to travelers of all ages, allows you to stay in HI-affiliated hostels at member rates; one-year membership is about $25 for adults (C$26.75 in Canada, £9.30 in the U.K., $30 in Australia, and $30 in New Zealand); hostels run about $10–$25 per night. Members have priority if the hostel is full; they're also eligible for discounts around the world, even on rail and bus travel in some countries.

➤ ORGANIZATIONS: **Hostelling International—American Youth Hostels** (✉ 733 15th St. NW, Suite 840, Washington, DC 20005, ☎ 202/783–6161, FAX 202/783–6171, hiayhserv@hiayh.org, www.hiayh.org). **Hostelling International—Canada** (✉ 400–205 Catherine St., Ottawa, Ontario K2P 1C3, Canada, ☎ 613/237–7884, FAX 613/237–7868, info@hostellingintl.ca, www.hostellingintl.ca). **Youth Hostel Association of England and Wales** (✉ Trevelyan House, 8 St. Stephen's Hill, St. Albans, Hertfordshire AL1 2DY, U.K., ☎ 0870/8708808, FAX 01727/844126, customerservices@yha.org.uk, www.yha.org.uk). **Australian Youth Hostel Association** (✉ 10 Mallett St., Camperdown, NSW 2050, Australia, ☎ 02/9565–1699, FAX 02/9565–1325, www.yha.com.au). **Youth Hostels Association of New Zealand** (✉ Box 436, Christchurch, New Zealand, ☎ 03/379–9970, FAX 03/365–4476, info@yha.org.nz, www.yha.org.nz).

HOTELS

Upscale hotel rooms on Bali and Lombok ($$ and above) usually have air-conditioning, queen-size beds, and showers; the best usually have bathtubs and pools as well. In budget hotels ($ and ¢), expect a simple room with a fan, a queen-size bed, and a *mandi* (a cold-water basin or bucket from which you dip water to wash yourself—much more refreshing than it sounds). Budget hotels usually have Indonesian squat toilets, while more expensive accommodations have typical Western-style toilets. All hotels listed have private bath unless otherwise noted.

Particularly in budget hotels and during the off-season, **check out more than one room before you move in.** If you like quiet, stay away from rooms by the street, shared rest rooms, and public chatting areas. Check to see that lights, air-conditioning or fans, toilets, and showers work; that windows open; and that doors lock securely.

➤ RESERVING A ROOM: When requesting hotel information by phone or using a letter, fax, or e-mail, make sure you ask for the following pieces of information: the nightly rate for and availability of the type of room you want; the rate for a similar room with a shared bath; whether a weekly rate or low-season discount is offered; whether there's an extra charge for a room with a view of the ocean/surroundings; whether there's an extra charge if extra adults/children also stay in the room; whether there's an extra charge for a rollaway bed/crib. When making your reservation, be sure to specify the following: upper or lower floor; the type of room and the number of adults/children; private or shared bath; and any extras, such as a rollaway bed or cot, that you need; be sure to note if you'd like a room away from the street or other noise.

➤ TOLL-FREE NUMBERS: **Best Western** (☎ 800/528–1234, www.bestwestern.com). **Choice** (☎ 800/221–2222, www.hotelchoice.com). **Four Seasons** (☎ 800/332–3442, www.fourseasons.com). **Hilton** (☎ 800/445–8667, www.hilton.com). **Holiday Inn** (☎ 800/465–4329, www.basshotels.com). **Hyatt Hotels & Resorts** (☎ 800/233–1234, www.hyatt.com). **Inter-Continental** (☎ 800/327–0200, www.interconti.com). **Ramada** (☎ 800/228–2828, www.ramada.com). **Ritz-Carlton** (☎ 800/241–3333, www.ritzcarlton.com).

MAIL & SHIPPING

Indonesian addresses are straightforward. All you need for a proper address are the name, street address (Jl. stands for *jalan*, or road), number (though many addresses in small towns won't have this), town, island, and postal code. Finally, be sure to follow all this information with "Republik Indonesia."

Expect postcards, letters, and packages to take 10 days by standard mail to North America and Europe and about a week to Australia and New Zealand.

OVERNIGHT SERVICES

Federal Express and DHL both serve Bali and Lombok.

➤ MAJOR SERVICES: **DHL** (✉ Jl. Hayam Wuruk, Denpasar, Bali, ☎ 0361/222526). **Federal Express** (✉ Jl.

Bypass 100X, Jimbaran, Bali, ☎ 0361/701727).

POSTAL RATES

Two kinds of airmail are available: *pos udara* (regular) and *kilat* (express). Kilat rates to the United States and the United Kingdom are Rp 1,600 and Rp 1,700 for letters weighing 1 gram (.035 ounce). Postcards are Rp 600 to all foreign countries. Pos udara letters less than 21 grams are Rp 1,600 to North America and Europe and Rp 1,200 to Australia and New Zealand.

RECEIVING MAIL

To receive letters or packages, have them sent to the main post office in a major town, which will usually be open Monday through Thursday 8–4, Friday 8 AM–11 AM, and Saturday 8 AM–12:30 PM. Letters should be addressed with your surname followed by your first name, then "Poste Restante" and the post office address. You may have to pay a small fee to pick up a letter. Most hotels will also accept mail and hold it. Do not have anyone send cash.

SHIPPING PARCELS

You can ship packages from post offices on Bali and Lombok; the trick is to wrap them securely, but simply enough that they can be opened for inspection and sealed again if necessary. Service is notoriously slow, so expect to spend at least a half-hour getting your package properly stamped and recorded. Most post office employees are honest, but you may find those who will get their hands on your package before it reaches its destination, so **never mail anything valuable.** You can generally trust recommended city shops and mail services to ship valuable items for you. For an even more secure mailing service, use an international overnight company.

MONEY MATTERS

Prices on Bali and Lombok depend on what you're buying. The basic cost of living is low and domestic labor is cheap, but you pay a premium for anything imported. Thus, wine is expensive, rice is not. Costs rise in direct relation to tourism and business development. Prices at deluxe hotels and restaurants in resort areas such as Jimbaran and Nusa Dua are relatively high; prices in Kuta and Ubud and most of Lombok, by contrast, are bargains.

Kuta, Denpasar, and Nusa Dua have shopping complexes and department stores where prices are fixed, but at small shops and street stalls in other tourist areas—and in markets and villages throughout Lombok—bargaining is not only expected but is part of the whole shopping experience. Bargaining is an art, so try to develop your own technique. Start by offering half the asking price, even a third in the tourist areas; you'll finish somewhere in between. If the seller refuses to budge from his or her first offer, move on—he or she may just call you back and offer a lower price. Shops with higher-quality merchandise are likely to take credit cards, but payment in cash puts you in a better bargaining position.

Prices throughout this guide are given for adults. Substantially reduced fees are almost always available for children, students, and senior citizens. For information on taxes, *see* Taxes, *below.*

➤ SAMPLE PRICES: Cup of coffee: 25¢–$2; small bottle of beer, $1–$4; small bottled water, 25¢–$2; can of soda: 50¢–$3; bottle of house wine: $7–$15; sandwich: $2–$7; ½ km (1 mi) taxi ride, 75¢–$3 (depending on traffic); city bus ride: 10¢–$2; museum: 25¢–$3.

For suggested temple donations, *see* Etiquette & Behavior, *above.*

ATMS

ATMs are found in tourist-area banks, hotels, supermarkets, and malls. Cirrus and Plus cards, as well as credit cards, are usually accepted—but make sure that your card and your PIN number are set up for international service. Also ask your bank if there is a charge for taking out cash from and depositing funds into an international terminal. ATMs are for the most part reliable. Make sure to **take out enough cash well before holidays,** however, because the machines may run out of money.

CREDIT CARDS

All major credit cards are accepted at most higher-end tourist hotels, restaurants, and travel operators. In smaller establishments Visa is the most widely accepted card. Some establishments add a 1%–3% fee for credit card transactions.

Throughout this guide the following abbreviations are used: **AE**, American Express; **DC**, Diners Club; **MC**, MasterCard; and **V**, Visa.

➤ REPORTING LOST CARDS: To report lost or stolen credit cards, call the following toll-free numbers in the U.S.: **American Express** (☎ 800/327–2177); **Diners Club** (☎ 800/234–6377); **MasterCard** (☎ 800/307–7309); **Visa** (☎ 800/847–2911).

CURRENCY

Indonesia's unit of currency is the rupiah. Bills come in denominations of Rp 100, 500, 1,000, 5,000, 10,000, 20,000, 50,000, and 100,000, coins in Rp 25, 50, 100, 500, and 1,000. The exchange rate at press time was Rp 7,595 to the U.S. dollar, Rp 5,144 to the Canadian dollar, Rp 12,059 to the U.K. pound sterling, Rp 4,535 to the Australian dollar, and Rp 3,780 to the New Zealand dollar.

Because of the unstable economic situation in Indonesia, there have been large fluctuations in the value of the rupiah; thus, prices in the book are almost always given in dollars. You can check the current exchange rate using the Universal Currency Converter at the Xenon Laboratories Web site (www.xe.net).

CURRENCY EXCHANGE

For the most favorable rates, **change money through banks.** Although ATM transaction fees may be higher abroad than at home, ATM rates are excellent because they are based on wholesale rates offered only by major banks. You won't do as well at exchange booths in airports or rail and bus stations, in hotels, in restaurants, or in stores. To avoid lines at airport exchange booths, **get a bit of local currency before you leave home.**

➤ EXCHANGE SERVICES: International Currency Express (☎ 888/278–6628 for orders, www.foreignmoney.com). **Thomas Cook Currency Services** (☎ 800/287–7362 for telephone orders and retail locations, www.us. thomascook.com).

TRAVELER'S CHECKS

Do you need traveler's checks? It depends on where you're headed. If you're going to rural areas and small towns, go with cash; traveler's checks are best used in cities. Lost or stolen checks can usually be replaced within 24 hours. To ensure a speedy refund, buy your own traveler's checks—don't let someone else pay for them: irregularities like this can cause delays. The person who bought the checks should make the call to request a refund.

OUTDOORS & SPORTS

BICYCLING

Bicyclists continue to be drawn to the island of Bali, where road conditions range from the flat, sunny terrain of the south to the twisted, forested roads around Ubud and Gunung Batur. Most bike travelers **choose one small island or region to explore,** as the busy highways and extremely rugged back roads make long-distance travel impractical except for the very experienced. Outside the major cities you won't find bicycle supply or repair shops, so **bring everything you might need for emergencies.** Although you can rent bikes for day trips in tourist areas, if you're planning a longer trip around the island, the best plan is to **bring your own bike with you.**

GOLF

Golf has become a major passion on Bali. There are four 18-hole championship courses in prime locations: the Bali Handara Kosaido Country Club, near Danau Bratan; the Bali Beach Golf Course, in north Sanur; the Bali Golf & Country Club, in Nusa Dua; and the new Le Meridien Nirwana Golf & Spa Resort, near Uluwatu. Lombok's only 18-hole course is at the Rinjani Country Club, in Narmada.

HIKING

Bali is a hiker's delight: trekking experiences vary from mountain slopes and forested tracks to foot-paths through mangroves and quiet beach trails. There are many short trails that can be walked in a day, as well as longer circuits in Bali Barat National Park that are punctuated by *pondoks* (open sleeping huts). The park office in Bali Barat can provide information on necessary permits, as well as the availability and cost of guides, supplies, and nearby accom-modations. Ubud has wonderful walking trails, as well as guided bird walks; the areas around Gunung Agung, Gunung Batur, and the Batur and Bratan lakes also make for lovely and easy day treks.

Lombok's Gunung Rinjani, the third-highest mountain in Indonesia, at-tracts hikers and backpackers with its magnificence and beauty. If you plan on hiking up to and around the rim, you should be in good shape and allow yourself several days to explore the area's hot springs and waterfalls.

➤ LOCAL CONTACTS: **Bali Barat National Park** (✉ Headquarters, Cekik, Bali, ☎ 0365/61060). **Lotus Asia Tours** (✉ Jl. Raya Senggigi 1 G, Meninting, Lombok, ☎ 0370/636781) for Rinjani treks.

SCUBA DIVING & SNORKELING

There's an underwater paradise off Bali and Lombok. Bali's most famous dive site is the wreck off the coast of Tulamben, and there are wonderful reefs off Amed, Sanur, Lovina, Nusa Lembongan, and Menjangan Island in Bali Barat National Park. For snorkelers the reefs off Sanur, Amed, Menjangan Island, and Lombok's Gili Islands are tame and full of color. Equipment and repair shops can be found in Kuta and Legian, on Bali, and in Senggigi and the Gili Islands, on Lombok; tourist hotels in Tulam-ben and Amed, on Bali, cater to divers and live-aboard dive boats. If you're planning to do a lot of diving outside these areas, **bring your own equipment** because you can't trust the safety standards of the small opera-tors in more remote locations.

➤ DIVE OPERATORS: For more infor-mation on local dive operators *see* the Outdoor Activities and Sports sec-tions *in* individual chapters. **Bali Club Diver** (✉ Jl. Tamblingan 110, Sanur, Bali, ☎ 0361/287263). **Bali Diving Perdana** (✉ Jl. Danau Poso, Gang Tanjung, Sanur, Bali, ☎ 0361/286493). **Baruna** (✉ Jl. Raya Seririt, Lovina, Bali, ☎ 0362/41084). **Geko Dive** (✉ Jl. Silayukti, Padangbai, Bali, ☎ 0363/41516). **Nusa Dua Dive Center** (✉ Jl. Pratama 93A, Tanjung Benoa, Nusa Dua, Bali, ☎ 0361/774711). **Sea Star Dive Center** (✉ Jl. Bypass Ngurah Rai 45, Sanur, Bali, ☎ 0361/286492).

SURFING

You'll probably see several surfboards tumble off the baggage-claim belt when you arrive on Bali, for the island is the domain of international surfers. It all started here with a little left break off Kuta Beach, then the hot spots branched out to include Uluwatu, Canggu, Medewi, and Nusa Lembongan. There is a prominent counterculture here, and if you're a surfer, you'll fit right in. Beginners should start at Kuta, where the equip-ment and instructors are top-notch; the experienced can move wherever the waves take you. Lombok and the Gili Islands have terrific breaks for more experienced surfers, but they're not always easy to get to.

PACKING

Pack light because porters can be hard to find and baggage restrictions are tight on international flights; **check your airline's luggage policies before you pack.** And either leave room in your suitcase or bring ex-pandable totes for all your souvenir purchases.

If you'll be traveling through several different climates, bring clothes you can layer. Light cotton or other natu-ral-fiber clothing is appropriate for any destination on Bali or Lombok; drip-dry items are an especially good idea because the tropical sun and high humidity encourage frequent changes of clothing. Avoid exotic fabrics because you may have difficulty getting them laundered.

Bali and Lombok are generally infor-mal: a sweater, shawl, or lightweight linen jacket will be sufficient for dining and evening wear except at top international restaurants, where men will still be most comfortable in—and may be required to wear—a jacket and tie. A sweater is also a good idea for overly air-conditioned restaurants or cool evenings in the mountains. An umbrella can be helpful for shielding against both rain and sun.

The paths leading to temples can be rough; in any case, a pair of sturdy and comfortable walking shoes is always appropriate when traveling. Slip-ons are preferable to lace-ups, as shoes must be removed before you enter most temples. For more about temple dress, *see* Etiquette & Behavior, *above.* Pack a flashlight and extra batteries for trips to caves—and for when the occasional power outage turns your hotel room into a cave.

It's wise to **bring your favorite toilet articles** (in plastic containers to avoid breakage and reduce the weight of luggage). To combat the tropical sun, bring along a hat and sunscreen. Mosquito repellent is a good idea, and small tissue packets are handy since toilet paper is not always supplied in public places. Moist towelettes are great for cleaning off tropical grime and sweat while traveling, as well as for quick washups before meals in more remote establishments, where soap and water aren't always available.

In your carry-on luggage **pack an extra pair of eyeglasses or contact lenses** and **enough of any medication you take** to last the entire trip. You may also ask your doctor to write a spare prescription using the drug's generic name since brand names may vary from country to country. In luggage to be checked, **never pack prescription drugs or valuables.** To avoid customs delays, carry medications in their original packaging. And don't forget to carry with you the addresses of offices that handle refunds of lost traveler's checks.

CHECKING LUGGAGE

How many carry-on bags you can bring with you is up to the airline. Most allow two but not always; make sure that everything you carry aboard will fit under your seat or in the overhead bin, and get to the gate early. Note that if you have a seat at the back of the plane, you'll probably

board first, while the overhead bins are still empty.

If you are flying internationally, note that baggage allowances may be determined not by piece but by weight—generally 88 pounds (40 kilograms) in first class, 66 pounds (30 kilograms) in business class, and 44 pounds (20 kilograms) in economy.

Airline liability for baggage is limited to $1,250 per person on flights within the United States. On international flights it amounts to $9.07 per pound, or $20 per kilogram, for checked baggage (roughly $640 per 70-pound bag) and $400 per passenger for unchecked baggage. You can buy additional coverage at check-in for about $10 per $1,000 of coverage, but it excludes a rather extensive list of items, shown on your airline ticket.

Before departure, **itemize your bags' contents** and their worth, and label the bags with your name, address, and phone number. (If you use your home address, cover it so potential thieves can't see it readily.) Inside each bag, **pack a copy of your itinerary.** At check-in, **make sure each bag is correctly tagged** with the destination airport's three-letter code. If your bags arrive damaged or fail to arrive at all, file a written report with the airline before leaving the airport.

PASSPORTS & VISAS

When traveling internationally, **carry your passport** even if you don't need one (it's always the best form of I.D.) and **make two photocopies of the data page** (one for someone at home and another for you, carried separately from your passport). If you lose your passport, promptly call the nearest embassy or consulate and the local police.

ENTERING INDONESIA

The Indonesian government stipulates that passports must be valid for at least six months from arrival date, and all travelers must have proof of onward or return passage. For stays up to 60 days, visas are not required for citizens of the United States, Canada, the United Kingdom, Australia, or New Zealand, as long as you **enter Indonesia through one of the major gateways**: the airports at Ambon, Bali, Balikpapan, Bandung, Batam, Biak, Jakarta, Kupang, Manado, Mataram, Medan, Padang, Pekanbaru, Pontianak, and Surabaya, as well as the seaports of Ambon, Balikpapan, Batam, Belawan, Benoa, Jakarta, Kupang, Manado, Padangbai (Bali), Pontianak, Semarang, Surabaya, and Tanjung Pinang. The only international land crossing allowed is between Kuching, Malaysia, and Pontianak, Kalimantan. Other ports of entry may require a visa. Lombok is not a major gateway, and most visitors to this island arrive in Bali first and arrange transport from there.

PASSPORT OFFICES

The best time to apply for a passport or to renew is in fall and winter. Before any trip, check your passport's expiration date, and, if necessary, renew it as soon as possible.

➤ U.S. CITIZENS: **National Passport Information Center** (☎ 900/225–5674; calls are 35¢ per minute for automated service, $1.05 per minute for operator service; www.travel. state.gov/npicinfo.html).

➤ CANADIAN CITIZENS: **Passport Office** (☎ 819/994–3500; 800/567–6868 in Canada; www.dfait-maeci. gc.ca/passport).

➤ U.K. CITIZENS: **London Passport Office** (☎ 0870/521–0410, www. ukpa.gov.uk) for fees and documentation requirements and to request an emergency passport.

➤ AUSTRALIAN CITIZENS: **Australian Passport Office** (☎ 131–232, www.dfat.gov.au/passports).

➤ NEW ZEALAND CITIZENS: **New Zealand Passport Office** (☎ 04/494–0700, www.passports.govt.nz).

REST ROOMS

The Indonesian toilet may at first be a challenge to Western travelers. There are several models: the long porcelain bowl in the floor, which flushes; the usual Western throne; its seatless cousin, often used in mid-price hotels, which is flushed with a dipper of water; and the hole in the ground. Instructions for floor toilets: squat

and go. This can be hard on the knees, and requires balance, but most people actually find it easy with practice. Most tourist hotels and restaurants have Western-style toilets. Note that the sink is often outside the room with the toilet, and there is sometimes a nominal charge (Rp 100) for rest room use in such public places as bus terminals. If you need to find a bathroom, ask for the WC (*way*-say).

SAFETY

If you're a hiker or diver, be aware that these islands are home to a number of dangerous and poisonous snakes, spiders, scorpions, and rodents—know what to watch out for before you head into the wild.

The large public demonstrations and riots that have occurred in major cities throughout Indonesia have not bothered Bali; this is the one tropical haven foreigners kept visiting, even during the country's darkest times of upheaval. Lombok suffered from three days of riots in January 2000, but things have been calm since. Tourists should be safe in any case, but be wary of the social climate before you travel, pay attention to travelers' advisories, and steer clear of areas embroiled in political upheaval, especially during elections.

Crime against travelers is rare on Bali and Lombok. Still, small-time thieves, especially pickpockets and con artists, prey on unseasoned visitors, so a little caution in how you act can go a long way. **Dress modestly and don't flash your money around.** Carry traveler's checks and keep large amounts of cash in a hidden money pouch or locked in the hotel safe.

LOCAL SCAMS

Scam artists draw in naive travelers in Kuta, Legian, and Sanur on Bali. Check out what you buy before you lay down the money—fake jewels, fake name-brand items (handbags, shoes, perfume), bait-and-switch gifts "prewrapped" for customs, and bogus shipping promises are the typical tricks of this region.

A new highway scam has appeared in northern Bali, in which a car will pull up, its occupants waving their arms, implying that something is wrong with your car. **Ignore them.** This is likely to be a scam in which they will have you pull over, "fix" a problem that doesn't exist, and then charge you for it. **Pay attention to similar warnings** that come from car rental operations.

WOMEN IN INDONESIA

Although the stereotype of the rich, aggressive, and loose female is less prevalent among the Balinese than in Islamic Indonesian cultures, Western women traveling here will still probably find that they have a few negative images to dismantle. Bali is probably the easiest island in Indonesia for getting around alone or in a group of females, but because this is a society where women are still secondary and it is uncommon to be alone, you may find yourself the subject of unwanted attention. If a man is hovering around or following you, look him in the eye and ask what he wants, then firmly excuse yourself and walk away. If someone touches you in an unwelcome way, tell him, "No!" in a loud voice and push his hand away; the embarrassment may do the trick. If he still bothers you, immediately go to a public place or enlist help from someone nearby. The best tactic is to make friends with Indonesian women wherever you go, as they will guard you from wandering fingers.

SENIOR-CITIZEN TRAVEL

Bali is an excellent destination for active, well-traveled senior citizens on an independent (but prebooked) holiday, an escorted tour, or an adventure vacation. Before you leave home, however, determine what medical services your health insurance provider will cover outside the United States; note that Medicare does not provide for payment of hospital and medical services outside the United States. If you need additional travel insurance, buy it (☞ Insurance, *above*).

To qualify for age-related discounts, **mention your senior-citizen status up front** when booking hotel reservations (not when checking out) and before you're seated in restaurants (not when paying the bill). When renting a car, ask about promotional car-rental

discounts, which can be cheaper than senior-citizen rates.

➤ ADVENTURE TRAVEL: **Overseas Adventure Travel** (✉ Grand Circle Corporation, 625 Mt. Auburn St., Cambridge, MA 02138, ☎ 617/876–0533 or 800/221–0814, ℻ 617/876–0455).

➤ EDUCATIONAL PROGRAMS: **Elderhostel** (✉ 75 Federal St., 3rd floor, Boston, MA 02110, ☎ 877/426–8056, ℻ 877/426–2166, www. elderhostel.org) coordinates trips to Indonesia, Malaysia, the Philippines, Thailand, and Vietnam.

SHOPPING

Shopping is a major part of the fun of being in Bali and Lombok, for even if you're on a tight budget, you can find beautiful, high-quality crafts that you can afford. There are shopping malls in Kuta, Nusa Dua, and Denpasar, on Bali, but the best places for finding a range of handmade goods and foodstuffs are the open markets and villages of both islands. Except where fixed prices are marked, bargaining is an expected part of the exchange between shopper and vendor (☞ Money Matters, *above*). For information on shipping goods home, *see* Mail & Shipping, *above*.

SMART SOUVENIRS

The most memorable and significant souvenirs from Bali and Lombok are handicrafts, and the best of these come in four classes: jewelry, textiles, carvings, and performance-art items. The center for elaborate silver filigree is Celuk, Bali, but you can find silver jewelry and ornaments sold all over the island. If you like textiles, you can pick up beautiful *ikat* (multicolor fabric woven on a loom) and *songket* (ikat interwoven with gold) blankets and sarongs at most markets on both islands. Batik, or dyed fabric, is a well-known type of local cloth, and you can purchase everything from batik sarongs to T-shirts and skirts to scenic murals suitable for framing. Many locals are expert carvers; particularly stunning are the detailed wooden statues, furniture, and pictures from the village of Mas, on Bali. Performance-art items—such as masks, musical instruments, and costumes—can be the most fun to shop for, especially if you've enjoyed a performance where such items were used.

WATCH OUT

The most prevalent shopping scam on Bali is the "tour guide" who attaches himself to you and then proceeds to drag you to all the stores of his friends and relatives (in hopes that you will buy something and make a commission for him in the process). If you feel that you're being pushed into a particular store, simply say you're not interested. Purchase gemstones and gold only from reputable dealers; otherwise you could get much less than your money's worth. Fake brand-name clothing items are often sold in the markets; if the bargain seems too good to be true, check to see that the Gucci label hasn't been sewn on over the original tag, or that the Prada name isn't misspelled "Pradda." Likewise, roving vendors with cases of fake Rolex watches and other upmarket goods sidle up to sunbathers and shoppers; if you don't want to buy anything, just say, *"Tidak mau"* ("I don't want it").

If you purchase something of value, store it in a place you know is secure, and keep it with you if your hotel's safe or staff has a less-than-honest reputation. And if you must send something of value home, consider mailing it overnight (☞ Mail & Shipping, *above*.). Some shops will offer to wrap and mail large purchases for you; use your credit card to protect against loss or damage.

SIGHTSEEING GUIDES

Most guides at tourist sites on Bali are either students trying to make a little extra money and practice their English or older citizens with vast knowledge about a particular place. Guides are rarely assigned; most of the time they will approach you, so you have the chance to find someone compatible with your interests and the level of your knowledge of the local language. Some guides can be quite persistent, though, and if one won't leave your side, politely—but firmly—say, "Tidak mau." Service charges are usually standard, with all guides charging about the same for a particular tour. Although tipping isn't expected, it's a nice expression of gratitude for someone who has done a good job of explaining the site; a few thousand rupiah will be sufficient.

STUDENTS IN INDONESIA

Travelers under 27 with Student I.D. (easily obtained in backpacker areas such as Kuta on Bali) can often get a discount on air- and train fare in Indonesia. However, policies seem to wax and wane depending on who's at the ticket counter or travel-agency desk. In any case, it can't hurt to ask when making your plans.

➤ I.D.s & SERVICES: **Council Travel** (CIEE; ✉ 205 E. 42nd St., 14th floor, New York, NY 10017, ☎ 212/822–2700 or 888/268–6245, FAX 212/822–2699, info@councilexchanges.org, www.councilexchanges.org) for mail orders only, in the U.S. **Travel Cuts** (✉ 187 College St., Toronto, Ontario M5T 1P7, Canada, ☎ 416/979–2406 or 800/667–2887 in Canada, www.travelcuts.com).

TAXES

High-end hotels charge 21% tax, of which only 11% is the regular government tax also seen on the bill at moderate hotels; the rest comprises various service charges. Departing passengers on international flights pay an airport departure tax of around $3. Domestic airport taxes are from 75¢–$1.50, depending on the point of departure.

TELEPHONES

Even at its best the Indonesian telephone system can be frustrating. Outside the largest cities, phones work only intermittently, and the lines often crackle with static. The best place to make long-distance and international calls is a *wartel,* short for *warung telekomunikasi* (telecommunications store). Wartels, which have at least one private phone booth (and often several), are where many Balinese make their calls; there are no added fees for phone calls, and you can usually send and receive faxes and packages as well. Most hotels place high surcharges on telephone calls from guest rooms, and the phones at post offices and transport stations—when available—don't always work.

Cell phones are available for rent in most tourist locations, including Kuta and Ubud. Your home model won't work unless you have international roaming for Indonesia or subscribe to a local service such as Telkomsel, Satelindo, or Excelcomindo. If you have international roaming, you can rent a *hand phone* and purchase a card to plug into your phone; this will also give you a local number. You can purchase Telkomsel's simPATI card at many groceries and photo shops in large cities. Satellite phones, although expensive, will work anywhere in the world. Pagers should work anywhere, but if you're staying in the country more than a week or two, subscribe to a local provider for a better deal.

AREA & COUNTRY CODES

To call Indonesia from overseas, dial the country code, 62, and then the area code, omitting the first 0. When calling long-distance on Bali or Lombok or between Indonesian islands, make sure to include the 0 before the area code. To call a mobile phone, dial the entire number, including the 0.

If you're calling home, the country code is 1 for the United States and Canada, 61 for Australia, 64 for New Zealand, and 44 for the United Kingdom.

DIRECTORY & OPERATOR ASSISTANCE

To reach an operator, dial 0. Most operators speak some English, but it is helpful to know at least the Indonesian versions of the numbers you want to call (☞ Vocabulary at the back of the book).

INTERNATIONAL CALLS

You can make collect calls to Australia, Europe, and North America; for other countries you need a telephone credit card. Reduced rates on international phone calls are in effect 9 PM–6 AM daily. For most Western countries, Indonesia also has special "home country" phones in its telecommunications offices and many hotels. With these you can contact an operator in your home country just by pushing a button. Like a collect call, the bill is charged to whomever you're calling, or you can use one of the calling cards that are sold everywhere.

Most of Bali's tourist areas are hooked into the International Direct Dialing (IDD) system via satellite. Dial 001 plus the respective country code. For towns without the IDD hookup, go through the operator. If you want to avoid using hotel phones, the most economical way to place an IDD call is from the nearest Kantor Telephone & Telegraph office. For international directory assistance, dial 102.

LOCAL CALLS

Although hotel phones offer the benefit of an operator to help with translation and information, your best chance of making a less expensive call is in a wartel. Some travel agencies have phones you can use for local calls.

For local calls, three minutes costs Rp 100. Older public phones take Rp 100 coins, but the newer ones accept only phone cards—a recent introduction restricted to the larger cities and tourist areas. For operator and directory assistance dial 108 for local calls, 106 for the provinces.

LONG-DISTANCE SERVICES

AT&T, MCI, and Sprint access codes make calling long distance relatively convenient, but you may find the local access number blocked in many hotel rooms. First ask the hotel operator to connect you. If the hotel operator balks, ask for an international operator, or dial the international operator yourself. One way to improve your odds of getting connected to your long-distance carrier is to travel with more than one company's calling card (a hotel may block Sprint, for example, but not MCI). If all else fails, call from a pay phone.

➤ ACCESS CODES: **AT&T Direct** (☎ 001–801–10). **MCI WorldPhone** (☎ 001–801–11). **Sprint International Access** (☎ 001–801–15).

PUBLIC PHONES

Phone cards (*kartu telepon*) and phone-chip cards (*kartu chip*) are widely used and can be bought at telecommunications offices, newsstands, grocery chains, and small shops. Regular phone cards have a magnetic strip, while the new hard-plastic phone-chip cards are embedded with an electronic chip. Most phones in tourist areas accept only phone cards (available in Rp 5,000, 10,000, 25,000, 50,000, and 100,000 denominations) or phone-chip cards; these phones are gray. Coin phones, which accept Rp 50 and Rp 100 coins, are blue. Green phones accept both coins and cards.

If a phone accepts coins, dial the number first, then drop the coin when you hear it ring on the other end. For card phones, swipe your card first, then dial.

TIME

Bali and Lombok are in Indonesia's central time zone, GMT + 8. When it's noon on January 1 in Bali or Lombok, it's 8 PM December 31 in Los Angeles, 11 PM on December 31 in New York, 4 AM January 1 in London, 2 PM January 1 in Sydney, and 4 PM January 1 in Aukland.

TIPPING

The more expensive tourist restaurants include a service charge; if service isn't included, tip 10%. Above the hotel service charge, plan to tip bellboys about $1 per bag; you may also want to tip room-service personnel if you request a special service. Porters at the airport should receive about 50¢ per bag. For a driver of a hired car, tip at least $5 for half a day. Taxi drivers aren't tipped on Bali or Lombok, although they always appreciate it if you leave them the small change. Private guides expect a gratuity, perhaps $3–$6 per day.

TOURS & PACKAGES

Because everything is prearranged on a prepackaged tour or independent vacation, you'll spend less time planning—and often get it all at a good price.

BOOKING WITH AN AGENT

Travel agents are excellent resources. But it's a good idea to collect brochures from several agencies, as some agents' suggestions may be influenced by relationships with tour and package firms that reward them for volume sales. If you have a special interest, **find an agent with expertise in that area**; ASTA (☞ Travel Agencies, *below*) has a database of specialists worldwide.

Make sure your travel agent knows the accommodations and other services of the place he or she is recommending. Ask about the hotel's location, room size, beds, and whether it has a pool, room service, or programs for children, if you care about these. Has your agent been there in person or sent others whom you can contact?

Do some homework on your own, too: local tourism boards can provide information about lesser-known and small-niche operators, some of which may sell only direct.

BUYER BEWARE

Each year consumers are stranded or lose their money when tour operators—even large ones with excellent reputations—go out of business. So **check out the operator.** Ask several travel agents about its reputation, and try to **book with a company that has a consumer-protection program** (look for information in the company's brochure). In the United States, members of the National Tour Association and the United States Tour Operators Association are required to set aside funds to cover your payments and travel arrangements in the event the company defaults. It's also a good idea to choose a company that participates in the American Society of Travel Agents' Tour Operator Program (TOP); ASTA will act as mediator in any disputes between you and your tour operator.

Remember that the more your package or tour includes, the better you can predict the ultimate cost of your vacation. Make sure you know exactly what is covered and **beware of hidden costs.** Are taxes, tips, and transfers included? Entertainment and excursions? These can add up.

➤ TOUR-OPERATOR RECOMMENDATIONS: **American Society of Travel Agents** (☞ Travel Agencies, *below*). **National Tour Association** (NTA; ✉ 546 E. Main St., Lexington, KY 40508, ☎ 859/226–4444 or 800/682–8886, www.ntaonline.com). **United States Tour Operators Association** (USTOA; ✉ 342 Madison Ave., Suite 1522, New York, NY 10173, ☎ 212/599–6599 or 800/468–7862, FAX 212/599–6744, ustoa@aol.com, www.ustoa.com).

TRANSPORTATION AROUND BALI & LOMBOK

BEMOS

A bemo is a converted pickup truck or minivan—a standard form of transport for short trips on both Bali and Lombok. Most bemos follow regular routes and will stop anywhere along the way to pick up or discharge passengers. You pay when you get out. Try to learn the fare (it varies according to distance) from another passenger; otherwise you'll be overcharged. An empty bemo will often try to pick up Western travelers, but beware: unless you clarify that it's on its regular route, you will be chartering it as a taxi.

SHUTTLES

Mid-size tourist shuttles regularly run between the main tourist towns and attractions on Bali. All large travel agencies post a chart of the schedules and fares; some agencies add their own fee, though, so check around before you book a ticket. Most buses seat 12–24 travelers. You should **reserve your place a day in advance**—or several days ahead of time if it's high season or a major holiday. If you're not planning to rent a car or take a guided tour and you like exploring towns and sites on your own, shuttles are an ideal way to get around: they're quick, inexpensive, and comfortable. In particular, travelers with children and travelers with disabilities will have a much easier time getting around by shuttle rather than public transportation.

TAXIS

Taxis are a cheap and quick means of getting around the tourist areas of Bali and Lombok. Registered vehicles, which are hailed on city streets, look just like Western-style taxis; the top outer TAXI light is on when the vehicle is empty and off when it's booked. There are taxi stands at most large hotels, as well as at both the Bali and Lombok airports. If you don't have a hotel shuttle or friend meeting you at Bali's airport, **use the taxi service outside the international arrival terminal** because the fares to tourist towns are fixed and the drivers speak English. In rural areas of Bali and Lombok, drivers with private vehicles cruise the streets as an informal taxi service; in this case (as well as for taxis with broken meters) **negotiate the fare with the driver before getting in the car.**

The 500-vehicle Bali Taksi fleet provides a comfortable, inexpensive way to get around Bali. The company also has a 200-vehicle sister fleet on Lombok, Lombok Taksi. Cabs run 24 hours and use a computerized reservation and map system; you can even book one ahead of time. The taxis are operated by English-speaking drivers and can be hired for day tours—or longer, if you pay for the driver's room and board. This is often a better option than renting a car, as you don't have to worry about parking, insurance, and driving (or paying a driver). Fares run from approximately 10¢ per kilometer (with an initial charge of 25¢) to around $30 for a full day. All Bali Taksi vehicles are robin's-egg blue; **look for the BLUEBIRD GROUP sticker** to make sure that the vehicle is part of the fleet, as several copycat operators are trying to coast on Bali Taksi's top-rated image.

➤ TAXI COMPANIES: **Bali Taksi** (☎ 0361/701111, www.bluebirdgroup. com). **Lombok Taksi** (☎ 0370/ 627000).

TRAVEL AGENCIES

A good travel agent puts your needs first. Look for an agency that has been in business at least five years, emphasizes customer service, and has someone on staff who specializes in your destination. In addition, **make sure the agency belongs to a professional trade organization.** The American Society of Travel Agents (ASTA), with 27,000 agents in some 170 countries, is the largest and most influential in the field. Operating under the motto "Integrity in Travel," it maintains and enforces a strict code of ethics and will step in to help mediate any agent-client disputes if necessary. ASTA also maintains a Web site that includes a directory of agents. (If a travel agency is also acting as your tour operator, *see* Buyer Beware *in* Tours & Packages, *above.*)

SMART TRAVEL TIPS A TO Z

➤ LOCAL AGENT REFERRALS: American Society of Travel Agents (ASTA; ☎ 800/965–2782 24-hr hot line, FAX 703/684–8319, www.astanet.com). Association of Canadian Travel Agents (✉ 1729 Bank St., Suite 201, Ottawa, Ontario K1V 7Z5, Canada, ☎ 613/237–3657, FAX 613/521–0805, acta.ntl@sympatico.ca). Association of British Travel Agents (✉ 68–71 Newman St., London W1P 4AH, U.K., ☎ 020/7637–2444, FAX 020/7637–0713, information@abta.co.uk, www.abtanet.com). Australian Federation of Travel Agents (✉ Level 3, 309 Pitt St., Sydney 2000, Australia, ☎ 02/9264–3299, FAX 02/9264–1085, www.afta.com.au). Travel Agents' Association of New Zealand (✉ Box 1888, Wellington 10033, New Zealand, ☎ 04/499–0104, FAX 04/499–0827, taanz@tiasnet.co.nz).

VISITOR INFORMATION

➤ OUTSIDE INDONESIA: Indonesia Tourist Board in the United States (✉ 3457 Wilshire Blvd., Los Angeles, CA 90010, ☎ 213/387–2078). Indonesian Embassy in Canada (✉ 287 MacLaren St., Ottawa, Ontario K2P 0L9, ☎ 613/236–7403). Indonesian Tourist Office in the United Kingdom (✉ 3 Hanover St., London W1R 9HH, ☎ 020/7493–0030). Indonesian Embassy in Australia (✉ 8 Darwin Ave., Yarralumla ACT 2600, ☎ 06/273–3222). Indonesian Tourist Office in Australia (✉ Level 10, S. Elizabeth St., Sydney NSA 2000, ☎ 02/9233–3630). Indonesian Embassy in New Zealand (✉ 70 Glen Rd., Kelburn, Wellington, ☎ 04/475–8697).

➤ WITHIN INDONESIA: Directorate General of Tourism in Indonesia (✉ Jl. Merdeka Barat 16–19, Jakarta, Java 10110, ☎ 021/386–7588). For regional tourist offices, see the A to Z sections in individual chapters.

➤ U.S. GOVERNMENT ADVISORIES: U.S. Department of State (✉ Overseas Citizens Services Office, Room 4811 N.S., 2201 C St. NW, Washington, DC 20520, ☎ 202/647–5225 for interactive hot line, 301/946–4400 for computer bulletin board, FAX 202/647–3000 for interactive hot line); enclose a self-addressed, stamped, business-size envelope.

WEB SITES

Do check out the World Wide Web when you're planning your trip. You'll find everything from current weather forecasts to virtual tours of famous cities. Fodor's Web site, www.fodors.com, is a great place to start your online travels. When you see a ☜ in this book, go to www.fodors.com/urls for an up-to-date link to that destination's site. For information on Bali and Lombok visit www.indonesiatourism.com.

WHEN TO GO

The best months to visit Bali are April and May and September through October, when crowds are lighter. The wet season, from late October through May, brings heavy rains. Lombok is drier, with a lighter rainy season that runs from October to March. Since most attractions on Bali and Lombok—temples, volcanoes, beaches, and outdoor festivals—lie under the open sky, the rainy season can very literally dampen your enjoyment. It can drizzle for several days in a row or pour half the day, with only occasional dry spells. Like many locals, you may want to keep an umbrella on hand at all times for protection from both rain and sun.

In the peak tourist months, July and August, popular areas are crammed with visitors. Hotels also tend to be fully booked around Christmas and New Year's; transport and accommodations in Bali are full around Balinese holidays and in Lombok are full around Muslim holidays. Unless you plan to stay only on Bali, consider carefully before visiting during Ramadan, the Islamic month of fasting, when many restaurants, offices, and tourist attractions are closed until sundown.

CLIMATE

The islands' lower regions are uniformly hot and humid year-round. Temperatures can reach 90°F (32°C) soon after midday, and they drop no lower than 70°F (21°C) at night. The weather at higher altitudes is up to 20°F (11°C) cooler.

➤ FORECASTS: Weather Channel Connection (☎ 900/932–8437), 95¢ per minute from a Touch-Tone phone.

1 DESTINATION: BALI AND LOMBOK

SUN, SEA, AND MYSTERY

FROM THE AIR, Bali rises fresh and green from the Indian Ocean, a verdant, glistening butterfly against a backdrop of gray. Just 145 km (90 mi) by 95 km (60 mi) at its widest points and 2½ km (1¼ mi) across at its narrowest, the island's lush forests and rice terraces gently rise up to a core of volcanoes whose ashes have rained down on the island over the centuries, making the soil fertile and rich. Gunung (Mt.) Agung, at 10,300 ft, is the highest and most sacred point on the island and is considered the Mother Mountain, the abode of the gods. Its sister summits—Gunung Batur (5,633 ft), Gunung Bratan (6,008 ft), Gunung Pohon (6,767 ft), and Gunung Catur (6,877 ft)—stretch across the center from east to west, with the placid waters of Danau (Lake) Batur, Danau Bratan, Danau Buyan, and Danau Tamblingan tucked in between. From these mountains tumble wild whitewater rivers, notably the Ayung, Pelang, Sangsang, Undu, and Balian. These waterways, along with the frequent rains of this humid region 8°–9° south of the equator, provide a way to irrigate the rice fields that produce three crops each year.

Although Bali seems to be covered with forests, only about one-fifth of the island has such natural vegetation. About 5% of the land is protected in Bali Barat National Park and other reserves. The mountain forests are but one of the island's three major environments; coastal swamps and beaches ring its outer edges, and rugged limestone hills form the core of Bukit Badung. Bali's satellite islands of Nusa Ceningan, Nusa Lembongan, and Nusa Penida are also slabs of limestone with dry, rough vegetation clinging to porous hills. The rains that bring Bali 100–120 inches of moisture annually rarely touch its edges except for brief daily storms during the October–May rainy season; in the mountains it may rain well into June. The dry season brings breezes beneath blue skies, as well as slightly cooler temperatures.

The island may be small, but it's home to numerous species of wildlife, most notably a rich variety of birds. White egrets, sandpipers, and cranes stand out in the green rice fields; the trees are alive with the chatter of sparrows and finches and the loud calls of hornbills; and the beaches host a variety of scavengers and waders. Bali's endemic star is the *jalak putih,* also known as the Bali mynah or Bali starling, a soft white bird with a band of azure feathers around its black eyes. Other creatures here include mouse deer, squirrels, lizards, and the brown *banteng* bovine; the Bali tiger has been extinct for nearly a century. The sea life around the island is more abundant, and snorkelers and divers are rewarded with the activity of a rainbow of sea creatures along the vast stretches of coral. Even aboard a ferry you'll spot flying fish, turtles, dolphins, and otters.

On a clear day, from the edge of eastern Bali you can see the green hills of Lombok, but the smaller island is far different from its internationally famous sister. Named by the Javanese for the *lombok* peppers so prevalent in the region's traditional curry sauces, Lombok is a dry, quiet island just 70 km (44 mi) across. The mountainous island is dominated by the 12,221 ft Gunung Rinjani volcano, the third-highest peak in the Indonesian archipelago, and fringed by tiny islands (*gili*), including Gili Air, Gili Meno, and Gili Trawangan. At its edges are pristine beaches and killer surfing bays, most of which are as yet undisturbed by tourism.

Lombok has fewer and very different species of flora and fauna than the wetter western islands of Indonesia, due in large part to the ocean trench that divides Lombok and Bali, known as Wallace's Line. This deep trench is characterized by treacherous currents and wicked winds, which prevented the continued migration of seeds and animals that made it from mainland Southeast Asia all the way down to Bali when the oceans were shallower. Such rain-forest species as the elephant, rhinocerous, tiger, and other large cats remained on the islands west of the Lombok Strait, while many smaller mammals, reptiles, and insects better suited to arid terrain never crossed over to the west from Lombok. This important boundary takes its name from naturalist Alfred Russel Wallace—a contemporary of Charles Darwin—who noted it in his 1869 book *The Malay Archipelago,* which is still an exemplary guide to the flora and fauna of Indonesia.

AS FOR HUMAN LIFE, based on fossil remains found on Java—which was once connected to Bali as part of the Sunda Shelf—some experts think early humans were here nearly 2 million years ago. Stone tools, prehistoric grave sites, and ancient jewelry confirm human presence on the island during the Paleolithic period. On Lombok archeologists are working to dig up evidence of the island's first settlers, but at this point little is known about about the early history of the island.

About 4,500 years ago a wave of seafaring, rice-growing migrants arrived on Bali from southern China, bringing with them a new Austronesian (Malay-Polynesian) language and a Neolithic technology that helped to create the rectangular stone adzes and ornate ocher pottery that have been discovered in eastern Bali and around Gilimanuk in western Bali. The first layered temples and other large works of stone, such as altars and oval sarcophagi, were built around this time. Between 800 BC and 300 BC, metalworking was developed, resulting in decorative bronze jars, musical instruments, and other items that are strikingly similar to those crafted by the Dongson culture in Vietnam. The most famous metal relic on Bali is a giant bronze kettledrum known as the Moon of Pejeng—the largest such drum in Southeast Asia—which today is housed in a small temple complex near Ubud.

By AD 700 the Javanese and Balinese cultures were interacting, tied together in part by religion and the Old Javanese language. Stories from Java's kingdom of Sri Kesari are recorded at the Sanur pillar, dated AD 914, in a unique Balinese-Indian script. Copperplate inscriptions and stone etchings reveal the linguistic advancements, while bas-reliefs and statues in temples and cave shrines from the era point to developing Hindu and Buddhist traits. The 10th century saw the rise of East Java's powerful king Airlangga, son of King Udayana of Bali and a queen from the Warmadewa dynasty of Java. The two islands' connection was further cemented under the rule of Jayasakti (1146–50) and Jayapangus (1178–81), two rajas from Java's royal Jaya family.

Ties to Java's Kediri kingdom were in place by AD 1200, and Bali's kings ruled autonomously until 1284, when the island was conquered by King Kertanegara of Java. In the mid-14th century Gajah Mada, ruler of Java's great Majapahit dynasty, ushered in Java's golden age while simultaneously overthrowing and organizing the kingdoms of Bali. Majapahit's power stretched from the Malay peninsula through eastern Nusa Tenggara, bringing to Bali, at the center of the kingdom, a structured caste system, rituals of royalty, and artistic and architectural advancement. As the influence of Islam swept southeast through the Indonesian islands from Aceh in northern Sumatra, many Javanese even moved to Bali to strengthen the island's Hindu traditions.

Under Javanese rule Bali's capital moved to Samprangan, then in 1460 to Gelgel. The mid-1500s witnessed a new golden age under King Waturenggong (or Baturenggong), whose spiritual guide, Danghyang Nirartha, would become a mythical figure in Balinese history. A healer, teacher, and soothsayer, Nirartha was also called "the Wandering Sage"; during his journeys he founded many of Bali's holiest temples, including Pura Uluwatu, at the southern end of the island. Those in the island's highest Brahman priest caste consider Nirartha a deity, and many Brahmans believe they are descended from him.

Bali's ruling kingdom fell into chaos after this golden age, though, as new rulers bubbled up and rebelled within Gelgel. The most destructive leader was Gusti Agung Maruti, a chief minister who threw out the rajas and then kept the region in upheaval until it was conquered by northern rulers and he was ousted. The embers of Gelgel became the new kingdom of Klungkung, which rose and then faded as other kingdoms took power in various parts of the island in the 17th and 18th centuries. Several new rulers from Klungkung established their own smaller kingdoms, including Karangasem in the east, Buleleng in the north, and Mengwi to the west. Although the latter two were reduced in size and power within decades, Karangasem took over more of Bali and conquered Lombok as well. By the end of the 18th century Bali was divided into nine centers of power: Badung, Buleleng, Jembrana, Klungkung, Karangasem, Mengwi, Tabanan, Gianyar, and Bangli.

The eruption of Gunung Tambora on Sumbawa in 1815 halted all this internecine fighting as famine took over Bali. However, as trade links with the rest of Southeast Asia grew stronger, the Balinese were able to rebuild core kingdoms rich enough to attract the eyes of the Dutch, who attacked northern Bali three times between 1846 and 1849, when they finally agreed to share power with the region's rulers. Bali's decade-long civil war, which began in 1884, kept the Balinese distracted enough that the Dutch were able to grab Lombok. By 1900 Gianyar and Karangasem were also under Dutch rule. The southern kingdoms, however, fiercely resisted takeover, their stoicism culminating in a series of *puputan* (mass suicides).

After their victory the Dutch neatly fashioned Balinese society into a European-type bureaucracy. They allowed some royal families to have power, but this was for show only; they also preserved the caste system, forced many Balinese into slavery, and romanticized the island as a tropical hideaway to their fellow Dutchmen at home. In spite of the eruption of Gunung Batur in 1917, tourists began to trickle onto an island that was becoming idealized as a utopia of golden beaches, clear seas, and nubile natives. Then all was brought to a halt when the Japanese entered into World War II and Bali—along with the rest of the country—formed an alliance with its Asian neighbor.

When the Japanese invaded in 1942, Dutch resistance was brief but not without bloodshed. Many Balinese actually welcomed the northern conquerers as their saviors from Dutch rule. In the following months, the Balinese realized that the Japanese were only intent on gaining power over the island in their quest to dominate the region. When the Japanese surrendered after the second atomic bomb was dropped on August 15, 1945, a breath of freedom swept through the Indonesian archipelago, giving the country's leaders the chance to stand up for Indonesian autonomy before the Dutch returned to reclaim the islands. Just 48 hours later, on August 17, Sukarno read the country's Declaration of Independence as the unifying red-and-white flag was raised.

But the fight wasn't over yet. On Bali, locals gathered leftover Japanese weapons to use against the returning Dutch troops. Famed Balinese guerilla leader Gusti Ngurah Rai was killed in a 1946 battle, and more than 1,400 Balinese died in the fight against Dutch forces. By 1947 Holland once again controlled Java and parts of Sumatra; a year later they controlled the whole archipelago. Bali then became the headquarters for the new Dutch state of Eastern Indonesia, under Gianyar's ruler Anak Agung Gede Agung—until he broke the newly minted Balinese-Dutch treaty. By the end of 1949 even the United Nations had turned against the Dutch, and on December 27 the Hague Agreement was signed, granting independence to all former territories governed by Holland except West New Guinea.

Sukarno and Mohammad Hatta became the republic's first president and vice president. Local kings still controlled their regions on Bali, and the next two decades brought political and economic confusion, as well as tragedy, to the island. Gunung Agung erupted in 1963 and brought famine once again, then in 1965 an attempted political coup by communists touched off riots throughout the islands. General Suharto, who stepped in to crush the revolt with his army, became the country's temporary leader until he was sworn into the presidency in 1968. During the years in between, however, the country was embroiled in chaos; it's believed that more than a half-million Indonesians and Chinese were killed by Suharto's troops in the anti-communist rampage that followed the coup.

UNDER SUHARTO'S LEADERSHIP, the country made great strides in developing health and medical care, education, and tourism—in fact Suharto is looked back on as the Father of Development. The tourist industry was a particular boon to Bali throughout the 1970s and 1980s. During the terms of the first and second Balinese governors, Brahman religious scholar Ida Bagus Mantra and Ida Bagus Oka, Bali carved a niche for itself as a peaceful, safe tropical retreat for tourists. Fortunately this image has remained strong despite the political and economic upheaval that ricocheted through the rest of the country in the late 1990s. Lombok, too, has been able to avoid most of the conflict that has torn apart other areas of Indonesia, developing into its own haven for travelers who want to get away from Bali's busy beaches. Although the end of the millennium saw anti-Chinese riots in the main trade areas of Mataram and Ampenan, the tourist areas of Senggigi, the Gili Islands, and Kuta remained safe for foreigners. Travelers are still drawn to Lombok for the challenge of climbing the active volcano Rinjani or for the charm of visiting the small Sasak villages tucked into the hills.

What is the new century bringing for Bali and Lombok? After the resignation of Suharto in 1997, the quick rule of B. J. Habibie in 1998–99, and the election of Abdurrahman Wahid and Vice President Megawati Sukarnoputri, Sukarno's daughter, in 1999, the Indonesian archipelago is politically insecure. The rupiah has slowly made its way back to a reasonable international exchange rate, and the fighting between political and religious foes is waning, for now. Lombok still has its conflicts, namely between the island's Islamic Sasak religions, Chinese immigrants, and Christians. Bali, however, has been a constant rock of serenity—a position that the Balinese maintain will not change. It is an island steeped in respectful religious traditions, with a society that revolves firmly around the family and concentrates its actions on the community. The Balinese are proud of their heritage and keep up even the smallest daily rituals. "As long as our eyes remain focused on Gunung Agung and our souls on traditional values," assures one local *bapak* (father), "the chaos around us cannot touch the good spirits within."

–Holly S. Smith

NEW AND NOTEWORTHY

Southern Bali

Many changes have been brewing in southern Bali over the past year, particularly along the west coast, where new restaurants and hotels have been slowly developing despite Indonesia's economic crises. The most notable addition is Le Meridien Nirwana Golf & Spa Resort, in Canggu, near Tanah Lot, with a beautiful Greg Norman–designed course spread over the hills and along the rugged cliffs of the coastline. The resort is a marvel, with upscale holiday rentals and time-shares and an opulent restaurant, Cendana, which looks out over the temple Pura Tanah Lot. Other promising new hotels include Tamukami and Pavilions, in Sanur, and Nusa Dua's Bali Aga. Private villa rentals are also a hot ticket now, and many top-of-the-line luxury properties are springing up amid the rice fields around Kerobokan and down little lanes along the west coast, just steps from beaches and shops.

Several new restaurants have opened along the main Seminyak–Kuta strip: Fabio's has excellent Italian cuisine; Pantarei has an eclectic Mediterranean atmosphere; Kori serves international dishes in a tropical setting; Veranda is a little place with the best European food on the island. In Jimbaran, Balangan is set over sweeping views of the western peninsula—and the food is superb. New dining spots have also cropped up along the east coast, namely northern Sanur's classy Jazz Bar & Grille and Kafe Wayang, next door; artsy Spago, in the middle of Sanur; and L'Oasis Restaurant & Bakery, on Jalan Bypass near Jimbaran.

Eastern Bali

The big news in eastern Bali is the number of new private villa properties and spas that have been built in the past couple of years. In the midst of the country's political and economic crises, local and international investors pushed ahead with construction plans to create several of the region's most unusual accommodations, including the Sacred Mountain Sanctuary ecoresort on the slopes of Gunung Agung; the Megah Log House, in the east near Semarapura; and the Emerald Tulamben Resort, on the northeast coast. The sounds of hammers fill the air as the older resorts upgrade their facilities to include new restaurants and spas; don't miss the elaborate rock carvings in the cavernous spa at the Tjampuhan hotel or the lovely lotus-pond setting for the new spa at the Amandari.

A few new restaurants have broken out of the crowd that vies for visitors to the

Ubud area. Terazzo serves Italian cuisine in a spacious, colorful setting; Bumbu Bali has a menu of Balinese and Indian dishes and an intimate garden; the Thai Food Restaurant cooks up top-notch Thai food (natch); and the Jazz Café has classy decor, good food, and local musicians.

The names of many of the region's streets and towns have changed recently. Klungkung, for example, is called Semarapura these days, out of respect for the town's revered palace, Puri Semarapura; Jalan Monkey Forest is now officially Jalan Wanara Wana, after the local name for the natural area in Ubud.

Northern Bali

At press time several new developments were planned in the coastal village of Air Sanih, about 15 km (9 mi) east of Singaraja. The owners of the two-bungalow Cilik's Garden hoped to take over the extremely rundown backpacker's hotel abutting cool springs next door and create a moderately priced guest house. A branch of the delicious Biyu Nasak restaurant of Lovina Beach was to open in Air Sanih under the same name, and the modern luxury resort Puri Bagus Lovina had plans to open a restaurant there, too.

Western Bali

Return visitors to Bali who were last here three or four years ago will be surprised at all the development around the village of Pemuteran. There used to be only one dive shop (Reef Seen Aquatics) and one place to stay (Pondok Sari), but now there are a number of luxury destinations, ranging from an upscale dive resort, Mimpi Menjangan Island, to the lavish Matahari Beach Resort & Spa, to the secret villas of Puri Ganesha. These resorts have also created some great new dining places, and travelers to this corner of western Bali will not be missing any of the cuisines and comforts of Ubud or Nusa Dua. Another worthwhile new resort in the wild west is the Waka Gangga, on Yeh Gangga Beach near Tabanan. Although the ocean here is not as ideal for swimming as it is near Kuta, you do have it all to yourself.

The recent resort developments in Bali Barat National Park are not so promising. When the Waka Shorea resort was allowed to build on park land, many farmers took this as a sign the land was available for cultivation. Another hotel, Menjangan Jungle Resort, is under construction in the park, although at press time its managers weren't sure what was to come of the project; environmentalists and concerned neighbors were hoping that the new government would do something to stop such commercial efforts on what is left of the only large area of undeveloped land in Bali.

Lombok

It took three days to shatter the image of Lombok as a placid, tranquil island. January 17, 2000, marked the start of three days of rioting, catalyzed by the yearlong religious conflict in the eastern Molucca Islands. According to newspaper reports, Lombok's extremist Muslims incited thousands to attack Chinese Christians in retaliation for the deaths of hundreds of Muslims in the Moluccas.

Christian churches and shops and houses owned by Christians were burned or looted; store owners resorted to displaying signs in Indonesian and Arabic saying MUSLIM-OWNED. Local police allegedly received orders to shoot troublemakers on sight, no questions asked, and they shot at more than a dozen people, killing three. Although they were never targeted, expatriates and tourists left Lombok for Bali. The general consensus among political leaders and Lombok residents was that the riots were provoked. Indonesian president Abdurrahman Wahid, then just three months into his term, declared that the unrest was part of a larger campaign to destabilize the country orchestrated by a handful of people who lost power in the transition to democracy. Some expats theorized that the rioting resulted in part from ethnic tension spurred by economic jealousy; although Christians make up less than 1% of the island's population, many successful businesses are owned by Chinese Christians.

At press time the investigation into the cause of the riots was still open. The only thing certain is that the uproar devastated Lombok's tourist industry. Of the 80,000 locals employed in this field, 8,000 workers lost their jobs as the island morphed into a ghost town. The January 2000 riots were an isolated incident, however, and the island's desertion has made it an even more peaceful retreat from touristy Bali.

WHAT'S WHERE

Indonesia is made up of five large and more than 17,000 small islands totaling more than 1,919,440 square km (741,052 square mi), with a population of 210 million. Bali, toward the center of the Indonesian archipelago, is only about 145 km (90 mi) long but has more than 3 million people and probably more than 10,000 temples. This is one of the very last completely traditional societies in which all facets of life—agriculture, economics, politics, technology, social customs, and the arts—are welded together by religion; this is the only Hindu stronghold in the predominately Islamic nation. To the east of Bali are the islands of Nusa Tenggara, which include Lombok, a tropical haven for those who find Bali too commercialized.

Southern Bali

Southern Bali is the tail of the butterfly-shape island, stretching from the capital, Denpasar, down to the temple of Uluwatu, at the southern end of the Bukit Peninsula. Bukit's landscape is arid all the way to its sand-fringed perimeter; at its core the hills are sculpted of golden limestone and pocketed with caves. The peninsula's edge has been thrashed into high, rugged cliffs by the Indian Ocean; here the crisp white sand beaches are the solitary havens of the world's best surfers. The eastern side of this region, around Sanur, is threaded with mangrove swamps and lined with coral reefs where turquoise *jukung* (outrigger fishing boats) cruise for the day's catch. The western side is tourist land, and the stretch from Jimbaran up to Seminyak is crowded with resorts and sunbathers. As the coast curves around to Tanah Lot, though, it regains its composure and becomes one of the prettiest sections of shell-strewn sand on the island.

Eastern Bali

Eastern Bali encompasses three of the island's most significant cultural sites: Ubud, the center for the arts; Pura Besakih, the holiest temple; and Gunung Agung, Bali's tallest and most sacred mountain. Most of this region is mountainous and covered with thick rain forest all the way to the coast. The area is defined by several volcanoes, with cool highland villages on slopes cut by deep river gullies. The rugged terrain becomes drier toward the edges, and many of the beaches are made of soft volcanic ash. This part of the island is fringed with coral reefs, making it an excellent place to dive and snorkel.

As a major cultural center Ubud is the region's most popular destination for travelers, but it's a smarter, quieter place than the southern tourist towns. Most visitors come here to learn about Balinese history and arts, and many linger longer than they originally intended. The town and surrounding crafts villages give off a subtle sense of magic that grasps nearly every visitor. Life here is slow and fulfilling, and the number of things to see and do draws travelers back again and again.

The interior is dotted with small towns, each with its own historic and artistic significance. Many were once centers of ancient kingdoms; others are gatherings of craftspeople that have grown into trade centers. These villages are guarded but friendly, proud of their heritage—and working hard to keep it alive—but very willing to share their stories with the interested visitor. The coastal towns are more casual, focused on diving and drinking, perfect for vacationers who want to skip the tourist scene.

Northern Bali

Northern Bali's mountainous interior, which stretches from the peak of Gunung Batur, in the northeast, to the crater lakes at Bali's center, isn't incredibly popular with non-Indonesian tourists. It has a completely different climate from the rest of the island: it's cool and damp year-round. Tourists won't find swimming pools at any of the hotels, but they will find a far more peaceful and less commercial existence. Agriculture is the most important activity, and the fruits and vegetables grown here feed the resort areas on other parts of the island. In addition to spectacular waterfalls, lakes, and an active volcano, the inland region is home to several of the island's most important temples.

Bali's northern coast is dry and hot like the south, but not nearly as developed. The string of coastal villages collectively known as Lovina is the main hub for tourists, particularly divers who like its accessibility to popular dive sites to the east and west. Lovina is also home to a tiny bit of nightlife, which is otherwise nonexistent in northern Bali. The north coast has natural springs for bathing and waterfalls, as well as small temples that display the fantastical carvings typical of the region.

Western Bali

Nature lovers and adventurers shouldn't miss Bali's rarely visited western end, with its long, dramatic black beaches (and dangerous ocean tides) and a large area of preserved land, Bali Barat National Park, with arid forests and mangrove swamps. A favorite destination of divers and snorkelers, the far west has some flourishing reef sites around Menjangan Island, off Bali's northwestern tip. There are a few fantastic resorts in this area, but shopping and nightlife are nonexistent. This is a place to bring a book, interact with the natural environment, and experience what Bali was like decades ago, before it was developed into a tourist center.

Lombok

Lombok lies in the middle of the Indonesian archipelago immediately east of Bali and west of Sumbawa. Bali and Lombok are only 43 km (27 mi) apart, but they are on opposite sides of Wallace's Line, an imaginary boundary that marks the separation of Asia and Australia. As you travel eastward across the island, Australian species increase, and you see less Asian flora and fauna. Sasaks call Lombok Bumi Gora, or "the Dry Farmland," and you won't find tropical forests here. The island is drier than Bali, with a rainy season from October to March and a dry season from April until September. Rainfall flows south from Mt. Rinjani to irrigate tobacco farms and rice paddies. The island has a bonnetlike shape that resembles the roof of a *lumbung,* the traditional rice storage barn. On the southern coast the crags that frame stretches of beach remind travelers of Ireland and New Zealand.

PLEASURES AND PASTIMES

Arts

Bali's artistic spirit resides in the eastern part of the island, with its heart in the area around Ubud. Here you find small gatherings of villages that have preserved and refined traditions over the centuries, where only one dance or music troupe knows one particular performance, where craftsmen who once worked for royalty still pass their secrets on to their sons. The town of Ubud presents artistic works in tourist shops, but you can easily find the real thing in the small towns just minutes down the road: Mas is the center for wood-carvers; Celuk is a town of silversmiths; Batubulan is the home of stonecutters; Batuan is the painting center; and Sukawati is home to painted mobiles and chimes. Kamasan, near Semarapura, is also a town of painters, and you'll find craftspeople in the villages along the eastern coast. While you're here, be sure to take in a dance or music performance—if possible at a temple at night, when gods are said to be in the audience.

On Lombok there's a popular dance that helps the reserved Sasaks overcome their shyness—the *gandrung.* The word means "love," and the ritual is like a Sadie Hawkins dance. Accompanied by a gamelan, a young girl flutters a fan as she sings and dances. The audience encircles the dancer, who eventually taps a boy with the fan; he then joins her for a duet that includes theatrics and even some dirty dancing. If you're interested in glimpsing this ritual dance, contact the Regional Office of Tourism in Ampenan.

Beaches

Southern Bali lives up to its legend as a tropical paradise, with powder-soft sand and tall coconut trees brushed by soft breezes coming off the jade-and-sapphire sea. These treasures can be found in the secluded resort beaches of Canggu, Berewa, and Jimbaran, as well as on Bukit Badung. The best span with public access runs for about 10 km (6 mi) between Seminyak and Kuta, and all the action is here: sunning, surfing, and the selling of everything from batik sarongs to massage and hair plaiting. Now lined with huge international hotels, the once-serene sands of Tuban also bustle with activity. Along the east coast the seaside stretches of Nusa Dua and Sanur have coarse brown sand and offshore reefs that provide some of the island's most convenient snorkeling; most beaches here are private, part of the resorts that stand side by side. Around the Bukit Peninsula, though, down the small back roads, lie hidden coves where your footprints will stand alone on the white sand—we'll let you find these on your own.

Lombok beaches are what postcards are made of. The beaches of the southwest are crescent stretches of white crystal sand. Along the coast near Kuta, the beaches Tanjung A'an and Selong Blanak offer coconut groves, sweeping seascapes, and seclusion. The Gili Islands' beaches are equally picturesque, though more crowded, especially during the summer months; still you can usually find a secluded spot by venturing away from the bungalows that dot the shore. Lombok's beaches aren't as developed as Bali's, so amenities like cabanas and soda vendors are scarce, though you may find an occasional pineapple or sarong seller.

Dining

Bali's newest crop of restaurants has expanded the variety of first-class dining opportunities, particularly in southern Bali. You'll find every type of food here, with imported French, Australian, and American chefs heading the kitchens. Gone are the fusions of Asian entrées flattened into pretty but tasteless gourmet packages. Today's chefs aren't afraid to dazzle diners with new dishes based on traditional recipes or to simply dress up well-known ethnic fare. Rather than trying to satisfy every customer, the new restaurants are choosing one cuisine and going all the way with it, whether it's French, Indian, Italian, or simply Balinese. Mediterranean cuisine has become particularly prevalent, and what's offered here can rival the best restaurants in Asia. Little Japanese diners have sprung up everywhere as well. Kerobokan and Seminyak are where you'll find the truly good dining spots, as this area is home to a number of the island's upscale resorts and villas and many expatriates. Sanur is building up a base of eclectic modern eateries, many of which have art galleries and live jazz. Denpasar is the best place to go for authentic Chinese cooking.

Golf

Southern Bali has three of the island's four golf courses, and they're all considered world class. The top spot is the new Le Meridien Nirwana Golf & Spa Resort, which lies between rice paddies and the rugged cliffs of Bali's rocky southwestern coastline. The tried-and-true Bali Beach Golf Course backs the Grand Bali Beach hotel, in north Sanur. The Bali Golf & Country Club, in Nusa Dua, is a favorite of resort guests in the south. On Lombok the course at the Rinjani Country Club, in Narmada, has female caddies and attracts Japanese businessmen.

The Natural World

Eastern Bali draws adventurers who want to climb its volcanic peaks, hike in its rain forests, raft its rough rivers, and dive the coral reefs that line its coasts. Gunung Agung, the island's highest peak and its most famous landmark, is surrounded by lesser summits such as Gunung Lampuyang, to the east, and Gunung Batur, to the northwest. Major waterways include the Ayung, Oos, and Unda rivers, which flow south from the mountains through deep ravines surrounding Ubud. Rain forest blankets these areas all the way to the coast, where drier terrain takes over. Although there are no national parks in this region, there are several notable wildlife havens. The most famous is the Bali Bird Park, about 10 minutes southwest of Ubud in Singapadu, Indonesia's largest collection of avian life and one of the top bird parks in Asia. Next to it, the Bali Rimba Reptile Park houses lizards from the islands, including Komodo dragons. The Bali Butterfly Park, west of Ubud, contains many of the archipelago's most brilliant and rare species. The Elephant Safari Park, north of Ubud, gives you a chance to explore the forest on one of these magnificent creatures.

The western end of Bali may not have much in the way of cultural performances, nightlife, or shopping, but it's a great place to escape from traffic, hawkers, and other tourists and do some exploring. Much of the region is taken up by Bali Barat National Park, which offers diving, snorkeling, and trekking—and a chance to see the rare Bali starling, which scientists are trying to save from extinction in the park's breeding area. The coral reef drop-off surrounding uninhabited Menjangan Island, recovering from the ravages of coral-eating starfish and dynamite fishing, now bubbles with sea life.

GUNUNG BATUR ➤ The area around Bali's Mt. Batur was formed more than 30,000 years ago by a gigantic volcanic eruption. The resulting crater lake in the center, Danau Batur, is surrounded by several rugged peaks. Gunung Batur, though not the highest peak, is still active and has four craters of its own. It has erupted more than 20 times in the past 200 years; its most recent activity was in 2000, when it spewed hot rocks for several months. In 1917 a major eruption killed more than 1,000 people living in the crater, in what was then Batur village on the lake's western edge. The lava flow stopped just outside the village temple, which was viewed as a positive omen, so the survivors remained even after the eruption. Six years later, however, another eruption wiped out most of the village and temple, and the people were forced to move up to the crater rim. Bringing with them as many shrines and relics as they were able to salvage, they rebuilt the temple, Pura Ulun Danu Batur, which honors Ida Batara Dewi Ulun Danu, the goddess who controls the water for the irrigation systems throughout the island. During the ritual sacrifices still made to Dewi Danu regularly, animals are thrown into the lake or into the volcanic craters.

The lava flows that wind through the lower part of the crater (dating from a 1974 eruption) give the area an otherworldly look, but Gunung Batur is not considered dangerous. Climbing it to watch the sun rise is for many visitors the most memorable experience of a trip to Bali. The simple breakfast cooked in the steam holes at the top of the volcano isn't bad, either.

DOLPHINS ➤ There has been some controversy over the boat trips that leave Lovina Beach in northern Bali each morning in search of dolphins. The frolicking animals have become an inseparable part of Lovina's lore (and lure), but in recent years many visitors have complained that the experience is unfair to the animals. The outrigger boats that transport small numbers of passengers are powered by outboard motors that sputter and growl. There was a time when mobs of these boats would desperately chase after the occasional dolphin fin, leading many to liken the so-called dolphin cruises to whale hunts. Although it's not clear how bothered the dolphins are by the noise, Lovina's boatmen must have gotten word of the tourists' horror because the operation has settled down considerably. Boats now keep a respectful distance from the dolphins and stay as far away from each other as possible. If you concentrate on the water, the sunrise, and the nearby dolphins, you may hardly notice the other boatloads of tourists with whom you're sharing the experience.

Nightlife

Bali's best nightspots are all in the south, the traditional gathering place for young and restless travelers. On the southwest coast, Canggu, Kerobokan, and Seminyak are where the rich, refined, and beautiful gather at eclectic bars and ethnic restaurants for quiet drinks, live jazz, and worldly conversations. Legian has become the club town, with discos and after-hours bars that keep night owls going until dawn. Kuta and Tuban reverberate 24 hours with the sounds of pop and heavy metal from big bars and international restaurants where tourists start the day's drinking at noon. Nusa Dua's nightlife is quieter, limited mostly to resort bars and clubs, with a few cocktail spots along Jalan Pantai Mengiat. Sanur's nightlife takes place in hotel and restaurant bars, except for a couple of clubs on Jalan Tamblingan. Though Denpasar rocks all night, it's mostly Balinese, Chinese, and Japanese at the night markets, in the karaoke bars, or on after-hours city tours.

Shopping

High-quality crafts, low prices, and professional shipping services make Bali one of the best places in Indonesia to shop. You'll find the ultimate in open-air market browsing in southern Bali, where traditional Asian-style shopping still thrives. Denpasar, which didn't become the island's capital until after World War II, is still very much a market town, as evidenced by the enormous Pasar Badung central market, the Pasar Kumbasari art market, and the Pasar Burung bird market—to say nothing of the numerous night markets throughout the city. The main strip from Seminyak to Kuta was once one long open-air shopping mall; today many of the stores are enclosed in glass and air-conditioned. A few small outdoor markets remain in Kuta, including the Pasar Pagi morning market, the beachside Pasar Seni art market, and the Pasar Malam night market, near the bus terminal. One of the south's most colorful markets is the Pasar Ikan fish market, in Jimbaran, where fishing boats line the shore and *warung* (food stalls) give off the smells of smoked seafood. Sanur probably has the best markets for a tourist center; look for the Pasar Sindhu morning market, the Pasar Pantai Sindhu beach market, the Pasar Seni art market, and the Pasar Pantai Sanur crafts market.

Unless you're heading into these main markets, shopping in southern Bali means a more Western-style stroll through air-conditioned shops with neatly arranged fixed-price items. You'll pay more—at least twice as much as in the markets—for this more familiar experience, but it's a far easier option for those with little time and no haggling experience. Canggu, Kerobokan, and Seminyak have a variety of boutiques and furniture and jewelry showrooms that sell high-quality handcrafted items. Much of the same can be found in Legian, Kuta, and Tuban, and at lower prices—although you really have to sort through the junk to get to the gems. Resort shops are your only option around the Bukit peninsula and along the beaches of Nusa Dua and Sanur, unless you're comfortable with comparison shopping and bargaining; if you are, then head for Jalan Pantai Mengiat and Jalan Nusa Dua. Better still, check out Sanur's main road and back streets, where you'll find the same goods for less. The island's largest mall is the Nusa Dua Galeria, an enormous open courtyard of sleek upscale shops and restaurants; everything from crafts to clothing is sold here, but you'll pay dearly for the same goods you'd find in Kuta. Denpasar has many indoor malls that are exact replicas of those found in the West.

On Lombok shopping is largely limited to locally made handicrafts, fabrics, and the like, and if that's what you're looking for, you can go right to the source to find skillfully made pieces. Prices are a little lower than they are on Bali. In addition to local baskets, pottery, and textiles, you'll be able to find crafts from islands farther east. You can shop for these things in the bustling city markets, such as the daily market in Cakranegara. Better yet, go to the villages where the crafts are produced; you'll find higher-quality goods and have a chance to see masters at work. Before shopping, check out the displays of knives, tools, *songket* fabric, basketwork, and masks at the Museum Negeri Nusa Tenggara Barat, in Ampenan, to get acquainted with local objets d'art.

Surfing

Bali is one of the world's original surf haunts, and the south takes pride in having some of the best waves you'll find anywhere. There's a definite surfing subculture here that includes young and old, men and women, and travelers from Australia, the United States, Europe, South America, and Japan. Annual competitions draw crowds to the remote beaches around the Bukit Peninsula. Hotels arrange surfing tours, and lessons have become a popular addition to daily resort activities. Everything a surfer needs can be found in southern Bali: board and repair shops, equipment and clothing stores, specialized tour offices, and, in all the bookstores, surfing books and magazines.

Except for Desert Point and Gili Air, the surf breaks in Lombok are not on a par with those in Bali. They tend to be more erratic and more inaccessible. Kuta is the place to station yourself, since the reputable breaks are mostly off the southern coast. Desert Point, off Bangko-Bangko Beach in the southwest, is a mecca for tough, experienced surfers. Not only is the break a fast, evasive left-hander, but the road to the beach is quite rough. Diehards will charter a boat from Bali just to surf Desert Point.

Temple Carvings

Spend a little time in Bali and you'll begin to think that unadorned surfaces are an endangered species. Nowhere are the decorations more exuberant than in the temple carvings along the northern coast. The carvings are mostly done in *paras,* a soft, pumicelike gray stone that is easy to carve but highly susceptible to the effects of weather. Great carvings are sometimes difficult to make out because they literally melt from the dampness. When paras is newly carved, it is pale gray and resembles cement—and in fact some carvings you see in restaurants and hotels will actually be cement casts meant to look like paras. Paras darkens with exposure, however, and can become covered entirely by moss or lichen within a few years. Some northern temples are carved from pale pink sandstone, another soft and malleable medium.

Although temples in the south are made primarily of redbrick with some small areas of carved paras, northern temples are nearly all carved stone, with little if any brick. Temple walls and archways practically heave under the weight of layers of detailed carvings. One particularly unusual temple is Sangsit's Pura Dalem. The depictions you'll see here aren't your typical religious imagery; soft porn might be a more accurate description. Of course, it's all done in the name of religion, with the various body parts demonstrating the pleasurable rewards due the faithful and the torturous life awaiting evildoers. Jagaraga's Pura Dalem is small and worn, but the front panels tell a fascinating and poignant story of the Dutch invasion from the Balinese perspective. Pura Maduwe Karang at Kubutambahan is surprisingly small and modest, considering how well known it has become for one of its carved panels, which shows a bicycle with wheels made from giant flower petals, thought to be a picture of the first actual bicycle on Bali.

Weddings

On Lombok, if you are fortunate enough to wrangle an invite to a local wedding, you'll learn about the island's tradition of "runaway marriage," or *kawin lari*. When families disapprove of a couple's intent to marry, the bride is "kidnapped" by the groom, who then must report the kidnapping to the village chief. Another messenger tells the bride's family where the girl is being kept and when the couple ran away. The next day the couple is married according to Islamic religious custom, then there are two days of festivity while the bridegroom's family determines a "bride price," based on how much it will cost to throw a reception.

GREAT ITINERARIES

Even a short holiday on Bali is worthwhile for the opportunity to relax on an inexpensive tropical island and experience its vivacious society. For lazy days sunning and shopping, head to the southern peninsula, where each town has a different character and focus. The large resorts are on the beaches of Sanur and Nusa Dua, in the southeast, as well as in Jimbaran, on the neck of the Bukit Peninsula. For rice-paddy and beach views in the midst of island life, try one of the villas of western Kerobokan; for upscale shopping and dining head for Seminyak; for day-and-night activity go to Legian, Kuta, or Tuban. If you'd rather just get away from

it all, make your vacation on one of the islands southeast of Bali in the Badung Strait.

If you have more time, and especially if you like to dive, drive around the east coast through Candidasa, Amed, and Tulamben. To experience island culture, stay near Ubud, where you can catch daily dance and music performances, explore museums and art galleries, hike to mountain temples, and visit villages that still do things the old-fashioned way. The northern coast is a pleasant black-sand alternative to the busy southern beach scene; here you can also swim with dolphins and hike to stunning waterfalls. Rugged western Bali is for the more intrepid traveler; its Bali Barat National Park is worth a trip if you're into hiking, diving, snorkeling, or observing wildlife.

Lombok makes an excellent side trip, but plan to spend at least three nights here to really make the most of it. Among your options are relaxing on the white sand beaches of Senggigi, the Gili Islands, and the south coast; backpacking on Gunung Rinjani; and taking cultural expeditions to Sasak crafts villages in the interior.

If you enjoy leisurely days and want to keep your own schedule, rent a vehicle—and hire a driver if you haven't mastered the twisting, steep, two-lane roads. Whether you're driving or on day tours, you should place as many of these must-see stops in Bali on your itinerary as you can: Pura Besakih, the island's holiest temple; Tanah Lot, the sacred temple of the southwest coast; Pura Uluwatu, the Bukit Peninsula's most famous shrine; the long shopping strip from Seminyak to Kuta; and Ubud, the center of cultural learning. Those with more time can peruse the historical sights of eastern Bali, such as the palaces of Gelgel and Semarapura, as well as the natural wonders of Gunung Agung, Gunung Batur, and the other volcanoes and lakes at Bali's core.

If You Have 3 Days

Fly into **Bali** and base yourself at the southern beach of your choice, then spend the first day sunbathing and browsing through the shops, but don't buy anything yet—just learn the prices. On day two take a day trip to **Ubud** and **Pura Besakih,** passing through the **crafts villages** along the way. Use day three to work on your tan and pick up a few souvenirs now that you know what you want and how much it should cost.

If You Have 6 Days

Spend the first two days at the beach—perhaps with a day trip to **Nusa Lembongan** or **Pulau Serangan** on the second day—then head up to Ubud for three days, where you can take short trips to the crafts villages, explore the museums, and watch nightly temple ceremonies and dance performances. On your last day return to the beach to absorb what you saw and learned before flying home.

If You Have 10 Days

Make your base in Ubud for four days, with a day each for the crafts villages, area temples, a mountain tour, and shopping downtown. On day five cruise or fly to **Lombok** and spend two nights in **Senggigi**, from which you can explore Sasak villages and seek out mountain views; or you can just relax in seclusion at one of the small hotels on the **Gili Islands.** On day seven return to Bali. If north-coast beaches or west-coast trekking interest you, make your way to **Lovina** to see the area's temples and dolphins, or spend a couple of days hiking and diving in **Bali Barat National Park.** Otherwise, head for Bali's southern beaches and spend your last few days enjoying the sun and taking day trips to **Denpasar,** the **Badung Strait Islands,** and the east coast before flying out.

If You Have 14 Days

To have two full weeks on Bali is a traveler's fantasy, for the whole island can be dipped into in this time. Begin in Ubud, and spend three days exploring Bali's crafts and culture. Then take a clockwise drive around the coast: go around the west end and Bali Barat National Park, travel along the north coast through Lovina, and then continue around the east end through **Tulamben, Amed,** and **Candidasa,** spending one night at each compass point. On day seven cruise or fly to Lombok and spend three days here sunning on the beach, trekking the interior, or visiting craft villages. On day 10 return to Bali and stay in the south, where you can sun, shop, and temple- or market-hop until it's time to fly home.

FODOR'S CHOICE

Beaches

★ **Berewa, southern Bali.** Hunt for little seashells at sunset along this lovely white stretch of sand.

★ **Buitan, eastern Bali.** This little-known resort beach is on a perfect arc of cliff-sheltered bay looking out over boats making their way across the sea from Padangbai.

★ **Jimbaran, southern Bali.** Lined with colorful fishing boats and filled with the aroma of sizzling grilled fish, this beach is the perfect spot for a morning walk or an evening meal.

★ **Mawun, Lombok.** The best thing about this half-moon-shape beach surrounded by rocky headlands is its isolation.

★ **Samudra Indah, southern Bali.** This is the classic picture of tropical paradise, with white sand, warm azure waves, soft breezes, and stands with simple but delicious Indonesian food.

★ **Selong Blanak, Lombok.** Vendors sell fresh coconuts from the plantations surrounding this snow white beach.

★ **Tulamben, eastern Bali.** The shell-strewn beach may seem ordinary—until you see the brilliant offshore reefs and the shipwreck just under the surface.

Dining

★ **The Damai, northern Bali.** Danish and Balinese chefs whip up a nightly four-star, five-course dinner served under the glow of a green glass chandelier. $$$$

★ **Balangan, southern Bali.** At this intimate restaurant high in the Jimbaran hills, diners are treated to fine Continental fare and a sunset panorama that stretches from the west coast to the central volcanoes. $$–$$$

★ **Indus, eastern Bali.** Sitting at the edge of a deep river gorge, this classy restaurant offers an eclectic Continental menu and soaring rice-paddy views. $$–$$$

★ **Telaga Naga, southern Bali.** Dress up and dine on fantastic Chinese fare at this pavilion-style restaurant set in estatelike gardens off Sanur's main road. $$–$$$

★ **Bumbu Bali, eastern Bali.** A romantic garden ambience and top-notch Indian and Balinese fare make this restaurant a standout. $–$$

★ **Veranda, southern Bali.** This kitschy little tropical restaurant in upscale Seminyak has perfectly prepared Continental cuisine and flawless service. $–$$

★ **Ayu's Kitchen, eastern Bali.** Homemade Balinese cooking is the specialty of this quaint little restaurant, and there's a tasty dessert case, too. $

★ **Biyu Nasak, northern Bali.** This cozy spot in Lovina's central Kalibukbuk area stands apart from the others with fresh, hearty, and very tasty dishes. $

★ **Lombok Coconut, Lombok.** The best pizza in Lombok comes with a money-back guarantee. $

★ **Taman Griya, Lombok** Head here for a taste of Lombok spice without too much bite—and be sure to take home a recipe. $

★ **Tutmak, eastern Bali.** The atmosphere of this inexpensive dining spot is bookstore kitsch, the menu is extensive and eclectic, and the food is outstanding. $

★ **Warung Batavia, southern Bali.** It's just a ramshackle roadside warung, but the basic Indonesian fare is terrific and the clientele ranges from locals to famous resort guests. $

★ **Warung Kopi at Puri Lumbung, northern Bali.** This quiet raised bungalow overlooks the green hills of central Bali. Ingredients are plucked from the surrounding hills, and the resulting dishes are eye-opening and mouth-watering. $

Lodging

★ **Amandari, eastern Bali.** This intimate luxury resort, designed to look like a Balinese village, lives up to its reputation as one of Southeast Asia's top small hotels. $$$$

★ **Ambara Ulangan, southern Bali.** Sitting atop a mountain summit in Jimbaran, this opulent villa complex affords sweeping views of both coasts from tiered infinity pools. $$$$

★ **Hotel Tugu Bali, southern Bali.** At this peaceful boutique hotel near Canggu, Balinese-style bungalows commemorate the island's artists. $$$$

★ **Pool Villa Club, Lombok.** The staff here manages to anticipate your every need without being obtrusive. The villas are so luxuriantly cozy guests are reluctant to leave the nest. $$$$

★ **Puri Ganesha Villas, western Bali.** This idyllic secret hideaway has spacious individual villas with private pools. If you want to see the "real" Bali, the owner is one of the best guides on the island. $$$$

★ **The Oberoi, Lombok.** Sunsets are sublime from this hotel's two-level stretch limo of a pool. The architectural details are perfect, down to the fish-filled lotus pond in every bathroom. $$$–$$$$

★ **Matahari Beach Resort & Spa, western Bali.** This resort in Pemuteran has one of the most impressive spas in Bali, with endless fountains and stone carvings (not to mention the addictive four-handed massage). $$$

★ **Waka Gangga, western Bali.** This luxurious yet simple resort isolated on the wild beach of Yeh Gangga is a welcome newcomer to the island, perfect for both romance and relaxation. $$$

★ **Umalas Stables, southern Bali.** Sleep above the stables—in luxury—at this hotel in the Kerobokan rice fields. Beginners and pros can ride here, and there are many activities for children. $$–$$$

★ **Puri Lumbung, northern Bali.** Guests here can interact with Balinese people, learn to craft offerings and cook traditional dishes, and take guided walks to see local plants and spices. $$

★ **Sacred Mountain Sanctuary, eastern Bali.** Bali's first ecoresort is nestled high in the forests of the Gunung Agung volcano, but it has the comfort and service of the best hotels. $–$$

★ **Amarta Bungalows, southern Bali.** With a convenient location between the beach and the shops, plus an upscale look, these two-story bungalows are a bargain. $

★ **Rambutan Beach Cottages, northern Bali.** In the heart of Lovina's busiest area, this hotel is a little oasis of friendliness. Accommodations run from budget to luxury, and Lovina Beach and scores of restaurants are within a few minutes' walk. $

★ **Honeymoon Guesthouse, eastern Bali.** Teak and marble make the rooms look expensive, but the rates are strictly budget.

This is the headquarters of one of Bali's best cooking schools and bakeries. ¢

Museums

⭐ **Agung Rai Museum of Art, eastern Bali.** It's not just a museum; this is Ubud's all-inclusive cultural center, with exhibits, art and dance classes, and weekly performances at the on-site temple.

⭐ **Museum Negeri Nusa Tenggara Barat, Lombok.** If you will be going shopping for local handicrafts and antiques, get to know the real thing through this museum's exhibits of weapons, arts, and crafts.

Outdoor Activities

⭐ **Gunung Batur, northern Bali.** With good weather, the pre-dawn climb up the island's active volcano allows a view clear across the island at sunrise. If you're not the climbing sort, view the 5,632-ft-high mountain and its crater lake from the cozy Lakeview restaurant.

⭐ **Gunung Rinjani, Lombok.** Trekkers will want to spend a few days exploring this volcano, the third-highest summit in Lombok. The panoramic view of the island from its caldera is breathtaking.

⭐ **Lovina's dolphins, northern Bali.** The sunrise is spectacular when viewed from a small boat in the Bali Sea. Add dolphins frolicking at arm's length and you've got one of Bali's best-loved attractions.

⭐ **Trekking around Munduk, northern Bali.** The village of Munduk is far enough off the beaten path to be thoroughly unaffected, and a hike through the area gives you an up-close look at everything from coffee trees and vanilla vines to out-of-the-way waterfalls.

Sacred Spots

⭐ **Narmada Taman, Lombok.** This water palace is a spa in more ways than one. It contains a well that's believed to be a fountain of youth.

⭐ **Pura Besakih, eastern Bali.** High on the slopes of the great Gunung Agung volcano, the island's holiest temple is the one sight you shouldn't miss.

⭐ **Pura Lingsar, Lombok.** Amid the nation's ethnic tensions, this temple is a landmark of harmony, a place where both Hindus and Muslims worship.

⭐ **Pura Puncak Penulisan, northern Bali.** Bali's highest temple is nearly always shrouded in cool mist. The fog may block the view, which on a rare clear day can be clear to the coast, but it adds to the atmosphere of a structure that houses sculptures more than 10 centuries old.

⭐ **Pura Rambut Siwi, western Bali.** This is one of the more beautiful temples in Bali, with sunsets as lovely as at Pura Tanah Lot, without the huge crowds.

⭐ **Pura Tanah Lot, southern Bali.** Perched on a rocky island just off the west coast, this sacred temple has classic sunset views.

⭐ **Pura Ulun Danu Bratan, northern Bali.** This is one of Bali's most photographed scenes: shrines sit on tiny islands along the edge of shimmering Danau Bratan, with Gunung Batur rising up in the distance.

⭐ **Pura Uluwatu, southern Bali.** This temple complex set high in the cliffs at the southern edge of the island looks out on a world-renowned surf spot.

2 SOUTHERN BALI

It's 6:30 PM at Kuta Beach, and across the gray ocean a copper-skinned surfer ducks under the silver curve of a wave. Tourists stroll barefoot along the wide sweep of honeyed sand; others pack up their bottled water and beach towels as they enjoy the last embers of sunshine. The scent of jasmine lingers along the busy beach road, where cruising taxis beep sharply and hucksters call out "Want massage? Change money?" to chattering shoppers. Amid all this a young Balinese woman clad in a gold-threaded sarong and lace jacket slowly places a small leaf-basket offering onto the sand, a testament to the timelessness of all that is still worshiped on Bali.

By Holly S.
Smith

S OUTHERN BALI USED TO BE just a string of little coastal villages trickling down from the bustling market hub of Denpasar. Today many of Bali's 3 million inhabitants have migrated to this region, with dreams of becoming rich through enterprises staked on the reliable influx of tourists. However, this end of the island wasn't always a magnet for international jet-setters and weary backpackers looking for a pretty beach and a cheap beer. The Chinese discovered Bali as early as 2500 BC, the Javanese arrived around AD 800, and the Dutch came in 1597. But it wasn't until the latter group conquered the island piece by piece in the early 1900s that this region was promoted as paradise. The first travelers indeed arrived to find gorgeous white beaches and azure seas, although this idyllic seascape was backed by an unattractive section of swamps and dry coconut groves. Yet now the original landscape has all but disappeared, swallowed up into the sunny shopping strips and manicured grounds of the modern mega-resorts built in the last century.

The land underneath the clusters of hotels, shops, and restaurants that have overtaken the rice fields from Denpasar south is an extension of the massive volcanoes that arise from Bali's center. Moving away from the mountains, the land becomes flat and dry, and the forest gathers into arid patches between clusters of civilization. Beaches dust both sides of Bali's southern tip: gray, shell-strewn shores off the eastern reefs of Sanur and Nusa Dua, and a golden expanse of sand stretching down the west coast from Canggu to Jimbaran. The slender neck of the Bukit peninsula slopes into the hills at its core, where bulldozers shave the chalky limestone walls into crumbled stones used for building the finest resort villas. At the peninsula's last edge, rugged cliffs rise hundreds of meters above the thundering ocean. This is one of Bali's most dramatic coastlines.

This area is rich with wildlife, particularly beneath the sea, but even on land there are many interesting plant and animal species. The brilliant hues of Bali's tropical flora will catch your eye first. Magenta and peach bougainvillea, rose-red hibiscus, pearl-drop tuber roses, and fragrant, snowy frangipani flowers blossom everywhere. Look above to find a natural feast. Banana, coconut, papaya, jackfruit, and star fruit trees are tucked into every garden. A half-dozen species of palm tree provide more than just shade: Leaves of the lontar palm are used for basket weaving and the pages of traditional books. The sago palm's leaves are used for thatch roofs and walls; its sap is used in rice wine.

Among these leaves and flowers you'll find a surprising variety of small creatures, notably butterflies, insects, and lizards. White and yellow moths are common, but you may also spot the iridescent emerald- or azure-and-black wings of a swallowtail butterfly. Giant green grasshoppers leap out to escape children's eager fingers during the day. After dark the songs of crickets and bullfrogs color the night air. You'll see lizards at all hours, from the tiny *cecaks* (pronounced *chee*-chaks) that scramble up the walls to the larger, colorful *gekkos* and the still larger *tokays*—you can tell each by its call, which mimics its name.

The former hunting grounds of the Mengwi kings, Bukit Badung was once a forested peninsula teeming with deer and wildlife. Today there aren't many large mammals left, but you can sometimes spot macaques in the trees and dainty brown mouse deer in the forests early in the morning. The south is still an excellent area for bird-watching, however. Along the beaches you'll find white terns, gray-brown boobies, and black frigate birds, and the rice fields are dotted with white herons and muddy brown ducks nibbling up mosquito larvae.

Underwater, a stellar collection of creatures lives along southern Bali's fringing reefs, which is why the area—particularly around Sanur, Nusa Dua, and Nusa Penida—is a thriving international dive center. Corals, sea cucumbers, urchins, starfish, sand dollars, crabs, and sea snakes are among the smaller creatures you'll find in the reefs and grasses. Colorful fish inhabit the southern waters, and you may also encounter sea turtles, sharks, rays, and dolphins. If you're shell seeking, head east to Sanur or west to Berewa and Canggu, where the shores remain ripe for combing. A tide table is a helpful tool for anyone interested in the region's beach walks; booklets are available at most hotels, groceries, and bookstores.

Southern Bali's earliest foreign visitors were attracted to the profit potential of this sea life, as well as to the island's convenient location for trade. The Dutch were the first to set up a formal trading post, which ultimately failed due to lack of interest in the main products: rice and slaves. A Dane named Mads Lange arrived in the mid-1800s to restore European interest by building a new post, as well as a lavish residence and cultural center, and by establishing relations between the ruling Badung kings and the west.

By 1891 the Pemecutan dynasty had risen to power, although its reign was cut short by the Dutch, who conquered the island at the beginning of the next century. Balinese sovereignty had already been all but ignored by the Chinese and Bugis traders who had long before settled the region. By 1904, when a Chinese ship hit a reef off the southeast coast and the goods inside disappeared, tensions between the Dutch and the Pemecutan ruling house were high. No one knows who stole the treasures, but it was the end of feigned peace between the Dutch and the Balinese, and when Dutch troops arrived two years later, the Badung rulers staged a *puputan* (mass suicide). A boy rescued from the burning palace was the last survivor of the royal dynasty; today his grandson lives at Pemecutan Palace, in Denpasar, and is considered to be the Pemecutan *cokorda* (king).

After their takeover the Dutch drew Europeans to Bali with promises of a tropical utopian setting. Americans Robert and Louise Koke set up the first real tourist hotel, the Kuta Beach, in 1936 as a pit stop for weary Western travelers. Modernization slowly continued through the Second World War, when Denpasar was made the island's capital. The 1960s brought hippie crowds on the tie-dye tour from Bangkok to Bombay; many stayed on in Bali when they found that easy trade schemes could support their cheap lifestyle. Slicker developments came two decades later with the onslaught of government-led resort planning in Sanur and Nusa Dua. Although Kuta remained the tourist center, in the next decade the crowded road spread so far north that it reached the capital, and the villas of Kerobokan and Sanur popped up on either side of Denpasar.

The rich cultural ambience of Bali hasn't been erased by the foreign crowds, though; it's just hidden from obvious view. Look between the bars and you'll spot stone temple figures. Look above the polished glass windows of the new upscale shops to see braided-leaf decorations hanging from slender bamboo poles. Watch truckloads of gamelan players rumble down the road to perform at village ceremonies, and catch the scent of jasmine incense at dawn and dusk. Admire textiles and wood and stone carvings created decades ago, visit the small museums, and take in a temple ceremony if you can. These are the best ways to discover Bali's magic on this end of the island.

EXPLORING SOUTHERN BALI

A Good Tour

The best way to become familiar with the compact area of southern Bali is to take a drive around its edges and explore the little sights along the way. Start early, perhaps even at sunrise, at **Pura Tanah Lot** ①, one of the island's most sacred temples. The crowds come here for the sunsets, so the sunrise view is quiet and uninterrupted by hawkers and foot traffic, giving you ample opportunity to explore the rocky shores and stone buildings (provided the tide is low). Next head southeast over the hilly rice-field roads to **Pura Petitenget** ② and take a few moments to explore the temple. From here turn inland on Jalan Kayu Aya, then take a sharp right on Jalan Seminyak, a crowded two-lane, shop-lined street that continues south from Seminyak all the way through Legian and Kuta, switching names as it enters each neighborhood. Because you have an early start, you can either cruise the strip slowly, hopping out to inspect the shops as you like, or park and walk through each different area. If shopping isn't your idea of fun, drive south down the strip, following the one-way signs, turn right on Jalan Kuta, and follow this road around as it turns into Jalan Pantai Kuta (usually just called Jalan Pantai), then take your pick of beaches as you go north along the road.

Numbers in the text correspond to numbers in the margin and on the Southern Bali and Denpasar maps.

After lunch stop at the **Mads Lange Tomb** ③ and the **Pasar Seni Kuta** ④ art market before driving south on Jalan Uluwatu. Stop in at the **Pasar Ikan Jimbaran** ⑤, a fish market along the beach, then drive through town past the Pasar Jimbaran market. Just down the road you can take a peek in the town's 11th-century **Pura Ulun Siwi** ⑥. Take a break at Garuda Wisna Kencana (GWK), a new performing-arts complex in the Jimbaran hills that has fantastic views of the peninsula all the way to the central volcanoes. Continue south, stopping at one or two smaller temples: Pura Balangan, Pura Masuka, and Pura Batu Pageh are ancient places of worship along this route. Catch the sunset at **Pura Uluwatu** ⑦, then head back to the main western strip for dinner.

You can cover the east coast the next day, beginning at Pura Geger, in Nusa Dua. Take a drive through the small strip of restaurants and shops on Jalan Pantai Mengiat, then browse through the upscale stores and eateries at the Nusa Dua Galeria shopping plaza. Cruise up the wide resort road to Tanjung Benoa, where you can explore the **Pasar Benoa** ⑧ and the **Chinese temple** ⑨ at the peninsula's northern end. From here drive around Benoa Harbor and take the coastal road to Sanur, stopping for a mangrove walk and a look at the ships. At Sanur's southern end you'll find the Pura Mertasari and Pura Belanjong temples. Continuing north you pass the **Pasar Sindhu** ⑩ art market, the **Pasar Pantai Sindhu** ⑪ beach market, and a host of shops, hotels, and restaurants in between. Take an hour to view the exhibits at the **Museum Le Mayeur** ⑫, the artist's former home and studio, and then visit a second beach market, **Pasar Pantai Sanur** ⑬, nearby. If you weren't up early enough to see the west coast's Pura Tanah Lot on the first day, this is a good jumping-off point to view it at sunset with the crowds (a main highway that cuts west across the island leads straight to it). Otherwise, enjoy the kite-strewn evening skies here.

On the third day put on good walking shoes and start at Denpasar's **Pasar Badung** ⑭ morning market, in a five-story cement-block building at the edge of the Ayung River. From here walk north to Jalan Gajah Mada, take a left, and continue west a half-block to reach the **Pasar**

Kumbasari ⑮, where you can spend an hour perusing crafts from all over the island. Cross the street and continue a block and a half west along Jalan Wahidin to **Pura Maospahit** ⑯, a temple honoring the former Majapahit kingdom. Turn around and walk east a half block to Jalan Thamrin, cross to the southeast corner of the intersection, and continue two blocks south to the **Puri Pemecutan** ⑰ palace and hotel. Take 15 minutes to explore the grounds, then head east on Jalan Batur—which becomes Jalan Hasanuddin—and walk four blocks to Jalan Udayana. Turn left here, walk a block, then cross the street to reach Puputan Square. Continue east a block and cross to the **Bali Museum** ⑱, where you can wander around for a couple hours before heading next door to the **Pura Jagatnatha** ⑲ with its lotus-throne shrine. From here take a left on Jalan Suprapati and walk a block to the Catur Muka statue, then walk north six blocks on Jalan Udayana—which turns into Jalan Veteran—to **Pasar Burung** ⑳. You can end your day here with a bouncy *dokar* (pony-cart) ride. Or if you're feeling ambitious, you can take a taxi to **Pura Kesiman** ㉑, in Abiankapas; visit Renon, southeast of the center, where you'll find mansions, government offices, and an enormous limestone carving in Lapangan Puputan Square; then finish off the day shopping at one of the modern complexes in Denpasar. In the evening catch a performance at the **Werdhi Budaya Art Center** ㉒.

If you have an extra day or two, consider taking a trip to Bali's eastern trio of islands: Nusa Ceningan, Nusa Lembongan, and Nusa Penida. Only the latter two have any infrastructure set up for tourists. Nusa Lembongan's reefs are a popular dive-and-snorkeling destination. On Nusa Penida the coastal mercantile town of Toya Pakeh is a good base for exploring the island. Start at **Pura Peed** ㉓, just outside town, then travel southeast to **Goa Karangsari** ㉔, a large cave that is probably the island's best-known tourist sight. Continue around the central mountains to reach the waterfall **Air Terjun Sebuluh** ㉕, pausing along the way for a look at local temples and village life, then continue on to Toya Pakeh.

TIMING

You can tour southern Bali any time of the year. Although beach and temple photos turn out better during the dry season (from May to October), it's much easier to travel in the cooler, cloudier rainy season—and it usually doesn't rain much on this end of the island anyway. If you have more time, you can easily break this three-day tour into half-days and string it out for a week. Alternatively, you can connect this tour with Chapter 3's trip around Ubud and the east coast for a full experience of the southern half of the island.

The West Coast

Kuta was once the core of this bustling, burgeoning area where sunning and shopping prevail by day and dining, drinking, and dancing rule the after-dark hours. However, in the past decade the growing tourist industry has spawned an extension of restaurants, hotels, villas, and boutique shops running up along the coast through Legian, Seminyak, Kerobokan, Batubuleg, Berewa, and northwest to Canggu—and the farther north you go, the finer the clientele. Still, between these tourist neighborhoods there are numerous cultural sights and clusters of traditional villages where you can catch a glimpse of pretourist Bali.

Sights to See

❸ **Mads Lange Tomb.** In the midst of a modest Chinese cemetery, this tall black-and-white monument pays homage to Mads Lange, a brash Danish trader of the 1820s and 1830s. As the story goes, Lange assisted the wrong side of a civil war on Lombok, then hopped over to

Bali—showing up at the palace his first day on a fine steed, no less—to set up a trading post and a coconut-oil factory, among other enterprises. His home was not only a fortress but also a makeshift cultural center and one of Bali's first true luxury villas. Gradually he became something of an ambassador to the local Balinese kings, the Dutch rulers, and the impressive array of international visitors he entertained. ⊠ *Jl. Tanjung Mekar, Kuta,* ☎ *no phone.* ⊠ *Free.* ☉ *Daily sunrise–sunset.*

❹ **Pasar Seni Kuta.** The Kuta Art Market is a small, busy collection of crafts and kitsch stalls where you can generally find better bargains than in the surrounding shops. Know the price ranges for items you're interested in, arrive early, and don't show too much enthusiasm, and you'll usually get a good "morning price" for your purchase. ⊠ *Jl. Bakungsari, Kuta,* ☎ *no phone.* ⊠ *Free.* ☉ *Daily 8–4.*

❷ **Pura Petitenget.** Sitting beside the ocean amid a breathtaking landscape of rice fields, the Petitenget Temple was the final journey point for 16th-century priest Danghyang Nirartha before he died at Pura Uluwatu. The temple is named for the priest's magically powerful (*tenget*) betel-nut box (*peti*) and has been partially restored since a downed banyan tree destroyed several of the shrines in 1993. ⊠ *Jl. Petitenget, Kerobokan,* ☎ *no phone.* ⊠ *Free.* ☉ *Daily sunrise–sunset.*

★ ☜ ❶ **Pura Tanah Lot.** The stunning evening panorama of rocky shores and scarlet sunsets at the southwestern curve of the island supposedly inspired Danghyang Nirartha to build this beautiful seaside temple, one of the island's six most sacred. Its name means "Temple of the Earth (*tanah*) and Sea (*lot*)," an appropriate title, as it neatly straddles both worlds. The dramatic setting draws crowds to these shores every evening, and at low tide you can walk up on the rocky outcrop where the temple sits over the ocean. The entrance walkway is clogged with souvenir shops, and hawkers selling postcards, shell turtles, and other small items will tug at your shirttails, but it's all part of the experience. For less hustle and fuss, come for the sunrise instead and get a more peaceful view of the temple. ⊠ *Jl. Tanah Lot, Canggu,* ☎ *no phone.* ⊠ *Donation required.* ☉ *Daily sunrise–sunset.*

Jimbaran and Bukit Badung

Best known for its long western strip of clean, golden sand, Jimbaran is a medium-size fishing village settled along an isthmus between two coasts less than 2 km (1 mi) apart. The eastern edge is made of mud-flats that lead around to Benoa Harbor. South of Jimbaran, great limestone hills rapidly rise to the center of Bukit Badung, where thousands of caves in the rugged cliffs provide evidence of prehistoric cultures. Criminals from the northern Badung and Mengwi kingdoms were once banished to this harsh environment.

In the dry season the land is overtaken by low, bedraggled brush, while the rains bring up fields of corn, peanuts, and soybeans. Needing additional enterprises besides farming to support even their often meager lifestyle, the villagers on the east coast cleverly resorted to spreading seawater over the mudflats, where it dries—the dirt is subsequently dried again by fires beneath metal pans—to produce salt; lime is also gathered from the leftover pieces of coral. On the west coast fishing is the primary occupation, and you'll see the *jukung* (wooden outrigger fishing boats, usually painted in bright pastel hues with black eyes on the front) returning with huge nets early each morning.

Sights to See

☜ ❺ **Pasar Ikan Jimbaran.** The Jimbaran Fish Market is the best place on the island to find fresh seafood, as proven by the crowds sitting and

Southern Bali

- **1** Pura Tanah Lot
- Canggu
- Kerobokan
- Canggu
- Berewa
- Berewa
- **2** Pura Petitenget
- Denpasar **14** — **22** See Detail Map
- Seminyak
- Seminyak
- Legian
- Legian
- Suwungbatankendal
- Pesanggaran

S E L A T

B A L I

(Bali Strait)

- **Kuta**
- *Teluk Kuta (Kuta Bay)*
- Kuta
- **4** **3** Mads Lange Tomb
- **Pasar Seni Kuta**
- PULAU SARANGAN (TURTLE ISLAND)
- Benoa Harbor
- Tuban
- **Ngurah Rai International Airport** ✈
- **Chinese Temple**
- **Pasar Benoa** **8** **9** Tanjung Benoa
- Tanjung Benoa
- **5** Pasar Ikan Jimbaran
- **Pura Ulun Siwi** Jimbaran **6**
- *Teluk Jimbaran (Jimbaran Bay)*
- *Teluk Benoa (Benoa Bay)*
- **Jimbaran**
- Jenggala Keramik Bali
- *Tanjung Balangan*
- Garuda Wisna Kencana (GWK)
- Celu
- **Balangan**
- **Pura Balangan**
- Cengiling
- **Pura Geger**
- **Uluwatu**
- **7** Pura Uluwatu
- Ungasan
- N D
- Sam Inda
- Pecatu
- **Pura Masuka**
- **Pura Batu Pageh**

N ↑

0 ——— 3 miles
0 ——— 4 km

KEY

① Exploring Sites

⚓ Beaches

🌲 Temples

⚓ Anchorage

Tohpati

Ketewel

Jalan Hang Tuah
Pasar Pantai Sanur
Museum Le Mayeur
Sanur ⑬ ⑫ **Pura Segara**
⑪ Pasar Pantai Sindhu
⑩ Pantai Sindhu

Pasar Sindhu

🌲 **Pura Blanjong**

Pura Mertasari

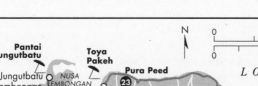

S E L A T   B A D U N G

(Badung Strait)

N   0 — 4 miles
0 — 6 km

**Pantai
Jungutbatu**   **Toya
Pakeh**   *L O M B O K*

Jungutbatu ○ *NUSA
Lembongan*   *LEMBONGAN*   **Pura Peed**   *S T R A I T*
○   ㉓
Sheraton   ○ Toya Pakeh
Laguna   **Mushroom** *NUSA CENINGAN*
Pantai   **Bay**
Nusa   ㉔ **Goa Karangsari**
Dua   **Pantai
                                                           Semaya**
              N U S A   P E N I D A   Semaya ○
        Batu Madeg ○ ㉕ **Air Terjun Sebuluh**   **Pura
                                                         Batu
                                                         Kuring**
                                                   🌲
B A D U N G   **Pura
                                                Batu
                                                Madan**
S T R A I T

B A D U N G   S T R A I T   I S L A N D S

sipping drinks at the lines of stalls along the beach every evening. In the morning, you can wander among the buckets, boats, and tanks to find just-caught fish, crabs, shrimp, squid, and other sea fare to take home. Otherwise, come for a stroll down the beach at sunset amid the smoky scent of fish sizzling on the grill, then choose a picnic bench and sit down for one of the best meals on Bali. ⊠ *Jl. Pantai Sari, Jimbaran,* ☎ *no phone.* 🎫 *Free.* ⊙ *Daily sunrise–sunset.*

❻ **Pura Ulun Siwi.** The Ulun Siwi Temple, founded by Javanese priest Mpu Kuturan in the 11th century, is one of Bali's earliest and holiest Hindu shrines. Its foreign origins are particularly evident in three unique traits: the temple faces west, toward Java's holy Gunung Semeru, rather than south; its spirits are thought to guard the welfare of both the wet and the dry rice fields; and it has only two courtyards, while most temples on Bali have three. The ornate brick entrance gate is similar to that of Pura Uluwatu, at the end of the Bukit peninsula; in fact, the ritual is to pray here first before worshiping at the latter temple. Farmers often visit both shrines to pray for prosperity and protection for their fields. ⊠ *Jl. Uluwatu, Jimbaran,* ☎ *no phone.* 🎫 *Free.* ⊙ *Daily sunrise–sunset.*

NEED A BREAK?   For a change of scene stop in at **Jenggala Keramik Bali** (⊠ Jl. Uluwatu II, Jimbaran, ☎ 0361/703310), an enormous, modern, air-conditioned ceramics factory with sleek displays of works by talented artists from Bali and elsewhere in Indonesia. The front room holds artifacts from the country's past (all for sale), while the cavernous right wing of the building houses contemporary dishes, cups, general kitchen and house wares, and other handy ceramic pieces. There is also a workshop where you can throw and paint your own pottery and a café serving delicious baked goods, sandwiches, drinks, and desserts. Through a big window upstairs in the back you can actually watch the wares being spun, fired, and painted before they line the shelves. The factory is open Monday through Saturday 9–5.

OFF THE BEATEN PATH   **GARUDA WISNA KENCANA (GWK) –** The GWK cultural park, designed around a massive statue of Garuda Wisna, is an enormous natural theater dedicated to Balinese culture, its meticulous landscapes carved out of the rugged limestone hills at the peninsula's center. A wide, winding road leads to an upper level of restaurants and shops. Climb several hundred steps to reach the highlight of the attraction: a windy overlook that has views all the way to the sea at the southern end of Bukit Badung. Or just sip an expensive drink and enjoy the same views at a lower level. At press time an amphitheater for cultural performances, a museum, and more shops and restaurants were in the works.

★ ❼ **Pura Uluwatu.** Perched over the sea, this temple is one of Bali's most famous sights. Its name means "Heavenly Place of Worship at the Head of the Rock": the temple's three courtyards stretch across a narrow finger of rugged limestone cliffs high above white surf and roiling blue waters. Uluwatu is one of Bali's six major *sad kahyangan* (territorial temples). Like Jimbaran's Pura Ulun Siwi (☞ *above*), it was reputedly built in the 11th century by the holy priest Mpu Kuturan. It was renovated 500 years later by the spiritual guide of the Gelgel kingdom's golden age, Danghyang Nirartha, who gave the temple its present style.

A sense of solitude envelops you as you enter the split wing-shaped gate to the outer courtyard. Inside, dual elephant-head Ganesh figures and a Kala head guard the second entrance archway. An open pavilion sits in the last inner courtyard, and a three-tiered temple stands watch over the very edge of the cliff. Late afternoons here are balmy and breezy, perfect for exploring the temple grounds and watching the monkeys—considered sacred—leap along the gray temple walls and between the trees. Remember your camera: the crimson sunset against a backdrop of silver waves, the dark silhouette of the temple in front of the scene, is one of Bali's perfect shots. ⊠ *Jl. Uluwatu, Bukit Badung,* ☎ *no phone.* 🎫 *Donation required.* ☉ *Daily sunrise–sunset.*

Nusa Dua and Tanjung Benoa

Once a wide, airy expanse of flat terrain and coconut trees, Nusa Dua was slowly altered—by the Indonesian government, with guidance from the World Bank—into a huge estate of self-contained international hotels. Today it is the ultimate upscale resort playground, with hotel complexes sprawling along the east coast of the Bukit Peninsula. The area was established to keep tourists corralled in the south, providing them with all the pleasures of a tropical holiday while minimizing their impact on local culture throughout the rest of the island.

But though Nusa Dua is *the* place to be for business (Bali's only convention center is at the Sheraton Nusa Indah) and upscale shopping (the island's largest mall, the Nusa Dua Galeria, is also located here), the area has preserved some of its early roots. Small temples, many established by the holy priest Danghyang Nirartha, are found in the outer villages and on hotel grounds. Even the entrance to the resort area bears a reminder of Bali's cultural focus: an enormous gate of carved stone straddles the highway to separate the complex from the outside world, and a modern fountain gate symbolically links the tourist area to the rest of the island.

Tanjung Benoa, the slender peninsula jutting up into the bay north of Nusa Dua, has less expensive resorts and a muddy eastern coast lined with dive shops and cruise headquarters. This area was once the mercantile hub for southern Bukit Badung and the eastern islands, and many Chinese and Bugis descendents of these traders still live in the area. The back streets are rabbit warrens of alleys pocketed with small shops, market stalls, and cheap homestays. Here you can explore local life—but early or late in the day, when the heat and the dust are less riled by the traffic lumbering along the main road. If you're driving to this area from the north, be sure to take the exit for Tanjung Benoa, not Benoa Harbor, which is the port on the opposite side of the bay.

Sights to See

❾ Chinese temple. You can't miss the brilliant hues of Tanjung Benoa's Chinese temple, an eye-catching artwork of neon red, yellow, and orange topped by red-and-yellow-striped roof arcs. Sitting in quiet grounds at the northern tip of the peninsula, this shrine is an interesting architectural contrast to the area's numerous small Hindu shrines. ⊠ *Jl. Pratama, Tanjung Benoa,* ☎ *no phone.* 🎫 *Free.* ☉ *Daily sunrise–sunset.*

OFF THE BEATEN PATH

BENOA HARBOR – If you drive northeast along the Jalan Bypass and take the right turnoff for Benoa Harbor, you'll be in for a few wonderful surprises. Just after the entrance you'll come to the lovely **Bali Mangrove Park** (⊠ Jl. Pelabuhan Benoa 7, ☎ 0361/729528), where you can wander along shaded paths over green mangrove pools or simply relax by the water. At low tide thousands of fiddler crabs, wading birds, and other wildlife scramble along the muddy embankments; at high tide you can take a journey on a colorful wooden boat to see the mangroves at eye level. Admission to the park is $4, and it's open daily 7 AM–9 PM. Continue down to the harbor, where you can stop at different docks to watch the ships—from towering international cruisers to beautiful *pinisi*-style sailboats to rickety Chinese fishing junks—as they make their way in and out of port. On the way back, stop at the **Marina Yacht Club** (⊠ Jl. Pelabuhan Benoa, ☎ 0361/726522), open daily 9 AM–11 PM, for lunch in the restaurant overlooking the harbor.

❽ **Pasar Benoa.** Take a few moments to browse through the little open-air Benoa Market, in the alleys of Tanjung Benoa's northwestern corner. This is an especially good place to pick up a bag of fresh tangerines, a juicy pineapple, or an enormous papaya if you don't like paying resort prices for a tiny fruit salad. ⊠ *Jl. Pratama, Tanjung Benoa,* ☎ *no phone.* ▦ *Free.* ☉ *Daily 7–4.*

Sanur

The east-coast resort area of Sanur may today be famous for its upscale hotels, shallow snorkeling reef, and colorful kites, but it is actually one of Bali's most richly historical areas. The Prasasti Belanjong pillar, dated AD 913, is one of the island's oldest artifacts, and stories of Sanur's holy men are told in historical texts of the 13th through 16th centuries. The town is still governed by members of the *brahman kuasa* (priest caste), and much of its history can be traced through the line of ancient coral temples along its coast. Sanur is actually a conglomeration of several smaller communities: the administrative center of Taman, the upscale centers of Intaran and Anggarkasih, and the fishing village of Belong. Its strong cultural roots and magic-steeped traditions add a dynamic element to the local artistry, making Sanur an excellent place to buy crafts and see dance performances.

Sanur was a bustling trading center in the 18th century, and it received positive notes in the journals of such entrepreneurs as Danish trader Mads Lange. Its reputation was tarnished, though, in 1906 when the local *perbekel* (leader) permitted troops from Holland, on their way to conquer Denpasar's Pemecutan kingdom, to land at Sanur, which led to the island's first horrifying puputan. Over the next three decades the coastal town turned its sights from trade to tourism, and its brown beaches became the prime target of real estate development for famed Western artists and expatriates such as writer Vicki Baum, choreographer Katharane Mershon, and anthropologist Jack Belo. Later residents included the multitalented artist Walter Spies, Australian artists Ian Fairweather and Donald Friend, and Belgian painter A. J. Le Mayeur de Merpres, whose former studio is now a museum.

While the town's expanding resort-style accommodations and reputation as an upscale tropical hideaway were attracting international playboys and movie stars, its leaders were working to preserve their rich coastal culture. Brahman leader Pedanda Gede Sidemen, one of Bali's foremost historical scholars, healers, and temple architects, was a pioneer in protecting and promoting this "Sanur style" of leadership, and his nephew, Ida Bagus Berata, integrated cultural and environmentally conscious practices into Bali's growing tourist industry—a model for modern-day Bali businesses. You'll find many of the island's most memorable artistic and spiritual traditions here: colorful ceremonial processions; a women's *keris* dance troupe; the magical Black Barong; and the practice of both black magic and white magic, the warring forces of good and evil symbolized by the checkered sarongs wrapped about the waists of temple statues. Even Ratu Ayu, the notoriously troublesome temptress spirit friend of the Black Barong, has her own temple here, in Room 327 of the Grand Bali Beach hotel. And be aware, while you're here, for stories tell of the strength of the town's spiritual powers: Room 327 was the only one left untouched by a fire that destroyed the rest of the hotel in 1993.

Sights to See

12 Museum Le Mayeur. Whether you're staying in Sanur or just shopping for the day, this modest little museum along the beach trail is worth a look for its intriguing island views by A. J. Le Mayeur de Merpres, one of Bali's most famous expatriate artists. This building is actually the Belgian painter's former studio and home. More of his works can be seen at the Puri Le Mayeur bungalow at the Hotel Tugu Bali (☞ Lodging, *below*). The temple court grounds are a pretty place for a picnic lunch after your tour. ⊠ *Jl. Hang Tuah,* ☎ *no phone.* 🎫 *50¢.* ☉ *Sat.–Thurs. 8–4, Fri. 8–1:30.*

13 Pasar Pantai Sanur. The popular Sanur Beach Market, at the north end of town, is where you can pick up everything from batik to kites to woven baskets. Come late on a Saturday night to snack at the food stalls and mingle with the locals. ⊠ *Jl. Pantai Sanur,* ☎ *no phone.* 🎫 *Free.* ☉ *Daily 24 hrs.*

11 Pasar Pantai Sindhu. Right next to the beach, near Jalan Pantai Sindhu, the Sindhu Beach Market is a gathering of small stalls selling batik clothes, sarongs, kites, crafts, and other tourist goods. If you've seen something you like in a resort shop, you can probably find it here for much less. ⊠ *Jl. Segara Ayu,* ☎ *no phone.* 🎫 *Free.* ☉ *Daily 8–5.*

OFF THE BEATEN PATH — **PURA SEGARA –** From Pasar Pantai Sindhu a five-minute stroll north will take you to the Segara Temple, whose outer gate is guarded by black-painted demons. The crumbling steps of the inner courtyard lead up a tri-level pyramid flanked by ancient carvings; a small thatch-roof temple sits atop the structure. It's open daily from sunrise to sunset.

10 Pasar Sindhu. Sanur's large Art Market is a gathering place for locals and tourists alike; the former bring their crafts from all over the east coast, and the latter snap them up for souvenirs. Great bargains include woven baskets, wind chimes, wood carvings, and kites—look for enormous, colorful sailboats, butterflies, dragons, frogs, and buffalo. The nearby produce market is open 4 AM–1 PM. ⊠ *Jl. Sindhu,* ☎ *no phone.* 🎫 *Free.* ☉ *Daily 8–5.*

OFF THE BEATEN PATH — **MERTASARI AND BELANJONG TEMPLES –** At the southern end of Sanur, at the edge of a pretty bay and surrounded by trees, the shady **Pura Mertasari** (Mertasari Temple), on Jalan Sekar Waru, is off the beaten track. It's worth a visit, particularly on its birthday, two weeks after the spring equinox, when you can see the *baris Cina* (Chinese baris) dance, a special after-dark performance by dancers who wear 20th-century battle helmets and carry bayonets—and eventually work themselves into a trance. A kilometer (½ mile) north, **Pura Belanjong** (Belanjong Temple), on Jalan Danau Poso, contains the famous Prasasti Belanjong pillar, discovered in 1932. Dated AD 913, this is one of Bali's earliest historical artifacts; it is inscribed with a combination of Sanskrit, Nagari, and Old Balinese characters, which confirms that Hindu traditions were prevalent on Bali at the time. The inscription chronicles the story of King Sri Kesari Warmadewa of Java's Sailendra dynasty, who founded a monastery and taught Mahayana Buddhism on Bali. Both temples are open daily from sunrise to sunset.

OFF THE
BEATEN PATH

PULAU SERANGAN – You can hire a colorful wooden jukung from Sanur Beach to take you on the 10-minute trip to Turtle Island, a small bit of land about ½ km (¼ mi) offshore. It is most famous for its turtle farms, but since the island is only about 3 km (2 mi) long, you can also walk through its few villages for a look at local life. Two temples are of interest here: **Pura Susunan Wadon**, which is similar in structure and decoration to central Javanese temples, and **Pura Sakenan**, which conflicting sources say was founded either in the 11th century by noted architect Mpu Kuturan or in the 16th century by the holy Javanese priest Danghyang Nirartha. If you're fit, you can save the boat fare and make the half-hour walk to the island across the mudflats at low tide.

Denpasar

The little town whose name means "East of the Market" has grown up into a capital city caught between the glitzy goals of modern development and the dusty ways of its ancient past. Since its inception as Bali's capital in 1958, the city has outgrown its market-town roots to spread east into Gianyar, southeast into Sanur, and southwest into Seminyak. It's a fascinating place, where shiny silver Mercedes slide through traffic past panting, slouching ponies pulling rickety wooden carts; where tourists in garish Hawaiian shirts and flip-flops rub shoulders with sarong-clad old women at the bustling central market; and where on Saturday night boom-box-toting teenagers with tattoos and earrings sidle up to candlelit pushcarts for a snack of *sate* (pronounced *sah*-tay—chunks of chicken threaded on thin wooden sticks and charcoal-grilled, served with spicy peanut sauce). It's a collection of contrasts—excellent cultural attractions, hot and noisy surroundings, beloved bargains, terrible traffic, eclectic restaurants, insignificant nightlife—yet Denpasar is the center of the island's trade activities. Farmers, merchants, businesspeople, homemakers, and tourists alike come here to get the best goods, the best prices, and the latest news about their neighbors elsewhere on the island. It's not a pretty place, nor is it particularly congenial or clean, but it has a likeable character and a host of interesting attractions.

Over the decades Denpasar has achieved an interesting cultural mix that includes descendents of the original Chinese traders who settled here in the 1700s, the Muslim Bugis who arrived shortly afterward, and the Arabs and Indian textile traders who discovered the town's lucrative markets in the 1930s. Since then Javanese workers have come looking for job and trade opportunities, and many have settled throughout the city. This combination of cultures has not only made Denpasar one of Indonesia's most eclectic shopping experiences; it has also made it one of the best places to find a variety of high-quality restaurants catering to tastes from all over Asia.

Sights to See

⑱ Bali Museum. A fascinating mix of typical Balinese temple and palace architectural styles, the Bali Museum is laid out across a large patch of gardens south of the Pura Jagatnatha (☞ *below*). The Dutch had the idea for the museum; they wanted to prove their interest in preserving Balinese culture, as well as repair some of the ill will directed at them after the puputan. Construction began in 1906, but it took more than two decades to finish the complex, which includes more than a dozen structures. Surrounded by a high brick-and-stone wall lined with bas-reliefs, the complex includes several pavilions that house ceremonial weapons, masks, musical instruments, paintings, sculptures, and textiles. The buildings themselves are examples of regional archi-

DENPASAR BY NIGHT

CAN'T SLEEP? Denpasar is a great place to while away the dark hours, for this market city never rests—and much of the action heats up just after sundown. Start with a small meal at one of the restaurants along Jalan Teuku Umar, where you can taste excellent Chinese and Balinese cooking. The street's small, brightly lit restaurants have window displays of fresh Padang-style dishes, billboards with enlarged pictures of menu items, and smartly dressed waitresses with comely smiles handing out sample menus. Otherwise head into town and stay near the market, Pasar Badung, dining on Jalan Gajah Mada at one of the Chinese-run clubs specializing in regional and seafood dishes. Little warung and noodle houses along Jalan Sumatra are just as good, and they're cheaper; these places are where the Balinese dine, so you can be sure of getting a good local meal. (If you stay late enough, you can test your vocal chords at one of the popular karaoke bars.)

After dinner go to the Werdhi Budaya Art Center to see a traditional dance performance or play. This is the center for the Denpasar arts, particularly in June and July, when the Bali Arts Festival is held. The streets around the center fill with noisy parades of crashing gamelan orchestras and lines of women dressed in gilded sarongs, holding pyramids of colorful fruit and small cakes high on their heads; and shows of music, dance, and fighting skills take place nightly. It's the annual conflux of island culture, and towns from all over the island hold competitions and plays. By day you can view painting and crafts exhibitions, and if you arrive early, you'll have time to explore the grounds.

After the performance head for the Pasar Malam Kereneng night market, on Jalan Gadung and Jalan Kemuning. After 8 PM the city workers arrive to shop for inexpensive clothing and to grab quick bites of Balinese food. Stalls of shirts and dresses line the street, so shop a bit and then work your way back to the food stands, where you'll find succulent *babi guling* (roast pig) stuffed with fragrant, spicy *lawar* and *urab* (Balinese spiced vegetables with coconut) served straight from whole pigs on the spit. This is a good place to try real Balinese cuisine if you dare. But beware: even the pork *sate* (skewered and grilled) has a bite to it. Choose your stall carefully, as some vendors are more particular about cleanliness than others. On the way out grab a colorful, sweet, sticky rice-paste cake.

Finally, stop by Pasar Badung again to watch the farmers bring their truckloads of goods. The inner market is closed at 6 PM, after which goods are sold right out of the trucks in the parking lot until dawn. A crew of security men directs the hourly rotation of vehicles so that everyone has a turn to sell and buy. The volume—and variety—of goods is amazing. There are bushels of lontar leaves for weaving offerings and bundles of bright flowers to fill them, baskets of eggs, bales of long string beans, and huge burlap sacks of rice. This is where merchants from all over the island come to trade their wares, and the action continues all night until the interior shops open for business again at dawn.

30

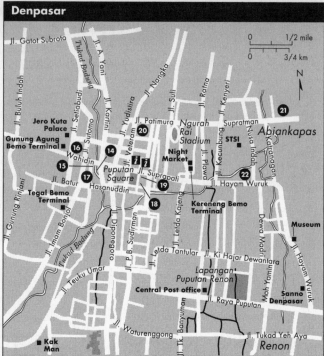

tecture: The **Tabanan Pavilion** has ornately carved and gilded posts that were once part of a Tabanan nobleman's home. The **Buleleng Pavilion**—which had previous incarnations at the 1914 Colonial Exposition in central Java, as a Singaraja museum, and as the Government Tourist Bureau office—represents the architecture of northern Bali. The **Karangasem Pavilion** was originally a palace audience hall in eastern Bali. ⊠ *Jl. Sudirman,* ☎ *0361/222680.* ☞ *$1.* ⊙ *Tues.–Thurs. 8–2, Fri. 8–11, Sat. 8–12:30.*

★ ☺ ⓮ **Pasar Badung.** A five-story cement-block building at the edge of the Badung River holds the lively, crowded, and colorful Badung Market, where you can view local bargaining tactics. The lower floor is for fish, meat, fruit, and vegetables; it's the place to buy luscious whole papayas, pineapples, and mangoes if you can store them in your hotel or villa. The second floor houses huge burlap sacks of spices and tables of home goods such as pots and pans, woks, dishes, Tupperware, and various sundries. The third floor has more spices, as well as textiles and T-shirts. You'll find a mix of everything on the upper floors, so if you like shopping, set aside at least two hours to go through it all. Be warned that the market is hot, hip-to-hip crowded, and often ripe with fumes, so the earlier you visit, the better. Come at night to watch the farmers pull up in pickups filled with produce headed for the local markets; you can buy bulk goods like rice, beans, flowers, and fruit straight off the trucks at rock-bottom prices. ⊠ *Jl. Sulawesi,* ☎ *no phone.* ☞ *Free.* ⊙ *Day market daily 6 AM–6 PM, night market daily 6 PM–6 AM.*

⓴ **Pasar Burung.** The Bird Market is one of Denpasar's most colorful merchant spectacles. Here songbirds—a precious commodity in Bali—are sold and traded. Note the intricate details on many of the carved, gilded cages. ⊠ *Jl. Veteran,* ☎ *no phone.* ☞ *Free.* ⊙ *Daily 9–6.*

⑮ **Pasar Kumbasari.** Around the corner from Pasar Badung is the Kumbasari Market, a four-story treasure chest of crafts from around the island. You probably won't find the low prices you would get in the villages, but the goods here are mostly direct from the craftspeople and cost much less than they do in tourist areas (although you have to bargain hard). As you wander the narrow aisles, look for wood carvings, masks, batik clothing, and textiles. ✉ *Jl. Gajah Mada,* ☎ *no phone.* 🎟 *Free.* ☼ *Daily 9–9.*

⑲ **Pura Jagatnatha.** The outstanding feature of the Jagatnatha Temple is its single, towering *padmasana* (lotus throne) shrine proclaiming loyalty to the deity Sanghyang Widhi Wasa, head of the godly gatherings on Bali. Because of its central location and power, this is a choice spot for observing full-moon ceremonies. Locals from around the city dress in their best traditional fashions—women in lacy pastel tops and sarongs, men in straight white jackets, sarongs, and headdresses—park their motorcycles out front, and kneel with *kwangen* offerings (flower petals wrapped in small leaf packets) between their fingertips as the bell for prayer echoes around them. ✉ *Jl. Sudirman,* ☎ *no phone.* 🎟 *Free.* ☼ *Daily sunrise–sunset.*

㉑ **Pura Kesiman.** The modern Kesiman Temple, once part of the royal family complex at the northeast corner of the city, has a beautiful example of a *candi bentar* (split gate). Today the shrine is part of a private mansion. ✉ *Jl. Supratman,* ☎ *no phone.* 🎟 *Free.* ☼ *Daily sunrise–sunset.*

⑯ **Pura Maospahit.** A quiet shrine tucked away behind a tall brick wall in the center of town, the 14th-century Maospahit Temple is the city's oldest shrine, built when Javanese and Balinese traditions were just beginning to intermingle. Of note are the large stone reliefs on the entrance gate, which were partially restored by the Archeological Service after a 1917 earthquake, and the delicate carvings on the wooden doors of the imposing inner arch. ✉ *Jl. Wahidin,* ☎ *no phone.* 🎟 *Free.* ☼ *Daily sunrise–sunset.*

⑰ **Puri Pemecutan.** Pemecutan Palace was long a center of Balinese history, and it is filled to the brim with artifacts from the turbulent conflict between local kings and the Dutch around the turn of the 20th century. Built in the 18th century, it housed the region's reigning families until the Dutch invaded the city in 1906. Today the jumbled grounds still contain many items and photographs from years past, including musical instruments, textiles, statues, and furniture. A mini zoo in the parking lot houses ducks, peacocks, and a forlorn pony; inside, amid the bric-a-brac of the main pavilion, is a stuffed tiger. Songbirds in cages, koi ponds, fountains, and potted plants line the grounds, creating a peaceful haven in the midst of one of the city's busiest blocks. There are very simple rooms for rent along the right side of the grounds; however, this is more a fascinating piece of history to explore for an hour than a place to spend the night. ✉ *Jl. Thamrin 2,* ☎ *0361/ 423491.* 🎟 *Free.* ☼ *Daily sunrise–sunset.*

㉒ **Werdhi Budaya Art Center.** The lush gardens, quiet paths, and smooth walking trails around the arts center by day belie the frenzy of activity it hosts during evening dance performances and the annual Bali Arts Festival. This is the place to view traditional and modern dances and plays, as well as arts and cultural exhibitions. A museum chronicles bits of Bali's arts history, and shops sell some of the island's better handicrafts, albeit at high prices. To browse the grounds and complex is free; otherwise, the admission varies depending on the exhibit and performance. ✉ *Jl. Nusa Indah,* ☎ *0361/222681.* 🎟 *Free.* ☼ *Daily 9–4 and for performances.*

The Badung Strait Islands

The stark, lushly covered limestone cliffs abruptly rise from the clear, swirling sapphire waters an hour's sail off Bali's southeast coast, the beauty of the scene a wicked contrast to the harsh reality of life in these quiet, coconut-covered islands. Nusa Penida, the largest, with only about two dozen villages, is believed to be the home of the notorious demon king Jero Gede Mecaling—who still sends disasters and diseases to mainland Bali. Nusa Lembongan, with two main settlements at Jungutbatu and Lembongan, is a center for seaweed farming and the island most developed for tourism. In between lies Nusa Ceningan, the smallest, with a single village inhabiting its rocky terrain.

Formerly under the reign of the Klunkung kings of the northeast, the islands used to be a place of exile for criminals, and their inhabitants are still regarded with an element of caution. Black magic is said to abound here, especially on Nusa Penida, and fearful residents along the Bukit Badung and Gianyar coasts still perform *sanghyang dedari* trance dances to exorcise the evil forces sent by Jero Gede Mecaling and his invisible soldiers. And perhaps magic—good or bad—is a necessary ingredient in handling the unfortunate circumstances handed those who live on these islands: a climate so dry that each drop of water is sacred; terrain so inhospitable that everything—even rice and farm animals—must be imported; and few opportunities for jobs or education. Roads are chiseled out of the rough earth, and limestone blocks are used to build one-room homes. The only semilucrative professions are fishing, cattle breeding, and seaweed farming. The tobacco, corn, and beans grown on the sparse hills are mostly for personal consumption, and cassava is the substitute starch for the rice used elsewhere on Bali.

Although the islands are poor, they are definitely worth seeing, and tourist funds are beginning to spark new life in the villages. The reefs around Nusa Lembongan draw day-trippers, divers, and snorkelers, and Jungutbatu has developed a small, thriving tourist base of inexpensive homestays and restaurants, which makes it a good jumping-off point for explorations of Nusa Penida. The busiest town on Nusa Penida is Toya Pakeh, in the north, a trading hub and stop for boats heading to the mainland and Nusa Lembongan. Only local jukung travel to Nusa Ceningan since there are no formal accommodations or restaurants there, although some enterprising travelers have managed to stay in the villages and camp along the shores.

Sights to See

㉕ **Air Terjun Sebuluh.** The Sebuluh Waterfall lies about 25 km (15 mi) south of Toya Pakeh on Nusa Penida; however, the only access is around the central mountain range via the twisted one-lane inland road. Just west is the village of Batu Madeg, where you can stretch your legs climbing the steps up to the **Pura Dalem Batu Madeg** (Madeg Temple Beneath the Stone), which has a unique coral entrance gate and interesting friezes of sea life. ⊠ *Jl. Batu Madeg, Nusa Penida,* ☎ *no phone.* ☏ *Free.* ☉ *Daily sunrise–sunset.*

㉔ **Goa Karangsari.** The Karangsari Cave, on the east coast of Nusa Penida, is perhaps the most famous of the island's many caverns. It reportedly tunnels 1 km (½ mi) underground and protects a sacred lake, where villagers come to make prayers and offerings during the Kuningan holiday. About 2 km (1 mi) south of here, near Sewana, are two local temples: **Pura Batu Madan** (Madan Stone Temple) and **Pura Batu Kuring** (Kuring Stone Temple). ⊠ *Jl. Timur Nusa Penida, Nusa Penida,* ☎ *no phone.* ☏ *Free.* ☉ *Daily 24 hrs.*

㉓ **Pura Peed.** Nusa Penida's Peed Temple, part of Jero Gede Mecaling's realm, shelters within a knotted old tree an ancient stone statue—supposedly the mouth of the giant's priest. If you're lucky, you might witness the grand pilgrimage of islanders who come here for a massive festival every 12th full moon. ✉ *Jl. Raya Nusa Penida, Nusa Penida,* ☎ *no phone.* ⌑ *Free.* ⊙ *Daily sunrise–sunset.*

BEACHES

Bali's southern beaches (called *pantai*) are world famous, and once you're on them, it's easy to understand why. There's a beach for every moment and every mood, from expanses of white to golden to brown-sugar sand, from the frenzied hubs for surfers, wandering sellers, and topless sunbathers to the most secluded, palm-fringed hideaways. The legendary white sands and gentle waters of photographs are to be found on the western edge of Bukit Badung. North of the peninsula, the crowds are biggest in Tuban and Kuta and shrink the farther north you go. The east coast has brown sand, shallow offshore reefs, and flat, quiet waters, although in the rainy season the winds can kick up a froth. The southern end of Bukit Badung isn't for swimming: here the rough ocean pounds against rugged limestone cliffs and rocky beaches, the dramatic views more than making up for the lack of places to dip your toes into the water.

Although the dress code is next to nothing in the surf and tour towns of Kuta and Tuban, swimming at most other beaches requires more modesty (that is, wear a swimsuit). Keep an eye on your things at any beach, especially those with crowds and wandering vendors, and firmly attach a waterproof, zippered pouch to your suit to hold any valuables you must bring with you. It's fine to walk the sand as the sun sets, but avoid the beaches after dark; if you're set on a midnight walk, stay with a crowd or on a guarded hotel beach. Most beaches don't have lifeguards, although riptide warning signs are posted in many places. If you're not a strong swimmer—and this especially goes for beginning surfers and children—stick close to the shore. Should you get caught in a riptide, don't fight against it; instead ride with it and slowly try to work your way out of it by moving parallel to the shore.

Most of these beaches are clearly marked with signs on the main roads. You'll also find them on every map. When in doubt you can always ask locals for directions.

The West Coast

This long string of coastline is the holiday base for the majority of tourists on Bali. It's the place to go for easy access to an array of shops, restaurants, and activities. You find all types here, from luxury villa dwellers in the northern suburbs to tourists on package deals rounded up in the big central and southern hotels. Kuta's strip, within steps of the cheap *losmen* (small hotels), simple dining places, and myriad souvenir sellers scattered throughout the town's back alleys, is the ultimate backpacker fantasy.

Berewa. This sloping golden beach covers the northern arc of the west coast as it turns into the southwestern province. Constant breezes result in big, slow waves, and low tide uncovers an abundance of seashells. The public shores are interspersed with private hotel and villa beaches, many of which are patrolled by security officers to keep off trespassers. Foreigners have been the targets of muggings here, so bring a friend to walk with if the beach is deserted.

Canggu. The shoreline between Berewa and Tanah Lot is a mix of brown sand, white sand, and rocky expanses, with good sunning spots and beautiful views. This is also one of the island's top surf spots.

☾ **Kuta.** It's true: Kuta's broad swath of golden sand and slowly curling tubes of aqua water are the picture of idyllic tropical pleasure. This is the ultimate place in Southeast Asia to kick back in the sand on a batik sarong, sip a cold drink, get a cheap massage, and watch the Speedos and string bikinis swagger past. At the shallow edges, children can wade, find crabs, and collect shells and sand dollars, while the gentle waves provide a baby course for beginning surfers. This is Bali's hub for the hip and happening, and you'll find that everything you could possibly desire for a day on the beach comes to you here via vendor: cold beer and soda, sarongs, surfboards, massage, hair braiding, and suntan lotions, watches, rings, souvenir bow-and-arrow sets, carvings, and silver jewelry. Just shake your head no, close your eyes, and absorb the ultimate cheap tourist fantasy.

Legian. A debatable boundary separates this continuing stretch of golden sand from Kuta Beach, but this area is mostly the domain of large, inexpensive resorts catering to package tourists. A wide dirt road separates the hotels from the sand, though, so the beach here is all public and somewhat more sedate than Kuta's casual, flirty beach scene.

Seminyak. The coast north of Legian continues into Seminyak, which has a mix of pretty, quiet yellow and brown beaches. The water becomes rougher the farther north you go, and many of these beaches are the property of private hotels or villas.

Tuban. This southern beach connects Kuta to the neck of the Bukit peninsula. Tuban is less famous than its sister beach, but the tourists, the hucksters, and the activities are found here too. More than a dozen high-rise international mega-hotels are based here, so shops, bars, restaurants, and accommodations are conveniently close at hand.

Jimbaran and Bukit Badung

There are beaches on both sides of the neck of the Bukit peninsula: the swampy eastern coast is better for fishing than swimming, and the stretch of western sand is perfect for sunning and sunset gazing. The beaches around the peninsula are mostly rocky, although there are pockets of perfect white sand. Because the waves are for the most part rough and unforgiving, the peninsula's beaches are good for scenic views only—unless you're a top surfer, in which case you'll find dozens of places to catch the perfect wave.

Balangan. Follow the signs down a slim dirt road, around rugged hills, and through small villages to this small southwestern beach. It's a top island surf spot—don't be surprised if locals call out, "Surfer! Surfer!" as you drive by.

Jimbaran. The town's western-facing strip of white sand is the ultimate place to view tropical sunsets. Dozens of open-air restaurants serve freshly caught seafood at rickety wooden tables next to the water. Come in the morning to watch the fishing boats returning with the day's catch.

Uluwatu. Look down from your perch over the roiling blue water to a smooth white beach far below you. Gorgeous and secluded at the end of the peninsula, Uluwatu is also probably Bali's most challenging surfing spot. It's where the best of the best come to hone their skills, and international competitions are staged here each year.

Nusa Dua

The huge holiday resorts lined up along this coast make most of the brown-gold sand inaccessible to all but guests, although you can walk the beaches if you're staying at one of the resorts. There's a public beach at the small bulb jutting out from the peninsula, but the rough service road makes travel there difficult, and its not always very clean. When the weather is calm, there are a few lovely places you can go for a picnic, swimming, and working on a tan.

Pantai Nusa Dua. If you're shopping at the Nusa Dua Galeria, take a five-minute stroll through the low, blossoming trees to the water's edge. This brown beach is a pleasant place for a picnic break after browsing the boutiques, but it gets crowded on weekends and holidays.

★ ⏱ **Samudra Indah.** This is what most travelers have in mind when they think of a tropical coastline: white sand, azure waters, and gentle waves, with colorful boats lining the shore. Several excellent *warung* (small open-air food stalls) behind the line of wooden lounge chairs serve simple Indonesian fare and sandwiches. Because it's down a bumpy little lane south of Nusa Dua, only a handful of tourists venture here—but it's worth the trip.

Sheraton Laguna. With sand the color of brown sugar, the beach at the Sheraton Laguna fits right in with the hotel's aquatic theme of lagoons, pools, and waterfalls. Catch the action of a daily volleyball game, look for treasures, or fly a kite. Or just recline in one of the wooden resting pavilions, sipping a drink and absorbing the perfect views. Hotel, restaurant, and spa guests can visit it for free; nonguests pay about $5.

Sanur

As in Nusa Dua, resorts occupy most of Sanur's beaches, which are brown, shallow, and swampy at times. During low tide you can walk out on the reef and look for sea life; in fact, this is one of the better places on the island to collect shells and snorkel.

Jalan Hang Tuah. The public beach at the end of this road is one of the most popular hangouts for locals and tourists. The brown sand is nothing to celebrate, but the trinket sellers, tour offices, and cheap food stalls make this a great place to browse for souvenirs, set up an island exploration, and sit down for a snack and watch the world wander by. The Museum Le Mayeur (☞ Exploring Southern Bali, *above*) lies a two-minute walk down the beach path to the south.

Pantai Sindhu. The town's busy beach market is alongside this public stretch of brown sand. Come here to shop rather than to work on your tan; it's one of the least expensive places to buy batik clothing and kites. Although the views are classic seascape, the waves are rough and the sand litter-strewn, so go elsewhere for peace and privacy.

The Badung Strait Islands

The reefs around Nusa Ceningan, Nusa Lembongan, and Nusa Penida attract divers and snorkelers, and several dive and day-tour companies have their own private beaches for tanning and barbecue lunch buffets. The waves off these islands, and particularly Nusa Lembongan, are well known on the international circuit. If you're a surfer, you can wander the coasts and find your own private haven. If you're just looking for a quiet place to nibble leisurely on picnic items or take an afternoon snooze, you'll find dozens of pristine beaches tucked between the tall limestone cliffs. Your only dilemma will be how to reach them.

Mushroom Bay. This small arc of white sand on Nusa Lembongan is tucked between high, rocky cliffs. A couple of snack and souvenir stalls stand out of the reach of the deep azure waves, which cover the beach during high tide. It's mostly a parking place for local fishing boats and a drop-off point for tourists on day trips to the island, but it's a terrific picnic site at low tide. The easy Playground surf break is about 1 km (½ mi) offshore, and the surrounding reefs are a favorite snorkeling spot.

Pantai Jungutbatu. This white sand beach stretches around the northwestern curve of Nusa Lembongan in front of more than a dozen small hotels and stores. At the southern end of the beach lies the seaweed-farming village of Jungutbatu, where you can observe local weavers and wood-carvers at work. At the northern end a coral reef teems with activity.

Pantai Semaya. The white beach off the small Nusa Penida village of Semaya is a quiet haven for picnics and sunning. Most travelers make it their lunch-spot stop after a dive along the offshore reef.

Pantai Toya Pakeh. Nusa Penida's main town, Toya Pakeh, has a pleasant white-sand beach where you can take in a panorama of cobalt sea and the smoky gray peak of Bali's famous volcano, Gunung Agung. This is the main stop for boats from Nusa Lembongan.

DINING

Southern Bali's restaurant scene is eclectic and inexpensive. Here you'll find Indonesian warung next to seafood grills, Korean barbecues next to French patisseries, steak shops next to Indian curry houses, and sushi bars next to Mexican cantinas. The range of cuisine is tremendous, and everything from caviar to seviche is available—often on the same menu. The best restaurants usually stick to one theme, though, whether it's Mediterranean, Thai, or southwestern U.S. style. Indonesian dishes are found on every menu, but the rule is the more upscale the restaurant, the more toned down the taste. If you like it spicy, go for a restaurant crowded with Indonesians or where an Indonesian is in charge of the kitchen. The best Balinese food is found at the markets, especially the *pasar malam* (night markets), and several Indonesian restaurants specialize in local dishes or have Balinese rijsttafel buffets.

If you enjoy spicy food, southern Bali will tempt you with an explosion of fiery tastes. There's *babi guling* (roast pork), *sate babi* (pork sate), and *babi kecap* (barbecued pork)—treats not found on Indonesia's Muslim islands. The traditional vegetable accompaniments are *lawar* (a green mix of bean sprouts, long beans, and spices, combined with shredded coconut, papaya, and star fruit) and *urab* (a red mix of vegetables, spices, and shredded coconut), both of which are usually used for stuffing the roast pig. Although *bebek betutu* (smoked duck with vegetable stuffing) and *bebek goreng* (deep-fried duck) are more common in central Bali, they're still served here, but they must be ordered a day in advance. For dessert look for the thin, crepelike Bali pancakes, often smothered in bananas and honey, and gooey *bubur injin* (black rice pudding).

You can find almost any type of cuisine in any town; it's more the atmosphere that varies from place to place. Seminyak has upscale dining in large terrace restaurants whose spic-and-span interiors, foreign chefs, and neatly clipped gardens create a safe, Western-style experience. Legian is more eclectic, its small, charming restaurants a mix of Seminyak's refined expectations and Kuta's daring, inexpensive dining establishments. Kuta and Tuban are clashes of cuisine and culture, where small, crowded diners sit on the same block as fast-food outlets, and where slim, unpolished alley restaurants share space with techno bars and elegant garden pavilions. Jimbaran's fish market is famous, but the town also has a few small restaurants on the roads to the larger hotels. The Bukit peninsula has pockets of good little restaurants between the resorts of Jimbaran and Nusa Dua, and Sanur's strip has a number of casual diners. Denpasar is the place to go for excellent Chinese, Indonesian, and seafood dishes, and there are numerous large, open-air seafood grills along the coast east of the city.

Of the Badung Strait Islands, Nusa Lembongan has the greatest variety of dining spots, mainly small beachside restaurants tucked in between the losmen-style hotels near Jungutbatu and Lembongan. For casual upscale fare, head to the resorts around Sanghiang Bay, which cater to guests on all-inclusive day and overnight packages from the main island of Bali. Nusa Penida has warung along the beach in Toya Pakeh; most losmen also have attached restaurants. On Nusa Ceningan you're limited to your host's cooking at the homestays and losmen—which actually might be the best option of all.

Though the selection of meals in this region is world-based, the preparation and service are rarely world-class, so don't expect perfection even at the top restaurants. Those recommended here will provide some of the region's best dining experiences, but even these establishments sometimes fall below Western standards of presentation and taste. Consider dining on Bali to be an adventure—and when things do go right, count it as a gift from the gods. And take a few chances: the best tiramisu you've ever tasted might come from the pastry counter at that scruffy warung in Kuta; the tastiest grilled fish might come from the Jimbaran market; and you just might be amazed at the succulent salmon terrine served at that tiny back-alley restaurant in Seminyak.

As for dressing up to dine out, the heat, sun, wind, and mosquitoes of southern Bali dictate that comfortable clothes are always appropriate. Decent shorts and clean T-shirts are the norm everywhere except at the finest hotel restaurants. But donning casual, elegant attire is always fun at the more refined places in Seminyak, Sanur, Nusa Dua, and Jimbaran. Few restaurants have air-conditioning, cloth napkins, or bathrooms that meet Western standards, so prepare accordingly. The good (or bad) aspect of this low-key dining environment is that families are welcome in all but the most austere resort establishments (most of which don't allow children on the premises anyway).

For general information and price categories, *see* Dining *in* Smart Travel Tips.

The West Coast

Cafés

$$ ✕ **Bali Bakery Patisserie & Café.** The busiest bakery in town is on Tuban's busiest road. You'll find it if you just follow the warm aroma of freshly baked bread. This bright, clean café is split into two sections: a wraparound bakery with baskets of rolls, bowls of long baguettes, and exquisitely designed cakes, and a café with little tables and cozy booths. The extensive menu lists such classic café choices as sandwiches and wraps, gourmet salads, and simple appetizers. Indonesian items and full dinners are also available. Afterward be sure to try one of the beautiful pastries. ✉ *Jl. Kuta 65, Tuban,* ☎ *0361/755149. AE, DC, MC, V.*

$$ ✕ **Taman Ayun Coffee House.** It's easy to miss this wonderful little restaurant in the Bali Padma hotel (☞ Lodging, *below*)—but it's worth the search. With a jazzy ambience and ice-cold air-conditioning, it's a great place to hang out on hot afternoons. The decor is cozy and comfortable, with rattan chairs, book-lined windowsills, and a polished wood floor leading to colorful mosaic stones bordering the curving marble bar. Try tea or coffee with one of the desserts: rhubarb crumble cake,

38

Ketewel

Tohpati

Denpasar

Jalan Hang Tuah

Sanur

Pura Segara

Pantai Sindhu

Pura Blanjong

Pura Mertasari

vungbatankendal

anggaran

PULAU
SARANGAN
(TURTLE ISLAND)

Benoa
Harbor

Badung

Strait

njung Benoa

Tanjung
Benoa

*Benoa
Bay*

Celuk

Sheraton
Laguna

Nusa
Dua

Pantai
Nusa
Dua

Pura
Geger

Samudra
Indah

geh

KEY

Beaches

Temples

Anchorage

coconut and sour cream cheesecake, ginger carrot cake, or chocolate mud cake. Appetizers, sandwiches, and tasty snacks are also served—to the sounds of live jazz in the evening—and this is a top choice for drinks before or after dinner. ⊠ *Jl. Padma, Legian,* ☎ *0361/752111. AE, DC, MC, V.*

$$ ✕ **Terrace Café.** This elegant 24-hour roadside café across from Kuta Beach, part of the Hotel Istana Rama, is a lovely little place for sunset drinks, an after-hours snack, or a sunrise breakfast. Small tables line several stone terraces, and waiters in white shirts, black pants, and bow ties add an element of formality to the beachside scene. The food is also a notch above average: poached mussels with cilantro, pan-seared tuna with green papaya salad, and shrimp, mango, and avocado salad join a range of pastas and Indonesian fare. Desserts in the back pastry case include peach sorbet with passion-fruit sauce, crème caramel, and apple pie. ⊠ *Jl. Pantai, Kuta,* ☎ *no phone. AE, DC, MC, V.*

$ ✕ **Kafe Moka.** The desert mural on the wall brings a North African feel to this bakery-restaurant, but the food is strictly simple gourmet. Small glass-top tables are crowded together in the little room, but it's fun to eavesdrop on the expatriates who come here for the French breakfast or afternoon coffee. The glass case in front shows off the day's specials, which range from leek salad to huge squares of pasta au gratin to thick rectangles of layered ground beef and mashed potatoes. Treats from the small bakery include truffles, cakes, and croissants. ⊠ *Jl. Seminyak, Seminyak,* ☎ *0361/731424. AE, DC, MC, V.*

$ ✕ **Kafe Teras.** This little French bakery has expanded into a large café, always a favorite of those staying along the main strip in Tuban. Fresh bread, rolls, and croissants are just teasers; beautiful cakes and sweets are also served. An extensive menu includes sandwiches, salads, and full dinners. Try the colorful antipasto focaccia, the tangy Reuben sandwich, a bittersweet coffee float, or a rich slice of mocha or chocolate cake to top off your day. ⊠ *Jl. Kartika Plz., Tuban,* ☎ *0361/751369. AE, DC, MC, V.*

Contemporary

$$$$ ✕ **Cendana.** Lavish decor and fabulous views make this spacious, opulent restaurant worth the price. The marble dining room spreads out into five pavilions separated from the adjacent rolling golf course by a lotus pond filled with ducks and fat koi. Dine inside between huge stone panels or out on the terrace for sunset views of the waves that pound the rocky beach behind the Tanah Lot temple. The gourmet European-style fare is meticulously prepared, presented, and served. Come on Sunday at sundown for the Indonesian rijsttafel (about $22), then work off your dinner with a lantern-lit stroll through the grounds of the Meridien Nirwana Golf & Spa Resort (☞ Lodging, *below*). ⊠ *Jl. Kediri, Canggu,* ☎ *0361/815900. AE, DC, MC, V.*

$–$$ ✕ **Made's Warung II.** This two-story, shop-encircled pavilion is a sister branch of Made's in Kuta, a classic hangout for budget travelers and expatriates that was under renovation at press time. Hence, everyone has migrated here—and the move may be permanent, for this is now one of the area's hottest nightspots, both for the food and the chance to see and be seen by the island's "in" clique. The long menu includes dishes from Europe, Indonesia, Thailand, and India. The Asian food, unfortunately, is bland; it's better to stick with Western fare and the terrific desserts. There's parking in back. ⊠ *Jl. Seminyak, Seminyak,* ☎ *0361/732130. AE, DC, MC, V.*

$ ✕ **Green Garden.** This big open-air establishment in the middle of Tuban's main road combines a popular bar with a good budget restaurant. It's a busy, relaxing place that people wander into for lunch during a day of shopping or for a snack after a dip in the rock-lined swimming pool of the adjacent Green Garden hotel (☞ *Lodging, below*). The large portions of Indonesian, Chinese, and Western fare are tasty and inexpensive. ⊠ *Jl. Kartika Plz. 9, Tuban,* ☎ *0361/ 754571. AE, DC, MC, V.*

Continental

$$$ ✕ **La Lucciola.** Perfect margaritas and sunsets are why most people come to this chic beachside restaurant, but the cuisine and service are top-notch as well. Set in front of the sea on the golden sands of Berewa, the open two-story building welcomes a casual, upscale crowd. By day families come to play on the private beach (around $6 per person) and snack on crisp spring rolls and sandwiches. In the evening a classier crowd settles in to sip wine by candlelight and take in the starlight and sea breezes. As for the food, the meaty chili squid curls are coated in a crisp, light batter and served sizzling hot; the baked chicken is succulent and tender; and the chocolate tart is crisp on the edges but richly moist in the center. ⊠ *Jl. Laksmana and Jl. Kayu Aya, Kerobokan,* ☎ *0361/730838. Reservations essential. AE, DC, MC, V.*

$$-$$$ ✕ **Kori.** Cross a little wooden bridge over a lotus pond and enter the restaurant, walk past the front bar, and you're in a cool, marble, two-story mansion with winding gardens behind it. Featured appetizers include chilled papaya gazpacho with coriander and lime salsa over fresh yogurt; Java corn chowder with fresh chives, cumin, and onion; and Balinese *sate lilit* (minced pork and spices molded onto sticks and grilled over hot coals). Outstanding main courses—Thai green curry, Singapore chili crab, and Indonesian beef stew—are followed by such exquisite desserts as Bavarian vanilla cheesecake on passion-fruit coulis, and a vanilla-chocolate mousse. The "Essentials for Expats" section of the menu, which lists standard burgers, steaks, and potatoes, gives you a clue as to who fills the tables nightly. ⊠ *Poppies La. II, Kuta,* ☎ *0361/758605. AE, DC, MC, V.*

$$ ✕ **Un's.** With its pebbled entryway, small trees strung with white lights, and U-shape pavilion lined with Balinese paintings, the feel here is that of a secret temple tucked away in the center of a bustling town. Margaritas are the happy-hour special, and entrées include both Indonesian and Western specialties: mushroom ravioli, Venetian chicken breast, cordon bleu, and grilled snapper and prawns. At day's end you can unwind in the bar at the center of the garden, where strolling Batak musicians from northern Sumatra occasionally perform. ⊠ *Poppies La., Kuta,* ☎ *0361/752607. AE, MC, V.*

$-$$ ✕ **Veranda.** This inconspicuous restaurant set back from the main
★ Seminyak strip serves the best European fare on the island. The experience begins with refreshing cold towels, then generous baskets of warm wheat rolls and baguettes—and it only gets better. Start with sliced avocado with pear cocktail sauce sprinkled with blue cheese or have orange-marinated cold roast-beef tenderloin with goat's cheese, aubergine mousse, and balsamic vinegar. Then sink your teeth into imported lamb chops with garbanzo Provençal sauce, served with a spinach and goat's cheese quiche, or try a spinach-and-salmon terrine wrapped in a soft fish fillet, topped with shrimp on a skewer and served with saffron sauce and garnished with caviar. Save room for dessert—you can even go back to the open kitchen and watch yours being created. The service is flawless, and although Veranda is an upscale place, the staff, menu, and facilities are very child-friendly. ⊠ *Jl. Seminyak 31B, Seminyak,* ☎ *0361/ 732685. Reservations essential. No credit cards. Closed Mon. No lunch.*

Cybercafés

$ ✕ **Bali@Cyber Café.** Polished wood tables and chairs fill the center of this large open-air space, and five state-of-the-art computers sit on fine teak desks against the back wall. Clever touches add to the upscale feel:

wood magazine racks with computer publications to borrow while you eat or wait for a terminal; screen savers with photos of Bali's most famous views; and CD-ROM coasters. But what makes this cybercafé a standout is the food, Balinese and Southeast Asian specialties done right. Try the Balinese lawar (vegetable salad mixed with grated coconut and spiced chicken), seafood *pepes bumbu Bali* (wrapped and grilled in banana leaves), or Malaysian pineapple curry. For a special treat, Malay *nasi lemak* (rice steamed in coconut milk) served with an egg and fried chicken is available Monday through Wednesday, and you can sample Singapore chicken rice Thursday through Saturday. ⊠ *Jl. Pura Bagus, Legian,* ☎ *0361/761326. AE, MC, V.*

$ ✕ **Krakatoa Café.** Tucked into the back of the Krakatoa Business Center, this informal restaurant is a gathering place for budget travelers. Choose from the daily blackboard specials—like vegetarian lasagna, grilled chicken with vegetables, or steak and potatoes—as well as breakfast items, Indonesian dishes, and gourmet salads. The food is a bit bland, but portions are large, and it's inexpensive. The front bakery has stellar desserts, including apple-carrot cake, lemon bars, and rich chocolate treats. Many travelers come just to check the information board, have a beer, and watch the nightly movies that start at 7 PM. ⊠ *Jl. Seminyak, Seminyak,* ☎ *0361/730824. MC, V.*

$ ✕ **Maccaroni Club.** This modern, airy restaurant seems more like a shopping mall than an Internet café, but the back terminals signify otherwise. The menu is on the light side: warm pork and mandarin salad; lime and chili coconut salad; a sandwich of smoked ham, cheese, artichoke, arugula, and tuna; a smoked beef, tomato, olive, and pâte combination. If you're waiting to dine here, you can use a terminal for free. ⊠ *Jl. Kuta, Kuta,* ☎ *0361/754662. AE, DC, MC, V.*

Eclectic

$$$ ✕ **The Living Room.** This snazzy new restaurant is the up-and-coming dining and nightlife spot for expats and local celebrities in the know. Upon entering the colonial-style Javanese pavilion you find an elegant dining room decorated with long hanging drapes, local paintings, and antique furniture. The large central area seats 70 diners, and a pleasant garden in back has tables for 50 more; the latter is the ideal place for a romantic drink by candlelight. Owners Dewi and Sri, who also established the Warisan (☞ below), use music to create a soothing ambience (they're so good at it that they've made a restaurant-soundtrack CD). The cuisine is Asian with a French flair, and waitresses clad in designer dresses made by Sri surreptitiously whisk dishes to and from the tables. The wine list is excellent, and you can choose the elements for your own after-hours party from the adjacent wine and spirits shop. ⊠ *Jl. Petitenget, Kerobokan,* ☎ *0361/735735. Reservations essential. AE, MC, V.*

$$$ ✕ **Warisan.** Dinner here is an elegant party: the island's elite expatriates, artists, and their often famous guests, dressed to the nines, leisurely smoke cigarettes and recount amusing tales of their international travels. The wine flows freely here—Warisan may have the best list on Bali, with fine labels from France, Chile, Argentina, South Africa, and Australia. The European cuisine complements the eclectic ambience. Precisely arranged escargots burst with freshness; rich Mediterranean fish soup has a light, lingering zest; the grilled rosemary chicken breast is meaty and succulent. It's also worth coming here for an afternoon treat and an espresso. If you're lucky, you might happen upon a special of juicy apple tart, or the triple chocolate threat: white chocolate, milk chocolate, and mocha layers of mousse-soft cake painted in dark chocolate and white caramel syrup. ⊠ *Jl. Kerobokan, Kerobokan,* ☎ *0361/731175. Reservations essential. AE, DC, MC, V. No lunch Sun.*

$$–$$$ ✕ **Poppies.** Surrounded by high-energy shops and dives, Poppies is a garden haven enclosed by tall, thin walls. Vines and blossoms tumble through trellises above the well-spaced tables, and the staff is quick to please. The relaxed alfresco atmosphere makes the bland Indonesian and Western dishes more enjoyable. Items range from Greek salads and *tom yam* (spicy Thai prawn soup) to grilled fish and succulent spareribs. Poppies is one of Kuta's main evening hangouts. ⊠ *Poppies La., Kuta,* ☎ *0361/751059. MC, V.*

$$ ✕ **Warung Kopi.** Marble-top tables facing the street and more in a rear garden provide an oasis from the chaos of the strip. The kitchen serves up Indonesian fish, vegetable and rice dishes, Indian curries, and Western beef and lamb. This is also a fine place to stop for just a beer and an appetizer or coffee and dessert. Try the wicked chocolate brownies or the spiced orange carrot cake. ⊠ *Jl. Legian Tengah 427, Legian,* ☎ *0361/753602. MC, V.*

$ ✕ **Santa Fe.** Even before you see the bright blue sign you can smell what's cooking in the wood-fired pizza oven in front. The look is rustic southwest U.S. style, with rough-hewn wood tables and chairs, and photos and knickknacks from the Wild West decorating the rugged beige walls. The menu includes international standards like rack of rosemary lamb and smoked salmon carpaccio; standouts are the colorful salads and terrific curries, served on a silver *thali* tray with chapati, rice, yogurt, dal, and chutney. Desserts, including tiramisu, Black Forest cake, and apple pie, are baked on-site. The restaurant is open 24 hours, so you can stop in whenever the mood strikes—perhaps after a show at the popular music club in back. ⊠ *Jl. Abimanyu 11, Legian,* ☎ *0361/731147. No credit cards.*

Indian

$ ✕ **Gateway to India.** This little dive has the best Indian food in southern Bali. A dozen wooden tables covered with red-checkered cloths spill out from the narrow cavern onto the patio overlooking the street, and Indian music blares from a boom box in the back kitchen. The best way to explore the cuisine here is to come in a group and share several dishes. Start with the garlic or cheese *naan* (flat, soft bread) or peppery *poppadams* (baked flour-dough chips); then choose from the rich chicken and beef curries, the tandoori chicken, and the succulent grilled dishes and vegetarian entrées, specifying a level of spiciness to suit your palate. A cold beer washes the heat down nicely, or you can soothe your fiery stomach with a cool dollop of *kheer* (sweet, creamy rice pudding). If you really want to try everything, come for the extensive—and immensely popular—buffet Sunday night from 7 to 10 ($5). ⊠ *Jl. Abimanyu 10, Legian,* ☎ *no phone. No credit cards. No lunch Sun.*

Indonesian

$ ✕ **Warung Batavia.** It's just a small thatch-roof warung by the road-
★ side at the edge of Kerobokan, but expatriates swear by the food. And they're right. It's real Indonesian fare, with spices that will make your eyes water. Old standbys include fried rice, noodles, and *gado-gado* (steamed spinach and cabbage, with thin slices of carrots, potatoes, and beans, tossed in a rich peanut sauce). If you can't decide, go for the *nasi campur,* steamed rice with a taste of everything on the menu around it. Portions are huge, so prepare to share or take some back to your hotel. Carryout service is available. ⊠ *Jl. Seminyak, Seminyak,* ☎ *no phone. No credit cards.*

$ ✕ **Warung Nasi.** This bright, clean little eatery along the main strip in Tuban serves up large portions at low prices, making it a great place to warm up to the country's cuisine. Long tables in front seat eight each on low stools, and in the middle of the restaurant a glass case holds some of your choices. If you're new to Indonesian fare, start with fried rice or noodles, stir-fried vegetables, or gado-gado; or have steamed rice with a piece of fried chicken, fish, or scoop of vegetables from the display case. ⊠ *Jl. Kartika Plz., Tuban,* ☎ *no phone. No credit cards.*

Italian

$$$ ✕ **Fabio's.** This classic Italian restaurant is open and breezy, with soaring ceilings and lots of marble and light. Red tile floors, white table-cloths, and blue glasses are a bold, businesslike contrast to the romantic greenery of the vine-shaded garden dining area in back. The menu ranges from pasta and pizza to risotto and includes an excellent selection of wines. Head for the windows in front of the large, clean kitchen to see your meal in progress. The savvy bar is busy every night, and there's live music on the performance stage on Wednesday and Saturday. ⊠ *Jl. Seminyak 66, Seminyak,* ☎ *0361/730562. AE, DC, MC, V.*

$$ ✕ **Teras.** Robin's-egg blue is the theme color of this restaurant, adding a cool Mediterranean feel to its third-story setting overlooking the main shopping avenue. Black-wire chairs with blue cushions sit at blue ta-bles amid the gold-washed walls of the enclosed section; wood and wicker chairs and tables fill the bougainvillea-encircled terrace. The thousands of photos lining the walls of the stairway signal that this is a popular place. You may even see some of those famous faces inside dining on specials of homemade fettuccine Alfredo with prawns, garlic beef sim-mered in white wine, or fresh octopus salad. Teras is perfect for sum-mertime drinks or a dollop of hazelnut ice cream. ⊠ *Jl. Seminyak 16A, Seminyak,* ☎ *0361/730810. AE, MC, V.*

$ ✕ **Spaghetti Jazz.** It's so tiny you'll miss it the first time, but you'll want to track down this restaurant for the fresh salads and huge portions of spaghetti, ravioli, and lasagna. Sit elbow to elbow at little tables on the stone terrace next to the road or in the dark dining room next to the bar. Spaghetti Jazz is open until 2 AM and almost always crowded and loud—traffic outside, music inside—so be in the mood to be part of the action. Otherwise, phone in your order from the delivery menu. ⊠ *Jl. Seminyak 16A, Seminyak,* ☎ *0361/730810. AE, MC, V.*

Japanese

$$ ✕ **Ryoshi.** Huge red lanterns hang in Japanese-style windows, guiding diners to this immensely popular restaurant. Polished wood tables and benches, a sushi bar, and raised floor-seating areas are the perfect com-plement to what's on the menu. Blackboard specials might include tem-pura, sukiyaki, or a sushi combination. Even though it's part of an island-wide restaurant chain, everything hits the mark here. ⊠ *Jl. Seminyak, Seminyak,* ☎ *0361/731152. AE, MC, V.*

$ ✕ **Hana.** Tucked into the Seminyak Galeria, this cute little place has been receiving raves from travelers since opening in 1999. Dark teak tables are on the right, and a raised seating area with cushions is on the left, or you can dine on the stone terrace. Blackboard menus in-clude the usual Japanese fare: salmon *siroyaki, kipiru,* miso soup, pumpkin *nimono, oshinko,* and *gohan.* ⊠ *Jl. Seminyak, Seminyak,* ☎ *0361/732778. AE, MC, V.*

$ ✕ **Inaka.** Quaint, quiet, and intimate, Inaka is exactly what you'd ex-pect a Japanese diner to be. The menu covers the basics, and portions are small but inexpensive, so you can sample a variety of things. If you've never eaten Japanese food, the friendly waitresses can help you decide. If you don't feel like going out, the diner happily delivers. ⊠ *Jl. Seminyak 18, Seminyak,* ☎ *0361/733398. AE, DC, MC, V. No lunch.*

$ ✕ **Yakiniku Fukutaro.** Upstairs at the Kuta Center, this classic Japa-nese buffet restaurant has lots of floor space and low tables with cush-ions. It's one of Kuta's most popular tourist hangouts; look for the huge banners around town. The food is inexpensive and filling, the atmo-sphere fun and casual, and it's right in the center of all the hotels. ⊠ *Jl. Kartika Plz. 8X, Tuban,* ☎ *0361/730810. AE, MC, V.*

Korean

$ ✗ **Kim Sat Gat.** This is a fun upstairs restaurant overlooking Tuban's shopping district. Relax on a cushion at a low table in the raised dining area, and try a sampler of inexpensive Korean dishes. A miniature charcoal cooker is brought to your table for grilling tender sliced meats. Vegetarians can choose from such specialties as *kim gui* (grilled seaweed), *neng myoun* (cold noodles with egg and vegetables), or *go chu beo sut jab che* (stir-fried vegetables). Call for free transport if you're staying in the area. ✉ *Jl. Bakung Sari, Tuban,* ☎ *0361/755130. AE, MC, V.*

Mediterranean

$$ ✗ **Pantarei.** A garden entrance wall shrouded in blossoming vines separates this elegant restaurant from the traffic noise. Inside, red tile floors lead through the bar to a koi pond and, beyond, a tree-lined terrace. Candlelit tables and colored glass lanterns overhead give Pantarei an ambience of international intrigue and romance. Warm up your appetite with a country-style Greek salad or light and tangy stuffed mushrooms with feta, cheddar, and blue cheese. If you're hungry, share the lobster spaghetti for two, or try the tagliatelle with diced beef, tomatoes, onions, and cinnamon in red wine sauce. End your meal with the sweet, airy baklava or the *loukoumades* (fried pastry puffs stuffed with honey-vanilla ice cream and sprinkled with cinnamon and cashews). There's free parking at Bintang Supermarket, a block north. ✉ *Jl. Seminyak 17, Seminyak,* ☎ *0361/732567. AE, DC, MC, V.*

$ ✗ **Daddy's Café.** Take the spiral staircase up to this sunny little second-floor restaurant, where diners sit at wooden tables and look out over Tuban's shopping action. The menu includes Greek dishes, as well as salads, curries, kebabs, and meat and vegetable grills. Try the baked potato stuffed with spinach, feta, and herbs, or the yogurt with dill, cucumber, and homemade bread. Come to Daddy's for snacks and happy hour—or for the daily "reggae breakfast." ✉ *Jl. Kartika Plz. 8X, Tuban,* ☎ *0361/762037. AE, DC, MC, V.*

Pizza

$ ✗ **White Stone Pizzeria.** Enter through a funky peach-color rock cave into a cavern filled with octagonal tables draped in lime-green fringed cloths and couches with huge cushions. The upstairs cave is cozy and clublike; downstairs the ceiling is draped with batik and hammocks that are suspended from the stalactites. This place is more for meeting than eating, with *arak* (palm wine) and a long list of drinks. There's plenty to eat, though, including pizza, pasta, salads, and basic Indonesian fare. It's allegedly a 24-hour restaurant, but there's no food from the time the cook goes home around 3 AM until he returns the next day at noon. ✉ *Jl. Arjuna 16, Legian,* ☎ *0361/733558. AE, MC, V.*

Seafood

$ ✗ **Bali Seafood Market & Restaurant.** You can both shop and dine at this well-known restaurant. Although gardens in front separate the huge inner space from the street noise, it's nearly as bright and busy inside as it is outside. The kitchen prepares fried and grilled seafood and many vegetarian dishes, and the main stage hosts live music every night and Balinese dancing on Monday. If you're here to shop, grab a cart out front before you head to the cases of iced seafood that line the left wall. ✉ *Jl. Kartika Plz. 92X, Tuban,* ☎ *no phone. AE, DC, MC, V.*

$ ✗ **Kuta Seafood.** This is one of Bali's famed dining spots, and you can't miss its multilevel terra-cotta roof and the blue jukung in front. The fresh seafood market to the left is lined with tanks and iced displays that exhibit what's on the menu. Large round tables, bamboo chairs, and thick columns give the restaurant the air of a ballroom, and the crowds come nightly for the steamboat special for two and the grilled seafood basket. If you don't like fish, there are plenty of Indonesian dishes available. The stage hosts Balinese dance performances nightly at 8 PM. ✉ *Jl. Kartika Plz. 92X, Tuban,* ☎ *no phone. AE, DC, MC, V.*

Singaporean

$ ✗ **Singapore Restaurant.** If you happen upon Singapore Restaurant, stop and watch the cooks at work in the roadside kitchen. The scents of thick, beefy fried noodles and fish-ball soup will entice you in for a meal. The warung in back dishes up large, spicy portions of Singaporean soups, noodles, and rice dishes, as well as Indonesian and Malaysian fare. As you may have guessed by the aromas of curry, chapati, and chicken tandoori, Indian cuisine is served as well. Just ask for whichever menu you want when you enter. The restaurant has a sister location on Jalan Kuta. ✉ *Jl. Kartika Plz. 188, Tuban,* ☎ *0361/ 761811. No credit cards.*

Thai

$–$$ ✗ **Kin Khao.** A glass storefront etched with a dancing Thai figure is the signature mark of this string of air-conditioned Thai restaurants, which give classy appeal to traditional Thai cuisine. Long garden vines drizzle over the glass ceiling and rock walls in front, and diners sit on soft cushions on the floor, Thai style. Portions are sample size, so you can try several dishes, such as *goong how pah* (shrimp wrapped in a thick, crispy pastry and served with sweet chili sauce), *yum reum-mit talay* (squid rings and shrimp with glass noodles and lemon juice, onion, and tomato), *pad preowwan goong* (stir-fried shrimp with vegetables), or the classic *how mok talay* (squares of steamed fish topped with red curry, coconut custard, and shrimp). Simple desserts, coffees, and alcoholic drinks are also served. Smoking is allowed inside, and when it's busy, the air can get heavy. ✉ *Jl. Seminyak 37, Seminyak,* ☎ *0361/732153. AE, DC, MC, V.*

Vegetarian

$ ✗ **Aromas.** The scents from this two-story travelers' favorite are exotic and savory. It's a fine place for breakfast, and many return in the evening for such unusual dishes as Bombay *bungkus* soup, a phyllo pastry with a split-pea-soup filling; Lebanese roll with tahini, falafel, hummus, and tabbouleh doused in barbecue sauce; and the huge East–West sandwich, a pita stuffed with barbecue tempeh and coleslaw and baked. After shopping drop by for coffee and a slice of lemon cheesecake, a taste of frozen chocolate-cream log, or a bowl of chocolate-raisin mousse. ✉ *Jl. Legian, Legian,* ☎ *0361/753602. MC, V.*

Jimbaran and Bukit Badung

Contemporary

$$–$$$ ✗ **L'Oasis Restaurant & Bakery.** This two-story restaurant is spacious and classy, with a cheery bakery and slick bar. Pastel hues and potted plants give L'Oasis a 1930s feel, and though the dining area is large, wood trellises between tables provide privacy. Appetizers include Roll Move (iced slices of grilled fish around sweet cucumber chunks, with tomato, red pepper, green onion, and sweet pickles); chili squid cilantro; and Giant Soup (a large bowl of hearty chicken-lemongrass broth with thick chicken slices and prawns). Main dishes are hearty: try the tangy pan-seared yellowfin tuna fillet with Moroccan lemon and capers, accompanied by a steaming square of au gratin potatoes. Desserts are just enough to top off a meal: a dome of frozen nougat, a scoop of mango parfait, or a small pear with raspberries. The service is leisurely enough to encourage conversation, but not so slow that you'll go hungry between courses. Winding stairs lead up to the popular jazz club. ✉ *Jl. Bypass, Jimbaran,* ☎ *0361/702669. AE, DC, MC, V.*

$ ✕ **Stiff Chilli.** In the hills of Jimbaran, this bi-level bamboo pavilion has the views without the high prices. Worn plank floors, splintered rails, and a ramshackle thatch roof can't deter regulars who show up here daily for the fluffy omelets, fresh bacon-and-cheese croissants, thick sandwiches, and top-notch salads. It's a neighborhood hot spot on weekends, and you can pick up fresh-baked bread at the counter. ✉ *Jl. Uluwatu, Jimbaran,* ☎ *0361/703517. No credit cards.*

Continental

$$-$$$ ✕ **Balangan.** Seemingly sitting up in the sky, this simple, thatch-roof
★ pavilion presides over a sweeping panorama of ocean from atop the forested Jimbaran hills. The atmosphere is intimate and refreshing, with just six tables and soft classical music in the background. The menu and wine list are limited, but what's there is excellent. Watch kites whip in the wind over the trees below as you nibble on French oysters or penne with vegetable-basil pesto and crispy goat-cheese croutons. Through the dusk, faraway planes silently glide into the airport as you dine on linguine with chorizo sausages, sweet peppers, and spicy tomato sauce; homemade pumpkin ravioli; or curried chicken broth with egg, tofu, and rice noodles. Roasted mango with caramel sauce is a sweet way to end an enjoyable evening. ✉ *Br. Cengiling 88, Balangan,* ☎ *0361/410711. Reservations essential. AE, DC, MC, V.*

$$ ✕ **Café Latino.** At night this enormous templelike building is so quiet it seems abandoned, but walk down the main hallway and you'll find four dining pavilions. Shining gold tablecloths add color to the gray stone pillars and floors, and fountains trickle into lotus ponds, enhancing the secluded atmosphere. The international dishes are well prepared: the bruschetta is perfectly crisp and garlicky; grilled vegetable kebabs are crisp outside and bursting with juicy flavor inside; the mixed seafood grill is generous; and the spaghetti carbonara is enormous, rich, and smoky. Make sure you have plenty of time, though, because waiting is part of the restaurant's relaxed ambience. ✉ *Jl. Uluwatu, Jimbaran,* ☎ *0361/703603. AE, DC, MC, V. No lunch.*

Indonesian

$$ ✕ **Pici-Pici.** It's advertised as a "warung Bali," but this restaurant at the GWK cultural park is actually an elegant two-story pavilion. Coral walls, teak tables, wicker chairs, and a stone floor provide an upscale setting for enjoying Balinese cuisine. Everything is offered here: *jukut nangka* (chicken-and-jackfruit soup), *urab kacang* (Balinese long-bean salad), *be siap menyet-nyat* (chicken simmered in aromatic spices), *be pasih sambal matah* (grilled whole fish in Balinese spices), and much more. For dessert choose the house favorite, *kolak biu* (bananas in palm sugar and *pandan* leaf syrup). ✉ *Jl. Uluwatu, GWK cultural park,* ☎ *0361/730604. AE, DC, MC, V.*

$$ ✕ **Restoran La Indonesia.** Stunning Balinese decor merges with wonderful island cuisine in this thatch-roof restaurant on Jimbaran's main road. The interior is elegant, and the back garden is romantic, the mood heightened by soft gamelan tones floating through the air. Try lawar, *tambusan be pasih* (diced fish roasted in banana leaves), or *saur kare* (vegetables in coconut milk curry). If you can't decide, ask for the individual rijsttafel sampler buffet. Note that Bali's famous dish, bebek betutu, must be ordered a day in advance. ✉ *Jl. Uluwatu 108, Jimbaran,* ☎ *0361/701763. AE, DC, MC, V.*

Nusa Dua and Tanjung Benoa

Chinese

$$ ✕ **Hann Chinese.** Nusa Dua's classiest Chinese restaurant is housed in a beige limestone building at the end of the shopping strip. The spa-

cious dining room is casual and comfortable, yet elegant enough to cater to upscale hotel groups that want to get out for the evening. The extensive menu covers the basics, and seafood is a specialty. This is also a good place to stop for drinks and sizzling hot appetizers. ⊠ *Jl. Pantai Mengiat 88, Nusa Dua,* ☎ *0361/776565. AE, DC, MC, V.*

Contemporary

$–$$ ✗ **Nyoman's Beer Garden.** Cold beer, Asian dishes, and hearty Continental fare are the favorites here. Always filled with chattering travelers, the patio has a busy international atmosphere. Portions aren't large, but you're really here to be part of the crowd, anyway. Have a game of pool in the back after your meal. ⊠ *Jl. Pantai Mengiat, Nusa Dua,* ☎ *0361/775746. AE, DC, MC, V.*

French

$$–$$$ ✗ **Escargot.** At this serene restaurant you can enjoy a romantic atmosphere and fine French cuisine. Small, closely spaced tables set with china are arranged under a large banyan tree and the stars. Besides the obvious escargots, the specialties include salad *niçoise*, chicken tarragon, lobster, and frogs' legs. In the Nusa Dua Galeria, Escargot has a wine bar where you can relax with a drink after shopping. ⊠ *Nusa Dua Galeria, Nusa Dua,* ☎ *0361/774906. AE, DC, MC, V.*

Mexican

$ ✗ **Poco Loco.** It's never quiet at this colorful Mexican restaurant above Nusa Dua's main shopping avenue. Peach walls and wood furniture complement the energetic ambience that brings the crowds in for happy hour. Though the food is bland, portions are large—and it's *the* place to be on the strip. The combination meals are the best deal; otherwise try the filling, cheesy nachos or the crisp tacos. ⊠ *Jl. Pantai Mengiat, Nusa Dua,* ☎ *0361/773923. AE, DC, MC, V.*

Seafood

$$$ ✗ **On the Rocks.** This gourmet seafood restaurant is prestigiously located at the front of the Nusa Dua Galeria. Imported Australian steaks and fresh-caught fish and lobster are the specialties. Try the succulent kebabs strung with thick chunks of meat and vegetables. Or go for the fresh pastas, which are sprinkled with a perfect mix of herbs. Don't miss desserts like the rich chocolate cake, drizzled with chocolate sauce and mango slices. ⊠ *Nusa Dua Galeria, Nusa Dua,* ☎ *0361/773653. AE, DC, MC, V.*

Sanur

Chinese

$$–$$$ ✗ **Telaga Naga.** Set way back off the main road in estate gardens, this
★   multipavilion restaurant surrounded by lotus ponds serves exquisite Cantonese and Szechuan cuisine. Dark teak beams, closely spaced tables, and candlelight add romance to the bustling atmosphere as waiters rush between smartly dressed diners. The portions are enormous, so order the "small" size unless you're very hungry. House specialties include sautéed chicken with dried red chilies and fried prawns with Szechuan sauce. ⊠ *Jl. Tamblingan,* ☎ *0361/2881234. Reservations essential. AE, DC, MC, V. No lunch.*

Contemporary

$$$ ✗ **Jazz Bar & Grille.** This two-story restaurant and club on the busy bypass is the east side's hangout for the beautiful people. Downstairs, patrons gather in intimate half-circle booths and at small round tables, while on the little stage jazz bands create a soothing, sexy atmosphere. Stairs lead up to a more casual club with pool tables. Standouts on the international menu include coconut-batter prawns; minicalzones stuffed with mozzarella, olives, and ham; grilled snapper marinated in olive oil and lime juice and served with papaya-onion salsa; and a huge appetizer platter of peppery black-and-blue tuna strips, lightly fried squid rings, and crisp-tender crab cakes. ⊠ *Jl. Bypass, Sanur Raya 15–16,* ☎ *0361/285892. Reservations essential. AE, DC, MC, V.*

$$ ✕ **Lotus Pond.** This thatch-roof restaurant, surrounded by gardens, has dining tables along one side, a cushioned lounge area along the other, and an extensive Indonesian buffet in the middle. The atmosphere is breezy and casual, the service amicable. Western offerings, such as club sandwiches and salads, are popular, as are the spiced-down Indonesian dishes. Dip into Bali's special cuisine at the nightly rijsttafel buffet. ⊠ *Jl. Tamblingan,* ☎ *0361/289398. AE, MC, V.*

Eclectic

$$ ✕ **Kafe Wayang.** Snuggled right up to the Jazz Bar & Grille (☞ *above*), this café-style restaurant and bakery is relaxed and quiet. It has a Mediterranean feel, with garden tables, mango-color walls, and lots of plants. The menu is a fusion of Continental and Indonesian cuisines. Try the huge grilled vegetarian sandwich, the chili-salmon wrap, or the excellent nasi campur; there's also a gourmet salad bar during lunch hours. For dinner you can't miss with the combination specials on the blackboard. Call for free transportation if you're staying in Sanur. ⊠ *Jl. Bypass, Sanur Raya 12–14,* ☎ *0361/287591. AE, DC, MC, V.*

$$ ✕ **Spago.** This spacious art house on Sanur's main road is one of the area's trendy hangouts, complete with a front bar, cozy sitting area, and works by local artists lining the walls. The cuisine mixes Western and Indonesian textures and spices, with such tasty results as rosemary spring chicken on couscous, pumpkin gnocchi with garlic sauce and crispy bacon, and pepper-crushed tuna with papaya-mint salsa. Wandering musicians strum jazz tunes most nights. ⊠ *Jl. Tamblingan 79,* ☎ *0361/288335. AE, DC, MC, V.*

$ ✕ **Tamarind.** This easygoing little restaurant is a favorite, both with the tourists who come for the breakfast specials and the expats who hang out here after dark and nibble on the simple fusion fare. Various Indonesian dishes are offered, but the curries and salads are better. Musicians perform most nights, sometimes spontaneously; if you're musically inclined, feel free to take down one of the guitars or accordions hanging up on the back wall and give an impromptu unplugged performance. ⊠ *Jl. Mertasari 2,* ☎ *0361/270572. No credit cards.*

Indonesian

$ ✕ **Warung Blanjong.** It's just a simple, thatch-roof roadside pavilion, but Warung Blanjong is a terrific place for Balinese and Indonesian food. The selections are basic—nasi campur, gado-gado, fried rice and noodles, curries—but it's all home-cooked fare. If you don't have time to sit down, grab a bite from the restaurant's take-out cart out front, or call and order delivery service to your hotel. ⊠ *Jl. Danau Poso 78,* ☎ *0361/285613. No credit cards.*

Italian

$ ✕ **Mamma Lucia.** It has a pink-and-green ice-cream-parlor look, but the hearty fare is definitely Italian. Start your meal by walking back to look at the pasta display, where you'll quickly learn to tell spaghetti from fettuccine and gnocchi from tagliatelle. The helpful staff can give you recommendations; go for the meaty lasagna, the pungent risotto, or the cheesy ravioli. ⊠ *Jl. Tamblingan 156,* ☎ *0361/289573. AE, DC, MC, V.*

Japanese

$–$$ ✕ **Kita.** Walk down the restaurant's gravel driveway, and you'll spot the glass case showing your dining options. The signs make it easy to name your selections: succulent yakitori, crisp tempura, or a big, steaming bowl of *udon* noodle soup. The best deals are the set menus, which include rice, miso soup, steamed vegetables, and a meat dish. Kita is large and clean and a favorite of Japanese travelers. ⊠ *Jl. Tamblingan 104,* ☎ *0361/288158. AE, MC, V.*

Pan-Asian

$$ ✕ **Penjor Restaurant.** Set back from the main street, this bamboo-wall restaurant surrounds an open courtyard where tables are set up in pavilions. A set menu rotates between Balinese, Indonesian, Chinese, and Indian dinners. Each night a different Balinese dance-drama is presented on the stage across the grassy garden. ⊠ *Jl. Tamblingan 140,* ☎ *0361/ 288226. AE, DC, MC, V.*

Denpasar

Café

$ ✕ **Sentana Bakery.** This inconspicuous bakery is where locals go to pick up treats on their way to work in the morning. Fresh loaves of bread, rolls, and pastries are basic and hearty. Try a cup of thick Bali coffee with an eclair sprinkled with shreds of mozzarella cheese. ⊠ *Jl. Sumatra 43,* ☎ *0361/226210. No credit cards.*

Chinese

$$ ✕ **Hong Kong Restaurant.** In front of the Pasar Kumbasari, this popular restaurant rocks during dinner hours. Chinese dishes are expertly cooked and could feed an army; it's best to bring a group so you can try several items. Seafood is a specialty, and you can have just about anything found in the ocean cooked any way that you like. The Hong Kong is also a party place where drinks come quickly; don't be surprised if you wind up at the second-floor karaoke bar later. ⊠ *Jl. Gajah Mada 99,* ☎ *0361/434845. AE, MC, V.*

Contemporary

$ ✕ **Thamrin Steakhouse.** Cheery red-and-black-checked tablecloths, a red tile floor, and Balinese bird pictures warm up this clean little steak house. The Western menu lists sandwiches, soups, chicken, and, of course, steaks. On weekends you can also get Chinese food, including sweet-and-sour chicken, crab-corn soup, and fried *bihun* noodles. The bar in the back can get busy at dinnertime. ⊠ *Jl. Teuku Umar 129,* ☎ *0361/ 239441. No credit cards.*

Eclectic

$–$$ ✕ **Gula Lunak.** This popular restaurant is a collection of indoor dining rooms, outdoor patio tables, and wood, wicker, and wire furnishings. The casual fare includes sandwiches, pasta, pizza, grilled items, and Indonesian dishes. On weekends live music is featured on the stage in back of the terrace. ⊠ *Jl. Teuku Umar 120,* ☎ *no phone. MC, V. Closed Sun. No lunch Fri. and Sat.*

Indonesian

$ ✕ **Kak Man.** This eatery along the capital's southern restaurant strip is a Bali institution. Don't be surprised if gregarious owner Nyoman—the Kak (grandfather) Man himself—sits down at your table to tell you all about it. A temple doorway leads into an open dining section; more tables and a karaoke bar are in the pavilions out back. The food is a mix of Indonesian, Chinese, and Balinese, all on the bland side, but it's a good place to taste traditional dishes like urab and *lawar daging* (cold vegetables mixed with pork or chicken). This is a rowdy local hangout on weekends. ⊠ *Jl. Teuku Umar,* ☎ *no phone. MC, V.*

$ ✕ **Mie 88.** There are no formalities at this busy, fluorescent-lit place. It's all about good Indonesian food, served hot and quick from the little roadside kitchen. Locals and travelers alike stop by for the thick noodles, as well as the steaming soups and rice dishes. ✉ *Jl. Sumatra 88,* ☎ *no phone. No credit cards.*

$ ✗ **Prambanan.** This two-story teak pavilion makes a beautiful setting in which to enjoy authentic Javanese food. The service is professional and meals are wheeled out on silver carts. Although the atmosphere is formal, the food is the warung style that makes lifetime travelers yearn for Jakarta. The curries are excellent, as are the fried dishes. Best of all is the nasi campur, which has a bit of everything: *opor ayam* (coconut-milk chicken), *nasi gudeg* (rice with rich jackfruit curry), mixed vegetables, a curried egg, and more. ✉ *Jl. Hayam Wuruk 30XX,* ☎ *0351/221909. No credit cards.*

$ ✗ **Warung Bandung.** This tiny diner, filled with locals from morning to night, is the place to eat if you like the cuisine of Bali and eastern Java. Browse the day's dishes at the side window and choose your nasi campur from warm vegetable salads, thick curries, spicy sate, and chunks of grilled meats. If you can't decide, look around; other guests will be happy to tell you what they're eating. ✉ *Jl. Sumatra,* ☎ *no phone. No credit cards.*

LODGING

🕮 *following the text of a review is your signal that the property has a Web site, where you will find details and, usually, images; for a link, visit www.fodors.com/urls.*

In southern Bali's circle of tourist towns visitors can find accommodations in enormous thatch-roof luxury villas with private plunge pools, tiny back-alley losmen rooms with fan and shared bath, and everything in between. But because hotels are much less expensive than comparable lodgings in the West—and because the island is still struggling to reclaim tourists lost during the last decade's political and economic crises—you'll find bargains in every town. Southern Bali is the place to splurge on accommodations, because for the price of a boring room in a midrange beach hotel, you may be able to get a charming private home. There are thousands of lodging options in the region, each offering unique bonuses, so carefully consider the amenities you need before making a decision.

The popular choice of savvy travelers to Bali has become the private villa rather than the upscale international hotel. Villas can range from sprawling, 10-bedroom beachside estates to intimate hilltop hideaways or quiet bungalows tucked away in rice fields. Most have the same facilities as the large hotels, including air-conditioning, modern electronics and entertainment systems, pools, laundry service, and cars with drivers. The majority also employ full-time staff who will arrange everything for you, from grocery shopping and daily meals to travel and business arrangements and special events. Because many villas have meeting rooms, computers, faxes, and Internet access, they're also excellent for executive gatherings or for businesspeople attending conferences elsewhere on the island. Most important, in a villa you're not just another tourist squeezed into a package hotel; you have your own tropical home with a corresponding level of comfort, service, and privacy—a perfect arrangement for families. You can find villas in nearly every price range, from $25 to $2,500 a night; they're a particularly good bargain if you're sharing with a few other couples or another family or using the rooms as a base for employees on a business excursion.

Most villa owners rely on an outside rental agent to take bookings for them. Bali's major villa rental agency is the efficient and reliable **Indovillas** (✉ Jl. Daksina 5, Batu Belig, Kerobokan, ☎ 0811/392985,

52

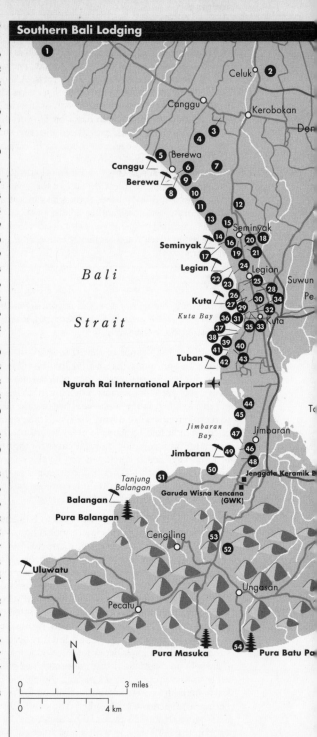

Southern Bali Lodging

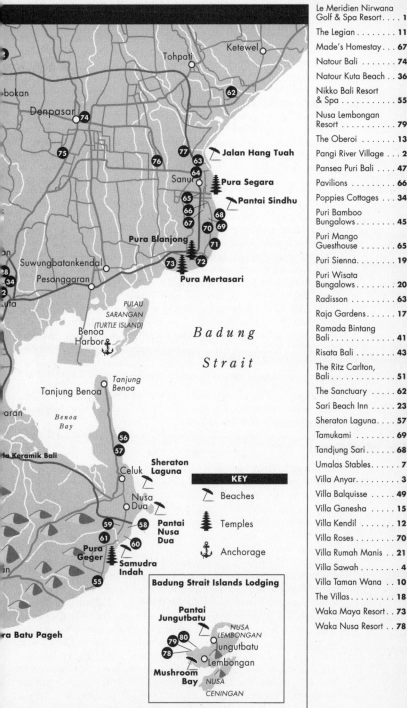

Ketewel

Tohpati

bokan

Denpasar

74

75

76

77

62

63 **Jalan Hang Tuah**

Sanur

64

Pura Segara

65

Pantai Sindhu

66

68

67

70 **69**

Pura Blanjong

71

an

Suwungbatankendal

73 **72**

34

Pesanggaran

Pura Mertasari

uta

*PULAU
SARANGAN
(TURTLE ISLAND)*

Badung

Benoa
Harbor

Strait

Tanjung
Benoa

Tanjung Benoa

aran

*Benoa
Bay*

a Keramik Bali

56

57

Celuk

**Sheraton
Laguna**

KEY

Beaches

Nusa
Dua

Temples

59

58

**Pantai
Nusa
Dua**

Anchorage

61

60

**Pura
Geger**

**Samudra
Indah**

55

Badung Strait Islands Lodging

ra Batu Pageh

**Pantai
Jungutbatu**

*NUSA
LEMBONGAN*

80

79

Jungutbatu

78

Lembongan

**Mushroom
Bay**

*NUSA
CENINGAN*

☎ ℻ 0361/733031, ✍). Many private villas listed in this chapter—all of which are top picks in their price ranges—use Indovillas as their booking contact. If you're interested in renting one of these villas, take a look at the Indovillas Web site, where your options are shown in full color with all the details. You can also have Indovillas's travel division do the planning for you, from booking accommodations to coordinating a personal cook and guide, a rental car, and tours and activities. Just e-mail the agency with your proposed dates of travel, the amenities you desire, and some ideas about what you'd like to do while you're there. Even if you'd like to stay in a traditional resort or hotel, Indovillas can provide deeply discounted accommodation and tour packages with Bali's best-known hotels and adventure companies, at prices from budget to ultra-expensive.

As for where to stay in southern Bali, if you'd like quieter lodgings, look north to the private villas around Kerobokan down through Seminyak, and south to the villas of Jimbaran. If you enjoy the constant buzz of activity in crowded hotels, you'll find plenty to choose from. The tourist hotels are clustered in Legian, Kuta, and Tuban, as are most of the small losmen—usually offering just a simple room with a bed, fan, and shared bath—preferred by budget travelers. The coasts of Jimbaran and the Bukit Peninsula are lined with luxury resort estates, although there are a few simpler hotels tucked into the alleys. Sanur has a mix of resorts, small hotels, and cheap losmen. The Badung Strait Islands have several midsize resorts and a handful of small hotels. Denpasar only attracts visitors on quick business trips, and thus it has only a half-dozen bland hotels; even if you plan to be in the city every day, your stay will be much more enjoyable if you base yourself in a nearby suburb, such as Sanur or Kerobokan.

All rooms in the listed hotels have bathrooms with tubs and hot water, unless otherwise noted. For general information and price categories, *see* Lodging *in* Smart Travel Tips.

The West Coast

Seminyak and North

$$$$ ☷ **Ele Bianco.** This two-story Italianate mansion sits at the edge of the sea near Berewa Beach. The spacious rooms are luxurious yet casual, tranquil amid the sounds of tumbling green waves and wind in the palm trees. Owners Giorgio and Pamela Kauten keep the decor tasteful and simple, adorning the graceful home with handwoven ikat and batik fabrics in shades of maroon, brown, and navy. The five light-filled bedrooms have floor-to-ceiling windows, polished plank floors, and oversize antique furnishings, including hand-carved teak canopy beds and wardrobes. The grand marble bathrooms have double sinks, dipping-pool-size sunken bathtubs with double showers, and adjacent teak walk-in closets. On the ground floor, the central living area is spacious and open, with a large-screen entertainment center and pool table. A long, open dining area—connected to the separate kitchen building by a bridge over a koi pond—is perfect for dinner parties. The breezy upstairs sitting area and terrace overlook the grassy palm grove, deep pool, tennis court, and beach. An organic garden provides the European-trained cooks with ingredients for gourmet fare such as spinach tortellini, baked fish, and homemade ice cream. The professional staff of 24 can service every whim, from assisting with shopping to whipping up an elegant dinner party at a moment's notice. At press time a spa, sauna, and fitness center were in the works. ⊠ *Berewa (Indovillas, Jl. Daksina 5, Kerobokan);* ☎ *0811/392985 for Indovillas reservation agency;* ☎ ℻ *0361/733031 to Indovillas. 5 rooms. Dining room, air-condition-*

ing, room service, pool, massage, tennis court, beach, billiards, baby-sitting, laundry service, travel services, car rental, free parking. MC, V. BP. ⊛

$$$$ ★ 🏨 **Hotel Tugu Bali.** The island's most memorable hotel is 11 km (8 mi) west of Denpasar in a bucolic landscape of rolling hills and rice paddies on the Indian Ocean. Nearly everything you see here is part of Balinese and Indonesian history—from the ornately carved teak doors and window frames and the reconstructed ancient Chinese temple to the 39 *boma* (faces) looking down from teak columns (39 is the number needed to show respect to and ask protection from the wrath of the gods). Each two-story villa has a back terrace with a plunge pool. Inside, you'll find marble floors, huge canopy beds, and exquisite antiques. Bath and toilet areas are small but have winning touches like stained-glass windows. You can also stay in (or just tour) the Puri Le Mayeur bungalow, a monument to Belgian artist A. J. Le Mayeur de Merpres, or the Pavilion, modeled after artist Walter Spies's home at the palace in Yogyakarta, Java. Other on-site attractions include an art gallery, the Puputan Museum, and a traditional medicine and spice stall. Even if you don't stay here, pop in for the delightful tea at the small Tugu Restaurant: crispy rice cakes, fried tempeh, spring rolls, fresh-fruit tarts, and chocolate cake squares. Don't miss the ginger tea—truly refreshing on a hot afternoon. ⊠ *Jl. Batu Bolong, Canggu,* ☎ *0361/731701,* ℻ *0361/731704. 25 villas. 2 restaurants, bar, air-conditioning, room service, pool, massage, spa, library, baby-sitting, laundry service, business services, meeting rooms, travel services, car rental, free parking. AE, MC, V. EP.*

$$$$ 🏨 **The Oberoi.** At the far-western end of Legian Beach, the Oberoi's 15 acres offer tranquillity and privacy. Guest quarters dot the gardens of bougainvillea, hibiscus, and frangipani. The thatched cottages have verandas, the villas have balconies and garden courtyards, and some of the luxury villas have private pools; all have traditional Balinese inner courtyards. Rooms are decorated with hand-carved teak furnishings and locally made silk-screen prints. Balinese dance is performed in the resort's amphitheater two or three evenings a week. Before the show, dine beneath the bamboo ceiling of the Kura Kura restaurant, where a Swiss chef and a Balinese sous-chef turn out an Indonesian buffet and à la carte items with a Continental flair. The bebek betutu is a standout dish. ⊠ *Jl. Kayu Aya, Basangkasa, Kerobokan (Box 3351, Denpasar 80033),* ☎ *0361/730361; 800/562–3764 in the U.S.;* ℻ *0361/730391. 60 cottages, 13 villas. Restaurant, bar, café, air-conditioning, in-room data ports, in-room safes, room service, pool, massage, sauna, spa, tennis court, health club, beach, windsurfing, shops, billiards, theater, baby-sitting, laundry service, business services, meeting rooms, travel services, car rental, free parking. AE, DC, MC, V. EP.* ⊛

$$$–$$$$ 🏨 **Bali Imperial.** This opulent glass-and-marble hotel has a distinct Japanese style, and it's just a 10-minute walk from Legian's shops. Rooms have high ceilings, light-wood furniture, shining wood floors, balconies that face the sea or the garden, and marble baths with separate showers. The resort is under the same management as the Imperial Hotel in Tokyo, and there's an emphasis on service (the staff-to-guest ratio is three to one). If you ring your butler for complimentary coffee or tea, he'll no doubt bring it to you immediately. ⊠ *Jl. Dhyanapura, Seminyak (Box 3384, Denpasar 80001);* ☎ *0361/754545; 212/692–9001 in the U.S.; 020/7355–1775 in the U.K.;* ℻ *0361/751545. 121 rooms, 17 bungalows. 2 restaurants, air-conditioning, room service, 2 pools, massage, 2 tennis courts, beach, baby-sitting, laundry service, travel services, car rental, free parking. AE, DC, MC, V. EP.*

$$$-$$$$ ⊡ **The Legian.** The stark Japanese style of the Legian will appeal to anyone who wants total serenity. Not a hint of bright color disturbs the muted brown, black, and white that highlight the sharp angles and rich wood trim of the three-story resort. Cool, elegant apartment-style suites are the ultimate in sleek, modern decor, with dark parquet floors, muted gray and grape cushions, and heavy wood trim. The terrace restaurant and pool overlook a white sand beach. ⊠ *Jl. Laksmana, Kerobokan 80361,* ☎ *0361/730622,* ℻ *0361/730623. 70 suites. Restaurant, bar, air-conditioning, minibars, room service, massage, pool, spa, health club, beach, baby-sitting, laundry service, business services, meeting rooms, travel services, car rental, free parking. AE, DC, MC, V. EP.*

$$$-$$$$ ⊡ **Le Meridien Nirwana Golf & Spa Resort.** Carved into the folds of Bali's southwestern coastline, this luxury resort fronts the island's newest and most spectacular golf course. Rooms have plush modern furnishings and Balinese art; even standard rooms have minibars, glass-wall showers, and wooden shutters that open the bathtub area to the rest of the room. The suites are apartment-size, with a desk and sitting area, separate bedroom, walk-in closet, and sumptuous marble bath. Twelve villas—six with one bedroom, six with two—each have a private plunge pool, terrace, courtyard with sitting pavilion, and garden shower. Pura Tanah Lot sits just below the estate, and ocean vistas are an essential part of dinner at the opulent Cendana restaurant (☞ Dining, *above*). Reserve a terrace table next to the duck pond for sunset views. ⊠ *Jl. Kediri, Canggu (Box 198, Tanah Lot 82171),* ☎ *0361/815900,* ℻ *0361/815901. 245 rooms, 21 suites, 12 villas. 2 restaurants, bar, grill, lobby lounge, air-conditioning, minibars, room service, 3 pools, massage, spa, 18-hole golf course, 2 tennis courts, health club, beach, baby-sitting, children's programs, laundry service, business services, meeting rooms, travel services, car rental, free parking. AE, DC, MC, V. EP.* ✍

$$$-$$$$ ⊡ **Villa Taman Wana.** After the rough drive from the airport to northern Kerobokan, step into the Taman Wana luxurious garden sanctuary. Cobbled paths lead through lush grounds under the shade of banana and coconut trees to ivy-laden stone archways with antique temple doors. Inside this jungle garden are three villa complexes. Villa Sumba's two separate bungalows are connected to the main living area by skylit boardwalks. The larger bungalow has two bedrooms, each with bath, and the single bungalow faces an 18 m lap pool. Villa Tioman has two single bungalows; one faces gardens, and the other faces a pool with a children's play area. Villa Lamu is a magnificent three-bedroom home with sweeping views of the forest. The free-form pool is an impressive feat of design, with a shallow beach end and a bridge arching over its middle. The master bedroom has a pool bubbling along the length of its deck; the single bedroom has a separate entrance; and the loft bedroom (not air-conditioned) has a marvelous "living picture window" of the surrounding foliage. The upstairs living area, connected to the lower level by a suspension bridge, is comfortable and spacious, with a wraparound couch and pool table. Each villa features modern kitchens, a dining and bar area, and garden bathrooms with huge terrazzo tubs. In addition to the three main villas, there are two smaller guest villas with showers only. The top-notch staff is unobtrusive yet ready to tend to your needs at a moment's notice. Airport transfers, laundry, a personal cook, shopping services, and other amenities are included in the price. Children are welcome, and you can take professional cooking classes on-site. ⊠ *Batu Belig, Kerobokan (Indovillas, Jl. Daksina 5, Kerobokan);* ☎ *0811/392985 for Indovillas reservation agency;* ☎ ℻ *0361/733031 to Indovillas. 7 rooms, 1 house. Dining room, air-conditioning (some), room service, 4 pools, massage, billiards, baby-sitting, laundry service, travel services, car rental, free parking. MC, V. BP.* ✍

$$-$$$$ ⊡ **Pangi River Village.** This collection of villas that spills over the hills
of Kerobokan has the elite, private feel of a gated community. Inside
high stone walls, separate estates provide the perfect environment for
business gatherings and families. Villa Pangi Gita, which has three dou-
ble-bed bungalows and three living-area pavilions, is the most formal,
with stark decor, wood floors, and antiques. Villa Frangipani has a larger
main building with three bedrooms and an indoor-outdoor living area
that looks out to a pool. Villa Bunga Wangi is casual and simple, with
polished wood floors, large bathrooms with sunken white tubs, a sep-
arate two-level office and bedroom, a raised *lumbung*-style (thatch-roof,
barn-shape) playhouse, and a comfortable sitting pavilion. This villa can
be connected to the Villa Bougainvillea complex next door, a family-
friendly place complete with toys for the pool. Although the estates are
close enough together to accommodate a large group, each complex is
separate and quite private. ⊠ *Kerobokan (Indovillas, Jl. Daksina 5, Ker-
obokan);* ☎ *0811/392985 for Indovillas reservation agency;* ☎ FAX
*0361/733031 to Indovillas. 5 villas. 5 dining rooms, air-conditioning,
room service, 5 pools, massage, baby-sitting, laundry service, travel ser-
vices, car rental, free parking. MC, V. EP.* ◈

$$-$$$$ ⊡ **Puri Sienna.** Located down a narrow alley between Seminyak's
main strip of shops and the beach, this villa is perfect for small groups
of friends, active couples, or families that want to explore, as well as
for business travelers who need access to the main roads but want a
quiet haven at the end of the day. Puri Sienna shows off owner James
Crow's building expertise and the travel industry experience of manager I Made Yudiantara. It's the little touches that make it stand out
from the other villas in the heart of Seminyak: soaps, shampoos, and
soft towels in the bathrooms; umbrellas, flashlights, and mosquito spray
in the large walk-in closets; Balinese-crafted notebooks and pens beside the beds. A lush lawn spreads out from the large central pool to
the main house, which has an upstairs bedroom and office, an open
downstairs dining room, a full kitchen, and a comfortable, well-
equipped living area. Six villas—four with three bedrooms, one with
two, and one with one—all have luxury bathrooms (with showers only)
and kitchens; all but the single have plunge pools. There's also an open,
thatch-roof dining pavilion next to the main pool with barbecue and
kitchen facilities. Across the alley, a new complex houses two-bedroom
Mediterranean apartments with large living, dining, and kitchen areas,
laundry rooms, private plunge pools on the first floor, and upstairs bedrooms. Breakfast and lunch are included in the price. ⊠ *Seminyak (Indovillas, Jl. Daksina 5, Kerobokan);* ☎ *0811/392985 for Indovillas
reservation agency;* ☎ FAX *0361/733031 to Indovillas. 7 villas, 13
apartments. Dining room, air-conditioning, in-room safes, refrigerators, room service, 2 pools, massage, baby-sitting, laundry service, travel
services, car rental, free parking. MC, V. BP.* ◈

$$-$$$$ ⊡ **Villa Anyar.** The Italianate look and Asian lines of this three-story
villa aren't the only reasons it's one of the most architecturally inter-
esting sites on the island: you can't help but notice its octagonal, top-
floor viewing pavilion that looks out over the Kerobokan rice fields
just at the height of the trees. The Australian owner's sense of fun is
evident in the long deck, which extends around three sides of the
house and has a pool table and entertainment and barbecue areas. The
downstairs has a kitchen, dining room, two bedrooms, and a spacious
bathroom with a sunken blue-terrazzo tub in a lush, private garden.
One of the bedrooms can be closed off to make a separate apartment,
and the lower area can be partitioned off from the wide foyer and stair-
case that lead to the second floor. Upstairs, the open-style living area
has a modern kitchen and bar, a huge daybed, and a deck overlook-

ing the rice fields. A bedroom to the side has a bathroom (with shower only), and a second bath with a tub sits off the living room. Up another flight of carved wooden stairs, in the octagonal tower, is the master bedroom, with a private (shower-only) bath and ocean-to-volcano views. First-class service, a trained private chef, a convenient location, and a tranquil setting make this a good pick if you want to get away from it all yet stay within reach of the action. ⊠ *Kerobokan (Indovillas, Jl. Daksina 5, Kerobokan);* ☎ *0811/392985 for Indovillas reservation agency;* ☎ FAX *0361/733031 to Indovillas. 4 rooms. Dining room, air-conditioning, room service, pool, massage, baby-sitting, laundry service, travel services, car rental, free parking. MC, V. BP.* ☜

$$–$$$$ 🏠 **Villa Sawah.** Lying in the verdant hills of Kerobokan, this clean, cozy country house, owned by a French novelist and lawyer, has a warmth that welcomes you immediately. A covered wooden walkway forms a bridge between the main house and a three-bedroom annex, all with floor-to-ceiling windows framing the rice fields. The sunny, spacious main building has a comfortable living area, a long dining table, and a modern kitchen, as well as two small bedrooms and a full bath. Glass walls slide open to reveal the large terrace, which has a full view of a sapphire-tile pool that runs along the outline of the rice terraces below it. In the annex, the master bedroom is nestled between a children's room (with three antique beds and lots of toys) and a guest bedroom; all have large outdoor bathrooms with enormous terrazzo tubs and garden showers. Throughout the villa, walls and floors are sponge-painted soft gold, and the ceilings are crossed by old whitewashed beams. In fact, the entire frame, built of sturdy wood, was imported from old houses on Java. Complementing the weathered teak and rural French coloring are antique Javanese pieces in matching muted colors that were hand-picked by the owner. A children's *bale* (Balinese-style raised pavilion) sits next to the pool. This is a wonderful place for families, with the comfort and privacy of home and a location close to beaches and cultural activities. ⊠ *Kerobokan (Indovillas, Jl. Daksina 5, Kerobokan);* ☎ *0811/392985 for Indovillas reservation agency;* ☎ FAX *0361/ 733031 to Indovillas. 5 rooms. Dining room, air-conditioning, room service, pool, massage, baby-sitting, laundry service, travel services, car rental, free parking. MC, V. BP.* ☜

$$–$$$ 🏠 **Umalas Stables.** This wonderful little hotel is one of Bali's best hidden delights. Walk through the entrance to find an enclosed courtyard lined with gardens and fountains, with a large free-form pool and a restaurant at the opposite end. Forming the left flank of the compound is a long two-story building. At ground level a line of stables houses bright-eyed horses; above are surprisingly elegant rooms. Guest quarters are done up in green floral fabrics and have high ceilings, green sectional couches, and compact desk areas. Bathrooms, though shower only, are large and accented with marble, with windows looking out to the surrounding rice fields. There are modern conveniences as well, including telephones, TVs, and minibars in every room. Most guests come to ride, though, for owners Ralf and Sabine Kaufmann have brought years of experience with them from Germany. Their horses are imported from all over the international circuit and receive first-class, round-the-clock care. A riding ring is next to the stables, and an indoor-outdoor arena is in back of the restaurant. Once a month on Sunday the owners host a daylong children's party, to which kids of all ages are invited to spend the day with the horses, play in the pool, and have fun at the playground. The restaurant, open 8–5 daily, has a limited menu, but what's there is good: pasta, curry, Indonesian dishes, and simple breakfast selections. ⊠ *Umalas, Kerobokan (Indovillas, Jl. Daksina 5, Kerobokan);* ☎ *0811/392985 for Indovillas*

★

reservation agency; ☎ FAX *0361/733031 to Indovillas. 4 rooms, 1 suite. Restaurant, air-conditioning, minibars, room service, pool, massage, horseback riding, baby-sitting, playground, laundry service, travel services, car rental, free parking. MC, V. BP.* ✍

$$-$$$ 🏠 **The Villas.** This eclectic congregation of bungalows with a seemingly clandestine location down a back lane in Seminyak is a unique alternative to traditional Bali accommodations. Its trademark is a blue-and-white yin-yang symbol, and the secluded, sexy ambience makes this a favorite of the young, rich, and single. There's no formal reception office, and the 7 one-bedroom and 15 three-bedroom villas are hidden behind a long, scalloped purple wall and wood doors marked with masks. Each two-story villa opens to lush, circular gardens and has a kidney-shape pool—with a yin-yang symbol under the water—a full kitchen, an upstairs daybed, and downstairs living and dining areas with dark furnishings. Next to the main villa, separate bedroom bungalows with garden bathrooms are surrounded by glass walls that look out to the pool. There's no restaurant, but the villas are down the street from the elite dining establishments of Seminyak. The Taj Mahal–style spa, with its intimate Indian architecture and colors, is one of the best on Bali. ✉ *Jl. Kunti 118, Seminyak,* ☎ FAX *0361/730840. 22 villas. Air-conditioning, refrigerators, room service, pool, massage, spa, baby-sitting, laundry service, travel services, car rental, free parking. AE, DC, MC, V. EP.* ✍

$$ 🏠 **Villa Rumah Manis.** The name means "Sweet House," and these luxury accommodations are just that: comfortable, convenient, private—and reasonably priced. Individual two-story, bungalow-style houses are gathered into a village connected by winding walkways yet separated by high stone privacy walls covered with ivy and blossoming vines. Enter a villa through one of the archways, and you'll find a garden sitting area with a beautiful plunge pool; inside, the lower floor has a bedroom, sitting area, and bathroom, while upstairs is a cozier bedroom under thatched eaves. Although the villas are filled with colorful, sturdy antiques, there are also TVs, refrigerators, and desks on both floors. The upstairs bath has a deep tub and sink of soft green terrazzo, while the downstairs bath has an outdoor shower that opens to the plunge pool. A larger pool, with a waterfall tumbling from stone dragons, separates the villas from the restaurant area and pool bar. The beautiful family villa—with a private pool and outdoor Jacuzzi, a full kitchen and pantry, three large bedrooms, and a private exit to the parking lot—is a steal. ✉ *Jl. Nakula 18, Seminyak,* ☎ *0361/730606,* FAX *0361/730505. 48 villas. Restaurant, bar, air-conditioning, refrigerators, room service, pool, massage, baby-sitting, laundry service, travel services, car rental, free parking. AE, DC, MC, V. EP.*

$-$$ 🏠 **Villa Ganesha.** This octagon-shape villa in the center of Seminyak was originally a bamboo house designed by a world-renowned fashion designer. The three-story main house—which was twice rebuilt and recently refined to luxury standards—includes a ground floor divided into living, dining, sleeping, and bathing quarters. Interestingly, the central dome is modeled after a spider; the eight "legs" of thick balsa, along with the ceiling and the floor, are inlaid with mother-of-pearl. The open second-floor apartment, all decked out in rich *bengkerai* wood, has a huge canopy bed, a double-sided wardrobe, a desk, and a private bath. The third-floor loft, up a wooden spiral staircase, has windows all around it and a skylight. A curving, stone-tile pool fronts the home, and four adjacent villas encircle it. Each two-bedroom villa has first-floor bedrooms with floor-to-ceiling windows, enormous canopy beds, and luxurious shower-only bathrooms; an upstairs living area and kitchen; and a plunge pool. Each one-bedroom villa has a front terrace, a pavilion kitchen, and a large sunken tub. The decor is highlighted by an excel-

lent collection of originals and prints by internationally known artists
Davina Stephens and Ashley Bickerton. Villa Ganesha is surrounded
by high privacy walls and conveniently located between the beach and
the shops. ✉ *Seminyak (Indovillas, Jl. Daksina 5, Kerobokan);* ☎ *0811/
392985 for Indovillas reservation agency;* ☎ FAX *0361/733031 to Indovillas. 4 villas, 1 house. Air-conditioning, refrigerators, room service, pool, massage, exercise room, baby-sitting, laundry service, travel
services, car rental, free parking. MC, V. EP.* ✜

$ ☷ **Ananda Bungalows.** If you want to stay on the beach in the north
and need extra space, these bungalows are a nice choice. Cream-color
buildings with terra-cotta roofs are surrounded by sculpted gardens
awash in pink blossoms. Choose from several layouts: Each two-story
Alamanda or Aselia bungalow has a living room, downstairs and upstairs bedrooms, a full kitchen, and two bathrooms. The Akasia studio, with one bedroom and an office, and the two-bedroom, two-bath
Akasia bungalow have Balinese and Javanese trimmings. ✉ *Jl. Kayu
Aya, Basangkasa, Kerobokan,* ☎ *0361/730526,* FAX *0361/731563. 12
bungalows. Restaurant, bar, air-conditioning, room service, pool, massage, sauna, spa, mountain bikes, shops, library, baby-sitting, laundry
service, business services, travel services, car rental, free parking. AE,
DC, MC, V. BP.* ✜

$ ☷ **Bolare.** If you want to escape the tourist frenzy of Seminyak and
places south but not pay resort prices, try this refreshing beachside hotel
in Canggu. The feel is that of a Mediterranean holiday spot: casual,
European, and right on a lovely stretch of golden, shell-strewn beach.
White brick bungalows with terra-cotta roofs house simple, bright rooms
with gem-color floral bedspreads, white tile floors, comfortable bamboo furniture, and plenty of windows to let in the western light. All
rooms have corner porches, kitchenettes, minibars, and large bathrooms
with tubs; suites have dark parquet floors and corner tubs. The pool
and play area are great for children by day, but it's the fantastic sunset panorama that brings most guests back again. ✉ *Bj. Berewa,
Canggu (Box 3256, Canggu),* ☎ *0361/730258,* FAX *0361/731663. 20
rooms, 8 suites. Restaurant, 2 bars, air-conditioning, kitchenettes,
minibars, room service, pool, massage, beach, baby-sitting, laundry service, travel services, car rental, free parking. AE, DC, MC, V. EP.*

$ ☷ **Sari Beach Inn.** From this budget inn set amid the expensive hotels
of Seminyak, it's just a walk through the breezy gardens and across
the street to the beach. Inside the thatch-roof buildings are rooms with
bamboo furniture, ikat bedspreads, woven floor mats, and full baths;
deluxe rooms have air-conditioning, minibars, and large marble bathrooms. All rooms have a porch or balcony sitting area. The European
and Australian clientele keeps things lively. ✉ *Jl. Padma Utara,
Seminyak (Box 2090, Seminyak),* ☎ FAX *0361/751635. 24 rooms.
Restaurant, bar, air-conditioning (some), room service, 2 pools, massage, baby-sitting, laundry service, travel services, car rental, free parking. AE, DC, MC, V. EP.*

$ ☷ **Villa Kendil.** At the north end of the main Seminyak road, within
walking distance of top neighborhood restaurants, lies this cluster of
two-story villas. The tree-shaded central pool, dining-bar area, and travel
office are separated from the surrounding guest buildings by a 10-ft-
thick wall. Each two-story villa has a private entrance leading to a secluded garden and covered exterior kitchen and dining area, a large
sitting room, an indoor bathroom with a sunken tub, an outdoor garden shower, and a romantic upstairs bedroom with a small balcony
and half-bath. With a friendly staff, this is a great option for families
on a budget. ✉ *Jl. Seminyak, Seminyak (Indovillas, Jl. Daksina 5, Kerobokan);* ☎ *0811/392985 for Indovillas reservation agency;* ☎ FAX *0361/*

733031 to Indovillas. 10 villas. Restaurant, bar, air-conditioning (some), minibars, room service, pool, massage, baby-sitting, laundry service, travel services, car rental, free parking. MC, V. EP.

¢ ▣ **Raja Gardens.** This is one of the region's best budget places, a little hotel within 10 minutes' walk of shops to the east and the beach to the west. The two-story complex is surrounded by rock gardens and strung with long vines, its quiet gardens kept company by the roaming house dog. Large rooms have canopy beds and brick tile floors. The downstairs rooms have lovely garden bathrooms but no hot water; if you prefer more contemporary accoutrements, it's just $5 more for an upstairs room with modern bath. All rooms have porches that overlook the 18 m pool. ⊠ *Jl. Abimanyu, Seminyak,* ☎ *0361/730494,* FAX *0361/732805. 6 rooms. Air-conditioning, room service, pool, massage, baby-sitting, laundry service, travel services, car rental, free parking. AE, DC, MC, V. EP.*

Legian

$$–$$$ ▣ **Alam KulKul.** A sunny resort redolent of sea breezes, the beachfront Alam KulKul has the quiet ambience of a Balinese village yet is in the heart of the west coast's tourist towns. Cottages and bungalows are gathered in cozy tropical gardens and kept private by high stone walls; standard rooms are in a large building at the back of the property. The breathtaking Bali villa, decorated with Balinese antiques, has a garden bathroom with a sunken tub, as well as a private garden and a little plunge pool. The two Java suites are decorated with beautiful island antiques, including canopy beds and huge wardrobes, and have large bathrooms with garden tubs. Superior suites have contemporary furnishings, green terrazzo floors and counters, and garden sitting areas— but note that because the rooms are all the same, those with the added view of the two-tier pool aren't really worth the higher price. Each of the two large Family Rooms has a sitting area, two extra beds, and big bathrooms. In front, the renovated Papa's Café serves exquisite Mediterranean cuisine. ⊠ *Jl. Pantai (Box 3097, Legian 80030),* ☎ *0361/752520,* FAX *0361/752519. 57 rooms, 23 villas. 2 restaurants, bar, air-conditioning, refrigerators, room service, 2 pools, beauty salon, massage, spa, shops, baby-sitting, children's programs, laundry service, business services, travel services, car rental, free parking. AE, DC, MC, V. EP.*

$$–$$$ ▣ **Bali Padma.** Sitting on a vast lawn under coconut trees across from the beach, this large hotel caters to a European clientele and feels more intimate than the international chains. Rooms have parquet floors, sand-color walls hung with Indonesian artwork, and soft floral bedspreads. The pavilion bar facing the ocean gets busy at sunset, and the elegant Taman Ayun Coffee House (☞ *Dining, above*) is a sleek spot for afternoon tea or after-dinner coffee and dessert to live jazz tunes. ⊠ *Jl. Padma (Box 1107, Legian),* ☎ *0361/752111,* FAX *0361/752140. 400 rooms. Restaurant, bar, coffee shop, air-conditioning, refrigerators, room service, pool, massage, spa, health club, beach, shops, baby-sitting, laundry service, business services, travel services, car rental, free parking. AE, DC, MC, V. EP.*

$$–$$$ ▣ **Jayakarta Hotel & Residence.** This enormous property lies steps from the beach and shops and has both hotel rooms and rental apartments. Rooms mix contemporary furnishings with Balinese decor; each has either a balcony or a terrace. Each apartment also has a kitchenette with a microwave and dishes and a sofa bed in the living room. ⊠ *Jl. Werkudara (Box 3244, Legian),* ☎ *0361/751433,* FAX *0361/752074. 271 rooms, 7 suites, 127 1-bedroom apartments, 20 2-bedroom apartments. 3 restaurants, 3 bars, coffee shop, air-conditioning, kitchenettes (some), refrigerators, room service, 3 pools, beauty salon, massage, sauna,*

tennis court, health club, mountain bikes, baby-sitting, playground, laundry service, business services, meeting rooms, travel services, car rental, free parking. AE, DC, MC, V. EP.

$$–$$$ ☒ **Risata Bali.** White tile floors, creamy brick walls and curtains, and splashy floral spreads of forest green and plum give the rooms in this small all-suites hotel a clean, modern feel. Deluxe rooms have terraces, and superior rooms have inner sitting areas. Each suite has contemporary furnishings with stylish Bali accents, and all have refrigerators and tubs. ☒ *Jl. Jenggala (Box 3207, Legian),* ☎ *0361/753340,* 𝔽𝔸𝕏 *0361/ 753354. 120 rooms, 26 suites. Restaurant, bar, lobby lounge, air-conditioning, refrigerators, room service, pool, massage, shop, baby-sitting, laundry service, travel services, car rental, free parking. AE, DC, MC, V. EP.*

$ ☒ **Amarta Bungalows.** At these new "boutique bungalows" on a quiet
★   street just down the lane from the beach, you can enjoy the atmosphere and luxury of a small private villa at a budget price. Centered around a stunning kidney-shape pool of sapphire blue, this collection of two-story thatch-roof bungalows has the graceful feel of a Balinese village. Tropical gardens flow around the outer walls of each villa; inside you'll find golden trim, hand-carved wooden furniture, and antique four-poster beds. Spacious garden bathrooms have stacked limestone-rock walls, deep bathtubs of mauve terrazzo, and lemon-color outdoor showers with sky-blue pebble floors. All villas have kitchenettes with microwaves and refrigerators, and breakfast and a daily fruit basket are included in the price. The hotel is willing to give deep discounts, so don't be afraid to ask. ☒ *Jl. Abimanyu 2000X, 80361,* ☎ 𝔽𝔸𝕏 *0361/ 734793. 8 villas. Air-conditioning, kitchenettes, refrigerators, room service, pool, wading pool, massage, baby-sitting, laundry service, travel services, car rental, free parking. AE, DC, MC, V. BP.*

¢   ☒ **Dewi Sri.** On a quiet lane in the middle of Legian, this surprising little gem has spent recent months in renovation, and its service and facilities shine anew. The rooms are clean, bright, and modern, with lacy curtains, blue trim, and ceilings overlaid with woven rattan. Amazingly, given the rates, all rooms have air-conditioning, minibars, tubs, phones, and TVs, and since there are just two rooms to a building, each has a large window. A new restaurant and pool were under construction at press time. ☒ *Jl. Legian and Gg. Batu Bolong,* ☎ *0361/751804,* 𝔽𝔸𝕏 *0361/751520. 98 rooms. Restaurant, bar, air-conditioning, refrigerators, room service, pool, massage, baby-sitting, laundry service, travel services, car rental, free parking. AE, DC, MC, V. EP.*

¢   ☒ **Puri Wisata Bungalows.** Walk down the alley leading north from the Goa 2001 cybercafé and through a tall, ivy-laden tunnel to reach an arched temple gate covered with green and gold faces. Inside you'll find a collection of brick-and-stone buildings surrounding a pool, with a used-book library and a bar to one side. The simple rooms at this quiet budget traveler base all have air-conditioning, refrigerators, bamboo furnishings, and porches. Standards are small, plain, and crowded; deluxe rooms have larger bathrooms, marble tubs, kitchen sinks in the main room, and TVs. Breakfast and all the coffee and tea you desire are included. ☒ *Jl. Legian Kaja (Box 1060, Legian),* ☎ *0361/730322,* 𝔽𝔸𝕏 *0361/730385, 27 rooms. Restaurant, bar, air-conditioning, refrigerators, room service, pool, massage, baby-sitting, laundry service, travel services, car rental, free parking. AE, DC, MC, V. BP.*

Kuta and Tuban

$$–$$$$ ☒ **Holiday Inn Resort Balihai.** It may be another Holiday Inn, but it is a nice place on the beach for families with children. Each of the three "Kidsuites" includes a theme bedroom (jungle, pirate, or outer space) equipped with bunks, TV, VCR, and Sony PlayStation—separated by a

sliding door from Mom and Dad's room—as well as a breakfast buffet and a Kid's Club membership. If you're sans children, you might prefer the upgraded facilities and more elegant furnishings of a deluxe room, suite, or villa. ✉ *Jl. Wana Segara 33, Tuban 80361,* ☎ *0361/753035,* FAX *0361/754548. 189 rooms, 8 suites, 2 villas. 2 restaurants, 3 bars, café, air-conditioning, minibars, room service, pool, beauty salon, massage, sauna, spa, tennis court, health club, shops, baby-sitting, children's programs, playground, laundry service, business services, meeting rooms, travel services, car rental, free parking. AE, DC, MC, V. BP.*

$$–$$$$ 🏨 **Kartika Plaza.** All rooms at this enormous Tuban hotel look out over the ocean. Garden bungalows have stone walls, thatch roofs, and wall panels enlivened with simple ink drawings of Balinese mythological characters. Standard rooms have parchment-color walls, rich wood trim, bright green floral spreads, and white tile floors. The facilities are so extensive you never need leave the hotel. ✉ *Jl. Kartika Plz., Tuban (Box 1012, Tuban 80361),* ☎ *0361/754067,* FAX *0361/754585. 294 rooms, 10 suites, 82 bungalows. 4 restaurants, bar, lobby lounge, air-conditioning, in-room safes, refrigerators, room service, 4 pools, massage, 3 tennis courts, health club, jogging track, squash, baby-sitting, children's programs, laundry service, business services, meeting rooms, travel services, car rental, free parking. AE, DC, MC, V. BP.*

$$–$$$$ 🏨 **Kuta Paradiso.** This bone-white building, gleaming in the sunlight, juts into the sky above Tuban Beach. The Kuta Paradiso has a busy, international feel, more like a metropolitan hotel than a place for a vacation. Standard rooms have pale walls and simple Balinese accents; deluxes are done in blue and bronze floral patterns and have polished wood floors, rich wood furniture, and spacious terraces. Windows look out over the lobby on one end and the ocean on the other. If you'd like more privacy, take a thatch-roof bungalow in back, in the coconut grove near the beach. The fabulous free-form pool is studded with rock and garden islands. ✉ *Jl. Kartika Plz., Tuban (Box 1133, Tuban 80361),* ☎ *0361/761414,* FAX *0361/756944. 233 rooms, 10 suites. 2 restaurants, bar, lobby lounge, air-conditioning, room service, pool, massage, health club, beach, baby-sitting, laundry service, business services, meeting rooms, travel services, car rental, free parking. AE, DC, MC, V. BP.*

$$–$$$$ 🏨 **Natour Kuta Beach.** There's nothing special about this large, overpriced, somewhat run-down hotel—other than that it occupies the best spot on Kuta Beach. The Natour can be counted on for cleanliness, excellent service, and lots of activities, and it has a variety of plain rooms and suites to choose from. ✉ *Jl. Pantai 1, Kuta (Box 3393, Kuta 80361),* ☎ *0361/751361,* FAX *0361/751362. 137 rooms. Restaurant, 2 bars, coffee shop, air-conditioning, refrigerators, room service, pool, massage, tennis court, beach, baby-sitting, playground, laundry service, business services, travel services, car rental, free parking. AE, DC, MC, V. BP.*

$$–$$$ 🏨 **Ramada Bintang Bali.** Set back from the road in the heart of Tuban, this international chain hotel has upgraded its facilities to rise a step above the other midrange hotels. With Balinese architecture and modern amenities, it's a stylish, relaxing place for a holiday. Rooms have parquet floors, pastel accents, and Balinese paintings. Everything you need is on-site, but if you want to venture out, the shops and beach are just steps away. ✉ *Jl. Kartika Plz., Tuban (Box 1068, Tuban 80361),* ☎ *0361/753292,* FAX *0361/753288. 391 rooms, 10 suites. Restaurant, 4 bars, coffee shop, lobby lounge, air-conditioning, minibars, room service, pool, beauty salon, hot tub, massage, sauna, 2 tennis courts, health club, shops, recreation room, baby-sitting, laundry service, business services, meeting rooms, travel services, car rental, free parking. AE, DC, MC, V. BP.*

$$ ⛩ **Aneka Beach Hotel** This clean, contemporary midsize hotel sits right on the beach road across from Kuta Beach, the island's most popular sunset-viewing spot. The stone-and-brick buildings have grass roofs and are surrounded by simple gardens. All rooms have refrigerators, and bungalows and suites have TVs. The family suite is actually a three-bedroom house with a living room, kitchen, and private pool. ⊠ *Jl. Pantai, Kuta (Box 2010, Kuta 80361),* ☎ *0361/752067,* ℻ *0361/752892. 39 rooms, 5 bungalows, 9 suites. Restaurant, bar, air-conditioning, refrigerators, room service, pool, massage, baby-sitting, laundry service, business services, travel services, car rental, free parking. AE, DC, MC, V. EP.*

$$ ⛩ **Hotel Bali Rani.** Step through the bustling lobby of this three-story hotel at Tuban's busiest corner into a tropical holiday setting. Comfortable rooms are soaked in warm colors, and each has a terrace or balcony. At the center of the grounds, wicker chairs sit in a library pavilion encircled by a lotus pond—a quiet haven for reading. Next to it are the central free-form pool and tropical gardens cut by winding walkways. This is a nice hotel for families, and it's also a popular place for business travelers who like the combination of a convenient location and a fun, modern atmosphere. ⊠ *Jl. Kartika Plz., Tuban (Box 1034, Tuban 80361),* ☎ *0361/751369,* ℻ *0361/752673. 101 rooms, 3 suites. Restaurant, 2 bars, café, coffee shop, air-conditioning, refrigerators, room service, 2 pools, beauty salon, massage, spa, health club, shops, billiards, library, baby-sitting, playground, laundry service, business services, meeting rooms, travel services, car rental, free parking. AE, DC, MC, V. BP.*

$$ ⛩ **Poppies Cottages.** At Poppies, one of Kuta's top small hotels, you can stay in a traditional thatched cottage for a fraction of the cost of a larger resort. Tucked into fragrant gardens, each cottage has one double bed or two single beds and a large, secluded balcony. Private garden bathrooms have sunken tubs. Pools, with landscaped sunbathing terraces and waterfalls, flow through the garden, and a pavilion houses a small library and game area. Convenience is another advantage here: Kuta's shops and beaches are a five-minute walk down the road. ⊠ *Poppies La., Kuta (Box 3378, Denpasar 80033),* ☎ *0361/751059,* ℻ *0361/752364. 20 cottages. 2 restaurants, bar, air-conditioning, room service, 2 pools, massage, library, baby-sitting, laundry service, travel services, car rental, free parking. AE, DC, MC, V. BP.*

$-$$ ⛩ **Green Garden Bali.** Also known as the Puri Hijau (Green Palace), this small hotel sits behind the Tuban shopping strip and the popular Green Garden restaurant (☞ Dining, *above*), a pleasant haven in the midst of the neighborhood's shops, restaurants, and nightlife. Rooms are centered around a pool, where a waterfall tumbles from a high, rocky escarpment frothing with greenery. The decor is simple: white tile floors, floral spreads, and wood trim. All rooms have desks, TVs, refrigerators, and bathtubs. The attached spa adds to the busy international feel of the place. ⊠ *Jl. Kartika Plz. 9, Tuban 80361,* ☎ *0361/761023,* ℻ *0361/754570. 25 rooms. Restaurant, bar, air-conditioning, refrigerators, room service, pool, beauty salon, massage, spa, baby-sitting, laundry service, business services, travel services, car rental, free parking. AE, DC, MC, V. BP.*

$ ⛩ **Bali Sumer Hotel.** This casual two-story hotel lies at the center of Kuta near the Matahari shopping complex, within a five-minute walk of the beach. Rooms are quiet and clean, with bamboo furnishings, Indonesian decor, and a businesslike green-and-brown color scheme. Standard rooms are upstairs and have hot water and tubs; for $5–$10 more, first-floor deluxe rooms have TVs and refrigerators. All rooms have patios. Next to the pool sits the restaurant, which serves inexpensive Indonesian and Western fare. ✉ *Jl. Pantai 38, Kuta 80361,* ☎ *0361/751503,* ℻ *0361/755637. 48 rooms. Restaurant, bar, air-conditioning, room service, pool, massage, baby-sitting, laundry service, travel services, car rental, free parking. AE, DC, MC, V. EP.*

¢–$ ▦ **Bounty Cottages.** Set back in an alley between the beach and the shops, this large hotel caters to a more upscale, well-traveled crowd than most other area accommodations. It's affordable, though, and the rooms are nicer than most in this class. Two separate sections of rooms are connected by a breezy walkway under an ivy-covered trellis; one side has a cool, quiet feel, while the other, with the pool and 24-hour bar, has more activity. All rooms have desks, pastel bedspreads, lacy curtains, and private balconies overlooking the pool or garden. For families there are seven triple rooms and two quadruples. ✉ *Jl. Segara Batu Bolong 18, Kuta (Box 2064, Kuta 80361),* ☎ *0361/753030,* ℻ *0361/752121. 100 rooms. Restaurant, bar, air-conditioning, minibars, room service, pool, massage, baby-sitting, laundry service, travel services, car rental, free parking. AE, DC, MC, V. EP.*

¢–$ ▦ **Bounty Hotel.** This rowdy place in central Kuta is for those who like to party, and the action here lasts 24 hours. Rooms have sitting areas, refrigerators, TVs, air-conditioning, terraces, tubs, and hot water. First-floor superiors are bigger and have larger terraces; two-story superior duplexes have stylish bathrooms with stone-tile walls. A loud crowd rallies around the pool bars by midafternoon. ✉ *Jl. Segara Batu Bolong 18, Kuta (Box 2064, Kuta 80361),* ☎ *0361/753030,* ℻ *0361/752121. 165 rooms. Restaurant, 2 bars, air-conditioning, minibars, room service, 2 pools, massage, baby-sitting, laundry service, travel services, car rental, free parking. AE, DC, MC, V. EP.*

¢ ▦ **Fat Yogi Cottages.** This backpackers' hotel is terrific for budget travelers who spend little time in their rooms. It's cheap as can be, with a great location amid shops and nightlife and close to the beach. Some rooms have air-conditioning, private baths with tub, and hot water. Cheaper rooms have fans and private baths with shower. The attached Locanda Latino restaurant serves large portions of Western and Indonesian fare and has a busy bar that gets crowded as night descends. The pool is a bonus, and though there's no laundry service, you'll find several laundry places just down the street. ✉ *Poppies La. I, Kuta 80361,* ☎ *0361/751665,* ℻ *0361/757231. 24 rooms. Restaurant, bar, air-conditioning (some), room service, pool, massage, baby-sitting, travel services, car rental, free parking. AE, DC, MC, V. BP.*

¢ ▦ **Hotel Lusa.** Hidden away on a quiet paved lane, this simple white-brick hotel is a good deal for budget travelers. It also has an excellent location, between Kuta's shops and the beach. The pink-and-cream rooms are a little rough around the edges, but they're large and have air-conditioning and tile tubs. Renovations to the gardens and pool are scheduled to be completed by early 2001. ✉ *Benasari La., off Jl. Pantai, Kuta 80361,* ☎ *0361/753714,* ℻ *0361/76591. 30 rooms. Air-conditioning, room service, pool, massage, baby-sitting, laundry service, travel services, car rental, free parking. No credit cards. BP.*

¢ ▦ **Komala Cottages.** Another popular budget place, this hotel sits on developing Benasari Lane, which is already inhabited by a few bars, restaurants, and surf shops. A path through a coconut grove leads to a simple building with a long white porch. Inside, rooms have wooden furniture, yellow walls, fans, and private cold-water showers. In this quiet location you waken to the sound of the breeze in the trees—a pleasure rare at this end of town. ✉ *Benasari La. off Jl. Pantai, Kuta 80361,* ☎ *no phone. 8 rooms. Room service, pool, massage, baby-sitting, laundry service, travel services, car rental, free parking. No credit cards. BP.*

¢   ⊡ **La Walon Bungalows.** With its white tile floors, bamboo furniture, Balinese decor, and large windows to let in the breezes, this clean, quiet place is popular with backpackers and families. All rooms have tubs and a porch or balcony; some also have air-conditioning, refrigerators, and TVs. ⊠ *Poppies La. I, Kuta 80361,* ☎ *0361/757234,* ℻ *0361/ 752463. 40 rooms. Bar, air-conditioning (some), refrigerators (some), room service, pool, massage, baby-sitting, laundry service, travel services, car rental, free parking. AE, DC, MC, V. BP.*

Jimbaran and Bukit Badung

$$$$ ⊡ **Ambara Ulangan.** This hilltop luxury resort affords a stunning
  ★   view of the entire northern isthmus of the Bukit peninsula, past the airport, Kuta, and Denpasar, and all the way to Bali's classic line of gray volcanic peaks. High on the hill sits Villa 1, which has a large bedroom walled by 30-ft tall windows. Just below it, Villa 2 has a loft bedroom and a spacious living area. Both villas have antique canopy beds, walk-in teak wardrobes, powder-blue terrazzo bathrooms with plunge-pool-size sunken tubs, stereos with compact disc players, private bamboo gardens, and windows all around. The spacious dining building, farther down the hill, is ready for dinner parties, with a large modern kitchen and a gray marble bar. A deck leads to the two-story shared main living room. This comfortable social area, centered around an extended sectional couch, has a large-screen television, a state-of-the-art stereo system, and a collection of videos and music. Extra guests can be accommodated in a small loft bedroom (without air-conditioning) tucked under the thatched eaves. Villa 3 is the owner's abode, which is rented out most of the year. This architectural masterpiece was built entirely for luxury, with marble floors, a cavernous walk-in closet, and a contemporary office above a curving wood staircase. An ivy-shaded Jacuzzi area overlooks the stacked infinity pools, which, in turn, face the stunning northern panorama. The best time to soak or swim is just after sunset, when the shimmering lights of the coastal resorts outline the island below as the sounds of the neighborhood gamelan musicians tinkle across the darkness. ⊠ *Ungasan, Jimbaran (Indovillas, Jl. Daksina 5, Kerobokan);* ☎ *0811/392985 for Indovillas reservation agency;* ☎ ℻ *0361/733031 to Indovillas. 1 room, 3 villas. Dining room, air-conditioning, room service, 2 pools, hot tub, massage, baby-sitting, laundry service, travel services, car rental, free parking. MC, V. BP.* ✆

$$$$ ⊡ **Four Seasons Resort.** Spread over 35 acres, this village of luxury bungalows rises from the shore some 150 ft up a hill. The most elevated bungalows have terrific bay views, and you needn't worry about hiking down to the public areas from them—an electric taxi will shuttle you to and fro. Once you enter your villa courtyard (through a pair of painted Balinese doors), you're in your own personal oasis. Stepping stones surrounded by luminous green pebbles lead to a private pool where water splashes gently in a fountain. The living-dining pavilions look onto the pool and bay beyond. Bedrooms have peaked bamboo-and-thatch roofs; bathrooms have huge tubs and separate showers—one inside and one in a small courtyard garden. Down by the beach, the pool spills over a 20-ft waterfall into a soaking area. The 10,000-square-ft spa features nine treatment rooms, a fitness facility, a refreshment center, and complete beauty services. ⊠ *Jl. Bukit Permai, Jimbaran 80361,* ☎ *0361/701010,* ℻ *0361/701020. 147 bungalows. 5 restaurants, air-conditioning, room service, pool, beauty salon, massage, spa, 2 tennis courts, health club, beach, snorkeling, windsurfing, boating, shops, baby-sitting, laundry service, meeting rooms, travel services, car rental, free parking. AE, DC, MC, V. EP.*

$$$$ 🖩 **The Ritz-Carlton, Bali.** The opulence of this luxury hotel is apparent as soon as you step into the entryway: a series of pools descends in falls toward a stunning view of the Indian Ocean. Unpolished marble surrounds the fountains and koi ponds, carved antique wooden benches adorn the hallways, and a replica of the painted panels from the Kerta Gosa Pavilion in Semarapura graces the lobby ceiling. The swimming area has a two-tiered pool and a grotto that leads through an 11,000-gallon saltwater aquarium. Most rooms in the four-story main building have ocean views; all have Western-style decor with a Balinese flair. The thatch-roof villas have striking Balinese accents, *bale bungong* (cushioned lounging areas), and private plunge pools. At the 130-seat Langit Theatre and open-air restaurant, you can watch Balinese dancing while dining. The intimate Padi's Restaurant, next to a pond lined with yellow and red heliconias, overlooks the bay. ☒ *Jl. Karang Mas Sejahtera, Jimbaran 80364,* ☎ *0361/702222,* 𝔽𝔸𝕏 *0361/ 702555. 277 rooms, 16 suites, 36 villas. 6 restaurants, 6 bars, air-conditioning, room service, pool, massage, spa, putting green, tennis court, beach, snorkeling, windsurfing, boating, baby-sitting, children's programs, laundry service, meeting rooms, travel services, car rental, free parking. AE, DC, MC, V. EP.*

$$$–$$$$ 🖩 **Hotel Inter-Continental Bali.** Five stone statues wrapped in black-and-white-checked cloths greet you from their posts in a large lotus pond at the entrance. Their brooding presence conveys a deeper sense of Indonesian formality than is found at other large resorts nearby. Here opulence readily mixes with tradition, from the intricately detailed pavilions to the carefully chosen decorations that highlight every room. Guest quarters are adorned with hardwood floors, light-wood furniture with cream and rose cushions, and stone and metal ornaments. A blue tile pool rests just over the bay; next to it a large thatch-roof pavilion with decorative fish dangling from its eaves is an ideal place for sunsets. ☒ *Jl. Uluwatu 45, Jimbaran 80361,* ☎ *0361/701888,* 𝔽𝔸𝕏 *0361/701777. 214 rooms. 2 restaurants, 2 bars, air-conditioning, room service, pool, massage, beach, snorkeling, windsurfing, boating, dance club, baby-sitting, laundry service, meeting rooms, travel services, car rental, free parking. AE, MC, V. EP.*

$$$–$$$$ 🖩 **Indio House.** Heading down the lane to Indio House, your first impression will be of an old Georgia estate: graceful, reserved, and luxurious. Follow the walkway, between weathered stone columns and a white trellis overflowing with blossoming vines, and the impression is heightened by the sight of the white Colonial-style mansion. A porch and a vine-covered gallery span the length of the house. The first-floor bedroom, decorated in muted greens, has a library annex that could be used as a children's room or reading area; a large, airy bathroom steps out to the gardens. Teak stairs lead to an open second floor, where contemporary furniture is arranged into entertainment and dining areas beneath high thatched eaves; a separate kitchen and a bedroom with bath are off to one side. A spiral staircase climbs up to a small attic bedroom that overlooks the living room. To the side of the main house are two cheery bungalows: one has a four-poster bed, a raised tile tub, and a large garden shower; the other has two double beds and a private garden shower. You can eat on the patio, adjacent to a little outdoor kitchen with a take-out window, or in the dining pavilion, at the west end of the estate near a path that leads right to Jimbaran Beach. The owner's one-bedroom villa, which sits across the pool from the bungalows, is occasionally rented out as well. ☒ *Jimbaran (Indovillas, Jl. Daksina 5, Kerobokan);* ☎ *0811/392985 for Indovillas reservation agency;* ☎ 𝔽𝔸𝕏 *0361/733031 to Indovillas. 2 bungalows, 2 houses. Dining room, air-conditioning, room service, pool, massage,*

tennis court, beach, baby-sitting, laundry service, travel services, car rental, free parking. MC, V. BP. ✎

$$$-$$$$ ⊞ **Nikko Bali Resort & Spa.** This huge resort at the eastern end of Bukit Badung has a splashy, energetic ambience. The open lobby and restaurants are set high above the ocean, and you can get a perfect view from the lookout tower or at close range from the beach. Rooms have polished wood floors, bathrooms with tubs, separate showers, and balconies. There are contemporary comforts and stellar views at every corner: a spectacular free-form pool with a network of bridges and slides; a pool bar in a cave, with a modern spa and fitness center on view through a glass window behind it; an amphitheater carved right out of the steep coastal cliffs. Nightly cultural performances and numerous activities keep guests busy; some never even leave the hotel grounds. ⊠ *Jl. Nusa Dua Selatan, Bukit Badung (Box 18, Denpasar 80363),* ☎ *0361/773377,* 𝔽𝔸𝕏 *0361/773388. 380 rooms, 15 suites, 6 spa villas. 4 restaurants, 4 bars, air-conditioning, refrigerators, room service, 4 pools, beauty salon, massage, sauna, spa, 3 tennis courts, volleyball, beach, snorkeling, windsurfing, shops, theater, baby-sitting, children's programs, playground, laundry service, business services, meeting rooms, travel services, car rental, free parking. AE, DC, MC, V. BP.* ✎

$$$ ⊞ **Bali Cliff Resort.** The grounds here are a little run down, but you can't beat the location on rough cliffs at the southern tip of the peninsula, 10 km (6 mi) southeast of Jimbaran. Rooms are done up tastefully in pastels. Suites and villas offer more space and elegance, with marble floors, hand-carved furnishings, sitting areas, spa baths, and balconies. You can stroll through mazes of gardens and fountains to an on-site temple. Frenzied *kecak* dances are performed on the lower beach as you dine by candlelight in a nearby cave—a memorable experience. A ride down a sloping, glass-enclosed tram takes you to the multilevel Ocean Restaurant, where tables in thatch-roof pavilions overlook the surf. If you're not a guest, you can still come for the exquisite and extensive Sunday buffet at the Coffee Shop restaurant, with free access to the infinity pool overlooking the ocean. ⊠ *Jl. Purah Batu Pageh, Ungasan,* ☎ *0361/771992,* 𝔽𝔸𝕏 *0361/771993. 180 rooms. 3 restaurants, 3 bars, coffee shop, air-conditioning, in-room safes, room service, pool, massage, spa, health club, shops, theater, baby-sitting, laundry service, meeting rooms, travel services, car rental, free parking. AE, MC, V. BP.* ✎

$$$ ⊞ **Pansea Puri Bali.** Luxury is reasonably priced at this resort at the edge of Jimbaran's beach. A black tile entryway dripping with ivy leads to a bridge between two ponds where large koi play follow-the-leader in packs. To the left of the bridge, facing the beach, is the dining pavilion. Scattered throughout the gardens are villas with straw roofs. Inside, marble floors and wood paneling complement the Balinese textiles, paintings, and carvings. Standard treats include wraparound terraces, spacious bathrooms with sunken tubs, and private gardens with open-air showers. A pool edges up to the beach and lagoon. ⊠ *Jl. Uluwatu, Jimbaran 80361,* ☎ *0361/701605,* 𝔽𝔸𝕏 *0361/701320. 41 villas. Restaurant, bar, air-conditioning, room service, pool, massage, beach, snorkeling, windsurfing, boating, library, baby-sitting, laundry service, travel services, car rental, free parking. AE, MC, V. EP.*

$$-$$$$ ⊞ **Villa Balquisse.** Walk through the stone temple doorway, and you're magically transported into a Mediterranean hideaway right in the middle of Jimbaran, just steps from the beach. There are two villa complexes here, each with a blue tile pool and a central dining pavilion decorated with unfinished antiques and colorful fabrics. One villa has a separate kitchen and three connected rooms: one room has a single canopy bed and a raised bathroom with a sunken tub; one has a canopy bed, a daybed, and a shower; and the two-story bungalow has a canopy bed and garden shower on the first floor and two double beds in the attic. The second villa has five double rooms. With a full-service business office and an enormous toy-filled playroom, Villa Balquisse makes an excellent base for small business groups or families. The small restaurant, which has a single long table beneath a poolside pavilion, serves exquisite but inexpensive gourmet fare, and you don't have to be a guest to eat here. ⊠ *Jimbaran (Indovillas, Jl. Daksina 5, Kerobokan);* ☎ *0811/392985 for Indovillas reservation agency;* ☎ FAX *0361/733031 to Indovillas. 7 rooms, 1 bungalow. Restaurant, air-conditioning, refrigerators, room service, 2 pools, massage, baby-sitting, laundry service, business services, travel services, car rental, free parking. No credit cards.* 🕸

$$–$$$ 🏨 **Keraton Bali Cottages.** The stone bas-reliefs and sparkling marble floors of the pagodalike entrance belie this hotel's reasonable rates. The "cottages" are actually rooms angled out to face the beach so that they have more privacy than typical hotel rooms. Standard rooms have garden views and showers. Suites have balconies, sitting rooms, and whirlpool tubs. The decor is simple and neat, and the large grounds and numerous facilities attract many European and Indonesian guests. ⊠ *Jl. Mrajapati, Jimbaran (Box 2023, Denpasar 80361),* ☎ *0361/701961,* FAX *0361/701991. 89 rooms, 10 suites. 2 restaurants, 3 bars, coffee shop, air-conditioning, room service, pool, massage, snorkeling, windsurfing, boating, billiards, theater, baby-sitting, laundry service, travel services, car rental, free parking. AE, MC, V. EP.*

$–$$ 🏨 **Bukit Inn.** This small hotel atop the Ungasan hill offers stellar views at budget prices. Rooms have wood furnishings, tile floors, and porches or terraces overlooking the ocean. The open-air restaurant serves up hefty portions of decent Western and Indonesian food. Though secluded, it's just a five-minute drive to Jimbaran Beach. ⊠ *Jl. Uluwatu, Ungasan,* ☎ *0361/702927,* FAX *0361/703361. 14 rooms. Restaurant, bar, air-conditioning, room service, pool, massage, baby-sitting, laundry service, travel services, car rental, free parking. AE, DC, MC, V. EP.* 🕸

$ 🏨 **Puri Bamboo Bungalows.** This small hotel doesn't have the opulent facilities that would jack up the cost, but it's comfortable and convenient. Each neat two-story cottage has four rooms—two upstairs and two down—all with small, simply furnished bedrooms and bathrooms with tubs and stone gardens. Superior suites have porches, and deluxe suites have sitting areas. A pool with a swim-up bar is the center of activity, even though the beach is just steps away. ⊠ *Jl. Pangeracikan, Jimbaran 80361,* ☎ *0361/701377,* FAX *0361/701440. 20 rooms, 18 suites. Restaurant, bar, air-conditioning, room service, pool, massage, beach, shop, baby-sitting, laundry service, travel services, car rental, free parking. AE, MC, V. EP.*

Nusa Dua and Tanjung Benoa

$$$$ 🏨 **Amanusa.** The rough, winding road that leads through the Bali Golf & Country Club and on to the Amanusa is at odds with the resort's opulence. Shining marble floors and thick columns welcome you into the main building, which towers above a reflection pond and a sapphire-tile swimming pool. From here the views of the forested peninsula stretch to the Indian Ocean, and most of the grand villas—built into the land's gentle folds—share this vista at least partially. Each also has checkered marble floors, rich teak furniture, a canopy bed, a garden, a sunken marble tub, and an outdoor shower. Eight villas also have plunge pools. You can toast the sunset beneath a canopy of bougainvillea beside the pool while gamelan music is played. Afterward, the candlelit tables of the Terrace restaurant provide a romantic dinner setting

above the peninsula's twinkling lights. Indonesian and Thai food are the highlights. ✉ *Jl. Nusa Dua Selatan, Nusa Dua (Box 33, Denpasar 80363),* ☎ *0361/772333,* ⅎ⅍ *0361/772335. 35 villas. 2 restaurants, air-conditioning, room service, pool, massage, spa, golf privileges, 2 tennis courts, windsurfing, boating, mountain bikes, library, baby-sitting, laundry service, meeting rooms, travel services, car rental, free parking. AE, DC, MC, V. EP.*

$$–$$$$ 🏨 **Bali Hilton International.** A spectacular floodlit waterfall in the middle of a huge lagoon sets the scene before a semicircle of five-story buildings. Rooms have a mix of modern furniture and Balinese trimmings; all have balconies that look onto the lagoon or the sea. A Japanese-speaking staff, Japanese newspapers, green tea, and slippers are available on request. ✉ *Jl. Nusa Dua, Nusa Dua (Box 46, Denpasar 80363);* ☎ *0361/771102; 800/445–8667 in the U.S.;* ⅎ⅍ *0361/771616. 538 rooms. 7 restaurants, air-conditioning, in-room safes, room service, 3 pools, massage, spa, 4 tennis courts, exercise room, squash, theater, baby-sitting, laundry service, meeting rooms, travel services, car rental, free parking. AE, DC, MC, V. EP.*

$$–$$$$ 🏨 **Grand Hyatt Bali.** Forty acres of gardens and cascading waterfalls are the setting for the Hyatt's four "villages," each with its own small lagoon or swimming pool. Most rooms have king-size beds and small sitting enclaves with banquette seats. Bathrooms have separate shower stalls and wooden shutters that open to the bedrooms. Regency Club rooms have balconies, marble bathrooms, private pools, and butler service. The hotel's Balinese flavor is enhanced by the open-air night market of food stalls and an amphitheater where traditional dances are performed. ✉ *Jl. Nusa Dua, Nusa Dua (Box 53, Denpasar 80363);* ☎ *0361/771234; 800/233–1234 in the U.S.;* ⅎ⅍ *0361/772038. 750 rooms. 5 restaurants, 4 bars, air-conditioning, in-room safes, room service, 6 pools, massage, putting green, 3 tennis courts, health club, squash, shops, theater, baby-sitting, children's programs, playground, laundry service, meeting rooms, travel services, car rental, free parking. AE, DC, MC, V. EP.*

$$–$$$$ 🏨 **Sheraton Laguna.** The Sheraton Laguna attracts an international crowd intent on relaxation and seclusion. The central courtyard has swimming pools, lagoons, and waterfalls connected by stone steps and wooden bridges. Ground-level suites sidle up to a free-form pool, which you can dive into right from your patio. Upper suites have bougainvillea-covered balconies, sitting areas, and marble baths with oversize tubs. The luxurious spa features indoor and outdoor whirlpool baths, a bathing pool with several waterfalls, and a massage and treatment villa. ✉ *Jl. Nusa Dua, Nusa Dua (Box 2077, Denpasar 80363);* ☎ *0361/771327; 800/325–3535 in the U.S.;* ⅎ⅍ *0361/771326. 211 rooms, 65 suites. 4 restaurants, air-conditioning, in-room safes, room service, pool, wading pool, 2 tennis courts, massage, spa, exercise room, baby-sitting, laundry service, business services, travel services, car rental, free parking. AE, DC, MC, V. EP.*

$$–$$$ 🏨 **Bali Aga.** Away from the beach crowds, this medium-size hotel—also known as the Swiss-Belhotel Resort—is a serene hideaway in the midst of Nusa Dua. Centered around twin L-shape swimming pools, the complex offers garden or pool views from its three-story buildings of gold limestone. The one-bedroom suites are large, with wood floors and furniture, marble bathrooms, and big windows; the bungalows have two bedrooms and private pools. The resort is right on the Bali Golf & Country Club, has an exquisite spa, and is within walking distance of the town's main shopping strip. ✉ *Jl. Nusa Dua Selatan 8, Nusa Dua (Box 97, Denpasar 80363),* ☎ *0361/776688,* ⅎ⅍ *0361/773636. 64 suites, 2 bungalows. 2 restaurants, bar, air-conditioning, room service, 2 pools, massage, golf privileges, spa, health club, shops, baby-*

sitting, laundry service, business services, travel services, car rental, free parking. AE, DC, MC, V. BP. 🍴

$–$$ 🏨 **Club Méditerranée.** Families with active kids—and parents who need alone time—are the target of this noisy, happy resort. It focuses on keeping kids of all ages busy, and there's plenty to do, from water sports to classes and games. The kid's club lets young ones try such activities as acrobatics and circus tricks, cooking and creative arts, treasure hunts, beach walks, and competitive sports. The staff is professionally trained, and baby-sitting hours are long to allow parents to get a break for themselves. Rooms are small, divided into compact areas with daybeds for parents and kids, and the bathrooms have showers only; but it doesn't matter because you spend most of your time outside. ✉ *Jl. Raya Nusa Dua, Nusa Dua (Box 1028, Nusa Dua 80363),* ☎ *0361/771210,* 📠 *0361/772617. 380 rooms. 5 restaurants, 2 bars, air-conditioning, room service, 3 pools, massage, spa, 7 tennis courts, recreation room, nightclub, library, baby-sitting, children's programs, playground, laundry service, business services, travel services, car rental, free parking. AE, DC, MC, V. All-inclusive.* 🍴

Sanur

$$$–$$$$ 🏨 **The Sanctuary.** Although grand in size, this white three-story mansion is quite casual—a villa set up for fun rather than idle luxury. The sunny living room, with light wicker furniture and a polished wood ceiling, is lined with pictures and shelves full of magazines, novels, games, and CDs. Across the room an expansive dining table and modern kitchen make entertaining easy. Both downstairs bedrooms have marble floors, baths with sunken tubs and double sinks, and sliding glass doors that open to separate garden entrances. The second floor has another living room, with a large-screen TV, a wraparound garden terrace, and a third bedroom with a large private deck and bathroom. The third floor is a lookout and party pavilion, complete with a kitchen and bar area, comfortable sofas, a pool table, and a telescope for gazing out over the rice fields to the ocean. A keyhole-shape pool is the highlight of the well-manicured grounds. There's also a separate private villa with a romantic canopy bed, a walk-through closet, and a marble bathroom with a sunken tub and indoor and outdoor showers; it also has its own small dining and kitchen pavilion, an infinity-edge plunge pool above the fields, and a thatch-roof *bale* overlooking the scene. Interiors have a pan-Asian feel, with Oriental rugs, Cambodian watercolors, and stone rubbings from Angkor Wat. If you don't feel like cooking, the professional staff can create gourmet meals, or you can have your food catered from one of the first-class restaurants in Sanur. A 21st-century business office and meeting rooms accommodate small groups of business travelers, and you can borrow the owner's golf clubs for a jaunt to one of three nearby courses. ✉ *Sanur (Indovillas, Jl. Daksina 5, Kerobokan);* ☎ *0811/392985 for Indovillas reservation agency;* ☎ 📠 *0361/733031 to Indovillas. 3 rooms, 1 villa. Dining room, air-conditioning, room service, 2 pools, massage, tennis court, exercise room, hiking, baby-sitting, laundry service, business services, meeting rooms, travel services, car rental, free parking. MC, V. EP.* 🍴

$$$–$$$$ 🏨 **Tandjung Sari.** This hotel, whose unique design has made appearances in books on architecture, is a peaceful village of Balinese-style bungalows on tropical grounds dotted with small stone temples and statues. The open-pavilion lobby is decorated with carvings, and the gardens overflow with blossoms year-round. Bungalows have split-bamboo walls and such touches as minibars, handwoven fabrics, and an antique or two. Most bathrooms have skylights. Prawns, curries, fritters, and a dozen other items are served in a romantic setting a stone's throw from the beach; Wednesday night features a superb rijsttafel. ⊠ *Jl. Tamblingan (Box 25, Denpasar 80001),* ☎ *0361/288441,* FAX *0361/ 287930. 24 bungalows. Restaurant, bar, air-conditioning, minibars, room service, pool, massage, beach, snorkeling, windsurfing, baby-sitting, laundry service, travel services, car rental, free parking. No credit cards. EP.*

$$$–$$$$ 🏨 **Waka Maya Resort.** At Sanur's southern edge, this collection of pavilion-style villas in sculpted grounds is a sanctuary by the sea. Surrounded by high walls, villas have a feeling of intimacy, with private courtyards, dark-wood floors, wicker and wood furniture, and thatched eaves. There's a shared kitchen area, and the beautiful stone-carved pool is reminiscent of Bali's sacred bathing places. The resort hosts a network of activities around the island and can organize packages with its sister hotels in Nusa Lembongan, Ubud, and Bali Barat National Park. ⊠ *Jl. Tanjung Pinggir Pantai (Box 80224, Sanur),* ☎ FAX *0361/ 289912. 7 bungalows, 7 villas. Restaurant, air-conditioning, room service, pool, massage, baby-sitting, laundry service, business services, travel services, car rental, free parking. AE, DC, MC, V. EP.* 🐾

$$–$$$$ 🏨 **Bali Hyatt.** For a hotel that's part of a large international chain, the Bali Hyatt has a surprisingly Balinese feel. Tropical gardens cover the expansive grounds to the 6 km- (4 mi-) long beach esplanade, where colorful jukung depart each morning. Rooms are in four-story buildings, and though slightly worn, each has island-style decor and a balcony. The most unusual feature is the green-tile pool with a waterfall replica of the entrance to the Goa Gajah (Elephant Cave) in eastern Bali. The hotel is within walking distance of local markets, shops, and restaurants. ⊠ *Jl. Tamblingan (Box 392, Denpasar 80001),* ☎ *0361/281234,* FAX *0361/287693. 390 rooms. 5 restaurants, 4 bars, air-conditioning, in-room safes, minibars, room service, 2 pools, massage, spa, 3-hole golf course, 2 tennis courts, jogging, beach, snorkeling, windsurfing, boating, baby-sitting, children's programs, laundry service, meeting rooms, travel services, car rental, free parking. AE, DC, MC, V. EP.*

$$–$$$ 🏨 **Grand Bali Beach.** Crowning the northern end of Sanur's line of big beach resorts, this hotel is among the most opulent. Fronted by a rolling golf course and backed by a span of soft brown sand leading out to a snorkeling reef, the resort's buildings are spread out in wings connected by covered walkways. Rooms are small but nicely furnished, with tile floors and a mix of contemporary and Balinese accents. Suites are a bit bigger, with bathrooms that are more luxurious. If it's space you require, go for a separate bungalow. This is a crowded place with lots of activities. Most of the major airline offices in Bali are here. ⊠ *Jl. Hang Tuah 58,* ☎ *0361/288511,* FAX *0361/287917. 400 rooms, 100 suites, 23 bungalows. 7 restaurants, 5 bars, air-conditioning, refrigerators, room service, 4 pools, beauty salon, massage, sauna, spa, 18-hole golf course, 4 tennis courts, health club, volleyball, beach, snorkeling, mountain bikes, shops, billiards, nightclub, recreation room, library, baby-sitting, children's programs, playground, laundry service, business services, meeting rooms, travel services, car rental, free parking. AE, DC, MC, V. EP.* 🐾

$$–$$$ 🏨 **Hotel Sanur Beach.** Most of the action here takes place around the pools, the beach, and the patio bars. All rooms have balconies, and most have huge double beds (a few in the older wing have twins); the best rooms face the pool. Twenty-six self-contained bungalows offer more privacy. The hotel hosts classical Balinese dance performances and buffet dinners most nights. ⊠ *Jl. Kalianget (Box 3279, Denpasar 80001),* ☎ *0361/288011,* FAX *0361/287566. 298 rooms, 26 bungalows.*

3 restaurants, coffee shop, air-conditioning, room service, 2 pools, massage, 4 tennis courts, badminton, beach, windsurfing, recreation room, baby-sitting, laundry service, meeting rooms, travel services, car rental, free parking. AE, DC, MC, V. EP.

$$–$$$ 🏨 **Radisson.** This hotel with its signature red terra-cotta roof stands on the busy northern corner of Sanur, but once inside, the grounds are surprisingly peaceful. Upper-floor rooms have views over the garden and pool, while first-floor rooms have private stone terraces. For just $5, the meal discount passport program entitles guests to half off all restaurant and buffet meals on-site. The proximity to Denpasar makes the Radisson a favorite of business travelers. If you need more room, ask about the Radisson Suites, five minutes south. ✉ *Jl. Hang Tuah 46, 80228,* ☎ *0361/281781,* 🖷 *0361/281782. 319 rooms, 10 suites. 5 restaurants, 4 bars, air-conditioning, refrigerators, room service, no-smoking floors, 2 pools, massage, golf privileges, exercise room, shops, recreation room, baby-sitting, children's programs, laundry service, business services, meeting rooms, travel services, car rental, free parking. AE, DC, MC, V.* ✎

$$ 🏨 **Pavilions.** A bamboo-lined lane leads deep into this quiet gathering of villas. The exquisite architecture is based on the palaces built during the golden age of Java's Majapahit empire. Inside, cream-color walls, rich teak trim, and elegantly carved furniture exude style while making guests comfortable. All the villas—with either one, two, or three bedrooms—have sunken baths, private dining patios, sundecks, and gardens. ✉ *Jl. Tamblingan 76,* ☎ *0361/288381,* 🖷 *0361/288382. 14 villas. Air-conditioning, in-room safes, in-room VCRs, room service, pool, massage, library, baby-sitting, laundry service, travel services, car rental, free parking. AE, DC, MC, V. EP.* ✎

$–$$ 🏨 **Tamukami.** This new little hotel, just steps from the main strip, combines the best of Bali's classic artistic styles with modern materials and comforts. It's built around a yellow terrazzo deck and free-form pool with a waterfall tumbling down to a shallow children's section. Rooms are furnished with carved antiques and have batik curtains and blue ikat bedspreads. Standards are upstairs in the main building. The superior rooms, which surround the pool, have inner sitting areas and porches; the studios have those amenities plus mini-bars and TVs. Two bungalows have more-businesslike furnishings (computers were on order at press time). A large conference room behind the lobby makes this an ideal base for small business groups. The colorful and cozy Alise Restaurant serves breakfast, mixed grills, and Western cuisine. ✉ *Jl. Tamblingan 64X,* ☎ *0361/282510,* 🖷 *0361/282520. 12 rooms, 7 suites, 2 bungalows. Restaurant, bar, air-conditioning, room service, pool, massage, baby-sitting, laundry service, business services, meeting room, travel services, car rental, free parking. AE, DC, MC, V. EP.* ✎

$–$$ 🏨 **Villa Roses.** Right in the middle of Sanur's back lanes, this compact villa offers a casual, family-friendly atmosphere within walking distance of the town's shops and beaches. A large azure pool nearly takes up the whole courtyard, which has a *bale* on one side and a modern cooking and dining pavilion on the other. The spacious kitchen, done in yellow marble, has a gas stove, barbecue grill, and huge pantry with an extra freezer. In the cozy main house, glass doors fold back to let in the breeze, and the living room is filled with modern electronics and bamboo furniture. The master bedroom has a large bathroom, with a tub that looks out to the garden. Down the hall three smaller bedrooms share a second bathroom with a corner tub and garden shower. A car and driver are included in the price. ✉ *Sanur (Indovillas, Jl. Daksina 5, Kerobokan);* ☎ *0811/392985 for Indovillas reservation agency;* ☎ 🖷 *0361/733031 to Indovillas. 3 rooms. Dining room, air-condition-*

ing, room service, pool, massage, baby-sitting, laundry service, travel services, car rental, free parking. MC, V. EP.

$ 🏨 **Made's Homestay.** Walk through Made's Pub and you'll find the extended gardens of this budget hotel. Bright, clean rooms, in white brick buildings with ornamental doors, are decorated with pastel fabrics and lace curtains; some have air-conditioning and hot water. The popular restaurant specializes in Indonesian and simple Western dishes. ✉ *Jl. Tamblingan 74,* ☎ FAX *0361/288152. 15 rooms. Restaurant, bar, air-conditioning (some), room service, pool, massage, shops, baby-sitting, laundry service, travel services, car rental, free parking. AE, MC, V. BP.*

¢–$ 🏨 **Puri Mango Guesthouse.** This quiet hotel is set back from the road and centered around a pretty little pool with a rock wall at one end. Rooms have ornamental temple doors, big front windows, bamboo furniture, ikat cushions, and colorful bedspreads. Upstairs rooms have fans and showers; downstairs rooms face the pool and have air-conditioning, bathtubs, TVs, and refrigerators. Because of the popular street-side restaurant and professional service, this is a well-known haunt of budget travelers. ✉ *Jl. Danau Toba 15,* ☎ *0361/288411,* FAX *0361/288598. 27 rooms. Restaurant, bar, air-conditioning (some), refrigerators (some), room service, pool, massage, baby-sitting, laundry service, travel services, car rental, free parking. AE, DC, MC, V. BP.*

Denpasar

$$–$$$ 🏨 **Hotel Tohpati Bali.** The hotel entrance resembles a temple facade, and umbrella-lined brick walkways lead to a surprisingly large property. Rooms have modern furnishings, refrigerators, terraces or balconies, safe-deposit boxes, and TVs. A tall volcanic-rock wall prevails over two free-form pools, alongside murals of mountains and underwater seascapes. Conference facilities make this a favorite of business travelers to the capital. A full-service spa is also on-site. ✉ *Jl. Bypass 28,* ☎ *0361/462673,* FAX *0361/462407. 41 rooms, 4 suites, 5 cottages. 3 restaurants, bar, piano bar, air-conditioning, refrigerators, room service, 2 pools, massage, sauna, spa, tennis court, baby-sitting, laundry service, business services, meeting rooms, travel services, car rental, free parking. AE, DC, MC, V. BP.*

$$ 🏨 **Hotel Sanno.** Surrounded by trees and neatly clipped gardens, this three-story hotel with a sloping terra-cotta roof is a quiet haven 10 minutes outside the capital. Rooms have floral prints and curtains, chipped wood furniture, and boring gray-tile bathrooms—but all have air-conditioning and refrigerators. Units are connected by a front terrace. ✉ *Jl. Hayam Wuruk 200,* ☎ *0361/238185. 56 rooms. Restaurant, bar, air-conditioning, refrigerators, room service, pool, massage, baby-sitting, laundry service, travel services, car rental, free parking. AE, DC, MC, V. BP.*

$$ 🏨 **Hotel Taman Suci.** If you must stay a few nights in the city, this comfortable hotel is an inexpensive way to do it. Rooms are spic-and-span, with bright tile floors and walls, contemporary furnishings, pastel floral bedspreads and cushions, and Balinese art. The quiet grounds are a nice place for a break in the afternoon. The efficient staff and professional atmosphere make this a favorite of Asian business travelers. ✉ *Jl. Imam Bonjol 45 (Box 3516, Denpasar 80116),* ☎ *0361/485254,* FAX *0361/484724. 72 rooms. Restaurant, bar, air-conditioning, refrigerators, room service, pool, massage, shop, baby-sitting, laundry service, business services, travel services, car rental, free parking. AE, DC, MC, V. BP.*

$–$$ ☒ **Natour Bali.** This modest hotel in the center of Denpasar offers extras that are quickly making it the top choice of travelers who want to stay in the city. Rooms, though a bit musty, have televisions, minibars, bathtubs, and sitting areas. Suites have canopy beds. Business groups are drawn to the meeting rooms, the semiformal ballroom-style dining room, and the expansive grounds (perfect for evening cocktails). A breakfast buffet is included. ☒ *Jl. Veteran 3 (Box 3003, Denpasar 80030),* ☎ *0361/225681,* ⅋⅋ *0361/235347. 69 rooms, 2 suites. Restaurant, bar, air-conditioning, room service, pool, massage, baby-sitting, laundry service, business services, meeting rooms, travel services, car rental, free parking. AE, DC, MC, V. BP.*

The Badung Strait Islands

$$ ☒ **Nusa Lembongan Resort.** Sitting above Sanghiang Bay, this resort is determined to take you away from it all. Everything you need is onsite—restaurants, bars, pools, and activities—and your job is simply to relax and explore the island. Spacious bungalows have antique furniture, marble bathrooms, and huge glass windows to show off the views. The white-sand beach is one of Bali's best; when you tire of sunning, you can snorkel, hike, cruise, or tour the island's villages. ☒ *Sanghiang Bay, Nusa Lembongan (Box 3846, Denpasar 80001),* ☎ *0361/ 725864,* ⅋⅋ *0361/725866. 25 bungalows. 2 restaurants, 2 bars, airconditioning, room service, pool, massage, hiking, volleyball, beach, dock, snorkeling, boating, shop, recreation room, library, baby-sitting, laundry service, travel services, car rental, free parking. AE, DC, MC, V. EP.* ✎

$$ ☒ **Waka Nusa Resort.** After a day of sailing on the Waka Louka catamaran, it's sheer pleasure to spend the evening relaxing at this resort. With a gorgeous setting on an azure bay tucked into the western edge of Nusa Lembongan, the grass-roof luxury bungalows are the perfect complement to island life. Large rooms have canopy beds, teak furniture, marble accents, and Balinese decorations; most have sea views. Walk on the white-sand beach, go for a glass-bottom boat ride, snorkel, or village tour—or just work on your tan. ☒ *Nusa Lembongan,* ☎ ⅋⅋ *0361/ 261130. 10 villas. 3 restaurants, bar, air-conditioning, room service, 2 pools, massage, hiking, volleyball, beach, dock, snorkeling, boating, shop, recreation room, baby-sitting, laundry service, travel services, car rental, free parking. AE, DC, MC, V. EP.* ✎

$ ☒ **Hai Tide Huts.** If you like the simple life, stay in one of these two-story, lumbung-style huts on the beach. Long grasses trickle down from the roof over the shady open-air patio; a wooden ladder climbs up to the cozy air-conditioned bedroom under the eaves. The setting is quiet, casual, and very romantic; tan by day and take your dinner under the stars in front of the surf. If you want more activity, though, there's plenty to do: the staff can organize water sports, games, and island explorations. ☒ *Nusa Lembongan (Box 3548, Denpasar 80001),* ☎ *0361/ 720331,* ⅋⅋ *0361/720334. 20 bungalows. Restaurant, bar, air-conditioning, room service, pool, massage, hiking, volleyball, beach, dock, snorkeling, boating, mountain bikes, baby-sitting, laundry service, travel services, car rental, free parking. AE, DC, MC, V. EP.* ✎

NIGHTLIFE AND THE ARTS

Southern Bali can rock, be romantic, or provoke resonant cultural insights. In Seminyak eclectic restaurant bars pipe in jazz or soft rock to soothe sleekly dressed patrons sipping martinis and wine. At the luxury hotel bars guests relax around small candlelit tables facing the sea. For the gregarious, Kuta and Legian are 24-hour party towns: restaurants start the day with "hangover breakfasts" and liquid lunches; happy hour arrives in the middle of the afternoon; bar-hopping buses lumber through the crowded streets just after sundown; disco beats pound through the darkness long past midnight; and after-hours parties continue through dawn. Around the Bukit Peninsula, including Jimbaran, Nusa Dua, and Tanjung Benoa, nightlife is limited to hotel bars and dance clubs, where the crowds are sedate and well-dressed. Sanur has a little of everything, from ornate resort bars on the beach to casual street-front watering holes and huge dance clubs. The Badung Strait Islands have no nightlife at all, and Denpasar attracts those who are more interested in noshing at the night markets or bargaining for produce than finding the next bar.

Although the south doesn't have the deep-rooted cultural traditions of the settlement of Ubud, to the north, you can still find cultural dances and performances here. The most accessible performances—and the most toned down for tourists—take place at the larger hotels, many of which schedule Balinese dance nights combined with an Indonesian buffet. The best place to see authentic Balinese dances and plays is the Werdhi Budaya Art Center, in Denpasar (☞ Exploring Southern Bali, *above*). If you'll be in Bali at the end of June or the beginning of July, try to take in some of the events at the annual Bali Arts Festival. Bali's shorter annual calendar, based on the lunar year, includes numerous holidays and temple ceremonies, and foreigners are welcome to attend most celebrations. You can pick up a schedule of dance and music performances, as well as a list of Balinese holidays, from most travel agencies. Many restaurants have impromptu live music, so check the outdoor blackboards when you're in the tourist areas.

Also look for the colorful bar-discount coupons that offer free drinks and a waived cover charge; they're distributed by numerous local bars and are a good way to try something different for free. Many restaurants and bars also provide free transport to and from area hotels, so call first and find out—it's a cheap and easy way to stay safe if you're heading out to the party scene.

Nightlife

The West Coast

BARS

The small, sparsely modern **A Bar** (⊠ Jl. Dhyanapura, Seminyak, ☎ 0361/733270) is where vodka lovers—the *A* stands for Absolut—suck back shooters and watch the street action. **All Stars Surf Café** (⊠ Kuta Center, Jl. Kartika Plz., Tuban, ☎ 0361/754134) books live rock bands on weekends. If you like Caribbean music, head to the funky **Apache Reggae Bar** (⊠ Jl. Legian 146, Legian, ☎ 0361/761212). There's always rogue action at the **Captain's Bar** (⊠ Jl. Kuta, Kuta, ☎ 0361/752529), in the New Bounty restaurant, one of Kuta's busiest watering holes; dancing in the cavernous ship-shaped club starts at 10 PM, and the south end's carefree youth keep it going until dawn.

Café Luna (⊠ Jl. Seminyak, Seminyak, ☎ no phone) has live music—and occasional go-go girls—on weekends, but the place rocks no matter what night it is. One of the area's best-known bars is the bustling **Goa 2001** (⊠ Jl. Seminyak, Legian, ☎ 0361/753922), at the casual seafood restaurant of the same name. For quiet drinks in elegant surroundings head to the bar at **Kori** (⊠ Poppies La. II, Kuta, ☎ 0361/758605); this is the neighborhood's best upscale option. The sleek, spacious bar at the **Maccaroni Club** (⊠ Jl. Kuta, Kuta, ☎ 0361/754662) is a popular spot for sipping before or after dinner.

The original **Made's Warung** (✉ Jl. Pantai, Kuta, ☎ no phone) was undergoing massive renovations at press time, but the updated version of the longtime beach icon should maintain its status as the perfect hangout for mixing with the crowd on summer nights. The place to grab a pint o' Guinness is the shamrock-accented bar at **Paddy's** (✉ Jl. Kuta, Kuta, ☎ 0361/752355). **Peanuts** (✉ Jl. Kuta, Kuta, ☎ 0361/754149) is a Kuta classic for the young and rowdy; hop aboard the Peanuts bus for a drinking tour of the area's best bars. The **Soda Club** (✉ Jl. Double Six 7A, Legian, ☎ 0812/3808846) kicks it off on Friday with a free buffet 9 PM–11 PM; the DJ-spun music grooves until 2.

DISCOS

Double Six (✉ Jl. Double Six, Seminyak, ☎ 0361/731266) is classy, with weekly fashion shows and other events that draw the trendy in-crowd of tourists and elite locals, but it's still *the* dance-party center. **Gado-Gado** (✉ Jl. Pantai, Legian, ☎ 0361/730955) is another haunt for the partying crowd. **Sari Club** (✉ Jl. Legian, Legian, ☎ 0361/754903), often called simply "SC," attracts the beautiful youth.

LIVE MUSIC AND EVENTS

The **Apache Surfers Bar** (✉ Jl. Kuta, Kuta, ☎ 0361/761212) hosts a live Top 40 band nightly at 10. The **Culture Club** (✉ Jl. Kartika Plz., Blok E-1, Tuban, ☎ 0361/757936) stages live music and cabaret shows. **Espresso** (✉ Jl. Kuta, Kuta, ☎ 0361/761212) presents live rock, jazz, pop, and blues bands nightly.

The bar at the **Hard Rock Hotel** (✉ Jl. Pantai Banjar Pande Mas, Kuta, ☎ 0361/761869) no longer is just a place to go drinking; it's also where you can catch unplugged local and international bands nightly on the center stage from 9 to 11 PM. Next door to the Hard Rock Hotel, the **Hard Rock Café** (☎ 0361/755661) has bands from 11 PM to 2:30 AM.

Jaya Pub (✉ Jl. Legian Kaja 2, Legian, ☎ 0361/730973), one of Legian's classic bars, also has live reggae, jazz, and Top 40 jam sessions weekly. **Puri Duyung Restaurant** (✉ Jl. Abimanyu 15X, Seminyak, ☎ 0361/730372) hosts live rock music and an Indonesian rijsttafel buffet every Monday—and provides free transport, as well. On weekends live bands take center stage in the back room at the renovated **Santa Fe** (✉ Jl. Dhyanapura, Seminyak, ☎ no phone). The **Southern Cross** (✉ Jl. Pantai, Kuta, ☎ 0361/753546), one of the busiest bars on the oceanfront strip, schedules live music nightly July through September and on weekends in other months.

NIGHTCLUBS

For a wild time in the dark, try the intimate upstairs dance floor of the **Club@The Villas** (✉ Jl. Kunti, Seminyak, ☎ 0361/730840), which also has an art gallery, patio, and pool hall; the 24-hour action includes fashion-model competitions, Afro-Cuban percussion and performance workshops, and Latin dance nights. **D'Angels** (✉ Jl. Abimanyu 23, 2nd Floor, Seminyak, ☎ no phone) is a cabaret club with a dance floor. **Hulu's Café** (✉ Jl. Legian, Legian, ☎ no phone) has cabaret-style entertainment. The trendy **Nero Bali** (✉ Jl. Legian 384, Legian, ☎ 0361/750756) hosts fashion shows that draw the young elite. Look for the two-story **Q Bar and Café** (✉ Jl. Dhyanapura, Seminyak, ☎ no phone), a busy, edgy nightclub with eclectic programs and cuisine.

Jimbaran and Bukit Badung

At the sleek upstairs club at **L'Oasis Restaurant & Bakery** (✉ Jl. By-pass, Jimbaran, ☎ 0361/702669) you can relax with drinks and a game of pool in the back room; on weekends come to mingle with the beautiful people and listen to first-class live jazz and blues bands.

Nusa Dua

BARS

Koki Bali (✉ Jl. Pantai Mengiat, ☎ 0361/772406) has Balinese dancing at 8 PM every Tuesday and Thursday. The jazz bar at **Poco Loco** (✉ Jl. Pantai Mengiat, ☎ 0361/773923) rocks on weekends in peak season. **Ulam** (✉ Jl. Pantai Mengiat, ☎ 0361/771590) is always crowded.

The bars in the **Nusa Dua Galeria** (✉ Jl. Nusa Dua, ☎ 0361/771662) offer free transport to and from area resorts.

LIVE MUSIC AND EVENTS

If you're in the mood to show off, **Club Taboh** (Nusa Dua Beach Hotel, Jl. Nusa Dua, next to the Sheraton Nusa Indah, ☎ 0361/977120) has karaoke and an all-night disco Tuesday through Sunday. Balinese cultural productions are held regularly at the **Galeria stage** (✉ Nusa Dua Galeria, Jl. Nusa Dua, ☎ 0361/771662); in summer live bands perform here on Saturday night. The pavilion at **Hann Chinese** (✉ Jl. Pantai Mengiat 88, ☎ 0361/776565) hosts Balinese dance performances and live bands nightly beginning at 7:30.

The Grand Hyatt's **Lila Cita** (✉ Jl. Nusa Dua, ☎ 0361/771234) presents fashion shows and live bands on the weekends. The **Melía Bali** (✉ Jl. Nusa Dua, ☎ 0361/771510) hosts a cultural show and buffet on Monday and Friday and cabaret on Tuesday, Thursday, and Saturday. The Melía also has nightly live music in the piano bar, and the Jungle Pub disco has one of the busiest dance floors on the strip. At the Sheraton Laguna, **Quinn's** (✉ Jl. Nusa Dua, ☎ 0361/771327) has live entertainment nightly.

Sanur

Bucu Warung (✉ Jl. Danau Toba 2, ☎ 0361/288462) schedules a mix of live Latin, rock, funk, and dance bands on weekends. The **Jazz Bar & Grille** (✉ Jl. Bypass, Sanur Raya 15–16, ☎ 0361/285892) hosts live jazz and blues bands on weekends and often schedules live performances during the week; call for updates, and be sure to make reservations, as this is *the* Sanur hot spot for the chic crowd. Saturday is ladies' night, when women receive 50% off all food and drinks after 10 PM. Next door to the Jazz Bar & Grille, **Kafe Wayang** (✉ Jl. Bypass, Sanur Raya 12–14, ☎ 0361/287591) has live jazz, blues, and rock music throughout the week, plus a jam session on Friday night; these are popular shows, so you'll want to reserve a seat in advance.

Mango Café (✉ Jl. Tamblingan, ☎ 0361/288411) presents live bands on Monday and *legong* dances by Balinese children on Wednesday and Friday. At **Spago** (✉ Jl. Tamblingan 79, ☎ 0361/288335), the classiest watering spot on the main drag, you can soak up the rich ambience to the sounds of wandering jazz musicians and live bands throughout the week.

The Arts

The West Coast

CLASSES

The owners of **Villa Taman Wana** (☎ 0811/392985 to Indovillas booking agency, ✍), in Kerobokan, have a thriving organic farm in Bedugul that supplies produce to many of the restaurants in southern Bali—as well as to their own Balinese cooking classes. The villa can arrange a day tour for just a few people or a full cooking school for groups, including a visit to the farm and local markets to learn about produce, complete cooking classes for every meal, special guest appearances by famed local restaurant chefs, and a wonderful celebration of food at the end. You don't have to be a guest at the villa to organize such a course.

You can learn Balinese dance and painting at the **Bali Plaza Shopping Center** (⊠ Jl. Bypass, Tuban, ☎ 0361/753301; ⊠ Ngurah Rai International Airport departure terminal, Tuban, ☎ 0361/757276). Classes can be scheduled a day in advance, or you can make a reservation while you're shopping. If you haven't reserved a space, teachers will also take students on a first-come, first-served basis.

CULTURAL PERFORMANCES

Acquaint yourself with Balinese dance at one of the free performances held at the **Kuta Center** (⊠ Jl. Kartika Plz., Tuban, ☎ 0361/756611). Shows take place every Tuesday and Saturday at 7 PM.

The **Jayakarta Hotel & Residence** (⊠ Jl. Werkudara, Legian, ☎ 0361/751433) plays host to a barbecue and Balinese *Ramayana* cultural show every Wednesday ($10); on Friday it's an Indonesian rijsttafel with legong dancing ($10). The **Legian Beach Hotel** (⊠ Jl. Melasti, Legian, ☎ 0361/751711) offers a legong performance from time to time; the show and a barbecue buffet cost $16. The **Mentari Grill** (⊠ Jl. Pantai 1, Kuta, ☎ 0361/751361), at the Natour Bali Kuta, schedules the occasional "Nusantara Night," with legong shows and an Indonesian buffet for $12.

At the **Nikko Bali Resort & Spa** (⊠ Jl. Nusa Dua Selatan, Nusa Dua, ☎ 0361/773377) there's a buffet and dance nightly in the Kupu Kupu Amphitheater: on Monday it's kecak dances and lobster ($35); Tuesday, Italian buffet ($20); Wednesday, "Desa Bali Night," with legong performances and a market-stall layout for tasting local cuisine ($27.50); Thursday, Asian satay buffet ($20); Friday, "Tour of Indonesia," with music, dances, and food from the various islands ($27.50); Saturday, *janger* and mask dances with a Balinese buffet ($27.50). Sunday's seafood buffet ($27.50) is at the Jala-Jala restaurant.

Sanur

Indonesian cooking classes are held on Wednesday in the Café Komodo at the **Radisson** (⊠ Jl. Hang Tuah 46, ☎ 0361/281781).

For cultural performances, head to the **Abian Boga Restaurant** (⊠ Jl. Kesuma Sari 5, ☎ 0361/287174), which hosts legong productions Sunday through Friday and *topeng* mask dances on Saturday. The **Penjor Restaurant** (⊠ Jl. Tamblingan, ☎ 0361/288011) is probably the most popular place on the main road for a meal and a cultural show, with performances of the frog dance on Monday at 8:15; legong on Tuesday, Thursday, and Saturday at 7:30; *joged* dance Wednesday at 8:15; and janger dance Friday at 8:15.

The **Hotel Sanur Beach** (⊠ Jl. Kalianget, ☎ 0361/288011) presents legong dances on Monday, *Ramayana* ballets on Wednesday, and frog dances on Friday, all beginning with a buffet at 7:30. On Saturday night the **Tajung Sari** hotel (⊠ Jl. Tamblingan, ☎ 0361/288441) has legong and gamelan performances at 7.

OUTDOOR ACTIVITIES AND SPORTS

Surrounded by water, with a center of massive shrub-covered hills, southern Bali was designed for almost every outdoor activity. The ring of reefs makes an ideal classroom for beginning divers and snorkelers; rugged west-coast waves lure surfers; and east-coast marinas provide boating and fishing opportunities. Hotels have modern ocean sports, from jet-skiing to windsurfing to parasailing. Resorts have every sports facility imaginable: fitness centers, running tracks, and courts for badminton, basketball, racquetball, squash, tennis, and volleyball. The region has three of Bali's four 18-hole golf courses, considered to be among the best in Southeast Asia. The numerous back roads make excellent tracks for mountain bikes, and the trails threading through the hills and caves of Bukit Badung are good for hiking. If you have a particular interest, you can usually ask for advice or make arrangements through your hotel—even if it's a small losmen—or through a travel agency in town.

Participant Sports

Bicycling

Because of the winding roads and relatively flat terrain, bicycling is a popular activity in southern Bali, particularly around the rice fields of Kerobokan. Mountain bikes are available at most of the larger hotels and private villas, and you'll find them for rent along the main streets in the tourist towns. Several companies organize cycling tours farther afield in the central mountains and rice paddies, usually for around $45. **Ayung River Rafting** (⊠ Jl. Diponegoro 150, Denpasar, ☎ 0361/238759) coordinates adventure trips on the popular Ayung River route. **Paddy Venture** (⊠ Jl. I Gusti Ngurah Rai 126, Sanur, ☎ 0361/289748) organizes trekking and cycling adventures in central Bali.

Boating and Sailing

The renovated marina at eastern Benoa Harbor is a hub for boating activities; here you'll find everything from sailboats to fishing vessels to catamarans. If you want to take a day or overnight trip, charter a full-crew ship, or rent a bareboat, this is the place to start looking. For day charters you can also head to Sanur or Tanjung Benoa, where many dive and island-cruise boats dock. For contacts *see* Cruises, *below.*

The large hotels along the coast sometimes have a few small speedboats available for guest use. If you want a thrill ride in a local fishing boat, look no farther than the public beaches at Sanur or Jimbaran.

Bungee Jumping

The increasing prevalence of young New Zealand and Australian travelers vacationing in Bali has prompted the construction of a couple of high-adrenaline parks that have bungee jumping and sky surfing—which is like bungee jumping, but you lie prone in a sleeping-bag type of getup. It's best to make reservations before you arrive, particularly in tourist season, as this is a popular group activity.

AJ Hackett (⊠ Jl. Double Six, Legian, ☎ 0361/731144) is the bungee jumping company that pioneered the concept on Bali. Services include free pickup from area hotels, night jumps on Saturday from 2 AM to 4 AM, and a pool that jumpers can use for free.

Bali Bungy Co. (⊠ Jl. Pura Puseh, Kuta, ☎ 0361/752658) offers four jump combinations daily from 9 to 9 for $49–$79. Free transport from local hotels is provided.

Camel Safaris

If you've ever wanted to ride a camel, contact **Bali Camel Safaris** (⊠ Jl. Nusa Dua Selatan, Nusa Dua, ☎ 0361/773377, ext. 210). They lead beach rides in the Nusa Dua area for $30–$80.

Cruises

Dozens of cruise companies ferry tourists to Bali's hidden coves and small offshore islands for snorkeling, picnics, and village visits. The most popular day and dinner cruises simply troll the coast to give guests the best opportunities for sunning, taking photos, and enjoying the scenery. If you prefer a more active trip, a dozen catamarans and sailboats depart each day for Nusa Lembongan in the morning and return that afternoon; these excursions include round-trip transport to

UNCONVENTIONAL CRUISING

SOUTHERN BALI is the natural starting point for cruises around the island, as well as to neighboring islands and through the rest of the archipelago. Benoa Harbor, just southwest of Sanur, is one of Indonesia's largest sea transport hubs, and though a few traditional cruise ships occasionally dock here, this is more a port for unique vessels. Here you can bargain your way aboard everything from a Chinese junk to a sparkling new catamaran.

A fine way to get acquainted with South Seas sailing is on a short catamaran cruise from Bali to Nusa Lembongan and Lombok, or on a sunset- and dolphin-watching cruise to the end of the Bukit Peninsula. Claim a place near the rail to watch the land disappear behind you; once you're on the way, grab a snack from the bar and a reclining seat. Most day-cruise companies have resort clubs near their docks at Nusa Lembongan, Senggigi, or the Gili Islands, where you can rest in a pavilion, swim, snorkel, take part in group activities or a village tour, and have a barbecue lunch on the beach before returning. Some resorts have bungalows where you can stay overnight if you can't bear to leave.

If you've ever had dreams of being an explorer—or a pirate—this is where you can bring that fantasy to life. The ultimate cruising experience is on the new line of teak Buginese schooners, modeled after ancient trading and pirate ships. Despite their antiquated appearance, these vessels are state of the art, with luxurious air-conditioned cabins (all with windows and private bathrooms), comfortable lounge chairs, sundecks, bars, and gourmet meals. You feel like you're on a sailing ship from centuries ago, especially when the wind billows the massive sails out before you as you stand on the deck in the salty sea spray—yet you have all the comforts of an upscale hotel.

A cruise on a traditional Bugis *pinisi* ship might take you to nearby Lombok and through Nusa Tenggara, or to Sulawesi, north of Bali. The trip can last for two days or for as long as three weeks. Most boats will pick you up midtrip from points on other islands (such as Komodo) with prior notice. Some companies specialize in charter trips, which allow your group to work with the company to hire a tour guide, cook, interpreter, and other special staff. Charter trips also have the bonus of traveling outside of the usual tour routes: up to Manado, Sulawesi, or out to Wasur, Irian Jaya, for example. You can also create your own specialized cruise—perhaps a dive tour or a visit to several of Indonesia's lesser-known wildlife havens. Priced by the day, the cost of these cruises comes to less than that of a moderately priced hotel, with all meals, transportation, and activities included. Your only extras are alcohol, souvenirs, and crew tips.

The trip begins the moment you set foot on the deck and stow your bags in your cabin. Have a welcome drink, chat with your fellow passengers, and get your sea legs before the boat leaves the dock (once it does, be prepared to handle the occasional strong wave). Go up on deck both for fresh air and the best views. Although these tours plan a combination of beach, trekking, and cultural activities by day, and most of the actual sailing occurs at night when passengers are sleeping, you'll still have plenty of chances to pretend you're looking for new territory while standing at the bow with the sails unfurling.

and from your hotel, snorkeling equipment, a village visit, and a buffet lunch on board. You can choose a fast catamaran cruise and spend more of your time on activities or take a leisurely sailing cruise and enjoy the ride and the scenery. If you decide to stay on the island—and many people do—accommodations can be arranged by each of the listed companies. The cruises are relatively cheap; accommodations, however, are as pricey as your preferences for luxury. If you want to venture farther afield, you can take a day cruise to Lombok or Gili Meno or a guided tour to Komodo or even Irian Jaya via Buginese schooner.

Bali Hai Cruises (✉ Benoa Harbor, ☎ 0361/720331) makes a one-hour journey to Nusa Lembongan in its high-speed catamaran, as well as a two-hour trip on the lovely *Aristocat* sailboat. The trips are $75 and include lunch, snorkeling equipment, and an island tour. You can stay overnight on Nusa Lembongan in their lumbung-style thatch-roof huts for $59 more.

Bounty Cruises (✉ Benoa Harbor; ☎ 0361/733333 on Bali; 0370/693666 on Lombok) hosts lively sunset cruises around Bali for $40 as well as trips to Senggigi and the Gili Islands of Lombok on their modern 500-passenger catamaran.

Island Explorer Cruises (✉ Jl. Bypass 622, Suwung, ☎ 0361/728088) sails to Nusa Lembongan on your choice of a 60-ft sailing yacht ($65, lunch included), a 65-ft power yacht ($59), or the superfast *Quick Cat* catamaran ($49). On Nusa Lembongan the outfit offers banana-boat rides ($5), glass-bottom boat trips ($5), dive packages ($49), and, if you decide you want to stay longer than a day, beach bungalows ($28).

The **Love Bird** (✉ Benoa Harbor, Benoa, ☎ 0361/281105) can be chartered for day tours and longer trips to area sights for $60–$98 and up, including gourmet meals and free drinks.

For cruising through the eastern islands of Nusa Tenggara, the volcanic archipelago east of Bali, the ultimate experience is on the lovely **Ombak Putih** (✉ Jl. Tirta Empul 14, Sanur, ☎ 0361/730191), a beautiful 120-ft, 24-passenger Buginese schooner. The design may mimic the centuries-old ships of explorers and pirates, but the decor is sleek, and the facilities are strictly modern. Spacious teak-accented cabins are air-conditioned and have private bathrooms. An upper-deck area is for lounging, and a large dining room on the main deck looks out over the ocean (healthful gourmet fare is served buffet style). The professional staff keeps the ship spotless and running smoothly, and the guides know their islands well. This is the way to experience the life of a former adventurer—but in modern-day comfort with superb service. A smaller boat for dive trips will be christened in late 2001.

Sea Trek (✉ Jl. Tamblingan 64, Sanur, ☎ 0361/286992) lets travelers experience the more adventuresome side to sailing in the 108-ft, 16-passenger *Katharina*, a comfortable, teak-finished Buginese schooner that sails the islands east of Bali all the way to Irian Jaya. Chartered tours and dive trips are the specialty. It's a favorite of film crews and sports teams, with such amenities as an all-electric kitchen (a rare safety feature) and an aluminum can compactor (to promote recycling). Included are an English-speaking crew of 12, professionally prepared meals, day trips to remote villages and beaches, and unexpected exploratory ventures along the way. Cruises last from one to three weeks and can be tailored to your particular wishes for adventure.

Sojourn (✉ Benoa Harbor, ☎ 0361/287450), a lovely four-mast yacht, makes day trips to Nusa Lembongan (for $49, including lunch) and overnight tours to Lombok.

Submarine Safaris (⊠ Jl. Segara Kidul 3, Tanjung Benoa, ☎ 0361/771977) gives underwater tours on the Beluga mini-submarine for $65.

Waka Louka (⊠ Benoa Harbor, ☎ 0361/484085) offers luxury cruises to Nusa Lembongan ($79), with an option of resort-style accommodations at the Waka Nusa Resort (☞ Lodging, *above*).

Golf

Southern Bali has three of the island's four major courses, and each combines a superb setting with world-class links. **Bali Beach Golf Course** (⊠ Grand Bali Beach hotel, ☎ 0361/288511), east of the Jalan Bypass in north Sanur, is a par 72 18-hole course. The **Bali Golf & Country Club** (⊠ Kawasan Wisata Nusa Dua, ☎ 0361/771791), in Nusa Dua, is a par 72 course with a sweeping view of the ocean; the club offers golf privileges to guests at most Nusa Dua hotels. At **Le Meridien Nirwana Golf & Spa Resort** (⊠ Jl. Kediri, Canggu, ☎ 0361/815930) you can see Pura Tanah Lot from the spectacular par 72 course, where 18 holes are nestled between terraced rice paddies and the rugged cliffs of Bali's rocky southwestern coast.

Mandalika Tours (⊠ Jl. Hang Tuah Raya 11, Sanur, ☎ 0361/287450) leads day tours to each course, or to a combination if you're feeling ambitious.

Pt. Bali Dirgahayu Wisata (⊠ Jl. Juanda, Tuban, ☎ 0361/761612) is a driving range and golf school at the airport with first-rate service and professional instructors. It's open 6 AM–10 PM. Fifty balls cost 75¢ before 6 PM and $1 after; you can rent clubs for $1–$4.

Hiking

Although there are no formal hiking trails in southern Bali, there are plenty of tracks that lead to the region's highlights. The narrow, muddy rice-paddy walkways and rickety bamboo river bridges of Kerobokan and north will take you into the midst of true village life. Dusty trails through the limestone hills of the Bukit Peninsula climb to spectacular 360-degree vistas from the edge of the sea all the way to the mountains. The opportunities for beach walks are endless—just check the tide tables first. Make sure to bring comfortable hiking boots and a sturdy sun hat, and plan your treks for the early morning or late afternoon hours.

Ayung River Rafting (⊠ Jl. Diponegoro 150, Denpasar, ☎ 0361/238759) offers day trips in the jungle and to rural villages for $37–$48 per person.

Paddy Venture (⊠ Jl. I Gusti Ngurah Rai 126, Sanur, ☎ 0361/289748) leads hiking trips around central Bali for $45 per person.

Horseback Riding

One of Bali's hidden treasures is **Umalas Stables** (⊠ Jl. Lestari 9X, Br. Umalas Kauh, Kerobokan, ☎ 0361/731402), a riding center with facilities for both pros and beginners. Owners Ralf and Sabine Kaufmann began their business in 1994 with six horses; they now have 30 competition-quality horses—including warmbloods, Thoroughbreds, Andalusians, quarter horses, and even a Grand Prix champion. Professional riders and trainers from Europe visit annually to teach short jumping and English-style riding to guests. The company maintains high standards of safety, and inexperienced riders are in good hands here. Every guest receives automatic insurance, and the ratio of guides to riders is one to one. Prices are very reasonable: $25–$60 for a lesson and a three-hour rice field tour.

Rafting and Kayaking

Although there aren't any rivers to run in southern Bali, several companies here lead excursions to central and northern Bali. Trips usually run $40–$80, depending on the company and the number of people participating.

Ayung River Rafting (✉ Jl. Diponegoro 150, Denpasar, ☎ 0361/238759) organizes white-water trips on the Ayung River ($63) as well as adventures on inflatable kayaks ($66).

Mega (✉ Jl. Bypass, Komplek Ruko Santi 126H, Sanur, ☎ 0361/289745) offers Ayung River trips.

The *Spirit of Adventure* (✉ Box 3212, Denpasar, ☎ 0361/221315) makes day trips down the Telaga Waja River.

Running

Joggers and runners will find plenty of space to stretch their legs in southern Bali. If you're on the west coast, avoid the potholes and open sewers of the main strip from Seminyak to Tuban and go for your run through Kerobokan's rice paddies or along the beach from Berewa to Canggu. Other scenic routes include the back trails of the Bukit Peninsula, particularly around the coastal temples and villages. Nusa Dua's wide roads and smooth sidewalks make running a pleasure.

Scuba Diving and Snorkeling

Whether you're a beginner or an instructor, you should try to fit in at least a day of diving. Trips of all levels are available from operators in Tanjung Benoa, Sanur, and Benoa Harbor. Any travel agent or hotel on the west coast can arrange a dive tour as well. Classes for beginning divers and refresher courses are widely offered; most of the outfits have PADI instructors. Experts can head for the Badung Strait Islands, north to Amed and the Tulamben wreck (☞ Exploring Eastern Bali *in* Chapter 3), or east to Nusa Tenggara. Shallow reefs rim most of southern Bali, so snorkelers can explore the sea life here as well, particularly off the east coast near Nusa Dua and Sanur. Depending on when you want to go and for how long, a one-tank dive will run $25–$40.

Bali Safari Dive (✉ Jl. Tamblingan 84A, Sanur, ☎ 0361/282656) has the ultimate dive shop: a neat, well-organized store that sells and rents books, tanks, underwater cameras, and other equipment.

Dive & Dive's (✉ Jl. Bypass 27, Sanur, ☎ 0361/288652) leads trips to a number of locations and has guides who speak a multitude of languages.

World Diving (✉ Jl. Tamblingan, Sanur, ☎ 0812/3900686) specializes in trips to Nusa Lembongan.

Surfing

For many travelers surfing is the highlight of a trip to Bali, and the island now has a bustling surfer trade, with specialty shops, tours, competitions, and lessons. Kuta is the classic starting place; as you wind your way through town you can't miss the stores lined with brightly colored boards and the modern, glass-front clothing shops touting the latest surf styles. Look along Jalan Kuta, Jalan Tanjung Mekar, and Benasari Lane for the best equipment and gear.

Experienced surfers bring their own boards and attire, then head for the waves at Canggu, Balangan, Bingin, Padang-Padang, Nyangnyang, Batu Pageh, and Nusa Ceningan. There are a couple of good breaks off the west coast of Nusa Lembongan, but Bali's ultimate challenge is at rugged Uluwatu, near the temple at the southern tip of the Bukit

Peninsula. All these places have basic local contacts for special orders, repairs, and basic necessities.

Swimming

If the ocean near your hotel is too rough for swimming, or if you just prefer to splash around in a pool, you won't have a problem finding a place for your dip. Except for the Kuta losmen, almost every hotel has at least one pool, and many of the large resorts allow nonguests to use their facilities for a daily fee.

On the west coast, **Waterbom** (✉ Jl. Kartika Plz., Tuban, ☎ 0361/ 755676) is the ultimate place for soaking. The water park includes water slides, pools, a full-service spa, towel and locker rental, restaurants, toddler facilities, and lifeguards. The park is open daily 9–6; admission is $2.

SHOPPING

Part of the fun of staying in southern Bali is exploring the long strings of crafts and clothes shops that decorate the main strip of each tourist town. Quality goods, low prices, and easy shipping options make this region the ultimate fantasy for die-hard shoppers—even those on a tight budget.

There are a few air-conditioned indoor malls in Legian, Kuta, Nusa Dua, and Denpasar where you can purchase fixed-price goods for a bland, Western-style buying experience, but otherwise, shopping is a totally different deal here. Along the main road of any tourist town, you'll find hundreds of shops crammed with textiles, clothing, carvings, household goods, kites, chimes, and kitschy souvenirs—pretty much the same stuff from store to store—in one open-air strip mall. The strategy is to take your time and explore as many shops as you can, find out the average price for your target purchases, and then go back to a store you like and drive a bargain. Start by offering half to two-thirds of what the vendor is asking; you'll usually meet somewhere in between. Note that many of the newer clothing boutiques in the upscale areas of Seminyak, Jimbaran, Nusa Dua, and Sanur now have fixed prices marked; look for signs stating this, or ask the salesperson before you start haggling. If you're on a tight budget, prices fall and exchange rates improve as you head into the alleys of Kuta and Tuban. Credit cards are usually accepted at mall stores and newer boutiques in resort areas, but small shops generally only take cash.

Good buys include batik sarongs, sheets, T-shirts, dresses, and shorts; ikat rugs and wall hangings; and woven baskets, purses, and mats. Women will be pleased with the number of boutiques selling two-piece sets and dresses for far less than in North America or Europe. Men can have dress pants, shirts, and suits made by professional tailors in just a few days. You can find high-quality silver pieces to complete any outfit in most towns; if you like gold, head for the line of shops in central Denpasar. Handbags, perfumes, aromatic oils and creams, soaps, and beaded jewelry are inexpensive purchases that make lovely gifts.

Wood carvings, stone carvings, and iron and bronze works make good souvenirs, although if you want to buy straight from the craftsperson, you'll need to head north to the villages around Ubud (Exploring Eastern Bali *in* Chapter 3). Unless you see something you really like or you're not planning to travel north, wait for Ubud to purchase paintings; the range of styles and the prices are much better there. There are dozens of new, large antiques and furniture stores in southern Bali where you can strike good bargains. And since many companies now offer full shipping services, you can get your purchases home safely.

Areas, Markets, and Malls

The West Coast

The two-lane, traffic-clogged stretch of main road that runs from Seminyak south through Tuban is packed with shops, restaurants, Internet hubs, and money changers. This is the best place to start looking for gifts and souvenirs, but know your prices before you start to bargain. Although the strip can be walked from end to end, it's too long and has too many shops to explore in a day. If you're short on time, the best shopping strategy is to drive or catch a taxi and cruise one direction, noting the shops of interest, then park or hop out at the opposite end of the strip and go to the nearest shop that caught your eye. Stop for a tea break, walk or take another taxi to the next store, and continue on until it's time to catch a taxi back to your vehicle or your hotel. You'll have a chance to explore the many shops without being overwhelmed, and you'll get an idea of restaurants and bars you might want to visit later.

For the best prices on fruits, vegetables, snacks, and crafts, try Kuta's open-air markets. The **Pasar Seni Kuta** art market is right next to the beach; it's open daily 8–4. The **Pasar Pagi** morning market, on Jalan Kuta, is open daily 4 AM–10 AM. The **Pasar Malam** night market, between Jalan Pantai Kuta and Jalan Bakung Sari across from the Chinese temple, is open nightly from dusk until around 10 PM.

The west coast also has numerous shopping complexes and supermarkets where you can pick up fresh meats and produce, sundries, clothing, and souvenirs.

Alas Arum Supermarket (✉ Jl. Seminyak, Seminyak, ☎ 0361/730706) is a small, crowded, and immensely popular store that carries fresh fruit, cereals, soda, snacks, alcohol, and souvenirs. It's right on the main road, with a money changer and a few parking spaces in front.

Bintang Supermarket (✉ Jl. Seminyak 17, Seminyak, ☎ 0361/730552), a block south of Alas Arum on the main road, is much larger, with a stationery department, household goods, a bakery, and a bookstore, as well as a big parking lot out back.

Gelael (✉ Jl. Kuta 105, Tuban, ☎ 0361/751082) is the best supermarket in the south. It has a huge grocery store and fast-food counters on the second level, and an enormous bookstore and stationery department are on the third floor.

Matahari (✉ Kuta Sq., Kuta, ☎ 0361/757588) has three stories of groceries, household items, clothing, and fast food, plus underground parking.

Surya Mas Mini Market (✉ Jl. Legian 478, Legian, ☎ 0361/753732) is a small store that carries basic groceries, toiletries, and household items.

Jimbaran and Bukit Badung

Because the Bukit Peninsula is mostly lined with resorts, you won't find the selection of inexpensive souvenir shops that there is along the coast to the north. There aren't any malls in this area, but the large hotels have pricey shops. You may find a few deals at the **Pasar Jimbaran,** on the main road, which runs from about 6 to 5.

Matahari (✉ Jl. Bypass, ☎ no phone) lies on Jalan Bypass at the north end of Jimbaran. In addition to the famed supermarket, this full-blown mall has an open arcade lined with dozens of name-brand clothing, shoe, and luggage shops, as well as a huge Gramedia bookstore on the second level.

Nusa Dua and Tanjung Benoa

This area's upscale resort environment has eliminated any chance for the survival of local markets, save for the small morning produce *pasar* in the back alleys of the surrounding villages. At the open-air **Pasar Benoa,** at the north end of Tanjung Benoa, you can buy fresh fruits and vegetables but not souvenirs.

Along **Jalan Pantai Mengiat,** in the center of town, clothing shops and trinket stalls filled with carvings and textiles are tucked between small open-air restaurants. Shops and bargains abound in the village of **Benoa,** a five-minute drive north of Nusa Dua along the eastern beach strip.

The big draw of this area, though, is the **Nusa Dua Galeria** (⊠ Jl. Nusa Dua, ☎ 0361/771662), the largest shopping complex on Bali, a single-level collection of more than 80 souvenir and clothing stores, restaurants, and entertainment venues. Everything is upmarket and expensive, but the neat gardens and clean, Western-style facilities are attractive and the fixed prices make shopping easy. If you only have a few days on Bali, this is probably the most convenient place to shop, for in just a few hours you can explore the stores, grab a bite at one of a dozen theme restaurants, and watch a nightly cultural or music performance on the main stage. Be sure to get a discount book from the information desk before you shop or eat. A free shuttle runs to all the Nusa Dua hotels, and you can get here cheaply by taxi from other parts of southern Bali. The Galeria is open from 9 AM–11 PM.

Sanur

Behind the town's resort section is a Kuta-like strip of restaurants, money changers, and small shops selling clothing and souvenirs. And, like Kuta's main road, this one could be walked in a long, dusty day; it's easier to take a taxi and cruise from one end to the other, with tea breaks in between bouts of shopping.

Sanur has several open-air markets where you can pick up produce and gifts: **Pasar Sindhu,** in the middle of town, is open daily 8–5. Nearby, on the beach, **Pasar Pantai Sindhu** is open daily 8–5. **Pasar Pantai Sanur,** at the north end of town, is open 24 hours. You can also try the art market, **Pasar Seni Sanur,** in the center of Jalan Tamblingan.

Alas Arum Supermarket (⊠ Jl. Tamblingan, ☎ 0361/289262) has, in addition to groceries, a huge selection of cassettes and compact discs. Longer-term visitors will be pleased to find Western cereals, snacks, and gourmet items for sale here, as well as soda, wine, and beer. Look in the cooler aisle for fresh meat and fruits.
Bagus Grocery (⊠ Jl. Tamblingan at Jl. Duyung, ☎ 0361/287794), a one-room supermarket, has groceries, compact discs and CDs, a good selection of books on Bali and Indonesia, and some popular novels.
Makro (⊠ Jl. Bypass 222X, ☎ 0361/723222) is the place to buy bulk food and household items if you'll be in Bali for a while. Like the U.S.-based Costco and Sam's Club warehouses, this outlet lets you stock up on cases of water and soda, boxes of ramen noodles and instant soups, bags of rice, powdered milk, and any other types of fruit, snacks, meats, and sweets you can think of. If you have small children, note that this is the only place on the island where you can buy cheap, good-quality diapers. Makro also has an enormous section of household items like dishes, towels, and toys. Children under 13 aren't allowed in the store. You can buy a full year's membership for $3—or just pay 75¢ and shop for the day.

Toko Wirasana (⊠ Jl. Tamblingan 13B, ☎ no phone) is a little shop that carries groceries, soda, and beer, as well as basic cosmetic items and toiletries.

Denpasar

The humid, buzzing capital city is an excellent place to shop—if you're daring enough to challenge the traffic fumes, upturned sidewalks, and close-set stores. Bolts of fabric, batik, and other textiles are along Jalan Kartini near Pasar Badung; gold shops line Jalan Hasanuddin and Jalan Sulawesi; and crafts shops are prevalent along Jalan Sulawesi and Jalan Gajah Mada.

Denpasar's biggest and best market is **Pasar Badung,** in the center of town. Its top floors hold clothing, carvings, textiles, and home goods; the lower floors have meat, produce, and spices. The inner market is open until 6 PM, when the night market begins in the parking lot. Across the river, **Pasar Kumbasari** is a multistory collection of crafts from all over the island; it's open daily 9–9. You can bargain for clothes and souvenirs at the **Pasar Malam Kereneng** night market, on Jalan Gadung and Jalan Kemuning, which runs from 6 PM to midnight.

The capital has the best of the region's shopping malls, all of which have department stores, music and electronics shops, restaurants, and entertainment venues such as movie theaters or video game rooms.

Hero Swalayan (⊠ Jl. Teuku Umar 38, ☎ 0361/262038) is a big Western-style supermarket that carries fresh fruits and vegetables, meat, frozen foods, and all sorts of chips, sodas, and beer.
Kerta Wijaya Plaza (⊠ Jl. Diponegoro 98, ☎ 0361/221160) is a combination grocery store, souvenir shop, clothing boutique, and fast-food outlet.
Libi Department Store (⊠ Jl. Teuku Umar 104–110, ☎ 0361/234667) is another Western-style supermarket with a bit of everything.
MA Department Store (⊠ Jl. Diponegoro 50, ☎ 0361/227201) has clothing and souvenirs as well as basic groceries.
Tiara Dewata Shopping Center (⊠ Jl. Mayjen Sutoyo 55, ☎ 0361/235733) carries food, souvenirs, clothing, shoes, and household goods.
Tragia Department Store & Supermarket (⊠ Jl. Hayam Wuruk 160, ☎ 0361/237295) has separate floors for groceries, fashion, and Bali mementos.

Specialty Shops

The West Coast

ANTIQUES AND SECONDHAND ITEMS

Tata Kayu (⊠ Jl. Laksmana 38, Kerobokan, ☎ 0361/735072) sells antique items made of wood and architectural pieces.
Warisan (⊠ Jl. Kerobokan 68, Kerobokan, ☎ 0361/733057; ⊠ Le Meridien, Jl. Kediri, Canggu, ☎ 0361/815900) has one of the area's best selections of antiques.

BOOKS

ABC Bookshop (⊠ Jl. Pantai Kuta 41E, Kuta, ☎ 0361/752745) is a busy little store selling used books.
Nirwana Bookshop (⊠ Jl. Legian Kelod 363, Legian, ☎ 0361/750697) sells new and used titles.
Toko Buku Karisma (⊠ Jl. Kuta 105, 2nd Floor, Kuta, ☎ 0361/765381) has a selection of hardcover coffee-table books and guides on Bali, Indonesia, and Asia, as well as popular paperback novels and children's books.

CLOTHING

Action Sports Retailer (ASR) (✉ Jl. Legian Kelod, Legian, ☎ 0361/762744) is the place to buy casual attire and sportswear.

Beach Bum Surf Shop (✉ Jl. Pantai, Kuta, ☎ 0361/756587) indeed carries clothing for beach bums.

Boko-Boko (✉ Jl. Seminyak, Seminyak, ☎ 0361/735386) sells women's outfits for both dressy and casual occasions.

Climax Swimwear (✉ Jl. Legian 363, Shop 1, Legian, ☎ 0361/761653; ✉ Jl. Pantai 42, Kuta, ☎ 0361/755734) is the place to go if you're in search of a swimsuit for the beach.

Covex's Shop (✉ Poppies La. I, Kuta, ☎ 0361/765678) fashions pastel satin party dresses and sequin bags. Owner Wayan Yuniari can make these items to order in a few days.

CV Sidoi (✉ Jl. Legian 363, Legian, ☎ 0361/752372) sells—and makes—tourist wear and souvenir clothing items.

Dynasty (✉ Jl. Legian, Legian, ☎ 0361/751844) is a wonderful three-story store where you can find classy women's clothes and dresses.

Hana Hou (✉ Jl. Seminyak 19, Seminyak, ☎ 0361/732768) has an eclectic collection of dresses.

Joe-Joe (✉ Jl. Seminyak, Seminyak, ☎ 0812/6581230) sells delicate little shell purses and other accessories.

Lucia (✉ Jl. Pantai 24A, Kuta, ☎ 0361/754462) attracts clothes hounds with its formal dresses and Chinese-style silks.

Reef Island (✉ Poppies La. I, Kuta, ☎ 0361/756771) sells a variety of surf and casual wear.

Studio Animale (✉ Jl. Pantai, Blok D1A 1–3, Kuta, ☎ 0361/753830) carries an extensive selection of casual wear and dress outfits for women.

The Surf Shop (✉ Jl. Legian 94, Legian, ☎ 0361/754915) has the usual range of surf wear and gear.

FURNITURE

Alamiah (✉ Jl. Seminyak 19, Seminyak, ☎ 0361/734214) has an enormous warehouse full of antique and reproduction Indonesian furniture. The company will also make pieces to order and ship furniture abroad.

Baliku Kayu (✉ Jl. Seminyak 18A, Seminyak, ☎ 0361/731448) creates beautiful reproductions of antiques.

Bambula Design (✉ Jl. Seminyak 50, Seminyak, ☎ 0361/733982) specializes in bamboo furniture, including dressers, woven privacy screens, and rocking baby cradles.

Kohe (✉ Jl. Double Six, Seminyak, ☎ 0361/734731) makes furnishings out of coconuts to order.

Panache (✉ Jl. Banjar Pengubengan Kauh, Kerobokan, ☎ 0361/732377) has a variety of high-quality contemporary pieces. The staff here will help you with design ideas.

GIFTS AND SOUVENIRS

Asana Asana (✉ Jl. Seminyak, Seminyak, ☎ 0361/732775) stocks Balinese coffee and tea.

Sari Artistik Foto (✉ Jl. Seminyak 504, Seminyak, ☎ 0361/730910) will take a sepia-tinted photograph of you dressed as a Balinese dancer, a Yogyakarta sultan, or a Timorese tribal chief—a memorable souvenir.

Studio Tas (✉ Jl. Pantai 25A, Kuta, ☎ 0812/3906163; ✉ Jl. Seminyak, Seminyak, ☎ 0361/750352) sells luggage and travel accessories.

Ticket to the Moon (✉ Jl. Double Six, Seminyak, ☎ 0812/3615314) has one-of-a-kind hammocks that make good souvenirs.

GOURMET FOODS

Dijon (✉ Jl. Setuabudi, Kuta, ☎ 0361/759636) stocks gourmet items. This is a favorite of expatriates for its cheese, deli meats, sauces, pickles, and wines.

HANDICRAFTS

Busana Indah (✉ Jl. Legian Kaja 502, Legian, ☎ 0361/751185) has a vast selection of cloth and batik.

Gunatama Textile (✉ Jl. Legian Kaja 504, Legian, ☎ 0361/730996) carries wonderful textiles. Have fun perusing the warehouse full of bolts of colorfully patterned Indonesian fabrics.

Isma'il Shop (✉ Jl. Dhyanapura 3, Seminyak, ☎ 0361/732737) weaves wonderful baskets and crocheted bags on site.

Mila Shop (✉ Jl. Seminyak, Seminyak, ☎ 0361/733462) sells hand-painted batik sheets, sheer fabrics, and sarongs.

One World Gallery (✉ Jl. Seminyak, Seminyak, ☎ 0361/735005), in Warung Made II, sells lovely pottery.

OXXO (✉ Jl. Legian Kaja 501, Seminyak, ☎ 0361/730787) carries *wayang* puppets and other Indonesian treasures.

Rumah Wayang (✉ Jl. Kartika Plz. 9X, Kuta, ☎ 0361/751650) has a not-to-be-missed selection of *wayang golek* (handmade wooden) puppets.

You'N'Me (✉ Jl. Pantai, Kuta, ☎ 0361/758698) specializes in hand-woven baskets and crocheted items.

HOUSEWARES

Adi Angada (✉ Jl. Seminyak, Seminyak, ☎ no phone) has a selection of pretty candles.

Bali Craft (✉ Kuta Sq. D41, Kuta, ☎ 0361/750386) is a beautiful shop where you can find little soap packets, baskets, aromatic oils, and small household items.

Grace Shop (✉ Jl. Legian Tengah 435–438, Legian, ☎ 0361/755920) sells unusual beaded candleholders and lampshades.

Ligora Interior (✉ Jl. Abimanyu 10A, Seminyak, ☎ 0361/733352) sells iron artworks and furnishings—including fish and geese, lizard CD holders, and other intriguing items—as well as leather lampshades.

Putri Dewata (✉ Jl. Legian Tengah 415, Legian, ☎ 0361/754496) carries iron and metal items like candleholders, compact disc racks, magazine holders, and wall decorations.

Surya Iron Works (✉ Jl. Legian 457, Legian, ☎ 0361/810773) has one of the region's most extensive ironwork collections, including candlesticks, picture frames, and lanterns.

JEWELRY

De Weer Terry (✉ Jl. LC Gatsu Barat 11X, Kerobokan, ☎ 0361/420685) creates original ebony and silver pieces, including chopsticks and napkin rings.

Mario Silver (✉ Jl. Seminyak, Seminyak, ☎ 0361/730977) has a large showroom with an extensive selection of jewelry and ornate silver items. They'll even pick you up and bring you to their office if you're staying in the area.

Ratu Silver (✉ Jl. Legian 372, Legian, ☎ 0361/756632) sells jewelry, as well as some larger filigree pieces.

LACE

Balinese handmade lace is of good quality and inexpensive, and many lace shops offer discounts of 25%–70%, depending on the item and the time of year.

Bunga and Lace (✉ Jl. Pantai 23D, Kuta, ☎ 0361/431273) is a good place to stop for an idea of what's available.

Lace Works (✉ Jl. Pantai 47B, Kuta, ☎ 0361/431273; ✉ Jl. Legian Kelod, ☎ 0361/431273) carries many types of lace tops and dresses.
Uluwatu (✉ Jl. Bakung Sari, Kuta, ☎ 0361/753428; ✉ Jl. Pantai, Kuta, ☎ 0361/755342; ✉ Poppies La. II, Kuta, ☎ 0361/758605; ✉ Jl. Legian, Legian, ☎ 0812/3804635) is a chain of stores specializing in handmade Balinese lace. Lace is more expensive here, but the quality is excellent, and Uluwatu can tailor custom outfits.

LEATHER

You'll find many talented leather workers hawking their goods on the west coast, particularly in Kuta.

Big Bear Leather (✉ Poppies La. I 5, Kuta, ☎ 0361/750598) specializes in leather jackets.
Janoko (✉ Poppies La. I, Kuta, ☎ 0361/765379) is a good place to go for leather jackets, pants, purses, and shoes.
21 Leather Fashion (✉ Poppies La. I 5, Kuta, ☎ 0361/765351) will work with clients to create unique, made-to-order leather items, including jackets and shoes.

MUSIC

Dynasty (✉ Jl. Pantai 47A, Kuta, ☎ 0361/755257; ✉ Jl. Padma Utara, Kuta, ☎ 0361/757171; ✉ Jl. Kartika Plz., Blok A3 12, Kuta, ☎ 0361/758531) carries a range of modern pop and old-time rock CDs and tapes.
Kuta Sparks (✉ Jl. Pantai 28D, Kuta, ☎ 0361/754117) sells all types of music on CD, including Balinese music and Indonesian pop.
Team Music (✉ Jl. Melasti 67, Legian, ☎ 0361/761238) has a large selection of world music, including American, European, and Indonesian pop and rock tunes from the 1960s onward.

TAILORS

There are many expert tailor's shops tucked into the shopping strips of southern Bali, so if you've ever wanted to have a dress or suit made to fit, this is the place to do it.

Martin Lassandy (✉ Kuta Center A8, Tuban, ☎ 0361/755555) is neat, clean, and well organized. You can have everything from casual clothing to a tuxedo made by hand, to your measurements, in 48 hours.
Rochman (✉ Jl. Pantai 11A, Kuta, ☎ 0361/756588) helps customers choose fabrics and styles for dresses and suits, which can be made in one or two days.
Suka Pandawa (✉ Jl. Seminyak 46, Seminyak, ☎ 0361/731167) can make any type of clothing for children and adults. Most items can be ready in two days.

Jimbaran and Bukit Badung

ART

Jenggala Gallery (✉ Jl. Uluwatu 2, Jimbaran, ☎ 0361/703310), with its remarkable selection of ceramics and art pieces, is a must for souvenir shoppers.

FURNITURE

If you're interested in purchasing antique or contemporary furniture from Indonesia, contact the specialists at **Equinox** (✉ Jl. Uluwatu 18X, Jimbaran, ☎ 0361/701695). Their extensive catalogs include wood tables, chairs, wardrobes, and carved canopy bed frames. They will also take clients on shopping expeditions to assist them in purchasing quality pieces—and they can take care of all shipping arrangements as well. Equinox is open daily 9–5.

HOUSEWARES

The **Shahinaz Collection** (✉ Jl. Uluwatu 18X, Jimbaran, ☎ 0361/701695), operating out of the same office as Equinox (☞ *above*), sells home wares and decorative items fashioned from local materials and fabrics. The owner designs items such as sofa spreads, bedcovers, pillowcases, and curtains, giving customers a massive catalog of textiles and styles from which to choose. Also available are handmade napkins, table sets, lamp covers, and a bright children's collection of bed linens, crib sets, and clothing.

Sanur

ANTIQUES AND SECONDHAND ITEMS

Ayu Shop (✉ Jl. Tamblingan 138, ☎ no phone) has an exquisite collection of hand-painted and hand-carved antiques from small villages around Bali.

Miralin Collection (✉ Jl. Tamblingan 136, ☎ 0361/286061) has an excellent selection of antique furniture, woodcarvings, and wall hangings. They can also make contemporary pieces to order.

CLOTHING

Animale (✉ Jl. Tamblingan 138, ☎ 0361/282646) is well known for its classy, contemporary dresses.

Mama & Leon (✉ Jl. Tamblingan 99A, ☎ 0361/288044) has its head office in Sanur. The store carries pastel dresses and outfits for women and girls. You can also make your own beaded bracelets.

Naga-Naga (✉ Jl. Tamblingan 56, ☎ 0361/286303) is a modern store with a variety of men's and women's clothing, all in black and white.

Tigresse (✉ Jl. Tamblingan 71, ☎ 0361/270005) is a new women's dress shop with floral and cotton outfits.

FURNITURE

CV Sari Utama Jaya (✉ Jl. Tamblingan 73, ☎ 0361/289092) stocks good-quality contemporary furniture and antiques. Pieces can also be made to order in less than a week.

Jawa Dewata (✉ Jl. Bypass 108, ☎ 0812/3901293) has both contemporary and antique furniture.

GIFTS AND SOUVENIRS

Bali Odina (✉ Jl. Tamblingan 60, ☎ 0361/286809) sells handwoven items—including pillowcases, wall hangings, place mats, and shawls—as well as Balinese handicrafts.

Bé (✉ Jl. Tamblingan 80, ☎ 0361/284076) carries a variety of handmade gifts, including paper products, notebooks, candleholders, and picture frames.

Gambir Art Market 2 (✉ Jl. Tamblingan 50, ☎ 0361/288779) is a huge indoor shop where you'll find every type of souvenir: batik sarongs and clothing, woven baskets, wood carvings, metal items, and tourist kitsch. The walls are covered with Balinese paintings, and there's even a jewelry shop up front.

Panca Sari Shop Kite Center (✉ Jl. Tamblingan 10, ☎ 0361/286050) is the place to buy one of Sanur's animal or boat kites—or have one made in a day.

Pesamuan Studio (✉ Jl. Pungutan 25, ☎ 0361/281442) has an excellent selection of ceramics, art pieces, and gifts.

HANDICRAFTS

Nogo Bali Ikat Center (✉ Jl. Tamblingan 98, ☎ 0361/288765) is a large shop where you can browse through hundreds of ready-made textiles and bolts of cloth. You can also have clothes and other items custom-made and learn about Balinese ikat weaving at the daily loom demonstration.

THE KITES OF SANUR

LOOK ABOVE YOU as you walk through Sanur in the late afternoon, and you'll see what appears to be a flock of huge, colorful birds hovering in the wide sky. These are in fact the fruits of the neighborhood's favorite pastime: kite flying. But the flying is only a small part of the fun. Much more goes into this traditional sport than meets the eye.

The kites start out in the imaginations of young girls and boys, who come up with inventive designs to try out over the fields. The simplest are geometric—squares, triangles, cylinders, and boxes that are easily lifted by the slightest breeze and are flown by the youngest of toddlers. Favored shapes are modeled after the island's main winged creatures: birds, bats, and butterflies. Other popular motifs include dragons, lizards, fish, and turtles. The kites are sewn by hand with any suitable fabric the maker can find. The insides are created out of light wood or sticks, gently curved beneath the material to catch the wind at the best angle. Simpler shapes are cut from old clothing; professional kites are made out of store-bought parachuting material. You also see large sheets of plastic creatively welded into flags, faces, and significant symbols (such as those of popular rock bands). Most animal kites are quite large, 3–6-ft wide, with nylon wings and papier-mâché bodies, downy, dyed feathers, and lifelike glass eyes. The most complicated are the competition kites, supported by long bamboo poles bound by thick ropes. Among the world's largest kites, each can be as big as a house, weigh as much as a small car, and require 20–30 men to carry it.

The kites take only a day to finish before they're taken to the family shops; some craftsmen can make as many as three in a day if they hurry. Those you see in the air every day, made by the children who fly them, are usually of a lesser quality than the competition kites—and yet they soar just as high. You'll be amazed at how they can pull nearly anything into the air, from miniature boxes to flags 12-ft high. Informal competitions take place on holidays and weekends, with prizes for those who can get the largest and the most creative shapes into the air. The crowning contest is the Bali Kite Festival, held over a weekend in July, which draws crowds of thousands to see which kite is champion of the skies. Villages can take months to create their entries, enlisting the help of every man and boy available. When finished, a kite is christened in a flurry of ceremonies, parades, and offerings. During the festival the beaches and streets of Sanur are crowded with onlookers and competitors, the latter of whom are often teams of men clad in identical uniforms—and soccer shoes, to get the best beach traction when hoisting the huge kites into the air.

If you buy a kite, don't just cart it home without testing it. Take it right to the beach, where you'll get expert flying advice. Particularly in Sanur, almost everyone knows how to make and fly kites, so you'll learn from the best. These unique toys are one of the most special (and fun) souvenirs you'll find on the island, and the experience of flying one here will give you a fond—and useful—memory to take home with your kite.

Sari Bumi (⊠ Jl. Tamblingan 152, ☎ 0361/284101), in the Café Batu-jimbar, has striking displays of pottery and other ceramics.

HOUSEWARES

Putih Pino (⊠ Jl. Tamblingan 182, ☎ 0361/287889) has a wonderful selection of decorative items and little gifts.

JEWELRY

Ispaknur Collection (⊠ Jl. Tamblingan 95, ☎ no phone) sells lovely beaded jewelry and seashells.

Suarti (⊠ Jl. Tamblingan 69, ☎ 0361/289092) is a smart shop that specializes in the beautiful handmade silver jewelry of Bali.

LIQUOR AND WINE

Bali Spirits (⊠ Jl. Bypass 622, ☎ 0361/728088) specializes in wines and hosts free tastings.

MUSIC

Vata Video CD (⊠ Jl. Pasar Sindhu, ☎ 0361/283020) has lots of cassettes and rents Sony PlayStations.

TAILORS

Franca (⊠ Jl. Tamblingan 97, ☎ 0361/288036) sells a variety of leather items and can make clothes and shoes to order in a day.

Full Collection (⊠ Jl. Tamblingan 24, ☎ 0361/283332) can make good-quality leather coats in three days for under $100. The shop also carries shoes, jackets, and purses.

Imba Leather City (⊠ Jl. Tamblingan 8, ☎ 0361/289565) has a selection of butter-soft leather coats, jackets, and purses. This shop's specialty is made-to-order clothing; tailoring services typically take 48 hours or less.

Royal (⊠ Jl. Tamblingan, ☎ 0361/288036), near the northern curve of Jalan Tamblingan, has dozens of bolts of cloth, as well as a selection of high-quality shirts, pants, dresses, and jackets that can be tailored to suit your measurements and style preferences.

Denpasar

Indonesian Export Gallery (⊠ Jl. Diponegoro 103, 3rd Floor, ☎ 0361/259363), in the Ramayana Bali Mall, is a good place to look for furniture and home decor ideas.

SOUTHERN BALI A TO Z

Arriving and Departing

By Airplane

Ngurah Rai International Airport, conveniently located 3 km (2 mi) south of Kuta off the Jalan Bypass, is Bali's only airport. Totally renovated in the mid-1990s, it is now a contemporary commercial enterprise, with a domestic terminal, an international wing, numerous shops and services, a line of fast-food outlets, and an organized taxi service. For details about flights, baggage, and weather conditions, contact **Airport Information** (☎ 0361/751011, ext. 1454). For more information about air travel to Bali, *see* Air Travel *in* Smart Travel Tips.

A number of international airlines have offices in Sanur's **Grand Bali Beach hotel** (⊠ Jl. Hang Tuah 58): **Air France** (☎ 0361/288511); **Ansett Australia** (☎ 0361/289636); **British Airways** (☎ 0361/288511); **Cathay Pacific** (☎ 0361/286001); **Continental** (☎ 0361/287774); **Japan Airlines** (☎ 0361/287576); **Korean Airlines** (☎ 0361/281074); **Malaysia Airlines** (☎ 0361/285071); **Quantas** (☎ 0361/288331); **SAS** (☎ 0361/288141); **Thai Airways** (☎ 0361/288141).

Other international carriers have offices at Ngurah Rai International Airport, in the Wisti Sabha building: **Air New Zealand** (☎ 0361/289636); **China Airlines** (☎ 0361/754856); **EVA** (☎ 0361/757295); **KLM** (☎ 0361/756126); **Royal Brunei** (☎ 0361/757292).

Singapore Airlines (✉ Jl. Dewi Sartika, Denpasar, ☎ 0361/261666) has an office in the Bank Bali building in the capital.

Several Indonesian airlines have offices in Denpasar: **Bouraq** (✉ Jl. Melati 51, ☎ 0361/223564); **Garuda** (✉ Jl. Melati 61, ☎ 0361/288011, ext. 1789); **Mandala** (✉ Jl. Diponegoro 98, Kerthawijaya Plz. D23, ☎ 0361/231659); **Merpati** (✉ Jl. Melati 53, ☎ 0361/285071).

FROM THE AIRPORT

Most hotels will send a shuttle when they know guests are coming, but you can also call for a shuttle from the information stand inside the international arrival hall. You can also catch or call a taxi at the stand directly outside the international arrival terminal. It's possible to flag down one of the minibuses circling the airport, but be aware that you'll be chartering the entire vehicle; it's usually easier and cheaper to take a taxi.

By Bemo

The cheapest way to get from point to point on the island is by local public minibus, or *bemo*. These frequently make rounds from the main airport arrival terminal to towns in a particular region, leaving whenever they fill up with passengers rather than on a set schedule. In southern Bali, the major bemo terminals are in Denpasar. The terminal **Batu Bulan** (✉ Jl. Raya Batubulan, 6 km [4 mi] north of Denpasar) is for bemos traveling to towns north and east of the capital. **Ubung** (✉ Jl. Cokroaminoto) is for bemos going to places west and north of the capital, including Java. A list of rates is posted at each terminal—make sure that the driver doesn't charge more.

By Boat

Bounty Cruises (✉ Benoa Harbor, ☎ 0361/733333) ferries passengers on its catamaran from Benoa Harbor to Senggigi and the Gili Islands of Lombok for $35 one-way and $70 round-trip. The boat departs at 8 AM, arrives at Senggigi at 10:15, and reaches Gili Meno at 10:45; the return voyage leaves Gili Meno at 1 PM, stops at Senggigi at 1:15, and arrives back at Benoa Harbor at 3:45.

Mabua Express (✉ Benoa Harbor, ☎ 0361/772521) is the main passenger-only express service to Lombok. Trips on the 130-ft catamaran depart at 8 AM from Benoa Harbor and return from Lembar Harbor on Lombok at 5:30 PM and take just two hours. This is a comfortable way to travel: on board are reclining seats, a bar, and handicapped facilities. Emerald Class or Lower Deck Class costs $30 and includes a snack, juice, coffee, and transfers; Economy Class, without the perks, is $25.

Pelni (✉ Benoa Harbor, ☎ 0361/721377) is a line of 1,500-passenger ships that travel between Bali and various points throughout Indonesia. For a schedule, contact the head office at Benoa Harbor.

Getting Around

By Bemo

Several bemo terminals in Denpasar will get you to other parts of the region. **Kereneng** (✉ Jl. Kamboja) is for bemos heading to Sanur, Batubulan, and around Denpasar. Head to the **Suci** terminal (✉ Jl. Diponegoro and Jl. Hasanuddin) for a ride to Benoa Harbor. **Tegal** (✉ Jl. Imam Bonjol and Jl. G. Wilis) is for bemos traveling to Kuta, Sanur, the airport, and Nusa Dua.

By Car

If you really want to get out and see southern Bali's sights, driving is the way to go. For the most part, roads are paved and in good shape, and the area is compact and easy to navigate. However, traffic can be abominable, temple festivals can cause complicated detours, and you're bound to run into delays wherever you go—so start early.

In southern Bali each tourist area usually has just one or two main streets, and parking is generally on the street up on the curb—and often the wrong way. You'll find several 24-hour gas stations in every tourist area. Roads can be crowded at rush hour and on weekends, so take your time, ease into traffic, and drive defensively. All vehicles have standard transmissions, so you need to be able to operate a stick shift up and down hills and around busy traffic circles. The Jalan Bypass highway, which runs from Nusa Dua through Jimbaran to Sanur, can be particularly tricky, as you have to make U-turns to reach parallel town roads.

Toyota Rent a Car (✉ Jl. Bypass Nusa Dua, Jimbaran, ☎ 0361/703333; ✉ Jl. Airport 99X, Tuban, ☎ 0361/763333; ✉ Ngurah Rai International Airport, Tuban, ☎ 0361/753744) is the most prevalent and highly recommended automobile rental and leasing service in Indonesia. You can rent everything from Toyota Land Cruisers and sport utility vehicles to compacts. The company's pluses include a top-notch fleet, on-site mechanics, reliable English-speaking drivers, competitive rates, and excellent service.

If it's high season and all of Toyota's vehicles are booked, you could try one of the many small car-rental agencies in the area. Beware, though, that many are fly-by-night operations that rent out the family vehicle, without insurance or mechanic options, and then charge double or falsely claim dents and scratches when the car is returned. If you must rent from a small company, make sure to check the vehicle before you sign anything—and document all prior damage with photographs and in writing. The following are some of the more reliable operators in southern Bali: **Bagus Rent Car** (✉ Jl. Tamblingan at Jl. Duyung, Sanur, ☎ 0361/287794); **Bali Baru Wisata** (✉ Jl. P. Ayu 7, Denpasar, ☎ 0361/221096; ✉ Jl. Legian 61, Legian, ☎ 0361/761155); **Calvin International Tours and Travel** (✉ Jl. Segara Batu Bolong 18, Kuta, ☎ 0361/751818); **Indo Trans Astri (ITA)** (✉ Jl. Kuta, Kuta, ☎ 0361/755518; ✉ Ngurah Rai International Airport, Tuban, ☎ 0361/757850); **Nusa Dua Rent a Car** (✉ Jl. Pantai Mengiat 23, Nusa Dua, ☎ 0361/771905); **Pt. Dirgahayu Valuta Prima** (✉ Jl. Tamblingan 66, Sanur, ☎ 0361/282657); **Sindhu Mertha** (✉ Jl. Tamblingan 20, Sanur, ☎ 0361/288354); **WBU Executive Travel** (✉ Jl. Tamblingan 2, Sanur, ☎ 0361/282594).

By Helicopter

Helicopters are a convenient—if expensive—way to get from point to point in a short amount of time. The premier service is **Bali Avia** (✉ Jl. Bypass 04X, Tuban, ☎ 0361/751257), which can take you on an entire circuit of Bali and the Badung Strait Islands or drop you off at a point on their route. Scheduled tours cost $550–$2,300, and charters run $1,150 per hour, with a maximum of four persons per flight.

By Motorcycle

You can rent motorcycles from any car rental agency (☞ By Car, *above*), as well as from most hotels and travel agencies. If you rent from one of the smaller agencies, the contract might be verbal, so be certain that the bike is in good condition before you hand out any money. In rural areas a motorcycle is the best way to get around; on Nusa Penida you can rent one at any small hotel.

By Shuttle

Thanks to southern Bali's ever-thriving tourist industry, there are now a number of shuttle buses for getting around without the expense of hiring a taxi, the hassle of a bemo, or the limits of a group tour. Most travel agencies post shuttle schedules and prices and can book tickets a day in advance. Or call one of the following shuttle companies: **CV Ganda Sari Transport** (☎ 0361/754383); **Cahaya Sakti Utama Tour and Travel** (☎ 0361/751875); **Perama** (☎ 0361/974772).

By Taxi

All cabs have meters, but not all of them work, so make sure your driver starts it before you depart. When you get in, ask what the approximate fare is to your destination, and make sure you have the appropriate denominations of cash ready, as drivers usually won't change large bills. The initial charge is 25¢, and then it's about 10¢ per kilometer; if you call, the minimum charge is 75¢. You don't need to tip, but it's customary to round up to the next 50¢ or so when you pay.

You should be able to easily flag down a taxi in any southern tourist town, or you can phone for one. A few reliable cab companies are listed here: **Airport Taxi** (☎ 0361/751011, ext. 1611); **Bali Taxi** (☎ 0361/701111); **Pan Wirthi** (☎ 0361/723355); **Praja Taxi** (☎ 0361/289090).

Contacts and Resources

Banks and Currency Exchange

You can find reliable banks throughout southern Bali, although unless you have an account, you probably won't need to go inside. All banks have ATMs, most of which take international bank and credit cards, and you'll find a machine on nearly every block in the tourist areas. Look for branches of **Bank Danamon** (✉ Jl. Gunung Agung 1A, Denpasar, ☎ 0361/436490); **Bank Lippo** (✉ Jl. Thamrin 77, Denpasar, ☎ 0361/436046); and **Bank Utama** (✉ Jl. Gajah Mada 112–114, Denpasar, ☎ 0361/423091).

You can use the free map handed out at supermarkets to find the ATMs of **Bank Bali** (✉ Jl. Legian 118, Legian, ☎ 0361/754291; ✉ Kuta Sq., Blok C16, Kuta, ☎ 0361/758377; ✉ Kuta Center A7, Jl. Kartika Plz. 8X, Tuban, ☎ 0361/761921; ✉ Poppies La. II, Kuta, ☎ 0361/761518; ✉ Jl. Pura Bagus Taruna 522, Kuta, ☎ 0361/761287).

Several major credit-card companies have offices in southern Bali: **American Express** (✉ Pan Indonesia Bank, Jl. Legian 80X, Legian, ☎ 0361/751058); **Diner's Club** (✉ Jl. Diponegoro 45, Denpasar, ☎ 0361/235559); **Visa** (✉ Bank Duta, Jl. Hayam Wuruk 165, Denpasar, ☎ 0361/226578).

Banks will change money, but money changers—also found on every block in the tourist areas—usually have slightly better rates. The following money changers are recommended: **Bali Maspintjinra** (✉ Jl. Seminyak, Seminyak, ☎ 0361/733202; ✉ Jl. Tamblingan 18, Sanur); **Central Kuta** (✉ Jl. Legian 165, Legian, ☎ 0361/751345); **Pt. Dirgahayu Valuta Prima** (✉ Jl. Tamblingan 66, Sanur, ☎ 0361/288787; ✉ Ngurah Rai International Airport, ☎ 0361/754251); **Rimana Valasindo** (✉ Jl. Tamblingan 32X, Sanur, ☎ 0361/283241).

Business Services

All the large hotels have business offices with basic telephone, fax, photocopying, and computer services. **CV Krakatoa** (✉ Jl. Seminyak 56, Seminyak, ☎ 0361/730824) will assist you with basic business services, including international calls and shipping, word processing, photocopying, faxing, and Internet access. **Primantara Business Center** (✉

Jl. Kartika Plz. 8, Kuta, ☎ 0361/752149) has computers, international phones, travel services, a money changer, and mobile phone rental.

A couple of companies will, for a fee, advise foreigners on setting up a business, purchasing property, and legally working for foreign and Indonesian companies on Bali. If you need guidance regarding work permits, licenses, management procedures, or other business concerns, contact **Pt. Bali Ide** (✉ Jl. Tukad Bilok 100, Denpasar, ☎ 0361/264749). **Bali Advisory Services** (✉ Jl. Danau Poso 108, Sanur, ☎ 0361/285336) can help with leases, contracts, and other business matters.

Emergencies

Southern Bali's 24-hour clinics are clean, reliable, and efficient. Many have a variety of doctors and services, including vaccinations, X-ray machines, and ambulances. The best is the **International SOS Clinic** (✉ Jl. Bypass 24X, Jimbaran; ☎ 0361/764555; 0361/755768 for emergency hot line), also known as Klinik SOS Medika, which is part of a worldwide health-care assistance organization. The Bali headquarters has a fully equipped emergency room, doctors on call around the clock, first-aid equipment, and general diagnostic facilities.

Pharmacies, called *apotik* or *farmacia,* are numerous in tourist areas and near clinics and hospitals. You'll also find them in the large supermarkets.

Ambulance (☎ 118). **Fire** (☎ 113). **Police** (☎ 110). **Search and Rescue** (☎ 111).

Hospitals: Rumah Sakit Kasih Ibu (✉ Jl. Teuku Umar 120, Denpasar, ☎ 0361/233036). **Sanglah Public Hospital** (✉ Jl. Sanglah, Denpasar, ☎ 0361/227911).

Clinics: Bali International Medical Center (✉ Jl. Bypass 100X, Jimbaran, ☎ 0361/761263). **Nusa Dua Medical Clinic** (✉ Grand Hyatt, ☎ 0361/771118).

24-hour clinics: Surya Clinic Jimbaran (✉ Jl. Uluwatu 31C, ☎ 0361/701272). **Surya Clinic Kuta** (✉ Jl. Padma Utara 517, ☎ 0361/761484). **Surya Clinic Tuban** (✉ Jl. Kartika Plz. 10XC, ☎ 0361/761207).

Pharmacies: Bali Farma (✉ Jl. Veteran 9, Denpasar, ☎ 0361/223132). **Farmasari** (✉ Jl. Banjar Taman, Sanur, ☎ 0361/288062). **Kimia Farma** (✉ Jl. Diponegoro 123–125, Denpasar, ☎ 0361/227812). **Maha Sandhi** (✉ Jl. Kuta, Kuta, ☎ 0361/751830). **Ria Farma** (✉ Jl. Veteran 43, Denpasar, ☎ 0361/223132).

English-Language Bookstores

You can find English-language publications throughout southern Bali's touristy parts. All the major supermarkets have bookstores, and all major hotels carry at least a few books and magazines in English. In Kuta, Legian, and Sanur many independent booksellers and used-book stores (☞ Specialty Shops *in* Shopping, *above*) sell used English-language books.

Event Planning and Catering

Amadea Florist (✉ Jl. Bypass 100X, Kuta, ☎ 0361/761262) creates fresh, dried, or silk flower arrangements—perfect for parties and events—and delivers them.

Bella Donna (✉ Jl. Pantai Berawa, Bj. Pelambingan, Canggu, ☎ 0361/739674) is an event-planning service that can organize dinners, parties, buffets, and special events for up to 100 people. Their eclectic international menu includes spring rolls, red bean soup, grilled chicken pâte, a mixed seafood barbecue, and gourmet lasagna. Salads, desserts, and baked goods are also part of the package, and the staff can even help plan birthday parties for adults and children.

Guided Tours

A guided tour will take you to the best of Bali's sights and is the most efficient way of seeing the island in a short amount of time. Most operators have private, air-conditioned vehicles and knowledgeable guides who can speak a variety of languages. Schedules usually cover a region's highlights and include lunch or dinner. You'll also find some unusual options, such as a sunset or night-market trip, or a theme tour that focuses on temples, crafts, or shopping. You can also see the island by helicopter (☞ Getting Around by Helicopter, *above*) or see the outer islands of Bali and Nusa Tenggara by boat (☞ Cruises *in* Outdoor Activities and Sports, *above*).

THE WEST COAST

Aerowisata Tours & Travel (✉ Jl. Bypass, Kuta, ☎ 0361/756769) leads a variety of tours around Bali and the islands of Indonesia. The agency can also book travel tickets and help with independent trips.

ANA Tourist Service (✉ Poppies La. I 2, Kuta, ☎ 0361/755221) has a knowledgeable staff that is always eager to help travelers. They can organize tours all over the island, including cruises, cultural day trips, treks, cycling routes, and river trips.

Bali Adventure Tours (✉ Jl. Bypass Ngurah Rai, Kuta, ☎ 0361/721480) organizes outdoor adventures, from hiking, trekking, cycling, and rafting to trips to the island's bird, elephant, and reptile parks.

Calvin International Tours and Travel (✉ Jl. Segara Batu Bolong 18, Kuta, ☎ 0361/751818) has the ultimate connections to the action around the island and targets the young crowd with special half- and full-day tours. Owned by the same management as the Bounty Hotel and the Gado-Gado and Double Six nightclubs, the agency attracts the kind of clientele that has energy to burn both day and night. Lively tours include cruises, beach trips, shopping dates, and cultural hops. The agency also plans parachuting, rafting, diving, and other adventures.

Mandalika Tours (✉ Jl. Hang Tuah Raya 11, Sanur, ☎ 0361/287450) organizes tour packages (including transportation) of Bali, Java, Lombok, Komodo, and Sulawesi. Day tours of the temples and mountains of eastern Java are approximately $225; Lombok day trips are $90 (overnights on the island are $175); three-day, two-night Komodo trips are $400; four-day, three-night Toraja packages are $525. Mandalika also coordinates sports and adventure tours, including golf packages to the island's four major courses.

SANUR

Bali Nagasari Tours & Travel (✉ Jl. Tamblingan 102, Sanur, ☎ 0361/288096) has a large open-air office where agents book tickets and help with independent trip planning. Here you can join a guided tour to the island's craft villages, hop on a river-rafting trip, hire a bicycle for tooling around the back roads, or sign up for a tour of the southern end's most popular local markets.

Dewata Journey Service (✉ Jl. Tamblingan 16, Sanur, ☎ 0361/286631) has a 24-hour reservations hot line that you can use to book a boat tour to Nusa Lembongan, a bus tour of the temples, or a river-rafting trip in central Bali.

Lila Cita Gaya Tours (✉ Jl. Tamblingan 6, Sanur, ☎ 0361/288023) has a fleet of tour buses for a dozen day trips that hit the island highlights: temples, beaches, craft villages, shops, and natural areas.

Health and Safety

These days about the most dangerous thing in southern Bali is a sunburn. Bali belly is pretty much a thing of the past as long as you stick to clean restaurants and take the usual precautions: clean produce before you eat it, and drink bottled water. Most hotels and restaurants have been educated in cleanliness and hygiene and have trained staff that take proper precautions before serving food. Ice supposedly is processed from purified water. Should you become sick or have an accident, there are excellent 24-hour clinics and pharmacies throughout this part of the island (☞ Emergencies, *above*).

There are still pickpockets and occasional muggings on the beach and in busy tourist areas, but if you don't wander around alone or drunk after dark you shouldn't have any problems. Transportation hustlers and wandering vendors can be aggressive, but just smile, tell them, "No, thank you," and let them move on.

Laundry

Most hotels have reasonably priced laundry services that do a far better job than scrubbing in the sink, albeit for double or more the price you'd pay to your average street-side laundry service. On the street you can expect to pay about 50¢ per shirt, blouse, pair of pants, or skirt and about 25¢ for smaller items and children's clothing.

Photography

The **Fuji Image Plaza** (✉ Jl. Kuta 117, Tuban, ☎ 0361/753194), across from the Gelael supermarket, has photo-processing services and sells film and some camera equipment.

For a reliable and quick place to develop film, head to one of the numerous branches of **Mercy Photo** (✉ Jl. Petitenget, Kerobokan, ☎ 0361/730777; ✉ Jl. Padang Luwih 3B, Kuta, ☎ 0361/426561; ✉ Jl. Tamblingan 58, Sanur, ☎ 0361/288603; ✉ Jl. Brigjen Ngurah Rai, Sanur, ☎ 0361/289631; ✉ Jl. Gatot Subroto 18H, Denpasar, ☎ 0361/435642).

Telephones, Internet, and Mail

LOCAL AND INTERNATIONAL CALLS

A few of Bali's public phones still take coins, but more take phone cards, which are available in various denominations. Not all public phones work, though; it's better to head for the ubiquitous *wartel,* where you can make local and international calls, send faxes, and often change money and use the Internet as well.

For local calls you don't need to dial the area code. When calling long-distance on the island or between Indonesian islands, you do dial the area code, including the 0 before it. The phone lines aren't great, even in the larger towns: there's often static on the line, and you may be cut off unexpectedly. Mobile phones are a hot trend; you can rent them from travel agencies and business centers, as well as from some of the larger hotels.

Satelindo (✉ Jl. Gatot Subroto Barat, Denpasar, ☎ 0361/412008; 021/5438–8888 for 24-hr information) sells cards to add minutes to your mobile phone. The cards can easily be reloaded via phone or ATM.

INTERNET SERVICES

A number of places along the main western strip from Seminyak to Kuta and a couple of establishments in Sanur allow you to hook up to the Internet. If these places are busy, try a business center in one of the large hotels, where nonguests can usually use the equipment and services for a fee.

Bali@Cyber Café (✉ Jl. Pura Bagus Taruna, Legian, ☎ 0361/761326, ✆) is one of the area's most pleasant Internet cafés.
Goa 2001 (✉ Jl. Seminyak, Legian, ☎ 0361/731178) has an air-conditioned office with a half-dozen computer terminals.

Hello Internet Café (✉ Jl. Diponegoro, Denpasar, ☎ 0361/246181) provides Internet and e-mail access.

Kapotajaya Wartel (✉ Jl. Seminyak 16A, Seminyak, ☎ 0361/733202) offers both international phoning and Internet access.

Kubu 2000 (✉ Jl. Pantai, Kuta, ☎ 0361/750090), in front of the Kuta Jaya Cottages, has Internet, faxing, and scanning services.

La Zale Internet Bar & Café (✉ Jl. Kartika Plz., Blok A3-2, Kuta, ☎ 0361/765202; ✉ Jl. Legian 363, Legian, ☎ 0361/754422) has two locations where you can surf in comfort.

Ocha Internet Café (✉ Jl. Tamblingan 84, ☎ 0361/284185) lets you make international calls and access the Internet.

Pt. Dirgahayu Valuta Prima (✉ Jl. Tamblingan 66, Sanur, ☎ 0361/282657) is a wartel with international phone service and public Internet access.

MAIL AND SHIPPING

You can buy stamps at and mail letters from local postal agents and most supermarkets and large hotels. The main post offices in southern Bali are: **Central Post Office** (✉ Jl. Raya Puputan, Denpasar, ☎ 0361/223566); **Kuta Post Office** (✉ Gg. Selamat off Jl. Kuta, Kuta, ☎ 0361/754012.

Several international couriers have offices in the region: **DHL** (✉ Jl. Hayam Wuruk, Denpasar, ☎ 0361/222526); **Federal Express** (✉ Jl. Bypass 100X, Jimbaran, ☎ 0361/701727); **Tiki JNE** (✉ Jl. Bypass 65, Jimbaran, ☎ 0361/286294); **TNT** (✉ Jl. Teuku Umar 88E, Denpasar, ☎ 0361/238043).

For shipping try one of the following companies: **Angkasa Jaya** (✉ Jl. Kuta 105A, Kuta, ☎ 0361/751390); **Bali Delta Express** (✉ Jl. Kartini 58, Denpasar, ☎ 0361/701727); **Pacific Express** (✉ Jl. Arjuna 21, Denpasar, ☎ 0361/235181); **Pt. Sumiando Graha Wisata** (✉ Jl. Padma Utara, Kuta, ☎ 0361/753425; ✉ Jl. Tamblingan 22, Sanur, ☎ 0361/288570); **United Parcel Service** (UPS; ✉ Jl. Imam Bonjol 336K, Denpasar, ☎ 0361/431870)

Visitor Information

You can find travel brochures and get general tourist information at several tourist offices. **Bali Tourist Information** (✉ Century Plaza, Benasari La. 7, Legian, ☎ 0361/754090) has a considerable selection of brochures and a staff that will be happy to help you plan your time on the island. **Kuta Tourist Information** (✉ Jl. Legian 37, ☎ 0361/755424) also has a helpful staff and numerous brochures to give you ideas about what to do while you're here. The **Bali Tourism Office** (✉ Jl. S. Parman, Renon, Denpasar, ☎ 0361/222387), a government office, has only a limited number of publications and isn't worth visiting.

Top Holiday Tour & Travel (✉ Jl. Legian Kaja 465, Legian, ☎ 0361/763087) is an excellent one-stop shop for booking tours and buying tickets, making reservations, mailing letters, changing money, and simply picking up information on Bali.

3 EASTERN BALI

A full moon shines high in the night sky, illuminating the crumbling brick walls of the ancient Pura Besakih, a temple nestled in the rugged folds of the volcano Gunung Agung. Tonight the place is filled with women dressed in their best gold brocade sarongs, pyramids of fruit piled high on their heads, who slowly move upward toward the summit to make ritual offerings. This is a special night, when the deities descend from the heavens to take part in the party. The shrines have been cleansed by the priests, the spirits appeased by the offerings and prayers. Now it's time for the guests of honor to arrive.

By Holly S. Smith

SHROUDED BY THE SHADOWS OF MOUNTAINS with rain forests and rice fields folded into their slopes, eastern Bali is the domain of gods and volcanoes. Deep caves are lined with statues of princes and gods, and crumbled stone temples and palaces allude to stories of the island's great kingdoms. This region is the historical center of Bali, a place of knowledge and power. Here steep rock walls are carved with images of court life from centuries past, and age-old Hindu shrines are adorned with carvings dating from the 11th century. This land evokes magic black and white from the spirits that inhabit its hills—and a quiet drive down the dusty back lanes of Ubud at twilight is all it takes to believe in their power.

With the 10,300-ft-high volcano called Gunung Agung silently watching over all that takes place here, eastern Bali is indeed the abode of the gods. As the island's highest peak, this Mother Mountain not only shelters Bali's holiest temple, Pura Besakih, but also casts a shadow over the other volcanoes in the region. The forces said to reside inside these mountains are feared by all who live beneath them: Gunung Agung's 1963 eruption was considered a sign of divine displeasure, and the Balinese subsequently went through a great reformation to appease the gods' seeming evil spells. Still there is beauty in even the darkest of forces, and the churning lava brought another rich layer of soil and made the fields even more fertile. Even the dark brown beaches are the result of the volcanic ash fallout, and the reefs ringing the coast also benefited from the tumbling porous limestone.

The region's aggressive geography has also dominated its history, for it took centuries for nomads and traders to find Bali's hidden kingdoms. These were clever societies, as evidenced by the bronze molds and artifacts found east of Ubud near the village of Pejeng. Balinese society inherited some of its characteristics from the Javanese, who crossed the strait sometime in the 8th century and set up royal links to Bali's eastern kingdoms in the 10th century. The marriage between Prince Udayana of Bali and a Warmadewa dynasty queen produced Airlangga, Java's famed king, and cemented the close connection between the two islands. Eastern Bali's court life and Hindu religious traits began to develop around this time; cave etchings and artifacts attest the growing importance of Javanese religion and royalty in Bali's eastern kingdoms.

The Javanese eventually grabbed power from the Balinese rulers, first in 1284 when King Kertanegara conquered Bedulu, just east of contemporary Ubud, then a half-century later when Java's Majapahit kingdom took control of the island. But Majapahit rule turned out to be a good thing, because by 1350 Bali was flourishing in a golden age similar to that occurring on Java. The capital was moved to Samprangan, a village on the border of today's political and administrative capital of Gianyar, and a sister dynasty was established on Bali to connect Java's Majapahit rulers with those to the west. Arts and cultural pursuits were encouraged, *meru* (tiered pagodas) were added to many island temples, and *topeng* (masked) dances spun tales of the rich times.

By the 15th century Majapahit had given way to the forces of Islam on Java, and the rising kingdom of Gelgel was able to take over Bali. A new capital was placed at today's city of Gelgel, and a second golden era peaked around 1550 under King Waturenggong, whose holy advisor, Danghyang Nirartha, is credited with establishing a caste system and founding a series of holy temples throughout Bali. Known as the "Wandering Sage," Nirartha's powers were so great and his reach so extensive that he is considered the ancestor of all Brahman priests on the island. Even contemporary noblemen of eastern Bali trace their roots to this kingdom, which remained the central power of Bali until the mid-1600s.

But by the turn of the century Gelgel had fallen to the kingdoms at Klungkung, Batuan, and Buleleng. The next 50 years brought battles between many of the smaller kingdoms, with Karangasem grabbing the west half of Lombok in 1740 and north and west Bali in 1768. Meanwhile, the Cokorda dynasty of Sukawati was establishing its own kingdom, which stretched from Peliatan to Tegallalang between the Petanu and Ayung rivers. However, in 1793 the Dewa and Anak Agung dynasties of Gianyar retook control of the region and turned it into one of the island's most powerful forces.

Sukawati held its own, though, and throughout the early 19th century Gianyar had to concede some of its power to the smaller kingdom's center at Batuan, now called Negara. Small battles still flamed, and in 1815 the region was thrown into even more chaos during the eruption of Sumbawa's Gunung Tambora. Power struggles between Gianyar and Sukawati temporarily ebbed over the next decades as Ubud became the center for Gianyar's *punggawa* (feudal lords). However, all were members of the Sukawati clan, and it's no surprise that in 1884 the Sukawati dynasty overthrew the kings of Gianyar.

Civil war broke out on Bali over the next decade, and the distracted kingdoms missed the warning signs of Western ambitions for their island. At first the continued presence and trade footholds of the Dutch, whose explorers first arrived on Bali in 1597, were readily accepted by local rulers. In 1849, after three battles in three years, the Dutch finally conquered north Bali, but it wasn't until they added Karangasem-ruled Lombok to their domain in 1894 that the eastern region perceived the real threat to their own kingdom. By the turn of the 20th century the Dutch had a firm grip on Gianyar and Karangasem—but the Balinese ruling families refused to concede power, leading to the horrifying *puputan* (mass suicides) of Badung in 1906 and Klungkung in 1908.

Over the next three decades the Dutch focused on the opposing interests of promoting Bali as a tourist destination and of keeping hold of their territory during the First and Second World Wars. When the Japanese arrived with promises of freedom, Bali—like the rest of the Indonesian islands—sided with its Asian neighbor, and the Dutch were dumped from the archipelago in 1942. On August 17 of that same year Bali was instituted as part of the republic of Indonesia, and the power of the island's eastern kingdoms was once again recognized within the larger span of the nation.

Yet somehow, through all the chaos and changes in power, the cultures of central and eastern Bali have managed to maintain their identities. In the 1930s the central villages became a center for artists and painters who celebrated the region's cultural heritage, thanks in many ways to the late Ubud ruler Cokorda Sukawati (who died in 1978), who promoted Ubud's arts and crafts to the outside world. Anak Agung Gede Agung, Bali's great political leader of the 1940s and 1950s, carried this focus further, promoting the island's merits on an international scale while focusing its citizens on maintaining their cultural roots. And though the region has since exploded with tourism, its focus has remained true to its origins: live a life with respect to the gods, be a good example for your family and village, and have a responsible existence in order that your next one might be better. You can't help but dream that life will continue this way beneath the great mountain shadows.

EXPLORING EASTERN BALI

A Good Tour

The mountainous center of Bali is the island's cultural core, one that requires time to explore slowly and savor. Make your base in Ubud, the virtual crossroads for crafts, traditions, and tourists, and spend at least one day exploring the town. You won't need a car here, for all the main sights are reachable on foot—and it's fun to browse through the many crafts shops along the way.

Numbers in the text correspond to numbers in the margin and on the Eastern Bali and Ubud maps.

Start your first day early with a stroll to the **Pasar Ubud** ①, where you can browse through the shops for textiles, crafts, and batik. Cross the street and peek into the royal palace, **Puri Saren** ②, along with the **Pura Pamerajaan Sari Cokorda Agung** ③ and the **Pura Saraswati** ④. Return to Jalan Ubud and walk a half-block west to the **Museum Puri Lukisan** ⑤, where you can spend an hour or so. Pop into one of the open restaurants lining the street for a cup of tea and a snack to fortify you for the climb to **Antonio Blanco's Gallery** ⑥. If you're ambitious, you can continue up the winding road to the shops and galleries of the Penestanan artist community and have a meal in one of the small restaurants there. Otherwise, turn around and head back to the main road and flag a shuttle or taxi to the **Neka Museum** ⑦, at the top of Jalan Campuhan.

After lunch catch public transportation to the **Agung Rai Museum of Art** ⑧, on Jalan Pengosekan, and spend an hour or two touring the exhibits and grounds. If you have time, cross the road and walk a minute west to visit the Nyoman Batuan Artist Community. Continue to the intersection with Jalan Hanoman, turn right, walk north 1 km (½ mi), turn left on Jalan Wanara Wana (also known as Jalan Monkey Forest), and walk for another ½ km (¼ mi) to reach the famed **Monkey Forest** ⑨. Finish your day by strolling north along the strip of shops and restaurants of Jalan Wanara Wana. After dinner watch a traditional dance at the Agung Rai Museum of Art or one of the area temples.

On your second day you'll need a vehicle to travel to historic and cultural sights on the outskirts of Ubud. Begin with a drive north into the mountains to the **Pura Sakenan** ⑩, then head west to view the sacred springs of **Pura Tirta Empul** ⑪ and the rock carvings at **Pura Gunung Kawi** ⑫. From here head south toward Pejeng, then take the small side road southeast just before Sanding; along this road you'll find more reliefs cut into the rock at **Krobokan** ⑬ and caves at **Goa Garba** ⑭. Follow the road south to Kelusu, turn right toward Pejeng, take a left at the market square, and stop 300 ft farther at the **Pura Penataran Sasih** ⑮ to see the enormous Moon of Pejeng bronze kettledrum, one of Bali's earliest artifacts. In the next 1 km (½ mi) you can also visit the **Pura Pusering Jagat** ⑯ and the **Pura Kebo Edan** ⑰ temples, as well as the pretty gardens and simple displays of ancient tools and sarcophagi at the **Museum Gedong Arca** ⑱. As you approach the intersection with Jalan Pengosekan, note the colorfully painted figure outside the temple called Pura Samuan Tiga. Turn right and continue 1 km (½ mi) to reach the ancient stone reliefs of **Yeh Pulu** ⑲ and, 1 km (½ mi) farther, the famous cave and temple at **Goa Gajah** ⑳ before returning to Ubud.

Have lunch in Ubud, then drive south on Jalan Hanoman and spend the afternoon shopping in the crafts villages—when the lines of tour buses have long left town. Start at the stone-carving center of **Batubulan** ㉑, then browse through the silver shops of **Celuk** ㉒ and the dis-

GIFTS FOR THE GODS

ON BALI the smallest offerings are signs of dedication to the gods—and art forms in their own rights. To create their offerings, the Balinese begin with basic natural materials, sometimes grown in the home compound, sometimes bought at the market, sometimes taken from the family kitchen. The most common offerings you see are canang, leaf trays held together by toothpicks; these are filled with carefully arranged pinches of rice, bright bougainvillea or marigold petals, and tidbits of food from the family's last meal. Canang for the higher gods are placed morning and evening within slots at the small family temples, on upper shelves in shops, and even on car hoods. Offerings for the lower deities are placed on the doorsteps of homes and businesses, though the mangy stray dogs that roam Bali's streets often devour these. Canang sari are small pinwheels of leaves with a central bouquet of blossoms; these are offerings for recent good luck and future prosperity. Kwangen—tiny, triangle-shape packets of palm strips carefully wrapped around a flower blossom, a fresh-picked leaf, and perhaps a Chinese coin—are held between the tips of both hands as the Balinese bow their heads and pray at the temples.

Look along the roadsides for penjor, bamboo poles that rise into the sky and curve into braided decorations that sway in the breeze like horse's tails. These signify a major celebration, such as the Balinese holidays of Galungan and Kuningan or a wedding, shop opening, or temple birthday. The upper curve of the pole mimics the soft silhouette of Gunung Agung; the braided tail is similar to that of the shaggy dog-lion Barong, symbol of good luck. Beneath each penjor is a sanggah cucuk, a small "mailbox" shrine in which offerings are placed during the celebration. A long red stick of jasmine incense is placed in the offering; the wisps

of fragrant smoke symbolize prayers being carried upward to the deities. You often can catch the scent of these offerings even before you see them.

The most recognizable offerings are the towering gebogan creations carried by village women during temple processions. To the crashing sounds of a marching gamelan, the women walk single file, balancing a tower of fruit, baked goods, and eggs—topped with carefully arranged frangipani petals—on top of their heads with just one hand. Different regions have different artistic styles: some of the towers have vertical stripes of fruit, sweets, and flowers; others have layers; others are wrapped in large leaves or strung with lamak (banners made of dyed and woven palm leaves). The most elaborate gebogan can rise 3 ft or more in height and weight more than 40 pounds.

On very special occasions look for sarad, elaborate offerings made from rice dough. Artists roll and shape the rainbow-hue dough into geometric shapes, flower petals, mythical creatures, and faces of people and gods—particularly that of Boma, a protector of all earthly beings. Pula gembal offerings start with a palm-leaf basket, into which small rice-dough figures are placed. Jajan (rice-flour cakes) can be modeled into miniature sculptures that interact in dioramalike scenes of good and evil between humans and gods.

Ready-made canang offerings are sold at the markets and shops. Yet at the night and morning markets, palm leaves and flower blossoms are among the best-selling items, and many Balinese arise to buy the freshest cuttings when the markets open at 4 AM. In the late afternoons groups of teenagers gather along the sidewalks crafting canang. At dawn and dusk the aroma of jasmine fills the air as the offerings are replaced yet again, continuing the circle of worship on Bali.

plays of mobiles and wind chimes dangling from the crafts outlets of **Sukawati** ㉓. Stop in the historic village of **Batuan** ㉔ and stroll past its temples before continuing on to the wood-carving shops of **Mas** ㉕. If you'd like to see more Balinese crafts, circle back to the Gianyar turnoff between Mas and Batuan and head through Kemenuh, **Blahbatuh** ㉖, and Bona on the way back to Ubud.

Use your third day in the region to step into the culture and history of Bali's eastern kingdoms. Just after sunrise drive out to the town of Gianyar, and take an hour or so to explore the **Puri Agung Gianyar** ㉗ and the temple next door, **Pura Langon** ㉘. Next drive to Semarapura, where you can walk through the grounds of the **Puri Semarapura** ㉙ to see the pavilions that tell stories of gods and man. While in Semarapura pay a visit to the **Pura Jero Agung** ㉚, the gardens of **Pura Taman Sari** ㉛, and the Pasar Klungkung market. Afterward, a detour 5 km (3 mi) south will take you to the former kingdom of **Gelgel** ㉜ and the traditional painting community of Kamasan. Return to Semarapura for an early lunch, or pack a picnic and stop along the road to enjoy the mountain scenery on the way to **Pura Besakih** ㉝, Bali's most sacred temple. If you started the day early, you'll be able to spend a few hours wandering through the massive complex of shrines and still make it back to Ubud just before dark.

On the fourth day take a road trip along the edge of eastern Bali, where you'll encounter rugged scenery, offshore reefs, and colorful coastal villages. Start along the road to Gianyar, continuing on through Semarapura and past Sampalan and Kusamba, to reach the bat cave called Goa Lawah. Keep going east and take the turnoff for the small ferry town of Padangbai, where you can walk through the market and shops to the beach lined with *jukung* (fishing boats, usually painted in bright pastel hues, with black eyes). You'll make it to Candidasa in time for an early lunch, after which you could visit the **Pura Candi Dasa** ㉞, in the center of town by the lagoon, and then drive north to see the ancient Balinese village of **Tenganan** ㉟. Alternatively, you could drive straight to Amlapura to view the **Puri Kaningan** ㊱ and then visit the **Puri Taman Ujung** ㊲ royal house just outside town. From Amlapura head north along the pass between Gunung Agung and Gunung Lampuyang to reach **Tirtagangga** ㊳ and the royal pools of Tirta Ayu, where you can cool off with an afternoon dip. For a quick snorkel take the turnoff to **Amed** ㊴ or continue north to **Tulamben** ㊵, where you can dive or snorkel around the wreck of the SS *Liberty Glo* sunk during World War II. If you began the trip very early, you'll have time to return via the back-road crafts villages of Budakeling, Bebandem, Sibetan, and Salak, turning south 1 km (½ mi) after Duda and continuing through Iseh and Sidemen until you reach Semarapura and the main road back to Ubud.

TIMING
Although the distances in this tour look short, the mountain roads are narrow, winding, and often clogged with trucks and tour buses, making travel impossibly slow at times. It's important to get a very early start each day to beat the heat and the crowds, even if you're just walking around Ubud. For the driving trips make sure to take along enough food and water, extra clothes, umbrellas for rain and sun, good walking shoes, and other basic necessities, because you probably won't make it back to your hotel until after dark. Check with Ubud Tourist Information (☞ Visitor Information *in* Eastern Bali A to Z, *below*) to find out when temple ceremonies are being held, because during these times roads to major shrines become clogged with local traffic and foreigners may not be permitted inside.

Eastern Bali

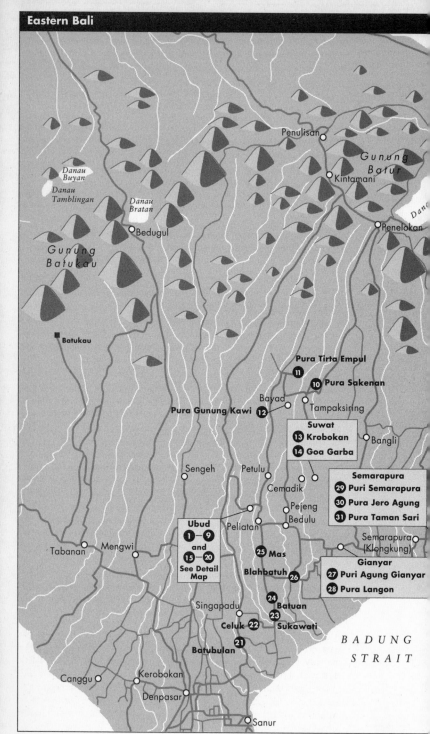

Penulisan

Gunung Batur

Kintamani

Danau Buyan

Danau Tamblingan

Danau Bratan

Bedugul

Penelokan

Gunung Batukau

Batukau

Pura Tirta Empul

11

10 **Pura Sakenan**

Bayad

Tampaksiring

Pura Gunung Kawi 12

Suwat

13 **Krobokan**

14 **Goa Garba**

Bangli

Sengeh

Petulu

Cemadik

Pejeng

Bedulu

Semarapura

29 **Puri Semarapura**

30 **Pura Jero Agung**

31 **Pura Taman Sari**

Ubud

1 — 9

and

15 — 20

See Detail Map

Peliatan

25 **Mas**

Blahbatuh 26

Semarapura (Klongkung)

Gianyar

27 **Puri Agung Gianyar**

28 **Pura Langon**

Tabanan

Mengwi

Singapadu

24 **Batuan**

23

Celuk 22 **Sukawati**

21

Batubulan

BADUNG STRAIT

Canggu

Kerobokan

Denpasar

Sanur

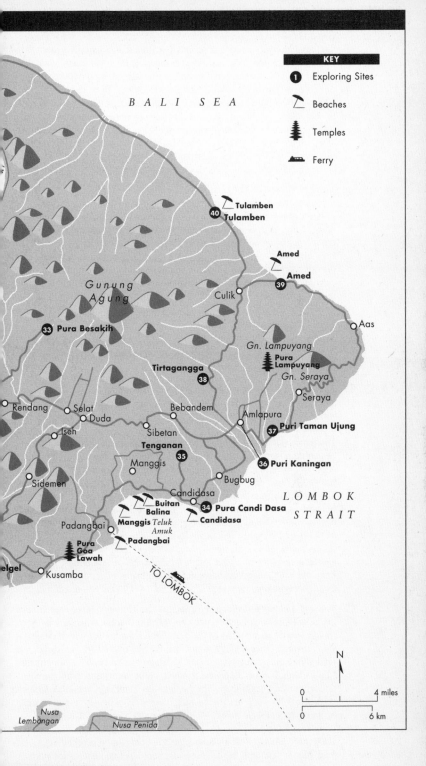

KEY

1 Exploring Sites

Beaches

Temples

Ferry

B A L I   S E A

40 Tulamben
Tulamben

Amed
39 **Amed**

*G u n u n g
A g u n g*

Culik

Aas

33 **Pura Besakih**

Gn. Lampuyang
**Pura
Lampuyang**

Gn. Seraya

Tirtagangga
38

Seraya

Rendang   Selat
          Duda

Bebandem

Amlapura

37 **Puri Taman Ujung**

Iseh   Sibetan

Tenganan

Sidemen   Manggis   35

36 **Puri Kaningan**

Bugbug

L O M B O K

Candidasa

**Buitan
Balina**   34 **Pura Candi Dasa**

Manggis *Teluk
Amuk*   **Candidasa**

S T R A I T

Padangbai
          **Pura
          Goa
          Lawah**   **Padangbai**

elgel   Kusamba

TO LOMBOK

N

*Nusa
Lembongan*

Nusa Penida

0   4 miles

0   6 km

Ubud

Ubud (pronounced oo-*bood*) has long attracted travelers with its casual artistic communities and has thus almost accidentally grown into the island's center for cultural experiences. It may be a small town, but it's bursting at the edges with temples, museums, and palaces that trace the colorful history of Bali's eastern kingdoms. Even those who prefer beaches can find solitude here amid the cool, rushing rivers and peaceful rice-paddy scenes. There is a gentle serenity here that slowly settles on even the most skeptical of visitors—during a quiet morning walk along thick, grassy terraces, while listening to a fountain gently trickling into a lotus pond, or after dark amid the scent of frangipani blossoms and the creaking calls of crickets and frogs.

Ubud is surrounded by records of the high points of Bali's history, from the ancient artifacts and caves of Pejeng and Bedulu to the remains of palaces and temples left behind by the great kingdoms of Gianyar, Klungkung, and Gelgel. Museums and galleries trace the more modern history of the international artists who settled here in the mid-1900s; they also highlight the works of the many Balinese artists whose traditions were born in this region. Classes allow visitors to dive into the culture, learning how to dance Balinese style, play gamelan instruments, make local crafts, and cook Balinese dishes. Ubud is a healing place, a salve for the soul, a small town that welcomes all and opens minds.

Sights to See

following the text of a review is your signal that the property has a Web site, where you will find details and, usually, images; for a link, visit www.fodors.com/urls.

★ ☺ ⑧ **Agung Rai Museum of Art** (ARMA). This well-organized museum, along with the **Agung Rai Gallery** around the corner on Jalan Hanoman, is one of the best places on Bali to learn about the island's artistic traditions. Part of an enormous compound of pavilions, ponds, temples, and gardens, the tall, white museum building is the center for exhibits of contemporary paintings, historic artifacts, and objects connecting the centuries in between. Many of the paintings are owned by Agung Rai himself, who—despite his heritage as a Peliatan prince—wound up hawking paintings by friends and family on Kuta Beach and eventually became one of the island's top art dealers. His vast collection of paintings spans the decades, as well as the Indonesian islands, although most of the finer pieces are works by Balinese artists and expatriates. Daily dance, music, and art classes are held in the compound, which also houses a café, a restaurant, and a hotel. At night the ornate temple gates are lined with flickering candles that light traditional dance performances. ⊠ *Jl. Pengosekan,* ☎ *0361/976659.* 🎫 *1$.* ◷ *Daily 9–6.* ✏

⑥ **Antonio Blanco's Gallery.** Housed in the timber-beam, thatch-roof home of Filipino-American painter Antonio Blanco, who died in 1999, this gallery displays many of the nudes and sketches for which the artist was famous. Once a stage magician, Blanco moved to the island and settled in Campuhan in the early 1950s to pursue his love of painting. "Bali's Dali," as he described himself, soon became an admired artistic force in the community. The gardens and buildings are adorned with traditional Balinese art pieces he gathered over nearly a half-century of living here. ⊠ *Jl. Ubud,* ☎ *no phone.* 🎫 *50¢.* ◷ *Daily 9–5.*

OFF THE
BEATEN PATH   **ELEPHANT SAFARI PARK –** Long ago Bali had its own subspecies of
☺   pachyderm. Although the Balinese elephant has been extinct for more than a century, you can ride a Sumatran elephant at this little park. Nestled into the Payangan hills north of Ubud, the park offers half-hour to

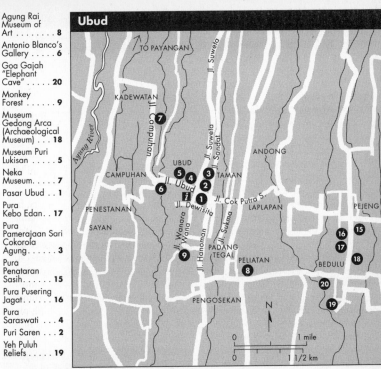

half-day journeys along rugged trails that cut through trees and rice fields. The elephants are actually quite light-footed, and this is an excellent way to see the countryside from tree level. Elephants of all sizes are available, and children are welcome. The park, open 9–5 daily, is a popular stop for adventure tour packages, but you can easily get here on your own by driving north on Jalan Campuhan, turning right onto Jalan Payangan, then following the signs to the turnoff 1 km (½ mi) after the town of Payangan. Admission is about $15.

❾ Monkey Forest. Tucked into Ubud's southeast corner, this shady, hilly expanse is filled with dozens of mischievous macaques. The walkway through the trees is a prime tourist hangout. Just remember: the monkeys are greedy—don't tempt them with food bits or they'll come over and grab your purse or glasses. These are wild animals, and they will bite, so keep an eye and a firm grip on small children and babies. ⊠ *Jl. Wanara Wana,* ☎ *no phone.* ☑ *25¢.* ☉ *Daily sunrise–sunset.*

NEED A BREAK?

The **Ubud Deli** (⊠ Jl. Dewi Sita, ☎ 0361/977984) is a roadside shop near the soccer field that's a popular stop for a snack during games.

❺ Museum Puri Lukisan. Founded in 1953 to showcase the works of Ubud's creative communities, the Palace of Paintings is a quiet haven where you can observe the works of some of the island's finest visual artists. The idea for the museum came from some of the era's most powerful talents: Balinese prince Agung Sukawati, the famed Pita Maha artisans, and Dutch painter Rudolph Bonnet. Housed in three pavilion-style buildings, the collection includes works from the 19th century to the present, most of which were donated by famous local artists or European arts investors who requested that their Balinese paintings be returned to the island upon their deaths. Notable exhibits include works by painters Anak Agung Gede Sobrat, Dewa Nyoman Batuan, and Ketut Budiana,

THE STRUCTURES OF BALINESE LIFE

I N BALI FAMILY IS SECOND only to religion, and the neatly structured layout of the home reflects the emphasis on worship, interaction, and privacy. Most homes still have traditional entrances through narrow double doors made of wood, which is often ornately carved and painted with gold-accented floral designs. The entrance is always on the right side of the high stone wall that surrounds the compound, a necessary element for privacy in the crowded neighborhoods. On either side of the doorway mailbox-size shrines are just the size for square *canang* offerings, placed here each morning and evening to welcome the higher gods. Evil spirits—which are believed to have trouble turning corners—are thwarted by an *aling-aling*, a short parallel wall just inside the entrance. This wall not only offers more privacy for the family, it is also said to prevent the lower deities from stumbling straight into the yard.

In the family compound the *bale*, or raised pavilion, denotes the connection between the gods (symbolized by the sloping roof), humans (symbolized by the central sitting area), and the land beyond death (symbolized by the thick base). The construction is strong, simple, and elegant: a cement or limestone foundation, widely spaced teak or jackfruit posts, and an *alang-alang* (palm leaves) roof—note that the shaggy black *ijuk* (sugar palm thatch) is reserved for temples. Walls, when used, are usually very thin and made of woven leaves to let in air and light.

The puzzling array of buildings in the Balinese compound begins to make sense when you realize that they are placed according to the directional rules of Balinese Hinduism. The house shrine is always *kaja* (at the side closest to the sacred peak of Gunung Agung), while the structures with the dirtiest functions—such as the pig sty—are placed *kelod* (on the side closest to the ocean). The *bale dingin* (east pavilion) is the most popular building in the compound, traditionally used for meetings and ceremonies. The *bale dauh* (west pavilion) is a multifunctional place used to house guests, to hold family gatherings, or simply to chat and craft offerings in the late afternoon. The *paon* (kitchen) lies to the south, the direction in which the fire god Brahma sits. The four-post *jineng* and six-post *lumbung* barns are for keeping rice and other dry goods; the platform below the storage area is often used as a napping place for children and animals during the day.

Next to the family compounds, community temples are the most important buildings in the Balinese village. Temple entrance gates are built in two main styles. *Candi bentar* are open, split gates with steps in between; double-door *kori agung* are more ornate, built of brick and limestone, with a fancy archway connecting both sides of the gate. Three courtyards lie inside the temple walls: the *jeroan*, which has shrines for the gods; the *jaba tengah*, which houses public meeting and music pavilions; and the *jaba pura*, where priests appease the underground deities. A temple has an odd number of *meru* (tiers); the more tiers, the more powerful the temple. The maximum number is 11, reserved only for the island's holiest shrines, such as Pura Besakih.

and wood-carvers Anak Agung Gede Raka of Peliatan and I Leceng of Nyuhkuning. ⊠ *Jl. Ubud,* ☎ *0361/975136.* ⊠ *$1.* ☉ *Daily 8–4.*

❼ Neka Museum. It's fitting that Indonesia's largest privately owned art museum stands atop the Campuhan hill overlooking the heart of Bali's artistic community. Opened in 1982 by Suteja Neka, a private art dealer who wanted to show off his vast collection, the museum exhibits more than a century of Balinese, Indonesian, and expatriate paintings. On display are works by Rudolph Bonnet and Walter Spies and the Balinese artists Affandi, Ida Bagus Rai, I Gusti Ketut Kobot of Pengosekan, and the great I Gusti Nyoman Lempad (1862–1978), whose own gallery is just 1 km (½ mi) to the southeast. ⊠ *Jl. Campuhan,* ☎ *0361/975074.* ⊠ *1$.* ☉ *Daily 9–5.*

❶ Pasar Ubud. This colorful little two-story market on the main road is a gathering place for local merchants and tourists. Bright sarongs and batik shirts hang from the rafters, painted masks line the walls, and piles of woven baskets crowd the small tables. Although the goods here aren't all that much cheaper than in the shops, it's a nice place to bone up on your bargaining skills and figure out what's available. ⊠ *Jl. Ubud,* ☎ *no phone.* ⊠ *Free.* ☉ *Daily 8–6.*

NEED A
BREAK?

If your legs need a break and you're near the soccer field between the Monkey Forest and Pasar Ubud, stop at the **Pondok Pekak Library and Resource Center** (⊠ Jl. Wanara Wana, ☎ 0361/976194), on the east side of soccer field, which has more than 4,000 travel guides, novels, and children's books in a dozen languages. This is also a cultural center where you can take language, music, and dance classes, watch a performance on the stage in the back, hook up to the Internet, have a drink and a pizza or sandwich, store baggage, fill up your water bottle for free, or simply climb up to the second-floor pavilion and stretch out on a cushion to read into the twilight. The library is open Monday through Saturday 9–9 and Sunday 11–7, and it costs about 50¢ to borrow a book.

❸ Pura Pamerajaan Sari Cokorda Agung. The Grand Cokorda Temple, which towers above the road behind the Puri Saren, is the private palace shrine of the royal family and the storehouse for their heirlooms. Stop for a look at the elaborate entrance arch with its stacked *boma* (faces). ⊠ *Jl. Ubud,* ☎ *no phone.* ⊠ *Donation suggested.* ☉ *Daily sunrise–sunset.*

❹ Pura Saraswati. Although the palace of its namesake has been gobbled up into the grounds of the Saraswati Hotel, the Saraswati Temple is still a testament to the region's talented artisans. Dedicated to Saraswati, the goddess of wisdom, learning, and the arts, the shrine has fine examples of ornately chiseled stone statues and stupas, particularly those on the tall lotus throne. These were carved by Balinese who came from all over the island to train with famed artist Lempad, who himself carved the statue of the demon giant Jero Gede Mecaling. The lotus pond and shimmering fountains in front of the temple make a lovely place to sit and reflect on the day. ⊠ *Jl. Ubud,* ☎ *no phone.* ⊠ *Donation suggested.* ☉ *Daily sunrise–sunset.*

❷ Puri Saren. At the town's heart sits its royal family palace, which encompasses a collection of shrines and pavilions inside high brick-and-stone walls. Destroyed when Gunung Batur erupted in 1917, the palace was quickly rebuilt and enhanced with new pavilions and arches. Today the inner courtyards are the home of the current *cokorda* (nobility). Of particular interest is the inner gate, an elaborate *kori agung*-style doorway (made of brick and limestone, with double doors) carved by noted Ubud artist Lempad. ⊠ *Jl. Ubud,* ☎ *no phone.* 🎟 *Donation suggested.* ☉ *Daily sunrise–sunset.*

Around Ubud

The little villages around Ubud are filled with exquisite crafts shops and crumbling historic sights. Although it would take months to see them all, many are accessible in just a short drive from town, so you can make half- or full-day trips, choosing from mountain temples, ancient archaeological relics, sacred caves, ornate rock carvings, crafts villages, and natural parks.

Sights to See

⑳ Goa Gajah. Bedulu's Elephant Cave is one of the region's most famous tourist sights, as well as one of its most significant historical markers. In addition to the caves hand-tunneled through the face of the mountain, the complex above the Petanu River includes temples, statues, pavilions, and three bathing pools (one for women, one for men, and a central pool for the gods). The exterior of the cave is an elaborately carved demonic head, and worshipers enter through the wide-open mouth. The archaeologists who discovered the face in 1923 originally thought it to be that of an elephant—hence the cave's name. Inside is a four-armed Ganesh carving, and carved into the walls are smaller statues and long niches, believed to have once been sleeping places for wandering travelers. Steps at the back of the complex lead down through overgrown gardens and lily ponds. A trail to the right crosses the river and leads to **Yeh Pulu** (☞ *below*). ⊠ *Jl. Bedulu,* ☎ *no phone.* 🎟 *50¢.* ☉ *Daily sunrise–sunset.*

⑭ Goa Garba. An inscription dated 1194 marks the temple at the top of this stone complex. Another 12th-century inscription is carved into one of the three hermits' caves at the lowest level. Look for the simple carvings of Ganesh and snakes decorating the shrine. ⊠ *Sawah Gunung,* ☎ *no phone.* 🎟 *25¢.* ☉ *Daily sunrise–sunset.*

⑬ Krobokan. This 12th-century site at the junction of the Krobokan and Pakerisan rivers has another of the region's hand-hewn hermit's caves. An 18-ft shrine is chiseled into the rock face next to it. ⊠ *Cemandik,* ☎ *no phone.* 🎟 *25¢.* ☉ *Daily sunrise–sunset.*

⑱ Museum Gedong Arca. This pleasant, well-organized little open-air museum along the main road has two courtyards, the first with four buildings housing originals and replicas of Bali's oldest archaeological relics, the second an open yard with pavilions displaying huge stone sarcophagi around a lotus pond. Although the displays aren't professionally labeled, they do cover the whole of the island's history and include ancient tools, Chinese pottery fragments, early jewelry, and wood and stone carvings. The helpful security guards will give you a quick tour if you like; or bring a drink and a snack, explore the inner displays, then sit back and relax in the open courtyard *bale* (pavilion) by the fountain. ⊠ *Jl. Pejeng,* ☎ *no phone.* 🎟 *50¢.* ☉ *Daily 8–2.*

⑫ Pura Gunung Kawi. This is the famed Temple on the Mountain of the Poet, which celebrates the Hindu god Siva. Here you'll find a fascinating complex of 11th-century temple shrines and royal tombs chiseled straight out of the sides of the hills. A steep climb leads to the entrance, where temple faces line either side of the rocks; the complex then extends into a monastery and several caves. It is believed that some of the monuments may be dedicated to King Airlangga of Java, son of Prince Udayana of Bali, although legend has it that a giant named Kebo Iwa carved the structures in one night with his fingernails. Look for the spring-fed pool filled with sacred koi, said to be the guardians of the water spirit. ⊠ *Tampaksiring,* ☎ *no phone.* 💳 *Donation required.* ☉ *Daily sunrise–sunset.*

⑰ Pura Kebo Edan. The Crazy Buffalo Temple is the last in Pejeng's holy triad. It is named for its 10-ft-tall statue of a demonic giant. Another statue of a chunky, crouching demon is also carved out of the rock here. ⊠ *Jl. Pejeng,* ☎ *no phone.* 💳 *Donation required.* ☉ *Daily sunrise–sunset.*

⑮ Pura Penataran Sasih. The Moon Temple is the most important of Pejeng's triad of holy shrines, for this one houses the ancient bronze **Moon of Pejeng**, a giant kettledrum decorated with elaborate etchings. Not only is this one of Indonesia's oldest artifacts, it's also the largest such drum in Southeast Asia. Although the Vietnamese produced similar relics, bronze molds found in this area prove the Balinese developed their metal skills independently. The Balinese have a story about the Moon of Pejeng's origin: the chariot wheel of the moon god (or the earring of the giant Kebo Iwa, depending on the legend) fell out of the sky, and its brilliance attracted a thief, who urinated on the drum to dim its light while he stole it, which consequently turned its exterior green. ⊠ *Jl. Pejeng,* ☎ *no phone.* 💳 *Donation suggested.* ☉ *Daily sunrise–sunset.*

⑯ Pura Pusering Jagat. Pejeng's Navel of the World Temple is the second in the triad of shrines along this road. This one features several intriguing stone statues of Hindu-based gods and demons. Look for the intricate reliefs of Hindu *Mahabharata* tales decorating the 14th-century stone jars in the rear pavilion. ⊠ *Jl. Pejeng,* ☎ *no phone.* 💳 *Donation suggested.* ☉ *Daily sunrise–sunset.*

⑩ Pura Sakenan. The Sakenan Temple is one of Bali's most important historical sites because it has one of the island's earliest examples of written language. An inscription from AD 960 describes the twin bathing pools of **Pura Tirta Empul** (☞ *below*), founded in that year. ⊠ *Manuk,* ☎ *no phone.* 💳 *Donation suggested.* ☉ *Daily sunrise–sunset.*

⑪ Pura Tirta Empul. The site of what is considered Bali's holiest spring, the peaceful, shady gardens and clear pools of the Tirta Empul Temple were once the bathing places of eastern Bali's kings. Legend has it the god Indra, whose army had been poisoned by the evil king Mayadanava, pierced a stone here to produce magical waters that would revive his men. Today a public pond lies in the outer courtyard, and the central compound has two rectangular pools lined with spouting fountains. The inner courtyard is home to nearly two dozen small, ornately carved temples and two large pavilions dedicated to the gods. During the annual Purnama Kapat celebrations, which take place on the anniversary of the temple's founding as recorded at **Pura Sakenan** (☞ *above*), the grounds come alive with colorful figures of the dog-lion Barong, brought here for ritual bathing ceremonies. The palace of Indonesia's first president Sukarno lies on a hill above the temple. Across the road and down a steep set of steps are the bathing pools of **Pura Mengening** (Mengening Temple), where many Balinese bring their curved *keris* (daggers) for washing. ⊠ *Tampaksiring,* ☎ *no phone.* 💳 *Donation required.* ☉ *Daily sunrise–sunset.*

⑲ Yeh Pulu. The origins of the extensive reliefs carved into the rock walls of this ancient site are a source of argument among experts, some of whom believe they were the work of a single 14th-century hermit who lived in a small cave nearby, while others think they were made by multiple artists from the 10th to the 19th centuries. Whatever the source, the 80-ft-high etchings recount stories of the Krishna, the charming goatherd and divine incarnation of the Hindu god Vishnu. ✉ *Jl. Bedulu,* ☎ *no phone.* 🎫 *50¢.* ⊘ *Daily sunrise–sunset.*

The Crafts Villages

In Bali you'll have a rare opportunity to actually view high-quality crafts as they're being made by the artists. From Denpasar north to Ubud and east to Gianyar, the traffic-clogged two-lane highways are jammed with craft shops standing shoulder to shoulder, their wares are laden with whatever type of wares are the area specialty. Because shops with one type of creation will be crammed into up to a mile of road, it's easy to shop: find the strip with item you want, then walk from shop to shop until you find the right artist and price.

㉔ Batuan. This once-powerful village was the administrative center for southern Bali's ruling family, the Gusti Ngurah Batulepang clan, during the 17th and 18th centuries. It was also gathering place and spiritual center for Bali's Buddhist Brahman priests, some of whom left to establish southern shrines but many of whom stayed and whose descendants live here today. The west side of town is still called Negara, a remnant of the 19th-century Sukawati kingdom that broke away from the ruling Gianyar house and overthrew it in 1884; the Dutch, however, folded it back into the Batuan domain in 1900 when they took over the region. Batuan's most famous former resident, though, is the evil giant Jero Gede Mecaling, who eventually crossed the strait to reside on Nusa Penida, although the temple named after him, **Pura Gede Mecaling,** remains.

Batuan is also a significant artisan village, for it is here that the Batuan style of black-and-white sketchlike painting originated. The intricate images of Balinese life were the inspiration of I Ngendon and I Patera, brothers from the village of Den Tiis who experimented in the 1930s with the classic pen-stroke style. This village also hosted the original performances of Bali's courtly *gambuh* dance dramas, believed to be the island's first palace dances. Today just two troupes present the gambuh, which is at its most powerful when performed to the sounds of the special gamelan gambuh under a full moon at the **Pura Puseh Batuan** (Batuan Temple Origin). A third temple, **Pura Desa Batuan** (Batuan Village Temple), holds one of the island's oldest inscriptions, 11th-century lettering in stone that records the kingdom's severance and subsequent independence from Sukawati in 1022.

Sights to See

OFF THE BEATEN PATH

BALI BIRD PARK – This park holds one of Southeast Asia's largest and most diverse bird collections. The tropical gardens provide a natural environment for more than 1,000 members of some 250 species, including birds from Africa, Australia, South America, and Asia. The Indonesian collection ranges from colorful cockatoos and birds of paradise to cranes, herons, and the rare Bali starling. Other park highlights are a rain forest aviary and a petting area. On Friday book a seat at the spacious Rainforest Bar and Café for a special dinner followed by a *kecak* dance performance. From Ubud head north on Jalan Campuhan to Kedewatan, take a left at the T junction, then drive south about 12 km (7 mi); the park entrance is on the right side of the road. ✉ *Jl. Serma Cok Ngurah Gambir, Singapadu,* ☎ *0361/299352.* 🎫 *$5; $9 for combined ticket with the reptile park.* ⊘ *Daily 8–6.*

BALI RIMBA REPTILE PARK – Before or after a trip to Bali Bird Park stop in to see the small but well-maintained collection of reptiles at the park next door. Housed here are a variety of lizards—including Komodo dragons—snakes, turtles, and frogs. The park is run by the Komodo Foundation, which uses the funds to promote awareness of endangered species and to support and research the surviving populations. ✉ *$5; $9 for combined ticket with the bird park.* ⊘ *Daily 9–6.*

㉑ Batubulan. Elaborate gray statues stand outside the many shops that line the main road through the town of Moon Stone. As you walk down this road, you can hear the taps of hammers and chisels and the scrapes of files as the artists fashion their crafts inside. Many of the carvings are made from *paras,* a soft, gray-black rock made of compressed volcanic ash. This material is easy to shape but tends to decay in a century or less, so many of the region's temples are under constant renovation. Antiques stores that carry treasures from around Asia are now tucked between the shops of stone-carvers. You can catch daily performances of the Barong and Rangda dance at the **Pura Puseh Bendul** (Bendul Temple of Origin) or behind the **Pura Desa Batubulan** (Batubulan Village Temple).

㉖ Blahbatuh. The highlight of this village is the collection of 17th-century Javanese masks kept in the **Pura Penataran Topang** temple. These masks, taken as souvenirs during Gelgel king Gusti Ngurah Jelantik's war against the western half of the island, are believed to be the inspiration for Bali's masked dances. Some of the island's most talented dancers performed in court ceremonies here during the late 1800s and early 1900s.

㉒ Celuk. Coming from Denpasar, the highway veers to the east after Batubulan, and you're suddenly surrounded by shops displaying intricate silver jewelry and filigree. This is Celuk, originally settled by *pande* (silver- and goldsmiths), clever magicians who supposedly stole the secrets of fire starting and metal forging from the gods. The creation of elaborate jewelry was once entrusted only to this clan of alchemists, although today many apprentices from outside the clan have been trained in the art. Gold-, bronze-, and ironworks are found here, although the prevalent metal is silver. Many stores open their backroom workshops so visitors can watch the artists melt, hammer, and curl the delicate filigree fibers.

㉕ Mas. Although this town gets its name from the Balinese word for gold (*emas*), it is the gathering place for Bali's best wood-carvers, who sit together on open porches that face the rice fields, chiseling rough stumps into tall, slender goddesses and Balinese masks. The secrets of the craft are passed from father to son, and artisans still mostly use axes, hammers, and chisels rather than drills to refine their shapes. The artists of centuries past only worked on sacred decorations for temples or ruling courts; today's carvers create whatever inspires them.

The town's history is just as intriguing as the works of its woodcarvers, for this was the home of the wandering 16th-century priest Danghyang Nirartha, who founded sacred temples throughout the island. It was here that he married the daughter of a local prince and rose to become the companion and high priest for the powerful king of Gelgel. The **Pura Taman Pule** (Pule Garden Temple), next to the town's central field, is a shrine to Nirartha built on the site of his former home. Legend has it that a tree in the center, possibly planted by the priest himself, once blossomed with a flower of gold, hence the town's name.

㉓ Sukawati. In the 18th century Sukawati was known as Timbul and was the second most powerful kingdom on Bali. It received its current name when the king of Mengwi and I Dewa Agung Anom, a prince of Klungkung, overthrew the evil ruler Ki Balian Batur using magical weapons from the courts of Klungkung. I Dewa Agung Anom then built a palace and proceeded to chisel into its walls the features of his own fantasy kingdom, modeled on the stories and ruins of Java's Majapahit. The *legong,* danced by young girls in gold-trimmed brocade, is said to have first been performed here; the kingdom was also the birthplace of many of the island's best *dalang,* the *wayang kulit* (leather shadow puppet) masters. The name Sukawati supposedly originated from the exclamations of the court guests, who upon viewing the elaborate palace and grounds would gasp, "*Sukahatine!*" ("My heart's delight!"). Today many of the island's most talented dalang still make their homes here. Sukawati is also the place to buy colorful mobiles and wind chimes.

Gianyar

Gianyar, now the region's administrative center, was once one of eastern Bali's most powerful kingdoms. Its palace is built on a former priest's home, and it is one of the best-preserved royal structures remaining on the island—parts of it even survived demolition and arson by neighboring Klungkung during Bali's 19th-century war of the rajas. The city may take its name from the palace's subsequent renovation, when it was dubbed the *griya anyar,* or "new priest's home."

When the Dutch arrived at the turn of the 20th century, the Gianyar kings forged an alliance that granted them special status as Dutch troops marched through the rest of the island. As a result, the town kept an element of independence throughout the years of Dutch rule. Gianyar was also the hometown of Anak Agung Gede Agung, Bali's famous political leader of the mid-20th century.

Sights to See

㉘ Pura Langon. Gianyar's Temple of Beauty, which sits next to the palace, is one of the region's state shrines. It's a major place of worship during island religious holidays and also the main worshipping place for the kingdom's royal family. ⊠ *Jl. Raya,* ☎ *no phone.* ▨ *Donation suggested.* ☉ *Daily sunrise–sunset.*

㉗ Puri Agung Gianyar. The Grand Palace of Gianyar is the former ruling place of King Anak Agung Gede Agung. Unfortunately, visitors aren't allowed within the grounds (except by appointment), but you should at least take a walk around its walls and peek inside the grand gate. You'll be able to view many of the massive carved walls and arches, as well as the original *bale bengong* (relaxation pavilion), which survived the city's thrashing by Klungkung. The kingdom's sacred banyan tree stands in the town square across from the palace. ⊠ *Jl. Raya,* ☎ *no phone.* ▨ *Donation suggested for appointment-only tours.* ☉ *By appointment only.*

Semarapura and Environs

The kingdom of Klungkung actually started off in Gelgel, the town from which the Dalem dynasty presided over much of the east—including parts of Java, Lombok, and Sumbawa—until 1651. The uprising of a local leader caused the royal members to flee, and it wasn't until three decades later that a new Klungkung prince returned to build a palace just 5 km (3 mi) north of the dynasty's original domain, in what is now the town of Semarapura. Java's 13th-century Majapahit kings may have been the ancestors of the ruling Dalem family, who changed their name to Dewa Agung (Great Deity) in the early 1700s after the move to the new capital.

Throughout the centuries—including during the civil war of the rajas and defensive battles against the Dutch—the Klungkung kings maintained a reputation of grace and wisdom. The rituals here are among

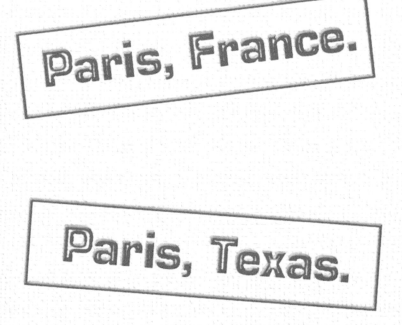

When it Comes to Getting Local Currency at an ATM,

Same Thing.

Whether you're in Yosemite or Yemen, using your Visa® card or ATM card with the PLUS symbol is the easiest and most convenient way to get local currency.

For example, let's say you're in France. When you make a withdrawal, using your secured PIN, it's dispensed in francs, but is debited from your account in U.S. dollars.

This makes it easy to take advantage of favorable exchange rates. And if you need help finding one of Visa's 627,000 ATMs in 127 countries worldwide, visit **visa.com/pd/atm**. We'll make finding an ATM as easy as finding the Eiffel Tower, the Pyramids or even the Grand Canyon.

It's Everywhere You Want To Be.®

SEE THE WORLD
IN FULL COLOR

Fodor's Exploring Guides bring all the great sights vividly to life with hundreds of photographs, fascinating historical background, and colorful anecdotes. Detailed maps and practical information keep you headed in the right direction.

Pair a **Fodor's** Exploring Guide with your trusted Gold Guide for a complete planning package.

the island's most intricate, the language the most formal, and the temples the most elaborate; for centuries only Klungkung architects were permitted to build the 11-tier cremation biers for the holiest people. The 1908 puputan in response to the Dutch takeover, two years after the Badung rulers' mass suicide in Denpasar, was a testament to the ruling clan's willpower: As the palace burned behind them, the royal family marched en masse to the center of town, where the king defiantly drove his magical keris into the ground in hopes of creating a deep crevasse into which the Dutch troops would fall. Instead, the Dutch fired their rifles point-blank, killing the king as behind him each of his wives committed suicide by plunging her dagger into her heart.

It is hard to imagine that this scene happened just a century ago, on the main street where motorcycles and tour buses park today. Although the town's name was officially changed to Semarapura in 1992 to commemorate the Puri Semarapura palace in the center of town, the Balinese—and many road signs—still call the community Klungkung in memory of the great kingdom.

Sights to See

32 **Gelgel.** As the former center of Bali's remarkable golden age, the town of Gelgel, 5 km (3 mi) south of Semarapura, has many important historical sites. The **Pura Jero Agung** (Great Palace Temple)—the ancestral shrine of the Gelgel royal family's elaborate original palace—is where King Dalem Seganing hosted the island's first Dutch visitors in 1597. The **Pura Jero Kapal** (Head Palace Temple), next door, is the last relic from Gelgel's second-largest palace. Ancestor gods are believed to descend from the heavens above Gunung Agung to attend temple festivals at the ancient **Pura Dasar** (Base Temple), to the east. Some archaeologists believe that the large, flat stones across the road are megalithic alters that precede all Balinese shrines. The **Mesjid Gelgel** (Gelgel Mosque), 300 ft to the east, is the oldest mosque on the island. *Temples and mosque free. Temples and mosque daily sunrise–sunset.*

OFF THE BEATEN PATH

KAMASAN – Adjacent to Gelgel, the village of Kamasan is where the two-dimensional *wayang* style of painting began. In this type of art, which also graces Semarapura's Kerta Gosa, figures have the same one-dimensional look as the intricate Javanese wayang kulit puppets. It was once the choice style of art for the region's royal families, and a special *banjar sangging* (painters' neighborhood)—where artists gather to work on pictures for the palace—still operates today. You can watch the progress of the three-step painting process: a master first draws the fine black-and-white figures; his children or relatives color them in; and the lines are retraced and embellished upon by the original artist. Kamasan was also once a training center for shadow-puppet masters, who worked with the artists as they created the characters. In addition, the town's *banjar pande mas* (goldsmiths' neighborhood) is where the gold- and silversmiths, descendants of Klungkung royal family servants, still practice their crafts and guard their secrets.

31 **Pura Taman Sari.** The Flower Garden Temple, on the northeast end of town by the Unda River, was a favorite meditation site of the royal family. It features an open pavilion surrounded by a large lotus pond. *Jl. Gunung Semaru, no phone. Donation suggested. Daily sunrise–sunset.*

30 **Pura Jero Agung.** Built in 1929, the Grand Palace Temple stands west of the original throne and replaces an earlier palace razed by the Dutch in 1908. It became the home for royal family members who survived the terrible puputan and battle, after they returned from exile on Lom-

bok. ✉ *Jl. Puputan*, ☎ *no phone.* ⧉ *Donation suggested.* ◷ *By appointment only.*

㉙ **Puri Semarapura.** Once the home of the Klungkung kingdom's powerful rulers, the Palace of the God of Love sits at the center of what is now Semarapura. The city's most famous site is the **Bale Kerta Gosa** (Hall of Justice Pavilion), famous for the elaborate ceiling painted in the muted pen-and-ink style that originated in the nearby village of Kamasan. Plan to spend some time here with your neck craned back, looking up at the great tales of the trial realms of the universe: modern life, the heavenly water gardens, and the world of the gods. There are 267 panels in all, arranged in nine sections to relate the Javanese and Balinese stories of *Tantri*—based on India's *Pancatantra* tales—as well as the adventures of Bima, a demigod from the legends of the *Mahabharata.* Also on the grounds is the **Bale Kambang** floating pavilion, once the gathering place for the kings' royal guards, which boasts eight Kamasan-style painted panels. The stories painted here are mostly of the semidivine Sutasoma; another panel tells the tale of Pan and Men Brayut, a couple with 18 children, and another shows an astrological calendar. Although most palace buildings were destroyed by the Dutch, you can also still see the original kori agung gate, guarded, ironically, by two Dutch-like figures, one swilling wine and the other counting money. ✉ *Jl. Puputan*, ☎ *no phone.* ⧉ *1$.* ◷ *Daily 8–4.*

Pura Besakih

★ ㉝ High up on Gunung Agung, the 30-temple complex of **Pura Besakih** is the most sacred of all of Bali's religious shrines—so revered, in fact, that it's known as the Mother Temple. It is thought to have been built even before Hinduism reached the island and then subsequently modified to fit newer beliefs as the religion gained power. Much of the original temple area was destroyed in 1963 when Gunung Agung erupted, but these areas have been restored over the years.

Although Pura Besakih is probably the number-one tourist spot in the mountains, it's worth fighting the throngs to see the splendor of the ornate stone-and-brick passages rising 2 km (1 mi) up through the forested mountain slopes. The parking lot is lined with souvenir and snack stands, and past these are the split entrance gates. Besakih lies on seven terraces that step toward the peak (the crowds grow thinner as you climb upward). Three main sections are dedicated to the gods: the south, painted red for the god Brahma; the center, painted white for Siva; and the north, painted black for Vishnu. Each temple section has courtyards and alleys filled with decorative arches and walls, and even on busy days you can usually find a spot for savoring the beauty of the setting. Although the inner courtyard is sacred, the rest is open to visitors—except on religious holidays; so check with the tourism office before you head up here.

Pura Besakih is 40 km (25 mi) northeast of Bangli, 45 km (28 mi) north of Semarapura, and 60 km (37 mi) northeast of Denpasar. The temple can be reached from Bangli (if you're coming from Gunung Batur), Semarapura (the best route if you're coming from Ubud, Denpasar, or points south), or Candidasa (take the road inland to Amlapura, where the road splits, continue along to Rendang, then turn right to climb the 11 km [7 mi] to the temple).

Padangbai and Environs

This cute little ferry town is actually Bali's biggest eastern transportation hub. Every day, around the clock, enormous car ferries chug their

INDULGING YOURSELF: BALINESE BEAUTY TREATMENTS

ONE OF THE GREAT LUXURIES of a vacation on Bali is being able to try one or several of the beauty treatments the island is known for—particularly a traditional massage. Massage has been an intrinsic part of Balinese healing and medicine for centuries. Newborn babies are massaged several times a day, which the Balinese believe encourages proper growth and formation. Many Balinese claim that massage by a traditional healer (or *balian apun*) fixes a broken bone more quickly and successfully than the Western method of using a cast. Unlike Westerners, the Balinese do not view massage as a relaxing treat but as a way to help cure certain physical or mental health problems.

A mix of deep tissue and acupuncture massage, traditional Balinese massage is offered almost anywhere on the island and can cost from $5 to $100. The cheapest deals are found on Kuta Beach, where upon arrival visitors are almost immediately approached by Indonesian women, and occasionally men, proffering their massage skills. An hour-long rubdown can be as little as $5 and takes place right there on the sand. If you are lucky you'll be in the hands of a real pro, but it's wise to test out a masseuse (or masseur) before you decide to commit to a full hour. A little more upscale is La Lucciola Beach Club, in Seminyak, which has a masseuse on staff. An hour of massage on one of the lounge chairs costs about $8, and afterward you can relax for a few hours under the sun.

If you're willing to spend a little extra for more privacy, almost all the hotels in Bali offer traditional massage to guests. In fact, one of the biggest trends at Bali's hotels in the past few years has been to add spa facilities. Nowadays there are almost as many spas in Bali as there are in New York City or Los Angeles, but most

Bali spas are considerably less expensive. Among the best are the spa at Hotel Tugu Bali in Canggu; the Bodywork Center in Ubud; and the Matahari Beach Resort & Spa in Pemuteran in the northwest (the Matahari's four-handed massage is the ultimate in relaxation).

Many resorts also offer a traditional Indonesian treatment called the *mandi lulur* (*lulur* is a Javanese word meaning "coating the skin"). This treatment has been practiced in the palaces of central Java for four centuries; today wealthy Javanese will have it done every day for a week before their wedding day. It usually begins with an hour-long massage, followed by a spice and yogurt scrub that exfoliates and moisturizes the skin, and then a bath of flowers; the treatment ends with an allover application of moisturizing cream.

Another common body treatment is a Balinese *boreh*, similar to a body mask or scrub. It's an age-old remedy used by the Balinese to treat everything from fever to arthritis to skin problems. Consisting of a mix of herbs and spices—the concoction will differ depending on the problem—a boreh is usually administered by a traditional doctor. At a spa the technician will use a basic recipe of herbs and spices that helps to increase blood circulation and soften the skin.

Also popular throughout Indonesia are *jamu,* or *djamoe*: herbal concoctions ingested in either liquid or pill form, similar to the herbal supplements now popular in the United States. Some claim to cause weight loss; others purportedly give energy and detoxify the body. You can find jamu all over the country in warungs, supermarkets, and drugstores.

—Gisela Williams

way across the Lombok Strait and back, shuttling passengers between Bali and the port of Lembar, on Lombok. On a clear day the silhouettes of Gunung Agung and Lombok's taller Gunung Rinjani vie for space in the skyline. Between ferries Padangbai is a pleasant market town, with just a few dusty streets, lots of small shops, and a stretch of brown beach lined with colorful wooden jukung that sail out before dawn each morning.

Most travelers skip Padangbai on their way to other island attractions or view it as merely a hub for boats to the Badung Strait Islands, but the town actually has a few merits of its own, including hotels and restaurants. The foremost attractions here are diving and snorkeling along the vast offshore reefs. The town also has historical significance: the Pura Silayukti temple is fabled to have been the home of the 11th-century priest Mpu Kuturan. As one of Bali's few natural harbors, it's also where Dutch ships first landed on Bali and later attacked to take power over the island. Take a motorcycle up the steep road at the north of the bay, and you'll find a forest-lined lookout facing a stunning ocean panorama.

The rocky shoreline north of Padangbai gives way to the smooth, golden beaches and rich coral reefs of Balina, Buitan, and Manggis. Along this hidden coast small hotels attract divers and sunbathers. There's not much to do but sun and snorkel—which is exactly why most people stay here.

OFF THE
BEATEN PATH
PURA GOA LAWAH – The Bat Cave Temple indeed lives up to its name, for the three-tier structure stands at the entrance to a large cave. The cave is inhabited by thousands of flying foxes that hang from the rocky ceiling by day and depart on food hunts in an explosion of black wings every evening. These large fruit bats are believed to be the temple's guardians and are considered sacred—as are the large pythons that live in the neighboring rocks. The bats' lair is rumored to lead underground all the way to Pura Besakih; other stories have it tunneling beneath the Badung Strait to the Pura Peed temple, on Nusa Penida. ✉ *Donation suggested.* ⊙ *Daily sunrise–sunset.*

Candidasa and Environs

This one-road tourist town takes its name from the Pura Candi Dasa, which lies at the eastern end of town next to a large lagoon. In the 1980s developers discovered the offshore reefs and then the white-sand beaches beside the lagoon, and soon the area was built into a coastal escape from Bali's overcrowded southern peninsula. The beach has since washed away, replaced by an ugly cement breakwater, and even the lovely sea views have vanished with the construction of chunky hotels. Still, Candidasa has the most modern and extensive facilities of any east-coast town north of Sanur. If it's serenity you seek, stay in southern Balina or northern Manggis and come here only for shopping and dinner.

Sights to See

34 **Pura Candi Dasa.** A 12th-century complex at the east end of town, the Monument Temple of Ten—referring to 10 holy Buddhist scriptures—has one of the most pleasant natural settings on Bali. The main temple overlooks a section of golden sand and a palm-fringed azure lagoon. A temple dedicated to Siva sits in an upper courtyard; a shrine to Hariti, a fertility goddess, is carved out of the rock face below. ✉ *Donation suggested.* ⊙ *Daily sunrise–sunset.*

35 **Tenganan.** The coastal road north of Candidasa passes through patchwork rice fields in different stages of cultivation. Men ankle-deep in mud plant and weed while ducks paddle and dip for their lunch. Out in the fields are shrines to Dewi Sri, the rice goddess, and raised wooden platforms where farmers rest and eat. In the village of Tenganan, 3 km (2 mi) north of Candidasa, artisans of the Bali Aga (original Balinese) clan weave intricate ikat fabrics and carve designs into palm-leaf panels. These are the ancestors of the original immigrants who settled the island more than 1,000 years ago, and they have protected their traditions throughout the years by marrying only within their village. The professional guides here will take an hour to lead you through their village homes, shops, and festival grounds, where you can observe Balinese life little changed from ancient times. A number of shops sell woven textiles and carved calendars and books; you can watch the artisans at work and marvel at the craftsmanship.

Amlapura

Formerly the center of the Karangasem kingdom, Amlapura is Bali's easternmost town. Called Karangasem originally, the settlement was comfortably nestled into the foothills of Gunung Agung until 1963, when the volcano's eruption and subsequent earthquakes wiped out everything in it. The rebuilt city was named Amlapura and stands as the Karangasem district's capital today.

This is a land of colorful legends, many of which debate the origin of the kingdom. As one story goes, the god of Gunung Agung came down from the mountain and impregnated a woman from town. She gave birth to a son named Karangasem, or God of the Eastern Hill, who became the founder of the royal dynasty. Another tale follows the 17th-century Gelgel court minister I Gusti Arya Batanjeruk, who was killed while escaping the kingdom with his wife and nephew, I Gusti Pangeran Oka. His widow later met a local prince in the Karangasem market and married him on the condition that her nephew would become the next ruler—and founder of a new kingdom—upon his death. The former ruling family of Karangasem, and many who live here today, claim they are descendants of the Majapahit rulers as well as of the 16th-century Balinese prime minister Batan Jeruk.

Whatever its origins, the original Karangasem dynasty built up power over eastern Bali and took over Lombok in the 17th century. The Dutch took control in 1894, although the rajas still held onto a bit of figurative independence and the royal house survived until the late 1970s. Today this mild-mannered administrative and trade center lies around the collection of temples that were once the focus of life in the royal family.

Sights to See

③⑦ Puri Taman Ujung. Atop green and gold hills, with the lavender silhouette of Gunung Agung in the distance, the Last Garden Temple quietly glows in the late afternoon sunlight. This elegant complex is one of three water palaces built by Karangasam's king Anak Agung Anglurah Ketut as a retreat for his family. Constructed in 1919, it originally was centered on a large enclosed *bale* of stucco and stained glass, with smaller open pavilions and a large pond around it. Most of the complex was destroyed in the 1963 eruption of Gunung Agung, but you can still wander among the statues and between the ghostly pillars and arches. ⊠ *Jl. Raya Ujung,* ☎ *no phone.* ☑ *Donation suggested.* ⊙ *Daily sunrise–sunset.*

③⑥ Puri Kaningan. The gardens, lotus ponds, and floating pavilions of the town's Eastern Temple are a wonderful place for a morning walk. Although they were the quarters for Balinese royalty, the buildings have

European and Chinese characteristics; the **Bale Maskerdam,** for example, is an enormous closed building with Continental decor, and in the **Bale London hall** a British royal crest sits amid the Balinese furnishings. Although the inner courtyard is only for royal guests, you can peek in and see the large lake and floating **Puri Amsterdam pavilion.** The temple has hosted famous guests such as the American writer and choreographer Katharane Mershon, who visited in 1937; rooms are still for rent if you'd like to stay. The temple is currently the only one in town open to the public. ⊠ *Jl. Raya,* ☎ *no phone.* ⊠ *25¢.* ⊙ *Daily 9–2.*

38 Tirtagangga. This water palace, whose name means "Ganges Water," takes its inspiration from the holy river of India. The complex of pools here, **Tirta Ayu,** is fed by a sacred spring, and the lush gardens, splashing stone fountains, and sweeping views of stacked rice terraces surrounding the area make this a refreshing place for a break. The retreat was built in 1948, and though many of the early features were lost 15 years later when Gunung Agung erupted, some have been restored. A large central pool and another closer to the spring are open for swimming, trails thread through the grounds and surrounding rice fields, and there's a small homestay inside the palace. ⊠ *Jl. Tirtagangga,* ☎ *no phone.* ⊠ *25¢.* ⊙ *Daily sunrise–sunset.*

The Northeast Coast

Heading north around the eastern wing of butterfly-shape Bali, the land is mostly a hard, dry patchwork of olive- and saffron-color shrubbery, occasionally punctuated by low green forest and chunky rice terraces. This is a road that nobody travels—save for locals making weekly trips to and from the larger markets in Tulamben and Amlapura—for a good reason: it is a rugged ribbon of crumbled asphalt and fallen rocks that winds through the mountain folds and clings to the cliffs. Passing the close-set peaks of Gunung Lampuyang and Gunung Seraya, the narrow highway reveals brown sand beaches and clusters of fishing villages. Huge metal pans of seawater line the shores here, as salt processing is the only alternative to fishing for making a living. Men balance lontar-leaf water buckets on their shoulders, bringing in ocean water to evaporate in the bins on the beach.

Sights to See

39 Amed. Over the past decade this fishing and salt-panning village has drawn a steady stream of tourists to its pristine offshore reefs. The town is small, but the market carries basic goods, and a few hotels and restaurants cater to divers and snorkelers that use Amed as a base for daily boat trips. It's the quieter alternative if you want to dive the Tulamben wreck (☞ *below*) but don't want to bunk with the tourist crowds.

40 Tulamben. For centuries this was just a modest fishing village—until the Japanese torpedoed a U.S. warship offshore in World War II. Since then the reefs have built up around the wreck, which has been discovered by divers, turning Tulamben into a tourist hub of modern shops, hotels, and restaurants. It's still small by Kuta standards, but it's a good place for an introduction to Bali's underwater beauty, since the shallow wreck is easy to reach even for the most timid snorkelers. If you enjoy more land-based pleasures, a few trails lead through the dry countryside and the rough volcanic beach has lovely eastern views.

Just 100-ft off Tulamben Beach—and in water less than 18-ft deep—lies the **wreck of the SS** *Liberty Glo,* Bali's most famous dive site. The steamer was torpedoed in the Lombok Strait by the Japanese on January 11, 1942; the vessel snapped in half two decades later when Gunung Agung erupted, which is how the ship rests today. Over the years the Tulamben wreck has become host to a thriving reef that shelters more than 400 types of fish, as well as dolphins, sharks, rays, and turtles. ✉ *Wreck free.* ⊘ *Wreck daily 24 hrs.*

BEACHES

Amed. The fine ashen grains of this volcanic beach are all right for strolling if you don't mind grubby toes, but the major attraction is the offshore reef. Still, the views are lovely, and the breeze is constant, making it a nice place for a picnic.

Balina. Four kilometers (2½ miles) east of Candidasa, this stretch of white sand against sapphire blue waves was once the hidden delight of a few backpackers and divers. But the news slowly spread, and today the coastline has a dozen or so small hotels and luxury villa complexes vying for business. It's quiet, though, and is mostly the haunt of divers and those who want to relax in total peace—perfect if you want a scenic setting for finishing that spy novel.

Buitan. Immediately east of Balina Beach, and just steps south of the town of Buitan, this beach is reserved for the exclusive resorts. If you're lucky enough to stay here, you'll have a perfect arc of bay to jog along while watching the ferries and fishing boats cross from Padangbai to greater seas. Shells, driftwood, and other treasures are scattered along the brown beach, which is framed by high, forested cliffs.

Candidasa. There's no real beach to speak of here—it has eroded away over the past two decades and been replaced by a cement breakwater—but you can find pockets of sand here and there in front of various hotels, particularly as you head away from town. The area around the lagoon has a few hidden stretches of brown beach as well, but you have to walk to find them.

Manggis. Settled up against the western edge of Buitan, this is one of Bali's newer—and more upscale—sweeps of coastline, and its soft, light-brown beauty befits the expensive resorts that are beginning to build up along its shores. This beach has one of the island's most dramatic backdrops, particularly at twilight, when the setting sun casts amethyst shadows over the mountainous curves of the bay and the lights of Padangbai and ferries crossing the wide strait glitter across the water.

☺ **Padangbai.** This brown-sugar beach is really too small, public, and crowded with jukung for private sunbathing, but it's one of Bali's most colorful beaches. It also has a very convenient location, right across from the town's little lane of hotels and restaurants.

Tulamben. The coffee-grounds sand here is a reminder of Bali's recent volcanic past. It's not that scenic or pleasant to walk on, but it really doesn't matter because Tulamben's main attraction is the shipwreck offshore. If you must have a sunning beach, try one of the resorts, where you'll find groomed sand, umbrellas, chairs, and drink service.

DINING

Eastern Bali's best dining experiences are concentrated around Ubud, in classy new restaurants, ethnic diners, and decades-old tried-and-true eateries. You can find every type of cuisine here, though not on the grand scale of southern Bali. In the mass of restaurants at Ubud's core you'll find Italian, Japanese, Mexican, Indian, Greek, and Indonesian food, usually all stuffed onto the same menu.

Unfortunately, since many of these places try to be all things to all people, their menus are often a jumble of ho-hum international dishes, and none of the restaurants—or meals—are particularly memorable. If you think dining out is about more than just sustenance, look for places that stick to one type of cuisine. For a nice ambience and fine European dishes, try one of the resorts along the Sayan terrace, most of which have world-renowned chefs and excellent service. At the large eclectic restaurants, pass up the watered-down Indonesian fare and go for the house specialties and desserts, two things that rarely miss the mark. For true Indonesian food, head to the lighted windows of a Padang-style *warung* (open-air food stall) or to one of the more modest specialized restaurants. Look on the menu for the warm, spicy vegetable salads *lawar* (a green mix of bean sprouts, long beans, shredded coconut, papaya, and star fruit) and *urab* (a red mix of vegetables and shredded coconut), indicating that there are Balinese cooks in the kitchen making island food the traditional way.

Although you can find real Balinese food in small restaurants throughout eastern Bali, Ubud is the best place on the island to try *bebek betutu* (smoked duck) and *bebek goreng* (crispy fried duck), two of Bali's traditional ceremonial dishes. You usually must reserve these meals a day in advance because they take several hours to prepare. Also note that although most international restaurants offer smoked and fried duck, this does not mean that they specialize in Balinese food. Other Balinese delicacies found in the region are *babi kecap* (barbecue pork), *sate babi* (pork skewered on wooden sticks and grilled, served with a spicy peanut sauce), and *babi guling* (roast suckling pig, usually stuffed and served with urab and lawar). The cooler mountain areas have more types of hot dishes, including meat and vegetable curries with spicy coconut gravy.

In the coastal fishing villages your dining options are pretty much limited to warung and hotel restaurants. Indonesian fare is the main staple, although the hotels dish up Western-style fare: eggs, sandwiches, fried foods, pizzas, and pastas. If you don't like spices, you can't go wrong with the seafood in most places. In the town of Amed, which hasn't yet developed into a major tourist hub, the food is prepared with Balinese flair. Tulamben has a greater variety of restaurants and even a few upmarket resort establishments where you can expect good service amid tropical elegance.

As throughout the island, meals in eastern Bali are casual, and the dress code is as well. No eateries require jackets, and you'll probably want no more than a nice skirt or light slacks for even the most posh resorts. If you want to dress up in Ubud, though, you won't be out of place, for it's a come-as-you-are sort of town that attracts everyone from scruffy wandering souls in tie-dyed T-shirts to the worldly rich in pressed silk shirts and sapphires. In Ubud brunch is more common than early breakfast, lunches are light, and dinner doesn't get started until after dark, even though many places shut down by 10 PM.

For general information and price categories, *see* Dining *in* Smart Travel Tips.

Ubud

Cafés

$ ✕ **Chantique.** Always busy, this bakery at the crossroads near the Monkey Forest displays an array of beautiful treats behind the glass-front counter. The cozy coffeehouse inside is the perfect place to curl up with a book, a pot of tea, and a treat on a rainy afternoon. This is also the place to order a fancy cake or dessert for that special day. ✉ *Jl. Wanara Wana,* ☎ *0361/349181. No credit cards.*

$ ✕ **Honeymoon Bakery.** Hidden down a narrow alley in Penestanan, this tiny bakery does a brisk catering business with Ubud's best restau-

Ubud Dining

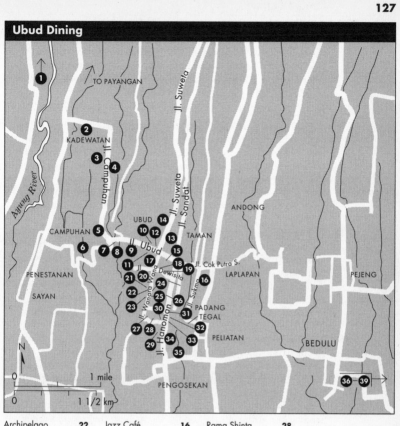

rants. It's open to walk-in customers as well, and if you go early you'll probably find a line of tourists perched along the picnic table out front sipping coffee and munching fresh croissants and cookies. Stay at the Honeymoon Guesthouse (☞ Lodging, *below*) and get the goodies free every morning. The bakery is open daily 8–4. ✉ *Jl. Bisma, Penestanan,* ☎ *0361/973282. No credit cards. No dinner.*

Contemporary

$$ ✕ **Café Lotus.** This large, busy restaurant in the center of Ubud is part of the courtyard gardens of a royal temple. Stone floors, intimate tables, and small waterfalls set the scene against the backdrop of a magnificent lotus pond. The standard Western and Indonesian fare—roast chicken, homemade pasta, fried rice—is bland, but the portions are sizable. If you're just stopping in for a drink and a peek at your guidebook, sit on a floor cushion in the raised pavilion in back. ✉ *Jl. Ubud,* ☎ *0361/975660. AE, MC, V.*

$$ ✕ **Kádek.** The yellow limestone exterior gives this elegant two-story restaurant an eye-catching prominence on the busy road. The lower level resembles a Borders bookstore with its fine wood tables, wicker-and-wire chairs, and muted colors. Upstairs is a large dining pavilion and an Internet café. The Indonesian and Western specialties are tasty and substantial. Kádek is a popular place for group parties and events and can cater outside functions as well. ✉ *Jl. Pengosekan,* ☎ *0361/978374. AE, DC, MC, V.*

$$ ✕ **Murni's Warung.** This multilevel restaurant overlooking the forested Ayung River valley is one of Ubud's original travelers' haunts. The rustic street-level dining room bustles with activity. Reserve a table above the river for the best views. The Singapore-style bar below, with its comfortable wicker couches, is the place to sip tony cocktails. The menu includes Western and Indonesian items like pasta, curries, seafood, and sandwiches. Although the food is fair at best, the portions are large, and the ambience is classic "travelers' Bali." ✉ *Jl. Campuhan,* ☎ *0361/975233. AE, MC, V.*

$ ✕ **Kafe Batan Waru.** Expats favor this cozy café for its relaxed atmosphere and well-prepared international fare. The pale walls are hung with classic William Farquhar sketches of Asian fruits, adding an element of colonial Singapore to the interior. Outside tables edge the sidewalk, where blackboards announce the day's specials: perhaps a grilled eggplant and tofu sandwich smothered in caramelized onions, chicken and pineapple curry, or pasta with candlenut cream sauce topped with grilled shiitake mushrooms. The staff is quick to deliver drinks and plates of food, even at the busiest times. ✉ *Jl. Dewi Sita,* ☎ *0361/977528. AE, MC, V.*

$ ✕ **Nomad Bar & Restaurant.** This longtime backpacker favorite has been upgraded and expanded, but the food is as good as ever. It's a place to kick back any time of day, with comfortable bamboo furniture, checkered tablecloths, and friendly service. The Balinese fare is among the best in town, and the Indonesian dishes taste like they're straight from the warung. Because it's along the main road, it's also a popular stop for drinks after temple dances. ✉ *Jl. Ubud 33,* ☎ *0361/ 977169. No credit cards.*

Continental

$$$ ✕ **Bridge Café.** Next to the Campuhan Bridge at the bottom curve of Ubud's main road, this multilevel restaurant has the best river views in town. The small main dining room is accented with polished marble and wood. A curving staircase leads up to a level lined with large cushions for floor seating and down to a dark, formal cave overlooking the river. The European menu includes main courses of steak, chicken, and lamb, as well as salads and soups. Although the food is

on the bland side, the portions are healthy and the service excellent. ⊠ *Jl. Campuhan,* ☎ *0361/975085. AE, DC, MC, V.*

$$$ ✕ **The Restaurant.** A sweeping vista of the lush Ayung River valley, squeezed between the blue of the sky and the infinity pool of the Chedi hotel (☞ Lodging, *below*), greets diners who step into this formal pavilion. Dark tables line the marble floors, and the clink of forks on china and the rustling of international newspapers are the only sounds above the whisper of wind in the trees. It's a perfect place for breakfast, when sumptuous Western food fills the plates, or for dinner by twilight, when the menu changes to a selection of delicate European and Indonesian specials. European ingredients mix with Balinese flavors in dishes like spiced calamari with fern tips and taro; grilled mackerel with ginger, basil, and jackfruit; and roast pork with sweet-and-sour sauce and long beans with turmeric and coconut. For dessert try the Indonesian sampler plate, with sticky rice and pandan almond ice cream. ⊠ *Desa Melinggi Kelod Payangan,* ☎ *0361/975963. AE, DC, MC, V.*

$$–$$$ ✕ **Ary's Warung.** This Ubud classic sits on the busiest spot on the main road. Don't expect warung food, though: the limited menu now has only trendy, upscale fare, with prices to match. The odd twists on such traditional cuisine as pasta Alfredo, smoked duck, and seafood kebabs aren't always well balanced, and although dishes are artfully presented, portions are small. Service is slow and not always sharp, and waiters avoid making extra treks up to the second-level dining room. But the restaurant has a bustling international feel that turns romantic by evening candlelight, making it a good place to stop for a drink after shopping or an evening dance performance. ⊠ *Jl. Ubud,* ☎ *0361/975053. AE, MC, V.*

$$–$$$ ✕ **Mai-Mai.** Tour buses line up outside this spacious restaurant at lunchtime, and—for once—you should follow them. With a bi-level seating area beneath the enormous pavilion, there's plenty of room. The food ranges from pastas and salads to breakfasts and sandwiches. However, the tourists are here for the set menu of Balinese and Indonesian dishes: spicy seafood and coconut soup, vegetarian curry, and shredded lemongrass chicken. The large koi pond in back is a great place for children to play while you linger over coffee and dessert. ⊠ *Jl. Hanoman,* ☎ *0361/977195. AE, DC, MC, V.*

$$ ✕ **Komaneka Café.** This small, open restaurant in back of the Komaneka Gallery offers simplicity and perfection in the color, style, and taste of its meals. The attentive waitstaff is there to serve every request, and the delicate portions are presented with artistic flair. Even something as common as *gado-gado* (steamed vegetables tossed in a rich peanut sauce) turns up precisely done and arranged in a floral pattern. The few wines available are well chosen. This is a nice place to linger after a walk through the gallery. ⊠ *Jl. Wanara Wana,* ☎ *0361/976090. AE, DC, MC, V.*

Eclectic

$$–$$$ ✕ **Indus.** Stone steps between fountains lead down into this museum-
★ size restaurant on the cliffs above the Ayung River. Vast panoramas of forest and rice terraces can be seen from every table in the marble-floor first level and from the breezy upper-level terrace that hangs out over the edge. The fare is wholesome and filling. Balinese paella has fragrant yellow rice; char-grilled beef is served with mushroom gravy; the sweet-potato soup is made with fresh coconut milk; and Chinese greens with tofu and mushrooms are served on red rice. Far more sinful are the desserts: fudgelike banana-chocolate cake, thick tiramisu, and creamy lime tarts. ⊠ *Jl. Sanggingan,* ☎ *0361/977684. AE, DC, MC, V*

$$ ✕ **Casa Luna.** With dining rooms set back from the main road, this popular restaurant is one of the top places for brunch and teatime treats.

Besides whole-wheat pancakes, omelets, and Indonesian breakfast items, the menu provides tastes of the American Southwest and India. Choose from entrées like spicy grilled chicken served with corn fritters and papaya-lime *sambal* (Indonesian chili sauce); feta chimichangas; chili-coconut fish served with saffron rice; and a tandoori chicken pita with yogurt dressing. You can dine on the sunny upper terrace or on the more boisterous lower level. If you're in the mood for homemade ice cream, try the creamy black rice, rum, and raisin. ⊠ *Jl. Ubud,* ☎ *0361/973283. AE, DC, MC, V.*

$–$$ ✕ **Jazz Café.** Black-and-white photos of Louis Armstrong, Billie Holiday, and John Coltrane look on as music from the stage eases over the candlelit bar. This cozy café, filled with dark wood tables, entertains an eclectic crowd with live jazz and exquisite cuisine. Tasty selections include thick carrot soup, colorful pasta primavera, and spicy Thai curry. The desserts are an added reason to linger: try the lemon crumble cake or the thick fudge-nut brownie. A raised area in back and two garden pavilions offer more-private seating around low square tables on ikat floor cushions. ⊠ *Jl. Sukma 2, Tebesaya,* ☎ *0361/ 976594. AE, MC, V.*

$ ✕ **Funky Monkey.** Eclectic modern decor and a cozy space indeed create a funky coffee-shop atmosphere near the Monkey Forest. The surprisingly savory menu features classic Continental dishes given an Asian twist: pumpkin soup with lemongrass and coconut milk, fettuccine with Kalamata olives and chili, and spinach-and-snapper ravioli with pesto. It's a popular stop for lunchtime appetizers and sandwiches—all the breads and pastas are homemade—or an afternoon gelato. ⊠ *Jl. Wanara Wana,* ☎ *0812/3903729. No credit cards. Closed Sun.*

$ ✕ **Tutmak.** This travelers' favorite has expanded from a tiny coffee shop
★ into a full-blown deli/restaurant that gets everything right. Wood and iron tables are staggered on wide steps up from street level. Take your time reading the extensive menu, and be prepared to change your mind several times. Huge sandwiches, such as the succulent Greek chicken salad with homemade mayonnaise and capers, come with chips or organic salads. Vegetarian choices include lasagna, Middle Eastern plates with *babaganoush,* hummus, couscous, and falafel; and Indian coconut fried rice with almonds, peanuts, spinach, and spices. Save room for desserts such as mango or lime mousse, Scottish shortbread cake, or a thick slab of chocolate cake garnished with prunes and marinated in marsala. ⊠ *Jl. Dewi Sita,* ☎ *0361/975754. No credit cards.*

Indian

$–$$ ✕ **Bumbu Bali.** On one of Ubud's busiest corners, this modest thatch-
★ roof restaurant has made its mark serving excellent Indian and Indonesian cuisine. Indonesian music creates a romantic ambience, and trickling fountains erase the sound of horns honking outside. The candlelit inner dining room is a place to escape from the rain; for more intimacy sit in one of the small garden pavilions by the green lotus pond. The Indian *thali* is served on a silver tray with pockets for rice, curry, dal, chutney, chapati, and yogurt. The Balinese meal, served on a traditional *wanci* ceremonial tray, is complete with sate, jackfruit curry, vegetable salad, and a cone of fragrant yellow rice. Other dishes combine unusual flavors with remarkable results: cranberry chutney flavors gingerbread-pumpkin soup; lemon fettuccine is tossed with a green olive and pistachio pesto. If you don't have room for dessert, come back again for a slice of moist cardamom coffee cake, cool piña colada cake, or—the sweetest, most sinful treat ever—chocolate and caramel pecan pie. ⊠ *Jl. Suweta,* ☎ *0361/974217. AE, DC, MC, V.*

$ ✕ **Rama Shinta.** Quaint and kitschy—with sherbet-green walls trimmed with pink paint and dark wood—this little café by the Monkey Forest is perfect for coffee, cocktails, and snacks. Try the rich Bombay beef or the chicken-potato curry tray, both served with rice, banana slices sprinkled with shredded coconut, a hot chapati, and cucumber yogurt. If you're just here for coffee, top it off with a thick slab of carrot or mocha cake. ⊠ *Jl. Wanara Wana*, ☎ *0361/732097. No credit cards.*

Indonesian

$$ ✕ **Bebek Bengil.** The Dirty Duck is one of Ubud's classic dining spots, a pavilion-style restaurant set against a backdrop of rice fields. It's a place to get lost in the ambience of Bali, with raised seating areas and private pavilions that seem intimate even when the restaurant is full. Ponds and fountains are interspersed throughout the large courtyard, and a long bar area links the front and back sections. The special, of course, is bebek betutu, whole smoked duck wrapped in betel palm leaves served with sate, warm vegetable salad, and yellow rice. Or you can sample the Indonesian rijsttafel for two, which includes sate, curried eggs, chicken curry, crispy fried duck, lawar, saffron rice, and coconut cream pie. International choices round out the menu. Save room for a slice of beautifully decorated strawberry cake, pungent black Russian pie, or warm apple crisp. ⊠ *Jl. Hanoman*, ☎ *0361/975489. AE, DC, MC, V.*

$
★ ✕ **Ayu's Kitchen.** Duck into this dark, cozy restaurant for some of the best local food in town. This is the place to try Balinese specialties like warm coconut vegetable salad with chicken, pork, egg, or vegetables; rich jackfruit curry; and tender chicken baked in banana leaves. Vegetarian dishes are served as well. Don't pass up the desserts in the front pastry window. ⊠ *Jl. Wanara Wana*, ☎ *0361/975439. No credit cards.*

$ ✕ **Café Biang Lalah.** This pavilion that opens up to the rice fields serves traditional Balinese fare in a perfectly Balinese setting. Polished tables, colorful decor, and smart service dress up the restaurant's casual elegance. Warm salads, pork dishes, and duck entrées are the specialties, but the regular Indonesian and Western fare is also memorable. ⊠ *Jl. Wanara Wana 100XX*, ☎ *0361/977871. AE, DC, MC, V.*

$ ✕ **Café Wayan.** Behind the baked goodies in the front window is a plain dining room lined with floor cushions. Move past this, and you'll stumble upon the back terrace, with four small tables and a separate pavilion. Although the garden ambience is pleasant enough, the Western fare is average and the snooty service impossibly slow. However, the restaurant's reputation is saved by the fantastic Sunday-evening Balinese buffet, set to live gamelan music, with dozens of top-notch (and spicy) island samples. ⊠ *Jl. Wanara Wana*, ☎ *0361/975447. AE, DC, MC, V.*

$ ✕ **Kafe Anyar.** This restaurant in a raised, open pavilion over the road is a pleasant place to sample Balinese dishes. An enormous paper lantern hangs over the tile-studded stone floor, and wood tables and deck chairs complete the casual decor. Specialties include warm vegetable salads, *serombotan* (boiled vegetables in spicy sauce), *ayam bumbu rujak* (stir-fried sweet-and-sour chicken in coconut milk), and *ayam bakar bumbu pecel* (grilled chicken in peanut sauce)—and all dishes here have a kick. If you want to try frog, a long list of varieties is available. For dessert don't miss the *dadar* (grilled banana with cheese and honey). ⊠ *Jl. Suweta 6*, ☎ *0361/974007. No credit cards.*

$ ✕ **Sehati Guest House.** This simple pavilion restaurant occasionally hosts a traditional four-course dinner of Balinese dishes in conjunction with *jegog* and *joged* dances (performed by groups of men and women accompanied by wooden musical instruments). The meal begins at 7 PM and costs about $3; add $3 more for the dance afterward. ⊠ *Jl. Wanara Wana*, ☎ FAX *0361/976341. No credit cards.*

$ ✕ **Warung Nuri.** You can smell the grill smoking outside this little roadside warung long before you reach it—and by the time you do your mouth is watering. The lunch cook serves up *nasi campur* (steamed rice with a little of everything from the menu) with all the spices, as well as the usual fried rice, noodles, and sate. With its Western breakfasts, hot dogs, thick steaks, and cold beer, Naughty Nuri's is a far cry from your traditional warung—it's a hangout for tourists rather than Indonesians. ⊠ *Tromol Pos 219,* ☎ *0361/977547. AE, DC, MC, V.*

Italian

$$–$$$ ✕ **Terazzo.** This local favorite is upbeat and upscale, with mango-color walls adorned with works by the island's leading painters and sculptors. A back terrace overlooks both the scene on the first level and the green terrazzo bar, for which the restaurant was named. The specialty is Italian cuisine—the pastas are superb—but the kitchen also dabbles in Indonesian and international fare. Try smoky black bean soup, tangy gazpacho, spicy Thai beef stir-fry, or fresh-grilled *tenggiri* (tuna). ⊠ *Jl. Suweta,* ☎ *0361/978941. AE, DC, MC, V.*

$ ✕ **Pesto.** Hidden in the corner of the Jalan Campuhan curve, this new little restaurant strives hard to get customers—and it deserves them. A half-dozen brightly polished tables are tucked into a shelter from the main road, and smartly dressed waiters are quick to bring fresh salads and pastas from the corner kitchen to your table. You can also grab a menu while shopping and call for takeout or delivery later. ⊠ *Jl. Campuhan,* ☎ *0812/3810292. AE, DC, MC, V.*

$ ✕ **Pizza Bagus.** It's just a tiny room off Jalan Hanoman, but it's one of the most popular places in town. You can't beat the 12-inch pizzas, thick slices of homemade lasagna, and fresh-baked desserts (order a day in advance). If you can't decide on your pizza toppings, let the cooks put together something unusual like pizza *cantik,* with asparagus, egg, and spinach, or pizza *sole,* with shrimp, zucchini, and garlic. On weekends book early for takeout and delivery orders. ⊠ *Jl. Hanoman,* ☎ *0361/978520. AE, DC, MC, V.*

Mexican

$ ✕ **Kura-Kura.** Icy margaritas, crisp nachos, and cheesy tortillas keep travelers coming back to this casual two-story restaurant. The upstairs tables with floor cushions overlooking the balcony are the best, although at ground level you're nearly part of the street action. The menu covers all the Mexican standards. ⊠ *Jl. Hanoman,* ☎ *0361/975669. AE, DC, MC, V.*

Seafood

$ ✕ **Archipelago.** A simple open-air pavilion with a large-screen TV blaring rock videos, this is actually one of Ubud's best seafood restaurants. Grilled, baked, fried, or curried—you can get it all here, and with any spices you like. The casual atmosphere attracts a young crowd, and movies are shown nightly. Dances and live music are sometimes scheduled as well. ⊠ *Jl. Wanara Wana,* ☎ *0812/3969077. AE, DC, MC, V.*

Thai

$$ ✕ **Kokokan Club.** Tucked into rice terraces in the Oos River valley, this two-story, thatch-roof pavilion offers memorable views and terrific Thai cuisine. Candlelight and river breezes make this a popular dinner place, although the views are best in the late afternoon. Though the service is quick and abrupt, water glasses are always full. Recommendations include *yam hed huni* (black and white mushroom salad), *por pat sod* (steamed spring rolls smothered in peanut sauce), *goong ob woonsen* (layers of ginger- and lemongrass-soaked glass noodles, vegetables, and shrimp served in a ceramic hot pot), and *gaeng phed ped fuctong* (roast duck and pumpkin curry). Every dish has a spicy zip that comes on slowly and lingers—but it can be washed away by a serving of thick steamed pumpkin with custard and vanilla ice cream. ⊠ *Jl. Pengosekan,* ☎ *0361/975742. AE, MC, V.*

$ ✕ **Thai Food Restaurant.** Once you spot the stone dragon, follow it back through an ivy-covered tunnel to reach private raised pavilions scattered around a vine-laden courtyard. The atmosphere is romantic even by daylight, with traditionally arranged meals served amid colorful blossoms and the buzzing of oversize bumblebees. The dishes are superb and fit for two—even the appetizers of crispy fried noodles with shredded chicken or steamed spring rolls. For a main dish try the dried beef or green chicken curry served in a coconut shell, steamed fish in banana leaves, stir-fried shrimp with spring onions, or minced chicken wrapped in a pandan leaf basket. ✉ *Jl. Wanara Wana,* ☎ *0361/ 977484. MC, V.*

Vegetarian

$ ✕ **Kukuruyuk.** This small restaurant north of town is a good stop for bicyclists wanting a fresh-squeezed juice and a snack. The basic fried rice and noodles are spicy and filling, but it's the rich curries that are the house specialty. Take a rest in the garden with a book before continuing your ride. ✉ *Jl. Sanggingan,* ☎ *0828/360252. No credit cards.*

$ ✕ **Monkey Café.** Decorated with graffiti and casually strewn with a mishmash of chipped chairs and tables, this restaurant in an alley off the main road to the Monkey Forest attracts a diverse crowd. The all-vegetarian menu includes salads, hot vegetable dishes, pastas, and curries, and the upstairs pavilion is a popular gathering spot in the evening. ✉ *Jl. Wanara Wana,* ☎ *0361/973246. No credit cards.*

Candidasa and Environs

The long strip of hotels and restaurants that parallels the shoreline of Candidasa is like a mini Kuta. There are no real specialty restaurants, and even the Indonesian dishes tend to be on the bland side because most eateries cater to the fickle tastes of the Western tourists in town. There are a few gems, but you have to choose the right dishes. Don't expect class or great service in the main town; for such things, head to the experts at the Manggis resort restaurants.

Eclectic

$$$$ ✕ **The Terrace.** The restaurant at the cliff-side Amankila resort gives you three menus to choose from: Indonesian, Nonya (Malay), and Western. The chef comes to your table to make recommendations tailored to your tastes, and the rest of the staff maintains this high level of service throughout your meal. Savory appetizers include a Thai-style crab and coconut salad and *bosonboh,* a light, crispy stir-fried salad with squid, tofu, bean sprouts, and vegetables. Succulent pork satay, juicy beef *rendang,* and curry *kapitan* (a wild-chicken curry flavored with lemongrass) are standout entrées. Each night a gamelan trio plays as the sun sets. ✉ *Pantai Buitan (3 km [2 mi] northeast of Padangbai turnoff), Manggis,* ☎ *0366/21993. AE, DC, MC, V.*

$$$–$$$$ ✕ **The Serai.** At the Serai resort's restaurant, small tables and butterscotch wicker chairs are arranged in a sheltered pavilion surrounded by a lotus pond. Must-try Asian dishes include steamed duck breast, spicy prawn mango curry with yellow rice, and Thai green chicken curry. If you crave a Western dish, try the mushroom wild-rice risotto or the grilled peppered tuna. ✉ *Pantai Buitan (6 km [4 mi] northeast of Padangbai turnoff), Manggis,* ☎ *0363/41011. AE, DC, MC, V.*

$ ✕ **TJ's.** Don't let the dressed-down setting (chipped blue chairs, a jumble of tables, and scuffed brick floors) put you off, because the food here is terrific. The cooks serve up Asian and Western cuisine, and the popular bar mixes every drink you can imagine. Among the best dishes are Thai green chicken curry, spicy Thai red prawn curry, and nasi campur. ✉ *Jl. Raya, Candidasa,* ☎ *no phone. AE, MC, V.*

$ ✕ **Warung Candi Agung.** Fresh food at very affordable prices has
made this eatery popular with travelers. The decor is very basic, and
motorcycles and trucks fly by, but the list of Western, Indonesian, and
seafood dishes is lengthy; the service is prompt; and the staff is eager
to please. The restaurant hosts free legong performances, usually on
Friday and Saturday, and operates a complimentary shuttle to and from
town. ⊠ *Jl. Raya, Candidasa,* ☎ *0363/41157. No credit cards.*

LODGING

It's not hard to find a place to stay in eastern Bali. Hotels are abundant in the region, particularly around Ubud, and the only difficulty
is choosing one. If you're visiting the area for culture and quiet, stay
outside the bustling small towns and instead head for the serene and
enchanting surroundings of the mountains. The many expensive resorts
and private villas tucked into out-of-the-way places make peaceful bases;
all you need is a vehicle (and driver) for day trips. If you're on a budget, inexpensive *losmen* (small hotels) are strung throughout Ubud and
the surrounding communities, and every town in the region has cheap
hotels and homestays. It's very difficult to find interesting midrange
accommodations. There are hundreds of one-room bungalows with red-
tile roofs for around the same price—the trick is to find something a
little different.

Padangbai has a strip of simple losmen and bungalows with attached
restaurants and a few basic services. Most are clean and friendly, and
all can set you up on boat and dive trips, which are the reasons most
travelers stay here. There are numerous accommodation options in and
around Candidasa, from the dive hubs and laid-back bungalows of southern Balina to the bland chockablock hotels along the water in town to
the ultra-luxury resorts of northern Manggis. It's generally less expensive
to stay in Candidasa than in southern Bali or Ubud, but you won't have
easy access to a beach unless you're willing to pay dearly for it. Many
hotels have pools, though. Travelers go to the small fishing town of
Amed for the diving and snorkeling, and accommodations are in simple hotels with adjoining restaurants. Except for a couple of large resorts, there's not much difference between them, but most have the basic
travel and dive services you'll need—and they're a great place to meet
other travelers who enjoy wandering off Bali's well-beaten path. Tulamben's growing tourism has led to the development of several large
hotels over the past few years, and the number of private villas being
built in the hills is a telltale sign of the northward march of foreign
habitation. With plenty of small, inexpensive losmen, as well as a few
dive resorts, Tulamben makes a nice base for diving and exploring the
mountains, especially if you want to see the central peaks but prefer
to stay at the beach rather than inland.

You won't find air-conditioning in the cool mountain areas, except at
the expensive resorts. Most hotels have hot water, but many rooms don't
have bathtubs, so ask first. Most rooms don't have phones, televisions,
or refrigerators either. An excellent alternative to a resort or hotel is a
private villa, where you'll find the Balinese-style charm and Western
comforts of a luxury resort combined with the seclusion of a private
home. These places have attentive service and more amenities than typical hotels, including private pools, air-conditioning, minibars, modern electronics, bathtubs, and cooking facilities. Over the past few years
dozens of villas for almost every price range have been built in the region, from quaint bungalows surrounded by rice paddies to sprawling Balinese palaces overlooking windswept river ravines. Most villas
are around Ubud, although new rentals are popping up along the east

coast near Manggis and Tulamben. You can usually rent out one bungalow in a villa compound, or you can share the estate with other friends or family. Like luxury hotels, most villas have full-service options available but without the exorbitant 10%–25% taxes. Many actually provide such services as a professional cook and housekeeping staff, unlimited laundry, a car and driver, travel and business resources, and computer access and Internet hookup free to guests.

Bali's major villa rental agency is **Indovillas** (✉ Jl. Daksina 5, Batu Belig, Kerobokan, ☎ 0811/392985, ☎ FAX 0361/733031, ✎), which is the booking agent for some of the private villas listed in this chapter. If you're interested in renting a villa for a vacation, group tour, or business function, check out the Indovillas Web site to view your options or send an e-mail to Indovillas's travel division, which can book transportation and accommodations and arrange guides, rental cars, activities, and whatever else you might need. They can also provide special deals on hotel accommodations.

All rooms in the listed hotels have bathrooms with tubs and hot water unless otherwise noted. For general information and price categories, *see* Lodging *in* Smart Travel Tips.

Ubud

Most of Ubud's luxury resorts lie along the ridge of the Ayung River, but there are a few in the Campuhan basin, the curves of Jalan Wanara Wana, and Peliatan. Midrange hotels, many marked by split brick-and-stone entrance gates, dot Jalan Hanoman, Jalan Wanara Wana, Jalan Kajeng, and Jalan Suweta in the center of town. Cheap losmen are tucked into the pockets and alleys between shops—but in the off-season look in the Penestanan and Kedewatan rice fields for midsize bungalows that can be bargained down to losmen prices.

$$$$ 🏨 **Amandari.** This gathering of luxury villas is the ultimate in Balinese
★ elegance, consistently topping *Condé Nast Traveler*'s annual international Gold List of small hotels. Local culture is reflected in the resort's traditional architecture, from the stone paths between lotus ponds to the high curving walls. Most of the thatch-roof bungalows overlook the forested Ayung River valley. Light-filled suites have marble floors, heavy cream-color upholstery, and enormous bathrooms with outdoor sunken tubs. Six villas have private plunge pools. The open-air lobby leads to a comfortable library, and the restaurant stands above an arresting infinity pool over the river. It's one of the island's most romantic dining spots, where nary a sound but the whisper of wind in the trees and the distant notes of a neighborhood gamelan accompanies the European and Indonesian fare. ✉ *Jl. Kedewatan (Box 33, Ubud 80571);* ☎ *0361/975333; 800/447–7462 toll-free in the U.S.; 212/223–2848 in the U.S.; 0800/282–684 in the U.K.;* FAX *0361/975335. 30 suites. Restaurant, bar, air-conditioning, refrigerators, room service, pool, massage, spa, tennis court, health club, hiking, bicycles, library, babysitting, laundry service, travel services, car rental, free parking. AE, DC, MC, V. EP.*

$$$$ 🏨 **Four Seasons Resort at Sayan.** The journey to this 17-acre property begins with a walk along a wooden bridge above terraced mountain slopes and the Ayung River. The path ends at a large elliptical lotus pond on the roof of the central three-story structure. A polished-wood staircase descends to the reception area and a lounge with a spectacular 180-degree vista. The main building holds two-story suites, and villas are set into the hillside all the way down to the riverbank. On a curving terrace, two sunken whirlpools seem to hang out over the valley. Inside, the rooms are accented with rich teak and stone and have

136

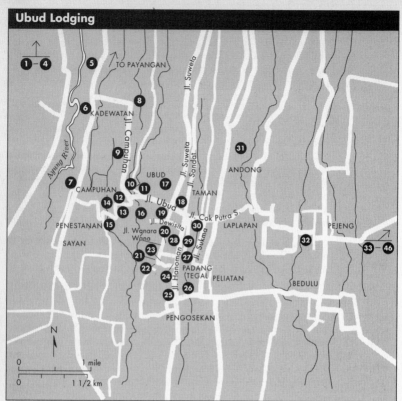

custom-made furnishings and tapestries from Bali and Java. ⊠ *Desa Sayan, 80571,* ☎ *0361/977577,* ℻ *0361/977588. 18 suites, 28 villas. 2 restaurants, bar, air-conditioning, refrigerators, room service, 2 pools, 2 hot tubs, spa, massage, health club, shops, library, baby-sitting, laundry service, meeting rooms, travel services, car rental, free parking. AE, DC, MC, V. EP.*

$$$$ 🏨 **Villa Pasti Indah.** At twilight this small complex in the Payangan hills looms like a dark castle. The property is nestled into a cleft in between rice paddy terraces, with a brown river curving around its base. Stone steps lead up to the thatch-roof, Japanese-style villas, which are surrounded by crushed limestone walls and low bamboo fences for privacy. The villas are enormous, with marble floors, stone walls, sunken sitting areas, VCRs and DVD players, and two king-size beds each. Cavernous marble bathrooms have garden showers and Jacuzzi tubs. The lower villa has a plunge pool, a little yard, and a large tree house overlooking the busy road; the upper villa's plunge pool has an infinity edge and a lush rice-paddy view. There's a kitchen guests can use, and the small restaurant serves basic, though expensive, Indonesian and Western fare. Service at both the hotel and restaurant is meticulously professional; staff members live at the property and rotate jobs so that each is a jack-of-all-trades. Breakfast, laundry, and a car and driver are included in the price. ⊠ *Payangan (Indovillas, Jl. Daksina 5, Kerobokan);* ☎ *0811/392985 for Indovillas reservation agency;* ☎ ℻ *0361/733031 to Indovillas. 2 villas. Restaurant, air-conditioning, in-room VCRs, refrigerators, room service, 2 pools, massage, shop, baby-sitting, laundry service, travel services, car rental, free parking. MC, V. BP.* 🐾

$$$–$$$$ 🏨 **Ibah Luxury Villas.** Tucked into the hills of Campuhan along Ubud's main road, Ibah is an unexpected pleasure. To reach the thatch-roof villas, you walk through stone archways, follow stepping stones across lily ponds, and hike trails that wind up the slopes. Rooms have heavenly views, wood floors, and bathrooms with marble tubs and garden vistas. Along the pools, cushioned seating areas are carved into a stone wall built into the hill. The spa above the restaurant is cozy and intimate, with treatment rooms right beneath its eaves. ⊠ *Jl. Campuhan (Box 193, Ubud 80571),* ☎ *0361/974466,* ℻ *0361/974467. 11 villas. Restaurant, bar, air-conditioning, refrigerators, room service, 2 pools, hot tub, massage, spa, health club, laundry service, baby-sitting, travel services, car rental, free parking. AE, MC, V. EP.*

$$$–$$$$ 🏨 **Kamandalu Resort.** A gathering of stone characters and animals welcomes guests to this ornate Balinese hideaway on the east side of town. The guiding principles here are relaxation and energization, which are the twin effects, in the Hindu *Mahabharata* story, of the elixir contained in the sacred *kamandalu* gourd, from which the resort takes its name (and as the elixir was created of holy water, the resort is surrounded by holy springs). Connected villas, clustered in groups throughout the estate, have temple entrances, high thatch ceilings, antique furniture, marble floors, large windows, and rice-paddy or forest views. Some decks lead to private plunge pools; the rest share the central pool by the spa. ⊠ *Jl. Tegallalang, 80561,* ☎ *0361/975825,* ℻ *0361/975851. 58 rooms. Restaurant, bar, air-conditioning, refrigerators, room service, pool, massage, spa, shops, baby-sitting, laundry service, travel services, car rental, free parking. AE, DC, MC, V.*

$$$–$$$$ 🏨 **Kupu Kupu Barong.** This complex of connected villas is spread out on a precipice over a deep valley, with glorious views of rice terraces and the Ayung River. Bungalows blend with the landscape and have decorative Balinese furnishings and small marble baths. Duplexes have pretty antique sitting areas, lofts with wayang-style paintings over the beds, and indulgently large garden bathrooms. Strong legs are required, as it's quite a walk—up and down stone steps, through gar-

dens, tunnels, and across bridges—from the reception area to the rooms and the restaurant. ⊠ *Jl. Kedewatan, 80571,* ☎ *0361/975478; 800/561–3071 in the U.S.; 020/7742–7780 in the U.K.;* 𝖥𝖠𝖷 *0361/ 975079. 19 suites. Restaurant, 2 bars, air-conditioning, refrigerators, room service, 2 pools, massage, bicycles, baby-sitting, laundry service, travel services, car rental, free parking. AE, DC, MC, V.*

$$$ 🏨 **Waka di Ume Resort.** Named for the rice fields (*ume*) that surround them, these villas copy the best of Balinese design. Close-knit thatch-roof bungalows are surrounded by high walls, mimicking the layout of a typical village. Rooms are luxurious, with marble floors, canopy beds, antique furnishings, and huge bathrooms with sunken tubs and garden showers. Each villa has a private terrace where you can relax, sip a glass of wine, and listen to the bullfrogs under the stars. The gorgeous stone-lined swimming pool, set in lush gardens, is modeled on the sacred bathing springs of Pura Tirta Empul. ⊠ *Jl. Suweta, 80571,* ☎ *0361/973178,* 𝖥𝖠𝖷 *0361/973179. 16 villas. Restaurant, bar, air-conditioning, minibars, refrigerators, room service, pool, massage, hiking, library, baby-sitting, laundry service, business services, travel services, car rental, free parking. AE, MC, V. EP.* 🕭

$$–$$$$ 🏨 **The Chedi.** This austere resort overlooking the forested hills is strictly for absorbing the peaceful surroundings—you won't find TVs, VCRs, or CD players in the rooms. Eight two-story blocks are laid out like a Balinese village, with panoramas on all sides. Although small, the rooms have a luxury-hotel feel. First-floor quarters have private terraces, back courtyards, and garden bathrooms with bathtubs, while the upper floors have showers only but have balconies with better views. A long pool with a central island and infinity edges hangs over the green valley; behind it sits the two-story Restaurant (☞ Dining, *above*). ⊠ *Desa Melinggi Kelod Payangan, 80572,* ☎ *0361/975963,* 𝖥𝖠𝖷 *0361/ 975968. 54 rooms, 4 suites. 2 restaurants, bar, in-room safes, refrigerators, room service, pool, massage, spa, shops, library, baby-sitting, laundry service, business services, meeting rooms, travel services, car rental, free parking. AE, DC, MC, V. EP.*

$$–$$$$ 🏨 **Villa Tugu.** Unusual combinations of light, angles, and color give this local artist's home an intriguing beauty. The focal point is a stunning saltwater pool whose surface forms a seamless horizon with the rice fields beyond. Awash in gold light, the main house includes a large living area, three sizable bedrooms, and a two-story artist's studio. The villa has a Japanese-style bedroom and living area with sliding shoji screens; the second bedroom has a canopy bed; and a bridge connects the second-floor office to a tower with breathtaking views of the rice paddies. If you want to eat in, there's a modern kitchen painted in muted pastels and an open dining pavilion. ⊠ *Jl. Tugu Pahlawan (Indovillas, Jl. Daksina 5, Kerobokan);* ☎ *0361/978558; 0811/392985 for Indovillas reservation agency;* ☎ 𝖥𝖠𝖷 *0361/733031 to Indovillas. 1 villa, 1 house. Dining room, air-conditioning (some), saltwater pool, massage, baby-sitting, laundry service, travel services, car rental, free parking. MC, V. BP.* 🕭

$$–$$$ 🏨 **Champlung Sari Hotel.** Conveniently located across from the Monkey Forest, this classic Ubud resort has maintained its international standards over the years. The high walls tower over the road like a castle; inside are traditional walled gardens, thatch roofs, and entryways of brick and stone. Standard rooms have wood floors, modern furniture, and pale walls hung with contemporary Balinese paintings; deluxes add beamed ceilings and marble bathrooms with tubs. The Parkit restaurant serves Indonesian and Western food—and the occasional Balinese buffet—in a thatch-roof pavilion at the hotel entrance. ⊠ *Jl. Wanara Wana (Box 87, Ubud 80571),* ☎ *0361/975418,* 𝖥𝖠𝖷 *0361/975473. 58 rooms. Restaurant, bar, air-conditioning, in-room safes, refrigerators,*

room service, pool, massage, library, baby-sitting, laundry service, business services, meeting rooms, travel services, car rental, free parking. AE, DC, MC, V. EP.

$$–$$$ 🏨 **Kokokan Hotel.** The stone-and-brick buildings of this hotel are scattered in the hills above the sacred Tirta Tawar River like forgotten temples. Standard rooms, adorned with lively hand-carved wooden doors and window panels and Balinese textiles and paintings, have marble floors, terraces, and huge shower-only bathrooms. Deluxe rooms have carved sandstone walls and sliding door panels that separate the large bedroom area from the shower-only bath. You can dine in the poolside café or at the nearby Kokokan Club (☞ Dining, *above*). Guests receive a 25% discount on classes at the on-site museum, which teaches arts such as gamelan playing, puppet and mask making, weaving, and dance—a great opportunity for parents to learn about Bali with their children. ⊠ *Jl. Pengosekan, 80571,* ☎ *0361/975742,* ℻ *0361/975332. 15 rooms. Restaurant, café, air-conditioning, room service, pool, massage, hiking, baby-sitting, children's programs, laundry service, travel services, car rental, free parking. AE, MC, V. BP.*

$$ 🏨 **Komaneka Resort.** Behind the white limestone facade of the Komaneka Gallery you'll find the breezy lobby of this new hotel. Rooms wrap guests in elegance, from the marble floors to the rich wood trim and classic Balinese art pieces. Suites, on the top floor, look out over the rice fields; the huge villas have glass walls, canopy beds under thatched eaves, sunken marble tubs next to lotus ponds, and outdoor garden showers. The sunny little Komaneka Café (☞ Dining, *above*) offers a limited menu of Indonesian and European dishes. ⊠ *Jl. Wanara Wana, 80571,* ☎ *0361/976090,* ℻ *0361/977140. 12 rooms, 2 suites, 6 villas. Restaurant, air-conditioning, room service, pool, massage, shop, baby-sitting, laundry service, travel services, car rental, free parking. AE, DC, MC, V. EP.*

$$ 🏨 **Puri Bunga Village Hotel.** This quiet oasis has the same views as the Amandari and the Kupu Kupu Barong hotels, but for a fraction of the price. Although the furnishings aren't that interesting, the rooms are spacious, and all but two face the Ayung River valley. The two junior suites have whirlpools, and the honeymoon suite is luxurious and private. You're better off with your own wheels here; otherwise it's a 10-minute taxi ride into Ubud's center. ⊠ *Jl. Kedewatan (Box 141, Ubud 80000),* ☎ *0361/975448,* ℻ *0361/975073. 14 rooms, 3 suites. Restaurant, air-conditioning, room service, pool, massage, baby-sitting, laundry service, travel services, car rental, free parking. MC, V. EP.*

$$ 🏨 **Tjampuhan.** Just steps west of the town bridge, the Tjampuhan was once an artists' colony, and the grounds still contain the house that was once the home of German painter Walter Spies. The bungalows sit in lovely gardens and have carved and gilded wood doors, woven bamboo walls, bamboo furniture, and handwoven fabrics and batiks. Trails between buildings and the pools are very steep and lined with rough rocks, so this hotel is only for the nimble-footed. At the spa, hot tubs lie between the trees of a stone-carved forest, and hillside massage rooms open to the riverine setting below. A spa café serves healthy eclectic and vegetarian dishes, and the more formal restaurant offers contemporary and Indonesian fare. ⊠ *Jl. Campuhan (Box 15, Denpasar 80364),* ☎ *0361/975368,* ℻ *0361/975137. 63 bungalows. Restaurant, bar, café, air-conditioning, room service, 2 pools, 2 hot tubs, massage, spa, 2 tennis courts, bicycles, baby-sitting, laundry service, travel services, car rental, free parking. MC, V. BP.*

$–$$ 🏨 **Jalan-Jalan Villa and Spa.** Staying at this miniresort is like having your own home in Ubud. The large light-filled rooms all combine modern facilities with traditional Balinese art and furniture. Each duplex has a first-floor bedroom with a woven-leaf ceiling, an alcove bathroom with a tub, a half-bath, a dining area, and a full modern kitchen; curving wood stairs lead up to a sitting area and a sanctuary-style bedroom with a peaked ceiling. Deluxe rooms have everything but the upstairs bedroom. The spa's tranquil, green swimming pool is fronted by a carved stone wall, similar to a royal bathing pool; a green marble Jacuzzi sits in a pavilion just above it. ⊠ *Jl. Pengosekan (Box 23, Ubud 80571),* ☎ *0361/979008,* ℻ *0361/979005. 2 suites, 2 1-bedroom bungalows, 2 duplexes. Coffee shop, air-conditioning, refrigerators, room service, pool, beauty salon, hot tub, massage, spa, health club, shop, baby-sitting, laundry service, business services, travel services, car rental, free parking. AE, MC, V. EP.*

$–$$ ▣ **Padma Indah.** You'd never find this hotel high in the Penestanan fields unless you were looking for it, and at this price it's definitely worth the search. The two-story *lumbung*-style (barn-shape) homes are like split-level apartments, with life-size carved-stone dogs to greet you. The first-floor living area has a marble floor, a big teak couch with orange floral cushions, a teak desk, a huge bathroom with a sunken corner tub and white-and-blue-tile shower, and a stone patio. Upstairs is the loft, where a wayang-style story panel hangs above a big canopy bed, and a big window overlooks the gardens. There are two apartments per building, and though only two have air-conditioning, the constant breezes keep the rooms cool. ⊠ *Jl. Penestanan, 80571,* ☎ *0361/ 975719,* ℻ *0361/975091. 10 apartments. Air-conditioning (some), refrigerators, room service, pool, massage, baby-sitting, laundry service, travel services, car rental, free parking. AE, DC, MC, V. EP.*

$–$$ ▣ **Pringa Juwita.** The Water Garden cottages are very Balinese and very romantic, removed from the main section of hotels yet close enough to walk to the shops. Strolling through the unusual grounds is like exploring an ancient temple: in the overgrown foliage you'll find high stone walls and hidden stone statues. The best deal here is a deluxe two-story cottage: Downstairs is an open living area with a red tile floor, a teak daybed and couch, and a bathroom with a sunken tub. The upstairs has a sitting porch with a wall of bamboo-framed miniature batik paintings that glow in the afternoon sunlight; doors slide back to reveal a small upstairs bedroom. Standards and a single superior are confined to one unimaginative building; all have red tile terraces, dark teak furniture, and sunken baths, but the superior has air-conditioning for twice the cost. ⊠ *Jl. Bisma, 80571,* ☎ ℻ *0361/ 975734. 12 rooms, 1 suite, 4 cottages. Bar, room service, pool, massage, baby-sitting, laundry service, travel services, car rental, free parking. AE, DC, MC, V. BP.*

$–$$ ▣ **Puri Gong.** The front of this place is an art gallery, and through a narrow stone doorway a path leads back to three large villas overlooking rice terraces. Rooms are bright, spacious, and breezy, with tile floors, teak canopy beds, and private bathrooms. (Each villa houses four rooms, two on the upper level and two on the lower.) Downstairs rooms have verandas, and upper ones have wonderful views through large windows that pull in the afternoon light. ⊠ *Jl. Hanoman, 80571,* ☎ *0361/975343,* ℻ *0361/298269. 12 rooms. Restaurant, bar, air-conditioning, room service, pool, massage, baby-sitting, laundry service, travel services, car rental, free parking. MC, V. BP.*

$–$$ ▣ **Siti Bungalows.** This compact collection of bungalows was once the haunt of artist Hans Snel. The atmosphere—and the standards—are a throwback to the 1920s, when things were much simpler on Bali. There's no air-conditioning and the service is surly, but the grounds are well-groomed, clean, and quiet. The buildings, made of crumbled gray limestone and brick, have thatch roofs, antique doors, and red tile porches. Bungalows 5 and 7 have terraces, while Bungalows 7 and 8 overlook the pool and the river valley. Bungalow 6 has twin beds on separate sides of the room, each with a closet, desk, and window. The restaurant serves good Indonesian and Continental fare. ⊠ *Jl. Kajeng 3 (Box 175, Ubud 80571),* ☎ *0361/975699,* ℻ *0361/975643. 8 bungalows. Restaurant, bar, fans, room service, pool, massage, library, babysitting, laundry service, travel services, car rental, free parking. AE, DC, MC, V. EP.*

$–$$ ⊞ **Ulun Ubud Cottages.** This long-time Ubud favorite was undergoing renovations at press time, but the steep hillside setting still affords the same river and rice-field views. The original carved wood-and-stone panels and polished antiques keep the shaggy grass-roof bungalows warm and comfortable feeling; the updated decor adds a slick modern touch. Updated studios have porches, air-conditioning, minibars, and televisions. Newer suites and family rooms are larger but unimaginative, with plain bamboo furniture and huge modern bathrooms. Standard rooms, all with classic furniture and wonderful views, are the best value. The pools here are among the loveliest places for a swim in the area. ⊠ *Sanggingan (Box 333, Ubud 80001),* ☎ *0361/975024,* ℻ *0361/ 975524. 11 rooms, 3 bungalows, 2 family rooms, 5 suites. Restaurant, bar, air-conditioning (some), in-room safes, minibars (some), room service, massage, baby-sitting, laundry service, travel services, car rental, free parking. AE, DC, MC, V. EP.*

$ ⊞ **Ananda Cottages.** At this quiet hotel set amid the rice paddies of Campuhan, gardens overflow with red and lavender hibiscus blossoms. The rooms—eight in each brick bungalow—have ornamental doors and windows, marble floors, antique furnishings, and ikat bedspreads. The top-floor superiors are nestled under the eaves, with air-conditioning, refrigerators, and views of the rice fields. First-floor standard rooms have porches and garden bathrooms with tubs; some have air-conditioning, and you can add a refrigerator on request. ⊠ *Jl. Campuhan (Box 205, Denpasar 80364),* ☎ *0361/975376,* ℻ *0361/975375. 57 rooms, 1 suite. Restaurant, bar, air-conditioning (some), refrigerators (some), room service, pool, massage, baby-sitting, laundry service, travel services, car rental, free parking. AE, DC, MC, V. EP.*

$ ⊞ **Munut Bungalows.** Sitting atop the Penestanan hill, this classy Balinese-style hotel has rooms in two tall stone buildings. Standard rooms in the front building have garden showers. In the back building the air-conditioned deluxe rooms have wood floors, large wooden terraces, and open blue-terrazzo bathrooms with hot water. If you're planning a trip between February and April, book early; this is where university groups come to stay and learn about Balinese art, dance, and music. ⊠ *Jl. Penestanan (Box 59, Ubud 80571),* ☎ *0361/975039,* ℻ *0361/977152. 13 rooms. Air-conditioning (some), room service, pool, massage, Ping-Pong, baby-sitting, laundry service, travel services, car rental, free parking. MC, V. BP.*

$ ⊞ **Pande Permai.** This hotel, hidden above the Ayung River valley near the Monkey Forest, has luxury rooms at budget-traveler prices. The best deals are the second-floor superior rooms, with lemon-sorbet walls, marble floors, canopy beds, and terraces that hang out over the treetops; two even have sunken corner tubs. Smaller superiors have fans only, but they have better views and cost slightly less. Standard rooms, in a three-story building next to the pool, have polished wood floors, porches, and showers (no tubs). ⊠ *Jl. Pengosekan, 80571,* ☎ *0361/ 975757,* ℻ *0361/975546. 12 rooms. Restaurant, air-conditioning (some), room service, pool, massage, baby-sitting, laundry service, travel services, car rental, free parking. MC, V. EP.*

$ ⊞ **Prada Guesthouse.** The charm of this hotel is that it's built right on the grounds of the Puri Saren in the center of Ubud. This is the place from which rajas once ruled the region, and the royal grounds have long been Ubud's artistic center. The back of the lobby connects to the palace, and visitors are welcome to observe ceremonies on the grounds with prior permission. Although it's part of a historical landmark, the hotel has a contemporary international feel. Rooms are unexpectedly modern and clean, with businesslike furnishings, and computer terminals are lined up in the lobby. Guests have access to the Saraswati Hotel pool across the street. ⊠ *Jl. Kajeng 1, 80571,* ☎ *0361/975122,* FAX *0361/ 974291. 22 rooms. Restaurant, bar, fans, room service, massage, mountain bikes, library, baby-sitting, laundry service, business services, travel services, car rental, free parking. No credit cards. EP.*

¢–$ 🏠 **Nick's Pension II.** Although it's a bit far from the center of town, this backpacker favorite is one of Ubud's best budget options. A narrow trail leads from Penestanan's main road past the restaurant and pool to tall brick buildings in neatly trimmed gardens. Rooms are bright and clean, simply furnished with canopy or bamboo beds, colorful spreads, tile floors, and hot showers. There's no air-conditioning, but upper rooms grab nice breezes and have views of the rice fields. Newer one-story bungalows have larger rooms with tubs. The busy pool is always surrounded by Europeans with tropical drinks, and the popular restaurant bustles with travelers who come for the filling, inexpensive Indonesian specialties. ⊠ *Penestanan, 80571,* ☎ FAX *0361/975636. 22 rooms. Restaurant, fans, room service, pool, massage, baby-sitting, laundry service, travel services, car rental, free parking. AE, DC, MC, V. BP.*

¢ 🏠 **Artini 2.** This small hotel is the best one in the Artini chain and a good choice if you want to stay on Jalan Hanoman. Neat walkways lead through manicured grounds to the restaurant, shop, and pool. Simple standard rooms are in an old brick building with a thatch roof, while a newer building in front houses modern deluxe rooms—with polished wood floors, bamboo furniture, and blue-and-white-tile baths—on its ground floor. Suites cost twice as much as deluxe rooms because they have air-conditioning and views. ⊠ *Jl. Hanoman, 80571,* ☎ *0361/ 975689,* FAX *0361/975348. 22 rooms, 2 suites. Restaurant, bar, air-conditioning (some), fans, room service, pool, massage, shop, baby-sitting, laundry service, travel services, car rental, free parking. AE, MC, V. BP.*

¢ 🏠 **Dewi Sri Bungalows.** A large stone goddess at the templelike entrance welcomes you to this busy hotel. Ignore the life-size stone fornicating pigs by the reception pavilion and you'll be able to spot the garden lined with two-story bungalows. Each bungalow has an open sitting area, a dining table, a garden bathroom, and a cozy second-floor bedroom under the eaves. Suites, also in individual bungalows, have front porches, antique furniture, and large garden bathrooms. Standard rooms are in an ugly brick building back by the pool and have showers only. ⊠ *Jl. Hanoman 69 (Box 23, Ubud 80571),* ☎ *0361/975300,* FAX *0361/975777. 16 rooms, 4 bungalows. Fans, refrigerators, room service, pool, massage, baby-sitting, laundry service, travel services, car rental, free parking. AE, DC, MC, V. BP.*

¢ 🏠 **Guci Guest Houses.** This quiet European-run guest house is down a coconut-tree-lined walkway at the intersection of Jalan Pengosekan and Jalan Hanoman. The three rooms are large, with woven walls, canopy beds, garden bathrooms with shower, and porches. The open-air house has a sitting area, dining room, and kitchen, and a large upstairs bedroom that looks out over the gardens. This is a favorite of budget travelers, so book early in high season. ⊠ *Jl. Pengosekan (Box 103, Ubud 80571),* ☎ FAX *0361/975975. 3 rooms, 1 house. Fans, shop. No credit cards. BP.*

¢ 🏠 **Honeymoon Guesthouse.** These colonial-Singapore-style mansions
★ and adjacent guest quarters are indeed the perfect place for a honeymoon. Far down a back alley in Penestanan, the quiet grounds are also home to a cooking school. Fan-cooled standard rooms are cozy and clean, with bathtubs and shelves of used books in the hallways. The

best deals are the deluxe rooms, which are painted in soft greens and blues and have marble baths with sunken corner tubs and antique beds, dressers, and mirrors (true romantics should take a room snuggled under the thatched eaves). The price includes a breakfast of fresh-baked croissants and other goodies from the Honeymoon Bakery across the alley (☞ Dining, *above*). ✉ *Jl. Bisma, Penestanan, 80571,* ☎ ℻ *0361/ 973282. 12 rooms. Coffee shop, air-conditioning (some), fans, room service, pool, massage, baby-sitting, laundry service, travel services, car rental, free parking. AE, DC, MC, V. BP.*

¢ 🏨 **Monkey Forest Hideaway.** Lying behind the shops at the edge of the Monkey Forest, this collection of villas around a lotus pond is one of Ubud's best accommodations deals. Enter your room through ornamental doors, and you'll find a lovely bedroom beneath thatched eaves, with a view over the forests surrounding the Ayung River valley. All rooms have sitting porches with wicker furniture; the four on the upper level have the best views. Bathrooms have hot showers. The restaurant in front serves simple Indonesian and Western dishes, and there's also an Internet café on-site. ✉ *Jl. Wanara Wana, 80571,* ☎ ℻ *0361/975354. 12 rooms. Restaurant, air-conditioning (some), room service, pool, massage, baby-sitting, laundry service, travel services, car rental, free parking. AE, MC, V. BP.*

¢ 🏨 **Oka Kartini Bungalows.** These bungalows, just east of town on the main road, are also home to a local dance school. The nicest rooms are the standards, which surround the pool and have porches and tubs. The larger deluxe bungalows, away from the noisy entrance and restaurant, stand alone in ornamental Balinese-style buildings and have tubs but are crowded with worn furniture. Wayang kulit shows are held here every Wednesday and Sunday. ✉ *Jl. Ubud, 80571,* ☎ *0361/975193,* ℻ *0361/975759. 15 rooms. Restaurant, fans, room service, pool, massage, baby-sitting, laundry service, travel services, car rental, free parking. AE, MC, V. BP.*

¢ 🏨 **Oka Wati Hotel.** Sitting way back off the road, this longtime travelers' favorite has two separate sections, each of which spans a rice paddy. The older brick-and-stone buildings, next to gardens and a free-form pool, house large rooms with antique furniture and black-marble sinks and tubs. The newer two-story building is closer to the road; its sizable rooms have woven walls, sitting areas, and showers (no tubs). All rooms have fans, and there are computer terminals in the reception area. ✉ *Jl. Wanara Wana, 80571,* ☎ *0361/973386,* ℻ *0361/975063. 5 rooms, 14 suites. Restaurant, fans, room service, pool, massage, baby-sitting, laundry service, travel services, car rental, free parking. MC, V. BP.*

Semarapura and Environs

$–$$ 🏨 **Megah Log House.** Traditional Balinese style meets contemporary comfort in this spa resort on Gunung Agung just east of Rendang. Cozy rooms have a rustic feel, with wood floors, walls, and furniture. Private sitting alcoves have large windows: choose from garden, river, or valley views. The Bukit Sari restaurant serves Western and Indonesian dishes in a pavilion overlooking the forest. ✉ *Desa Yangapi, Muncan 80571,* ☎ *0361/462673,* ℻ *0361/462407. 16 rooms, 1 suite. Restaurant, bar, air-conditioning, refrigerators, room service, massage, spa, hiking, bicycles, billiards, shops, library, baby-sitting, laundry service, travel services, car rental, free parking. AE, DC, MC, V. BP.*

$–$$ 🏨 **Sacred Mountain Sanctuary.** Bali's first ecoresort sits alongside the
★ beautiful Unda River on the slopes of Gunung Agung. Lumbung-style cottages with sloping thatch roofs overlook the lush estate, built around a spring-fed lap pool. Villas have wood floors, woven walls, mountain views, and garden bathrooms with marble and terrazzo fixtures and

sunken tubs. Two-story villas have private plunge pools. The restaurant specializes in organic Balinese and Thai cuisine. The resort is near Sideman, about 13 km (8 mi) northeast of Semarapura. *Bj. Budimanis, Sideman 80864, ☎ 0366/24330, FAX 0366/23456. 19 villas. Restaurant, air-conditioning, room service, pool, massage, hiking, baby-sitting, laundry service, meeting rooms, travel services, car rental, free parking. AE, DC, MC, V. EP.* 🍽

Candidasa and Environs

$$$$ 🏨 **Amankila.** This hillside resort has views of the Badung Strait Islands. Luxurious thatch-roof pavilions are connected by raised cement walkways. Each guest villa has a terrace, a bedroom with a king-size canopy bed, and a spacious bath with a sunken tub and separate shower; some villas have private pools. You'll feel like royalty basking in the sun beside the shared tri-level pool, whose waters rush down in falls from one level to the next. It's a stiff downhill climb to the beach—or you can ride there in a chauffeured Jeep. The library has an extensive collection of books on regional travel and history; in its sitting area, experts give slide shows and talks on topics related to local culture. The Terrace restaurant (☞ Dining, *above*) serves Asian and Western cuisine. ⊠ *Pantai Buitan (3 km [2 mi] northeast of Padangbai turnoff), Manggis 80871; ☎ 0366/21993; 800/447–7462; 212/223–2848 in the U.S.; 0800/282–684 in the U.K.; FAX 0366/21995. 35 villas. 2 restaurants, bar, air-conditioning, room service, pool, massage, hiking, beach, snorkeling, windsurfing, library, baby-sitting, laundry service, travel services, car rental, free parking. AE, DC, MC, V. EP.*

$$$–$$$$ 🏨 **The Serai.** When sunlight washes over the pale golden walls and marble floors, you can't help but fall under this resort's spell of enchantment. Superior rooms may not have tubs (only showers), but they have outer sitting areas that face the pool and beach. The more expensive deluxe rooms have full baths and balconies with built-in sofas overlooking the pool and gardens. The Serai encourages you to experience the local flora, fauna, and culture through various outdoor activities and tours, and at the cooking school you can learn more about Indonesian cuisine. ⊠ *Pantai Buitan (6 km [4 mi] northeast of Padangbai turnoff), Manggis 80871, ☎ 0363/41011, FAX 0363/41015. 58 rooms. Restaurant, bar, air-conditioning, room service, massage, beach, dive shop, baby-sitting, laundry service, travel services, car rental, free parking. AE, DC, MC, V. BP.*

$$ 🏨 **The Watergarden.** Terraces overlook lily ponds at these thatch-roof cottages, which have high ceilings, marble floors, brick walls, and simple island furnishings. Each dwelling is nestled into tropical gardens, with rushing waterfalls and koi ponds around every corner. Seven rooms have air-conditioning, and there's one deluxe suite with two bedrooms. From the beach across the road you can enjoy the view of Gunung Agung. ⊠ *Jl. Raya, Candidasa 80871, ☎ 0363/41540, FAX 0363/41164. 13 rooms. Restaurant, bar, air-conditioning (some), fans, room service, saltwater pool, massage, library, baby-sitting, laundry service, travel services, car rental, free parking. AE, DC, MC, V. BP.*

$ 🏨 **Balina Beach Bungalows.** Popular with scuba and snorkel enthusiasts for its diving club, this hotel of one- and two-story thatched cottages lies near a sandy beach 3 km (2 mi) west of Candidasa. All rooms have private baths and ceiling fans. The best rooms, upstairs in the two-story bungalows, have sitting areas and terraces. The one-story garden-view rooms have open-air bathrooms and large corner tubs as well as cushioned *bales* overlooking the rice fields. ⊠ *Pantai Buitan (8 km [5 mi] northeast of Padangbai turnoff), Manggis 80870, ☎ 0363/41002, FAX 0363/41001. 42 rooms. Restaurant, bar, fans, room service,* *pool, massage, beach, dive shop, baby-sitting, laundry service, travel services, car rental, free parking. AE, DC, MC, V. BP.*

$ 🏨 **Fajar Candidasa Beach Bungalows.** Whistling songbirds and chuckling mynahs welcome you to this small hotel, where dozens of birdcages decorate the back of the reception area. All rooms in the tall, templelike bungalows have small terraces and oversize sunken tubs, but only deluxe rooms have air-conditioning. The small swimming pool is right next to the ocean breakwater. The facilities here are clean and the grounds are quiet. ✉ *Jl. Raya, Candidasa 80871,* ☎ *0363/41539,* 📠 *0366/41538. 33 rooms. Restaurant, bar, air-conditioning (some), fans, room service, pool, massage, beach, boating, baby-sitting, laundry service, travel services, car rental, free parking. AE, MC, V. BP.*

Amed

$$–$$$$ 🏨 **Indra Udhyana.** Amed's first resort has all the perks and facilities of the larger hotels of Tulamben. Spacious rooms have Balinese decor and sea views, as well as air-conditioning. The restaurant serves drab Indonesian, Chinese, and Western cuisine. In tourist season dance performances are staged at the restaurant. ✉ *Bunutan (Box 119, Karangasem 80852),* ☎ *0370/26336,* 📠 *0370/36797. 33 rooms. Restaurant, air-conditioning, room service, pool, massage, beach, dive shop, snorkeling, bicycles, shops, baby-sitting, laundry service, travel services, car rental, free parking. AE, DC, MC, V. BP.*

$$ 🏨 **Wawa-Wewe II.** Sitting in the rocky Lipah hills and overlooking serene Papuan Bay, this place supplies basic comforts to those who want to get away from it all. The spacious bungalows sleep four to six and are perfect for families. Morning views of local fishermen setting out to sea in outrigger canoes and evening panoramas of Gunung Agung are a bonus. At the beach restaurant you can dine on seafood, barbecue, Indonesian dishes, and home-baked goods. ✉ *Jl. Raya Papuan (Box 124, Karangasem 80852),* ☎ 📠 *0363/22074. 10 bungalows. Restaurant, air-conditioning, room service, massage, baby-sitting, laundry service, travel services, car rental, free parking. No credit cards. BP.*

$–$$ 🏨 **Hidden Paradise Cottages.** This clean, modern place is a favorite of travelers, who like the access to diving and snorkeling sites, as well as the good service and activities like beach walking, boating, and bicycling. The quiet restaurant has a simple list of salads, soups, and hot dishes, and the popular bar gets going after hours. ✉ *Amed 80852,* ☎ *0361/431273,* 📠 *0363/21044. 16 rooms. Restaurant, air-conditioning (some), fans, room service, pool, massage, beach, snorkeling, bicycles, baby-sitting, laundry service, travel services, car rental, free parking. MC, V. BP.*

¢ 🏨 **Wawa-Wewe.** These rough-hewn but clean double bungalows sit in a garden 150 ft from Lipah bay, near Lipah village. Families like Wawa-Wewe for the toy collection, library, and local hiking and cultural activities. The restaurant here serves up Indonesian, Western, and vegetarian dishes, as well as special children's items and baked goods. ✉ *Jl. Raya Lipah (Box 124, Karangasem 80852),* ☎ 📠 *0363/22074. 4 bungalows. Restaurant, fans, room service, massage, shop, library, baby-sitting, laundry service, travel services, car rental, free parking. No credit cards. BP.*

Tulamben

$$–$$$$ 🏨 **Emerald Tulamben Resort.** Settled in between the slopes of Gunung Agung and a white-sand beach about 5 km (3 mi) south of Tulamben, the Emerald Tulamben is the region's premier upscale hotel. The two-story cottages that line the hillsides are surrounded by gardens of blossoming bougainvillea. Rooms have canopy beds, bamboo furniture,

air-conditioning, refrigerators, and private patios; many have views of the three circular pools that step down toward the ocean. Guests can enjoy, and get around on, the cable car that runs along the edge of the property; other attractions include an aquarium and a glass-bottom boat. The restaurant specializes in seafood but also serves Western and Indonesian dishes. ⊠ *Tulamben 80852,* ☎ *0361/462673,* 𝐅𝐀𝐗 *0361/ 462407. 50 rooms. Restaurant, bar, coffee shop, pizzeria, air-conditioning, refrigerators, room service, pool, massage, beach, dive shop, snorkeling, library, baby-sitting, laundry service, travel services, car rental, free parking. AE, DC, MC, V. EP.*

$–$$ 🏨 **Mimpi Resort.** Probably the most famous—and popular—hotel in the region, the Mimpi was one of the original hubs for serious divers. Lying between the sea and the foothills of Gunung Agung, with Balinese-style buildings mixed with modern amenities and excellent service, it's still one of the best places in town. All rooms are air-conditioned and have outdoor garden showers. The restaurant serves up Asian and Western specialties, and the bar is a great place to rub shoulders with other divers and get the scoop on their favorite underwater sites. ⊠ *Desa Kubu (Karangasem 80852),* ☎ *0363/21642,* 𝐅𝐀𝐗 *0363/21939. 40 rooms. Restaurant, bar, air-conditioning, fans, room service, pool, massage, spa, beach, dive shop, snorkeling, baby-sitting, laundry service, travel services, car rental, free parking. AE, MC, V. BP.*

$ 🏨 **Bali Sorga.** These thatch-roof bungalows in the northern part of town are a great deal: clean and spacious accommodations at budget prices. All have tubs or showers, but only four have air-conditioning and hot water. The hotel is the home of the prestigious Dive Paradise Tulamben dive shop, and it's just a quick walk to the Tulamben wreck. The beach restaurant serves up hearty contemporary dishes and basic Indonesian fare. ⊠ *Jl. Raya Tulamben (Box 111, Amlapura 80811),* ☎ *0363/41052. 24 bungalows. Restaurant, bar, air-conditioning (some), fans, room service, massage, shop, baby-sitting, laundry service, travel services, car rental, free parking. AE, DC, MC, V. EP.*

NIGHTLIFE AND THE ARTS

For the most part the central and eastern sections of Bali are part of a quiet, refined cultural realm with deep roots in the arts, so you won't find the wild nightlife here that you would in the south. What you will find are cultural performances, temple ceremonies, and market festivals—and the occasional late-night club where you can listen to jazz and sip a decent glass of wine. Most restaurants close around 10 PM, even in Ubud, although the town center does have a few bars where you can chat and swill drinks into the wee hours. Look for live music and dance performances on weekends in the tourist towns and more often during the July and August high season and over the Christmas holidays.

Nightlife

Ubud

Ary's Warung (⊠ Jl. Ubud, ☎ 0361/975053), in the heart of Ubud, is a jazzy, candlelit gathering place for the beautiful people in town. Although the **Beggar's Bush** (⊠ Jl. Campuhan, ☎ 0361/975009), one of Ubud's classic original expatriate hangouts, was undergoing massive renovations at press time, the top-floor bar was still open, and the pub is always a good place to kick back and have a beer with fellow travelers. At the lively **Do Drop Inn** (⊠ Jl. Wanara Wana, ☎ 0361/ 975309), next to the football field, you can hang over the terrace and watch the games, then throw back a beer with the rowdy winners af-

BALINESE DANCE: THE MOVEMENTS OF MOONLIGHT

IN THE RICH DARKNESS of the temple gardens, flickering candles on moss-covered stones illuminate the outline of an ancient royal shrine. The only sound is the abrupt belching of bullfrogs and the occasional yelp of a dog, then shimmering gamelan music arises out of the night. The silver clouds slide away to reveal a full moon at the very moment a flash of gold appears in the stone archway. Two young dancers, dressed alike in gold brocade, their heads crowned with a gold wreath of flowers, glide down the steps to the stone terrace, where they begin the precise, age-old dance movements of the *legong*.

This is a scene typical of central Bali, where centuries-old temples are still the sites for dances and plays that have developed over the ages. Although a few are staged for tourists, most of these performances celebrate the island's many religious rituals and festivals. Temple rites are performed at every full and new moon, each temple has its own annual birthday celebration, and Bali's many gods mean there's a ceremony somewhere every day. These dances also connect modern life to the days of the rajas, when court performances were a highlight of visits to the region's elaborate royal palaces.

The *gambuh* is the island's original dance-play. Its stories of how Prince Panji loses and reclaims Princess Galuh are based on tales of Java's Majapahit kingdom. Classical performances still use the Javanese tongue of the time, and they feature the *gamelan gambuh*, a special orchestra that incorporates ancient drums, flutes, and the unique two-stringed *rebab*. Other gambuh dances are based on the Javanese Malat stories, which are also the basis for the dances of the legong. In a legong performance two young girls perform stilted, synchronized steps, finger movements, head tilts, and turns to the crashing sounds of a gamelan. A third girl—dressed like the others in gold-threaded fabric, with a gold crown and a cluster of frangipani blossoms encircling her head—plays the role of a servant.

In other performances *topeng* (masks) are used. Most masks are made of painted wood and fit over the forehead, eyes, nose, and cheeks, leaving the mouth and chin area exposed for characters that can be quite realistic. Mask performances are more recent, probably only a few hundred years old, and are based on various stories from the Balinese kingdoms, although local plays sometimes tackle popular topics from the country's current events. In some performances one actor takes on all the roles, changing into more than a dozen masks. Other tales utilize separate players for the king, elders, servants, and plebeians—the latter of whom often take on a humorous role.

One of the most popular dance-dramas is that of the Barong, a shaggy creature that looks part lion, part dog and symbolizes good luck. It takes two actors to hold up the coconut-fiber costume, which is adorned with small mirrors and bright ribbons. The players usually inject humor into Barong's mannerisms, in the way he playfully snaps his jaws open and closed at the enemy or wiggles his rear as he makes his exit. His magical powers help the royal army fight off the evil witch Rangda, who hypnotizes a group of soldiers dressed in black-and-white-checked sarongs that symbolize the battle between good and evil. The men turn their swords on themselves, but Barong's powers keep the blades from piercing their skin. It's a vivid and memorable performance (although the end may prove a bit frightening for young children).

Bali's most famous play is the *kecak*, a ritual dance invented by expatriate painter Walter Spies and choreographer Katharane Mershon in the 1930s. The unique feature of this drama is the music, which is simply a chant, "*Kecak-kecak-kecak-kecak.*" The low, frantic words are a fitting background for the battle between good and evil, which ends in a fiery blaze of coconut husks tossed across the stage by warring groups. Many kecak performances are staged in the Ubud area throughout the week, but the dance is most exciting when performed in front of a candlelit temple stage at night.

terward. **Kafe Batan Waru** (✉ Jl. Dewi Sita, ☎ 0361/977528) has grown from an eclectic little restaurant into one of Ubud's major expat hangouts—a Singapore-style café-bar where you can sip wine and savor the exotic environment. The new **Terazzo** (✉ Jl. Suweta, ☎ 0361/978941) is proving to be another of Ubud's classy haunts, where the slender and stylish linger after dinner.

Archipelago (✉ Jl. Wanara Wana, ☎ 0812/3969077), with its large-screen TV, collection of movies and concert videos, and occasional live bands, is a longtime favorite nightspot. The **Funky Monkey** (✉ Jl. Wanara Wana, ☎ 0812/3903729) has DJ theme parties Monday through Saturday 9 PM–1 AM; depending on the night, the music might be anything from funk and worldfest to hip-hop, rhythm and blues, or acid jazz. Terrific live jazz by local musicians is the highlight at the new **Jazz Café** (✉ Jl. Sukma 2, Tebesaya, ☎ 0361/976594). **Sai Sai** (✉ Jl. Wanara Wana, ☎ no phone) has weekly live rock music and the occasional gamelan; call or check the outdoor blackboard for a schedule.

Candidasa and Environs

Nightlife here is centered around the small, open bars at the hotels along the main seaside strip (the fuller the hotel, the busier the bar). The always popular **TJ's** (✉ Jl. Raya, Candidasa, ☎ no phone), in front of the Watergarden hotel, is the best spot on the southern end of the road.

For a more stunning, and expensive, setting try one of the resorts. The sleek bar at the **Amankila** (✉ Pantai Buitan, Manggis, ☎ 0366/21993) has spectacular views over the bay. The spacious, open-air bar at the **Serai** (Pantai Buitan, Manggis, ☎ 0363/41011) is a relaxing place to unwind after a day of snorkeling or hiking.

The Arts

Ubud

CLASSES

The **Agung Rai Museum of Art** (✉ Jl. Pengosekan, ☎ 0361/976659) offers a wide array of daily Balinese dance, arts, and music classes. The museum specializes in children's programs.

The **Bumbu Bali** (✉ Jl. Suweta, ☎ 0361/974217) holds classes in Balinese cooking. The restaurant's staff will take you to the market and help you prepare a selection of dishes for lunch. A recipe book and a "Bumbu Kitchen Team" apron are included in the $10 price.

Jalan-Jalan Villa and Spa (✉ Jl. Pengosekan, ☎ 0361/979008) teaches Balinese dance for $3 per hour. You can have your photo taken in traditional Balinese ceremonial costume and makeup for $30, but book at least a day in advance.

Oka Kartini Bungalows (✉ Jl. Ubud, ☎ 0361/975193) holds weekly Balinese dance classes.

Honeymoon Guesthouse cooking classes take place at the guest house (☞ Lodging *above*) and the Indus and Casa Luna restaurants (☞ Dining, *above*). There are three classes a week from 9 to 2; each costs $10: Monday is spiced fish in banana leaf, spinach salad, tuna curry, carrot and cucumber pickles, and black rice pudding; Tuesday, market shopping tour, fried noodles, and green coconut crepes; Wednesday, satay, vegetable salad, gado-gado, corn fritters, and fragrant yellow rice.

GALLERIES

The **Agung Rai Gallery** (✉ Jl. Hanoman, ☎ no phone) displays the works of Agung Rai, as well as many valuable pieces from his international collection.

The **Komaneka Gallery** (✉ Jl. Wanara Wana, ☎ 0361/976090) exhibits modern pieces by local artists.

Be sure to make time to tour the **Lempad Gallery** (✉ Jl. Ubud, ☎ no phone), which celebrates the semierotic paintings and delicate pen-and-ink drawings of nudes by Ubud's most famous artist. Interestingly, Lempad was believed to have psychic powers, and the tale of his death (at age 116) is famous: He gathered his descendants from around the island, asked them to cleanse him and dress him in funeral clothing, requested that they complete his unfinished duties in life, said good-bye, and died. You'll find more of Lempad's works throughout town, notably at the Pura Saraswati.

The **Seniwati Gallery** (✉ Jl. Sriwidari 2B, ☎ 0361/975485), a small place just off the main road, has long been a source of support for Ubud's women artists, whose works are represented here.

PERFORMANCES

You can pick up a complete weekly schedule of traditional Balinese dances, music, and puppet shows at **Ubud Tourist Information** (✉ Jl. Ubud, ☎ 0361/973285).

The **Agung Rai Museum of Art** (Stage: ✉ Jl. Hanoman, ☎ 0361/976659) is the site of kecak dances—including an exciting battle with blazing palm branches—performed by candlelight during every full moon and new moon. The show begins at 7 PM and costs around $3. Peliatan dancers perform the legong here each Sunday at 7:30 PM, also $3.

Kertha Accommodation (✉ Jl. Wanara Wana, ☎ 973188) holds wayang kulit performances every Tuesday, Thursday, Saturday, and Sunday from 8 PM to 9 PM for about $3.

Oka Kartini Bungalows (✉ Jl. Ubud, ☎ 0361/975193) puts on shadow-puppet shows by firelight against a little screen in the back of the complex. You can catch these performances on Wednesday and Sunday from 8 PM to 9:15 PM; tickets are around $2.

At the **Puri Mandala Peliatan Stage** (✉ Jl. Peliatan, ☎ 0361/975026), the dancers and musicians of the famed Genta Bhuana Sari group, all of whom are just 10–17 years old, perform classical Balinese dances every Tuesday at 7 PM. The performance costs roughly $2; free transport from central Ubud is included.

Ubud's royal palace, **Puri Saren** (✉ Jl. Ubud, ☎ no phone), hosts classical Balinese dances and plays nightly throughout the week. These performances all start at 7:30 and cost about $2. Monday night is legong; Tuesday, *Ramayana* ballet; Wednesday, legong and Barong; Thursday, Gabor; Friday, Barong; Saturday, legong; and Sunday, legong of the *Mahabharata*. You can also watch the children of the Sadha Budaya Troupe practice their dance steps at the palace for free, Tuesday 3–5:30 and Sunday 9:30–noon.

Sehati Guest House (✉ Jl. Wanara Wana, ☎ FAX 0361/976341) occasionally schedules Balinese jegog and joged dances for $3; add the four-course traditional Balinese buffet for about $3 more.

Candidasa and Environs

Balinese cooking classes can be a highlight of a stay at the **Serai** (Pantai Buitan, Manggis, ☎ 0363/41011), which offers half-, two-, and five-day programs that take you into the heart of island life, from going to the market and fields to preparing the goods you found for a feast. This is a rewarding experience that will have you wielding a mortar and pestle like a local. The courses cost $75–$550 and are open to nonguests.

GET PAMPERED, BALI STYLE

BALINESE MASSAGES, body wraps, and fragrant baths have long been a favorite pastime of visitors to the island. It's no surprise then that dozens of small operations doing these treatments have sprung up in the past five years. On every street you'll find small spas that offer inexpensive massages, aromatherapy, hair and scalp treatments, manicures and pedicures, and holistic and herbal healing methods. Ubud, the main center for culture on Bali, is the ultimate place to receive such royal treatment, and all the spas listed below are here.

Jalan-Jalan Villa and Spa (✉ Jl. Pengosekan, ☎ 0361/979008) has massage, a salon, a terrific pool setting, and an upstairs fitness room with cardio equipment and weights.

Jelatik (✉ Jl. Wanara Wana, ☎ 0361/978307) provides various scrubs, massages, and aromatherapy.

Padi Prada (✉ Jl. Wanara Wana, ☎ 0828/381207) does baths, body wraps, massages, facials, as well as combination packages.

Tino Beauty Center (✉ Jl. Ubud, ☎ 0361/978623), in Toko Tino grocery, offers a range of basic treatments.

The **Tjampuhan Spa** (Jl. Campuhan, ☎ 0361/975368) has one of the most fabulous settings of any spa on the island. To reach the spa, you walk on stepping-stone paths through little man-made streams running alongside the Ayung River ravine. The entrance is guarded by enormous stone creatures carved by some of the island's most talented craftsmen. The walls and ceiling of the cave-like spa are carved into an elaborate forest of stone figures; whirlpools are settled into deep crevices between stone tree roots laden with stone blossoms and frogs; and massage rooms are natural shelters tucked into the forested hillside.

Ubud Sari Health Resort (✉ Jl. Kajeng 35, ☎ 0361/974393) is a quiet place, with massage and beauty treatment rooms, mud baths that use volcanic ash from Gunung Agung, and a terrazzo Jacuzzi in a peaceful garden setting by a river.

Other, smaller spas have basic massage, facial, and beauty treatment services:

Maria Beauty Salon (✉ Jl. Wanara Wana, ☎ 0361/975622) provides help with Balinese costumes and makeup in addition to its regular beauty services.

The **Meditation Shop** (✉ Jl. Wanara Wana, ☎ 0361/976206) is a quiet little place that offers simple massages and herbal products, as well as five free meditation lessons.

Mentari Massage Service Center (✉ Jl. Ubud 8X, ☎ 0361/974001) does massage, acupuncture, and reflexology and specializes in treatment for men.

Milano Salon (✉ Jl. Wanara Wana, ☎ 0361/973448) has masseuses that will come to your hotel.

Nikki Tradisional Salon (✉ Jl. Dewi Sita, ☎ 0361/977546) does massages, manicures, facials, and hair treatments.

Panorama (✉ Jl. Pengosekan, ☎ 0361/973336) offers haircuts and coloring as well as massage.

OUTDOOR ACTIVITIES AND SPORTS

If you like adventure, make eastern Bali your base: your options run from mountain climbing, cycling, river rafting, and elephant riding to scuba diving, kayaking, and parachuting. You can plan just about any trip from any of the tourist towns in the region. Note, however, that although there are a number of companies advertising adventure trips and tours, not all are well organized, and the cheaper options are almost never the best. If you're shopping for a tour company, go with one that has been recommended and that specializes in the adventure you want, whether it's rafting, diving, trekking, or cycling.

Participant Sports

Boating and Sailing

The majority of hotels along Padangbai's beach road can arrange boat trips to neighboring islands, including Nusa Penida, Lombok, and the Gili Islands. Try one of the following: **Pantai Ayu** (☎ 0363/41396); **Puri Rai Beach Inn** (☎ 0363/41386); or **Topi Inn** (☎ 0363/41424).

Charters and day cruises can be booked from most hotels in Candidasa and Tulamben. In Tulamben call one of these places: **Bali Sorga** (☎ 0363/41052); **Emerald Tulamben Resort** (☎ 0361/462673); or **Mimpi Resort** (☎ 0363/21642).

General Adventures

Bali Adventure Tours (✉ Jl. Bypass Ngurah Rai, Kuta, ☎ 0361/721480) is a reliable multiactivity agency that organizes mountain biking, rafting, and trekking tours in the region, as well as trips to the elephant and bird parks.

Sobek (✉ Jl. Tirta Ening 9, Jl. Bypass, Sanur, ☎ 0361/287059) has years of adventure experience in Indonesia. The skilled guides lead one-day and multiday cycling, rafting, and hiking trips in eastern Bali.

The Trekker (☎ 0361/725944) will take you on the "Indiana Jones Adventure," a half-day of canoeing, biking, and trekking through the mountains for $44.

Hiking

Numerous companies lead hikes in the rice paddies and rain forests around Ubud and in the mountains. Many resort hotels also organize picnic day trips to hidden waterfalls and scenic spots.

Bali Bird Walks (✉ Jl. Campuhan, Ubud, ☎ 0361/975009) offers tame strolls with Victor Mason, author of numerous bird books and articles and founder of the Bali Bird Club. The $33, three-hour walks begin at 9 AM outside the Beggar's Bush pub and include lunch and drinks afterward.

Herb Walks in Bali (✉ Jl. Ubud, Ubud, ☎ 0361/974865) takes you out into the forest with Balinese healers Ni Wayan Lilir and I Made Westi. The walks, scheduled Monday through Thursday, begin outside the Museum Puri Lukisan at 8:30 AM and last until noon. The $18 cost includes herbal tea and a snack.

Jero Wijaya Tourist Service (✉ Jl. Andong 9X, Andong, ☎ 0361/973172) can plan a trip tailored to your preferences and fitness level. The agency offers sunrise treks to Gunung Agung, as well as hikes in other areas of Bali, for $60–$100. Make sure to bring comfortable hiking boots and a sturdy sun hat, and schedule your trek for early morning or late afternoon.

Rafting

The region's many mountain rivers provide excellent opportunities for white-water rafting. One of the most professional outfits is **Unda River**

Rafting (Jl. Kajeng 33, Ubud, ☎ 0361/975366), which organizes a unique trip along the Unda River out of Semarapura. This is a particularly notable excursion because it focuses on a rarely rafted section of waterway (and doesn't involve the 100-step climb to and from the road necessary for trips on other rivers). Plus, the price includes a hearty buffet lunch after the trip.

Other companies cover the well-traversed Ayung River. **Ayung River Rafting** (✉ Jl. Diponegoro 150, Denpasar, ☎ 0361/238759) organizes white-water trips on the Ayung ($63) as well as adventures on inflatable kayaks ($66). **Baleraf** (Jl. Tamblingan 82, Sanur, ☎ 0361/287256) can tailor group trips to different levels of rafting skill and experience. **Bali International Rafting** (Jl. Tirta Ening 7, Bypass Ngurah Rai, Sanur, ☎ 0361/281408) offers several half- and full-day trips, with lunch included.

Scuba Diving and Snorkeling

Padangbai is a major departure point for dive trips, and all of the hotels have dive tour services. On the hill overlooking town, the popular hotel **Pantai Ayu** (✉ Jl. Silayukti, ☎ 0363/41396) has a travel center that can organize a variety of dive trips. The largest hotel in town, the **Puri Rai Beach Inn** (✉ Jl. Silayukti, ☎ 0363/41386), has a dive shop with experienced pros; you can book tours and rent equipment here too. The **Topi Inn** (✉ Jl. Silayukti, ☎ 0363/41424), a favorite of budget travelers, has a travel office that offers less expensive dive trips.

In Candidasa, **Barrakuda** (✉ Jl. Raya, ☎ 0363/41214) is one of the most popular places to book a dive trip. **Baruna** (✉ Jl. Raya, ☎ 0361/753820) is one of the most experienced outfits on the island, and the experts here can organize multiday dive tours to many locations around eastern Bali and Nusa Tenggara. **Stingray** (✉ Jl. Raya, ☎ 0363/41063), in the Puri Bali Bungalows, is another well-known dive outfit in Candidasa.

Tulamben has several high-quality dive operations. **Dive Paradise Tulamben** (✉ Jl. Raya Tulamben, ☎ 0363/40132), in the Bali Sorga hotel, leads dives to the wreck of the *Liberty Glo* and to other dive sites along the east coast. The **Emerald Tulamben Resort** (✉ Tulamben, ☎ 0361/462673), the largest hotel in town, has a private reef right off its beach; the pros at the dive shop here can take you to the wreck and to many other area reefs. The Denpasar-based **Ena Dive Center** (☎ 0361/287945) is one of the top bets for booking dive trips in the Tulamben area. Probably the best-known outfit in town is the **Mimpi Resort** (✉ Desa Kubu, ☎ 0363/21642), which has an excellent selection of modern dive equipment for rent, as well as several professional dive instructors who lead trips and teach certification classes. Any of these companies can also arrange snorkeling trips.

SHOPPING

One of the pleasures of visiting this region is browsing for eclectic clothing and crafts. You'll find hundreds of handmade items to choose from, and most are quite inexpensive. You can usually watch the artisans at work carving, painting, weaving, or forging. All prices are negotiable, except in the upscale shops, where prices are marked. The best places to find inexpensive high-quality goods are the local markets, where you can shop and take in local life.

Shops carry a wide variety of items, but you can also usually order something special—though it may not be ready by the time you leave the island. If you have something particular in mind, talk with your hotel manager or one of the major travel agencies; someone is certain to know of an artist who can do the job in the specified time and for the right price.

Areas, Markets, and Malls

It's hot, crowded, and bustling with locals and tourists, but the **Pasar Ubud** market, at the corner of Jalan Ubud and Jalan Wanara Wana, is the best place to get a taste of the local trade process; the produce market held every three days only adds to the din, but you can pick up cheap fruits and vegetables here. At the **Pasar Malam** night market, two blocks east of Pasar Ubud, you can buy sundries and tasty snacks. You'll find other small morning produce markets and night food-stall markets in every town from Ubud to Tulamben.

The streets of Ubud are lined with shops filled with handmade clothing and crafts. Candidasa has many of the same wares, though in lesser supply. To purchase works straight from the artists, head south of Ubud to the crafts villages: **Batubulan** is the center for stone carving; **Celuk** is where intricate silver and gold jewelry is made; **Mas** is a hub for wood-carvers; **Peliatan** has painted mobiles and wind chimes. You'll find beautiful handmade quilts hanging from shops along the sides of the road in **Sayan,** west of Ubud, and in the mountains around **Besakih,** to the northeast.

Specialty Shops

Ubud

ANTIQUES AND SECONDHAND ITEMS

Oman Gallery (✉ Jl. Sanggingan, ☎ 0812/3906610) has an extensive display of antique crafts.

Panen Collection (✉ Jl. Dewa Sita, ☎ 0361/977734) carries beautiful antiques, textiles, and batik.

Papadun (✉ Jl. Sanggingan, ☎ 0361/975379) is a good place to buy antiques, especially old textiles and wood carvings from Sumatra.

Rococo Antiques (✉ Jl. Ubud, ☎ 0361/974805) is a fantastic place, full of lovely furniture, textiles, and masks.

Tegun (✉ Jl. Hanoman 44, ☎ 0361/973361) has all sorts of collectible Indonesian crafts and cloth.

Tips Handicraft Center (✉ Jl. Dewa Sita, ☎ no phone) sells beautiful antiques, *wayang golek* (wooden puppets), masks, and baskets.

ART

Gajah Mas Gallery (✉ Jl. Hanoman at Jl. Pengosekan, ☎ 0361/976283) is two stories of traditional and modern Balinese paintings. You can't miss the two large elephants outside.

Seniwati Gallery (✉ Jl. Sriwidari 2B, ☎ 0361/975485) has a shop that sells crafts made by women, some of whom also have works displayed in the gallery.

BOOKS

Ary's Bookshop (✉ Jl. Ubud, ☎ 0361/978203) has a good selection of guidebooks and coffee-table books on Balinese culture and wildlife. Here you can also find novels, current newsmagazines, maps, and volumes on Indonesia and Southeast Asia.

Dewa Mas (✉ Jl. Hanoman 88, ☎ 0361/978786) carries a basic selection of books about Bali and Indonesia.

Igna Book Shop (✉ Jl. Wanara Wana, ☎ no phone) sells both new and used titles.

CERAMICS

Juli Shop (✉ Jl. Wanara Wana, ☎ 0361/977983) has tangerine-color walls that highlight its specialty ceramics.

Keramik (✉ Jl. Pengosekan, ☎ no phone) was undergoing renovations at press time, but the expanded store will carry more of the usual teapots, candleholders, and mugs.

CLOTHING

Ada-Ada (✉ Jl. Wanara Wana, ☎ 0361/298459) carries upscale accessories and jewelry for women.

B & F Collection (✉ Jl. Hanoman, ☎ 0361/240987) has a selection of lovely dresses and can also make clothes to order.

Baliso Tailor (✉ Jl. Wanara Wana, ☎ 0812/3910395) sews men's and women's clothing.

Dayu (✉ Jl. Wanara Wana, ☎ 0361/977981) sells pretty white and pastel cotton dresses, as well as bath products and oils.

Ini-Itu (✉ Jl. Wanara Wana, ☎ 0361/298459) has the beautiful dresses, shoes, sarongs, and handbags to wear with the accessories sold at sister shop Ada-Ada (☞ *above*).

Mama & Leon (✉ Jl. Wanara Wana, ☎ 0361/944060), one of an upscale chain of shops, sells professional-looking tropical dresses and suits that fit Western sizes.

Meianti Shop (✉ Jl. Ubud, ☎ no phone), tucked into the main strip between Ubud Music and Toko Tino, specializes in handmade batik dresses and casual clothing.

Mr. Bali (✉ Jl. Wanara Wana, ☎ 0361/975310) specializes in menswear and carries shirts, pants, suits, and shoes.

Mutiara (✉ Jl. Ubud, ☎ 0361/975145) is a nice men's shop with a good selection of high-quality shirts, shorts, and boots.

Noe (✉ Jl. Wanara Wana, FAX 0361/975115) is the place to head for kids' clothing. You'll find this store by looking for the unmissable Pondok Frog sign across the street.

Opiq (✉ Jl. Wanara Wana, ☎ 0361/943951), in Toko Tino grocery, specializes in children's clothing, particularly bright batiks.

Puspita (✉ Jl. Hanoman 53, ☎ no phone; ✉ Jl. Suweta 5, ☎ no phone) carries nice dresses, shirts, and basic jewelry.

Pt. Ayu Orchid (✉ Jl. Dewi Setia, ☎ 0361/977733) has an excellent collection of elegant, high-quality dresses, shoes, and outfits for women. Ask for a catalog.

Rasa Sayang (✉ Jl. Wanara Wana, ☎ 0361/977593) is a bright shop with very helpful service and a selection of gorgeous dresses.

Sama Sari Shop (✉ Jl. Hanoman 19, ☎ 0361/975927) sells frog, fish, and turtle zipper purses to go with the fabrics at the Sama Suka Shop (☞ *below*).

Sama Suka Shop (✉ Jl. Hanoman 19, ☎ 0361/975927) has wonderful ikat and batik clothes and scarves.

Sely (✉ Jl. Hanoman, ☎ 0361/977805) sells bright plaid handbags.

Studio 22k (✉ Jl. Ubud, ☎ 0361/975624), next to the Oka Kartini Bungalows, sells women's dresses and jewelry, as well as classy sarongs and textiles.

Toko (✉ Jl. Wanara Wana, ☎ 0361/95046), in Toko Tino grocery, carries dresses, hats, and jewelry, as well as fabric and bath products.

Uluwatu (✉ Jl. Wanara Wana, ☎ 0361/977557) is part of an island chain that sells women's clothing and home accents made of handmade Balinese lace.

FURNITURE

Gophir Furniture & Craft (✉ Jl. Bima 19, ☎ 0361/978667) makes and carries woven rattan and imitation wood furniture. It's possible to bargain here.

Mandalika (✉ Jl. Pengosekan, ☎ 0361/978339) specializes in art and interiors, selling hand-carved wooden crafts and furniture.

Rindang Homestyles (✉ Jl. Ubud, ☎ 0361/975087), in the Campuhan basin, has a wonderful collection of items to add to your home, including antique reproduction furniture, art, and collectibles.

GIFTS AND SOUVENIRS

Ani's Collections (✉ Jl. Campuhan, ☎ 0361/975431), near the Campuhan bridge, carries a variety of Indonesian crafts.

Dhyma's Dream (✉ Jl. Hanoman, ☎ no phone) sells little household items, handmade pillowcases, and small antiques.

Eama Gallery (✉ Jl. Wanara Wana, ☎ 0361/973232) has hand-carved antiques and lovely trinkets and decorations.

Kites Center (✉ Jl. Wanara Wana, ☎ 0361/298709) is where to go for the big, colorful kites you see flying over the rice fields. You can buy a kite straight from the shop or have one made to order.

Wayan's Shop (✉ Jl. Ubud, ☎ 0361/977721) has a wonderful selection of wayang kulit and wayang golek puppets.

GROCERIES

Andalan (✉ Jl. Lungsiakan, ☎ 0361/979087), a new little shop along the main road between Sayan and Campuhan, is an organic grocery carrying everything from produce and dairy products to spices and vitamins—just make sure to bring your own bags. The store also makes daily deliveries. A small café serves sandwiches, pasta, drinks, and Indonesian dishes.

Cahaya Intan (✉ Jl. Campuhan 88X, ☎ 0361/975901) is a medium-size grocery shop that also carries a good assortment of household items, as well as baby and children's clothes and toys.

Toko Tino (✉ Jl. Ubud, ☎ 0361/975020) is a three-story supermarket with household items in the basement and an Internet café and spa upstairs.

HANDICRAFTS

Amnesia (✉ Jl. Wanara Wana, ☎ 0812/3933433), in spite of its name, is a gallery of unforgettable creations, from butterfly batiks to mobiles, painted boxes, and little glass candleholders.

Kunang-Kunang (✉ Jl. Campuhan, ☎ 0361/975714; ✉ Jl. Ubud, ☎ 0361/975716) stores are museumlike shops where you can discover all sorts of crafts from Bali and the rest of Indonesia.

Le Chat (✉ Jl. Wanara Wana, ☎ 0811/388925) carries women's shirts and basic Balinese souvenirs.

Oleh-Oleh (✉ Jl. Ubud, ☎ 0361/973466) is a good place to pick up Balinese and Indonesian crafts.

Panorama (✉ Jl. Pengosekan, ☎ 0361/96336) carries the gamut of basic Bali kitsch.

Pondok Frog (✉ Jl. Wanara Wana, ☎ 0361/975565) sells T-shirts and wood carvings and also makes souvenirs to order.

HOUSEWARES

Alam (✉ Jl. Ubud, ☎ 0361/975087) sells contemporary nature-theme crafts for the home.

Casa Lina Homewears (✉ Jl. Ubud, ☎ 0361/977406) carries little items like bright cushions, fabrics, and soap dishes. Look for the colorful Japanese paper lanterns hanging outside the entrance.

DesianEko (✉ Jl. Bima, ☎ 0361/978623), just west of the Agung Rai Museum of Art, is a small wholesaler of lontar palm pens, lamp shades, stationery, and cards. There are also items created articles palm bark and recycled paper.

Rindang Homestyles (⊠ Jl. Ubud, ☎ 0361/975087) is a wonderful shop full of beige- and cream-color fabrics, woven rattan crafts, and muted cotton and tropical batiks.

Wei-Wei (⊠ Jl. Wanara Wana, ☎ 0812/3900646) sells soaps, candles, stationery, and other elegant accents for the home.

JEWELRY

Aget (⊠ Jl. Wanara Wana, ☎ 0812/3931465) sells beautiful jewelry and stonework. You can select from displayed items or work with the smiths to make your own designs.

Alit's Silver (⊠ Jl. Wanara Wana, ☎ 0361/298101) can create gold and silver jewelry to order.

Budhi Ayu (⊠ Jl. Celuk, ☎ 0811/385563) specializes in made-to-order gold and silver pieces.

Dewi Sri Silver (⊠ Jl. Wanara Wana, ☎ 0361/975938) carries classic silver pieces as well as Balinese souvenirs.

Hari Ini Silver (⊠ Jl. Wanara Wana, ☎ 0361/974009) is home to Balinese artists who blend traditional designs with more modern materials and motifs.

Karang Silver (⊠ Jl. Pengosekan, ☎ 0361/975445) has a shop full of silver items.

Treasures (⊠ Jl. Ubud, ☎ 0361/976697) lives up to its name: it's one of the best places in Ubud to find gold jewelry.

MUSIC

Era 21 (⊠ Jl. Wanara Wana, ☎ 0812/3906568) has a large assortment of CDs.

Pandawa (⊠ Jl. Wanara Wana 65, ☎ 0361/975698) carries CDs and cassettes.

Ubud Music (⊠ Jl. Ubud, ☎ 0361/975362), on the main road, is one of the largest music sellers in town.

TEXTILES

Batik Work Shop (⊠ Jl. Wanara Wana, ☎ no phone) is a little place where you can buy batik or make your own.

Ketut Suta (⊠ Jl. Penestanan Kaja, ☎ 0361/976091) is a painter whose shop lies on the devilish hill from Campuhan to Penestanan. Out front you'll find beautiful ikat fabrics and gorgeous hammocks.

Lotus Studios (⊠ Jl. Ubud, ☎ 0361/975363) has a boutique that displays classic Indonesian textiles and sarongs.

Low Art Batik (⊠ Pasar Ubud, Lantai III, Blok C89, ☎ 0812/3942393) carries a basic selection of colorful batik sarongs and tourist clothing.

Pithecanthropus (⊠ Jl. Ubud, ☎ no phone) has a nice selection of batik fabrics.

Sunari Art Gallery (⊠ Jl. Sanggingan, Br. Lungsiakan, ☎ 0361/977273), a batik painting house, sells beautiful sheets and quilts. You can also watch the women at work in the back.

WOOD CARVINGS

Cha Cha (⊠ Jl. Wanara Wana, ☎ 0361/977781) is a charming shop that carries all sorts of wood-carved and painted cats.

Dewa Dewi (⊠ Jl. Pengosekan, ☎ 0361/978427), a wood-carver, has a shop just west of the Agung Rai Museum of Art. Here you'll find a team of women weaving baskets, as well as a back shop full of gorgeous wood dressers, cupboards, and boxes, both raw and painted in bright pastels with flowers, dragons, and birds.

Putri Shop (⊠ Jl. Wanara Wana, ☎ no phone) is crammed with wood-carved mobiles, picture frames, notebook covers, and the like. The shop can also make objects to order.

Candidasa

The town's main road is lined with shops selling crafts from around the island and handmade clothing, much of it of the same quality you'd find in Ubud and the small villages—although at higher prices. In particular, look for shell-accented items such as purses and picture frames.

EASTERN BALI A TO Z

Arriving and Departing

By Airplane

Bali's only air hub is Ngurah Rai International Airport, in Tuban in southern Bali, and all airline offices are there or in Sanur or Denpasar (☞ Southern Bali A to Z *in* Chapter 2). If you need to change reservations or reconfirm bookings, a local travel agent or your hotel can call the airlines for you.

FROM THE AIRPORT

No matter how you travel from the airport, it takes at least an hour to reach Ubud, 1½ hours to reach Candidasa, and 2½ hours or more to reach Amed and Tulamben. Most hotels and villas have free pickup services, but be sure to reserve a ride before you arrive. Otherwise, your best bet is to travel by taxi, which you can arrange at the Bluebird window, right outside the arrivals hall: just state your destination, pay the set rate for your ticket, and off you go without worrying about haggling over prices. If you have a big group or a lot of luggage, you can hire a minivan for about the same cost, but you'll need to bargain hard. There are also shuttles (☞ Getting Around, *below*) available to Ubud and the coast, but these must be booked ahead.

By Boat

Padangbai is the only port in the region, and it's used mostly to shuttle passengers between Bali and Lombok. Rusty car ferries make the four-hour trip to Lembar every two hours round the clock. Schedules often change due to weather and rough seas, though, so contact the **harbor office** (☎ 0363/41840) to find out when the next boat departs and what the current cost is for passengers and vehicles. If you're taking your car across, make sure you have a permit from the car rental office to take the car off the island.

If you're adventurous, you can also get to Nusa Penida from Padangbai by hiring one of the private fishing boats lined up on the beach east of the ferry terminal between 7 AM and noon. It costs about $5 to charter a boat, which can carry 20–30 people, for the half-hour trip.

Getting Around

By Bicycle

Central and eastern Bali are threaded with back roads that wind through spectacular mountain and rural scenery. Mountain bikes are the perfect way to see it all up close, whether on a day trip or a week-long circuit. You can rent bikes from the following places in Ubud: **Akira Bali** (⊠ Jl. Pengosekan, ☎ 0361/973131); **Jineng Wisata** (Jl. Hanoman 22X, ☎ 0361/976006); **Pande Wayan Ardana** (⊠ Jl. Pengosekan, ☎ 0361/974615).

By Car

Although it's convenient enough to walk to Ubud's shops and see other towns and sights on day tours, if you'll be in the area for more than a few days a car gives you added freedom to roam the countryside. It's actually quite inexpensive to negotiate a private driver into the deal, which lets someone else handle the directions and parking while you sit back and enjoy the surroundings. If you choose to drive your-self, make sure you're comfortable handling a manual transmission on very steep hills and in tight, fast-moving two-lane traffic. Most hotels and villas have free parking; most restaurants and sights do not, so you're limited to squeezing in on the street. North and east of Ubud and Se-marapura, gas stations are few and far between, so fill up before you depart.

A main road runs north from Denpasar to Ubud and then up into the mountains; another runs east from Ubud through Gianyar and Se-marapura to the coast; another runs north along the coast from Padang-bai, cutting inland toward Amlapura, to Amed and Tulamben. All thoroughfares are two lanes—or less, depending on road work, street parking, and ceremonial processions. Always allow time for delays, and keep a sense of humor at all times.

Toyota Rent a Car (✉ Jl. Bypass Nusa Dua, Jimbaran, ☎ 0361/703333; ✉ Jl. Airport 99X, Tuban, ☎ 0361/763333; ✉ Ngurah Rai International Airport, ☎ 0361/753744) is the island's premier car rental service. Their offices are in southern Bali, however; so you'll either have to book a vehicle through them and pick it up at the airport when you arrive or rent one from a local agent.

Ubud is the only place in this region to find professional rental companies, and your best bet is probably **Jineng Wisata** (✉ Jl. Hanoman 22X, ☎ 0361/976006; ✉ Jl. Hanoman 69, ☎ 0361/976477; ✉ Jl. Ubud, ☎ 0361/976104; ✉ Jl. Wanara Wana, ☎ 0361/977518). This agency has a fleet of international vehicles, a crew of professional drivers, and an array of motorcycles and mountain bikes for hire, and they also have mechanics available 24 hours.

The following rental companies are also in Ubud: **Arwana Tourist Service** (✉ Jl. Pengosekan, ☎ 0812/3959791); **Kori Car Rental** (✉ Jl. Pengosekan, ☎ 0361/977688); **Manacika Bali** (✉ Jl. Penestanan, ☎ 0361/979131); **Pudja Arsri Car Rental** (✉ Jl. Pengosekan, ☎ 0361/974676).

By Motorcycle

It's cheap and easy to rent motorcycles anywhere in the region, usu-ally from someone's brother's uncle's cousin's friend. Most are in good shape, but if you get a bum bike, you can usually just laugh it off and owe nothing. You can also rent motorbikes from any car rental agency and from most resorts. You do need to know how to drive one through rough terrain.

In Ubud, **CV Ubud Wisata** (✉ Jl. Ubud, ☎ 0361/975498) rents mo-torcycles and can provide additional services, such as planning trips. You can also rent motorbikes at **Jineng Wisata** (✉ Jl. Hanoman 22X, ☎ 0361/976006; ✉ Jl. Hanoman 69, ☎ 0361/976477; ✉ Jl. Ubud, ☎ 0361/976104; ✉ Jl. Wanara Wana, ☎ 0361/977518).

By Shuttle

One of the most popular ways for tourists to travel between towns is by shuttle. The bus makes a round of stops at specific travel agencies and hotels at set times throughout the day and generally takes a direct route between towns and the airport. Most travel agencies and hotel desks have their particular shuttle times posted, so all you have to do is figure out which one costs the least and which pickup point is most convenient.

Approximate shuttle rates from Ubud are: airport, $10; Amed or Tu-lamben, $30; Bedugul, $13; Candidasa, $20; Denpasar, $10; Kintamani,

$13; Kuta, $10; Lovina or Singaraja, $22; Padangbai, $15; Pemuteran, $30; and Sanur, $10.

By Taxi

You won't find many taxis in central or eastern Bali; the main modes of travel are private vehicle, minibus, and crowded public minivan. You'll see men driving slowly up and down the main streets shouting, "Transport?!"—you can flag them down and bargain your fare. If you do find a real taxi, make sure that the driver turns on the meter or that you agree on a price before you begin the trip.

Contacts and Resources

Banks and Currency Exchange

You can find branches of every major Indonesian bank—and ATMs—along the main streets of Ubud and Candidasa. Most ATMs are new and thus fairly reliable, although rates are slightly worse than in the south.

In Ubud you can change money at the following places: **Pertiwi Radyaartha** (✉ Jl. Wanara Wana, ☎ 0361/978180); **Pande Wayan Ardana** (✉ Jl. Pengosekan, ☎ 0361/974615).

Business Services

All major hotels and most private villas have computers, faxes, and modem lines; many also have photocopying, graphics, and translation services.

Ary's Business and Travel Service (✉ Jl. Ubud, Ubud, ☎ 0361/973130) is an international travel, telephone, and Internet office. It's a clean, air-conditioned place to make calls and check e-mail.
Jineng Business Center (✉ Jl. Hanoman, Ubud, ☎ 0361/975300) is a professional operation with Internet, fax, translation, and typing services, as well as Web page and brochure design.
Trio (✉ Jl. Andong, Petulu, ☎ 0361/976709) has a business center that offers a full range of business, shipping, and legal services. There are also a couple of computers for Internet access and a café.

Emergencies

Ambulance (☎ 118). **Fire** (☎ 113). **Police** (☎ 110).

Ubud has an excellent base of emergency services, including round-the-clock assistance for medical and dental problems. Several 24-hour clinics offer specialized services for children's care. **BMA Medical Assistance** (✉ Jl. Hanoman 100X, ☎ 0361/978360) provides 24-hour medical care. **Ubud Clinic** (✉ Jl. Campuhan 36, ☎ 0361/974911), at the bottom curve of the Campuhan road, has experts on hand 24 hours for every medical need.

English-Language Bookstores

Although there are no major English-language chain bookstores in Ubud, you can find novels, travel guides, and coffee-table souvenir volumes at small bookstores such as **Ary's Bookshop** (✉ Jl. Ubud, ☎ 0361/978203), **Dewa Mas** (✉ Jl. Hanoman 88, ☎ 0361/978786), and **Igna Book Shop** (✉ Jl. Wanara Wana, ☎ no phone). Many large groceries, including **Toko Tino** (✉ Jl. Ubud, ☎ 0361/975020), have large book sections. Also look in stores that sell film and music shops such as **Ubud Music** (✉ Jl. Ubud, ☎ 0361/975362).

Guided Tours

If you're short on time or you don't want to rent your own vehicle, guided tours are a good option for seeing eastern Bali's sights. Most of the region's tours offer comfortable transportation, English-speaking guides, a range of sights to visit, and, usually, a lunch stop and a free snack.

Almost all tour companies run the same routes around the island. Price and services can vary, so check if lunch, a guide, and tour admission are included. Many of the little street-side tour and travel services are simply booking offices for other companies, so make sure you get the company you want, preferably one that has been tried and recommended by other travelers. The name of the bus company and the name of the tour office that sold it are on the ticket; you give your contact info so that the office can let you know about any changes. If you have a particularly wonderful or terrible experience, let the folks at **Ubud Tourist Information** (✉ Jl. Ubud, ☎ 0361/973285) know about it.

Listed here are the main tours of the region, along with their general costs according to the Ubud Tourist Information office (you may pay much more or less depending on the company you select): **Kintamani** includes a morning temple dance performance and stops at the crafts villages, Goa Gajah, Tampaksiring, and Gunung Batur ($25); **Besakih** includes a temple dance and stops at the crafts villages, Goa Gajah, Gianyar, Semarapura's Kerta Gosa, Pura Besakih, and Pura Bangli ($25); **Bedugul** includes the Bali Bird Park and Bali Rimba Reptile Park, the royal temple at Mengwi, the botanical gardens at Bedugul, and Lake Bratan ($30); the **East Coast** includes Gianyar, Semarapura, Goa Lawah, the Bali Aga villages, Candidasa, and Pura Besakih ($40); the **Shopping Tour** includes the crafts villages and Denpasar's Bali Museum and markets ($25); the **Uluwatu Tour** includes the crafts villages, Pulau Serangan, and Pura Uluwatu ($25).

The following tour companies are in Ubud:

Akira Bali (✉ Jl. Pengosekan, ☎ 0361/973131) covers all of the main daily tours.

Jalan-Jalan Wisata (✉ Jl. Pengosekan, ☎ 0361/976101) leads tours on air-conditioned buses to all of the island's attractions; these range in price from $4 to $7. The agency can also help with shuttles to other towns, car rental, and air tickets.

Manacika (✉ Jl. Penestanan, ☎ 0361/974405) does the basic Bali day tours. They'll also rent cars, provide shuttles to other towns in the region, change money, and do your laundry.

Nominasi Tour & Travel Service (✉ Jl. Wanara Wana 67–71, ☎ 0361/975067) offers inexpensive, good-quality tours of Bali and other Indonesian islands and can help you with air and land tickets.

Roda Tourist Service (✉ Jl. Bisma 3, ☎ 0361/976582) has been recommended by travelers for its tour and transportation services.

Sanggingan Tourist Service (✉ Jl. Sanggingan 36, ☎ 0361/978363) can help you plan and book tours. The company also rents vehicles and bikes and can assist with ticketing and overseas shipping.

Health and Safety

Make sure to take precautions against mosquitoes, particularly in the rainy season or if your lodgings are around the rice paddies, including sleeping within a net and burning coils at night (these precautions apply especially to children). It's also a good idea to drink only boiled or bottled water and make sure that meals are hygienically prepared. Make your way slowly along crumbling sidewalks and around luxury hotels and villas where steep stairs, deep ponds, and slick marble floors are the norm. Other than the occasional pickpocketing attempt, crime isn't really a concern in the region.

Laundry

All hotels and villas provide laundry service, if not on-site then at the nearby laundromat (to which you can deliver your clothes yourself for a far better price). Look for the simple, hand-painted LAUNDRY signs on the main roads of each town. In Ubud, **Indah Laundry Service** (✉ Jl. Kedewatan, ☎ 0361/975504) offers a full range of clothes-cleaning services with one to two days' turnaround time. **Super Laundry** (✉ Jl. Pengosekan, ☎ 0361/97837) makes the same promise.

Photography

Your photographs' worst enemies in this region are rain and heat, so keep your cameras and film in waterproof containers at all times. Photos of lush rice fields are best in midmorning and late-afternoon light, when the green saturates the terraces to turn them emerald and gold. Note that if your camera or video camera has been inside an air-conditioned room, the lens will be foggy for a minute or two after you take it out of the case.

You can get film developed quickly—in an hour or two, sometimes even within a half-hour—at dozens of outlets in Ubud. Try **Era 21** (✉ Jl. Wanara Wana, ☎ 0812/3906568); **Indah Photo** (✉ Jl. Ubud, ☎ 0361/975152); or **Pandawa** (✉ Jl. Wanara Wana 65, ☎ 0361/975698). Photo shops in Candidasa and Tulamben can usually provide one-day service.

Telephones, Internet, and Mail

For local calls you don't need to dial the area code. When calling long-distance on the island or between Indonesian islands, make sure to include the 0 before the area code.

Ubud has reliable international communications systems, and you can usually make phone calls, send faxes, or retrieve e-mail at any hour. Your best bet for such services, though, is at a *wartel* (telephone office), which will charge less than a hotel or villa. The least-expensive calling option is to use a phone card, which you can buy at many shops and groceries throughout the region. There are few street-corner public phones, but many wartels have phones that accept the cards. There are also dozens of Internet cafés in Ubud and Candidasa. The following places in Ubud offer telephone or Internet services or both:

Ary's Business and Travel Service (✉ Jl. Ubud, ☎ 0361/973130) is a clean and cool place where you can book tours, then make international calls and send e-mail to tell everyone all about what you saw.
CV Nyoman Nomad Telecommunications Services (✉ Jl. Ubud 33, ☎ 0361/977169), above the Nomad Bar & Restaurant, lets you cheaply and conveniently make international calls while you wait for your food.
Bali 3000 (✉ Jl. Ubud, ☎ 0361/978538) is the ultimate Internet café: the large, bright store has a bank of busy terminals, plenty of cushioned benches and little couches to wait on, and a nice little eating area in the front. Even if you have to wait a bit for a terminal, this is a great place to chat and meet other travelers.
B'li Bar (✉ Jl. Wanara Wana 71, ☎ no phone) combines Internet services with a grocery shop.
Desak Tourist Service (✉ Jl. Wanara Wana, ☎ 0361/973276) has five Internet terminals.
Gebxe Net (✉ Pasar Ubud, ☎ 0361/974675), at the Pasar Ubud parking lot, has a few computers where you can get your e-mail.
Kadek Restaurant & Internet (✉ Jl. Pengosekan, ☎ 0361/978374) has computers you can use while you wait for your food.
MM Net (✉ Jl. Suweta 7, ☎ FAX 0361/976355) has a half-dozen terminals that are always busy.

Roda Tourist Service (✉ Jl. Bisma 3, ☎ 0361/976582) is a clean, friendly place to surf the Internet and send e-mail.

Tino Café Net (✉ Jl. Ubud, ☎ 0361/975020), upstairs in the back of the Toko Tino grocery store, has several computer terminals, fax services, and international phone lines.

Trimanunggai Net (✉ Jl. Pengosekan, ☎ 0361/975446) is the place to check e-mail near the Agung Rai Art Museum.

You can mail letters at any orange postal box on the main road (provided that the envelope is already stamped). Groceries and some money changers sell postage, and many hotels will mail letters and packages. The **main post office in Ubud** (✉ Jl. Jembawan 1, ☎ 0361/975764) will hold general delivery mail for up to a month. **Candidasa's post office** (✉ Jl. Raya, ☎ no phone) will do the same.

Because many tourists purchase souvenirs too large to take home on the plane, there are many professional shipping services in Ubud. **Nominasi Chandra Wisata** (✉ Jl. Wanara Wana, ☎ 0361/975067) has reliable cargo shipping, courier, and mail services—and a few Internet terminals, too. The following companies also can ship cargo overseas: **Ayumas Bentala Cargo** (✉ Jl. Mas, ☎ 0361/975286); **CV Berata** (✉ Jl. Wanara Wana 88, ☎ 0361/976644); **DV Wahyu Dewata Agung** (✉ Jl. Wanara Wana, ☎ 0361/975704); **Pandawa Sari Sejati Cargo** (✉ Jl. Wanara Wana, ☎ 0361/978206).

Visitor Information

Ubud Tourist Information (✉ Jl. Ubud, ☎ 0361/973285), also known as Bina Wisata, is one of the most informative and helpful tourist offices in Indonesia. Not only can they provide schedules of events, tourbus routes and times, and lists of *bemo* shuttles to other towns, they can also give you maps and guidance on how to reach area attractions and what to do when you get there.

4 NORTHERN BALI

Northern Bali's interior is a cool, damp, mountainous region that lures intrepid visitors with an active volcano ripe for climbing, beautiful lakes formed in the craters of long-dormant volcanic peaks, and treks through lush vegetation and past tumbling waterfalls. The north coast is tame in comparison, with black sand beaches, the unassuming resort area of Lovina, and temples with some of Bali's most ornate—and amusing—carvings.

By Margaret
Feldstein

NORTHERN BALI IS MADE UP OF two distinct areas that have little in common other than their geographic proximity. The interior is lush, with giant crater lakes and a cool, damp climate, and is where many of the island's vegetables, fruits, and spices are grown. Volcanoes collect water in their craters and their eruptions enrich the soil; the temples erected near these tremendous natural forces are some of the holiest in Bali. On the shore of one of the volcanic lakes, Danau Batur, lies one of the island's only traditional Bali Aga villages, where ancient Balinese customs and burial practices are still observed. In contrast, the narrow strip of the northern coast is flat and dry, with a climate much like the rest of the island: hot and sunny year-round. The coast is a place of brown and black beaches, natural springs (both hot and cold), and spectacular waterfalls. The busy city of Singaraja reveals signs of past foreign influence all around, and the sleepy resort area of Lovina is the north coast's tourist center, attracting backpackers, students, and luxury-inclined tourists alike.

Undoubtedly the interior's most prominent characteristic is its misty climate, which lingers in the memories of visitors after they leave. The weather is cold compared to Bali's coastal areas, and as soon as your car begins the climb up into the mountains it's time to put away the sunglasses and get out a sweater. Most likely it's the cooler temperatures that make the area far less popular with foreign tourists, who tend to stick to the sunnier shores. The absence of a fully developed tourist network can be both a blessing and a curse. On the one hand you may have sights entirely to yourself (except in the lakes district and at the nearby Bali Botanical Gardens, both of which are incredibly popular with Indonesian tourists), and village streets aren't lined with touristy shops like you find in the south. However, facilities are sometimes not up to the standards of the busier areas, and because there aren't as many tourist dollars flowing in, hawkers can be very aggressive when they do spot a visitor. This is particularly true in the Gunung Batur region, where locals are desperate for any added income. Their behavior can be annoying and upsetting, but try to be understanding of the circumstances that create it.

The inland region supplies the rest of the island in two important ways: For one, the high rainfall in the mountains and the numerous crater lakes provide fresh water for the elaborate irrigation system that stretches throughout the rest of the island. For this reason farmers make regular pilgrimages to Pura Ulun Danu Bratan, on the shore of Danau Bratan, to honor the goddess of the lake, Dewi Danu. Secondly, the extremely fertile land in the area (made richer by occasional volcanic eruptions) supports a wide array of vegetables and fruit—most noticeably corn and strawberries—that are consumed elsewhere. You'll also see truckloads of blue hydrangea blossoms being carted away to be sold for use in small daily offerings around the island.

Bali's northern coast has rich agricultural land as well. All the island's major crops are grown here, including coffee, rice, and copra, the dried coconut flesh from which coconut oil is extracted. In addition to miles of coconut palms you'll see giant heaps of discarded coconut husks. A newer crop being cultivated along the coast is grapes, which are grown both for export to other parts of Asia and for making Balinese wine.

The northern coast has a rich culture heritage, and a distinct regional style is evident in many places. With their wild temple carvings, northern Bali's temples are some of the best known on the island. The Sapi Gerumbungan bull races, in Lovina, are unusual for valuing style as much as speed. Northern Bali also is home to several renowned dance troupes, and the *janger* style of dance originated in the region. Similarly, *kebyar,* a form of music derived from the traditional gamelan, was created in the north during the 1920s.

The northern coast's tourist hub—the laid-back gathering of beach villages known as Lovina—is nothing compared to the converging chaos and luxury of the crowded resort areas in the south. It's hard to believe that the first tourist hub in Bali was in fact Singaraja: boats from Java began to bring travelers to the area in the mid-1920s. Ten years later the first cluster of guest bungalows was built on empty Kuta Beach, and the southward exodus began. Today Singaraja is not a major stopping point for tourists, although any trip along the north coast will inevitably pass through the town since the major roads converge there. Though the second-largest city in Bali, Singaraja is mostly interesting to visitors for the visible remnants of its colonial past. In contrast to the rest of the island, it's easy to see the Dutch influence in the city's tree-lined streets and colonial houses. Evidence of the Dutch presence is strong because Singaraja was the seat of Dutch power until less than 50 years ago. The first military expeditions to the island landed off the coast of the Buleleng district, as the north is known, during the mid 19th century, and the north was the first part of Bali to fall under Dutch control. (It was nearly a half-century before the south fell, too.) Muslim and Chinese traders left their mark as well, particularly near the city's old port, where there's a cluster of tiny shops that are likely owned by descendants of the original merchants. Today Singaraja is an educational center, with two universities and the world's only library of *lontar* leaf manuscripts.

Numbers in the text correspond to numbers in the margin and on the Northern Bali map.

EXPLORING NORTHERN BALI

A Good Tour

Start early on the first day and drive north to the Taman Rekreasi Bedugul, on the edge of majestic **Danau Bratan** ①. Take a rowboat out on the lake or try your hand at a water sport like parasailing or waterskiing. Next head to the **Bali Botanical Gardens** ②, where flora freaks can explore thousands of species of trees and plants; for others, a quick drive through to check out the highlights will be enough. Afterward stop in at the bustling Bukit Mungsu market, about 1 km (½ mi) south of the turnoff to the gardens, to buy fruit, spices, or a sarong to wear into the temples.

Next travel north to **Pura Ulun Danu Bratan** ③, one of of Bali's most beautiful—and most photographed—temples. Dedicated to Dewi Danu, goddess of water and fertility, it is the directional temple for the northwest and consists of several shrines, some situated on the shore of the lake and some sitting on small islands. For lunch try As Siddiq (☞ Dining, *below*), on the left side of the street about 350 ft north of the temple, or Bukit Stroberi (☞ Dining, *below*), in the other direction just south of the lake. If you play golf, you'll want to hit the greens at the Bali Handara Kosaido Country Club, one of Asia's top courses. Finally, travel west—passing around the area's other crater lakes, Danau Buyan and Danau Tamblingan—to the village of **Munduk** ④. Here you can stay the night at the charming Puri Lumbung (☞ Lodging, *below*), in a wooden bungalow modeled after a traditional barn.

Spend the early part of the next day hiking to a nearby cluster of waterfalls; on the way you'll see crops of produce and spices that supply the entire island. In the afternoon head northwest to the town of Seririt and the coast. From Seririt take the main coastal road east for about 4 km (2½ mi) and then turn off to the south; after 2 km (1 mi) you come to the **Air Panas Banjar** ⑤, where you can soak in the sulfuric pools if you're so inclined. Roughly 8 km (5 mi) farther east is the **Lovina** ⑥ resort area, where you can get a good night's rest.

Rise with the sun the next morning for a ride in an outrigger canoe to see the famous dolphins that frolic just offshore (be sure to make the arrangements the night before). After breakfast, drive 30 minutes east to reach the city of **Singaraja** ⑦, where you can see the lontar leaf manuscripts of the Gedong Kirtya library and watch ikat weavers at work. Then grab your sarong and pay a visit to the temples that dot the landscape east of Singaraja: **Pura Beji** ⑧, **Pura Dalem** ⑨, **Pura Dalem Jagaraga** ⑩, and **Pura Maduwe Karang** ⑪.

If you're game for the exhilarating climb up Bali's famous **Gunung Batur** ⑫, you'll want to spend the night in a town on the volcano's rim so you can start your trek very early and see the sun rise. Arrive at the Lakeview hotel (☞ Dining *and* Lodging, *below*) in Penelokan in time for dinner and head to bed early to rest up for the following morning's hike. You'll be awakened in the wee hours for a quick breakfast and then driven down to **Danau Batur** ⑬, where the ascent begins. When the weather's good, the view over the crater lake encompasses the surrounding hills clear to the north coast. When you've made it back down, exhilarated but exhausted, you'll welcome the stop for a dip at Tirta Sanjiwani, the pleasantly hot sulfuric spring on the edge of Danau Batur. Since the day started so early, you'll be finished by late morning, giving you plenty of time to see the area's atmospheric temples, **Pura Ulun Danu** ⑭ and **Pura Puncak Penulisan** ⑮.

TIMING

Four days is just enough time to cover all the sights in one giant loop. But if you're short on time, a two-day tour will allow you to see, if not explore, the high points. For an abbreviated tour spend one day visiting Pura Ulun Danu Bratan and the waterfalls at Gitgit (north of Danau Bratan on the road to Singaraja), then drive straight up to Lovina to spend the night. After visiting the dolphins early in the morning, drive to Gunung Batur for lunch at the Lakeview restaurant. On your way back to southern Bali, be sure to stop at the Elephant Safari Park near Ubud (☞ Exploring Eastern Bali *in* Chapter 3).

The Lakes District

The lakes district is very popular with Balinese vacationers and other Indonesians, who flood the area on weekends and holidays. When you arrive you'll see why: there are lush, green mountains, shimmering lakes, and gorgeous vistas around every corner. With a shrine to the goddess Dewi Danu, who is believed to provide water to the entire island, this is one of the holiest areas in Bali.

Sights to See

❷ **Bali Botanical Gardens.** At the roundabout in Candi Kuning, you'll come to an unmissable homage to the local crop: a giant corn cob. Appropriately, it's here that you turn off to reach Bali's extensive botanical gardens. The cool green lawns are popular with the Balinese, who bring picnics on Sunday and holidays. If you're a true plant lover, you'll want to spend some time here perusing the hundreds of species of orchids, trees, and cacti from around the world. Unfortunately the gardens don't offer much to the layman, since the plants are sometimes scraggly and often unlabeled. If a greenhouse you're interested in viewing is locked,

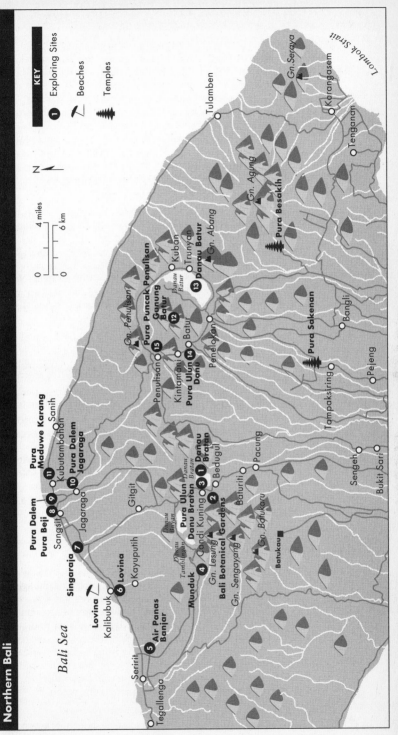

Northern Bali

Bali Sea

Lombok Strait

KEY

1 Exploring Sites

Beaches

Temples

N

4 miles

6 km

0

0

Tulamben

Gn. Seraya

Karangasem

Tenganan

Gn. Agung

Pura Besakih

Gn. Abang

Danau Batur

Kuban

Trunyan

13 Danau Batur

Pura Sakenan

Bangli

Pura Puncak Penulisan

Gunung Batur

12

Batur

Gn. Penulisan

15

14 Pura Ulun Danu

Penelokan

Pejeng

Pura Maduwe Karang

Sanih

Kubutambahan

11

10 Pura Dalem Jagaraga

Kintamani

Penulisan

Tampaksiring

Pura Dalem

Pura Beji

8 9

Singaraja

Sangsit

Jagaraga

Gitgit

3 1 Danau Bratan

Bedugul

Pura Ulun Danu Bratan

Danau Bratan

Pacung

Sengeh

Bukit Sari

7

Lovina

6 Lovina

Kayuputih

Danau Buyan

Candi Kuning

2

Baturiti

Gn. Batukaru

Batukaru

Kalibubuk

Danau Tamblingan

4

Gn. Lesung

Bali Botanical Gardens

Munduk

Gn. Sengayang

Seririt

5 Air Panas Banjar

Tegallenga

ask a groundskeeper to open it for you. ⊠ *Candi Kuning,* ☎ *0368/ 21273.* ⊠ *60¢ per car, 25¢ per person.* ☉ *Daily 8–6.*

❶ Danau Bratan. At the southern end of shimmering Lake Bratan is an area known as Bedugul, which encompasses the **Taman Rekreasi Bedugul** (Bedugul Recreational Park) and adjacent facilities, including a concession stand, a gift shop, a modest restaurant, and, above the restaurant, even a few hotel rooms that overlook the lake. If you're dead-set on staying right by the lake, though, the Bedugul Cottages, run by the same management, are a better bet (☞ Lodging, *below*). The lake's main draws are boats and water sports, but on a pleasant day it's also a nice place to stop for a drink or snack. With the exception of the restaurant, which stays open until 9 PM, the whole place shuts down fairly early—around 4 PM or 5 PM, depending on how much business there is. ☎ *0368/21197 for park office.*

★ ☕ ❹ Munduk. On the drive from Danau Bratan to the village of Munduk you'll get spectacular views of Danau Buyan and Danau Tamblingan. (Those lakes, surrounded by marshy land, are not developed like Bratan is, so the view from above is the best you'll get.) Munduk is a fantastic place to experience rural Balinese life. Good hiking paths lead to waterfalls and past many of Bali's native crops—coffee, vanilla, cloves, papaya, pineapple—growing in the wild. Guides for the treks are available at the Puri Lumbung hotel (☞ Lodging, *below*). ⊠ *About 16 km (10 mi) west of Danau Bratan.*

★ ❸ Pura Ulun Danu Bratan. The Temple of the Lake Goddess at Bratan is one of Bali's most visited—and most spiritually important—temples. Dedicated to Dewi Danu, the goddess of the waters, it is the focus of numerous ceremonies and pilgrimages to ensure supplies of water. A temple sits on the shore of the lake, but visitors cannot enter it. It's the multitiered thatch-roof shrines, or *meru,* perched on tiny islands just offshore that are best known. The unforgettable setting is typically Balinese: At the edge of Danau Bratan irises bloom in shades of yellow, fuchsia, and magenta; young girls and old men fish in clusters among the tiger lilies; the misty peak of a dormant volcano emerges in the distance. In the gardens surrounding the temple trees drip with trumpet flowers. Also on-site are a children's playground and a restaurant featuring mostly Indonesian food. ⊠ *Off the Singaraja-Denpasar road, on the western shore of Danau Bratan.* ⊠ *Donation required.* ☉ *Daily 8:30–6.*

The North Coast

Bali's north coast shares the same good weather as the south but is mercifully without the overdevelopment and crowds. Singaraja, though the original arrival point for Bali's early tourists before there was even a hotel on Kuta Beach, doesn't offer much in the way of accommodations or entertainment for tourists today. It's the Lovina resort area that has the amenities. Much of the land along the coast is covered by vineyards; the grapes are exported to Hong Kong and Japan and used to produce Balinese wine. The north coast has a more sizable Muslim population than elsewhere on the island, and you'll hear calls to prayer emanating from the pastel-painted mosques dotting the road.

Sights to See

☕ ❺ Air Panas Banjar. Even if you don't crave a soak in the natural hot springs in the village of Banjar, it's worth the short trip from Lovina just to see the lush grounds and pale green pools of water. A strong sulfur smell floods your nostrils as you approach the tiered pools, which are enjoyed by Balinese and foreign tourists alike. The water feels like a warm bath. Since the pools lie directly in the sun, the early morning or late afternoon might be the best times for a dip. Swimsuits must be worn in the pools; you can change and shower on the premises. A basic, very inexpensive restaurant overlooks the pools and is a nice spot for a cool drink. ⊠ *Banjar,* ☎ *no phone.* ⊡ *35¢; parking 5¢.* ⊙ *Daily 8–6.*

★ ❻ **Lovina.** The most popular place on the north coast is Lovina, a catch-all name for the resort area that encompasses a group of villages along the coast: **Pantai Happy, Anturan, Kalibukbuk,** and **Temukus.** Lovina has the region's largest selection of hotels and restaurants and its only upscale facilities—thus it makes a great base for traveling to the other coastal areas and even the inland regions, especially if you prefer luxury accommodations. Kalibukbuk is where you'll find the area's best beach, Lovina Beach, which is also the departure point for a small armada of outrigger canoes that head out every day at dawn in search of dolphins. Kalibukbuk is popular with backpackers and students, who come for the economical accommodations and food; there's also some low-key nightlife to be found, from bars and live bands to Internet outposts and the nightly movies that some of the inexpensive restaurants project during dinner. Kalibukbuk is dense enough that it's easy to walk around among the establishments, but you'll need your own transportation to get around in some of the other parts of Lovina.

❽ **Pura Beji.** Made of pink sandstone rather than the typical gray volcanic stone, the unusual Seed Temple, dedicated to the goddess of agriculture, is a great example of northern Bali's wild architectural style. The temple walls and archways are densely covered with carvings of the faces of exaggerated, cartoonlike demons and serpents sprouting fangs. Once painted in vibrant colors, many of these faces have faded over the years. The temple guard can walk you over to the nearby Pura Dalem. ⊠ *1,000 ft north of main road, Sangsit (8 km [5 mi] east of Singaraja),* ☎ *no phone.* ⊡ *Donation suggested.* ⊙ *Daily 8–4.*

❾ **Pura Dalem.** Just a short walk from Pura Beji (about 1,200 ft across the rice fields) is Sangsit's Temple of the Dead, best known for its somewhat pornographic carvings depicting scenes of punishment and reward in the afterlife. Although many of the carvings are worn down, it's hard to miss the male and female sexual organs, which practically drip off the temple walls. ⊠ *Sangsit (8 km [5 mi] east of Singaraja),* ☎ *no phone.* ⊡ *Donation suggested.* ⊙ *Daily 8–4.*

❿ **Pura Dalem Jagaraga.** Dedicated to Siva the Destroyer, the Temple of the Dead of Jagaraga is famous for the reliefs on its outside wall depicting the early Dutch invaders, particularly the image of a Ford Model T driven by a troll-like Dutchman. The carvings are very badly eroded and thus hard to make out, so it helps to know what you're looking for. To the far left of the entrance are scenes of bucolic Balinese life before the invasion: kite-flying, fishing, and climbing coconut trees. The near left and the right panels show the arrival of the Dutch in cars, bicycles, and planes. The temple sits right on the main road running through the small village of Jagaraga, so in visiting it you'll also be able to observe local life—from fighting cocks pecking angrily inside their cages to women returning home balancing baskets of fresh coconuts on their heads. ⊠ *Jagaraga (5 km [3 mi] southeast of Sangsit),* ☎ *no phone.* ⊡ *Donation suggested.* ⊙ *Daily 8–4.*

⓫ **Pura Maduwe Karang.** The Temple of the Owner of the Land is one of the most impressive in northern Bali, thanks to its beautifully carved panels, including one depicting a man riding a bicycle with wheels of flower petals. It is thought that the cyclist is Dutch artist W. O. J. Nieuwenkamp, who arrived on Bali in 1904 with what was probably the island's first bicycle. If you're lucky, your guides to the temple will be two young boys, sons of the temple guard, who earnestly recite the historical information they've memorized. The temple is in Kubutambahan, a largely untouristed village with a welcome steady pace. No sarongs are available for rent, so be sure to bring your own. ⊠ *Kubutambahan (1 km [½ mi] east of Kintamani turnoff),* ☎ *no phone.* 🖃 *Donation suggested.* ⊘ *Daily 8–4.*

❼ **Singaraja.** Singaraja, Bali's second-largest city, has a significant history. It was the center of Dutch power from the mid 19th century until the 1940s, and the influence of the Dutch is still visible around the city. It was also the most popular arrival point for Bali's early tourists in the second decade of the 20th century. Nonetheless, the busy city holds little of interest to today's tourists and is not a popular stopping point, perhaps also in part because the busy city is difficult to navigate. The best spot to stop is the open plaza by the water, where you can enjoy the cool breezes and see some of the old Dutch buildings that once made up a market area; a quiet Chinese Buddhist temple sits nearby.

One area of interest lies south of Singaraja's center. Here you'll find an important cultural site, the **Gedong Kirtya library,** which houses the world's only collection of manuscripts made of the leaves of the lontar palm. Just behind the library there's a weaving workshop, **Puri Sinar Nadi Putri,** where you can watch ikat being made and then purchase it. ⊠ *Library: Jl. Veteran 20.* ☎ *0362/22645 to library.* ⊘ *Library: Mon.–Thurs. 8–2, Fri. 8–11, Sat. 8–12:30; appointment suggested. Workshop: daily 8–4.*

OFF THE BEATEN PATH

GITGIT – Roughly 10 km (6 mi) south of Singaraja, the **Air Terjun Gitgit** (Gitgit Waterfall) is well known for its impressive height (130 ft) and beautiful setting. What's not so beautiful, however, is the way the area has been built up. It's packed with tourist facilities such as restaurants, souvenir stalls, and even hotels. If you've had the chance to check out some of Bali's other waterfalls (such as those near Munduk), take a pass on Gitgit. If you do visit, it's open daily 8–5:30, and a donation of 60¢ is suggested. More peaceful is the deceptively named **Air Terjun Bertingkat** (Multitier Waterfall), off the same road 2 km (1 mi) farther south (same hours as Gitgit; $1 donation).

AIR SANIH – On the north coast about 15 km (9 mi) east of Singaraja is Air Sanih (also known as Yeh Sanih), a small village popular with the Balinese for its natural freshwater cold spring. The shallow rock pools are full of frolickers of all ages; they're also incongruously (to Western tastes) surrounded by stone altars—actually small temples—loaded with offerings. Admission to the pools, which lie on the north side of the road by the ocean, is 25¢ for adults. The restaurants along the road aren't worth a special stop, except for the the branch of Biyu Nasak (Lovina's best casual restaurant) that's scheduled to open here in 2001; the bungalows at Cilik's Garden are a great place for longer-term stays in isolation (☞ Lodging, *below*).

Gunung Batur and Environs

The area around Bali's dramatic, still-active volcano is unlike any other place on the island. For one, the weather is dramatically different—cooler, damper, and frequently foggy or rainy (though it's more drizzle than heavy downpour most of the time). The air is wonderfully clean and moist, which is why this is where most of the produce for the island is grown. Driving through you'll see fields of corn (which are terraced like rice fields), lettuce, and strawberries. In Penelokan you'll find lots of local produce for sale along the road. Of course, the volcano, Gunung Batur, is the real reason to visit the region.

If you're short on time, at least stop to admire the view, perhaps over a meal or a drink at the Lakeview hotel and restaurant. If you have more time, arrive at the Lakeview in the afternoon or evening and spend the night in order to rise before dawn and climb the looming volcano. And don't miss the area's temples, filled with mist and so remote they're often deserted. Be sure to bring some warm clothes to this area: at the very minimum you'll need a light sweater and long pants. Many of the region's sites are marred by extremely aggressive hawkers who badger visitors to pay for their services or wares. Try to bear in mind that this is one of Bali's poorest regions, with tourist dollars less plentiful than in other areas. However, you needn't give in to hawkers' pleas if you're not interested in what they're selling; instead try to ignore them.

Sights to See

⑬ Danau Batur. Bali's largest lake, Lake Batur, actually sits in an ancient volcanic crater. On the drive down, the landscape recalls images right out of *Planet of the Apes*: old lava flows are dotted with stubborn plants pushing up among the rocks. At the shore of the lake is a public hot spring, and a few basic restaurants and hotels in the area serve as bases for some very aggressive hawkers. From the village of Kedisan you can catch a boat ride across the lake to the unusual villages of Trunyan and Kuban (☞ *below*).

★ **⑫ Gunung Batur.** Mt. Batur is one of Bali's active volcanoes, and rocks were spewing out of the peak's crater as recently as April 2000. It's also a holy site, which the Balinese visit and make offerings to on a regular basis, as well as whenever anyone is killed on the volcano. Offerings come in the form of live animals such as cows, pigs, chickens, and ducks, which are thrown directly into the crater to placate the gods.

Gunung Batur is beautiful to admire from afar and truly memorable should you choose to undertake the early morning climb to view the sunrise from its peak. The ascent is not for the faint of heart, however: the so-called path is really a series of lava rock footholds, and the climb begins in the pitch black. A good guide is essential. There is a local association of guides, but the most civilized way to make the climb is to let the Lakeview hotel arrange the details for you. Aside from the hassles it saves you, there isn't much of a premium for this service—arranging a guide yourself will cost at least $20, and through the Lakeview it's $35—especially when you consider the extras the hotel throws in. You'll be awakened around 3:30 AM so that you can have a light breakfast before embarking on the 20-minute van ride to Toya Bungkah to begin the climb. Your guides will bring flashlights and a bottle of water for you, something you'll be very glad of after the first 30 minutes or so.

It's best to wear layers (a long-sleeve shirt over a T-shirt will do), and you'll need good climbing shoes or sneakers. The climb up takes a few hours, depending on your pace, and when you reach the top, you'll have a chance to enjoy what will probably be the only meal of your life cooked in a volcano. Raw eggs and bananas are tucked into one of the steaming holes and covered with a bundle of straw; 10 minutes later breakfast is ready. After the scramble down the volcano you'll be driven to the Lakeview-owned **Tirta Sanjiwani**, a hot spring on the edge of Danau Batur that is fed into a large pool with warm and cold sections, for a leisurely dip. This isn't Club Med—the changing rooms are extremely run-down—but the soak feels fantastic after the climb. (If you want to try out the pool but aren't part of the Lakeview's climbing group, you'll pay $15.) ☎ *0366/52362 for local guide association; 0366/51464 or 0366/31394 for Lakeview hotel.*

OFF THE BEATEN PATH	**TRUNYAN AND KUBAN –** One of the island's Bali Aga villages, Trunyan, has turned into a major tourist attraction because of one of the ancient practices it still observes: instead of cremating the deceased, as is done everywhere else in Bali, or burying the body, the people of Trunyan leave the dead out in the open air to decay (the holy banyan tree in the cemetery supposedly prevents any odor). Fascination with this macabre-sounding practice has brought many visitors to Trunyan's cemetery, in the nearby village of Kuban, which is accessible only by boat. What there is to see, however, often disappoints. The bodies are left in pits and covered with cloth and bamboo, so at most you'll see a few old bones left out for the tourists' benefit. The heavy haggling required to secure a boat ride and just to maneuver through Trunyan (where frequent donations are expected) can be brutal, so again it's best to arrange your visit through the Lakeview hotel.

★ ⑮ **Pura Puncak Penulisan.** The Temple of Penulisan Hill is usually completely deserted, which adds to its serene beauty. Sitting up high in the mountains and surrounded by evergreens, it was once the highest point in all of Bali—until a TV tower was built nearby. Reaching the temple requires a hike up a few hundred fairly steep steps, but you'll be rewarded with a quiet, misty courtyard full of ancient *lingga* (the rather phallic symbol of the god Siva) draped in celebratory swathes of fabric. ⊠ *Penulisan,* ☎ *no phone.* 🎫 *Donation suggested.* ☉ *Daily sunrise–sunset.*

⑭ **Pura Ulun Danu.** Filled with mist and ceremonial parasols, this Temple of the Lake Goddess is considered very holy—it's second only to Besakih in importance—and is thus a popular place of worship for the Balinese. Nonobservant visitors can look into the inner courtyards but are not permitted to enter. The parking area opposite the temple is often full of aggressive hawkers, so bring your own sarong and *selendang* (sash) in order to avoid haggling with them. ⊠ *Batur (about 2 km [1 mi] south of Kintamani),* ☎ *no phone.* 🎫 *Donation suggested.* ☉ *Daily 8–6.*

BEACHES

Although the northern coast is certainly something to look at, the beaches are sadly not much to lounge on. The volcanic sand is often a sooty-looking shade of gray, and many areas are very rocky, making wading a difficult proposition. In addition, during the rainy season runoff from the mountains can make the ocean water dirty. Lovina is renowned for its beach, which is certainly a nice place to watch the sunset or even to swim. Ultimately, though, the best sunbathing and swimming may actually be found in swimming pools.

The main beach in **Lovina** is at the end of Jalan Bina Ria in Kalibukbuk, and it's easily identified by the large dolphin statue where the road meets the beach. Stretching on for hundreds of yards, it's an excellent place for strolling. For swimming, find a spot west of the dolphin statue, where the beach is wider and there's more sand. Toward the east, scores of small boats wait to take tourists to catch a glimpse of the area's dolphins. Other than the Sea Breeze restaurant and the souvenir stalls by the beach (and the plentiful free parking), there are no facilities to speak of.

DINING

Northern Bali is not a gourmand's paradise. Once you leave the resort areas of the south and Ubud, your dining options lessen considerably.

The Lovina area offers better restaurants and more choices, from tasty Indonesian standbys such as satay and *gado-gado* to plenty of Western favorites. But other than the superb European-Asian fusion cooking at the Damai restaurant, none of the cuisine is really remarkable.

The lakes district has one standout, Warung Kopi at the Puri Lumbung hotel in Munduk, which is unusual in offering Balinese (as opposed to Indonesian) dishes that use local ingredients. Since Danau Bratan is quite popular with Indonesian tourists, you can get some very good—and very cheap—typical fare at local spots by the lake. Gunung Batur has little to offer in the way of food—which in this area is more of a necessity than an indulgence.

For general information and price categories, *see* Dining *in* Smart Travel Tips.

The Lakes District

$ ✕ **As Siddiq.** Just north of Bedugul, this very basic restaurant is the Indonesian equivalent of a country truck stop in the United States: it may not be much to look at, but it serves up delicious Indonesian favorites at low prices (a dish of steamed rice is only 15¢!). Try the *gado-gado*, steamed vegetables with a very spicy peanut sauce. ⊠ *Bedugul, 300 ft north of parking area for Pura Ulun Danu Bratan, on west side of street,* ☎ *no phone. No credit cards.*

$ ✕ **Bukit Stroberi.** With the same owners as the famous Poppies in Kuta, this restaurant has the feeling of a country inn—just substitute batik for gingham—and serves up tasty Western and Indonesian food. Be sure to try the pancakes or milk shake featuring the local strawberries (the restaurant's name means "Strawberry Hill"). Downstairs you'll find a pool table and fireplace, while upstairs has a more intimate feeling, though it can be noisy when the muffler-free motorbikes speed along the twisting mountain roads below. Don't confuse this establishment with the awful Strawberry Stop near Pancasari. ⊠ *Bedugul,* ☎ *0368/21265. No credit cards.*

$ ✕ **Pacung Indah.** This ideally located Australian-owned eatery has the area's best view of the valley of rice fields, farms, and trees. It's fairly new (opened in 2000), very clean, and offers decent food (the usual mix of Indonesian and Western cuisine), but has a somewhat homogenized, sterile feel. Not surprisingly, busloads of tour groups are regularly deposited here. The best tables are in the back, where there's an area that opens to the valley. ⊠ *Pacung,* ☎ *0368/21207. MC, V.*

$ ✕ **Warung Kopi at Puri Lumbung.** This restaurant serves mouth-wateringly delicious authentic Balinese food inside the lush gardens and ★ rice-barn-style cottages of the Puri Lumbung hotel (☞ Lodging, *below*). The open-air eating area overlooks the dense valley, and tables are lighted by small oil lamps. The extensive menu is translated in detail and includes regional specialties made with fresh, flavorful local produce. Be sure to try *aras ayam,* a hearty chicken soup with thin slices of tender young banana stems, and *urap paku,* sautéed baby ferns with fresh grated coconut, a very typical Balinese dish. The *bubuh injun* (black rice pudding) is divine and can be enjoyed at breakfast, as the Balinese do, or as a dessert. You can take a cooking class from the chefs, choosing the dish you want to learn how to make; call at least 24 hours in advance to sign up. ⊠ *Munduk,* ☎ *0362/92811 or 0362/92810. AE, MC, V.*

The North Coast

$$$$ ✕ **The Damai.** The five-course prix-fixe dinner, which changes each night, ★ is the best food you'll have in northern Bali and perhaps the entire island. The food is European-Asian, but chances are you've never had

WAYAN, MEET WAYAN

WHAT'S IN A NAME? In Bali a lot more than you'd imagine. When you first arrive, you'll probably notice that a surprising number of the people you meet are named Wayan, Made, or Nyoman. You'll also find that many cafés and shops bear one of those names. This is because all Balinese, regardless of sex, are given one of four names corresponding to their birth order: Wayan for the firstborn, Made for the second, Nyoman for the third, and Ketut for the fourth. If there are more than four children in a family, the names are repeated. (In some areas in northern Bali it is customary to give the name Ketut to all children from the fourth-born onward.)

In recent years, however, a family-planning campaign in Bali has resulted in smaller families, which means the names Ketut and Nyoman are being used less frequently. Of course, so many people with the same first name can make communicating in group situations pretty complicated. But many Balinese, particularly men, also have a nickname that is used casually by their coworkers and friends. These nicknames are usually given by parents during childhood and often refer to something the child resembled: Frog, Thermos, and Chubby are a few examples.

In addition to the publicly used names, Balinese have a unique private name that is given by a *balian* (priest) at the *tebulan* ritual that occurs three months after birth. Very often this name is unknown, even to people who have daily contact with each other. Even if this name is known, it is usually considered impolite to call someone by it. A further layer is added because of Bali's caste system, which adds titles that precede full names. Members of the highest caste, the Brahman (priests), use the title Ida Bagus (for males) or Ida Ayu (for females). The higher nobility, who were former warrior-prince rulers of the island and are now part of the Satria caste, use titles such as Anak Agung, Dewa, and Cokorda. The Wesya, members of the former lower nobility reserved for merchants, use the title Gusti. These three upper castes are collectively known as the Triwangsa. All other Balinese, or about 90% of the population, are part of the caste of farmers and artisans known as Sudra, which translates to "Outside the Court" (of course members of this caste aren't always farmers or artisans these days). The titles used in this caste are I for males and Ni or Luh for females.

The caste system was brought to Bali in the 15th century by the Majapahit rulers, and today all Balinese except the Bali Aga, who retain ancient Balinese customs, are born into one of the four castes. (Some Sudras argue that because the system is not indigenous to the island, it should be eliminated.) Three different varieties of the Balinese language correspond to the caste differences between speakers. High Balinese is used when speaking to superiors (who use Low Balinese to reply); Middle Balinese is the polite form, used to address strangers; and Low Balinese is used when speaking to friends and equals. In order to determine which form of the language to use, some older Balinese will ask a new acquaintance, "Where do you sit?" (meaning "What is your caste?"), instead of asking for a name.

anything like it before—unless you've had roast fillet of red grouper with bok choy and red beet, saffron, and potato puree, or chocolate fig cake with pineapple sorbet. The setting, Damai's open-air dining room, which centers on a fantastic green-glass chandelier, is nearly as stunning as the food. There's an extensive list of international wines, a rare thing in Bali. Breakfast and lunch are served here, in the restaurant or by the pool, but dinner at the Damai is the real coup. ⊠ *Kayuputih (10-min drive southeast from Kalibukbuk),* ☎ *0362/41008. Reservations essential. AE, MC, V.*

$ ✗ **Biyu Nasak.** This unassuming restaurant, an easy walk from Lov-
★ ina Beach, is by far the best in the immediate Kalibukbuk area. Owned by an Australian expat married to a Balinese man, the Ripe Banana specializes in vegetarian dishes and seafood, consistently serving up delicious versions of travelers' comfort food: homemade garlic bread, tasty chocolate cake, grilled cheese sandwiches with tomato and avocado, and muesli and homemade yogurt for breakfast. It's cozy and calm, with a large selection of books, magazines, and children's' toys available for customers to use for free. ⊠ *Jl. Raya, Lovina Beach, Kaliasem,* ☎ FAX *0362/41176. No credit cards.*

$ ✗ **Café Lumbung.** On the road that leads to Lovina Beach, Café Lumbung is modeled after a Balinese rice barn (*lumbung*). The large, high-ceilinged room is set back from the street a bit, and the superpolite waitstaff is well versed in English. The menu of Indonesian and Western dishes includes an excellent chicken satay, served over its own mini-hibachi of coals and accompanied by a rich, chunky peanut sauce. ⊠ *Jl. Bina Ria, Kalibukbuk,* ☎ *0362/41149. AE, MC, V.*

$ ✗ **Kakatua.** One of a number of inexpensive restaurants that line Kalibukbuk's main street, Kakatua is named after the cockatoos that live (seemingly quite contentedly) in the large cage at the front of the restaurant. The service is extremely friendly, and it's a great vantage point from which to observe the heart of Lovina Beach. If you sit on the restaurant's left side, you'll also be able to watch the goings-on in the restaurant's small kitchen. The menu lists Mexican, Thai, and Indian dishes. ⊠ *Jl. Bina Ria, Kalibukbuk,* ☎ *0362/41144 or 0362/41344. No credit cards.*

Gunung Batur and Environs

$ ✗ **Lakeview Restaurant and Hotel.** The Lakeview is undoubtedly the best outlook from which to admire the crater lake and volcano. The kitchen prepares both Western and Indonesian dishes, and the food is all right. An extensive buffet lunch is popular with tour buses passing through the area. If possible, secure a table along the massive wall of windows, and be patient if the view is obscured by fog. The weather can change dramatically in a matter of minutes, and the fog may roll out by the time your meal arrives. ⊠ *Jl. Raya, Penelokan,* ☎ *0366/ 51464 or 0366/31394. AE, MC, V.*

LODGING

Lovina has good hotel options in all price ranges, from budget to luxury. The lakes district has a number of hotels and guest houses, but the quality is uneven; the best have a rustic charm that is complemented by the cool, damp weather. The climate in the interior makes air-conditioning unnecessary and can result, unfortunately, in musty-smelling rooms since linens and carpets never fully dry out. The area around Gunung Batur is the least developed in terms of accommodations; there's no reason to stay the night unless you plan to make the early morning climb.

All rooms in the listed hotels have bathrooms with tubs and hot water, unless otherwise noted. For general information and price categories, *see* Lodging *in* Smart Travel Tips.

✎ *following the text of a review is your signal that the property has a Web site, where you will find details, and, usually, images; for a link, visit www.fodors.com/urls.*

The Lakes District

$$ 🏨 **Puri Lumbung.** You'll feel as though you're staying with a Balinese
★ family at this cluster of cottages in the village of Munduk. The hotel's staff is not just immensely (and genuinely) friendly; they're also happy to involve you in the patterns of Balinese culture and everyday life. Classes are offered in cooking and crafts (sign up 24 hours in advance), and the staff can accompany you on hikes to nearby waterfalls or through the plantations of local fruits and spices. Lumbung-style cottages, raised on wooden stilts, are cozy but rustic, with wooden furniture, sheer mosquito netting over the beds (necessary since windows don't have screens), and small balconies overlooking private lily ponds. In clear weather the view often extends over the hills to the ocean and even the island of Java. Discounts are available if you stay for several nights and can be combined with stays at Villa Ratu Ayu, near Lovina (☞ *below*). ⊠ *Munduk (Box 3603, Denpasar 80036),* ☎ *0362/ 92810,* 🖷 *0362/92514. 15 cottages. Restaurant, hiking, shop. AE, MC, V. BP.*

$–$$$$ 🏨 **Bali Handara Kosaido Country Club.** This enormous hotel sits on the edge of one of Asia's best golf courses. You enter through a traditional stone gate and drive down a tree-lined lane and then through the course itself. But the pastoral idyll ends when you reach the hotel and clubhouse. The circa-1970 buildings look like pods from outer space that landed in Bali's green hills. The hotel rooms are equally alien, done up '70s style, with wall-to-wall carpet, plus wet bars and mini-saunas in the most expensive rooms. The hotel, geared toward a Japanese clientele, lacks a true Balinese feel. If you're a golf fanatic, it may be worth the high prices to be staying on the course (you'll also get 50% off the $100 fee for 18 holes). Otherwise you'll feel like screaming, "Beam me up, Scotty." ⊠ *Pancasari (Box 3324, Denpasar);* ☎ *0361/288944 for reservations line in Sanur; 0362/22646 for hotel. 39 rooms, 4 suites. Restaurant, Japanese baths (men only), massage, sauna (men only), tennis courts, exercise room, pro shop. AE, MC, V. BP.* ✎

$–$$$ 🏨 **Pacung Mountain Resort.** Despite its proximity to the main road, this resort is very peaceful—so peaceful the Kuta-based Bali Usada Meditasi (Bali Health Meditation) Foundation uses it for a retreat for one week every two months. If you wind up sharing the resort with the group, you won't be bothered (they don't speak out loud for the entire week), but they do take over the best accommodations, the cozy thatch-roof cottages. Each cottage has a balcony overlooking the rice fields and is enveloped by the sound of running water from the complex natural irrigation system. The hotel rooms are not as spacious or charming; the best are Rooms 120 and 123, which have nice views. The weather here is a bit drier and warmer than elsewhere in the region, and the only hotel swimming pool in the area is here. The hotel's biggest surprise is undoubtedly the gondola—the only one in Bali— that ferries guests from their rooms to the lobby and pool areas. The main drawback is vastly inflated rates (bungalows are $165); try negotiating if business is slow. ⊠ *Jl. Raya Pacung, Baturiti 82191,* ☎ *0368/21038, 0368/21039, 0361/262461, or 0361/262462,* 🖷 *0368/ 21043. 30 rooms, 10 cottages. Restaurant, bar, coffee shop, pool, minibars. MC, V. BP.*

$ **Bukit Jegegg.** The area's best bet for luxury accomodations is this
new hotel, which opened in 2000 (and already has plans to change its
name—to Kalaspa, from the Indonesian word for health, *kala*). From
the huge, modern lobby a wooden spiral staircase leads up to a small
restaurant, where you can take in the view of the surrounding mountains and fields. The traditional Balinese-style villas sit among well-land-
scaped grounds, and each has a small front courtyard behind carved
doors. Inside you'll find Javanese furniture and modern amenities; the
larger villas have two floors, each with its own bedroom and bathroom.
Don't miss Bukit Jegegg's unusual welcome drink, a warm ginger and
palm-sugar tea that tastes a bit like spicy maple sugar. ⊠ *15 km (10
mi) northwest of Bedugul on road to Munduk (Box 2000, Denpasar
80114A),* ☎ ℻ *0361/419606 or 0361/419607. 6 villas, 2 family villas. Restaurant, bar, spa. MC, V. BP.*

¢–$ **Enjung Beji Resor.** The real advantage of this hotel, whose name means
"Close to Holy Place," is that it sits right on the edge of Danau Bratan.
You can even fish from the hotel grounds or take a canoe out for a
paddle. It's popular with Indonesians for its low rates, but you'll want
to avoid the cheapest cottages, called Superior Cottage II, which sit in
an odd bunkerlike row along the driveway. Each pleasant Superior Cottage I has a double bed plus a window seat that easily doubles as a bed
for one; each family cottage has two rooms, one with a double bed
and one with twins. In good weather guests can enjoy meals in the large
open pavilion by the lake. ⊠ *Candi Kuning,* ☎ *0368/21490 or 0368/
21491,* ℻ *0368/21002. 2 penthouses, 21 cottages. Restaurant, coffee
shop, fishing, shop. MC, V. BP.*

¢   **Bedugul Cottages.** Bedugul is not a fantastic area, but if you want
to be within walking distance of recreational facilities, this place is the
best option—especially if you can stay in Cottage 16, a one-room cottage with two twin beds and glass on three sides for a spectacular view
of the lake. In all cottages, tile floors mean there's no mildew smell (a
common problem in this damp region), and the vast bathrooms are ser-
viceable but shabby. This place books up, so be sure to reserve in advance. The related Bedugul Hotel on the edge of the lake has adequate
dormlike rooms. ⊠ *By recreation park, Bedugul Tabanan,* ☎ *0362/
21366,* ℻ *0368/21198. 16 cottages. Restaurant. No credit cards. BP.*

The North Coast

$$–$$$$ **Puri Bagus Lovina.** This comfortable midsize hotel, popular with tour
groups, is part of a Balinese chain and not the place to go for an "au-
thentic" Balinese experience. Though these are some of Lovina's only
upscale accommodations, the staff at times can be downright unhelp-
ful. Rooms are spacious and have both indoor and outdoor showers.
A large free-form swimming pool sits on the edge of the shallow beach
and is surrounded by the café and restaurant. The hotel provides a weekly
program of guided sightseeing tours in nearby areas and hosts cultural
activities on-site. Occasional performances of traditional dance are ac-
companied by a large buffet of Indonesian, Western, and sometimes
Japanese food. If you're not staying at the hotel, it's worth stopping
by for dinner on one of these nights; call ahead to see if a performance
is scheduled. ⊠ *Jl. Singaraja-Seririt, Lovina (Box 3419, Denpasar
80361),* ☎ *0362/21430,* ℻ *0362/22627. 40 villas. Restaurant, bar,
café, refrigerators, room service (24 hrs), pool, snorkeling, travel ser-
vices. AE, DC, MC, V. BP.*

$$–$$$ **The Damai.** Opened in 1998, this tiny luxury hotel is Lovina's most
★   elegant and romantic. Up in the hills about a 10-minute drive from
Kalibukbuk, the Damai has a great view of the ocean and the sunset.
With only eight bungalows, the atmosphere here is intimate and re-

laxed, and guests often gather around the pool for after-dinner drinks. (The exceedingly helpful staff is likely to bring preheated blankets to the poolside gathering if the night air is cool.) Bungalows have lovely dark wood furnishings and outdoor showers; deluxe bungalows also have Jacuzzis. An added draw is the incredible food: the nightly five-course dinner ($38) is not to be missed under any circumstances (☞ Dining, *below*). The hotel provides free transportation within Lovina. ⊠ *Kayuputih, Lovina,* ☎ *0362/41008,* ℻ *0362/41009. 8 bungalows. Restaurant, bar, minibars, spa, driving range (open 2001), badminton, travel services. AE, DC, MC, V. BP.* ☙

$–$$ 🏨 **Hotel Mas Lovina.** Also known as Las Brisas Cottages, these two-story, bullet-shape, thatch-roof cottages are made of dark wood but painted pastel pink. Each cottage has a redbrick terrace, bamboo furniture, and a large shared backyard with fruit trees. Bedrooms are upstairs and have views of the pool and the bay. Some cottages have a living area downstairs, while others have a kitchen, so be sure to specify your preference when booking. A restaurant serving Indonesian, Western, Chinese, and Japanese food catches the breeze off the water. Children under 12 can stay with parents at no extra cost or can share their own room for half price. *Jl. Raya Seririt, Kalibukbuk 81151,* ☎ *0362/41237,* ℻ *0362/41236. 20 rooms. Restaurant, bar, pool, beach, dive shop, travel services. MC, V. BP.* ☙

$–$$ 🏨 **Villa Ratu Ayu.** The owners of Munduk's Puri Lumbung (☞ *above*) opened this property in June 2000. The look is similar: individual raised cottages resemble Balinese rice barns and have thatch roofs and open-air bathrooms. Each cottage's balcony affords a gorgeous view of rice fields, vineyards, and the glint of the ocean beyond. The resort is about 300 ft from the beach, a somewhat slippery five-minute walk through the rice fields. The beach itself is rocky and dirty, however, so the best way to enjoy it is to take a horseback ride along it. Villa Ratu Ayu emphasizes meditation and spiritualism, and guests are encouraged to learn about Balinese Hinduism; the staff can help you craft offerings to take to the area's many shrines. The new restaurant here will undoubtedly be as good as Puri Lumbung's. Discounts are available for stays of several nights and can be combined with stays at Puri Lumbung. ⊠ *Umaanyar, near Seririt (Box 3603, Denpasar 80036),* ☎ *0361/413679, 0361/92810, or 0361/93437,* ℻ *0361/437071, 0361/92514, or 0361/ 93437. 3 cottages (more may be added in 2001). Restaurant, horseback riding. AE, MC, V. BP.*

$ 🏨 **Cilik's Garden.** Co-owned by a German and a Balinese (that's Cilik), this unique property offers incredible privacy with just two spacious bungalows in large tranquil gardens right on the ocean. Long-term guests are encouraged (most stay for at least two weeks), and the bungalows have all the amenities of home. Each bungalow is wired for Internet access—guests can borrow a computer and printer or bring their own—and the master-bedroom-cum-living-room has a CD player and collections of CDs and books. The bungalows are shaded by coconut palms, and cool nights make air-conditioning unnecessary, although each has a small room, with twin beds, that's fully air-conditioned. Cilik's doesn't have a swimming pool, but the stretch of pristine beachfront (no hawkers here) makes up for it nicely. Cilik and his family live on the premises, giving guests a chance to peek into Balinese family life. Book as far in advance as possible. ⊠ *Air Sanih 81172,* ☎ ℻ *0362/26561. 2 bungalows. Restaurant, air-conditioning, in-room data ports, refrigerators, beach, snorkeling, laundry service. No credit cards. BP.* ☙

$ 🏨 **Rambutan Beach Cottages.** An oasis smack in the middle of Kalibuk-
★ buk's busiest area, Rambutan was opened by an Australian who now lives on the property with his Balinese wife and their young children. It's a particularly welcoming place for kids, who will enjoy the seesaw,

swing set, and slide. From here you can reach Lovina's casual center on foot, not to mention walk along the area's best stretch of beach. Accommodations run the gamut from budget rooms with cold water only and standard hot-water rooms to deluxe rooms and new luxury villas with fantastic stone mosaic bathrooms. The two large and attractive pools and acres of lush grounds make the hotel the best value in Lovina. ⊠ *Jl. Ketapang, Kalibukbuk 81152,* ☎ *0362/41388,* ℻ *0362/ 41057. 33 rooms. 2 restaurants, bar, 2 pools, badminton, Ping-Pong, playground. DC, MC, V (3% extra charge to use credit card). BP.* ❧

¢–$ ▦ **Bali Taman.** It's Las Vegas meets Bali at this unintentionally wacky beachside hotel where the grounds are liberally decorated with elaborate whitewashed cement sculptures of mythical figures. This is old-school Lovina, and the decor is traditional Bali guest house: light bamboo furniture, an open-roof bathroom, and a tile front porch that overlooks the grounds' fishponds and fountains. There's a restaurant on the premises, plus a small stage where traditional Balinese dancing and gamelan performances are occasionally held. The sandy beach is remarkably free of aggressive hawkers. Special tours of a nearby coffee mill can be arranged. ⊠ *Jl. Raya Lovina, Anturan, Lovina,* ☎ *0362/ 41126 or 0362/41194,* ℻ *0362/41840. 20 rooms. Restaurant, bar, pool, wading pool, tennis courts, snorkeling. MC, V. BP.* ❧

¢ ▦ **Aditya Beach Bungalows.** This hotel's ornate reception building, right on the main road in central Lovina, has an Indian feel but is actually an old Balinese structure. Guest quarters are down long paths through well-maintained gardens, and many have yards just steps from the sand. Rooms are large and open, with back entrances, raised front porches, tile floors, and very basic furnishings. Check the toilet, tub, and refrigerator to make sure they're working, and keep food wrapped up, as ants can be a problem in this area. The staff is very helpful and friendly, and a breakfast buffet is included in the price. ⊠ *Jl. Raya Lovina, Lovina (Box 134, Singaraja 81101),* ☎ *0362/41059,* ℻ *0362/41342. 80 rooms. 2 restaurants, café, bar, refrigerators, pool, wading pool, spa, tennis court, putting green, travel services, car rental. AE, MC, V. BP.* ❧

¢ ▦ **Rini Hotel.** Hidden back on Kalibukbuk's quieter street, this small hotel is very basic but looks brand new despite being more than 10 years old. Cheaper rooms have cold water and are fan-cooled, while the more expensive rooms have hot water and air-conditioning. Rooms are sparsely (but nicely) furnished and immaculate, and bathrooms are covered in sparkling white tiles. A small pool has a shallow children's area and is surrounded by a deck and several palm trees. The Kalibukbuk location means proximity to numerous restaurants and nightlife options, as well as the area's best beach for swimming, snorkeling, or dolphin-watching. ⊠ *Jl. Ketapang, Kalibukbuk 81152,* ☎ ℻ *0362/ 41386. 30 rooms. Restaurant, air-conditioning (some), pool. No credit cards. BP.*

Gunung Batur and Environs

¢ ▦ **Lakeview Restaurant and Hotel.** Of the cluster of small, inexpensive hotels and restaurants in the Gunung Batur area, the Lakeview, in Penelokan, is the best and most popular. The staff is friendly, and the rooms are clean, but the accommodations are very basic. The only reason to stay here is if you plan to undertake the morning hike to the top of the volcano. Superior quarters come with hot water (but have showers only) and double or twin beds; deluxe rooms have double beds and bathtubs. The restaurant (☞ Dining, *above*) has decent Indonesian fare and memorable views; tour buses often stop here for the buffet lunch. The hotel can arrange a guide for Gunung Batur (including a swim in the hot springs afterwards) for $35 per person. ⊠ *Jl. Raya,*

Penelokan 80652, ☎ FAX 0366/51464 or 0366/31394. 20 rooms. Restaurant, bar, laundry service. AE, MC, V. BP.

NIGHTLIFE AND THE ARTS

Northern Bali is not particularly rich in nightlife, and you won't find as many organized dance and music shows as in the more developed tourist hubs of the south and Ubud. Lovina, popular with tourists who usually stay at least a few days, has the most options. Many area hotels bring in dance troupes to perform for guests during dinner, and there is an outdoor dance stage in Kalibukbuk. For information about upcoming cultural performances, ask at your hotel. The only nightlife you'll find is in Lovina, and it's nothing compared to the swinging scene in Kuta.

Nightlife

Lovina is not a real party town: the few Internet establishments can be at least as packed as the bars, and the dress code everywhere is less than casual. The one exception to that rule is the Damai hotel, where the incredible nightly five-course dinner qualifies as entertainment in itself. To take in Lovina's after-dark dynamic, have a drink in one of the restaurants along Jalan Bina Ria, the main street leading down to the beach in Kalibukbuk, as the sun starts to set. You'll see the marked change between the town's daytime and nighttime personalities, from the old man walking home from work with his long bamboo fishing pole and basket of fish to the bars setting up shop as the young Balinese men wearing Harley-Davidson T-shirts arrive on their motorbikes.

Movie watching is a popular nighttime diversion in Lovina. Several of the inexpensive restaurants in Kalibukbuk show movies—usually recent American blockbusters—at dinner time.

Malibu (⊠ Jl. Seririt-Singaraja, east of Jl. Bina Ria, Kalibukbuk, ☎ 0362/41671) is a bit out of Lovina's hub—though still walking distance from the beach—which may explain why on some nights it's dead empty while other nights find it full. (At press time Saturday night was when you could find Lovina's roving party crew at Malibu.) The atmosphere is pizza-parlor-meets-disco, with red-checked tablecloths and a sizable parquet dance floor. A cover band plays favorites, food and a nightly movie are offered, and until midnight the staff will pick up patrons at their hotels and deliver them back at no cost.

Poco Bar (⊠ Jl. Bina Ria, Kalibukbuk, ☎ no phone), a newcomer that opened in 2000, lies right in the middle of Lovina's main drag next to the Spice Dive Internet office. A local band plays covers nightly (think Lynyrd Skynyrd and Bob Marley), and the lively scene spills out of the tiny space onto the sidewalk. The kitchen here serves up Italian food.

Sea Breeze (⊠ Lovina Beach, ☎ 0362/41138) has Lovina's best sunset-watching location, right on the sandy beach to the west of the dolphin statue. Food, including nightly specials, is served in a large, airy space that rocks on late into the night. A Balinese band plays covers for Westerners and Indonesians sitting at tables or gathered around campfires on the beach. An enthusiastic crowd forms when European football games are shown. If you're looking for action, Sea Breeze is the place—but if you're a single female, beware the attention of Lovina's local lotharios.

The Arts

Senggol Lovina (⊠ Jl. Singaraja-Seririt, Kalibukbuk, ☎ 0361/41169 or 0361/41293) is an outdoor stage that offers Balinese dance performances a couple times a week, usually on Thursday and Saturday, for $1.50 per person. Stopping by the stage isn't the best way to find out about the schedule, since often no one is around; inquire at your hotel instead.

OUTDOOR ACTIVITIES AND SPORTS

Northern Bali has outdoor activities for every kind of person. If you're looking for a challenge, there's nothing like scrambling over volcanic rocks in the darkness, with only a flashlight to guide you, to reach the summit of Gunung Batur for the sunrise. Fun seekers may want to try out a water sport on Lake Bratan or off Lovina, which is also a north-coast hub for one of Bali's best-known activities, scuba diving. If your favorite activity is sitting back and taking in the sights, you can do so on a morning boat ride from Lovina to see the area's most popular residents, the dolphins.

Participant Sports

Bicycling

Cycling is a popular activity in the Lovina area, where you can bike along the coastal road and to nearby villages. Bicycles are available for rent at many of the car rental businesses along Lovina's main road; you can expect to pay about $3 per day.

Golf and Tennis

Golf connoisseurs will want to pay a visit to the **Bali Handara Kosaido Country Club** (⊠ Pancasari, ☎ 0362/22646), in the lakes district. The 7036-yard, par 72 course is one of the best in Asia. Greens fees are $100 (including a caddy); rental of a full set of clubs is $20. The weather can get cold and foggy by 1 PM, so get an early start. The country club's tennis court costs $10 per hour; racket rental is $5 a day.

Hiking

The lush hills of Munduk are a great place for low-key hiking. You'll get the most out of your walk—and won't get lost on the winding paths—if you have a guide, which can be arranged through the charming **Puri Lumbung hotel** (⊠ Munduk, ☎ 0362/92811 or 0362/92810). Call ahead to reserve a guide, and plan your schedule so that you can stop for lunch or dinner afterward at Puri Lumbung's Warung Kopi. Expect to pay—or offer a donation of—at least $2.50, depending on the length of your tour.

Gunung Batur is, naturally, a main attraction in the region. This hike is not for the timid, and it shouldn't be attempted without proper footwear. The best way to make the trip is through the **Lakeview hotel** (⊠ Jl. Raya, Penelokan, ☎ 0366/51464 or 0366/31394).

Jero Wijaya Tourist Service (⊠ Jl. Andong 9X, Andong, ☎ 0361/973172), in the Ubud area in central Bali, organizes hikes around Gunung Batur's caldera and jungle walks around Danau Tamblingan for $60–$100.

Scuba Diving and Snorkeling

Lovina's proximity to the popular dive spots of Menjangan Island, to the west, and Tulamben, to the east, makes it a good base for divers who want to visit Bali's underwater corals and schools of tropical fish—and for anyone looking to get certified. You can also go snorkeling just off Lovina Beach; the small boats on the beach will take you out and loan you snorkel gear for $2.50 a person.

Most of the area's dive operations are in Kalibukbuk. **Spice Dive** (⊠ Jl. Bina Ria, Kalibukbuk, ☎ 0362/41305 or 0362/41509; ⊠ Café Spice,

Jl. Singaraja-Seririt, ☎ 0362/41969) was the first dive shop established in Lovina and is the most respected operator in the area. The shop offers introductory dives, tours to Menjangan and Tulamben, and night dives. Full courses are available in open-water ($250) and advanced open-water ($225) diving.

Water Sports

Visitors to Danau Bratan can enjoy water sports such as jet skiing, parasailing, and waterskiing. All the lake's recreational facilities are in or around **Taman Rekreasi Bedugul** (✉ Bedugul, ☎ 0368/21197), open daily from 9 until 4 or 5. It costs about $15 for 30 minutes of any of the water activities, which can be arranged through the ticket window at the park.

In Lovina, the Café Spice location of **Spice Dive** (✉ Café Spice, Jl. Singaraja-Seririt, ☎ 0362/41969) rents equipment for a number of water sports, including parasailing, waterskiing, windsurfing, and wakeboarding.

Spectator Sports

Lovina has long been popular with visitors for the dolphins that frolic offshore in the early morning. In the last decade the "sport" of dolphin-watching got a bit out of hand, with a huge fleet of small motorboats chasing desperately after dolphins every morning; in recent years the locals have decided not to pursue the creatures so aggressively, making the experience far more relaxing. You can arrange your trip through your hotel or by simply asking the operator of one of the boats on Lovina Beach to take you out. Expect to pay about $3 per person (more if you go through your hotel), and be sure to arrange your trip the day before so you aren't stranded on the beach at 5:30 AM. The trip starts just before dawn to accommodate the dolphins' schedule and takes about an hour. It's likely, though not guaranteed, that you'll spot some dolphins—but even if you don't, seeing the sunrise over the Bali Sea is a lovely experience in itself.

The Sapi Gerumbungan bull races races take place at the track in Kaliasem, Lovina, on March 31 and August 17, and sometimes on other dates. For race information ask at **Ubud Tourist Information** (✉ Jl. Ubud, Ubud, ☎ 0361/973285) in eastern Bali or **Kuta Tourist Information** (✉ Jl. Legian 37, Kuta, ☎ 0361/755424) in southern Bali.

SHOPPING

Northern Bali has little in the way of shopping. Some of the better resorts have gift shops, which have small selections and slightly inflated prices. A notable exception is the tiny shop at **Puri Lumbung** (✉ Munduk, ☎ 0362/92811 or 0362/92810), which sells local products at good prices. Much of it you will find elsewhere in Bali, but there are some unusual items, like miniature Balinese houses, complete with working window shutters, made from bamboo (about $30).

Lovina Beach's stalls offer the usual down-market items such as poor-quality sarongs and T-shirts. Lovina also has a couple of shops, where prices are fixed. The charming **Global** (✉ South side of Jl. Singaraja-Seririt, just west of intersection with Jl. Bina Ria, ☎ 0362/41230) carries wares made of natural materials from the area: lamps made from coconut shells, bamboo place mats, and the like, all reasonably priced. The tiny shop inside the restaurant **Biyu Nasak** (✉ Jl. Raya, Lovina Beach, Kaliasem, ☎ FAX 0362/41176) sells all sorts of crafts, plus everyday items, such as altar decorations, used by the Balinese.

ONE LAST TRAVEL TIP:

Pack an easy way to reach the world.

123 456 7891 2345
J.D. SMITH

Wherever you travel, the MCI WorldCom Card℠ is the easiest way to stay in touch. You can use it to call to and from more than 125 countries worldwide. And you can earn bonus miles every time you use your card. So go ahead, travel the world. MCI WorldCom℠ makes it even more rewarding. For additional access codes, visit **www.wcom.com/worldphone**.

MCI WORLDCOM.

EASY TO CALL WORLDWIDE

1. Just dial the WorldPhone® access number of the country you're calling from.

2. Dial or give the operator your MCI WorldCom Card number.

3. Dial or give the number you're calling.

China (A)	108-12
Hong Kong	800-96-1121

Indonesia ◆	001-801-11
Japan ◆	00539-121▶
Korea	00729-14
Malaysia ◆	1-800-80-0012
Philippines ◆	105-14
Singapore (A)	8000-112-112
Taiwan ◆	0080-13-4567
Thailand (A) ★	001-999-1-2001
Vietnam (A) ❖ ●	1201-1022

(A) Calls back to U.S. only. ◆ Public phones may require deposit of coin or phone card for dial tone.
▶ Regulation does not permit intra-Japan calls. ★ Not available from public pay phones. ❖ Limited availability.
● Local service fee in U.S. currency required to complete call.

EARN FREQUENT FLIER MILES

Bureau de change

Cambio

外国為替

In this city, you can find money on almost any street.

N O - F E E   F O R E I G N   E X C H A N G E

The Chase Manhattan Bank has over 80 convenient
locations near New York City destinations such as:
>   Times Square
>   Rockefeller Center
>   Empire State Building
>   2 World Trade Center
>   United Nations Plaza

Exchange any of 75 foreign currencies

◯ CHASE

THE RIGHT RELATIONSHIP IS EVERYTHING.®

For life's necessities head to the minimarket called **Mailaku** (✉ Jl. Bina Ria, Lovina, ☎ 0362/41163), which carries a good selection of pharmaceutical items and is open until midnight. **Asri Photo** (✉ Jl. Bina Ria, Lovina, ☎ 0362/41357) sells and develops film; you can get a roll of 36 printed in 25 minutes for about $6.

NORTHERN BALI A TO Z

Arriving and Departing

By Airplane

Bali's only air hub is Ngurah Rai International Airport, in Tuban in southern Bali, and all airline offices are there or in Sanur or Denpasar (☞ Southern Bali A to Z *in* Chapter 2). If you need to change reservations or reconfirm bookings, your hotel can call the airlines for you.

FROM THE AIRPORT

Most travelers will spend at least a night in Kuta or Ubud before proceeding to northern Bali. Car-rental prices are cheapest in Kuta, so if you want to have your own vehicle, get it there and drive here. Otherwise, call the hotel at which you'll be staying and ask to be picked up. Most are more than happy to send a car and driver to retrieve guests from the airport or other towns around the island. Depending on the distance, this service will cost $15–$30.

Getting Around

By Bemo

Every town has at least one *bemo* (local public minibus) stop. However, there often aren't direct routes to more remote places in the region, making it necessary to travel through major hubs farther south. The tourist shuttles (☞ *below*) are a better budget option.

By Car

Cars can be hired with or without a driver, most easily in Lovina. A number of agencies are on the main road in Kalibukbuk, Jalan Bina Ria, and many hotels can arrange a rental car for you. Cars are also available in the smaller towns near the lakes and volcano; inquire at a local hotel. It should cost about $10 per day for a car and another $5 for a driver (perhaps more if you arrange it through a hotel). Hiring a driver is recommended if you're uncomfortable driving Bali's winding roads on your own. The easiest method is to hire a car and driver for only the particular routes you want to travel, such as for a day trip to a few temples in neighboring towns or to take you from one hotel to the next. If you are transferring to another hotel, call ahead because some provide free pickup.

By Shuttle

Shuttle buses head from the tourist hubs in southern Bali to northern Bali on a regular basis, usually daily. A popular shuttle service is **Permama** (✉ Jl. Seririt-Singaraja, Kalibukbuk, ☎ 0362/41104), whose office on the main road in Kalibukbuk is next to the tourist office and police station. Permama makes trips to hubs like Kuta, Sanur, and Ubud as well as to Kintamani and Bedugul. Fares are only a few dollars per person for any of the above routes.

Contacts and Resources

Banks and Currency Exchange

At press time Lovina had two ATMs, both east of Kalibukbuk on the Singaraja-Seririt road. You can change money and cash traveler's checks at most hotels in northern Bali. Some businesses along Jalan Bina Ria in Kalibukbuk will also exchange currency.

Emergencies

Without a doubt the first thing you should do if you have an emergency is contact your hotel's front desk. They will be able to arrange for a doctor to come to your room or, if necessary, take you to the region's only hospital, in Singaraja. Most important, they will be able to translate for you.

Lovina's 24-hour **clinic** (⊠ Jl. Raya Seririt-Singaraja and Jl. Desa Kalibukbuk, Kalibukbuk, ☎ 0362/41106) provides care for minor traumas and assists in medical evacuation; the clinic is designed for travelers from abroad, so English is spoken. **Rumah Sakit Kerta Usada** (⊠ Jl. Jen Achmad Yani 108, Singaraja, ☎ 0362/22396) is a private hospital with a dentist on-site. **Rumah Sakit Umum** (⊠ Jl. Ngurah Rai, Singaraja, ☎ 0362/22046) is a public hospital.

Basic medicines are relatively easy to come by in Lovina, which has two well-stocked pharmacies, including **Mailaku** (⊠ Jl. Bina Ria, Lovina, ☎ 0362/41163). You can find aspirin (try asking for headache medicine) in even the smallest villages—it's sold in the little warung.

Lovina's **police station** shares the same building as the tourist office. It's on the Singaraja-Seririt road between Jalan Bina Ria and Jalan Ketapang.

English-Language Bookstores

Two minimarkets in Lovina sell used English-language paperbacks: **Mailaku** (⊠ Jl. Bina Ria, ☎ 0362/41163) and **Lovina Art Shop** (⊠ Jl. Singaraja-Seririt at Jl. Bina Ria). Magazines are virtually unavailable in the region. The best bets for buying newspapers are the gift shops of the larger hotels—some of which deliver complimentary copies of the *International Herald Tribune* or the *Jakarta Post* to guests each morning.

Guided Tours

Most hotels offer tours of area attractions and even of sites that are a few hours away. If you're staying in a resort in Lovina, for example, you can go on a day trip to the lakes or the volcano. It's generally best to ask fellow travelers which tour guides they recommend (or don't), since the quality of your experience will depend on your guide.

In Munduk, the **Puri Lumbung** hotel (⊠ Munduk, ☎ 0362/92811 or 0362/92810) leads a number of great walking tours to the area's plentiful waterfalls and plantations of vanilla, coffee, cloves, papayas, snake fruit, and other exotic plants.

Health and Safety

Like the rest of Bali, the northern areas are essentially crime-free and very friendly. The hawkers (mostly women) around Gunung Batur and Danau Bratan can be very aggressive, though, which makes getting into the temples aggravating. If you have your own sarong and selendang, however, they won't have much to harass you about.

One surprising recent problem is a car-repair scam on the main road leading north from Gunung Batur to the coast. Two men will attempt to flag down a car by pulling up alongside it and gesturing wildly or pointing, implying there's a problem with the vehicle; after magically "fixing" the problem, they'll ask for payment for their services. Ignore them: they won't follow you for long. Pay attention to any such warnings that come from the car-rental operations.

Telephones, Internet, and Mail

You don't need to dial the area code when calling locally. When calling long-distance on the island or between Indonesian islands, make sure to include the 0 before the area code.

In general, phone service in northern Bali is reliable, although there are often problems with Internet access in the Lovina area. Most better hotels have direct-dial service in the rooms, but it may be worth visiting a *wartel* (an office with private phone booths) to make your phone calls. This is the cheapest way to make a call since no fees are added on; a computer printout will show the length of your call and how much you need to pay for it.

In Lovina you'll find a wartel and Internet services at **Spice Dive** (⊠ Jl. Bina Ria, Kalibukbuk, ☎ 0362/41305 or 0362/41509).

The **Lovina post office** (⊠ Jl. Singaraja-Seririt, about 1 km west of Kalibukbuk) is open Monday through Thursday and Saturday 8–3, Friday 8–1. To receive mail here, have it addressed to you at "Post Office, Jalan Raya Singaraja, Lovina, Banjar, Singaraja 81152, Bali, Indonesia." Hotels, guest houses, and wartels will often be able to help you mail letters and packages.

Visitor Information

Unfortunately, Lovina's primary **tourist office**, on the Singaraja-Gilimanuk road in Kalibukbuk, has almost nothing to recommend it. Maps aren't available, and the staff can't be particularly helpful since their English is poor.

The tourist office in Penelokan, **Yayasa Bintang Danu** (☎ 0366/23370), open daily 9–3, can provide limited information on local transportation and trekking.

5 WESTERN BALI

The least-developed area of the island, the west is Bali's last frontier. Home to the endangered Bali starling, traditional water-buffalo racing, and an expansive national park, this region is worth a trip if you have the time or the inclination for adventure. The waters around and near Menjangan Island have some of the best diving and snorkeling in Bali, and several unique luxury resorts have recently sprouted up to accommodate the growing number of travelers.

By Gisela
Williams

N WESTERN BALI THE CROWDS of tourists, street vendors, and resort chains typical of the south seem very far away. Here you'll find expansive undeveloped parkland, rice fields, empty black beaches that meet rough seas, and a mix of cultures from across Indonesia. Much of what is known as western Bali today is the regency of Jembrana. Once called Jimbar Wana, which means "the Great Forest," this area has always been wilder and less populated than the rest of the island. A 15th-century civil war between the area's two ruling princes brought down both kingdoms, and the thriving court culture that is present to this day in the rest of Bali never developed as fully or elaborately here. Many non-Hindus make their home in the Jembrana region, which is just a half-hour from Java by boat; mosques are plentiful, and one of the largest Catholic churches in eastern Indonesia is here. The area is given flavor by the mix of religions and communities of settlers from Java, Madura, and Sulawesi, who have come here because there is space and because the region isn't overwhelmingly Hindu; many of them make their living farming or fishing.

The Bali Barat National Park, with almost 200,000 acres of forested mountains, palm savannas, and mangrove swamps, takes up much of western Bali. It was created in the 1970s to protect the Bali tiger. The tiger has since become extinct, but the park is still home to the endangered Bali starling (there are less than 40 left in the wild) and several species of monkeys and deer. This is a fairly popular hiking area, and the waters that surround the park's Menjangan Island draw scores of divers and snorkelers. Until recently Bali Barat National Park was one of the few areas left untouched by farmers and developers. A few years ago, though, a hotel was developed on park land, leading some farmers to feel that they should be allowed to cultivate some of the park. Unfortunately, with the country facing larger political problems, the government has been unable to make regulation of the park a priority.

Most hotels in western Bali are not far from where the main road along the northern coast enters the park. Many are clustered around the village of Pemuteran, which has been developed only in the last few years. This is the most visited part of western Bali, largely because it is a major diving destination. From here it is a fairly quick boat ride to the corals and colorful schools of fish around Menjangan. However, now that a few unique luxury resorts have moved in, it's not just divers or backpackers who are staying around Pemuteran. You're just as likely to see well-heeled Europeans and American baby boomers exploring this part of the island, searching for the Bali of their past.

One major road runs along the southwestern coast between Denpasar and Gilimanuk, a port town and gateway to Java. This road is mainly used by large trucks and busses carrying passengers and cargo to and from the ferries. Along this road are a few unique tourist attractions, but few places to stay. Some tourists find the trip worthwhile just to see the dramatic traditional bull racing in Perancak. Visitors also come to see performances of the gamelan *jegog*, a type of bamboo orchestra found only in western Bali.

Several black beaches run along the southwestern coast. Most are difficult to get to and thus are frequented only by surfers. Though the tides can be fatal for swimmers, these isolated beaches are lovely to look at and stroll upon. The most beautiful stretch is near Pura Rambut Siwi, an important Balinese temple. Near the village of Yeh Gangga, the Waka Gangga hotel—one of the few luxury hotels in southwestern Bali—overlooks a black-sand beach that during low tide leads all the way to Tanah Lot.

Like its beaches, western Bali can be at once breathtakingly beautiful and inhospitable. It takes an adventurous spirit and some hard work to find the best of this region. The experiences you have here will reflect your willingness to have an open mind when dealing with a foreign culture—to get a bit lost and ask for advice from the locals. If you can travel without a map, western Bali holds many fascinating encounters in store: there are still places here that have rarely seen outside visitors. Many claim that this region takes you back to a Bali of 20 years ago, but Bali's western end is and always has been a bit disconnected from the rest of the island. With its Muslim and Catholic communities, western Bali is more like Java or Lombok than like the rest of Bali, but that only makes it more intriguing.

EXPLORING WESTERN BALI

A Good Tour

You can see much of the west by driving along the coastline on the one main road, which connects Denpasar, in the south, to Gilimanuk, at the northwestern tip of the island. Just south of Gilimanuk a road heads east along the north coast toward Lovina and Singaraja. The following tour assumes you are starting near Lovina Beach; you can follow it backward if you are coming from Kuta or Nusa Dua. Make the tour by car; either rent a car or hire one with a driver. A driver may be preferable because stretches of the road, especially in the northwest, are in need of repair and maneuvering around the large buses and trucks that frequent this route can be tricky.

Numbers in the text correspond to numbers in the margin and on the Western Bali map.

Heading west on the northern coastal highway, your first stops should be two temples that are within a mile of one another: **Pura Melanting** ① and **Pura Pulaki** ②. Pura Melanting is off the main road before you reach Pura Pulaki. Pura Pulaki is famous for the gregarious monkeys that live within the safety of its walls. Soon after Pulaki you reach Pemuteran, the site of many of the best resorts in the west. If you can't stay for a night or two, at least pay a visit to **Reef Seen Aquatics and Pemuteran Stables** ③, a small dive shop and horse stable that also sponsors a turtle sanctuary.

Continue west to reach the **Bali Barat National Park** ④ and Labuhan Lalang, where you can catch a boat to **Menjangan Island** ⑤. It's best to reserve a full day to explore this area. The shortest hike through the park takes about two hours, and if you want to go snorkeling or diving, the boats usually leave in the morning and return around 2 or 3. Not far after Labuhan Lalang, stone steps on the left side of the road lead up to **Pura Jayaprana** ⑥. Here you find the grave of Jayaprana, a local hero who, along with his wife, met a fate reminiscent of Romeo and Juliet. From the top of the temple site you can see out over much of the park.

At Cekik you'll see signs to Gilimanuk, which is a ferry port and not of great interest. Instead go south for about 16 km (10 mi) and then follow the signs for **Palasari** ⑦, turning left onto a smaller road. This road eventually leads to the Catholic community, in the middle of which lies one of the largest Catholic churches in eastern Indonesia. Getting here and then back to the main road can be confusing, so be prepared to ask for directions.

Back on the main road, heading southeast, you'll soon reach the large bustling town of **Negara** ⑧, where you can visit a cash machine or grab

NO SARONG, NO SASH, NO SERVICE

MOST BALINESE people have become accustomed to the "strange" ways of tourists and are not usually offended or surprised by a Westerner's ignorance of Balinese customs and beliefs. But a little knowledge of such things is valuable, especially in the more remote villages. When entering a temple or witnessing a religious ceremony, you should wear the customary sarong and *selendang* (sash) over appropriate clothing (no shorts or miniskirts); usually someone outside the temple will be willing to rent or lend these items to you. If you plan to visit several temples during your stay, buy yourself a sarong and a sash at a market beforehand. A selendang should cost you less than $1, while a sarong, depending on the quality of the fabric, can range in price from $3 to $75. In a temple it is considered rude to walk directly in front of people praying. It's generally acceptable to take photographs, as long as you are a reasonable distance away from people and don't use a flash. According to an ancient law still strictly adhered to today, a person with a bleeding cut or a menstruating woman is not allowed to enter a temple because blood on holy soil is taboo. And always make a donation at any temple you visit or any ceremony in which you take part. If the ceremony is at a private house, it's acceptable to offer a gift of sugar, tea, or coffee instead of money.

Indonesians consider the left hand to be unclean because it is the hand used in the bathroom. Always use your right hand to give or receive something. If you accidentally use your left hand in a transaction, acknowledge your mistake by saying, "*Ma'af tangan kiri*," which means "Excuse my left hand." In Bali the head is considered sacred, the feet unclean. Avoid touching adults or children on the head. Exposing the sole of your foot to someone is considered insulting, as is stepping over someone's food or person.

Before you enter someone's house, it is customary to take off your shoes. It is also polite to always sit a bit lower down than your host (the higher someone sits, the more important they are). This is especially true in the temples or during a ceremony: make sure you are seated at a lower level than the priest or the offerings.

Finally, making the okay sign with your fingers does not mean "OK" in Bali; it is a sexual gesture. Motioning to someone with an upturned hand is considered aggressive; Balinese people will do that only when they want to fight. Pointing at someone with your index finger is rude as well (Indonesians point with their thumbs, with the palms turned upward and fingers curled in). Making one of these hand gestures isn't exactly like flashing a middle finger at a stranger in Times Square, but it's always good to know how your body language is perceived in a different culture. Fortunately, the Balinese are forgiving and polite people who generally respond with a "*Tidak apa-apa*" ("No problem") to our faux pas.

some snacks. You can also take a quick side trip to **Loloan Timor** ⑨—less than 2 km (1 mi) south of town—a small, traditional Buginese village, with architecture that's very different from what you see in the rest of Bali.

From Negara it's roughly a 3-km (2-mi) drive east on the main road to the town of **Jembrana** ⑩, which is the place to take in a gamelan jegog (bamboo orchestra) performance. Almost 16 km (10 mi) past Jembrana you'll see signs for **Pura Rambut Siwi** ⑪, one of the most important temples of the region. Sunset is the ideal time to visit the temple, which hangs over an empty black-sand beach.

Continue along the main road for about 15 minutes to reach **Medewi Beach** ⑫. This beach is black and rocky near the entrance road, but it turns to sand and stretches on for quite a distance. The ocean here is not very swimmable but is appreciated by surfers for its long left-hand wave. There are two or three places to eat and stay, but it's best to continue on to **Lalang Linggah** ⑬, another 22 km (14 mi) east. Here you will find the Sacred River Retreat, a small hotel that specializes in meditation and has comfortable bungalows as well as a good vegetarian restaurant. The waters of the nearby beach are extremely dangerous to enter, but it's another popular surfer destination.

The road soon leaves the coast and the Jembrana region and heads inland toward the region and town of Tabanan. Just before leaving the coast you'll pass by Soka Beach. The restaurant and recreational area here have seen better days and are now only frequented by big tour buses. About 15 km (9 mi) later, before entering the town of Tabanan, you'll see signs for Krambitan. If you're interested in checking out the village's palace, **Puri Anyar** ⑭, take a right off the main road. Although the royal family still lives here, guests are allowed. The best reason to visit is to attend one of the nighttime dance performances.

In Tabanan you'll find a rather interesting tribute to Balinese rice agriculture, the **Subak Museum** ⑮, which is worth a short visit. Finally, stop in the town of Mengwi, about 15 minutes to the east, to check out **Pura Taman Ayun** ⑯, surrounded by a wide moat, which was the main temple of the former Mengwi kingdom.

TIMING

This tour can be completed in one very long day—if you skip Bali Barat National Park and Menjangan Island. To explore the region's attractions more thoroughly, give yourself at least two days: spend one day hiking or snorkeling in the park, stay the night at a hotel near Pemuteran, and spend the next day driving south and taking in a few sights.

The Northwest

Many travelers arrive in northwestern Bali by car from Lovina. This area is worth a trip just for the great snorkeling and diving around Menjangan Island in Bali Barat National Park. Another worthwhile sight is the small center in the national park that is trying to keep the Bali starling from disappearing in the wild by releasing birds bred in captivity.

The northwest is a popular destination for tourists who want to be far from the crowds of Sanur, Kuta, and Ubud. Although the region has a few first-class hotels, you won't find much in the way of shops, bars, or cultural activities. Here visitors have nothing to do except relax, sunbathe, and maybe go for a dive or bike ride.

Sights to See

❹ **Bali Barat National Park.** Created in the 1970s in an attempt to save the endangered Bali tiger, the Bali Barat (West Bali) park has since

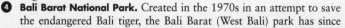

Western Bali

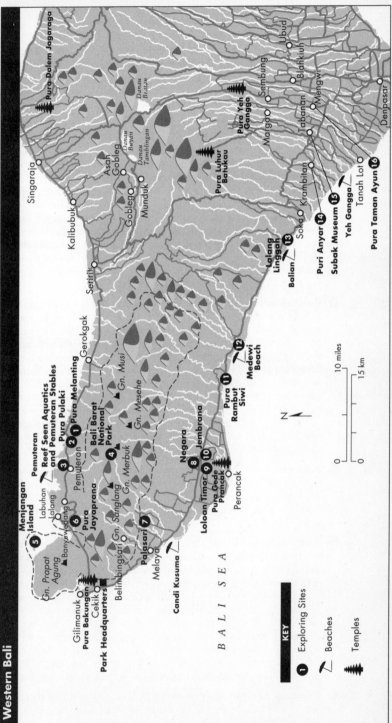

Singaraja

Kalibubuk

Seririt

Gerokgak

Pemuteran
Reef Seen Aquatics
and Pemuteran Stables
Pura Pulaki
Pura Melanting

Labuhan
Lalang

Menjangan
Island

Gilimanuk
Pura Bakungan
Cekik
Park Headquarters

Gn. Prapat Agung

Banyuwedang

Pura Jayaprana

Belimbingsari
Gn. Sangiang

Melaya

Candi Kusuma

Palasari

Gn. Merbuk

Bali Barat
National
Park

Gn. Musi

Gn. Mesehe

Negara

Loloan Timor
Pura Gede
Perancak

Perancak

Jembrana

Pura
Rambut
Siwi

Medewi Beach

Balian

Lalang
Linggah

Soka

Krambitan

Puri Anyar
Subak Museum
Yeh Gangga
Tanah Lot

Pura Taman Ayun

Tabanan

Marga

Sembung

Pura Yeh Gangga

Pura Luhur
Batukau

Munduk

Goblerg
Asah
Gobleg

Danau
Tamblingan

Danau
Buyan

Danau
Bratan

Pura Dalem Jagaraga

Mengwi

Blahkiuh

Ubud

Denpasar

BALI SEA

KEY

Exploring Sites ①

Beaches

Temples

0   10 miles
0   15 km

grown in area, though the tigers no longer exist. Now almost 200,000 acres, the park encompasses jungle and mangrove swamps that are home to wild boar, several species of monkeys and deer, and a large number of bird species, including the rare Bali starling. To hire a hiking guide or arrange a tour of the Bali starling conservation project, go to the park headquarters. ⊠ *Park headquarters: Cekik (at junction of northern coastal road and western coastal road),* ☎ *0365/61060.* ☒ *30¢ entrance fee; $10 for hiking guide for 2 hrs for up to 3 people.* ☉ *Daily 8–3.*

❺ Menjangan Island. A very popular dive and snorkeling destination, Deer Island is part of ☞ **Bali Barat National Park.** The small, uninhabited island is home to one of Bali's oldest temples, dating from Indonesia's golden age, the Javanese Majapahit period, which peaked in the early 14th century. Most visitors, however, are more interested in the surrounding corals and fish than the island itself. For years sea life suffered due to a coral-eating starfish and explosives used by fishermen, but park rangers and local divers have rallied together to save the coral, and life on the reef is thriving. Divers encounter creatures like lionfish and reef sharks, and snorkelers are awed by the colorful drop-off just feet from the shore. You can hire a boat to the island from the jetty at Labuhan Lalang; the cost is about $10 round-trip, including snorkeling gear. ☒ *Donation suggested for temple.*

❻ Pura Jayaprana. Jayaprana Temple is the gravesite of a fabled local hero. A foster son of the region's royal family in the 18th century, Jayaprana, according to legend, married a very beautiful woman the king wanted for himself. The jealous king invented a story that pirates had invaded the northwest and sent Jayaprana to defend the area, but waiting for Jayaprana instead was one of the king's men, who murdered him. The king's plan backfired when, rather than accepting his advances, Jayaprana's widow committed suicide. To reach the temple from Labuhan Lalang, walk west for about five minutes; on the south side of the main road a long stretch of stone steps leads up to the temple, which affords views of the sea and the park. ⊠ *1 km west of Labuhan Lalang,* ☎ *no phone.* ☒ *Donation suggested.* ☉ *Daily sunrise–sunset.*

❶ Pura Melanting. The large Melanting Temple has a dramatic setting in the foothills and is usually empty of tourists. Merchants make offerings here in order to secure good luck for their businesses. ⊠ *East of Pulaki, off main road,* ☎ *no phone.* ☒ *Donation suggested.* ☉ *Daily sunrise–sunset.*

❷ Pura Pulaki. Pulaki Temple is said to be on the site of an old village whose inhabitants were taught the art of becoming invisible by Danghyang Nirartha, a wandering 16th-century priest. Some Balinese believe the invisible villagers, known as *gamang,* still exist and occasionally become visible (they are apparently recognizable by the absent upper lip and bag over the shoulder). The temple, completely rebuilt in the early 1980s, is well known for its monkeys. You can buy grapes or bananas to give them, but be on your guard: sometimes the somewhat aggressive monkeys—spoiled by the visitors and locals who feed them— don't like to wait and will grab food right out of your hands. ⊠ *Pulaki,* ☎ *no phone.* ☒ *Donation suggested.* ☉ *Daily sunrise–sunset.*

★ ☺ ❸ Reef Seen Aquatics and Pemuteran Stables. Australian Chris Brown was one of the pioneers of the Pemuteran area, opening a dive shop here in 1993. Since then he has branched out: he now also runs a large horse stable and a turtle sanctuary and sponsors a local girls' dance troupe. Brown is actively involved in the preservation of the local environment, especially the nearby coral reefs. If you don't have time to explore the waters or go horseback riding, stop by to release a baby turtle into the sea. And if you happen to be in the area on a Saturday night, don't miss the dance performance. ⊠ *Pemuteran (between Matahari and Pondok Sari hotels),* ☎ *0362/92339.* ⊠ *To release turtle $8.* ☉ *Daily 8–8; dance performance Sat. 7:30 PM.*

The Southwest

Even less traveled than the northwest, southwestern Bali is home to the *mekepung* (traditional bull races) and the gamelan jegog. The only reasonable places to stay here—comfort-wise—are two well-kept bungalow hotels and the Waka Gangga resort; there are also a few surfer homestays. Surfers make the trip to the rough black beaches at Medewi and Lalang Linggah for the good break. Although some of the black sand beaches along the coast are quite beautiful, the tides and surf can be fatal, and visitors are warned not to swim at most of them.

This area is made up of two separate regions, Jembrana, to the west, and Tabanan, to the east. Tabanan is full of rice paddies and farms, while Jembrana is less cultivated and less peopled.

Sights to See

❿ **Jembrana.** This small town used to be the capital of the region and is now the center of the gamelan jegog, a type of orchestra found nowhere else on Bali. A gamelan jegog is made up of 14 large bamboo instruments, some of which are so big it's necessary for the musicians to sit on top of them to reach the keys. The instruments resonate deeply, and you can hear, and feel, the music from quite a distance. In the occasional competitions called *jegog mebarung,* the winner is the group that plays the loudest. ⊠ *On main road 3 km (2 mi) east of Negara.*

⓭ **Lalang Linggah.** The Balian River cuts a pretty path to the ocean through this tiny village, named for the wide-blade grass used to construct thatch roofs. There are two places to stay here, a surfer homestay and a more upscale spiritual retreat with a vegetarian restaurant, Café Louisa (☞ Dining, *below*), that is a great place to stop for a meal. There's not much to do except eat and find your way to Balian Beach. Don't try to swim, though: several people have died here in the past few years. ⊠ *44 km (27 mi) east of Negara.*

❾ **Loloan Timor.** This little village is populated by Bugis people from South Sulawesi, who have a strong tradition of living off the sea and who had a reputation—for most of the last millennium up until recently—for being fearsome pirates. With its Buginese architecture the village looks different from the rest of Bali. Homes, usually raised on platforms, are made of wood and painted in a variety of bright colors. ⊠ *Less than 2 km (1 mi) south of Negara.*

⓬ **Medewi Beach.** Mostly visited by surfers, this black beach is rocky near the road entrance but becomes nice and sandy as you walk north along the shore. If you want to do a little exploring, you can rent a boat from one of the fishermen. The village of Medewi, settled in 1912, is not much more than a few houses. It gets its name from the Balinese word for thorny, *meduwi,* which describes the *ketket* trees that once covered the area. ⊠ *22 km (14 mi) east of Negara.*

❽ **Negara.** This is the largest town in Jembrana, though tourists won't find much to do here except get cash out of an ATM or stop at a typical Indonesian department store, like Hardy's on Jalan Ngurah Rai, to buy some snacks or cheap flip-flops. Negara is predominantly Muslim, and mosques pepper the area. The town is known best for the traditional buffalo races, mekepung, that take place from August to November. Check with any tourist office for race dates and locations.

OFF THE
BEATEN PATH

PERANCAK RACECOURSE – Head southwest from Negara, following a very small road through rice fields for about 40 minutes, to reach the village of Perancak. Once there follow the signs for MEKEPUNG to get to the racetrack. Much of the region's bull racing takes place on this newly restored track run by I Gusti Ngurah Hartono, owner of the Kuta disco Peanuts. (It is also used for motorcycle races and other events.) Not far from the track are a small temple called Pura Gede Perancak, a fishing harbor, and a small crocodile zoo. Hartono, who grew up here, is your best guide to the area; he organizes frequent tours here from Kuta. Call Peanuts (☎ 0361/754149) for racetrack and tour information.

⑦ Palasari. Somewhat difficult to find, this small village is home to one of the largest Catholic churches in eastern Indonesia. Palasari was settled by Balinese converts to Christianity who in the early and mid-1900s were exiled to the wild west. The **church** would not stand on its own in the West, but because this imposing European structure lies in the middle of a small, traditional Balinese village, its sense of grandeur is exaggerated. The Dutch priest here gives sermons in Indonesian and Balinese. Farther north, about 10 minutes by car, is the village of Belimbingsari, a primarily Protestant community. Belimbingsari's **open-air church** mixes Balinese and Western architecture. ✉ *18 km (11 mi) northwest of Negara.*

★ **⑪ Pura Rambut Siwi.** The most important temple of the Jembrana district is Pura Rambut Siwi, or the Temple for Worshiping Hair. In the 16th century the Hindu priest Danghyang Nirartha arrived on the southwest coast of Bali from Java and began preaching Hinduism. He declared a spot near Medewi to be holy and donated some of his hair to the local villagers. They erected a temple on the edge of a cliff overlooking a dramatic black beach, and they buried Nirartha's hair in a sandalwood box inside. Steep steps lead past several small shrines down to the beach. At dusk, when the dying sun reflects on the black sand below, a sense of mystery settles over the ancient temple. ✉ *Yehembang,* ☎ *no phone.* 🎫 *Donation suggested.* ☺ *Daily sunrise–sunset. Sarong and sash required.*

⑯ Pura Taman Ayun. Built in the early 17th century, the Taman Ayun Temple was the state temple of the old Mengwi kingdom, which remained powerful until 1891. The temple is surrounded by a moat, and a series of garden terraces leads to its center. The Balinese can worship other sacred sites and temples here, and there are shrines to the holy mountains Agung, Batur, and Batukau, among others. Across from the temple a faded and not very well organized **museum** displays different types of ritual offerings. ✉ *Mengwi,* ☎ *no phone.* 🎫 *Donation suggested.* ☺ *Daily sunrise–sunset. Sarong and sash required.*

⑭ Puri Anyar. Krambitan's New Palace belongs to a branch of Tabanan's royal family that made the village its home in the 18th century. The family's members, like those of other royal families, have looked to tourism to keep up their lifestyle—here they even rent out rooms. The rooms are very basic, and guests eat the very traditional Balinese food that the family eats. Although it is not a very comfortable place to stay, it can be an interesting place to visit. An eccentric prince who is a painter lives in the compound, and he or someone else may be able to guide you around, but don't expect a very organized tour. (If you don't call first, nobody may be around to help you.) Try to time your visit so you can attend one of the traditional dinners, featuring a dance performance, held for tour groups. A nearby palace, **Puri Agung Wisata** (Palace of Big Tourism), is owned by the same family; you can visit it for a small donation. ✉ *Krambitan (7 km [4½] mi west of Tabanan),*

☎ 0361/812668. ✉ *Puri Anyar, free; Puri Agung Wisata, donation suggested.* ✆ *Call before visiting; traditional dinners start at 8 PM.*

⑮ Subak Museum. It's somewhat rundown and doesn't attract many visitors, but this museum is a worthwhile stop if you're interested in Bali's complex system of rice agriculture. A museum guide will gladly take you through the exhibits, which include artifacts and pictures of the farming tools, rituals, and architectural systems that are part of cultivating rice. Like everything in Bali, there are many levels, spiritual and physical, to rice agriculture, the heart of which is the *subak,* or rice farmers' collective. This museum was founded by Ida Bagus Mantra, a former governor of Bali, and opened in 1988. ✉ *Jl. Gatot Subroto, Tabanan,* ☎ 0361/810315. ✉ *Donation suggested.* ✆ *Daily 8–4:30.*

OFF THE
BEATEN PATH

YEH GANGGA BEACH – You can reach Yeh Gangga Beach by turning south off the main road between Tabanan and the road to Krambitan (a sign marks the turn). Follow the smaller road for about 20 minutes. From the Waka Gangga hotel or the Bali Wisata Bungalows you can access the beautiful black beach, which stretches all the way to Tanah Lot.

BEACHES

There are several stunning black-sand beaches in the west. However, most of them are only frequented by surfers and are too dangerous for swimming. One of the safest and most visited beaches is a narrow strip of beige sand that runs along the northwest coast, by the cluster of hotels near **Pemuteran.** Not especially beautiful, this beach is hardly worth a trip from the south. But if you're passing by and want to take a break, you may access the beach from almost any hotel—so long as you have a meal at the hotel restaurant.

Some travelers make the trip to **Candi Kusuma Beach,** which is 13 km (8 mi) west of Negara. Signs lead you off the main road to the beach, which is isolated and bare of normal beach facilities. The **black beach** near Pura Rambut Siwi rarely sees a tourist and is a nice place for an early or late picnic or a quick swim. (This is one of the only southwestern beaches where it is reasonably safe to go swimming.) Like at Candi Kusuama, there are no facilities or food stalls here, and you may be the only tourist around. **Medewi Beach** is fairly rocky near the two worn-down places to stay in town, but it stretches on for a while and is popular with a few surfers. **Balian Beach,** farther south, is accessible from Balian Beach Bungalows and the Sacred River Retreat. It's especially beautiful where it meets the mouth of the Balian River. Resist the temptation to go swimming; these waters have proved deadly in the past few years.

Yeh Gangga Beach is another black-sand beach with rough waters. The beach stretches on for quite a ways, and during low tide you can follow it all the way to Tanah Lot—a worthwhile adventure that takes about an hour. Ask for directions at either of the two hotels, Waka Gangga or Bali Wisata Bungalows; unless you're a guest you won't be given a guide.

DINING

Many of the dining establishments in western Bali are in hotels, most of which are in the northwest near Pemuteran. Hotel restaurants generally serve both Western and Indonesian fare, although some menus reflect the nationalities of expatriate managers or owners. Fish is the typical specialty on the west coast, and you'll usually find at least two or three fish dishes on the menu.

All the listed restaurants are connected to resorts and hotels and serve nonguests. To find out more about the ambience of these places or the facilities they have for overnight guests *see* Lodging, *below*. For general information and price categories, *see* Dining *in* Smart Travel Tips.

The Northwest

$$$$ ✕ **Matahari Beach Resort & Spa.** For a special night out, ditch your sarong, put on something a little more elegant, and head to the restaurant at the Matahari for some fine dining. This is as close as it gets to an international scene in western Bali. The German chef and resort manager, Thomas Kilgore, serves a fusion of Indonesian and European dishes made with fresh ingredients from the resort's private farms. With its great service and extensive wine list, this restaurant is a treat, especially if you've had your fill of *nasi goreng* (fried rice). You can dine inside or on the patio, and there is live entertainment almost every night. The buffet breakfast is an endless spread of home-cooked German breads, fresh fruit, yogurt, and cereal, but at $18 it's one of the most expensive in Bali. ✉ *Pemuteran,* ☎ *0362/92312. AE, DC, MC, V.*

$$ ✕ **Mimpi Menjangan Island.** There are two places to eat at this upscale dive resort. The main dining room, near the public hot springs of Banyuwedang, has a menu of Western and Indonesian dishes and serves three meals daily. At the smaller café, which sits on the water and looks out onto a bay of mangroves, snacks and light meals are served throughout the day. The view from here is especially beautiful at dusk—a great time to sip a drink and watch the colors of the sunset reflect in the shallow waters. The food at both places is not especially remarkable, but the service and atmosphere are friendly and relaxed. ✉ *Banyuwedang,* ☎ *082/8361088. AE, MC, V.*

$$ ✕ **Puri Ganesha Villas.** This secret getaway has an intimate restaurant that is well worth a visit for lunch or dinner. Each day a small chalkboard lists several appetizers and entrées, such as arugula and goat cheese salad, seafood risotto, pumpkin curry, and *gado-gado* (steamed vegetables with peanut sauce). Every dish is prepared simply, with fresh ingredients, and has at least one whimsical detail—like a serving of rice shaped into a heart. You might follow your meal with an Arak Attack, a special cocktail made by the owner's Balinese husband, or a dessert treat like sweet and crispy mango wontons. The atmosphere is as delightful as the cooking. Cozy tables out on a balcony, funky artworks, and atmospheric lighting set the mood. The British owner and hostess, Diana von Cranach, is usually on hand and full of information and gossip about the island. ✉ *Enter through driveway of Taman Sari hotel, Pemuteran,* ☎ *0362/93433. Reservations essential. AE, MC, V.*

$ ✕ **Taman Sari.** This popular hotel has a large beachside restaurant that serves up a wide variety of Western and Indonesian eats, from pizza to grilled vegetables to nasi goreng. This is a relaxed, friendly place to grab some lunch and sit in the sun. For dinner a Thai menu is offered, which accounts for its reputation as the best (well, only) Thai food spot in the west. ✉ *Pemuteran,* ☎ *0362/93264. MC, V.*

$ ✕ **Taman Selini.** Popular with the expats, this casual restaurant has well-prepared Greek fare (the owner is Greek), a rare treat on Bali. The Country Salad is a favorite, and the feta cheese tastes like the real thing. The menu, several pages long, also includes Western and Indonesian cuisine. Diners are cozy under a thatch roof a minute from the sea. Service can be erratic, but it's worth the wait. ✉ *Pemuteran,* ☎ *0362/93449. No credit cards.*

The Southwest

$$ ✕ **Waka Gangga.** If you are in the Tabanan area, the food alone makes it worth the trip down the bumpy little road that leads to this isolated resort on Yeh Gangga Beach. The restaurant is in an open-air thatch-roof building that looks out over the black beach and the Indian Ocean. Starters include a flavorful corn-and-tomato soup with lemon and a good selection of hearty salads. Western and Indonesian influences show up in entrées like barbecue spareribs and roasted baby tuna with lemongrass sauce. Service is attentive, especially because it is not uncommon to have the whole place to yourself. The wind can be fairly strong at night, so bring a sweater. ✉ *Jl. Pantai, Yeh Gangga,* ☎ *0361/416256. AE, MC, V.*

$ ✕ **Café Louisa.** This open-air vegetarian restaurant is part of the Sacred River Retreat (☞ Lodging, *below*), on the Gilimanuk-Denpasar highway at the eastern edge of the Jembrana region. Hospitable and small, with about five tables, Café Louisa serves a wide variety of soups and salads, as well as entrées of pasta, curry, and tempeh. Alcohol is not served here, but there are plenty of hydrating options: tea, juices, and sodas. Order the Sacred River Muesli cookies and take some to go; you won't find tasty cookies like these elsewhere in western Bali. If you are here for lunch, take the time for a walk along the Balian River to the nearby beach. During dinner the restaurant often hosts some form of entertainment, such as Balinese dancers or gamelan. ✉ *Lalang Linggah,* ☎ *0361/730904. No credit cards.*

LODGING

There is not a huge selection of places to stay in the rarely visited west, but within the last few years some unique, quality resorts have arrived, mostly in the northwest. These resorts bring western amenities like spa facilities, gourmet chefs, and air-conditioned rooms to an area that until recently had only a scattering of simple bungalow homestays. But, however tasteful, they also mean higher prices and the occasional tour-group invasion. The bungalow homestays remain, and the budget backpacker can still find places to stay for less than $10 a night, while the luxury-minded can spend up to $400 for a private villa.

The southwest is still fairly resort-free, although it may just be a matter of time. Since the rest of Bali is starting to be almost overbuilt, quite a few hotel investors are looking this way. For the moment, however, there are only a few surfer homestays. These offer the most basic type of lodging: somewhat decayed rooms with fans and the typical pancake breakfast. Most are found near the surfer hot spots, Balian Beach and Medewi Beach. Obviously you don't have to be a surfer to stay in one of these places, but they're not for the timid.

Most hotels and resorts listed in this chapter are worth stopping at for their restaurants alone; *see* Dining, *above,* for detailed reviews of the best hotel eateries. All rooms in the listed hotels have bathrooms with tubs and hot water, unless otherwise noted. For general information and price categories, *see* Lodging *in* Smart Travel Tips.

✎ *following the text of a review is your signal that the property has a Web site, where you will find details and, usually, images; for a link, visit www.fodors.com/urls.*

The Northwest

$$$$ ▥ **Puri Ganesha Villas.** No detail has been overlooked in making Puri
★ Ganesha an idyllic home away from home. Each of the four two-story thatch villas has two bedrooms, an open-air garden bathroom, mag-

A HOUSE IN BALI

FOR MORE THAN 400 YEARS BALI has been a magnet for explorers, traders, and utopia seekers. Early Portuguese and Dutch visitors came for the spices, slaves, and conquering. In the early 20th century the first tourists arrived, and some of them fell deeply in love with their surroundings. One of the first records of such a love affair is a book of photographs of the island published in Europe in 1920 by Gregor Krause. The book was entitled *Bali,* and it—along with a smattering of films of the Balinese people and their exotic culture shot in the 1920s and 1930s—captured the imagination of several Europeans and Americans, who then made their way to the island in search of paradise.

One of the most influential and well-known expatriates of Bali at this time was the German artist and musician Walter Spies. Having made his way to Bali from Java in 1927, he created a home in Campuhan, near Ubud. In his years there Spies collaborated with Balinese dancers, painters, and musicians; co-founded Pita Maha, the first Balinese association of artists; and was the center of a glamorous scene of Hollywood guests and other expats. He introduced the anthropologist Margaret Mead to many of her contacts and hosted everyone from Barbara Hutton to Charlie Chaplin in his two-story bungalow, now part of the Tjampuhan hotel (☞ Lodging *in* Chapter 3).

The 1930s was a golden age for expatriates in Bali. Westerners who took up residence in the country included the Belgian painter A. J. Le Mayeur de Merpres, who fell in love with and then married his muse, the famous Balinese dancer Ni Polok; Canadian composer and writer Colin McPhee, who wrote the noted book *A House in Bali;* and Mexican cartoonist Miguel Covarrubias and his wife, Rose. Then there was the eccentric K'Tut Tantri (also known as Manx), a woman who was "adopted" by one of the Balinese royal families and then took on a Balinese name. (Her exotic and inspiring autobiography, *Revolt in Paradise,* received much attention upon publication in the 1960s.) She and Robert and Louise Koke, an American expat couple, were the first to build hotels on Kuta Beach, in 1936. At first K'Tut Tantri and the Kokes were partners, but they soon went their separate ways, opening two rival but very similar hotels next to each other—Manx's Rooms-Bungalows and the Kuta Beach hotel. Both were visited by many high-society tourists before World War II (during which the hotels were destroyed). Robert Koke, a fan of surfing, is given some credit for creating the Kuta of today, a surfer's destination. The bungalow style of the hotels (as well as Walter Spies's house) was copied for years and still exists today.

All these romantic characters helped to draw others to Bali. Later expatriates moved into houses in Ubud and Kuta, particularly during the 1960s and 1970s. Lorne Blair, the monocle-wearing coauthor of the classic book *Ring of Fire* and director of the documentary of the same name—not to mention *Lempad of Bali*—was one of the more recent Ubud expat characters (he died in 1995). Many Westerners live in Bali today, although most are hotel managers and other business types. There are still some eccentric expats around trying to keep the romance alive in Bali and in their own imaginations. If you're lucky, you might meet one or two of them during your travels.

azines to read while lazing at the villa's private saltwater plunge pool, and straw hats to wear while sunbathing. The British owner, Diana von Cranach, is a former interior designer, and her personality is what makes Puri Ganesha so unique. Her philosophy is to keep it simple, but use the best—which means searching for the rawest Indonesian silk with which to decorate a bedroom, driving for hours to gather spices from an organic farm, and collecting "the Evian of Bali" water from a local mountain spring. Guests can take meals on their terrace overlooking the ocean or join other guests and the owner in the dining room. Breakfast is cooked to order by the butlers assigned to each villa. Puri Ganesha can arrange Ayurvedic cooking classes, spice and rice tours to mountain farms and lively local markets, and studies of Bali's Hindu culture. There is no sign on the main road to direct you here; you have to enter through the driveway of the Taman Sari hotel and continue past it to find Puri Ganesha. ⊠ *Taman Sari entrance road, Pemuteran 81155;* ☎ ⅨX *0362/93433;* ⅨX *0362/23635 for reservations. 4 villas. Restaurant, air-conditioning, beach, travel services, airport shuttle.* AE, MC, V. EP. ⊛

$$$–$$$$ 🏨 **Waka Shorea.** In the Bali Barat National Park, with views of nearby Menjangan Island, this isolated luxury safari resort is reachable only by boat. The individual raised bungalows have large four-poster beds, and the decor is somewhat tribal. Fans are used instead of air-conditioning, and the bathrooms have showers but no tubs. Simple, delicious meals are served outdoors near the pool or the ocean. Just before dusk you may see harmless wild boars wandering into the property looking for food. The focus here is on participating in nature, whether hiking, snorkeling at Menjangan Island, or boating. On a rainy or lazy day take advantage of the resort's spa. ⊠ *Jl. Raya Gilimanuk, Labuhan Lalang,* ☎ *082/8361448,* ⅨX *082/8361341. 14 bungalows, 2 villas. Restaurant, pool, spa, hiking, dive shop, snorkeling, boating, travel services. AE, DC, MC, V. BP.* ⊛

$$$ 🏨 **Matahari Beach Resort & Spa.** Originally intended to be a dive re-
★ sort, the Matahari now competes with the top luxury resorts in Bali. Thanks to managers Maja and Thomas Kilgore, the Matahari has a top restaurant, a luxurious spa, and an efficient staff. Sixteen two-room bungalows are hidden among tropical gardens. The rooms are all pretty similar; the larger or closer to the ocean the room, the more expensive it is. Each has elaborate Balinese-style four-poster beds, air-conditioning, a comfortable balcony, and a large bathroom with an outdoor shower. The clientele is a mix of nationalities, mostly European. You'll find guests relaxing by the pool, surrounded by frangipani and hibiscus trees; having a drink beachside; or getting a four-handed massage amid fountains and stone sculptures in the luxurious spa. The more active might go for a spin on a resort bicycle or take advantage of David's Dive Sport Center. For guests interested in activities that are more mental than physical, the resort has a gallery of Balinese art and gives classes in cooking, carving, and music. ⊠ *Pemuteran (Box 194, Singaraja),* ☎ *0362/92312,* ⅨX *0362/92313. 32 rooms. Restaurant, bar, air-conditioning, room service, pool, massage, spa, tennis court, exercise room, beach, dive shop, baby-sitting, travel services, free parking. AE, DC, MC, V. BP.* ⊛

$$–$$$$ 🏨 **Mimpi Menjangan Island.** The word *mimpi* in Indonesian means "dream." This new resort 15 minutes from Menjangan Island by boat is certainly worthy of its name. It is described as a "luxury dive resort"— it has extensive scuba facilities—but as many nondivers stay here as divers. The standard patio rooms, small but well equipped, are a good deal. The more expensive villas are breathtaking. Each has a small exotic courtyard and an outdoor tub filled with the waters of the nearby ancient hot springs. Some villas come with a private cold plunge pool, but the best have a view of the lagoon. The property includes several pools—one surrounded by lotus ponds, a dive pool, two hot-springs pools, and a children's pool—as well as a large new spa. You can also sign up for activities such as hiking in the Bali Barat National Park and kayaking around the mangrove bay. At the moment this is the only resort in Banyuwedang, but others may soon follow. ⊠ *Banyuwedang 81151,* ☎ *082/8362729,* 𝔽𝔸𝕏 *082/8362728. 30 rooms, 24 villas. Restaurant, bar, air-conditioning, minibars, room service, 5 pools, spa, dive shop, boating. AE, MC, V. BP.* 🐾

$–$$ 🏨 **Taman Sari.** One of the best deals in the area, Taman Sari offers rooms from simple to luxurious in beautiful landscaped gardens near the ocean. The suites are individual thatch bungalows with exotic details like small lily ponds, outdoor showers, and private daybeds. The Junior and Butterfly Superior suites have spacious second floors where guests can relax or dine in privacy; the deluxe and standard rooms are much more basic. Not all baths have tubs, so ask about this when you book. The hotel has on-site dive facilities and also offers hiking and a full-moon temple tour. The beachside restaurant serves up decent fare and is especially noted for its Thai dinner menu. ⊠ *Pemuteran 81155,* ☎ 𝔽𝔸𝕏 *0362/93264. 21 rooms, 8 suites. Restaurant, hiking, dive shop. MC, V. BP.*

$ 🏨 **Pondok Sari.** Pondok Sari was the first hotel in Pemuteran and still has many loyal return guests, but these days the place is somewhat faded and rundown. It does have the distinction of being the cheapest place to stay in the area. The decently sized rooms, in thatch-roof bungalows, have simple bamboo furniture; each has a shower-only bathroom. Lounge chairs sit on the small beach under the shade of several large trees. The restaurant's food is mediocre, but its setting is a relaxed spot near the ocean. A dive shop leads trips to Menjangan, although beginning divers should go next door to Reef Seen Aquatics or another of the more professional dive shops in the area. ⊠ *Pemuteran 81155,* ☎ 𝔽𝔸𝕏 *0362/ 92337. 20 rooms. Restaurant, air-conditioning (some), fans, beach, dive shop. AE, MC, V (3% extra charge to use a credit card). BP.*

$ 🏨 **Taman Selini.** Hidden between Reef Seen Aquatics and the Pondok Sari hotel, this is the most recent of Pemuteran's hotel offerings. The rooms are in small thatch-roof bungalows scattered among the gardens. The more expensive rooms have an extra netted outdoor daybed, but all have small balconies, outdoor bathrooms, and romantic four-poster beds. This is a quiet, relaxing place to stay, especially for couples, with nothing to do except read on the balcony and take walks along the beach. (Taman Selini means "Garden of the Moon.") Water activities are usually organized through Reef Seen. The Greek owner has obviously influenced the menu at the hotel's restaurant. ⊠ *Pemuteran 81155,* ☎ 𝔽𝔸𝕏 *0362/93449. 11 bungalows, 6 with outside daybed. Restaurant, air-conditioning, hiking, snorkeling, boating. MC, V. BP.*

The Southwest

$$$ 🏨 **Waka Gangga.** The Waka Group, which owns several resorts in Bali, ★ searches out properties that are unique and slightly out of the way. Waka Gangga is on Yeh Gangga Beach, an isolated black-sand beach on the Indian Ocean. The large bungalows have conical thatch roofs and small terraces with dramatic views of the water and rice fields. The centerpiece of each room is a large wooden bed shrouded in white mosquito netting, and the large open-air bathrooms have sunken tubs and indoor and outdoor showers. Only two of the bungalows are air-conditioned; the rest are fan-cooled. The resort's narrow pool is surrounded by comfortable wooden lounge chairs. Guests can take a break from sunbathing to visit the nearby spa or dine at the hotel restaurant, which serves a satisfactory mix of Western and Indonesian fare. Other than the few hotels near Tanah Lot, this is the only luxury resort in southwestern Bali. ⊠ *Jl. Pantai, Desa Sudimana, Yeh Gangga, Tabanan,* ☎ *0361/416256,* FAX *0361/416353. 10 bungalows. Restaurant, air-conditioning (some), room service, pool, spa, laundry service. AE, MC, V. BP.* 🐾

$ 🏠 **Bali Wisata Bungalows.** More than 25 years ago, when German businessman Peter Falkenberg was scouting out a place for a picnic, he came upon Yeh Gangga Beach and immediately put down money to lease the land. He built a house for himself and several bungalows to rent out to the occasional tourist. Yeh Gangga is still as isolated as it was then and is a great destination for the adventurous traveler who wants to see a part of Bali that most do not. The bungalows here are very basic but clean, with bamboo furniture, thatch roofs, bathrooms with showers, and manicured lawns. In the restaurant Peter's wife serves up good home-cooked Indonesian and Western fare. ⊠ *Yeh Gangga (Box 131, Tabanan),* ☎ *0361/2613654,* FAX *0361/812744. 12 bungalows. Restaurant, pool. No credit cards. BP.*

$ 🏠 **Sacred River Retreat.** This unique retreat where the Balian River runs into the ocean mainly draws people interested in studying meditation. The creation of an Australian jewelry designer and her Balinese husband, the Sacred River Retreat is also a quiet, interesting place to simply relax for a day or two. Small one- and two-story cottages are scattered down a slope among jungle gardens; several look out over a snake-shape pool. The interiors are simple, with large mosquito-netted beds and small terraces, and the property is adorned with mosaics. Meditation sessions take place each night in a small man-made cave (these are not mandatory). A yoga class is taught each morning, and a horse-riding teacher is available for instruction. The restaurant, Café Louisa (☞ *Dining, above*), serves good vegetarian cuisine. Ask for a tour of the owners' dramatic house, which must be one of the tallest private dwellings in Bali. ⊠ *Gilimanuk-Denpasar Hwy., Lalang Linggah,* ☎ *0361/814993,* FAX *0361/732165. 15 cottages. Restaurant, 2 pools, spa, laundry service, meeting rooms. AE, MC, V. BP.* 🐾

NIGHTLIFE AND THE ARTS

If you are looking for a nightlife scene, the west is not the place for you. Most of the tourists who escape here enjoy it for that reason. The only bar scene exists in the hotels—and the word *scene* is hardly appropriate (although before dinner the Matahari's bar may have more than a handful of visitors). Arts offerings are also limited; your best bet is to ask your hotel to inform you of any nearby religious celebrations.

In the town of Jembrana you can occasionally take in a performance of the bamboo-instrument ensemble called gamelan jegog. Ask around in Jembrana or Negara for information on festivals or where you can find a group practicing.

Matahari Beach Resort & Spa (⊠ Pemuteran, ☎ 0362/92312) has live entertainment in its restaurant a few nights a week. On Monday the local dance troupe from Reef Seen performs, and on other nights the restaurant might present a local band.

Puri Anyar (⊠ Krambitan, ☎ 0361/812668) hosts occasional dinnertime dance performances for tour groups. The palace is renowned for its Barong-Rangda dance performances, which take place after a typical Balinese buffet meal. The combined price for dinner and the dance performance is $30. Call in advance to find out when the next show will be.

Reef Seen Aquatics (⊠ Pemuteran, between the Matahari and Pondok Sari hotels, ☎ 0362/92339) presents a dance performance each Saturday night at 7:30. The dancers are quite young and not especially professional or polished, but that makes the experience all the more authentic, and sweet—like checking out a pageant at your local junior high school. They do a sampling of several classic Balinese dances and end with a *legong* dance, bringing in members of the audience to join in. The donation you make at the end of the show (required) goes to paying the dancers' teacher and enabling the program to continue.

OUTDOOR ACTIVITIES AND SPORTS

Many visitors come to western Bali for the area's great snorkeling and diving. In fact, there are almost as many dive shops in Pemuteran as there are resorts. Hiking through the Bali Barat National Park is another popular activity. Some resorts offer bikes and kayaks to guests, usually for free. Experienced equestrians can go for a ride at Pemuteran Stables, while the truly daring can try the bulls at the racetrack in Perancak.

Participant Sports

Hiking

Hiking in western Bali is best done with a guide, and guides for the Bali Barat National Park are best found at the park's office in Cekik. There are also guides available at Labuhan Lalang, but they are not official park rangers and may not be as knowledgeable about the local wildlife. Hikes are usually organized by the hour, with a typical trek taking about two hours—enough time to give you a feeling for the terrain and to spot a few monkeys and a barking deer. When hiking in western Bali outside the national park, arrange a guide through your hotel.

Horseback Riding

Pemuteran Stables (✉ Pemuteran, between the Matahari and Pondok Sari hotels, ☎ 0362/92339) is run by Chris Brown, owner of Reef Seen Aquatics. Rides last for either an hour ($25) or an hour and a half ($30). An introduction to horses and horse riding lasts an hour-and-a-half and costs $30. The office is open daily from 7:30 to 6. Morning rides should be booked at least a day in advance; afternoon rides need to be booked by 2 that day. The horses here can be a little wild, so this is not the place to take up riding. Bring long pants and sturdy shoes.

Hot Springs

Although the Mimpi Menjangan Island resort offers a chance to experience the **Banyuwedang hot springs** in relative luxury, a public bathing area exists nearby. Frequented mostly by the locals, the public baths are not especially remarkable, although Banyuwedang has been compared to well-known thermal spring waters like those in Baden-Baden and Vichy. The basic temperature is 46°C (115°F), and regular bathing here is said to improve mild skin inflammations and joint and muscle pains. You pay a minimal entrance fee of about 50¢, and you should bring a bathing suit.

Scuba Diving and Snorkeling

David's Dive Sport Center (✉ Matahari Beach Resort & Spa, Pemuteran, ☎ 0362/92312) has a full assortment of scuba equipment for rent. Divemasters are available to take you out; a one-tank dive costs $65.

Easy Divers (✉ Pemuteran, near Taman Sari and Pondok Sari hotels, ☎ no phone), owned by a Slovenian couple, is a very professional operation. A one-tank dive costs $30–$35, depending on the location.

Mimpi Menjangan Island (✉ Banyuwedang, ☎ 082/8362729) has a dive center that is a great place to get certified. The resort has the most extensive dive facilities in the west, including dive pools, classrooms, numerous course offerings, and a large, professional staff—and it's a short boat ride from Menjangan Island. A basic one-tank dive at Menjangan Island costs $40.

Reef Seen Aquatics (✉ Pemuteran, ☎ 0362/92339) rents out everything you need for a day of snorkeling or scuba diving and also offers introductory dives. A single local dive is $30; to dive Menjangan Island you have to sign up for a minimum of two dives ($70).

Spectator Sports

Mekepung

It's best just to watch this traditional sport, although tourists can attempt to race the bulls. The official mekepung track is in the village of Perancak. Call **Peanuts** (☎ 0361/754149), a nightclub in Kuta, for information. The owner of Peanuts, I Gusti Ngurah Hartono, is the track's developer.

WESTERN BALI A TO Z

Arriving and Departing

By Airplane

Bali's only air hub is Ngurah Rai International Airport, in Tuban in southern Bali, and all airline offices are there or in Sanur or Denpasar (☞ Southern Bali A to Z *in* Chapter 2). If you need to make or change plane reservations, your hotel can make arrangements with the airlines for you.

Because of the growth of luxury resorts in the northwest, a small airport called Letkol Wisnu has been built recently in the village of Sumberkima, near Pemuteran. If you're interested in chartering a small plane to western Bali from Ngurah Rai International Airport, contact the **Matahari Beach Resort & Spa** (✉ Pemuteran, ☎ 0362/92312). The cost is about $140 per hour per person. (Currently there's a maximum of three people.)

FROM THE AIRPORT

Most resorts in the west will pick you up at Ngurah Rai Airport as long as arrangements are made in advance. You'll generally be charged $60–$80 one-way, depending on the size of your group. The trip from the airport takes three to four hours to Pemuteran and less than two hours to Yeh Gangga.

By Ferry

Ferries run hourly between the port of Banyuwangi, in eastern Java, and Gilimanuk. The journey takes just a half-hour and costs about 50¢.

Getting Around

By Car

The only way to explore western Bali thoroughly is by car. However, there are no rental car companies in the west, so you should rent a car before you get to the region. In the north the closest place to rent a car is Lovina (☞ Northern Bali A to Z *in* Chapter 4). If you're coming from the south, you can rent a car at the airport or through one of the small agencies in the region (☞ Southern Bali A to Z *in* Chapter 2).

If you get into an accident—not an uncommon occurrence on the poorly maintained roads of the northwest—be aware that, no matter where the fault lies, as the tourist you will probably be blamed and have to dole out quite a bit of money.

By Taxi

There are no cabs in the west, but several of the resorts in Pemuteran can make arrangements for a car and driver. These drivers will take visitors on day trips to the Bali Barat National Park and other nearby points of interest.

By Bemo

As in the rest of Bali, *bemos* are the local form of transportation, and it is possible to find and hail the vanlike vehicles on the main roads from Pemuteran to Tabanan. Traveling by bemo is not easy, however, especially if you have bags.

Contacts and Resources

Banks and Currency Exchange

You'll find banks in the towns of Negara and Tabanan, and you can exchange money at most hotels. The only ATMs in western Bali are on Negara's main road, Jalan Ngurah Rai. There are no American Express offices in this part of Bali.

Emergencies

Hospital (✉ Singaraja [1 hr from Pemuteran], ☎ 0362/22573). **Police** (☎ 0362/92999).

English-Language Bookstores

There are no English-language bookstores in the region, although many of the resorts and hotels have small libraries.

Guided Tours

Jero Wijaya Tourist Service (✉ Jl. Andong 9X Andong, ☎ 0361/973172), near Ubud in eastern Bali, can organize an individually tailored trip to Bali Barat National Park for $60–$100.

I Gusti Ngurah Hartono, owner of the nightclub **Peanuts** (✉ Jl. Kuta, Kuta, ☎ 0361/754149) in southern Bali, leads tours to the bull-racing track in Perancak and the surrounding area.

Health and Safety

Be especially careful if you are driving your own car, because the roads of the northwest are in rather poor shape.

Telephones, Internet, and Mail

Phone connections in the west are weak and unpredictable. It's best to make phone calls, especially international ones, from your hotel. You don't need to dial the area code for local calls; for calls to other parts of Bali or Indonesia, dial the area code, including the 0 in front of it.

There are no cybercafés in the region, and most hotels won't let you check or send e-mail unless it's an emergency. Hotels and resorts are the only locations where you can mail letters and postcards or have your mail held.

Visitor Information

The **Jembrana Government Tourist Office** (✉ Jl. Dr. Setia Budi 1, Negara, ☎ 0365/41060) is useful for tracking down gamelan performances but otherwise has little tourist information to offer. Office hours are sporadic.

The **Bali Barat National Park headquarters** (✉ Cekik, ☎ 0365/61060) also serves as a tourist office. It's open daily from 8 to 3.

6 LOMBOK

Lombok and the Gili Islands are where all good divers and snorkelers go to heaven. The surrounding crystal sea contains more species of fish than the Great Barrier Reef, and the coastline is a paradise for anyone who wants an exclusive slice of silken sand. In southern Lombok the beaches are surrounded by craggy limestone cliffs that are perfect for hiking. Visitors find history in the antique treasure shops of Ampenan's Arab quarter, while the city's dusty streets ring with the hypnotic warbling prayer coming from a paint-peeled mosque.

By Denise
Dowling

Y OU CAN SEE BALI IN LOMBOK, but you can't see Lombok in Bali."
As this popular local expression suggests, although you won't
encounter Lombok culture in Bali, Balinese traditions are evident in Lombok. Comparisons between the neighboring isles are in-
evitable, but the differences are more evident than the similarities.
Central Lombok resembles Bali, with alluvial plains and fields irrigated
by water from the mountains, but the terrain around Kuta has the stark-
ness of the Australian outback, with mountains that frame translucent
turquoise cays. Lombok, a mere 45 km (27 mi) east of Bali, lacks the
crowds and commercialism of its neighbor. The island seems to exist
several decades back in time and indeed is often described as "Bali of
the 1970s."

Named for its well-known *lombok* (chili pepper), Lombok is home to
two peoples: Balinese Hindus, who ruled the island until 1894, and
Sasak Muslims. Most of the Balinese live on the island's western side
around Ampenan, Mataram (the capital of West Nusa Tenggara, which
includes Lombok and Sumbawa), and Cakranegara. Here you find interesting Balinese temples, though none as architecturally intricate as
those on Bali. The Sasaks, descendants of 18th-century invaders who
came to Indonesia from northern India centuries ago, live mainly in
Lombok's central and eastern regions and comprise the majority of the
island's population of 2.5 million. Traditionally, Sasaks were agricul-
turists and animists who practiced ancestor and spirit worship. Although
they're included in the country's census of Islamic peoples, their religious practices are more animist and Hindu than Muslim, with the exception of the orthodox Muslim sect known as Wektu Lima. Although
the Wektu Lima (Five Prayers) sect stringently follows the guidelines
of Islam, the island's other Sasak sect, Wektu Telu (Three Prayers), practices a religion that mixes the elements of several beliefs.

Islam was first introduced on Lombok from Java in the 16th century.
In the 18th century the Balinese conquered western Lombok, aided by
the prime minister of a Sasak kingdom. And then in 1894, following
a Sasak revolt, the Dutch invaded Lombok on the pretext of restoring
order—despite previously pledging, in a signed treaty with the Balinese rulers of Lombok, never to annex the island. The Balinese were
worthy opponents, but after numerous battles the Dutch prevailed. The
Sasaks, who had requested Dutch intervention, found themselves ruled
by new masters far more severe than the Balinese. Indonesia finally gained
its independence from the Dutch in 1949, and Lombok was incorpo-
rated into the province of Nusa Tenggara, which includes more than
560 islands—from Sumbawa, Komodo, Sumba, Timor, and Flores to
some so tiny they remain nameless.

The island's economy still relies primarily on agriculture, although the
government is working to cultivate a thriving tourist industry. Common occupations are tobacco farming, cattle raising, and fishing.
Brightly painted fishing boats troll the waters early and late in the day;
after dark the fishermen lower their nets and use pressure lanterns to
attract schools of fish, and their boats become a flotilla of water candles. The majority of locals are subsistence farmers, constantly threat-
ened with land shortages and insufficient water supplies. A
transmigration program even ships some of the island's excess population to underpopulated islands. Poverty, drought, and bouts of famine
are the underbelly of this beautiful island.

Lombok remained free of the religious and political conflicts that led
to violence and looting in other parts of Indonesia at the end of the

20th century. However, in January 2000 rioting broke out in central Lombok after extremist Muslims incited people to attack Chinese Christians as a protest against the deadly violence happening in the Moluccas. The rioting lasted for only three days, and no further disturbances occurred, but the incident took a toll on the tourist industry. The island was deserted following the riots, making Lombok even more of a haven from the masses of tourists that inundate Bali. Several months later tourists started trickling back, but it will be a while before you'll need reservations at any local restaurant.

With a predominantly Muslim population, Lombok has a fairly conservative culture. Strolling around in a bikini and sarong will get you the deep-freeze; keep your shoulders and legs covered for a warmer reception. Compared with the quick smiles and joking manner of the Balinese, the people of Lombok seem reserved. It is often up to the tourist to initiate contact; knowing a few Indonesian greetings helps to thaw the ice. Like the Balinese, Sasaks dote on their kids, and acknowledging local children with a smile can ingratiate you to the shyest mother. Because poverty is a chronic problem in Lombok and tourism is a fairly new industry, there is a degree of wariness toward the *orang putih* (white people) with the fat wallets, which takes some getting used to if you've just been in Bali. Public outcrys and aggressive haggling from a foreigner are frowned upon, so remember that an argument over 10,000 rupiah is an argument over the price of a soda in the United States.

The rewards for dealing with Lombok's conservative culture and somewhat primitive accommodations and transportation include beachs that are often superior to Bali's (and which you may have all to yourself), traditional villages where time seems to have stopped centuries ago, and a dramatic contrast to Bali's lush terrain. To unlock the island's treasures, venture away from Senggigi's beach resorts. And don't leave without making the jaunt to one of the Gili Islands: as the outrigger, puttering through the brilliant blue water, approaches the silvery palm-fringed beach, you'll find yourself wishing for a shipwreck.

EXPLORING LOMBOK

A Good Tour

Many of Lombok's most visited temples, villages, and museums are clustered on the west coast; a few attractions lie farther east in central Lombok, and a handful are on the southern route to Kuta. The far-eastern and northern coasts are not easily accessible, and accommodations there are spartan. To reach many of the island's sights, it's helpful to have a four-wheel-drive vehicle, preferably with a local guide or driver.

Numbers in the text correspond to numbers in the margin and on the Lombok map.

Most people arrive via boat or plane in the tri-city of Mataram–Ampenan–Cakranegara. For your first couple of days stay in the Senggigi resort area, which makes a perfect base for day trips to other parts of Lombok. Even though the tri-city area is very spread out, with only a few attractions that are within walking distance of one another, you can still reach most of the temples and attractions in one day. A good starting point in the capital of Mataram is the **Museum Negeri Nusa Tenggara Barat** ①. After this introduction to Lombok's traditional crafts, hop in a vehicle and head east to Cakranegara to stroll through the palatial grounds of the former Balinese court, **Taman Mayura** ②. It's a quick walk southwest on Jalan Selaparang to Jalan Hanoman, where you'll find **Pura Meru** ③, with three courtyards of Hindu shrines. Drive 10 km (6 mi) east to **Narmada Taman** ④, where you can paddle a swan-shape boat around a lagoon made to look like the lake at Gunung Rinjani. From Narmada head north for 3 km (2 mi) to reach Batu Kumbung, where there's even more water—a creek purported to have healing powers. Continue west to **Pura Lingsar** ⑤, where two factions worship different gods under the same roof. To the east is **Pura Suranadi** ⑥, with its pools of holy eels.

The next day plan to explore the sights south of the tri-city. From Mataram take Jalan Bung Karno south for 5 km (3 mi) to Telagawaru; then head west on Jalan Nyamarai for 3 km (2 mi) to arrive at **Gunung Pengsong** ⑦ for some hiking and views. After your hike drive south on Jalan Ketejer and then east on Jalan Banyumulek to reach **Banyumulek** ⑧, where you can buy a water flask and cool off. It's a 20-minute drive southeast, on the main road through Kediri, to the weaving village **Sukarara** ⑨ and another 10 minutes, on the road through Praya, to **Penujak** ⑩, where potters use paddles to shape gray clay. From here drive another 20 minutes southeast to reach **Rambitan** ⑪ and **Sade** ⑫. Take the coastal route for scenic views on the hour-long drive back to Ampenan.

On your third day start off in Ampenan and drive north on Jalan Saleh Sungkar. Just north of Dayen, take the dirt road west to the beach temple of **Pura Segara** ⑬. Continue north on the coastal road, and as you near Senggigi, look for **Pura Batu Bolong** ⑭ perched on a cliff over the sea. It's a hilly drive of 65 km (40 mi) to **Bayan** ⑮, where you'll find the oldest religious structure on Lombok. From Bayan you can drive 8 km (5 mi) south to the village of Senaru Bayan and then walk for a half-hour to reach the waterfall **Sendang Gila** ⑯. Bayan is also a viable starting point to begin a climb of **Gunung Rinjani** ⑰, which will take 2–3 days, depending on your route.

On your way back from the Bayan area, stop in Tanjung on the northwestern coast and spend the night at the Oberoi resort (☞ Lodging, *below*). The next morning, head to Bangsal Harbor and catch a boat to Gili Trawangan. End your trip here, lazing about in the sun for a couple of days before returning home.

TIMING

This tour would take at least seven days to complete, even with your own vehicle, though you can shorten it by omitting the Gunung Rinjani climb. If you prefer a more leisurely pace, plan for two days to explore the tri-city area. If serious shopping is on the agenda, you'll want a full extra day to visit just the crafts villages south of Mataram. Taking public transportation to all the sites would require a few more days due to what the Indonesians call "rubber time": the elasticity of schedules, with buses, ferries, and planes frequently being late or canceled. Hiring a guide or four-wheel-drive vehicle and driver is the most time-efficient way to see the island. A local will know the layout of the roads, which can seem like a maze to foreigners.

With only a few days you could do an island-sampler-type itinerary: one day exploring the crafts villages in the south-central area near Kuta, another day living it up at a Senggigi resort, and a third day snorkeling or diving at the Gili Islands, with their picture-perfect beaches that cry out for a postcard to the boss. Instead of a tour of all three Gilis, choose one and stay a couple of days. Pretend you're stranded.

Central and Southern Lombok

Most visitors are introduced to Lombok by way of Ampenan, Cakranegara, and Mataram—the string of towns that make up the most populated area on this island. Each settlement has a separate function:

Ampenan, to the west, is the decaying port where travelers arrive by ship, ferry, and hydrofoil; Cakranegara, Lombok's former capital, is a trading center; and Mataram is the island's administrative core and the site of Lombok's airport. Although most tourists scurry from the city and head to Senggigi, this population center merits exploring. Ampenan's Arab and Chinese quarter is a labyrinth of narrow, crooked streets lined with antiques shops. In Cakranegara you can watch working weavers, who still use foot-powered looms, and get a history lesson while touring a Balinese temple.

Only about 25 km (16 mi) southeast of Mataram but years back in time is Praya, where villages of thatched palm have been constructed on hilltops to defend against thieves. Surrounded by fields of sweet potatoes and Muslim graveyards of small upright stones, Praya has a Saturday market that draws craftspeople from surrounding villages to sell their wares.

Due south of Praya, on the Indian Ocean, Kuta was once a tiny village. It's still a quiet town, but that may soon change: at press time the beach was slated to be the site of several new luxury hotels, though property disputes mean that construction has remained on rubber time. White crescent beaches with coconut trees for shade stretch out to the east and west of Kuta. If you hurry, you might have a beach to yourself.

Sights to See

⑧ Banyumulek. This town is famous for its earthenware. Its main street is lined with shops selling engraved and textile-covered vases as well as traditional urns and water flasks. Come in the morning if you want to watch potters at work. A fun way to get here is by horse cart from Lembar, on the western coast. ⊠ *2 km (1 mi) west of main road from Mataram to Lembar, 6 km (4 mi) south of Mataram.*

⑦ Gunung Pengsong. Mt. Pengsong gives you two views for the price of one hike. In the early morning you can see the majestic Gunung Rinjani from the peak; by late afternoon Bali's highest mountain, Gunung Agung, is visible in the distance (a panorama of rice fields is ever present). As you climb a concrete staircase to the mountain's **shrine**, bold monkeys chatter for a church offering. An altar holds a large egg-shape stone, symbolizing fertility. If you visit in the spring, ask about the Bersih Dasa ceremony to honor Dewi Sri, the rice goddess, which occurs following the harvest in March or April. Nonworshiping visitors can watch the ritual, during which a water buffalo is led to the top and sacrificed. ⊠ *Jl. Gajah Mada, 6 km (4 mi) south of Mataram,* ☎ *no phone.* 🎫 *Donation required.* ⊘ *Daily sunrise–sunset.*

★ ① Museum Negeri Nusa Tenggara Barat. The Museum of West Nusa Tenggara has intriguing exhibits of island weaponry, decorative arts, and artifacts. If you plan on shopping for antiques, this is a good place to get acquainted with the real thing. ⊠ *Jl. Panji Tilar 6, Ampenan,* ☎ *0370/637503.* 🎫 *25¢.* ⊘ *Tues.–Sun. 8–2, Fri. until 11 AM.*

★ ④ Narmada Taman. Lombok's most famous temple-palace complex, Narmada Park, was built in 1727. The architecture is an interesting mix of Hindu, Islamic, and Sasak, but the temple is most notable for its man-made **lagoon**, a miniature replica of Segara Anak, the lake that fills the interior of Gunung Rinjani in northern Lombok. The faithful say the replica's purpose was to permit an aging king to fulfill his religious obligations—tossing offerings into the mountaintop lake—when he became too old to make the climb. More likely it was built so the monarch could spy on the maidens washing in the pool and choose the fairest for his concubines. The site is now secular; you can get a

Gili Islands

Bali Sea

N

Blue Coral
■ Area

■ **Lighthouse**

Telephone■

*Gili
Trawangan*

*Danau
Meno*

*Gili
Meno*

■ **Snorkeling**
■ **Coral Garden**
Area

*Gili
Air*

Telephone■

Hospital
Telephone■

■ **Pearl
Farm**

0   1 mile

0   2 km

Bali Sea

Selen

Kayangan

**Gili Islands
see detail map**

Gondang

■ **Tiu Pupas
Waterfall**

Tanjung
Sokong

Gn. Bangketaji

*Gn.
Mursatas*

Gn.

Gn. Buc

Bangsal

Pemenang

Bt. Jangkar

▲ *Bt.*

**Monkey
Forest**

Gn. Duduk

Senggigi

Senggigi

Pura Batu Bolong

*Gn.
Pusuk*

▲ *Bt. Peluntak*

*Gn.
Sebiris*

Gn. Masjidbor ▲

Gn. Muteran

*Gn.
Meninting*

Gn. Pelola

Bt.

B

Bt.

14

S E L A T   L O M B O K

(L O M B O K

S T R A I T)

Pura Segara

13

Gunungsari

Mambalan

Ampenan

Pura Lingsar

Mataram

5

Pura S

6

Batukumbung

Museum Negeri Nusa Tenggara Barat

1

Cakranegara

Pura Meru

2 **Taman Mayura**

3

Sweta

4

Narmada

Narmada Tam

Gunung Pengsong

7

8 **Banyumulek**

Kediri

Jagaraga

Pringgarata

Sukarar

9

TO
BALI

Gili Anyaran

Gili Rengit

Gili Layar

Gili Asahan

**Bangko-
Bangko**

Bangko-Bangko

Gn. Gua ▲

Gili Nanggu

Gili Tangkong

Gili Nanggu

*Gili
Sudak*

Gerung

Lembar

Penu

10

*Gili
Gede*

Sekotong Indah

Sekotong Barat

Sekotong Timur

Ungga

Pelangan Barat

Sekotong Tengah

▲ *Gn. Mereje*

▲ *Gn. Raruna*

Gn. Marmadi ▲

Montongsapah

Gn. Tebuik

▲

KEY

1 Exploring Sites

Beaches

Ferry

Gn. Blongas ▲

*Gili
Wayang*

Gn. Panggang ▲

*Gili
Sarang*

Gn. Bremi

*Gili
Kawu
Anakewok*

Gili Batupayung

**Selong
Blanak**

Gn. Barbojot

Mawun

*Gn.
Pengulu*

*Gil
Nu*

Mawun

Are Goleng

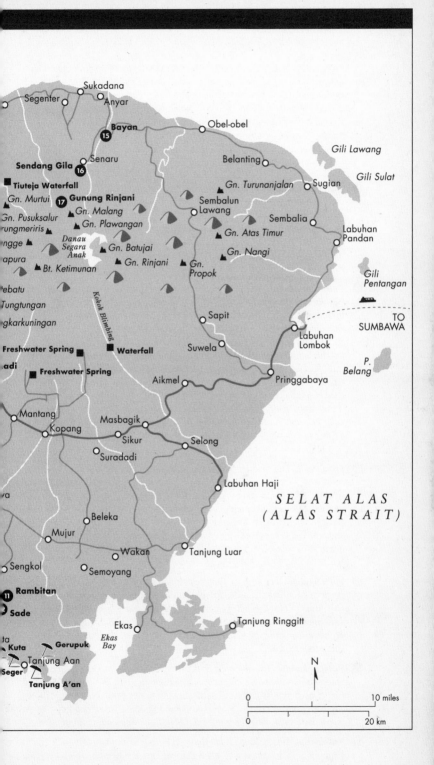

Sukadana
Segenter
Anyar
Bayan
15
Obel-obel
Belanting
Gn. Turunanjalan
Gili Lawang
Gili Sulat
Sugian
Sendang Gila
Senaru
16
Labuhan
Pandan
■ **Tiuteja Waterfall**
▲*Gn. Murtui*
17 **Gunung Rinjani**
Sembalun
Lawang
Sembalia
▲ *Gn. Malang*
Gn. Pusuksalur
▲ *Gn. Plawangan*
▲ *Gn. Atas Timur*
rungmeriris ▲
Danau
ngge ▲
Segara
▲ *Gn. Batujai*
▲ *Gn. Nangi*
Anak
apura ▲
Gili
Pentangan
▲ *Bt. Ketimunan*
▲ *Gn. Rinjani*
Gn.
Propok
ebatu
Tungtungan
gkarkuningan
Sapit
TO
SUMBAWA
P.
Belang
Suwela
Labuhan
■ Freshwater Spring ■ **Waterfall**
Lombok
adi
Aikmel
Pringgabaya
■ **Freshwater Spring**
Mantang
Masbagik
Kopang
Sikur
Selong
Suradadi
Labuhan Haji
va
SELAT ALAS
(ALAS STRAIT)
Beleka
Mujur
Wakan
Tanjung Luar
Sengkol
Semoyang
11 **Rambitan**
Sade
Ekas
Tanjung Ringgitt
ta
Ekas
Kuta **Gerupuk**
Bay
Tanjung Aan
Seger
Tanjung A'an

N

0   10 miles

0   20 km

beer, paddle a swan-shape boat around the lake, or take a dip in the public swimming pool. ⊠ *Jl. Air Awet, Madan, Narmada (10 km [6 mi] east of Cakranegara),* ☎ *0370/672490.* 🎟 *10¢.* ⊙ *Daily 8–5.*

OFF THE
BEATEN PATH   **BATU KUMBUNG –** This rarely visited Sasak village near Narmada is locally famous for its music ensemble and dance troupe, both of which perform at weddings and other celebrations, and its creek, reputed to possess healing powers. You can watch ikat being woven on back-strap looms, and although the villagers are shy, no one will gape at you. Because it's not as visited as other traditional villages on the tourist circuit, Batu Kumbung has less of a Disneyland feel. ⊠ *Jl. Batu Kumbung, 3 km (2 mi) north of Narmada.*

⑩ Penujak. In this village lovely terra-cotta *gerabah* pottery is created from red clay; it is molded by hand, using a paddle but no wheel. This is where Sasaks purchase immense water containers and tourists buy smaller, more portable pitchers. Cruise the main street to get a sense of design, selection, and quality. You'll also find *gentong* (clay vessels used for food storage), *jangkih* (traditional stoves), and wooden masks here. ⊠ *6 km (4 mi) south of Praya.*

★ ⑤ Pura Lingsar. Built in 1714 by the first immigrant Balinese, Lingsar Temple was reconstructed in 1874 as a symbol of unity with Sasak Muslims. Hindus and Muslim followers of the Wektu Telu tradition worship on separate levels. The facade is showing its age, but with two levels the ornate temple is the most striking model of religious architecture on the island. An **eel pool** is fed by the spring waters of Gunung Rinjani; legend has it that if you drop in an egg in and an eel surfaces to eat it, you'll have good fortune. In late November or early December the temple is the sight of the Pujawali ritual, the highlight of which is a full-moon food fight, with Sasaks and Balinese pelting each other with *ketupat,* leaf-wrapped grenades of steamed rice. ⊠ *Jl. Lingsar, 5 km (3 mi) northwest of Narmada,* ☎ *no phone.* 🎟 *Donation suggested.* ⊙ *Daily 8–6.*

③ Pura Meru. The Multiroof Temple is the largest Balinese temple on Lombok. It was constructed in 1720 in an attempt to unite the island's various Hindu factions by giving them a central place to gather for festivals. Look for the scenes depicting stories from the *Ramayana.* The temple is arranged around three courtyards filled by 33 multitier shrines. The three most important—those to Siva, Vishnu, and Brahma—are in the central courtyard. ⊠ *Jl. Hanoman and Jl. Pejanggik, Cakranegara,* ☎ *no phone.* 🎟 *10¢.* ⊙ *Daily 8–5.*

⑬ Pura Segara. The Segara Temple rests on a black-sand beach. The view is more of a lure than the temple itself, although it is brightly colored in imitation of the *jukung* (fishing boats) that dock here with their wing sails outstretched. ⊠ *Just north of Ampenan; take dirt track west off Jl. Saleh Sungkar,* ☎ *no phone.* 🎟 *10¢.* ⊙ *Open daily sunrise–sunset, but often locked.*

⑥ Pura Suranadi. Indonesians and foreigners alike make pilgrimages to the lush hillside town of Suranadi, where an ancient temple is nestled into a garden with Balinese baths. Spring-water pools (not for bathing) are filled with eels; the waters and the fish are considered holy. ⊠ *Jl. Raya Suranadi,* ☎ *no phone.* 🎟 *Donation required.* ⊙ *Daily 8–6.*

⑪ Rambitan. In this town a *lumbung* (rice barn) sits next to each traditional Sasak house. Try to get a glimpse inside a house, which has two main areas: the outer area is where the men sleep, and the inner one is reserved for the women. A few of the villagers sell batik sarongs at surprisingly low prices. ✉ *Just north of Sade, 8 km (5 mi) north of Kuta.*

⑫ Sade. This village has been declared a historic preservation area. It still has many traditional thatch-and-bamboo homes with palm-leaf walls and bonnet-capped lumbung, symbols of pre-Western Sasak culture. The village is a pit stop on every package tour, and a fleet of little boys serve as escorts and architectural guides, explaining the buffalo dung foundations of each house. Women sell ikat in weaver cooperatives lining the main street, but you'll still be pestered to buy ikat—or to photograph people for a price. ✉ *6 km (4 mi) north of Kuta.*

⑨ Sukarara. Its fame as a traditional textile center has made Sukarara something of a theme park—the costumed weavers at the looms in front of the shops are just for show, as the real weaving is done in the villages—but it's *the* place to see the creative, colorful works of Lombok artisans. It's fascinating to see ikat being woven on hand-and-foot looms and to watch the process of resist dyeing, a batik technique that involves drawing patterns in dye-resistant wax on fabric, dyeing the fabric, then stripping off the wax to expose the undyed areas. The village is home to several weaving showrooms and shops, all on raised wooden platforms. Bring your camera and a wallet; these weavers are also dexterous sellers, and prices are better than you'll find in the cities. ✉ *6 km (4 mi) northwest of Praya.*

② Taman Mayura. Once a water palace that served the Balinese court, Mayura Park has a large artificial pool filled with lotus plants. In the pool's center sits **Bale Kambang,** a floating pavilion similar to the one in Klungkung, Bali, but smaller and less ornate. The park includes Western playground equipment, of all things. ✉ *Jl. Selaparang, Cakranegara,* ☏ *no phone.* ▨ *15¢.* ⊘ *Daily 8–5.*

Northern Lombok

The narrow, curving strip of sand that is Senggigi was once a backpackers' escape from Bali's crowded beaches. Inexpensive accommodations are still available, but luxury resort hotels dominate the beach. Senggigi is a pleasant place to relax, but it's no longer a quiet hideaway. Mangsit, just north of Senggigi, is the place to stay if you want a respite from "downtown." Although new hotels continue to creep northward, Mangsit remains a bucolic hamlet of secluded sand and bovine farmland.

For sweeping vistas don't miss the coastal drive from Senggigi to Bangsal Harbor, where boats set off for the Gili Islands. The twisting road snakes past a river and bands of monkeys, with a view of coconut groves and candy-color boats bobbing in emerald cays.

Sights to See

⑮ Bayan. The area around this traditional village is notable for its tall spade-shape houses and rice barns. The settlements here are small, quiet clusters of life where men till the fields and women create beautiful textiles. Bayan is thought to be the birthplace of the island's indigenous Wektu Telu religion (the less stringently Muslim of the island's two Sasak sects). Wektu Telu followers live on the north side of the town's road, and orthodox Muslims live on the south. Bayan's classic three-tier Javanese **mosque** stands on a stone platform; it is said to be more than three centuries old, which would make it Lombok's oldest religious structure. The village's gamelan orchestra performs only on Muhammad's birthday and refuses to be coaxed into playing at any other time. ✉ *Mosque: Jl. Raya Bayan.* ▨ *Mosque donation required.* ⊘ *Mosque daily 8–6.*

★ ⑰ **Gunung Rinjani.** The third-highest mountain in Indonesia, after Puncak Jaya (16,564 ft), in Irian Jaya, and Kerinci (12,600 ft), in Sumatra, the 12,221-ft Mt. Rinjani is one of the most revered, and feared, summits in the country. It's revered because, like Bali's Gunung Agung, it's considered sacred, a place of the gods; it's feared because the mountain still occasionally shudders and spews fiery lava. Its beauty is stark and magnificent, a smoldering peak against blue sky and ocean, with the green crescent of **Danau Segara Anak** (Lake Child of the Sea) shimmering below the peak. The trek up the slope is breathtaking, both for the natural views and village scenes as well as for the physical effort.

Anyone in reasonable shape should be able to hike to the crater rim and down to the lake. However, you'll need stamina and experience to reach the summit of Rinjani. The trail to the rim begins at a settlement called Senaru, 8 km (5 mi) up the mountain from Bayan. The well-marked trail begins to the left of a small hotel, Bale Bayan Senaru, and winds through lush forest. Not far from the trail head a government office sells the first required permit for about 25¢; farther along the trail a forestry office sells the second permit you'll need, for around 50¢. This route winds from the village at 2,820 ft (some maps mark it "Position I") to a rest stop at 5,150 ft and then another stop at 7,544 ft. Each stop has a primitive shelter pavillion, but none offers much shelter for staying the night, so bring a tent. After the third rest position, the incline is steep up to the rim at 8,640 ft. Plan for around seven hours of hiking and an overnight unless you are in bionic shape.

After climbing to the rim, you can descend into the crater to the lake, Segara Anak, at 6,560 ft. The path is very steep and requires nimble steps, but upon arrival you'll be rewarded with a soak in the lake or in the hot springs along its shores. If you want to hike to Rinajni's summit, you'll exit a different route to a site called Plawangan II, at 9,512 ft; from here you can reach the peak in about seven hours, but you'll need a guide to lead the way.

Most trekkers plan on a three-day journey from Senaru, taking one day to explore nearby hot springs and falls—including ☞ **Sendang Gila**—hiking up to the crater the next, and returning the same way on the third day. You should take comfortable hiking boots, warm layers, a sleeping bag, a tent, a stove, cooking utensils, and a flashlight, most of which you can rent from the *losmen* (small hotels) that abound in Senaru and nearby Batu Koq. Stock up on foodstuffs and water in Mataram, where there's more variety and prices are lower. If you are just climbing from Senaru to the rim or to the lake, you won't need a guide—unless you want to lighten the load. Guides often act as porters, helping to cook and carry your food; you can hire a guide in Senaru for about $2 to $3 a day. If you'd rather not do the hike on your own, several outfitters arrange organized treks (☞ Guided Tours *in* Lombok A to Z *below*).

⑭ **Pura Batu Bolong.** As you approach Senggigi from Mataram, you'll spot the Rock with a Hole Temple from the road. Perched above the ocean on a huge outcrop that does, indeed, have a natural hole in it, the temple faces west toward Gunung Agung and the sunset. It is said that in ancient days beautiful maidens were tossed into the sea as divine sacrifices, reason enough for residents to claim that sharks haunt these waters. ⊠ *Jl. Saleh Sungkar, Senggigi, just south of Senggigi Beach,* ☎ *no phone.* ⊡ *10¢.* ☉ *Daily 8–5.*

★ ⑯ **Sendang Gila** (Sindanggile). In this Edenic setting water pours over the hillside and culminates in 80-ft-high falls that flow into the river,

Kokok Putih. It's cool and shady here, even during the hottest part of the day, making it a nice place for a picnic; if you can stand icy water, take a dip in the jade pool. From Senaru Bayan the falls are a half-hour walk on an unmarked path through the woods and along an irrigation canal; you can ask for directions at the Bale Bayan Senaru hotel. ⊠ *Senaru Bayan, 8 km (5 mi) south of Bayan.* 🔄 *50¢.* ⊘ *Daily sunrise–sunset.*

The Gili Islands

A 30-minute drive north of Senggigi brings you to the Bangsal ferry dock, near Pemeneng, where a small boat will zip you across to one of three islets, known collectively as the Gili Islands. Most losmen on the islands rent snorkeling equipment, and dive trips can be arranged through various operators. Bring cash to the Gilis: credit cards are rarely accepted, and traveler's checks can be difficult to exchange. Also bring plenty of sunscreen and a hat, as the islands don't offer much shade.

Gili Air is closest to shore and requires only a quick 20-minute sea crossing in a motorized *prahu* (outrigger). Here dazzling white sand meets crystal-clear water, and the coral reef dances with brightly colored tropical fish. The atmosphere is calm and uncluttered, the scenery simple and rural. It's a great place to clear your head.

The next atoll out, Gili Meno, has even more pristine waters and a greater abundance of sea life—red-lined triggerfish, starfish, five-lined damsel, and the occasional shark—and for scuba divers, unique blue coral awaits 50–80 ft below the surface. The best snorkeling is off the island's northeast coast; just inland from the west coast is a large salt lake, which is interesting to see, though no recreational activities are allowed. This is the quietest island, which makes it popular with families, and it has earned its place as a divers' haven. Its accommodations and restaurants are basic, but that's part of its charm.

Gili Trawangan, the farthest from Lombok (about an hour by boat), is the party island. Sybarites sunbathe topless on the beach, and longhaired locals are especially friendly to Western women.

BEACHES

The sea around Lombok melts into jeweled hues of emerald, jade, sapphire, and turquoise and is dotted with coral. Kuta has crescent-shape beaches with sand as fine as birdseed; as if the luminescent sea and beach weren't enough, all of it is surrounded by limestone cliffs and creek-fed rice fields. At Kuta's Putri Nyale Beach you can watch locals navigate the reef at low tide to collect *trepang,* a type of sea cucumber. Some of the southwestern beaches are not that conducive to swimming because they're shallow and rocky, but the Gili Islands have coconut palms and calm, clear water in which you can float on your back and dream of early retirement.

Are Goleng. Villagers' huts line this stretch of land behind the bay, but you can venture west through the coconut groves for more privacy. To reach the beach from Kuta, take the main paved road west. One mile out of Kuta, take the dirt track next to a MTM 64 sign; after 2 km (1 mi) you'll spot the seaweed beds in the shallows.

Bangko-Bangko. Surfers flock to this beach, which is part of a forest reserve. It can be reached by jeep or minibus. To get here from Lembar, take the road that rounds the harbor; after 20 km (12 mi) you'll reach a T junction at Sekotong. The road to the right runs along the coast of Lombok's southwestern peninsula and eventually leads to this beach. Nearby is Desert Point, one of the most popular surf breaks off Lombok.

Gerupuk. This small fishing village is a popular surf spot, and buyers from major hotels come here just to purchase lobster. You can charter a canoe or outrigger to cross the bay to Bumbang, a quaint fishing village on the eastern shore. This beach is easy to reach, even without a rugged vehicle. From Kuta head southeast, keeping to the paved roads, for nearly 10 km (6 mi) to reach the western shores of Gumbang Bay.

Gili Nanggu. If you've ever craved abandonment on a desert island, now you can have it. For around $5 you can charter a prahu from Lembar Harbor for the 10-minute ride to little Gili Nanggu. The crescent-shape beach here is empty of peddlers and other tourists. For fun you can rent a canoe or sailboat from a local fisherman.

Kuta. Also known as Putri Nyale, this beach extends alongside the coastal road to Tanjung A'an. Each year in February or March Kuta Beach is the scene of a fertility festival that draws thousands.

Mawun. Off the road between Kuta and Selong Blanak, this beach is sheltered by hills that are perfect for climbing and taking in the view.

Seger. About 2 km (1 mi) east of Kuta, a huge rock called Batu Kotak affords panoramic views of the countryside if you climb it in the morning. The waves at the beach here can be challenging, so it's not much of a swimming place.

Selong Blanak. This beach is worth a trip just for the drive through volcanic foothills and past valleys of premodern Sasak agriculture. The beach sits among coconut groves in a lake-shape bay between two hills. The best way to get here is by motorcycle, jeep, or minibus, as the roads are unpaved and rough. Travel west from Kuta for 10 km (6 mi); turn left at the sign for Selong Blanak Cottages.

Senggigi. The beach at Senggigi encompasses a vast stretch of coastline, with sweeping bays punctuated by towering headlands. Most of the major hotel resorts face the beach and take measures to ensure that guests are not pestered by hawkers. However, the strip of sand is narrow and many guests wind up lounging poolside, where they won't get swallowed by an incoming tide. As it crawls north, the beach is known as Mangsit Beach, and the span of sand becomes even narrower. Mangsit is more remote, though, with plenty of palm trees for shade.

Tanjung A'an. This is the celebrity beach of Lombok—known and loved because of its seclusion and good surfing and swimming. From Kuta follow the paved road east for about 6 km (4 mi). Tanjung A'an actually is two classic beaches with fine, powdery white sand on either side of a horseshoe-shape bay; on the east side a craggy peninsula juts out into the sea. The beach is usually deserted except for a few vendors and windsurfers.

DINING

The Indonesian word for chili pepper is *lombok*, and traditional Sasak cooking uses chili the way Westerners use salt. The irony is that finding genuine Sasak cuisine in Lombok requires some sleuthing, whereas you'll be tripping over places that serve Indonesian and Chinese food. Types of eateries vary, from dubious-looking food carts, which often serve up a quick bowl of *bakso ayam* (chicken soup with meatballs), to slightly more upscale *warung*. A warung, or a *rumah makan,* which literally means "eating house," may have a couple of scattered tables or may be a full-fledged restaurant.

The staple of most meals is noodles or *nasi* (cooked rice), often paired with chicken or fish—you won't find pork on these menus. Any dish with the word *pelecing* in it is served with chili sauce. A Lombok specialty is *ayam taliwang*, grilled or fried chicken served with chili sauce, a dish that originated in Taliwang on Sumbawa. *Kankung*, known as Asian watercress or water spinach because it grows in shallow water, is the ubiquitous side vegetable here; it's usually boiled and has a milder flavor than Western spinach. Fruit is common for dessert, as is a sticky, sweet rice concoction wrapped in a banana leaf.

Padang-style cuisine from Sumatra is also popular on Lombok, perhaps because it rivals Sasak cooking in fieriness. The food is served cold and piled on platters in the window of a *rumah makan Padang*. There's no menu; you point to the dishes you'd like and pay at the end of your meal. Several Padang dishes use curry, and the heat is not turned down for Western mouths.

For general information and price categories, *see* Dining *in* Smart Travel Tips.

Central and Southern Lombok

Eclectic

$$ ✕ **Impat Ikan.** Beneath a thatch roof and overlooking the Putri Nyale lagoon, this restaurant offers a nightly Indonesian buffet and Western foods à la carte. It has the most variety and the most gourmet offerings in Kuta: try the pesto pasta while enjoying a performance by a local dance troupe. Once a week, the management runs a night bazaar just outside the restaurant. ⊠ *Novotel, Mandalika Resort, Pantai Putri Nyale, Kuta,* ☎ *0370/653333. AE, DC, MC, V.*

$$ ✕ **Pondok Ampenan.** Housed inside Lombok's first bank building, this
★ restaurant has the feel of a traditional pub, with an old-fashioned billiards table, dart boards among black-and-white photos, and banquet-length teak tables. The menu is a global mix of surf and turf, Thai cuisine, barbecue fish, burgers, and Australian strip loin. There's outdoor seating around a brick pizza oven or overlooking Ampenan Harbor. Inside, bands play everything from traditional music to rock. ⊠ *Jl. Yos Sudarso, Mataram,* ☎ *0370/634353. No credit cards. Closed Mon.*

Indonesian

$–$$ ✕ **Denny Bersaudara.** This eatery's motto is A Taste of Tradition, and it's reputedly the place to go for authentic Sasak cooking. The menu is in English and Indonesian, and the waitstaff will gladly explain the ingredients and cool the spiciness to suit Western palates. The ambience is pure banquet hall and lacks intimacy—but after the first bite, who cares? Recommended dishes include the lamb satay and ayam taliwang. ⊠ *Jl. Pelikan 6, Pajang (near Pajang shopping center), Mataram,* ☎ *0370/633619. No credit cards.*

Pan-Asian

$ ✕ **Taman Griya.** The name means "Garden House," and this open-pavil-
★ ion restaurant feels like Sunday dinner at Mom's. Don't be surprised if the Surabayan owner visits your table to share a recipe for *pecal* (steamed vegetables with peanut sauce) or spicy crabmeat. For dessert there's homemade jackfruit ice cream. Don't expect atmosphere; a hunk of garden sculpture is the only decoration. But any local will tell you it's the best place to eat in Mataram—it has been a landmark for more than two decades. ⊠ *Jl. Pejanggik, across from hospital, Mataram,* ☎ *0370/632233. No credit cards.*

Northern Lombok

Cafés

$$ ✕ **Café Wayan.** Just south of Kafe Alberto, this cozy restaurant and bakery is owned by the daughter of the family that started the Café

Wayan in Ubud on Bali. Home-baked pastries, organic brown bread, soups, and homemade pasta are offered. For an entrée try the Balinese smoked duck, wrapped in betel-nut leaves and smoked with island spices. Desserts are the claim to fame here: go for the Death by Chocolate cake or a traditional black-rice pudding. ⊠ *Senggigi Batu Bolong, Senggigi,* ☎ *0370/693098. No credit cards.*

$–$$ ✕ **Kafe Alberto.** For a quick meal of barbecue, brick-oven pizza, sushi, or homemade ravioli, try this open-air beachside restaurant, where you can also watch traditional dance performances and even take dancing lessons. Tiki torches and tables by the water's edge make for a romantic dinner, and rowboats and changing rooms are available for a luncheon swim. There's also a karaoke room for those special occasions. Free transportation can be arranged from your Senggigi hotel. ⊠ *Jl. Raya Senggigi, Senggigi,* ☎ *0370/693313 or 0370/693039. MC, V.*

Eclectic

$–$$ ✕ **Princess of Lombok.** This place has the best Mexican food in Lombok—though there isn't much competition. In addition to the outstanding enchiladas, chili *con queso,* and burritos, the restaurant serves Thai *tum yum goon* (prawns in lemon broth with lemongrass, mushrooms, and chili peppers), burgers, and banana sundaes. The rattan pavilion overlooks a small garden; downstairs are a pool table and pub. If you want the same menu with an ocean view, head for Princess Lombok Too, at the art market. ⊠ *Jl. Raya Senggigi, Senggigi,* ☎ *0370/693011. No credit cards.*

$ ✕ **Lombok Coconut.** Over a meal of fresh seafood, gourmet pizza, or
★ pasta, you can chat about the dozens of stone carvings that decorate this restaurant's facade or the birds that twitter in their cages. Eavesdropping on the oft-interesting conversations of other travelers is also an option. There's a money-back guarantee with every meal. ⊠ *Jl. Raya Senggigi, Senggigi,* ☎ *0370/693195. No credit cards.*

Indonesian

$–$$ ✕ **Coco Loco.** Fish is the highlight of the menu at this seaside restaurant; don't miss the red snapper in green curry. The fare is traditional Indonesian, but the decor is international, with festive Mexican colors, Japanese paper lanterns, and bamboo place mats. Unfortunately, the peddlers who frequent the art market may come with your meal, but the waitstaff will run interference. ⊠ *Pasar Seni, Jl. Raya Senggigi, Senggigi,* ☎ *0370/693396. No credit cards.*

$–$$ ✕ **Graha Restaurant.** Red tile floors and red-check tablecloths add cheer to this thatch-roof restaurant. An outdoor terrace looks out over the sea, and soft jazz plays in the background. Specialties include grilled shrimp, *graha lumpia* (deep-fried spring rolls with sweet-and-sour sauce), and *ikan bumbu kuning* (fried fish with a yellow sauce). Entrées come with a choice of four kinds of *sambal* (Indonesian chili sauce). ⊠ *Jl. Raya Senggigi, Senggigi,* ☎ *0370/693101. MC, V.*

Pan-Asian

$–$$ ✕ **Bayan.** With etched terra-cotta walls and inlaid stone designs, this restaurant resembles a cave inhabited by artsy, stylish cavemen. Palm trees grow in the center, near a circular water fountain. The menu has Chinese (fried noodles or rice) and Indonesian dishes; specialties are grilled lobster and a spicy fried fish dish called *taliwang.* An acoustic band plays a global mix every night. ⊠ *Jl. Raya Senggigi Km 8, Senggigi,* ☎ *0370/693616. No credit cards.*

$–$$ ✕ **Restaurant Naga.** The Chinese lanterns and eye-popping yellow sign out front compel you to stop for a bite. Signature dishes are cashew chicken, Hong Kong duck, and Szechuan crab; nightly specials might include Japanese seafood stew or baked spareribs. Free transport is available to and from area hotels. ✉ *Jl. Raya Senggigi, Senggigi,* ☎ *0370/ 693207. MC, V.*

The Gili Islands

Gili Air

INDONESIAN

$ ✗ **Coconut.** Frequented by backpackers, this spartan restaurant attached
★ to a losmen is one of the few places where you can sample Sasak food.
Owned by a Scottish woman and her Indonesian husband, it caters to
Western tastes while still serving meals that are *pedas* (spicy). Try the
gado-gado (vegetables with peanut sauce) or the grilled catch of the
day with curry. ✉ *Gili Air,* ☎ *0370/635365. No credit cards.*

Gili Trawangan

ECLECTIC

$$ ✗ **Borobudur.** If you're seeking a table for two away from the island's
rowdier restaurants, Borobudur should be your destination. It's a bit
dressier than most local establishments, so you may want to iron your
shorts. An ocean view, vaulted ceiling, wood carvings, and classic
chandeliers make for a romantic dinner. The menu is a mix of Chinese,
Indonesian, and Western—it's unlikely you'll find schnitzel anywhere
else on the island—and includes tender lobster and tuna steak. ✉ *Gili
Trawangan,* ☎ *0370/634893. No credit cards.*

INDONESIAN

$$ ✗ **Vila Omback.** This open-air, candlelit restaurant is set by a pool and
the sea. A wood-burning oven makes New York–style thick-crust piz-
zas. You can watch chefs grilling the catch of the day, whether it's fresh
tuna, snapper, or barracuda. For real entertainment watch the sun set
against the backdrop of Gunung Rinjani while sipping something tropical and listening to the house salsa band. ✉ *Gili Trawangan,* ☎ *0370/
642753. MC, V.*

LODGING

With views of blood-orange sunsets and a frangipani tree outside your
window, even the island's simplest accommodations can seem luxurious. Most low-budget hotels are set in tropical gardens and have
rooms with terraces or verandas. Senggigi is thick with possibilities for
every wallet; outside Senggigi, however, lodging tends to be in losmen,
though there are a few Shangri-las with lagoon pools, coconut palms,
and jasmine-scented air. The Gili Islands attract backpackers because
of their primitive losmen, most of which are simple bamboo huts
($12–$23) with cold-water *mandi* (dip-bucket baths) and squat toilets.
On Rinjani you can find spartan accomodations in and around the village of Bayan. Most lodgings here are basic bamboo-and-thatch bungalows, but the garden and mountain views more than compensate for
the spare rooms.

Although a few of the island's losmen are homestays run by families,
most commonly they're simply small-scale hotels, usually one-story de-
tached cottages or bungalows built of rattan and bamboo. Yet losmen
are homey and can foster more intimacy between guests and staff than
can some of the mega-resorts. What's charming about them is returning to your room to find a pot of sweet tea just when you need an afternoon pick-me-up, or awaking in the morning to a simple breakfast
such as banana pancakes and fruit waiting on your terrace. Most losmen outside the Gili Islands have hot water and Western plumbing,
and a few even have air-conditioning—although the "air-conditioning"
may be a fan. Many have an attached restaurant similar to a warung.

According to a government decree, no hotel can be built higher than a coconut tree, so you won't see skyscraper resorts in Lombok. In the tricity area of Ampenan, Mataram, and Cakranegara a number of economy hotels cater to businesspeople; some are little more than concrete cubes, but they all have televisions and diet-breaking minibars. Most large hotels on the island have spas, fitness centers, and business facilities. Deluxe resorts such as the Oberoi also have suites of rooms for rent. Villas have kitchens and living rooms; a few have their own plunge pools for those who want the ultimate in privacy.

Many hotels and losmen have open-roof garden bathrooms, some with intricate mosaic floors and showerheads sculpted into the wall, where you have the luxury of bathing under the sky in complete privacy. Some losmen have squat toilets, and if that idea makes you squeamish, ask to see the bathroom first. Hot water showers are ubiquitous (except for on the Gili Islands). Bathtubs aren't common, but several deluxe hotels have sunken marble tubs. All rooms in the listed hotels have hot water and showers unless otherwise noted.

Book well in advance if you're planning to travel during peak season (from mid-June through August and from December through January). For online booking and detailed descriptions of various accommodations, check out www.lombokhotels.com. For general information and price categories, *see* Lodging *in* Smart Travel Tips.

✍ *following the text of a review is your signal that the property has a Web site, where you will find details and, usually, images; for a link, visit www.fodors.com/urls.*

Central and Southern Lombok

Central Lombok

$–$$ 🏨 **Sahid Legi.** This Arab-owned hotel, part of an Indonesian chain, has more character than the other area hotels that cater to businesspeople. The simple, immaculate rooms are done in turquoise and orange, and each has a minibar and marble bath with tub; executive suites have separate living rooms. The solicitous staff can steer you to the city's best Sasak restaurant and advise on which *bemo* (public minibus) to take to the Arab part of Ampenan. ✉ *Jl. Sriwijaya 81, Mataram 83231,* ☎ *0370/636282,* 🖷 *0370/636281. 100 rooms. 2 restaurants, bar, air-conditioning, minibars, pool, beauty salon, laundry service, travel services. AE, DC, MC, V. BP.*

¢–$ 🏨 **Wisma Soedjono.** This hotel is imbued with the color of its grandiose
★   past. Originally a guest house built by the Dutch in the 1920s, its grounds became the home of Pak Soedjono, the first doctor in eastern Lombok, and it is still run by his family. Accommodations range from very basic rooms in small lumbung to more appealing deluxe bungalows. An open-sided restaurant overlooks rice terraces and affords a lovely morning view of Gunung Rinjani, and the pool is purported to be the coldest in Lombok. The hotel rents motorcycles and cars, so you can use it as a base for exploring the area south of Gunung Rinjani. It's often booked up by tour groups, making reservations essential. To get here, head east through Narmada, Mantang, and Kopang; at the village of Montonggamang, turn north to Tetebatu. ✉ *Tetebatu,* ☎ *0370/ 622159. 13 rooms, 25 bungalows. Restaurant, fans, pool, travel services, car rental. No credit cards. CP.*

¢   🏨 **Hotel Suranadi.** You can escape the heat at this 30-year-old colonial-style landmark in the mountains east of Mataram. Some people find the hotel dreary, for the grounds and buildings show signs of neglect, but it's still the most comfortable hotel for a sojourn in Suranadi. The spring-fed pool and cracked tennis court are surrounded by tropical gardens. Each characterless room has chintz prints, a fan, and a small pavilion overlooking the gardens. You're better off in one of the two stucco cottages with verandas and air-conditioning. A stark warung-type restaurant serves Indonesian food. The owners are Chinese, and the hotel is popular with Japanese tourists. ⊠ *Jl. Raya Suranadi 1, Suranadi (Box 109, Mataram 83010),* ☎ *0370/633686,* FAX *0370/635630. 17 rooms, 2 cottages. Restaurant, bar, air-conditioning (cottages), fans, pool, tennis court. MC, V. EP.*

Southern Lombok

$$–$$$ 🏨 **Novotel.** Kuta's only resort has a menu of activities that rivals Club Med. Aqua aerobics, pottery lessons, wood-carving demonstrations, and Sasak dance performances are just a sample of what you can choose from—if you can be lured from the hotel's most enticing feature, Putri Nyale, a white-sand beach dwarfed by craggy limestone cliffs. The hotel is as dramatic as its setting, combining Sasak architecture with Sumbanese and African motifs. The rooms are sparsely furnished, with walls of coconut wood and teak bathrooms with showers; the bungalows have showers and tubs. ⊠ *Mandalika Resort, Pantai Putri Nyale, Kuta (Box 5555, Mataram 83001),* ☎ *0370/653333,* FAX *0370/653555. 85 rooms, 23 Sasak bungalows. 2 restaurants, bar, air-conditioning, 2 pools, spa, health club, beach, snorkeling, boating, library, travel services, car rental. AE, DC, MC, V. BP.* 🐾

¢–$ 🏨 **Matahari Lombok Hotel and Restaurant.** This friendly establishment caters mainly to budget travelers, although its lovely setting and cleanliness make it seem more upscale. Three houses are available, one with 12 double rooms, one with 4, and one with 3; all have basic but pleasant local furnishings, but only some rooms have private baths (with tubs). Deluxe one-bedroom villas with garden bathrooms are poolside; the most unusual is Lombok House, an A-frame with loft bed. The restaurant serves Indonesian and basic Western dishes. The hotel is in the village, but it's still within walking distance of the beach. ⊠ *Kuta Beach/Jl. Kuta, Kuta,* ☎ *0370/655000 or 0370/654832,* FAX *0370/654909. 26 rooms, 6 villas. Restaurant, air-conditioning (some), fans, pool. MC, V. EP.* 🐾

¢ 🏨 **Nanggu Cottages.** Gili Nanggu is the perfect desert island, an atoll, surrounded by a sea of jade and turquoise, that you can traverse in half an hour. The only accommodations are 10 sparsely furnished seaside bungalows on stilts, all with open-air baths that have Western plumbing. Fishermen stop by in the evening, and the friendly Balinese owner acts as liaison for guests who wish to bargain for fish or lobster, which is then cooked to order. You can charter an outrigger from Lembar for the hour-long journey to Nanggu. ⊠ *Gili Nanggu (Jl. Tumpang Sari, Cakranegara),* ☎ *0370/622898. 10 double cottages. Restaurant, fans, beach, snorkeling. No credit cards. BP.*

Northern Lombok

Senggigi

$$$$ 🏨 **Pool Villa Club.** The scent of coconut wood and teak greets guests
★ at these two-story villas on the grounds of the Senggigi Beach Hotel (☞ *below*). Each villa has two ivory marble bathrooms—one with a sunken tub—and a sundeck and whirlpool facing a riverlike swimming pool. An arched walk over the pool passes through frangipani and bougainvillea gardens guarded by Hindu goddess fountains. Guests can sip and swing at the swim-up bar with tree-house-style swing chairs. Three restaurants, open to nonguests, serve some of Senggigi's best Italian, Asian, and French food. ⊠ *Jl. Pantai Senggigi (Box 1001, Mataram 83010),* ☎ *0370/693210,* FAX *0370/693200. 16 villas. 3 restaurants, 2*

bars, air-conditioning, in-room safes, minibars, refrigerators, pool, spa, beach, snorkeling, windsurfing. AE, DC, MC, V. BP. ✪

$$–$$$ 🏨 **Lombok Intan Laguna.** Beside the ocean it may be, but the Intan Laguna's focal point is its curving pool and the thatch-roof bar next to it. Rooms in the two-story cottages have tile floors, wood furniture, and indoor-outdoor bathrooms with tubs. Less expensive rooms are in a more modern three-story building. At the open-air restaurant diners breathe in the scent of flowers carried from the gardens on the cooling sea breeze. The hotel is within walking distance of Senggigi's main shopping area. ✉ *Jl. Raya Senggigi (Box 1049, Mataram 83125),* ☎ *0370/693090,* FAX *0370/693185. 123 rooms. 2 restaurants, bar, air-conditioning, pool, 2 tennis courts, exercise room, beach, shops. AE, DC, MC, V. EP.* ✪

$$–$$$ 🏨 **Senggigi Beach Hotel.** Sitting on a peninsula that juts into the Lombok Strait, this resort has thatch-roof cottages, each with several guest rooms, on 25 acres of grass, coconut trees, and white-sand beach. The modest rooms have twin beds, tables, chairs, and TVs. Breakfasts and dinners are served buffet style in the open-sided dining room overlooking the pool. ✉ *Jl. Raya Senggigi (Box 1001, Mataram 83101),* ☎ *0364/693210 or 0364/693219,* FAX *0364/693200. 148 rooms. Dining room, air-conditioning, pool, spa, 2 tennis courts, badminton, beach, snorkeling, windsurfing, boating, travel services. AE, DC, MC, V. BP.* ✪

$$–$$$ 🏨 **Sheraton Senggigi Beach Resort.** The lobby of this resort hotel, with
★ its polished antiques and bay views, introduces you to the subtle elegance that pervades the place. Landscaped grounds thick with blossoms surround the three-story terraced buildings. Rooms have sumptuous wood and wicker furniture and are decorated with local wood-carvings and ikat; all look onto the gardens and the free-form pool, and many offer a glimpse of the beach. Two beachfront villas have private pools. The main restaurant has indoor and outdoor dining, and its stage is the site of traditional dance performances. ✉ *Jl. Raya Senggigi, Km 8 (Box 1154, Mataram 83015);* ☎ *0370/693333; 800/325–3535 in the U.S.;* FAX *0370/693140. 156 rooms, 2 villas. 3 restaurants, 3 bars, air-conditioning, pool, spa, 2 tennis courts, health club, beach, snorkeling, windsurfing, boating, business services, travel services. AE, DC, MC, V. BP.* ✪

¢–$ 🏨 **Graha Beach.** Sitting on the beach, the Graha is one of the best of several inexpensive hotels and losmen in Senggigi. Clean, air-conditioned rooms have twin beds, tile floors, and TVs. The hotel has a restaurant, small souvenir shop, and currency-exchange counter. The hotel can arrange a guide and driver for tours of Lombok; prices are negotiable. ✉ *Senggigi Beach,* ☎ *0370/693101,* FAX *0370/693400. 39 rooms. Restaurant, air-conditioning, beach, shop, travel services, car rental. MC, DC, V. EP.*

Mangsit

$$–$$$ 🏨 **Holiday Inn Resort Lombok.** This familiar Western establishment does
★ a good job of mixing local traditions with foreign comforts. It's a chain resort with a conscience; recycling and conservation measures are evident in the rooms and landscaping, and the management mingles with guests, fishing for feedback and making subsequent improvements. Stone walkways lead through gardens to guest rooms in connected chalets and bungalows with several rooms; both types of accommodations have porches and large garden bathrooms with tubs. A multilevel pool includes a swim-up bar and Jacuzzi; beside it is a dining terrace where local musicians stroll nightly. The adept travel staff can help arrange tours anywhere on the island. ✉ *Jl. Raya Mangsit (Box 1090, Mataram 83015),* ☎ *0370/693444,* FAX *0370/693092. 145 rooms, 14 bungalows. 2 restaurants, 3 bars, air-conditioning, pool, massage, spa, health club,*

beach, snorkeling, windsurfing, boating, shops, laundry service, meeting rooms, travel services, car rental. AE, DC, MC, V. BP.

$ ▦ **Alang-Alang.** This boutique hotel shuns the cookie-cutter design of most resorts. Thatch bungalows have the same amenities, but each is decorated with unique furnishings. Open-air marble bathrooms are inlaid with a mosaic of pebbles. At the center of the small pool is a three-tier waterfall with a cave-shape entrance to a hidden Jacuzzi. The hotel overlooks a crescent beach, and guests can watch the sunset from box seats—wooden benches shaped like hands—or from beneath the cathedral ceiling of the restaurant. A Chinese and Italian menu includes grilled lobster and homemade tagliatelle with Gorgonzola. Given Mangsit's seclusion and the hotel's laissez-faire staff, it's the place to stay if you want to be left alone. ⊠ *Jl. Raya Mangsit 888,* ☎ *0370/ 693518,* 🖷 *0370/693194. 20 bungalows, 1 villa. Restaurant, bar, air-conditioning, pool, beach. AE, DC, MC, V. EP* 🐢

¢–$$ ▦ **Puri Mas Hotel and Villas.** This hotel's name means "Golden Palace," and the architecture and furnishings are so ornate they border on campy. Bungalow doors and windows are painted with gold leaf or inlaid with mother-of-pearl, and canopy beds are gilded, carved, and veiled in netting. A wild garden path lined with water-lily ponds leads to a small swimming pool. Rooms are placed at all angles to ensure privacy, and Mangsit Beach lies at your feet. A separate branch of four villas is at the end of a secluded dirt road. The villas are much pricier ($250–$350 a night), but they're suitable for up to four people and have amenities and furnishings worthy of a raja. Each villa has a kitchen and half-enclosed stone-inlaid bathroom with tub, a minibar, a daybed, marble tables, two terraces, big windows, and French doors. Siegfried and Roy would feel at home on the grounds around the villas, where deer, monkeys, and cockatoos frolic among the coconut trees, bougainvillea, and frangipani and a narrow pool is lined with palms and Hindu fountains. ⊠ *Mangsit Beach (Box 1123, Mataram);* ☎ *0370/ 693023 or 0370/693831 to hotel; 0370/693596 to villas;* 🖷 *0370/ 693023 to hotel; 0370/693023 to villas. 17 bungalows, 4 villas. Restaurant, air-conditioning, 2 pools. MC, V. CP*

¢ ▦ **Santai Beach Inn.** This backpacker's hideaway is so popular it only
★ accepts reservations for deluxe rooms. Thatch-roof bungalow rooms resemble tree houses; guests climb into a loft where the only piece of furniture is a mosquito-netted bed. The deluxe rooms have open-air bathrooms with hot water and fans. Every bungalow has a terrace overlooking a gorgeous garden that is practically a jungle. Gurgling fountains line a path to the beachfront and dining pavilion, where guests feast family style. Dinners used to be strictly vegetarian, but there are now occasional lapses of barbecue fish and chili con carne. ⊠ *Jl. Raya Mangsit (Box 101, Senggigi 83355),* ☎ 🖷 *0370/693038. 10 rooms. Restaurant, fans (some), beach, travel services. No credit cards. BP.*

Tanjung

$$$–$$$$ ▦ **The Oberoi, Lombok.** Hidden away on Lombok's northwest coast
★ and within sight of Gili Air, this resort offers the ultimate in upscale seclusion. The spacious pavilions sit in well-groomed grounds and have terraces and lovely views. High stone walls enclose the private villas, which have gardens, fountains, and raised dining pavilions; some have plunge pools. Inside both are high thatch ceilings, marble floors, dark teak furniture, oversize canopy beds, and wicker seating areas. Good-size bathrooms have separate toilet and shower compartments, double marble sinks, large walk-through closets, and sunken tubs. Service is discreet and unobtrusive. Two large pools face the ocean, and a boat is available to take you snorkeling at nearby reefs or to the Gilis. ⊠ *Pantai Medana (Box 1096, Mataram 83001),* ☎ *0370/*

638444, FAX 0370/632496. 20 villas, 30 terrace pavilions. 3 restaurants, 2 bars, air-conditioning, in-room safes, pool, beauty salon, spa, health club, beach, snorkeling, windsurfing, library, laundry service, car rental. AE, DC, MC, V. EP. ✑

Gili Islands

Gili Trawangan

$ ☷ **Vila Omback.** Gili Trawangan's only resort caters to families and young couples seeking white sand and savage tans. Two-story lumbung huts offer more privacy than the interconnected bungalow rooms, which are closer to the pool. The grass A-frame huts are romantically minimalist, with rattan matting and futons under a netted canopy; deluxe bungalows are more spacious, with skylights and teak tables. All accommodations have hammocks for lazing beside garden-view terraces and lush bathrooms that open to the heavens. As of press time there was no hot water supply on the island. The hotel has its own speedboat to whisk guests from Bangsal Harbor and deposit them at its front door. ⊠ *Gili Trawangan,* ☎ *0370/642753 or 0370/642754, FAX 0370/ 642337. 24 huts, 12 rooms. Restaurant, bar, air-conditioning, pool, spa, beach, scuba diving, travel services. MC, V. BP.* ✑

¢ ☷ **Salobai.** You can't miss the hotel restaurant, which has a boat prow jutting toward the ocean. At the far north end of the island, Salobai is a great escape from the tourist throngs of the south side, a half-hour walk away. Accommodations are wooden lumbung-style bungalows with bonnet roofs and tall windows (a modern adaptation). The interiors have less character: quilted bedspreads, mirrored walls, and basic showers. Deluxe rooms have modern amenities, including satellite television and air-conditioning. The Asian and European restaurant hosts dance parties bimonthly. A remote stretch of beach is adjacent to the hotel. ⊠ *Gili Trawangan (Box 1161, Mataram),* ☎ *0370/643152, FAX 0370/643151. 16 bungalows. Restaurant, bar, air-conditioning (some), laundry, travel services. No credit cards. EP.*

NIGHTLIFE AND THE ARTS

Nightlife

Most locals work a six-day week, so Saturday is the night for going out. Senggigi used to be rowdier, but the dearth of tourists since the riots in January 2000 has meant a sleepier nightlife. Dancing queens will be disappointed, for discotheques are frowned upon in this conservative culture (Sasaks are teetotalers and fairly reserved). Even on Gili Trawangan, which is a constant party with no shortage of bars, there are few places to dance. A number of low-key bars have acoustic bands playing something harder than folk; karaoke's popular, too.

Compared to Senggigi, Kuta's nightlife is slumberous. **Mascot** (☎ no phone), at the western end of Kuta Beach, is the best venue for a drink and a dance, but only on Thursday and Saturday nights.

Senggigi's main strip, Jalan Raya Senggigi, has some small bars and dance places, which are busiest on Saturday nights. **Club Tropicana Bar and Restaurant** (☎ 0370/693463), at Senggigi Square, has a dance floor with bands and DJs spinning salsa, pop, and rock. The **Indigo Bar** (☎ 0370/693679), just north of the Pacific supermarket, is a sleek lounge with plush blue couches and a teak bar; an acoustic band plays on weekends. For karaoke and traditional dance shows and lessons try **Kafe Alberto** (☎ 0370/693313). The **Sheraton Senggigi Beach Resort** (☎ 0370/693333) hosts various cultural performances weekly.

For parties on Gili Trawangan look for flyers plastered around the island. Dance parties tend to be full-moon raves on the beach. **Vila Omback** (☎ 0370/642336) has techno and rock dance parties, either on the beach or at the hotel bar/restaurant. A couple of doors north of Vila Omback, **Tirnanog** (☎ no phone) opens at 10 AM, which isn't surprising on this island, although this bar tends to attract an older clientele—which means over 23. Owned by a hip Irish couple, the place resembles a European pub, with Celtic music, dark wood, and dart boards. Food is served here, too; try the margarita pizza or the barbecue chicken.

The Arts

Sasak traditions of poetry, song, and dance have been influenced by Hindu and Islamic forms, though most Sasak songs and poems are characterized by sadness. The Sasak gamelan, similar to that of Bali, is used in processions to announce life-cycle ceremonies such as birthdays, circumcisions, and weddings. Orthodox Muslim leaders have attempted to ban certain arts such as puppetry because depicting the human form is taboo for followers of Islam.

Unlike on Bali you won't see signs here advertising trance dances and other pay-per-view shows for tourist audiences. Witnessing an authentic dance, wedding, or music performance usually requires a special invitation. Some hotels, such as Kuta's **Novotel** (⊠ Mandalika Resort, Pantai Putri Nyale, ☎ 0370/653333), bring culture to your table, giving you the chance to watch an esteemed Sasak dance troupe during dinner.

The sacred gamelan *tambur* (a type of drum) ensemble accompanies the *batek baris,* a military processional with dancers in ill-fitting Dutch army uniforms carrying wooden rifles. The best place to see this is at **Pura Lingsar** (⊠ Jl. Lingsar, 5 km [3 mi] north of Narmada, ☎ no phone). For more information about the arts on Lombok, including a calendar of performances, contact the **Regional Office of Tourism** (⊠ Jl. Langko 70, Ampenan, ☎ 0370/631730).

OUTDOOR ACTIVITIES AND SPORTS

Water sports reign on Lombok, with its unsullied beaches, calm waters, jade lagoons, and coral reefs. You'll find snorkeling equipment and sit-on-top kayaks for rent at many resorts; some even have Jet Skis and sailboards. Or you can take a ride on a *bagan*; painted in cheery colors with eyes on the bow, these motorized outriggers skim the sea like water spiders. To arrange a trip, all you need to do is walk down to the water, any place where there are fishermen, and offer to charter one, or ask at the front desk of one of the larger hotels in Senggigi. For experienced surfniks, the Gili Islands—collectively known as G-land in surfspeak—are mecca.

Participant Sports

Boating and Sailing

Baruna Water Sports (⊠ Jl. Raya Senggigi, Senggigi, ☎ 0370/693210), at Senggigi Beach Hotel, arranges cruises and deep-sea fishing excursions, offers instruction in scuba diving, and rents sailboards ($8 an hour) and surfboards ($3 an hour).

Novotel (⊠ Mandalika Resort, Pantai Putri Nyale, Kuta, ☎ 0370/653333) has sit-on-top kayaks and sailboats available for guests. The kayaks are free; the sailboats cost about $8 an hour.

The Oberoi (⊠ Pantai Medana, Tanjung, ☎ 0370/638444), at Medana Beach, has kayaks and sailboats for guests.

Perama Travel (⊠ Jl. Pejanggik 66, Mataram, ☎ 0370/635928) organizes sunset cruises and a glass-bottom boat tour of the Gili Islands.

Golf

Rinjani Country Club (Booking: ⊠ Jl. Sriwijaya 39, Mataram, ☎ 0370/637316), in Narmada, has English- and Japanese-speaking female caddies and caters mostly to Japanese businessmen. A day pass for the 18-hole course is $40. The club has a pool, a tennis court, and concrete bungalows with rooms that give new meaning to the term *minimalism.*

Hiking

Nazareth Tours and Travel (⊠ Jl. Koperasi 62, Ampenan, ☎ 0370/631695) organizes treks to Gunung Rinjani. Founder Eddy Batubara, a walking guidebook, is fluent in English.

Satriavi (⊠ Senggigi Beach Hotel, Jl. Raya Senggigi, Senggigi, ☎ 0370/693210) leads a three-day, two-night trek around Gunung Rinjani that includes transportation from Mataram or Senggigi.

Rafting

For white-water rafting on the Segara River, with valley and jungle views, contact **Lombok Inter Rafting** (⊠ Jl. Raya Senggigi at Senggigi Sq., Senggigi, ☎ 0370/693202). Trips start at the base of Gunung Rinjani, and transportation from Senggigi is included.

Scuba Diving

Dive operators are plentiful in Senggigi and on the Gili Islands (some operators have dive shops in both places). Conservation efforts are under way to restore the reefs, which have been harmed by illegal dynamite fishing. Nature, however, has done even more damage than man. Coral cannot tolerate balmy temperatures for long, and Lombok's coral reefs suffered with the warm tides brought by El Niño. Despite these problems a menagerie of sea creatures can still be found around the reefs of the Gili Islands: moray eels, hawksbill sea turtles, zebra fish, angelfish, and lionfish, to name a few. A three-day open-water certification course runs $300–$400, while a single-tank dive is $50–$60.

Albatross (⊠ Jl. Raya Senggigi, Senggigi, ☎ 0370/693399; ⊠ Gili Trawangan, ☎ 0370/630134) offers dive trips as well as courses in English, Japanese, and several European languages.

Blue Coral (⊠ Jl. Raya Senggigi, Senggigi, ☎ 0370/693441; ⊠ Gili Trawangan, ☎ 0370/634497) claims to have been the first PADI representative on Lombok.

Blue Marlin Dive Center (⊠ Gili Trawangan, ☎ 0370/632424) makes daily dive trips around the Gilis for certified divers; a two-tank day trip is about $60. Introductory classes and full certification courses are offered.

Dream Divers (⊠ Jl. Raya Senggigi, Senggigi, ☎ 0370/693738) is owned by Germans.

Reefseekers Pro Dive (⊠ Gili Air, ☎ 0370/641008), at Gili Air Harbor, is an excellent place to learn technique and ocean ecology (the owners also run a sea turtle nursery). As of press time Reefseekers was planning to open an office in Senggigi.

Waterworld (⊠ Jl. Raya Mangsit, Mangsit, ☎ 0370/693444), at the Holiday Inn, rents scuba equipment.

Snorkeling

For snorkeling off the beach, most hotels will rent you fins and masks for about $10 a day. If you want to snorkel offshore, many dive operators will rent you the equipment and allow you to come along on a boat dive for about half the price of a dive ($20–$30).

SURFING LOMBOK

LOMBOK AND THE GILI ISLANDS have some great surfing, but accessing the reefs requires tenacity. Gili Air has a well-known break called Pertama, a hollow right-hander that breaks over shallow coral reef, but during the fierce trade winds of the wet season, this one can be tricky. Senggigi Beach has a couple of breaks, and several more are accessible on the other side of the island from the beach at Labuhan Haji, just south of Labuhan Lombok (you can get here by bemo from the towns of Selong and Tanjung Luar). Kuta Beach is most accessible by road, and boat owners will take you to the reef breaks for a fee. There's Kuta left, in front of the village, and Kuta right, at the eastern end toward Tanjung A'an. You can scramble up Batu Kotak to get an overview of the beach. Kuta village is an excellent base, with a good variety of accommodations. West of Kuta, Selong Blanak and Mawun Beaches are both decent, although the surf is erratic. Around the headland at Selong Blanak is a good left-hander that's at its best during the dry season, from April through September.

Desert Point is the island's best-known break. Near Bangko-Bangko, on the south-western peninsula, it's a fast left-hander over a coral reef. The area is difficult to reach by road, and there are no visitor facilities except for primitive huts, so you'll need to bring supplies. Most people access it via a surf tour or chartered yacht, either from Bali or Lembar. The break is erratic; it needs a good-size swell and a dry-season southeasterly trade wind. The wave can get shallow in the inside, so bring booties. It starts as a smaller peak and builds as it goes down the line into manageable tube sections, growing faster and shallower the farther you go.

East of Kuta the best breaks are off the coast of the southeast peninsula near Serewe, but you'll have to charter a boat. There are more breaks inside the southern headland of Awang Bay, and you can charter outriggers from Awang, on the west side of the bay, to reach the right-hander on the reef just south of the village. Gerupuk Bay has the potential for big waves at its shallow mouth and smaller ones in the middle and to the east of the bay. Farther east, Ekas Bay has a reef break accessible by boat.

Baruna Water Sports (✉ Senggigi Beach Hotel, Jl. Raya Senggigi, Senggigi, ☎ 0370/693210) leads snorkeling trips to the Gili Islands on outriggers for $35 and rents snorkel and fins for $3 an hour.

Ocean Blue (✉ Jl. Parawisata, Kuta, ☎ 0370/653911) rents snorkeling equipment.

Perama Travel (✉ Jl. Pejanggik 66, Mataram, ☎ 0370/693007) runs boat trips to the Gili Islands for snorkeling.

Sunshine Tours (✉ Jl. Raya Senggigi, ☎ 0370/693232), next to the Interlokal wartel, arranges snorkeling trips.

Surfing

Lombok and the Gili Islands have surf breaks that can break a beginner. Some resorts arrange for surfboard rental, but most aficionados bring their own. A good reference is the book *Surfing Indonesia* (Periplus Editions, 1999), by Lorca Lueras.

In Kuta, **Ocean Blue** (✉ Jl. Parawisata, ☎ 0370/653911) rents surf and boogie boards; surfboards start at $3 per day. The shop also organizes "surfari" trips throughout Lombok and Sumbawa. The longhaired locals who work here are happy to advise on the best breaks and the most deserted beach. And if you don't know a pop-up from a barrel, they teach the fundamentals, too.

Spectator Sports

Sasaks love displays of prowess and feats of strength, and many competitions of one-on-one combat take place on the island. Circumcision ceremonies are often accompanied by *peresehan,* ritual fights that make boxing look like child's play.

Horse Racing

Mataram's **Selakalas field** (✉ Off Jl. Gora; ☎ no phone to track; 0370/637828 to Regional Office of Tourism for schedules) hosts races on various holidays and the occasional Sunday (mostly in August). The jockeys are all young boys, who must retire by age 12—before they can be distracted by puberty or tempted by gamblers to hold back their mounts. Bareback riders whip around the 1,000-meter track wearing ski masks and helmets. The animals are actually ponies: pony racing is an honored tradition because the *cidomo* (pony-drawn cart) is so ubiquitous in Lombok. Jockeys are cheered by their home village, and the government offers them such prizes as televisions, motorcycles, and goats. The evening before a race villagers help the animals relax by massaging them, shooing mosquitoes away, and playing gamelan music, and the ponies are fed a special meal of eggs, honey, and ginger. Right before the race the ponies lap at a bucket of sweet coffee for that caffeine boost.

Martial Arts

Traditional fighting with rattan sticks and buffalo-skin shields is a rather violent display; in most cases the performance is not concluded until one combatant draws blood. These fights frequently accompany circumcisions, which are often performed in the Muslim month in which Muhammad's birthday is celebrated; they are also held in conjunction with national or local celebrations and occasionally as part of an agricultural ritual asking for rain. Although these contests occur in rural areas throughout the island, they're not formally scheduled and tourists aren't always welcome to watch, so ask locals or at the Regional Office of Tourism (☞ Visitor Information *in* Lombok A to Z, *below*) if one is planned that you'd be able to attend. You might catch a fight during August in Lendang Nangka, a Sasak village southeast of Tetebatu. Tamer versions are also put on for tourists in areas, such as Praya, that are rural but popular destinations on the tourist shopper's circuit; in these battles contestants stick to hitting the buffalo hide and not one another's skin.

SHOPPING

Lombok is an island of crafts. Fine art is hard to find, but basketwork, pottery, and textiles abound. Prices are lower than on Bali, and shops offer more crafts and intricate ikat from eastern islands like Sumbawa and Flores. If you're seeking souvenirs and quality isn't a priority, head for the Cakranegara daily market (☞ Areas, Markets, and Malls, *below*). City markets like this are always an adventure: every alleyway is crammed with vendors, buyers, and produce, and the ripe smells and chaos can be overwhelming. For a calmer shopping experience visit the shops and workshops in the areas where crafts are actually produced. You'll see how the crafts are made, and by perusing a wide variety of similar crafts, you can better compare prices and quality. Some shops close for a few hours in the middle of the afternoon and by noon on Fridays, for religious services.

In markets and villages, as the saying goes, "The price is whatever you'll pay for it." It's best to establish a rapport before asking the price. Indonesians enjoy nuanced negotiating, so smiles, jokes, and small talk go over big. To get an idea of what your beginning bid should be, hover around other shoppers and see what price they pay (but don't expect to pay as little as locals do). If your heart is set on a piece of painted pottery, deflect attention by initially focusing on something smaller. Once a price is agreed upon, you're expected to seal the deal, so don't bargain when you're truly just browsing. If a seller absolutely won't budge, try walking away; most times, they will yoo-hoo after you and agree to your final offer. Be aware that a guide, although often an effective liaison for bargaining, usually receives a commission from every purchase, driving up the price.

Areas, Markets, and Malls

The **Cakranegara daily market,** on Jalan Hasanuddin, is a great place for handicrafts. It starts at around 8 and ends at about 5. For the same goods minus the market chaos, try **Lombok Handicraft Center** (⊠ Jl. Hasanuddin, Sayang), just north of Cakranegara. Also called Rungkang Jangkuk, this complex of stores is one-stop shopping: if it's made in Lombok, you're guaranteed to find it here. The **Sweta market,** across from the Mandalika bus terminal in Bertais, 4 km (2½ mi) east of Cakranegara, runs daily 8–5. Here you can shop for spices and beautifully made cane baskets that entrepreneurs buy and take back to Bali to sell at inflated prices.

Gunung Sari is a village 6 km (4 mi) north of Mataram where craftsmen make "instant" antiques from wood, leather, bone, horn, and bamboo. **Praya,** a quaint town of gardens and colonial buildings southeast of Mataram, has a crafts cooperative and a large market on Saturday. The market, on the main drag, Jalan Raya Praya, features pottery and baskets woven from rattan, banana palm, and coconut leaf.

In Senggigi check out the cluster of shops at the art market known as **Pasar Seni,** just south of the Sheraton on Jalan Raya Senggigi. It's a smorgasbord of textiles, wood carvings, and small furnishings, and though the sellers are alpha males, the variety is worthwhile.

Pacific Supermarket (⊠ Jl. Raya Senggigi, Senggigi, ☎ 0370/652441) stocks basics such as coffee, cookies, and other dry and canned goods,

SMART SHOPPING ON LOMBOK

BRING EXTRA SUITCASES to Lombok for all the loot you'll have to lug home. You'll be tempted everywhere by intricate palm-leaf wedding trunks and armoires with mother-of-pearl inlays. Bone, wood, and bamboo are good buys, along with ikat and *songket*, a fabric with silver and gold thread running through it that was traditionally used for sarongs worn by royalty. Expect to pay dearly for antique songket, and inspect it for moth holes. Select wooden items carefully: Some woods such as teak are accustomed to humidity and can warp in dryer climates. Check for cracks before buying and ask if the wood was soaked in polyethylene glycol, which fills cracks before they widen. Look carefully for termite damage and dubious restoration.

When bargaining, tact is better than tenacity; remember that you may be bickering over a difference of 50¢. Upscale stores usually have fixed prices, although there may still be wiggle room. Ask whether something is *harga pas* (firm price) and keep in mind that the wiggle is wider with big-ticket items.

If you wind up buying more than you can carry home, numerous cargo companies can arrange for shipping. A reliable cargo company is Nominasi, whose Mataram branch is **WSA Lines Ltd.** (✉ Jl. Dr. Wahidin 3 Rembiga, ☎ 0370/632688). The usual price is about $250 per cubic meter.

but doesn't have a bakery or deli. You can pick up sunscreen, shampoo, and other sundries here, as well as T-shirts, sarongs, cheap handicrafts, and maybe a tour book or beach read.

Specialty Shops

Antiques

Indonesians have cornered the market on "made-to-order antiques." Many imitations are indistinguishable from genuine antiques, so it's best to buy something based on its appearance rather than its alleged history. Antiques and crafts shops are concentrated in the Arab quarter of Ampenan, on Jalan Yos Sudarso and Jalan Saleh Sungkar.

Freti (✉ Gg. Sunda 18, off Jl. Yos Sudarso, Ampenan, ☎ 0370/633835) is a two-story treasure chest of drums, mother-of-pearl wedding trunks, teapots, and armoires.

Hary Antiques (✉ Gg. Tengiri 2, off Jl. Saleh Sungkar, Ampenan, ☎ 0370/636958) specializes in intricate *songket* (fabric with silver and gold thread), Asian pottery, and hand-painted masks.

Pak Sudirman (☎ 0370/636315) received a presidential award for reviving Lombok's traditional crafts. He's well-known for his *jaran kamput*, festive wooden and mirrored horses modeled on those used to carry boys to their circumcision rituals. Sudirman will do custom orders, and he can handle shipping. His workshop in Ampenan and his Senggigi showroom have sporadic hours, so call for an appointment.

Clothing and Accessories

When it comes to clothing, Lombok is a far cry from Paris. Street stalls hawk T-shirts and sarongs, and you can find some unusual outfits and jewelry in resort boutiques.

Lotus Arts de Vivre (⊠ Pantai Medana, Tanjung, ☎ 0370/638444), in the Oberoi, carries polished teak boxes, gem jewelry, and antique Javanese sarongs. The quality is what you'd expect at a posh resort like the Oberoi.

Lumba-lumba (⊠ Jl. Raya Mangsit, Mangsit, ☎ 0370/693444), at the Holiday Inn Resort Lombok, sells snakeskin and feather purses, surfer shorts, swimwear, chunky sterling jewelry, and sarongs you won't find on the street.

Furniture

Asmara (⊠ Jl. Raya Senggigi, Senggigi, ☎ 0370/693109) sells tables and chairs carved from bamboo and coconut wood, silver jewelry, kitchenware, and antique glass pieces. The English owner can arrange shipping and accommodate orders for commissioned pieces.

Pamour Art Gallery (⊠ Jl. Raya Senggigi, opposite Senggigi post office, ☎ 0370/693104) has exhibitions of regional art, crafts-making demonstrations, and an extensive collection of crafts and furnishings.

Handicrafts

Lombok Pottery Centre (⊠ Jl. Sriwijaya 111A, Mataram, ☎ 0370/640351; ⊠ Galleria Senggigi, Jl. Raya Senggigi, Senggigi, ☎ 0370/693370) uses its profits to improve living conditions in pottery villages.

Slamat Riyadi (⊠ Jl. Tanun 10, Cakranegara, ☎ 0370/625387) gives visitors a glimpse into the making of the region's handwoven textiles. To see weavers at work on foot looms, visit in the morning.

Pearls

If you can't find diamonds, settle for pearls. Lombok has a couple of Japanese-run pearl farms along the east coast. View the crop at **Paloma Group** (⊠ Jl. Permuda 30, Mataram, ☎ 0370/635082).

LOMBOK A TO Z

Arriving and Departing

By Airplane

For a stay of up to 60 days visas are not required for citizens of Australia, Canada, New Zealand, the United Kingdom, and the United States—as long as you enter the country through one of the major gateways. Since Lombok lacks immigration facilities, most people fly to Ngurah Rai International Airport, in southern Bali, and arrange transport from there (☞ Southern Bali A to Z *in* Chapter 2). There is no direct service from North America to Lombok's **Selaparang Airport,** in Mataram. Singapore Airlines flies to Lombok via Singapore, and Garuda Indonesia has flights via Jakarta. Air Canada connects to Garuda Indonesia flights via Los Angeles; Cathay Pacific also has flights from Canada. From Australia add-on transfer flights to Lombok are possible on Garuda and Qantas. To reach the international carriers from Lombok, call their Bali offices: **Cathay Pacific** (☎ 0361/286001), **Garuda Indonesia** (☎ 0361/22782), **Malaysia Airlines** (☎ 0361/285071), **Qantas** (☎ 0361/288331), or **Singapore Airlines** (☎ 0361/261666).

Air Mark (☎ 0361/759769 in Bali; 0370/643564 in Lombok) and **Merpati** (☎ 0364/22226 in Bali; 0370/636745 in Lombok) run shuttle services between Denpasar and Mataram on small-seater planes, with flights every hour from 8 until around 5. You can buy tickets at the airport an hour before departure. The cost is about $30.

Bouraq (☎ 0370/627333) and **Sempati** (☎ 0370/621612) connect all major Indonesian cities and towns. However, because of decreased numbers of tourists in Lombok, at press time both carriers had reduced the number of their outgoing and incoming flights. Note that domestic flights tend to be late and are frequently canceled.

FROM THE AIRPORT

Some Senggigi hotels will have a minivan waiting for you at the airport if you ask in advance; others may reimburse the cost of a taxi. Taxi fares from the airport are fixed: it's about $2 to Senggigi (a 15-minute ride) and $7 to Kuta (which takes about an hour). You can also charter one of the private minivans lurking outside the airport. A public bemo is the cheapest option at roughly 10¢, but you'll have to change in Ampenan for Senggigi, and you won't be too popular if you lug five suitcases on board.

By Boat

Ferries make the four-hour crossing from Padangbai, east of Denpasar on Bali, to Lembar, south of Ampenan on Lombok, every two hours between 2 AM and 10 PM; the fare is about $1. Since the ferry docks some distance from the tourist centers on both Bali and Lombok (it takes three bemos to travel from Lembar Harbor to Senggigi), it's a good idea to take advantage of a bus-ferry package that goes between Ubud, Kuta, or Sanur on Bali and Mataram or Senggigi on Lombok. Fares are reasonable—it's about $4 from Kuta to Senggigi—and most travel agents can make the arrangements. Try **Dewi Sri Murni Tours** (☎ 0361/730272) in Kuta on Bali. On Lombok contact **Perama Travel** (✉ Jl. Pejanggik 66, Mataram, ☎ 0370/693007 or 0370/635928).

Two express ferries cruise from Bali to Lombok:

Bounty Cruises (✉ Benoa Harbor, Bali, ☎ 0361/733333) ferries passengers from Benoa Harbor to Senggigi and the Gili Islands on Lombok for $35 one-way and $70 round-trip. The boat departs at 8 AM, arrives at Senggigi at 10:15, and reaches Gili Meno at 10:45; the return voyage leaves Gili Meno at 1 PM, stops at Senggigi at 1:15, and arrives back at Benoa Harbor at 3:45.

Mabua Express (✉ Benoa Harbor, Bali, ☎ 0361/772521; ✉ Lembar Harbor, Lombok, ☎ 0370/625895) is the main passenger-only express service to Lombok; trips on the 130-ft catamaran depart at 8 AM from Benoa and at 5:30 PM from Lembar and take just two hours. Choose an Emerald Class or Lower Deck Class ticket, which includes a snack, juice, coffee, and transfers, for $30; Economy Class, without the perks, is $25.

Getting Around

By Boat

Don't be fooled by hawkers plying boat charters to the Gili Islands as you walk toward Bangsal Harbor, where the ferry office is located on the beach. Morning is the best time to catch the public shuttle boats. There is no fixed departure time; the shuttles leave about every half-hour starting at 7 AM until 9:30 AM, depending on how fast boats fill up. The fare to Gili Air is about 50¢; it's 60¢ to Gili Meno or Gili Trawangan. After 10 AM or so, if there aren't enough people for a public boat, you can arrange through the same office to charter a boat, which usually costs about $5.

By Bus and Bemo

Public transport in Lombok should be considered adventure travel. Buses and bemos are packed with women returning from the market laden with baskets of fruit and chain-smoking men on their way to work. Pop music blares, a stuffed animal swings from the rearview mirror, and the driver takes the van's racing stripes to heart.

Public minibuses, known as bemos, are the way to get around in town and to nearby sites. Trips cost 10¢ for short distances, though the government-regulated prices were due to increase at press time; bargain with drivers for longer jaunts. Beware an empty bemo as the driver will assume you're chartering the whole bus. Bemos are ubiquitous; you'll be harangued with "transport, transport" offers as they idle past. They also congregate around **Mandalika,** Lombok's central bus terminal, in Bertais, 2 km (1 mi) east of Sweta.

Bus schedules and government-set fares are posted at Mandalika. You can call the warung at the terminal, **Cantina** (☎ 0370/667017), and someone will check the board for you. Public buses are cheaper than renting a car, but they tend to be crowded and smoky.

By Car

Lombok's infrastructure is less developed than Bali's. The main road that runs west to east, from Mataram to Labuhan Lombok, is good, but roads in the far north, the southwest, and the southeast are potholed, and the horse carts that are still used in many places cause traffic congestion. Roads are narrow, only two lanes, and passing is allowed in both directions. The roads can be labyrinthine; some streets share the same name and are only distinguished by Roman numerals.

To reach remote coastal regions, it's best to rent a hardtop Jeep or a Kijang, a small utility vehicle. Any major hotel can arrange rental car or driver services. The average cost, excluding driver, is $18–$30 a day. There are also several reputable car rental agencies on Lombok. **Arwidas** (✉ Jl. Raya Senggigi, Senggigi, ☎ 0370/693843) charges $25–$35 a day for a four-wheel-drive vehicle. **Metro Rent Car** (✉ Jl. Yos Sudarso, Ampenan, ☎ 0370/632146) rents small Suzuki sport utility vehicles for $15–$25, including insurance. **Rinjani Rent Car** (✉ Jl. Bung Karno, across from Hotel Granada, Mataram, ☎ 0370/632259) is a reliable option. **Toyota Lombok** (✉ Jl. Adi Sucipto 5, Rembiga, Mataram, ☎ 0370/626363) is a good bet.

By Horsecart

The cidomo is still a popular form of transportation on Lombok, and it's the only transportation allowed on the Gili Islands. This pony-drawn cart seats four or five and costs roughly 15¢ per 1 km (½ mi); the fare is determined in advance. Ponies' necks are garlanded with flowers and bells, and the carts are usually jockeyed by young boys.

By Motorcycle

Motorcycle rentals aren't very common in Lombok, perhaps because the roads are intimidating. But motorbikes actually can be the best way to reach some of the rugged and remote coastal roads. A few dubious-looking shacks advertise rentals (usually a family member or friend doesn't need the bike that day). A safer way to procure a bike is to ask if your hotel can arrange for a rental or inquire at a car rental agency. The minimum charge is about $6. You may have to show an International Driver's License (IDL) or leave a passport. Some agencies may ask for a motorcycle license, which you can obtain at the police station.

By Taxi

In dense tourist areas like Senggigi, the sky-blue taxis cruise the streets, so just extend an arm to flag one down. You can also book a taxi from any hotel or restaurant. The initial charge is 20¢, then it's roughly 10¢ per kilometer; be sure the driver turns on the meter. Prices are fixed from the airport, and you can also hire a taxi for a flat fee to take a tour. In remote areas it's best to call for a cab in advance; the minimum fare is about 60¢ when you call a taxi. **Pt. Lombok Taxi** (☎ 0370/627000) serves all of Lombok.

Contacts and Resources

Banks and Currency Exchange

Lombok's exchange rates are slightly worse than those on Bali, so you may want to change money before arriving. Senggigi has plenty of exchange booths that offer more bang for your buck than hotels and banks. In general, banks are open 8–3 Monday through Thursday, 8–noon on Friday, and are closed weekends. Senggigi has two ATMs outside its two banks. ATMs give Jakarta rates, but the withdrawal maximum is minimal (about $66). Outside Senggigi and the Mataram district, ATMs and banks are an anomaly, although Praya has a few.

In Praya try **Bank Central Asia** (✉ Jl. Gajah Mada, ☎ 0370/654618). Mataram has a branch of **Bank Negara Indonesia** (BNI; ✉ Jl. Langko 64, ☎ 0370/622788). Senggigi has two branches of **Bank Negara Indonesia** (BNI; ✉ Jl. Raya Senggigi, next to art market, ☎ 0370/693333; ✉ Jl. Raya Senggigi, next to Pacific supermarket, ☎ 0370/693308).

A reputable money changer in Mataram is **Muara Lintu Artha** (✉ Jl. Pejanggik Cilinaya, ☎ 0370/622314). In Cakranegara you can exchange currency at **Pt. Sehat Usaha Mandiri** (✉ Jl. Sultan Hasanuddin 24, ☎ 0370/622367).

Emergencies

Try to avoid having a crisis in Lombok. There are no foreign representatives on the island; the closest consulates are in Bali. For medical problems hotel and tourist-area clinics cater to foreigners, and nearly every major hotel has a doctor and a dentist on call. A clinic should be your first stop because hospitals are undeveloped and may not have English-speaking doctors. It's wise to invest in medical insurance before visiting Lombok.

EMERGENCY NUMBERS
Ambulance (☎ 118). **Fire** (☎ 113). **Police** (☎ 110).

HOSPITALS AND CLINICS
In Mataram try **Klinik Risa** (✉ Jl. Pejanggik 115, ☎ 0370/625560). The **Public Hospital of Mataram** (✉ Jl. Pejanggik 6, ☎ 0370/621345) is centrally located.

The Senggigi Beach Hotel has a clinic, **Klinik Senggigi Medical Services** (✉ Jl. Raya Senggigi, near Pacific supermarket, ☎ 0370/693210). In Mangsit there's a clinic at the **Holiday Inn Resort Lombok** (✉ Jl. Raya Mangsit, ☎ 0370/693444). Gili Trawangan has a tiny clinic that's more of an infirmary.

PHARMACIES
Pharmacies, or *apotik,* are uncommon in Lombok, but they often dispense medication over the counter that would require a prescription in other countries. In Mataram there's a pharmacy at the **Mataram Supermarket** (✉ Jl. Pejanggik 129B, in the Mataram Plaza, ☎ no phone).

In Ampenan the **Police Office of Lombok Barat** (☎ 0370/631225) is on Jalan Langko. The **Senggigi tourist police station** (☎ 0370/693267 or 0370/693110) is open 24 hours; look for the POLISI sign immediately north of the art market. There are no police on the Gili Islands.

SCUBA-DIVING EMERGENCIES

The closest decompression chamber is at Bali's **Sanglah Hospital** (✉ Jl. Nias, Denpasar, ☎ 0361/227911).

English-Language Bookstores

Most major Lombok resorts have at least a few books, news magazines, and international papers available. Used bookstores come and go in the tourist areas of Senggigi and Kuta; ask at your hotel. Many losmen have collections of books that have been traded or donated.

In Kuta, **Kimen** (✉ Jl. Parawisata, next to Ocean Blue surf shop, ☎ no phone) sells used paperbacks, most in English and German.

The **Senggigi Supermarket and Department Store** (✉ Jl. Raya Senggigi, ☎ 0370/693738) sells guidebooks, maps, and novels.

Gili Trawangan has a couple of tiny used-book shops. **William Bookshop** (☎ no phone), across from the harbor, has beach reads and a smattering of highbrow novels in English.

Guided Tours

Dozens of operators provide tours, ranging from glass-bottom boat trips to the Gili Islands to studying Sasak cooking and staying at a farmhouse. There are also many fly-by-night businesses and hawkers whose definition of a tour is taking you to see their cousin's ikat shop. You can book a tour or find a knowledgeable guide through your hotel or by contacting one of the reputable and experienced companies listed below.

Bidy Tour and Travel (✉ Jl. Ragigenep 17, Ampenan, ☎ 0370/632127 or 0370/634095) offers treks up Gunung Rinjani, island cruises, dive packages, visits to cultural villages, and fishing trips.
Lotus Asia Tours (✉ Jl. Raya Senggigi 1 G, Meninting, ☎ 0370/636781) organizes handicraft tours, snorkeling excursions to the Gilis, Rinjani trekking, and golf tours. Giuseppe Marchesi, the Italian owner of Kafe Alberto, brings his charm and enthusiasm for *la dolce vita* to every Lotus trip.
Pt. Lombok Independent Tours (✉ Jl. Gunung Kerinci 4, Mataram, ☎ 0370/632497) arranges farmhouse stays, monkey walks, and Rinjani and rain-forest treks.

Health and Safety

Lombok's main tourist areas pose few health hazards to tourists—besides sunburns or scorched tongues from chili sauce. In the developed areas there's little risk of malaria although it does exist; as a precaution, sleep under mosquito nets and douse yourself with repellent. The currents around Kuta and the Gili Islands can be quite strong, so doggy-paddlers might want to stay on land. Ask at your hotel about jellyfish, which can be floating near shore depending on the time of year.

Since the nation's economic crisis, a spate of robberies has occurred at Gunung Rinjani. The pilfering usually happens while hikers are asleep. The best protection is to sign up with a reputable trekking company rather than hire locals on-site, and women should never climb alone. Outside Rinjani, women can comfortably travel solo.

Telephones and Mail

For local calls you don't need to dial the area code. When calling long-distance on the island or between Indonesian islands, make sure to include the 0 before the area code.

Local calls are very reasonable, about 3¢ per "pulse," with approximately one pulse per minute. Although urban areas have blue public phones that operate with phone or credit cards, these phones are usually good only for local calls, and service is sporadic. To avoid hotel surcharges, phone from a public or privately owned *wartel*. Note, however, that smaller wartels often lack the capacity for collect, long-distance, or overseas calls. Senggigi's full-service wartel, **Interlokal wartel** (✉ Jl. Raya Senggigi, just south of Princess Lombok), is open daily 8 AM–midnight.

Most hotels will hold mail for guests. The Mataram and Senggigi post offices have held-mail services; be sure that letters to you are addressed with your surname followed by your first name, then "Poste Restante" and the post office address. The **Kantor Pos Mataram** (✉ Jl. Sriwijaya, ☏ 0370/621838) is open weekdays 8–8 and Saturday 8–6. The **Kantor Pos Senggigi** (✉ Jl. Raya Senggigi, ☏ 0370/693711) is open Monday through Saturday 7:30–7 and Sunday and holidays 8–noon.

Visitor Information

The hotel reception desk is often the most accurate source of information for local events. The **Regional Office of Tourism** (✉ Jl. Langko 70, Ampenan, ☏ 0370/631730) is a bit out of the way, but it's stocked with brochures and a well-intentioned staff.

7 PORTRAITS OF BALI AND LOMBOK

BALI AND LOMBOK: A CHRONOLOGY

By Gisela Williams

7 million years ago Hominids occupy Java.

40,000 years ago Homo sapiens in Indonesia.

5000 BC Austronesian peoples emigrate from Philippines to Indonesian archipelago.

3000 BC Existence of pottery, beads, shell jewelry in Sulawesi and East Timor.

500 BC–AD 500 Bronze age on Bali. Existence of drums and axes ornamented with geometric, animal, and human figures.

400 Indian influence spreads to Southeast Asia. Hindu kingdoms established in Java and Kalimantan (present-day Borneo).

10th century Hindu kingdoms emerge in Bali.

991 Birth of Airlangga, son of Balinese king and Javanese wife, heralds union between the two kingdoms.

11th century Airlangga marries daughter of Javanese ruler, linking Java to Bali politically and cementing long Javanese cultural influence over Bali. Javanese replaces Old Balinese as court language in Bali.

1049 Airlangga dies. Bali independent kingdom for 235 years.

1343 Bali invaded by Javanese kingdom of Majapahit. Majapahit introduces changes to Balinese social system; most important is imposition of the Hindu caste system.

1515 Seeking exile from Islamic empires that now dominate Java, leading members of collapsed Majapahit kingdom emigrate to Bali, leading to further merging of Javanese and Balinese cultures.

1550 King Waturenggong ascends Balinese throne, inaugurating golden age of Bali. He conquers Blambangan, in eastern Java, and colonizes Lombok, creating a strong, centralized—and some say benevolent—kingdom.

1585 Portuguese ship planning to build fort and set up trading post on Bali founders off coast of Bukit Peninsula, leaving almost no survivors.

1597 First Dutch expedition to Bali, led by explorer Cornelius de Houtman. Record visit first substantial information about Bali to reach Western world.

17th century Time of tumult. Multiple, competing kingdoms replace single rule in Bali, signaling end of golden age and beginning of Balinese vulnerability to Dutch invasion and colonization.

1601 Dutch make overtures to Balinese rulers regarding possible trade agreements; Balinese decline.

1602 With goal of reaping great wealth from Indonesia, Dutch form Dutch East India Company.

1740 Bali conquers western Lombok.

1799 Indonesia officially declared a Dutch colony.

1815 Tambora volcano on Sumbawa erupts, killing 25,000 people.

Abundance of volcanic ash creates fertile soil, leading to surge in crop exportation to British colony of Singapore. Dutch fear British encroachment on Bali. Mudslide at Buleleng, Bali, kills 10,000 people.

1830 Resumption of Dutch overtures toward Bali regarding trade and slavery.

1841 In accordance with Balinese principle of reef rights, under which they are entitled to plunder shipwrecks off their coasts, Balinese strip a Dutch ship, *Overijssel,* further exacerbating tensions.

early 1840s Under threat by competing European powers for control of area and because of frustration with plundering of ship wrecks, the Dutch forge treaties with rulers of Badung, Buleleng, Klungkung, and Karagasem kingdoms, in which they promise to protect Mataram kingdom of Lombok in return for recognition of Dutch sovereignty.

1846 Dutch launch expedition against Buleleng for refusing to comply with new treaty banning plundering of ships; they are rebuffed.

1849 Dutch launch successful expedition against Buleleng, resulting in deaths of thousands of Balinese, some at hands of Dutch, others as a result of mass *puputan* (Balinese ritual in which suicide is committed as alternative to surrender.)

1850–1888 Bali hit by plagues of mice, which devastate food supplies and bring epidemics of cholera, smallpox, and dysentery.

ca. 1850 Mads Lange, Danish trader, negotiates new agreement in which Dutch are declared sovereign but separate from Balinese internal affairs.

1853 Buleleng rebels, prompting Dutch control of internal affairs.

1882 Dutch unite Lombok and Bali into single residency, bringing northern Bali under direct Dutch rule.

1894 Dutch troops take advantage of internal unrest on Lombok and take over island. In protest another great puputan takes place.

1904 *Sri Kumala,* a Chinese-owned Dutch trading ship, strikes reefs and is plundered by Balinese. Dutch demand recompense and are rebuffed.

1906 After two years of fruitless negotiations over the *Sri Kumala,* Dutch march on Denpasar. Rather than surrender, city's royal families commit puputan that results in deaths of more than 2,000 Balinese.

1908 Dutch impose monopoly on opium, cutting off Balinese from lucrative trade. Raja of Karangasem opposes act. Riots break out in Klungkung. Dutch send in troops, resulting in yet another puputan. Dutch now control the entire island of Bali.

1910 Founding of Indonesian Communist movement.

1917 Earthquake hits Bali, flattening villages and destroying temples and killing more than 1,000 people.

1920–1930s Westerners—including artists, sociologists, economists, dancers, and musicians—flock to Bali, spawning scholarship on Balinese history and promoting idea of Bali as "paradise."

1927 Sukarno founds political party with Indonesian independence as its goal.

1928   Bali Hotel in Denpasar, first high-end hotel on Bali, established.

1930s   Road connecting Gilimanuk to Denpasar built. Air travel becomes possible, although first survey flight crashes into Mt. Batukau and first airport only provides safe landing during calmest weather.

1936   First hotel built on Kuta Beach.

1942   World War II; Japan invades Indonesia. Small force of Japanese land at Sanur and take over from Dutch, ruling Bali for three years.

1945   Japan surrenders and departs, leaving power vacuum in Indonesia.

1945–1949   Indonesians battle Dutch for independence.

1949   Dutch capitulate, recognizing Sukarno as president of independent state of Indonesia.

late 1950s Period of growing political strife, during which Indonesian Communist Party (PKI) clamors for change and clashes with Sukarno's Nationalist Party of Indonesia (PNI).

1962   Rats infest Bali's fields and granaries.

1963   Urged by President Sukarno to perform sacred ceremony of Eka Dasa Rudra before proper calendar year, priests prepare island of Bali for centennial ritual. Soon afterward Gunung Agung erupts, killing about 1,600 people and leaving 86,000 without homes. Disaster confirms Balinese belief of being punished for not obeying rules of the gods.

1965   Abortive Communist coup against Sukarno. Massacres follow. Up to 100,000 people killed in Indonesia. Thousands killed on Bali alone.

1967   Suharto replaces Sukarno as president of Indonesia.

1967–1998   Suharto's reign characterized by corruption and inflation. In response to authoritarian rule and collapsing economy, riots—from which Bali is spared—eventually force Suharto out of office.

1970s   Tourism infrastructure created, contributing to economic growth on Bali.

1998   Former vice president B. J. Habibie becomes president. He promises to lift restrictions on political parties and hold free, democratic elections in 1999.

1998–1999   Throughout Indonesia protests and riots call for reforms.

1999   In country's first democratic elections, Indonesia names Abdurrahman Wahid as president. He inherits nation near economic collapse and plagued by religious and ethnic violence.

Oct. 1999   Three days of riots throughout Bali, mostly in the north, to protest Megawati Sukarnoputri's failure to be elected president of Indonesia. Soon afterward Megawati made vice president.

late 1999   A U.N.–supervised ballot on autonomy produces vote in favor of East Timorese independence from Indonesia, leading to violent backlash by pro-Indonesian militias.

Jan. 2000   Several killed when anti-Christian riots sweep through Lombok. Much of island's Christian community flees to Bali.

MEGA: INDONESIA'S REFORM QUEEN

Spend any time driving along the back roads of Bali, especially in the Tabanan region, and you're sure to see local tributes to the popular PDI-Perjuangan (Democratic Party of Struggle), painted in the party colors of red and black and often featuring its symbol, an angry-looking bull. Most often those signs will include the word *Mega*, the nickname of Indonesia's queen of reform, Megawati Sukarnoputri.

Megawati may have been a middle-aged housewife when she entered party politics just over a decade ago, but she had a political heritage that none could rival: her father, Sukarno, was Indonesia's first president, a revolutionary nationalist who established the country's independence from the Dutch in 1945. Because Sukarno's mother—Mega's paternal grandmother—was Balinese, Megawati is particularly popular on Bali.

Megawati was born January 23, 1947, and spent her childhood in the presidential palace in Jakarta. She was close to her father and as a teenager even traveled to overseas meetings with him. The privilege for Megawati and her seven siblings ended, however, when Suharto ousted her father in 1965. Megawati was forced to leave her university before finishing her degree, and the family was suddenly socially ostracized and poor. When Megawati married her first husband, Surendro, an air force pilot, her deposed father had to ask Suharto's permission to attend the ceremony.

Sukarno died in 1970, and friends say Megawati went into a depression. Soon after she had another tragedy in her life. When she was pregnant with her second son, Surendro disappeared during a mission over Irian Jaya. His body was never recovered, and Megawati still becomes emotional when talking about him. Her next marriage in 1972, to an Egyptian businessman, was very brief (depending on the source, it lasted from one day to three months) and ended in an annulment.

Megawati married her third and current husband, Taufik Kiemas, in 1973. By all reports, their civilian lives were very ordinary. The family of five lived in a modest Jakarta home, and Taufik ran a chain of Jakarta gas stations, while Megawati opened a shop where she arranged flowers. Some say Mega joined the political arena only because her ambitious husband urged her to, but whatever the reason, Megawati joined the PDI party in 1987. By most accounts Megawati's grasp of policy was limited at first, and she was uneasy in public meetings and showed little appetite for confronting president and PDI opponent Suharto. History might have turned out very differently if Suharto hadn't attacked Megawati first.

Spooked by the rising popularity of an offspring of his predecessor (Megawati became chairwoman of the PDI in 1993), Suharto schemed to manipulate a June 1996 PDI party congress and remove Megawati as chair, even though she was not a real threat in the rigged national elections staged every five years. When Megawati's supporters protested and occupied the party headquarters, Suharto had them forcibly removed, and five people died in the ensuing riots. Some say these events brought out a stronger side of Megawati, and though many advised her to compromise with the powerful president, she refused to give in and instead announced that she would sue the government and challenge her removal from the PDI. She filed a complaint in every courthouse that would accept one, and a new hero was born.

Despite winning only seven verdicts, the trials meant that Megawati was standing up for her rights, and with each court appearance she bolstered her popular support among the masses of Indonesians, who identified with her struggle against the repressive government. Suharto had created his own nemesis, a rare misstep for a man who previously had effectively sidelined any threats to his one-man rule. As Megawati led her party against Suharto's attacks, her stubborn resistance created a heroine with whom all the other victims of his corrupt regime could identify. By raging against her, Suharto furthered the image of Megawati as a victim, increasing her appeal to the populace and solidifying her resolve to stand up to the man who had bullied her, her family, and the entire nation.

After three decades of Suharto's iron-fisted rule—during which Indonesia watched him and his network of friends and family grow increasingly rich at the country's expense—people were finally fed up. In the spring of 1998 student protests broke out, and violence followed when Suharto's army opened fire on the crowds, killing many. Megawati, who was running for president, was harshly criticized for her noticeable absence at the protests and funerals. At the time she said she was staying off the streets to avoid inciting more violence, and many agree now that this was a wise choice. Crowds love Mega: more than a million people showed up for the final rally of her presidential campaign in 1999. Had she called people to the streets in 1998, the result could have been even bloodier.

Suharto did resign eventually, and in October 1999 Indonesia had its first democratic election in decades. Megawati lost the presidency to Abdurrahman Wahid and joined him as Indonesia's vice president. In the ever-changing Indonesian political climate, Megawati's role was redefined yet again only 10 months into her term. Faced with massive disapproval (not only was he criticized for his political and economic mishandlings of the country, the nearly blind leader dozed off while giving a speech), President Wahid officially made Mega responsible for running the government. Viewed as a cautious reformer, Megawati once said in an interview, "I don't like radical change—that creates problems." However, she is very clear about her desire for Indonesia to remain secular and united. What is most important about Megawati is that she understands and has come to symbolize the nation's aspirations for complete renewal, a feat that overshadows her shortcomings. With her new role effective until the next general election in 2004, Megawati is part of a common thread running through Southeast Asian politics, where female leaders in India, Pakistan, Bangladesh, Myanmar, and Sri Lanka have all followed their fathers in leading either the government or the opposition party of their respective countries. Perhaps Ibu (Mother) Mega knows it was her destiny to fuse with her father's legacy in a cult of personality. "I was born in the cradle of politics," she has said. "We eat, drink, bless politics in this house."

— Margaret Feldstein

BALINESE PAINTING: REFLECTIONS FROM AN ISLAND OF ARTISTS

The setting is a verdant tropical world, where diminutive kings dressed in gilded brocade preside over peasant communities of raised homes built from sticks. The backdrop is forest-covered volcanoes dotted with small, crumbling temples and drizzled with misty clouds. Near a quiet palace settled into the central hills, a half-dozen men sit in a semicircle on the cool wood floor of a village pavilion, shadows from the grass roof that protects from the rising tropical sun falling over their brown shoulders. The rustling of bristled paintbrushes stirs the moist air as the artists carefully make strokes across thick swatches of bark cloth. Wiry images of young, black-haired gods slowly emerge from each page. Above the soft, intermittent ringing of locusts, the rhythmic tapping and stroking of lines and muted colors continues until the canvases are awash in vibrant scenes of Bali's most revered religious stories.

Everyone on Bali is an artist in one way or another, and many of the island's inhabitants specialize in painting. No one knows when the tradition began, just that throughout the centuries slices of Bali's history have been carefully chronicled by numerous artists in a variety of styles and media. The earliest paintings focus on religious themes, using characters and following stories from the most popular tales of the times. These works were commissioned by the reigning rajas, who considered the palace artists so important that they were housed in adjacent complexes and kept on staff to create decorations for temple ceremonies and religious celebrations. One of the most famous artist communities is Kamasan, south of Gelgel near Klungkung, where artists who once served the rajas still paint in the old court style.

The history of Balinese painting is characterized by vastly different styles embraced by the artists of each era. Early artists, who worked on bark or cotton cloth, painted in the simplistic *wayang* style, so named for the characters' resemblance to the *wayang kulit* (leather shadow puppets) prevalent throughout Bali and Java. Two-dimensional figures were drawn with thin black lines and elaborate details, then filled in with soft shades of red, green, and gold. Characters, painted in three-quarter view, were from well-known Hindu epics—kings and heroes identified by their refined features, elaborate clothing, and shimmering jewelry and evil characters denoted by sharp canines and bulging eyes. These early works often feature several scenes to a painting, a space-saving measure, with each block subtly separated by decorative borders or back-to-back characters. The earliest such Balinese paintings are at Pura Besakih, the island's most sacred temple, located high in the eastern mountains. In the complex are two wooden planks dating from 1444 and 1458. Depicting Ganesha, the elephant-headed god, and a lotus flower, these old paintings can be found at the temples Pura Penataran and Pura Batu Madeg.

Before the 19th century, Balinese artists' subjects and styles were limited, for until then painting was used only to create religious decorations and ornaments. Just three styles existed: *iders-iders* were long, bannerlike paintings that gracefully scrolled downward from the high temple eaves; large rectangular *langse* paintings were often used as dividing curtains in temples and palaces; and calendars were painted with detailed dramas of the gods. The calendars were a particular favorite of the rajas, for their detailed astrological symbols were believed to foretell the future. Because the artists themselves were also believed to have mystic powers, their paintings were often regarded as magical accoutrements that lent power to the most important shrines and the rites that were held within them.

Creating these magic-filled paintings wasn't always a simple process of drawing with natural ink and colored dyes on paper or cloth. Often this was an intricate procedure, one that began with palm leaves, metal, and potsherds. A stylus was used to inscribe the materials, which were then blackened with ash. Today some of the old-school painters still prefer using natural materials, although many artists have switched to the Chinese paints and ink that have become widely available throughout the region.

In the 1800s European explorers and traders arrived and settled on Bali, bringing with them an abundance of paper. They continued to import the new medium as an ongoing gift to the rajas, who passed the paper on to their palace artists. Suddenly, provided with so much working space—and freed from the time-consuming process of creating bark- or cotton-cloth paper—Balinese artists were able to produce many more paintings. The loosening of traditional artistic boundaries, along with an influx of Western images, slowly pried open a creative crevasse that expanded into new painting styles and images. The earliest surviving painting on paper is an illustrated manuscript of the *Ramayana* epic. It's notable because each sheet includes a passage of text and a single scene, whereas earlier it was common to arrange many scenes on a single page. This liberation of space gave artists more room for detail and soon led to experimentation with more realistic and brighter colors. Another famous work of the new paper era was a Balinese–Old Javanese dictionary, commissioned by Dutch-Chinese linguist Herman Neubronner van der Tuuk, which included innovative, experimental illustrations by 14 Balinese painters. Some of the most famous artists of the day were I Ketut Gede, I Gusti Wayan Kopeng, and I Matjong, who produced many works for palace temples and developed their own wayang-type styles. The latter two artists, experimentalist painters from Krambitan, introduced stronger lines and bolder hues into the two-dimensional scenes.

A true revival of Balinese painting, however, came in the 1920s, when the Pita Maha painting community was established by a group of Balinese and Western artists. Pita Maha, also the name of the creator god Brahma, refers to the creation of a new painting style and era; the term also means "great-grandfather" in Old Javanese and thus points to the deep historical themes on which this style is based. The community combined the teaching and marketing skills of Western artists, who were settling on Bali and creating and promoting a demand for Balinese art in the West, and the power of the raja of the Sukawati house, Cokorda Sukawati, who encouraged the Europeans to motivate Balinese painters and develop their talents. Because of the Pita Maha community, artistic materials were soon distributed throughout the Ubud area, generating a renewed interest in creative expression. Finally Balinese painters had the freedom to experiment with new images and stories. This era was about painting for pleasure, a totally new concept on this god-focused island. What emerged were images of rural Balinese life. And Western buyers were interested, injecting money into the local economy and proving that painting for its own sake was a legitimate way of making a living.

A dozen or so Western writers and artists defined the Pita Maha era and became the guides for a young generation of Balinese painters who were hungry for new ways to develop their individual styles and skills. Dutchman W. O. J. Nieuwenkamp (1874–1950), a talented writer and painter, produced a series of romantic pen-and-ink sketchbooks that were among the first publications to present elaborate images of Bali and Lombok to Europe. Rudolf Bonnet (1895–1975), also from the Netherlands, used thick, simple strokes and shades, while fellow countryman Arie Smit (1916–) painted detailed scenes of Balinese life, including many colorful rural scenes. A. J. Le Mayeur de Merpres (1880–1958), of Belgium, painted gorgeous dappled pastel scenes similar in style to the works of Monet. German Walter Spies (1895–1957) captured sweeping dramas of rural Bali in muted blues, greens, and browns. Mexican Miguel Covarrubias (1904–1957), who wrote one of the quintessential early guides to Bali, painted bold figures in rich hues and deep shadows. Australian Donald Friend (1915–1989), who also wrote and illustrated several books on Bali and on art in general, painted detailed scenes in watercolors and oils. Each of these men added his signature skills to Bali's artistic mix, and local painters then copied elements of each style and built upon them in their own images.

Spies and Bonnet formally set up the famed Pita Maha Association in 1936, with the purpose of encouraging young Balinese artists and creating a world market for their works. Probably the most famous local painter who arose from this group was I Gusti Nyoman Lempad, whose elaborate ink sketches and paintings play on epic characters and themes. Other notable Balinese artists of the era included I Bagus Made Nadera, who developed shadowy tempera works; I Gusti Ketut Kobot, who worked in paint and ink; and A. A. Gede

Meregeg, who painted lively characters and scenes in detailed, convincing color. The painter Ida Bagus Made was a noted apprentice of Rudolf Bonnet, and A. A. Sobrat's works spanned the trends of Ubud style with characteristics of both his mentors, Bonnet and Spies.

Despite the unification of Balinese artists within the Pita Maha, two very different types of artists actually emerged from the organization. The Ubud painters created vibrant, realistic tropical scenes resplendent with jungle life, while the Batuan artists focused on more somber, shrouded mythological and modern scenes. A third, less prevalent group was the Mooi Indië painters, who visualized Bali in graceful, romanticized settings. The latter style was roundly criticized by many Balinese artists, however, who didn't like the way the paintings trivialized life on the island just to attract Western tourists. On the southeast coast a fourth painting group known as the Sanur school was raising a crop of talented painters whose black-and-white works used wide spaces and elongated wayang figures.

In the mid 20th century Balinese painters broke into a series of even smaller artistic communities. Dutchman Arie Smit inspired the Young Artists' School of Penestanan in the late 1950s, an east Ubud community of teenage boy painters who used bright colors, thick lines, and simple images to illustrate themes ranging from Hindu mythology to natural surroundings. South of Ubud, the Pengosekan school, a branch of the Pita Maha Association that specialized in wayang char-

acters in muted colors, developed under Balinese painters Gusti Ketut Kobot and Gusti Made Baret, who were originally tutored by Walter Spies. Soft shades and nature scenes were the hallmarks of the Padangtegal School, credited to Spies apprentice Dewa Ketut Rugan. The complex, three-dimensional scenes painted by those in the Batuan Miniaturist School tell stories that require contemplation and an examination of every element from facial expressions to finger positions.

And from these communities came modern Balinese artists, some of whom— known as the Acadameans—were also trained in Western-style schools on Java. Others, known as Adventurers, are untrained and work from their own inspiration, free from the influence of the former painting schools. Some of the most famous contemporary artists include Nyoman Tusan (1933–), Nyoman Gunarsa (1944–), Nyoman Wianta (1949–), and Nyoman Erawan (1957–), all of whom combine abstract geometric patterns, vivid colors, and repeated characters to create a sense of action and movement. Artists like Abdul Aziz, Chusin, and Dullah offer gentle realistic paintings that focus on the subtle emotions of their lifelike subjects and evoke the enchanting ambience of life on Bali. Given the freedom of expression and wealth of materials available on the island, these artists and their up-and-coming apprentices will have no trouble releasing their creative energies and further broadening Bali's artistic horizons.

— Holly S. Smith

BECOMING A GOD: THE RELIGION & RITUALS OF BALI

Life on Bali centers on a unique form of the Hindu religion and respect for the natural world. The mix of Hindu and Buddhist beliefs, known as Agama Hindu Dharma (Religion of the Hindu Doctrine), focuses on maintaining stability in life and the cosmos through a balance of good and bad gods, their vehicles (the creatures on which they ride around the heavens), their emotional colors, and compass directions. It sounds complicated, but charts, sold in shops around the island, list in detail which gods should be worshiped or appeased during which months.

Much of the island's mystery is derived from the deep religious focus evident in everyday rituals. This is best seen in the mountain areas, particularly around Gunung Agung, the highest point on the island and so sacred it's referred to as the Mother Mountain. Bali's holiest temple, Pura Besakih, is a stone-and-brick complex nestled in the volcano's northwestern slopes; it is called the Mother Temple, and it is believed that each lunar year the gods descend from the heavens to celebrate here. Each day Balinese from all over the island come to Besakih to pray. Offerings are presented at the temples at dawn and dusk, and the fragrant scent of burning incense—sending prayers up to the gods—is always in the air.

This religious focus even emerges through the cloud of tourist action that smothers the southern coast. Two of Bali's most important places of worship, the Tanah Lot and Uluwatu temples, are in the south, and you'll see smaller village and house shrines—with their statues swathed in ceremonial checkered skirts—tucked into the alleys of Seminyak and Sanur. Note the woven-leaf ornaments swaying from the end of long *penjor* (bamboo poles) outside shops and homes; these aren't just for decoration but are in fact symbols of celebration and prayers for prosperity. You'll see offerings to the higher and lower gods in the form of *canang*, little leaf baskets filled with bright flower petals and bits of rice, which are placed on temple walls, doorsteps, and even vehicle dashboards. You'll catch the fragrant scent of jasmine in the air each morning and afternoon as incense is burned, entwining prayers into the wisps of smoke making their way to the heavens. In the crowded streets you may happen upon a parade of villagers in festive sarongs going to celebrate the birthday of a local shrine—particularly if there's a full moon.

The frequent ritual celebrations add to Bali's magic. The *manusa yadnya* (life-cycle ceremonies) are performed to balance the material and spiritual sides; the purpose of every ritual is to cleanse people and things. Through evil actions, whether in this life or another, a soul becomes tarnished, and only by touching pure objects (ducks, geese, eggs, or special leaves) or washing in fire, ash, or holy water can the spirit be cleansed so it can be reborn as a god. Purification ceremonies occur throughout the year, during life passages and before temple birthdays, when the gods are believed to come down from above Gunung Agung to visit the material world.

Babies, who are believed to be living spirits descended from the heavens accompanied by big-brother or big-sister spirits, are considered little gods for the first year. At 12 days a blossom- and banana-filled shrine is placed by a child's bed for its spiritual keeper, Dewa Kumara, who is instructed by his father Siva to protect the baby until the first tooth emerges. At 42 days the older-sibling spirit departs, and a ceremony is held to cleanse the child's mother. A baby's feet never touch the ground for the first three months; on the 105th day the body and spirit are bound, and the baby receives a name and the feet are placed on the earth. The first birthday is celebrated at 210 days, when the baby's hair is cut for the first time and an offering is made to announce that the child is part of the village. At puberty teenagers undergo a tooth-filing ceremony to grind down the pointed canines, considered hallmarks of demons; today this is done more just for show and isn't the painful dental experience it once was. Marriage and death are the two other major events celebrated on Bali. For the former, elaborately dressed families gather in the village center to observe the couple's vows and partake in rituals for eternal bliss. The latter is a frenzied celebration of parades and burning pyres spun around and around to confuse the evil spirits who might follow the departed along their journey to the gods.

It is the neat, compartmentalized organization of religion and ritual in life that keeps traditional Balinese society thriving amid the influx of Western products and practices. Coming from countries where church is an afterthought, attended only on Christmas and Easter, where traditional cultural holidays have turned into odes to storewide sales, and vacations have all but disappeared into workaholic routines, tourists might see the Balinese way of life as too structured and too difficult to understand. But the basic principles are actually quite simple: Place the gods first, the family second, and the community third. Be responsible to them, respectful of them, and work hard to balance your own life. The reward? To become a god of your own.

— Holly S. Smith

VOCABULARY

Bahasa Indonesia is the language that allows for communication within the Indonesian archipelago of 300 or so regional dialects. There are several varieties of the Balinese language, based on the lingering caste system, but everyone speaks Bahasa—and usually a bit of English, too. Once you learn a few handy phrases, you shouldn't have any problems getting what you need.

In fact, you'll probably find that Bahasa is quite simple, because there are no past and future tenses as there are in English. The word *pergi*, for example, is used to say that you are going, you went, and you have gone; the word *makan* is used to say that you are eating, you ate, and you have eaten. The term *sudah* indicates that an action has already happened; *akan* indicates that it will happen in the future. (*Saya sudah makan* means "I already ate"; *Saya akan pergi* means "I will go.")

In two-syllable words the emphasis is usually on the first syllable: *na*-si (rice), *los*-men (small hotel). It's on the second syllable of three-syllable words: sel-*a*-mat (as in *Selamat pagi,* which means "Good morning"). And it's on the third syllable of four-syllable words: In-do-*nes*-ia. Spelling is phonetic, with a couple of twists: the letter *c* is pronounced "ch" (Candidasa is Chan-dee-*dah*-sa); the letter *y* is pronounced "j." The letter *c* is sometimes spelled *tj* (Tjampuhan versus Campuhan) and the letter *j* can also be spelled *dj* (Djakarta instead of Jakarta). There is no letter *v*; November, for example, is spelled *Nopember.* The vowel *u,* as in Ubud, is pronounced "oo"; the *i,* as in *dingin,* is pronounced "ee."

On Bali, as in the rest of Indonesia, older men are addressed as *bapak* and older women are addressed as *ibu,* while young women are called *nyonya.* Casual terms for friends are *adik* (younger sibling) and *kakak* (older sibling). As in the rest of the country, the Balinese appreciate your attempts to learn their language, because doing so shows respect for them and their island.

English	Indonesian	Balinese
yes	ya	
no	tidak/bukan	
please	silakang/tolong	
thank you	terima kasih	matur suksma
you're welcome/ back to you	kembali/sama-sama	ngiring/durusan
Good morning.	Selamat pagi.	Om swastyastu.
Good morning/ afternoon. (midday)	Selamat siang.	Om swastyastu.
Good afternoon.	Selamat sore.	Om swastyastu.
Good evening.	Selamat malam.	Om swastyastu.
How are you?	Apa khabar?	Sapunapi gatrane?
I'm fine.	Baik-baik saja.	Becik-becik manten.
Wow/Darn/ My goodness!!	Adu!!	
Excuse me.	Ma'af.	Nawegang.
Please help me.	Tolonglah saya.	
toilet	WC (way-say)	

Where is the toilet?	Dimana WC disini?	
What time is it?	Jam berapa?	
How much does it cost?	Berapa harga ini?	Aji kuda ajine?
It's too expensive!	Ini terlalu mahal!	
I don't understand.	Saya tidak mengerti.	
I don't speak Indonesian.	Saya tidak mengerti bahasa Indonesia.	
airplane	kapal terbang	
airport	bandar udara	
bicycle	sepeda	
boat	kapal laut	
bus	bis	
bus station	stasiun bis	
motorcycle	sepeda moto	
taxi	taksi	
train	kereta api	
train station	stasiun kerata api	
fast	cepat	
slow	pelan-pelan	
left	kiri	
right	kanan	
straight	terus	
far	jauh	
short	dekat	
street	jalan	
lane/alley	gang	
hotel	hotel, resort, villa, losmen	
Do you have a room?	Masih adda kamar kosong dising?	
How much is a room?	Berapa harga untuk kamar ini?	
hot	panas	
cold	dingin	
water	air	
big	besar	
small	kecil	
city center	kota	
neighborhood	banjar	
town	kampong	
village	desa	
temple	pura	
palace	puri	
beach	pantai	
hill	bukit	

hot spring	air panas	
island	pulau	
lake	danau	
mountain	gunung	
peak/summit	puncak	
river	sungai	
volcano	gunung api	
waterfall	air terjun	
food	makanan	ajengan
drink	minum	nginem
water	air	
coffee	kopi	
tea	teh	
milk	susu	
juice	jus	
soda	soda	
beer	bir	
wine	anggur	
drunk	mabuk	
rice	nasi	
noodles	mie	
bread	roti	
meat	daging	
beef	sapi	
pork	babi	
chicken	ayam	
egg	telur	
vegetables	sayur	
fried	goreng	
boil/steam	rebus	
grill	bakar	
hungry	lapar	
full	penuh	
enough	cukup	
I would like to pay/ I would like the bill	Saya mau bayar/ Saya minta bon	
day	hari	
night	malam	
morning	pagi	
midmorning to afternoon	siang	
afternoon	sore	
yesterday	kemarin	
tomorrow	besok	

day after tomorrow	besok lusa	
today	hari ini	
Sunday	Hari Minggu	
Monday	Hari Senin	
Tuesday	Hari Selasa	
Wednesday	Hari Rabu	
Thursday	Hari Kamis	
Friday	Hari Juma'at	
Saturday	Hari Sabtu	
Saturday night	Malam Minggu	
week	minggu	wuku
month	bulan	sasih
year	tahun	
January	Januari	
February	February	
March	Maret	
April	April	
May	Mei	
June	Juni	
July	Juli	
August	Augustus	
September	Septiember	
October	Oktober	
November	Nopember	
December	Disember	
0	koson	
1	satu	
2	dua	
3	tiga	
4	empat	
5	lima	
6	enam	
7	tujuh	
8	delipan	
9	sembilan	
10	sepuluh	
11	sebelas	
12	duabelas	
13	tigabelas	
14	empatbelas	
15	limabelas	
16	enambelas	
17	tujuhbelas	
18	lapanbelas	

19	sembilanbelas
20	duapuluh
30	tigapuluh
40	empatpuluh
50	limapuluh
60	enampuluh
70	tujuhpuluh
80	lapanpuluh
90	sembilanpuluh
100	seratus
1,000	seribu
10,000	sepuluh ribu
100,000	seratus ribu
1,000,000	sejuta

INDEX

NOTES

NOTES